PERSEVERANCE IN GRATITUDE

Perseverance in Gratitude

A Socio-Rhetorical Commentary
on the Epistle "to the Hebrews"

David A. deSilva

WILLIAM B. EERDMANS PUBLISHING COMPANY
GRAND RAPIDS, MICHIGAN / CAMBRIDGE, U.K.

Printed in the United States of America

05 04 03 02 01 00   7 6 5 4 3 2 1

Library of Congress Cataloging-in-Publication Data

deSilva, David Arthur.
     Perseverance in Gratitude: a socio-rhetorical commentary
on the Epistle "to the Hebrews" / David A. deSilva.
        p.   cm.
     Includes bibliographical references and indexes.
     ISBN 0-8028-4188-0 (pbk.: alk. paper)
     1. Bible. N.T. Hebrews — Socio-rhetorical criticism.   I. Title.

BS2775.2 .D475 2000
227'.8707 — dc21
                                      99-462192

For James Adrian deSilva
and John Austin Alexander deSilva,
sons of encouragement

Contents

Preface

Since many excellent books and comprehensive commentaries on Hebrews have already appeared in print, writing yet another requires some justification. What can this commentary contribute to a conversation that has already been significantly advanced by such scholars as Ceslaus Spicq, Harold Attridge, Lincoln Hurst, William Lane, H.-F. Weiß, Paul Ellingworth, and many other members of that cloud of witnesses who have made Hebrews an area of specialization? While the work of these scholars is foundational to my own reflection on Hebrews, I believe that there remains more to be discovered about that rhetorically complex and rich text, particularly when it is examined from the perspectives of rhetorical analysis, social-scientific criticism, cultural-anthropological perspectives, and ideological criticism. In short, the current conversation about Hebrews will be enriched as broader methodological approaches are brought to bear on this text. As new sets of questions are developed, new information can be gathered from our ancient witness. These insights, in turn, enhance and correct earlier interpretations of the text and call for a new integration with the findings from the more established approaches. The result, it is hoped, is a more richly textured, three-dimensional reading of Hebrews, written for the benefit not only of the professional scholar, but specifically also of the seminarian and pastor who will need to apply the word of Hebrews persuasively in new social and cultural situations.

The methodological framework within which this commentary locates itself is socio-rhetorical interpretation, an interpretive model developed by Vernon K. Robbins.[1] This model encourages interpreters to take full advantage

---

1. *The Tapestry of Early Christian Discourse: Rhetoric, Society and Ideology* (London: Routledge, 1996); *Exploring the Texture of Texts: A Guide to Socio-Rhetorical Interpretation* (Valley Forge, PA: Trinity Press International, 1996).

of the spectrum of methods of investigating texts and to do so in such a way as to invite conversation among the many disciplines that now make up that spectrum (e.g., literary and narrative criticism, rhetorical analysis, intertextual analysis, social-scientific criticism). The interpreter engages the text in detailed analysis, but he also engages the world that produced the text and on which the text seeks to have some kind of impact.

The model emphasizes the importance of inner texture, intertexture, social and cultural texture, ideological texture, and sacred texture. Inner texture focuses the interpreter on the patterns and progression of the text itself. Here, structural, literary, rhetorical, and narrative strategies for analysis come into play. One looks for repetitions in the text, which may signify anything from markers of sections (e.g., inclusions) to an important element of the author's strategy for shaping his audience's perception of their world. The argumentative texture of the text (elements of enthymemes, maxims, patterns of elaboration, and the like), as well as ways in which the text draws in the different senses or body zones of the audience into the experience of hearing, are also important elements of a close investigation of the inner texture.

Intertexture takes the interpreter to the conversation that exists or may exist between the text and other available texts, very broadly conceived. It inquires into the world of texts that resonate with the text under investigation and contribute to how that text seeks to make an impact and how it will be heard. Quotations and allusions to the Jewish Scriptures, intertestamental literature, and early Christian teachings are not only to be identified: the manner in which the author reshapes and applies these other "texts" so as to advance his goals is of primary importance. Robbins stresses, however, that the early church and its leaders were just as much members of the Greco-Roman culture as of Jewish and Christian culture (all the more as Christianity moved toward the inclusion of Gentiles). It is imperative, and fruitful, to investigate allusions and resonances created by a text with images and texts from that culture as well. Written or "oral" texts (oral-scribal intertexture), however, are not the only "scripts" that might be woven into the fabric of the text under investigation. Cultural and social roles (like patrons, clients, guests, kin), maps (like the Jewish purity maps), and codes (like honor) are also, in a broader sense, texts with which our text may interact. Reference to "real life" events — to a shared knowledge about the historical past — forms yet another kind of intertexture to be investigated.

Social and cultural texture moves from the world of the text to the world of the author and audience. How does the text orient its audience to the world of everyday life? How does it shape their relationships and interactions with one another? What kind of community does it seek to form? What discernible tensions exist between audience and non-Christian neighbors? Does sociology of religion or sociology of knowledge shed any light on the potential or intended social effects of the text? The first-century Mediterranean world was composed of a complex matrix of divergent and varied groups, each with their own set of values and conceptions of how those values were to be enacted. How does the author locate himself, and seek to locate his audience, in this complex cultural environment? Does he share the values of other groups, differing perhaps only in the means by which they are fulfilled? Does he reject the values of other groups, proposing different values for the core of Christian identity?

Ideological texture asks the interpreter to recognize that the text is not just a vehicle for ideas, but rather a vehicle by which the author hopes to achieve a certain goal.[2] What goal or goals drive the author? How does the author use the text to achieve this goal? This may involve changing the audience's perception of their situation, alerting them to dangers that are going unperceived, or drawing stark alternatives so as to move the audience to choose more readily the author's favored alternative. Successful analysis of the author's ideological strategy requires the integration of insights gleaned from exploring the other textures — repetition, argumentative texture, use of authoritative texts, employment of patron-client expectations, and the like can all serve the author's agenda for the hearers in their situation. Investigation of ideological texture, however, also asks that the interpreter look critically at the interests and commitments that have guided (frequently determined) the findings of other scholars in the history of interpretation, as well as one's own interaction with the text. In a sense, this is a methodological application of Paul's observation that "we see in a mirror, dimly" (1 Cor. 13:12) — a mirror that is, moreover, colored and contoured by our own experience, our religious and ideological commitments, our social location, and the like. There is, thus, no interpretation of a text that is "pure" in the sense that the interpreter has not read into the text what she or he requires to sustain his or her worldview.

Finally, socio-rhetorical interpretation acknowledges the importance of the religious dimension of these texts and what they can contribute to the interpreter's experience of the divine and to ethical reflection. In this regard, socio-rhetorical interpretation may help bridge the gap between biblical studies and theology, between exegesis and hermeneutics.

This commentary will not attempt to utilize all the resources of socio-rhetorical interpretation in every passage, nor even emphasize equally those re-

---

2. John H. Elliott (*A Home for the Homeless: A Sociological Exegesis of 1 Peter, Its Situation and Strategy* [Philadelphia: Fortress, 1981], 10-11) brings this to the fore of the exegetical task: "Strategy implies not simply the communication of ideas but the deliberate design of a document calculated to have a specific social effect on its intended hearers and readers. Sociological exegesis thus seeks to discover the manner in which a given document has been designed as a response to a given situation, and how it has been composed to elicit a social response on the part of its audience." Socio-rhetorical interpretation includes and broadens the goal of sociological exegesis.

sources it does employ. It will, however, honor the primary concern of socio-rhetorical interpretation, namely, that an investigator work at a text from aspects of each texture and bring the various levels into conversation with one another. Here the author's predilection for certain kinds of investigation makes itself known. My principal interest is in the rhetorical strategy of Hebrews (how the author seeks to persuade his audience to remain committed to the Christian movement)[3] and the social effects of accepting the author's ideology as one's own (i.e., what kind of church does Hebrews seek to create). Observations concerning repetitive texture, oral-scribal intertexture, and social and cultural intertexture (patron-client scripts, kinship language, honor discourse, purity codes, and rituals) will be incorporated primarily as these illumine the author's rhetorical strategy as well as the communal ideology the author seeks to promote among the hearers. Social and cultural texture will be examined primarily with a view to displaying the relationships within the group that the author seeks to sustain, as well as the dynamics in the relationship between the Christian group and their host society. It is primarily in these areas that this commentary seeks to make its contribution to reflection on Hebrews within the church and the academy.

The model suggests two avenues for the writing of a commentary — one that takes the reader through each of the various textures, and another that integrates insights gathered from the various perspectives and angles into a single reading. This book will follow the latter course as the more useful and reader-friendly format.

---

3. Elliott (*Home for the Homeless*, 107) likens the dynamics of author, text, and audience to "game playing or battle tactics," in which "strategy involves a plan calculated to have a specific effect." Those entrusted with the task of shaping and nurturing Christian communities now should find this approach to the NT texts helpful for their own work, which involves a similar challenge: How can the contemporary Christian community respond to new challenges while retaining the essence of the vision for the "people of God" attested in the Scriptures? Investigating how the NT authors used the resources at their disposal to motivate what they discerned to be a "faithful" response will open up new possibilities for their successors in church leadership.

Acknowledgments

This commentary is, in many ways, an expansion and a deepening of my earlier investigations of Hebrews, primarily my doctoral dissertation. I remember here with gratitude the formative influences, the encouragement, and the contributions of Luke T. Johnson, Vernon K. Robbins, and Carl R. Holladay to my thinking and methodology. I have profited much from continuing conversation with Professor Robbins and Duane F. Watson, as well as the new mentor and colleague I have found in the series editor, Ben Witherington III. The debt I owe to the magisterial commentaries on Hebrews by William Lane, Harold Attridge, and Paul Ellingworth will be apparent throughout this volume, and I thank them for their diligence and comprehensiveness in compiling what will continue to be foundational resources for investigating Hebrews.

The administration and faculty of Ashland Theological Seminary have continued to be sources of support and encouragement for me in my research and writing, as well as willing conversation partners (in particular L. Daniel Hawk, whose expertise in the Hebrew Bible has been a valuable resource for me), and I am thankful to have such colleagues as I have found here. Thanks are due as well to my teaching assistant, Brett Scott, whose help in grading numerous assignments contributed significantly to the timely production of this book. Four classes of students have wrestled with Hebrews alongside me, and their questions and objections have pushed me to formulate my position more clearly and compellingly at many points. It is for them and for all readers engaged in ministry that I have written the "Bridging the Horizons" sections, and I am glad to have had students who reminded me frequently of the ultimately primary question of relevance. I hope the present volume will contribute not only to the interpretation of Hebrews but to the positive shaping of communities of faith and individual disciples as a result.

The present volume incorporates material from my previous book on Hebrews, *Despising Shame: Honor Discourse and Community Maintenance in the Epistle to the Hebrews* (SBLDS 152; Atlanta, GA: Scholars Press, 1995) and an article entitled "Hebrews 6:4-8: A Socio-Rhetorical Investigation" published in *Tyndale Bulletin* 50/1 (1999): 33-57 and 50/2 (1999): 225-35. Several paragraphs from a devotional series on Hebrews 9–13 published in *Encounter with God* (Milton Keynes: Scripture Union, July-September 1997) now appear in the "Bridging the Horizons" sections. My appreciation goes out to Gregory Glover of the Society of Biblical Literature, Bruce Longenecker of Tyndale House, and Andrew Clark of Scripture Union for securing permission for me to incorporate these materials here.

I have worked from my own translation of Hebrews, but have also quoted from the Revised Standard Version (©1946, 1952, and 1971) and New Revised Standard Version (©1989 by the Division of Christian Education of the National Council of the Churches of Christ in the USA: All rights reserved; used by permission). Classical quotations generally are taken from the Loeb Classical Library.

I extend my gratitude to Dr. John Simpson at Eerdmans Publishing, who was a source of encouragement and guidance during the years between proposal and production, and to Jennifer Hoffman, Milton Essenburg, and others at Eerdmans, who worked painstakingly in the preparation of this volume.

Finally, I thank my wife, Donna Jean, for her commitment to the importance of the Scriptures, which enables her to support my endeavors, for her willingness to do more than her share of parenting during the months when I was in the throes of writing, and for her essential reminders not to lose sight of that higher priority — spending time with our two sons, James Adrian and John Austin, to whom I dedicate this volume.

Abbreviations

AB	Anchor Bible Commentary Series
ABD	*Anchor Bible Dictionary*
ACNT	Augsburg Commentary on the New Testament
AJT	*American Journal of Theology*
ALGHJ	Arbeiten zur Literatur und Geschichte des hellenistischen Judentums
ANF	The Ante Nicene Fathers: Translations of the Writings of the Fathers Down to A.D. 325 (ed. A. Roberts and J. Donaldson; 10 vols.; Grand Rapids: Eerdmans, 1951-53)
ANRW	*Aufstieg und Niedergang der römischen Welt*
BAGD	W. Bauer, W. F. Arndt, F. W. Gingrich, and F. W. Danker, *Greek-English Lexicon of the New Testament*
BBR	*Bulletin of Biblical Research*
Bib	*Biblica*
Bib Sac	*Bibliotheca Sacra*
BJRL	*Bulletin of the John Rylands University Library of Manchester*
BTB	*Biblical Theology Bulletin*
BZ	*Biblische Zeitschrift*
CBQ	*Catholic Biblical Quarterly*
CBQMS	Catholic Biblical Quarterly Monograph Series
CTJ	*Calvin Theological Journal*
ExT	*Expository Times*
FRLANT	Forschungen zur Religion und Literatur des Alten und Neuen Testaments
GTJ	*Grace Theological Journal*
HTR	*Harvard Theological Review*

HTRDS	Harvard Theological Review Dissertation Series
ICC	International Critical Commentary
IDB	*Interpreter's Dictionary of the Bible*
JBL	*Journal of Biblical Literature*
JBR	*Journal of Bible and Religion*
JJS	*Journal of Jewish Studies*
JSNT	*Journal for the Study of the New Testament*
JSNTSS	Journal for the Study of the New Testament Supplement Series
JSP	*Journal for the Study of the Pseudepigrapha*
LCL	Loeb Classical Library (London: Heinemann, and Cambridge, MA: Harvard University)
LEC	Library of Early Christianity
LSJ	Liddell-Scott-Jones, *Greek-English Lexicon*
LXX	Septuagint
MeyerK	H. A. W. Meyer, *Kritisch-exegetischer Kommentar über das Neue Testament*
MT	Masoretic Text
NASV	New American Standard Version
NICNT	New International Commentary on the New Testament
NIGTC	New International Greek Testament Commentary
NIV	New International Version
NJB	New Jerusalem Bible
NKJV	New King James Version
NovT	*Novum Testamentum*
NPNF[1]	A Select Library of the Nicene and Post-Nicene Fathers of the Christian Church, First Series (ed. P. Schaff and H. Wace; 14 vols.; Grand Rapids: Eerdmans, 1956)
NPNF[2]	A Select Library of the Nicene and Post-Nicene Fathers of the Christian Church, Second Series (ed. P. Schaff and H. Wace; 14 vols.; Grand Rapids: Eerdmans, 1956)
NRSV	New Revised Standard Version
NRT	*La nouvelle revue théologique*
NT	New Testament
NTS	*New Testament Studies*
OT	Old Testament
OTP	*The Old Testament Pseudepigrapha* (ed. J. H. Charlesworth)
PG	J.-P. Migne (ed.), *Patrologia cursus completa . . . Series graeca* (166 vols.; Paris: Petit Montrouge, 1857-83)
Rhet. Alex.	*Rhetorica ad Alexandrum*
Rhet. Her.	*Rhetorica ad Herennium*
RSV	Revised Standard Version
SBFLA	*Studii Biblici Franciscani Liber Annuus*

SBLDS	Society of Biblical Literature Dissertation Series
SBLSP	*Society of Biblical Literature Seminar Papers*
SBT	Studies in Biblical Theology
SJT	*Scottish Journal of Theology*
SBLMS	Society of Biblical Literature Monograph Series
SNT	Studien zum Neuen Testament
SNTSMS	Society for New Testament Studies Monograph Series
SNTU	*Studien zum Neuen Testament und seiner Umwelt*
TDNT	*Theological Dictionary of the New Testament* (ed. G. Kittel and G. Friedrich; 10 vols.; trans. G. Bromiley; Grand Rapids: Eerdmans, 1964-76)
Trin J	*Trinity Journal*
WBC	Word Biblical Commentary
WTJ	*Westminster Theological Journal*
VC	*Vigiliae christianae*

Abbreviations of classical literature follow the *Oxford Classical Dictionary* wherever possible.

Introduction

When we consider the situation to which the Letter "to the Hebrews" responds, we are without much of the supplemental data available for understanding, say, the Corinthian letters or Revelation. For those texts, extensive investigations of the city of Corinth or Ephesus (and the other six cities addressed in Revelation) provide a rich picture of the setting of the addressees and, in many cases, illuminate specific references in the text. With Hebrews, however, the identity of the author remains, after two millennia of speculation, unknown, and the locations of author and addressees remain unspecified. Many scholars advance arguments for a specific location, from Rome[1] to the Lycus Valley[2] to Jerusalem itself,[3] in an attempt to avoid "exegetical generality."[4] While some hypotheses certainly appear stronger than others, they remain precisely that — hypotheses. Even if we cannot, however, determine such particulars as the name of the author, the location of the addressees, and the like, we can elicit from the text a clear sense of the author's rhetorical agenda as well as a wealth of information concerning the audience, their history as a Christian community, and their current situation. "Exegetical generality" can thus still be avoided.

---

1. William L. Lane (*Hebrews 1–8* [WBC; Dallas: Word, 1991], lviii-lxvi) provides the strongest case for locating the addressees in Rome, which then leads him to a highly specific reconstruction of the community's history and present setting.

2. Robert Jewett, *A Letter to Pilgrims: A Commentary on the Epistle to the Hebrews* (New York: Pilgrim, 1981), 5.

3. This position is represented by the highly controverted hypothesis of George W. Buchanan, *To the Hebrews* (AB; Garden City, NY: Doubleday, 1970). A Jerusalem address has recently been proposed by Randall C. Gleason, "The Old Testament Background of the Warning in Hebrews 6:4-8," *Bib Sac* 155 (1998): 62-91.

4. Jewett, *Letter to Pilgrims,* 3.

The Recipients of the Letter "To the Hebrews"

Ethnic Background

One central question concerning the addressees is their ethnic composition. The majority of extant manuscripts bear the superscription ΠΡΟΣ ΕΒΡΑΙΟΥΣ,[5] and ever since Tertullian (*De pudic.* 20) referred to the text by this title, the assumption of a Jewish Christian audience has been predominant. With this assumption in place, numerous aspects of the letter can then be used to "prove" the conjecture.[6] Prominent among these proofs is the suggestion that the author's wide-ranging use of the OT, and the weight he places on arguments from the OT, would have been meaningful chiefly to an audience of Jewish origin. Moreover, the author's use of exegetical methods, which came to characterize rabbinic Judaism, suggests a Jewish environment for both author and recipients. The author's interest in the Jewish cult "would probably have left gentile readers cold."[7] Proving the obsolescence of the Old Covenant is thought to be a matter of importance for Jewish, not Gentile, Christians.[8] The result of this assumption is almost inevitably the suggestion that the problem addressed by Hebrews is a potential reversion to Judaism on the part of Jewish Christians who seek to avoid ongoing tension with their non-Christian Jewish families and neighbors.[9]

There is, however, nothing compelling us to view the Christian addressees as exclusively, or predominantly, Jewish in origin. Unlike the author of the Pauline letters (as well as books like 1 Peter and Revelation), the author of Hebrews identifies neither himself nor his readers. The title "To the Hebrews" represents an early conjecture concerning the addressees based on an estimation of the contents.[10] This ascription could well be ideologically motivated. As the move-

---

5. With varying degrees of elaboration, e.g., "To the Hebrews written from Rome" or "Italy," "To the Hebrews written from Rome by Paul to those in Jerusalem," and the like.

6. F. Delitzsch (*Commentary on the Epistle to the Hebrews,* 2 vols. [Edinburgh: T. & T. Clark, 1871-72], 1:4, 20-21) assumes without discussion that the audience is composed of Jewish Christians, and, moreover, that they must be resident in Palestine where the distinction between "Hebrew" and "Hellenist" Jews had meaning. A location near the temple is also inferred from the author's interest in the levitical cult (despite the fact that the author speaks wholly of the desert tabernacle and never the stone temple).

7. Paul Ellingworth, *Commentary on Hebrews* (NIGTC; Grand Rapids: Eerdmans, 1993), 25.

8. Thus Gleason, "Old Testament Background," 67.

9. David Peterson, *Hebrews and Perfection: An Examination of the Concept of Perfection in the 'Epistle to the Hebrews'* (SNTSMS 47; Cambridge: Cambridge University Press, 1982), 186; Philip E. Hughes, *A Commentary on the Epistle to the Hebrews* (Grand Rapids: Eerdmans, 1977), 18-19; Ray C. Stedman, *Hebrews* (Downers Grove, IL: InterVarsity Press, 1992), 11-13; Gleason, "Old Testament Background," 69.

10. Ellingworth, *Hebrews,* 21; Thomas Long (*Hebrews* [Interpretation; Louisville, KY:

ment developed and the gap between synagogue and church widened into an irreparable chasm, having a canonical "response" to the parent religion — a sort of indirect manifesto of supersessionism — would have been valuable as a witness to the legitimacy of the sect's existence and ideology. The literature of the early Church attests to the importance of the sect's self-definition over against Judaism,[11] and this letter, with its prominent use of the rhetorical device of *synkrisis* (comparison, here between Jesus and the mediators of the "old covenant"), could reinforce that task admirably. Not much weight, therefore, should be placed on "external attestation" on this point.

Arguments based on what would be appropriate or relevant to Christians of one race over another are even more specious. The Gentile entering the Christian community became an "heir of the promise," a "child of Abraham," the "Israel of God," the "circumcision," and the "royal priesthood, God's holy nation."[12] That is to say, the Gentile Christian was socialized to view himself or herself as the heir to the titles and promises that belonged to God's chosen people (historically, the Jewish people). The Gentile Christian was also enculturated to regard the Jewish Scriptures as the "oracles of God" (cf. Heb. 5:12, where these serve as the primary textbook of the Christian converts), and was taught to read those oracles, moreover, as the divine revelation that legitimated the Christian hope and shaped the Christian ethos.[13]

John Knox, 1997], 1) boldly but correctly suggests that the person "who attached a title to this document . . . was probably just speculating about its original recipients and was as much in the dark as we are."

11. Compare the *Epistle of Barnabas; Epistle to Diognetus* 3–4; Justin Martyr, *Dialogue with Trypho*.

12. Gal. 3:29; 6:6; Phil. 3:3; 1 Pet. 2:9. This is not to suggest that every Christian was introduced to all these epithets as the common property of the Christian culture, but merely to show the wide-ranging tendency to create the sect's identity out of the terms and concepts of the parent religion.

13. This point was well made by James Moffatt, *A Critical and Exegetical Commentary on the Epistle to the Hebrews* (ICC; Edinburgh: T. & T. Clark, 1924), xvi-xvii: "how much the LXX meant to Gentile Christians may be seen in the case of a man like Tatian, for example, who explicitly declares that he owed to reading the OT his conversion to Christianity (*Ad Graecos*, 29)." Justin (*Dial.* 8) has a similar testimony. William Robinson ("The Eschatology of the Epistle to the Hebrews: A Study in the Christian Doctrine of Hope," *Encounter* 22 [1961]: 37-51, 40) posits a mixed congregation, arguing that "the title is certainly misleading. Most probably it arose because of the interest in the Old Testament sacrificial system; but this need not necessitate a Jewish-Christian group of readers, as the Pauline Epistles show that Gentile converts to Christianity were assumed to be familiar with the Jewish Background." P. M. Eisenbaum (*The Jewish Heroes of Christian History: Hebrews 11 in Literary Context* [SBLDS 156; Atlanta: Scholars Press, 1997], 9) also contends that the volume of use of the OT in Hebrews does not speak to the ethnic identity of the addressees: "That the past for Christians amounts to the biblical history of Israel is indicative of two things not necessarily re-

Christian worship and proclamation involved the reading of these oracles and their exposition in the distinctive Christian manner. The canonical texts provide only a few windows into the lives of the early Christian communities. What happened in Christian communities in the "everyday" rhythm of assembling for worship and teaching was likely to be oriented toward instruction from the OT as well as from the teachings of Jesus (which were, themselves, largely concerned with deriving an ethic from the Jewish Scriptures). We must not allow the plight of so many modern Gentile Christians, with their relative lack of knowledge of the OT, to color our understanding of the first-century convert, for whom the OT was the revelation of God's will, the source (together with the experience of the Spirit) for the legitimation of the sect and the hope to which those converts clung.

Both Galatians and 1 Peter address audiences that are in some major part Gentile. The argument of Galatians (the exhortation against receiving circumcision, which would be a moot issue for those born Jews) is particularly pointed toward Gentile converts to Christianity.[14] That text employs an extended exposition from the story of Abraham in Genesis, as well as texts from Deuteronomy, Habakkuk, Leviticus, and Isaiah, and expounds these texts according to rules familiar from rabbinic exegesis. 1 Peter, addressing those who "no longer join" in with their Gentile neighbors, is even richer in oral-scribal intertexture with the OT, as well as allusions and references to OT figures and stories. 1 Corinthians 10:1-13 derives moral instruction from a string of events connected with the exodus generation but does so in an allusive manner that presumes a high degree of familiarity with these stories on the part of the largely Gentile Christian audience.

The use of the OT in Hebrews, then, does not necessitate or even suggest an audience made up primarily of Jewish Christians. Gentile Christians — especially those who have been attached to the Christian community for some time, as it seems likely that these have — would also be familiar with those texts and keenly interested in their interpretation. Since they were instructed to read

---

lated to the make-up of the community: the burgeoning religion's Jewish origins and the need of the first missionaries for Jewish scripture in their apologetics." She also concludes (*Jewish Heroes*, 8) that a mixed audience of Jewish and Gentile Christians is the best conclusion to be drawn.

14. Ellingworth (*Hebrews*, 23) claims that "the argument that Galatians proclaims to gentile Christians freedom from the law of Moses, and that Hebrews could therefore similarly use OT evidence in writing to gentiles, rests on the questionable presupposition that the Galatian Christians were all of gentile origin." This is a false analysis of the argument, however. The argument presumes that the Gentile Christians, who were most directly affected by the outcome of the Galatian debate, would have been adequately instructed in the OT to follow and accept Paul's argument. The presence of Jewish Christians in the audience is not relevant to this point.

them by Jewish Christians like Paul and his team, we should consider the likelihood that Gentile Christians would have been exposed, at least inductively, to rules of interpretation such as *gezera shawa* (which becomes a cardinal rule of Christian interpretation of Scripture as well, as "concordant Scriptures" in Augustine's *De Doctrina Christiana*) or *qal wahomer* (also part and parcel of Greco-Roman argumentation) in the course of this instruction.[15] Moreover, the interest in the levitical cultus in Hebrews would probably not, contrary to Paul Ellingworth's suggestion, leave Gentile Christians cold. Both Jewish and Gentile Christians were socialized into a sect that required both an acceptance of the OT as a record of divine revelation *and* a rejection of the contemporary validity of the covenant and priesthood therein described (or, better, commanded).[16] Hebrews strongly reinforces this dual orientation to the Jewish Scriptures. Gentile believers could "warm up" to the central exposition of Hebrews (7:1–10:18), as well as its other comparisons of the advantages of those belonging to the new covenant over those who labored under the old, as relevant for several purposes. First, the author gives them a salvation-historical perspective on their situation. As those who draw near to God through the new covenant, they are more privileged, more secure in their hope, and further along to the goal of God's deliverance and kingdom than the "people of God" had ever been. This enhances the significance of belonging to, and importance of remaining with, the Christian community, as well as stimulates gratitude and loyalty at being favored beyond their inherited predecessors.

Second, it serves the well-known need of sects to legitimate their existence by proposing the failings of the parent body (here, Judaism) and the ways in which the sect members have been given the advantage of "true" knowledge about how to approach to divine, what the divine plan entails, and the like. Hebrews supports group definition and identity through developing a contrast with an alternative group's ideology, stressing the superiority of Christian ideology as a means of sustaining commitment. As the Christian community

---

15. How the Scriptures are handled, however, says more about the author's background and training than the recipients' ethnic origin.

16. F. F. Bruce (*The Epistle to the Hebrews* [NICNT; Grand Rapids: Eerdmans, 1990], 6) believes that the author's use of the OT to sustain commitment to the group proves that Gentile Christians are not in view, for if these were tempted to defect from the church, they would also be prepared to throw away the OT as well, whereas Jewish Christians would not. If their temptation to defect, however, is primarily social (yielding to society's shaming techniques at last) rather than ideological (rejecting the message about Christ and the texts in which it was grounded), then the OT would remain a valid body of texts from which to elevate ideological considerations over considerations of social well-being. I do not, therefore, find Bruce's argument necessary, or even likely, on this point. The addressees need reminding that ideological integrity (commitment to the worldview and vision of the group) is ultimately more advantageous than social reintegration.

grows, it continues to engage in this sort of ideological warfare against both Judaism and paganism as part of the ongoing process of justifying why "we" are not "them" and why "they" are the worse for it. Much of the literature of the first three centuries treats the topic of why Christianity is superior to the Mosaic covenant and the teachings of Plato, to Jewish sacrifices and pagan worship. Hebrews responds very well to this need, mainly with regard to non-Christian Judaism.[17] There is no need to assume that, if Gentile Christians are in fact among the intended readers of Hebrews, they would necessarily be subject to the temptation to convert to Judaism in order for the author's message to have relevance.[18] All members of sects need to be assured that their approach to God is the more effective, the more valid, the more secure, and it is precisely this point that Hebrews reinforces.

I find, therefore, no reason to limit our reading of Hebrews as a sermon addressing Jewish Christians or even prominently interested in the Jewish Christians in the audience.[19] Neither would I push this in the opposite direction and suggest that Gentile Christians are either prominent or especially targeted. The letter, unfortunately named, would be equally meaningful to Christians of any ethnic origin, since both Jewish and Gentile converts are socialized into the same Christocentric reading of the same Scriptures. Just as Gentile readers have continued to find in Hebrews justification for their claim on God's promises and access to God's favor even while they worship apart from the synagogue and God's historic people, so the Gentile Christians in the first audience would not have been

---

17. We will explore below the purpose of comparison with the levitical cultus, if not to forestall "reversion" to Judaism, as well as the author's choice of facets of Jewish tradition, rather than Greco-Roman religion, for his demonstration of the unique efficacy of the Son's mediation of access to God.

18. Bruce (*Hebrews*, 6 n. 13) and Gleason ("Old Testament Background," 67) read too much into the nonmention of circumcision. The latter claims that "the lack of any reference to circumcision rules out the possibility that he was addressing Gentile Christians attracted to Judaism." Aside from the problematic assumption that all forms of Judaizing involved circumcision of Gentiles (that is to say, were as extreme as those of the Judaizing party encountered in Galatia), there is the more problematic commitment to the view that Hebrews is only meaningful as an attempt to forestall conversion/reversion to non-Christian Judaism. This commitment has long prevented readers of Hebrews from considering that the comparisons in Hebrews serve primarily to shape a communal ideology that would make any defection from the sect (whether to Judaism or traditional Greco-Roman religion) seem unprofitable.

19. A number of contemporary scholars have also expressed strong skepticism concerning the validity of hypothesizing a Jewish-Christian audience. See Harold W. Attridge, *Hebrews* (Hermeneia; Philadelphia: Fortress, 1989), 10-13 for a thorough review of the discussion as well as a balanced assessment of the evidence; Andrew H. Trotter, Jr., *Interpreting the Epistle to the Hebrews* (Grand Rapids: Baker Book House, 1997), 28-31. Some scholars, while opting for a mixed congregation, still put the emphasis on a Jewish-Christian majority. See V. C. Pfitzner, *Hebrews* (ACNT; Nashville: Abingdon, 1997), 25; Ellingworth, *Hebrews*, 27.

more prone to doze off during the reading of chapters 7 through 10 than their Jewish Christian sisters and brothers. Too much stock in the "Jewish Christian" audience hypothesis prevents us from seeing that the sustained *synkrisis* (comparison) with the levitical cult serves ideological needs of Gentile Christians as well and unduly limits our appreciation for the contribution of this letter to the world construction and group maintenance of the early Church.[20] In this commentary, therefore, we will be looking at how the sermon would be meaningful for Diaspora Jewish Christians and Gentile Christians, how the argument would impact and shape both elements of a typical Christian assembly.

History of the Community

Although we are without certain knowledge of the city within which the addressees resided, the author of Hebrews reveals several important aspects of the community's history, from which we may gather a solid picture of the formative influences on their identity and their situation. The author speaks of their conversion, the elements of their socialization into the new group, and a particular period of heightened tension between the converts and their neighbors. The rhetorical effects of reminding the hearers of these past events will be treated in the commentary below. For now, these passages will provide us with a window into the life and history of the addressees.

Hebrews 2:1-4 speaks of the conversion of the audience, or at least the core of that congregation, in response to the proclamation of the gospel by the witnesses of Jesus.[21] The author recalls that "God added his testimony by signs

---

20. It is frequently assumed that the author compares Jesus with respected figures celebrated in the Jewish Scriptures (angels, Moses, the levitical high priests) out of a polemical agenda. Stedman (*Hebrews*, 11), for example, misunderstands the function of these comparisons, leading him to posit a Jewish-Christian audience contemplating a return to Jewish traditions. As this commentary will demonstrate, these comparisons are not arguments against returning to Jewish practices (which, indeed, Jewish Christians need never have left behind), but rather serve to set up the exhortations, which are usually warnings based on a lesser to greater argument (common to both Jewish and Greek rhetoric). Christ is shown to be greater than the angels and Moses in order to set up the proof that undergirds the author's warnings against breaking faith with God: if the message spoken through the angels (2:1-4) and Moses (10:26-31) was valid and transgressors were duly punished, transgressions of the Word that came through Jesus must carry a proportionately stiffer penalty since Christ is more honorable than both angels and Moses. Careful attention to the author's development of his arguments is required before too much can be read into a comparison.

21. The author's inclusion of himself among those who came to faith through the preaching of the witnesses argues strongly against the attribution of this text to Paul, who vociferously stresses his conversion through a direct revelation and not through human agency (Gal. 1:11-17; 1 Cor. 15:3-10).

and wonders and various miracles, and by gifts of the Holy Spirit, distributed according to his will" (Heb. 2:4). This brief account is strikingly similar to Paul's reminiscences about the founding of the churches in Galatia and Corinth (Gal. 3:2-5; 1 Cor. 2:1-5), where again ecstatic or miraculous phenomena are emphasized as God's confirmation of the validity of the message. These times of community formation were highly charged with awareness of divine presence and power, an awareness that reinforced commitment to the Christian message as "divine word," God speaking "in a Son" (Heb. 1:1). The congregation should still have a memory, at least, of this time of firsthand experience of the "truth of the gospel." The author's reminders of the initiatory experiences may themselves provide the strongest legitimation for his challenge, as it did for Paul in Galatians (3:1-5).

Hebrews provides further evidence to suggest that the old dictum that sects, in general, "are connected with the lower class"[22] and that Christianity, in particular, recruited "mainly from the labouring and burdened, the members of the lowest strata of the people" and consisted of "slaves and emancipated slaves, of poor people deprived of all rights" is incorrect or at least overdrawn.[23] Linguistically, Hebrews is composed in very stylish and difficult Greek. The author uses extensive vocabulary (including more *hapax legomena* than any other NT author) and writes in a somewhat Atticizing style, with a syntax more independent of word order than that of other NT authors. This alone suggests an audience capable of attending meaningfully to such language and syntax, unless the author was simply a bad preacher who spoke over the heads of his congregation. The letter tells us also that a number of the community members possessed property worth confiscating, and we know from Tacitus and other historians that local or imperial authorities tended to seek out the well-propertied with poor social networks for confiscation. The community members are capable of charitable activity and hospitality (13:2; 10:33b-34a; 13:16: this is one of Gerd Theissen's criteria for higher social status) and even appear

---

22. Ernst Troeltsch, *The Social Teaching of the Christian Churches* (2 vols.; London: George Allen, 1931), 1:331.

23. Karl Marx and F. Engels, *On Religion*, ed. Reinhold Niebuhr (Atlanta: Scholars Press, 1964), 334, 316. Extensive critiques to this earlier view, as well as careful reconstructions of the social level of Christians in the Corinthian churches, can be found in Wayne A. Meeks, *The First Urban Christians: The Social World of the Apostle Paul* (New Haven: Yale University Press, 1983), and Gerd Theissen, *The Social Setting of Pauline Christianity: Essays on Corinth* (Philadelphia: Fortress, 1982). The state of the question is helpfully reviewed in Bengt Holmberg, *Sociology and the New Testament: An Appraisal* (Minneapolis: Fortress, 1990). Meeks (*First Urban Christians,* 53-72) and Theissen (*Social Setting,* 70-96) develop criteria for the evaluation of social status and apply these criteria to the Corinthian congregation, showing that half of the persons named in the letter come most probably from a higher social level.

to need warnings against overambition, with regard to both possessions (13:5) and status (13:14). The possibility of recovering wealth and prestige in the non-Christian society, which appears to be the principal motivation to hide or sever one's attachment to the Christian group, tells us that at least some of the recipients come from the "propertied" classes; not all came to Christianity as the "labouring and burdened." In all probability, the community was composed of people from a wide range of social strata, as in the congregations about which more is known (e.g., Rome, Corinth, or Thessalonica).[24]

The author refers also to the process by which the converts were socialized into the new group, or forged into a new community, the basic elements of the curriculum being given in 5:11–6:3. They were taught "the basic elements of the oracles of God" (5:12), namely, the Jewish Scriptures,[25] and "the basic teaching about Christ" (6:1), which would naturally involve an exposition of the Scriptures (particularly based on LXX versions) through the lens of the work of Christ. The author refers to a "foundation" of "repentance from dead works and faith toward God, instruction about baptisms, laying on of hands, resurrection of the dead, and eternal judgment" (6:1b-2). The converts thus appear to have been exposed to a rather comprehensive process of socialization. They were inculcated thoroughly into the Christian movement's construction of reality, as seen especially in the temporal dimension of apocalyptic eschatology (resurrection of the dead, eternal judgment, the age to come). While he uses Platonic vocabulary, the author mainly relies on the temporal dualism of apocalypticism (the distinction between the present age and the age to come) in shaping the response he calls for from the addressees, counting heavily on their acceptance of this worldview.

The converts also participated in a number of ritual acts that marked their entry into the new community, the value of which for their self-understanding should not be overlooked. The author refers to "baptisms" in the plural. It remains possible that "baptisms" here includes forms of "ablutions," purificatory rituals that persisted in the early Church from its Jewish heritage (but that are not elsewhere attested in the NT). It remains probable, however, that the hearers would recall their own baptism, which was the initiatory rite into the Christian movement.[26] What did that rite mean for the initiates? John's baptism as well as baptism in Acts (cf. Acts 2:38) is related to the

---

24. Holmberg, *Sociology,* 75; cf. Pliny (*Ep.* 10.96), who attests that the Christians came from "every social order."

25. Compare Rom. 3:2, which also speaks of the Scriptures as "the oracles of God" with which the Jewish people were entrusted.

26. The author of Hebrews speaks of partaking of the Holy Spirit in close proximity to the mention of baptisms and laying on of hands, which raises the possibility that the double baptisms featured prominently elsewhere in the epistles and in Acts, namely, water baptism and the baptism of the Holy Spirit, were part of the community's initiatory experiences.

forgiveness of sins; so also in Hebrews it is at least a sign of the washing away of past sins (10:22).

The rite of baptism was calculated to have an even more profound impact on the consciousness of those entering the waters. Paul's interpretation of the significance of baptism demonstrates that the ritual can effect a powerful change particularly in self-perception. Paul develops the significance of baptism through the language of dying and rising with Christ (Rom. 6:3-12), and it is probably with reference to this identification with the crucified Christ in baptism that he says "It is no longer I who live, but it is Christ who lives in me" (Gal. 2:20, NRSV). As Mary Douglas explains, the ritual provides a way for the initiates to "die to their old life" and be "reborn to the new."[27] Mircea Eliade expresses this in rather poetic phrases: "In water, everything is 'dissolved,' every 'form' is broken up, everything that has happened ceases to exist; nothing that was before remains after immersion in water. . . . Breaking up all forms, doing away with the past, water possesses this power of purifying, of regenerating, of giving new birth."[28]

Victor Turner's analysis of the "ritual process" provides a helpful cross-cultural perspective.[29] In his model of how rituals work (particularly status-transformation, status-reversal, or status-elevation rituals), the status and identity that a person had before the ritual began is broken down and abolished. He or she is now "marginal" or "liminal" with regard to society, not fitting into any of that society's lines of classification. During the ritual, a new status and identity is formed (sometimes in the context of a strong, common bond with other initiates), and the person is reintegrated into society at the completion of the ritual with this new status or identity (as well as the sense of camaraderie with the fellow initiates). Rites of passage from childhood to adulthood, or from common status to chieftain, fit this model very neatly.

Baptism also functions as a rite of passage separating initiates from their past life and associations — symbolically enacting their death and rebirth to a

---

27. Mary Douglas, *Purity and Danger: An Analysis of Concepts of Pollution and Taboo* (London: Routledge and Kegan Paul, 1966), 96. The author of Hebrews does not himself bring out this aspect of the significance of baptism, and there is some danger in introducing Pauline concepts at this point. We are not, however, here investigating the significance of baptism for the author, but rather for those converted by the witnesses (2:3) and subsequently. It appears likely from a number of data that the congregation was founded as part of the Pauline mission (the similarity of the description of its founding with the description of the founding of the Galatian and Corinthian churches and the indications that the author belongs to a Pauline circle together with Timothy, a close associate of Paul), and thus the addressees' understanding of the significance of their baptism need not be limited to what the author of Hebrews specifically includes.

28. Cited in Douglas, *Purity,* 161.

29. Victor Turner, *The Ritual Process* (Ithaca, NY: Cornell University Press, 1969), 94-165.

new life and set of associations. It possesses a quality of mortification, as the baptized are purified of that part of their past that they no longer wish to own. It enacts symbolically the renunciation of former allegiances, affiliations, and relations.[30] Whatever status or identity initiates had before the rite, the waters of baptism washed it away (cf. 1 Cor. 6:11). As they emerged from the waters, they were joined to a new community, the "sanctified," who are "washed with pure water" (Heb. 10:22). The main difference from Turner's model, however, is that this reintegration leaves them marginal or liminal with regard to the larger society. Their new identity and status is status within the sect, not a new status recognized by the society. The early Christian movement compels the converts "to inhabit the fringes and interstices of the social structure . . . and to keep them in a permanent liminal state, where . . . the optimal conditions inhere for the realization of communitas."[31] This is especially significant for the book of Hebrews, which develops at great length the theme of a pilgrimage faith and emphasizes the "passage quality of religious life,"[32] and so reveals as a major concern acceptance of the tensions surrounding and resisting "liminality" with regard to the larger social body as a "permanent condition."

Not only were the converts "ground down to a uniform condition to be fashioned anew" in water baptism, however, but they were also "endowed with additional powers to enable them to cope with their new station in life,"[33] namely, baptism in the Holy Spirit (2:4; 6:4). This new access to the power of God and experience of the "gifts of the Spirit" (2:4) served as a reminder that something significant had changed in the converts' lives. This immediate presence of the divine provided for a different experience of the world as far as the converts were concerned, such that the world could no longer be seen as objectively identical to what it was for the converts before initiation.[34]

The addressees, therefore, had undergone a rigorous process of socialization into the worldview of the sect and had experienced ritual and ecstatic markers of transition from their old identity and status to their new identity as the sanctified "people of God." Their rejection of their former values and associations, however, provoked significant counterreactions from their non-Christian neighbors. The community's confession brought them into a time of conflict with the larger society. While this did not lead to the deaths of the believers (12:4), they still "endured a severe contest of sufferings" (10:32). Some

---

30. R. M. Kanter, *Commitment and Community: Communes and Utopias in Sociological Perspective* (Cambridge: Harvard University Press, 1972), 73.

31. Turner, *Ritual Process,* 145.

32. Ibid., 107.

33. Ibid., 95.

34. M. J. Neitz, *Charisma and Community* (New Brunswick, NJ: Transaction Books, 1987), 153.

of the congregation were subject to reproach, and their trials were made a public spectacle. Others demonstrated solidarity with those who were so treated (10:33), even with those in prison (10:34). Some also suffered the seizure of their property, as a result either of an official decree or of looting and pillaging while the owners were in prison, exiled, or otherwise occupied (10:34).

What would motivate neighbors to respond in such negative ways to the Christians' newfound religious commitments? Those Gentiles who committed themselves to Christianity inherited Judaism's restrictions on participation in the Greco-Roman world. On account of their exclusive devotion to the One God and the accompanying refusal to acknowledge any other deity, most Christians avoided any setting in which they would be exposed to idolatrous ceremonies (see the stress laid on this abstinence in 1 Cor. 10:14-22; 2 Cor. 6:14–7:1; 1 Thess. 1:9). Since some form of religious worship comprised a part of almost every political, business, and social enterprise in the Greco-Roman world,[35] Christians adopted a lifestyle that, in the eyes of their pagan neighbors, would have been considered antisocial and even subversive. Loyalty to the gods, expressed in pious attendance at sacrifices and the like, was viewed as a symbol for loyalty to the state, authorities, friends, and family. Worship of the deities was something of a symbol for one's dedication to the relationships that kept society stable and prosperous. By abstaining from the former, Christians (like the Jews) were regarded with suspicion as potential violators of the laws and subversive elements within the empire. Those who did not acknowledge the claim of the gods on their lives and service could not be counted on to honor the claims of state, law, family, and the traditional values of the society. Christians were subjected to prejudice, rumor, insult, and slander and were even made the targets of pogroms and local legal actions. It was thus both dishonoring and dangerous to be associated with the name of "Christian."

Gentile Christians would be subject to the "discipline" of their Greco-Roman neighbors on account of their flagrant violation of the values of piety, gratitude, and civic unity; Jewish Christians would come under pressure from their non-Christian Jewish family and associates. The goal of all non-Christians was the same — to correct the dangerous and vicious errors of their former colleagues by any means necessary.[36] Indeed, it was essential to the commitment of

---

35. The pervasiveness of cultic activity throughout all aspects of life in Greco-Roman society has been demonstrated in such works as Ramsay MacMullen, *Paganism in the Roman Empire* (New Haven: Yale University Press, 1981), 38-39, 47.

36. 1 Thess. 2:13-16 provides an interesting correlation of pressures endured by Jewish and Gentile Christians from both the Roman citizens of Thessalonica and the Jewish residents of Judea. For more detailed analysis of the dishonorable stigma attached to the label "Christian" in the first-century Greco-Roman world, see D. A. deSilva, *Despising Shame: Honor Discourse and Community Maintenance in the Epistle to the Hebrews* (SBLDS 152; Atlanta: Scholars Press, 1995), 146-54.

the non-Christians to their own ideologies to undermine the critique of their worldview implicit in the conversion of their neighbors and explicit in the proclamation of the gospel. Their own sense of being "right" with God or the gods was at stake in the defection of their peers to this new sect. The recipients of Hebrews certainly felt the full force of this discipline. In the one experience of the community most fully described by the author, we find that these Christians have suffered significant loss of status and dignity as a result of their confession. This passage is all the more significant given the author's reticence in providing details about the community's history:

> But remember the former days in which, having been enlightened, you endured a hard contest with sufferings, in part being publicly exposed to reproaches and afflictions, in part having become partners of those being thus treated. For you both showed sympathy to the imprisoned and accepted the seizure of your property with joy, knowing that you possessed better and lasting possessions. (10:32-34)[37]

We cannot know how long ago the events of the "former days" transpired. All that we can say is that this period of public rejection, humiliation, and dispossession belongs to the community's past, and that the author perceives that the community must recover the same dedication and endurance that they displayed then but lack now. This description, moreover, shows that what was chiefly at stake was the honor of those who identified themselves with the Christian community in the eyes of their neighbors. These believers became the target of society's deviancy-control techniques, most notably shaming, which aimed at coercing the believers to return to a lifestyle that demonstrated their allegiance to the society's values and commitments.

The experience is described in terms of a public show: some portion of the Christian community was subjected to open reviling, being held up to ridicule and shame.[38] The term used to describe the experience evokes the image of the theater (arena), where games, contests, and public punishments occurred.[39]

---

37. All translations of passages from Hebrews are my own, unless otherwise indicated.

38. Commentators have consistently recognized this aspect of the addressees' experience (cf. Attridge, *Hebrews*, 299; Ceslaus Spicq, *L'Épître aux Hébreux* [Paris: Gabalda, 1952], 2:329).

39. Compare G. Kittel, "θεάομαι," *TDNT* 3:43: "The θέατρον is by human standards, not a proud [spectacle], but a sorry and contemptible [one]." Philo (*Flacc.* 74-75, 84-85, 95) recounts a vivid example of the public nature of punishment in his narration of the brutal actions taken against the Jewish inhabitants of Alexandria. Flogging and crucifixion of Jews formed a spectacle and show (ἡ θέα, τὰ πρῶτα τῶν θεαμάτων). Similarly, the record of Nero's execution of Christians in Tacitus's *Annals* 15.44 shows that derision was as crucial an element as pain in dealing with that marginal group. The recipients of Hebrews, of course, had not yet experienced such excesses (12:4).

The public imposition of disgrace constituted a device of social control by which the society sought to dissuade the afflicted from continuing in, and others from joining, the Christian counterculture. The Christians were subjected to "reproach" and "affliction" (τοῦτο μὲν ὀνειδισμοῖς τε καὶ θλίψεσιν). The first term suggests verbal assaults on honor and character, an experience shared by many early Christian communities.[40] Shaming and reviling were society's way of neutralizing the threat Christians posed to their view of the world and constellation of values and allegiances. The burning experience of humiliation and rejection was geared toward "shaming" the deviants into returning to their former convictions and obligations as members of the dominant culture.[41]

The society reinforced verbal "correction" with physical abuse, which not only involved the inflicting of physical pain but also underscored the degradation of the victim. Cultural anthropologists and their students have noted the close connection between a person's honor and the treatment of that person's body.[42] That such was the case in the first-century Mediterranean world is demonstrated, for example, in the way Philo of Alexandria speaks of the physical punishment suffered there by the Jews as a "disgrace" or "insult." ὕβρις, usually translated "outrage" or "insult," is used also to refer to "assault and battery." Exposed to verbal and physical attacks on their honor, the recipients of Hebrews had been subjected to what has been called a "status-degradation ritual,"[43] by which a society neutralizes the threat posed by deviants to the absolute and ultimate character of that society's values and social arrangements.

A noteworthy aspect of this experience was the solidarity shown by those who had escaped being singled out for this public punishment with those who were subjected to public humiliation. They voluntarily became "partners with those thus treated," that is, partners with the disgraced. This manifested itself in the care shown by the community to those members who were imprisoned. Prisoners in the Greco-Roman world relied on family and friends from the outside to provide even the most basic of needs (food, clothing, medicine). Lucian of Samosata, a second-century-A.D. writer of satirical prose, provides a moving (if somewhat mocking) description of the resources a Christian group would mobilize for one of its own (*On the Death of Peregrinus* 12-13). The community

---

40. Compare 1 Pet. 4:14-16 and Matt. 5:11.

41. John Chrysostom, commenting on 10:32, notes the power of such disapproval and grants of dishonor to affect judgment: "Reproach is a great thing, and calculated to pervert the soul, and to darken the judgement. . . . Since the human race is exceeding vainglorious, therefore it is easily overcome by this" (NPNF1[1] 14:461; *PG* 63:149).

42. Julian Pitt-Rivers, "Honour and Social Status," in *Honour and Shame: The Values of Mediterranean Society,* ed. J. G. Peristiany (London: Weidenfeld and Nicolson, 1965), 25.

43. Bruce Malina and Jerome Neyrey, "Conflict in Luke-Acts: Labelling and Deviance Theory," in *The Social World of Luke-Acts,* ed. J. H. Neyrey (Peabody, MA: Hendrickson, 1991), 107.

brought food and changes of clothing for their imprisoned brother, bribed the officers for special treatment, and kept the prisoner company, cheering him day and night. What Lucian describes in fiction can be seen in truth from Ignatius of Antioch's journey to execution at Rome. The apostle Paul, who was frequently in prison, similarly received gifts and encouragement from his communities.[44] Rather than be concerned for what the unbelieving society would think of those who identified with such criminal deviants, the believers consistently supported and maintained their bonds with their sisters and brothers who were in prison or who were suffering society's other "correctional" procedures.[45]

A final component of the addressees' experience alluded to by our author is the confiscation of the believers' property. The Greek term refers most often to plundering, the looting to which abandoned properties often fell victim.[46] Even an officially sanctioned act, however, could be regarded as "plundering" by those suffering the loss.[47] It is also difficult to assess from this passing reference what sort of property was taken. A court or local official might have ordered the seizure of land and house, or simply the imposition of a fine; unofficial plundering (while the believers were involved in trials or imprisonments) would involve the loss of movable property, but might nevertheless represent a substantial loss of wealth. "Plundering" could also indicate driving people from their homes in the context of a riot or pogrom.[48]

Whether the loss of property was occasioned by official or unofficial seizure, the loss of material wealth translates into a loss of honor and status. Inhabitants of the ancient world did not accumulate wealth and possessions for the sake of ownership or pleasure, but bartered material wealth for prestige and honor either through display at private banquets or through benefaction. When one lost material goods, one also lost the raw materials for building pres-

---

44. This was the mission, for example, of Epaphroditus (Phil. 2:25).

45. The imprisoned were aware of the sacrifice made on their behalf, as both "Paul" (2 Tim. 1:16) and Ignatius (*Smyrn.* 10) are aware that their visitors had to set aside the disgrace attached to the prisoners' bonds and risked further injuring their own reputation by associating with prisoners. Such association could even lead to the sympathizers falling prey to the same treatment, as it did for many Jews in the Alexandrian riots recounted by Philo (*Flacc.* 72).

46. Compare Lucian *Peregr.* 14; Josephus *J.W.* 4.168; Philo *Flacc.* 5.53-57.

47. Melito of Sardis, in his "Petition to the Emperor Marcus Aurelius" (cited in Eusebius, *Hist. eccl.* 4.26.5), bears witness to a sort of open policy for the pillaging of those denounced as Christians: "Religious people as a body are being harried and persecuted by new edicts all over Asia. Shameless informers out to fill their own pockets are taking advantage of the decrees to pillage openly, plundering inoffensive citizens night and day."

48. Compare 2 Esdr. 16:70-73, which includes such dispossession as part of the persecution of the righteous: "There shall be a great insurrection against those who fear the Lord . . . plundering and destroying those who continue to fear the Lord. For they shall destroy and plunder their goods, and drive them out of their houses."

tige. Jerome Neyrey has argued that such considerations applied not only to the wealthy landowner but even to the peasant in a village.[49] Such loss would further provoke contempt from others if the victim had brought the loss on himself or herself.[50] This would have been the case for the Christians in Heb. 10:32-34: through their own neglect of their obligations to society, state, and gods, they had justly earned their misfortune.

This loss of property could also have put the believers in an uncomfortable economic position. The Alexandrian Jews (Philo *Flacc.* 57) lost their houses and workshops in the course of the pogroms against them, with the result that they were at once impoverished but also removed from access to the very tools of their trade and their shops by which they could regain economic stability. The recipients of Hebrews may have suffered similar losses, and they have found themselves in a lower economic status with no means of recovery as long as they remained associated with a suspect group. As part of a disgraced "subversive" culture, they could not expect to regain the security of wealth through partnerships with non-Christian partners or benefactors.

In summary, the former experience of the community to which the author calls attention was one of humiliation, rejection, and marginalization. The Christians lost their place and standing in the society, stripped of their reputation for being reliable citizens on account of their commitment to an alternate system of values, religious practices, and social relationships. While the society intended this experience to draw the deviants back into line with the dominant culture, the believers remained steadfast in their loyalty toward God and the group, not allowing society's means of social control to deflect them from their faith. They sustained one another through mutual assistance and caring ("love and good works," 6:9-10), resisting society's attempts to discourage them in their new hope.

The Occasion of Hebrews

If the community was able to meet so great a challenge as described in 10:32-34, what could have befallen them to occasion the composition of the letter "To the Hebrews"? At the time of writing, the character of the community has changed. Some of them, at least, are in danger of "drifting away" (2:1) from the message that they received, of "neglecting" the message spoken by Jesus and attested by God (2:3), of "failing to attain" the promised rest (4:1), of falling through unbelief

---

49. J. Neyrey, "Poverty and Loss of Honor in Matthew's Beatitudes: Poverty as Cultural, Not Merely Economic, Phenomenon" (an unpublished paper delivered at the CBA Seminar in October 1992), 4.

50. Ibid., 7.

in the same way as the wilderness generation (4:12), of growing weary and losing heart (12:3). Even more strongly, they are in danger of falling into worse punishment than the transgressors of the Mosaic Law through "trampling underfoot the Son of God, regarding as profane the blood by which you are sanctified, and affronting the Spirit of grace" (10:29). Some have apparently begun to withdraw from the congregation (10:25), many have not lived up to what was expected from mature believers (5:12), and there appears to be a general faltering in commitment (see, e.g., 10:35-36, "Do not cast away your confidence," and 12:12, "Strengthen the weak knees and lift up the drooping hands").

What brought about this change? The letter is not explicit about this point, and scholars have engaged in varying degrees of mirror reading of the evidence in the letter to produce scenarios of varying degrees of plausibility. Some readers argue that the reference in 12:4, "you have not yet resisted to the point of blood," contains a shadowy implication of growing hostility against the believers and a coming persecution that the believers wish to avoid.[51] Others hold that the author's reliance on argumentation from the Hebrew Scriptures and his comparison of Jesus and the angels (who, in Jewish tradition, served as God's intermediaries when the Law was given to Israel), Moses, and the Jewish priesthood indicate that a strategic conversion or reversion to Judaism (which enjoyed a measure of toleration within the empire that Christianity did not) was a lively possibility.[52] Both of these theories, however, are equally intelligible as rhetorical strategies of the author rather than as indications of the nature of the occasion of Hebrews. Other scholars present a less dramatic picture, arguing that "moral lethargy" is the dominant problem that lies behind the epistle.[53] Some scholars prefer to allow a number of factors to stand side by side, understanding the author to respond here to one concern and there to another: "from the response that he gives to the problem, it would appear that the author conceives of the threat to the community in two broad but interrelated

---

51. Graham Hughes, *Hebrews and Hermeneutics: The Epistle to the Hebrews as a New Testament Example of Biblical Interpretation* (Cambridge: Cambridge University Press, 1979), 28.

52. William L. Lane, *Hebrews: A Call to Commitment* (Peabody, MA: Hendrickson, 1985), 22-25; Gleason, "Old Testament Background," 68-69. Ernst Käsemann (*The Wandering People of God: An Investigation of the Letter to the Hebrews* [Minneapolis: Augsburg, 1984], 24-25) strongly argued against perpetuating the old assumption that some Judaizing tendency or temptation to revert to Judaism was the presenting problem of Hebrews.

53. T. Schmidt, "Moral Lethargy and the Epistle to the Hebrews," *WTJ* 54 (1992): 167. A similar emphasis appears in W. G. McCown, *Ο ΛΟΓΟΣ ΤΗΣ ΠΑΡΑΚΛΗΣΕΩΣ: The Nature and Function of the Hortatory Sections in the Epistle to the Hebrews* (Ph.D. dissertation, Union Theological Seminary, 1970), 261. Alternative scenarios abound. Jewett (*Letter to Pilgrims*, 10-13) favors the situation of danger from heretical teachings. Buchanan (*Hebrews*, 256) creatively suggests an audience of pilgrims who arrived too late in Jerusalem to witness the ministry of Jesus but who are nevertheless urged to hold onto their Zionist hopes.

categories, external pressure or 'persecution' . . . and a waning commitment to the community's confessed faith."[54]

Of all these suggestions, that of Harold Attridge appears to be closest to the target. Viewing Hebrews against the cultural background of a society that takes as its pivotal values honor and shame leads to a new insight into both the nature of the "external pressure" and the cause of the "waning commitment" to Christian confession and involvement. Such an approach leads beyond the stereotyped picture of Christians being rounded up for execution in the arena, or denying Christ before the emperor's tribunal in order to save their lives, to a more highly nuanced sense of the pressures faced by early Christians in maintaining their confession and commitments to one another, and of the ways in which they might have succumbed to those pressures.

The author describes the addressees as if some are in danger of "failing to enter" the rest set before them (4:1-2), or of "selling their birthright for a single meal" as did Esau (12:16-17). The examples chosen and shaped by the author are particularly telling. The audience stands on the threshold of the promise (now an "unshakable kingdom" rather than the land of Canaan) as did the wilderness generation, but their lack of trust and obedience (particularly in the face of the hostility of human beings) threatens to rob them as well of their prize. Abraham, Moses, and Jesus (11:8-22, 24-26; 12:2) embraced marginalization and loss with regard to status and wealth in society for the sake of the prize of faith. After living a liminal existence for decades, Abraham never went back to the city where he once had status but kept his eyes on the heavenly city that God had prepared (11:13-16). Moses thought the loss of a throne and the endurance of reproach and maltreatment insignificant compared to the reward of God (11:26). Finally, the community's successful resistance to earlier attempts at social control becomes their own best example for their present situation. It is this earlier "assurance" or "boldness," which enabled them to endure loss of status and honor in society's eyes, that is now at stake and must be recovered.

The situation thus presented appears to be a crisis not of impending persecution, nor of heretical subversion, but rather of commitment occasioned as a result of the difficulties of remaining long without honor in the world. The danger of falling away stems from the lingering effects of the believers' loss of status and esteem in their neighbors' eyes, and their inability to regain a place in society, or approval from the outside world, by any means that would allow them to remain rigidly faithful to Jesus and the One God. The believers have experienced the loss of property and status in the host society without yet receiving the promised rewards of the sect, and so are growing disillusioned with the sect's promise to provide. As time passes without improvement, they begin to feel the inward pressure for their society's affirmation and approval. The fervor

---

54. Attridge, *Hebrews*, 13.

and certainty of their earlier life as a community (the effervescence of the ecstatic and charismatic experiences described in 2:3-4 and 6:4-5) have cooled
with their prolonged exposure to their neighbors, the witnesses of their degradation, who no doubt continued to disparage the believers and to regard them
as subversive and shameful.[55] They have begun to be concerned again for their
reputation before society. Though they were able to resist it at the outset, the
machinery of social control is in the long run wearing down the deviants' resistance. While they could accept their loss in the fervor of religious solidarity, living with their loss has proven difficult.

The author writes as if apostasy is a lively option for the addressees: "How
can we escape if we neglect so great a salvation?" (2:3, NRSV); "Take care,
brothers and sisters, that none of you may have an evil, unbelieving heart that
turns away (ἀποστῆναι) from the living God!" (3:12, NRSV); "For it is impossible to restore those who . . . have fallen away" (6:4-6, NRSV); "How much worse
punishment . . . will be deserved by those who have trampled upon the Son of
God, regarded as profane the blood of the covenant, . . . and outraged the Spirit
of grace?" (10:29). Neither the threat of violent persecution nor a new attrac-
tion to Judaism motivates this apostasy, but rather the more pedestrian inability to live within the lower status that Christian associations had forced upon
them, the less-than-dramatic (yet potent) desire once more to enjoy the goods
and esteem of their society. The price was now more on their minds than the
prize. In the eyes of society, and perhaps increasingly in the eyes of some believers, renouncing the "confession" that had first alienated them from the dominant culture might be a step toward "recovery."

The author encounters his audience at this point of wavering and challenges them with the claim that the real loss is not the deprivation of their place
in society but the forfeiture of their inheritance from God. They risk losing the
lasting honor that God grants them if they "shrink back" under pressure from
society:

> Do not throw away your confidence, which has a great reward. For you have
> need of endurance in order that, having done the will of God, you may re-
> ceive the promise. For yet "but a little while" and "the one who is coming will
> come and not delay; and my righteous one will live by faith, and if he or she
> shrinks back, my soul has no pleasure in that one." But we are not character-
> ized by shrinking back unto destruction but by faith unto the attainment of
> life. (10:35-39)

---

55. Aristotle (*Rh.* 2.6.27) indicates that people "are more likely to be ashamed when
they have to be seen and to associate openly with those who are aware of their disgrace." That
inhabitants of the Mediterranean world (as any society) were not above taunting their
undesirables is shown from such complaints as LXX Ps. 108:25: "I am an object of scorn to
my accusers; when they see me, they wag their heads."

The endurance of disgrace in the eyes of society has earned for the believers honor before God. Their commitment to Christ, their benefactor, through times of heavy social pressure will not go unrewarded. He urges them to understand their experience of marginalization as their obedience to God's will. They must continue in their "confidence" if they are to claim the promised "greater and lasting possessions" (10:34) and "glory" (2:10). Παρρησία, usually translated as "confidence," carries more the sense of boldness, candor, and openness. In this period, it often appears as the antonym for αἰσχύνη, or shame.[56] A refusal to feel "shame" before society, and a firm grasp on the certainty of God's promises, will lead the believers to attain greater honor than they could ever enjoy at society's hands.

Date and Location

The discussion of the date of the writing of Hebrews and the location of author and addressees must remain inconclusive due to the lack of internal evidence from the text. The use of Hebrews by Clement of Rome places the latest possible date of composition before 96 A.D.[57] I concur with those scholars who favor a date before 70 A.D. Even though the author is primarily concerned with the archaic cult of the tabernacle rather than the temple in Jerusalem, he asks the rhetorical question, "Would they [the sacrifices prescribed by Leviticus] not have ceased to be offered?" (10:2). After 70, they did cease to be offered, although for a different reason than the decisive removal of sins! Scholars in favor of a pre-70 date also point to the fact that there is no mention of the destruction of the temple, which might have played very well into the author's hands.[58] While arguments from silence (what the text does *not* say) are always tenuous, I would disagree with those who claim that the author would not allude to the temple's destruction out of sensitivity for his (Jewish) hearers. He is so unsparing in his critique of the inefficacy of the levitical cultus and in his affirmation

---

56. In both 1 John 2:28 and *1 Enoch* 97:1, 6; 98:10, these words are placed within the context of standing before the divine Judge at the parousia or the last day. The reward of those who have remained in Christ (or who have continued steadfast in the Law) is "confidence" or "open freedom" before God or Christ, which is contrasted to the shame of the wicked, who are unable to exercise any boldness or openness due to their disgrace before God.

57. P. Ellingworth, "Hebrews and 1 Clement: Literary Dependence or Common Tradition," *BZ* 23 (1979): 262-69; Donald Hagner, *The Use of the Old and New Testaments in Clement of Rome* (Leiden: Brill, 1973), 179-95; against G. Theissen, *Untersuchungen zum Hebräerbrief* (SNT 2; Gütersloh: Mohn, 1969), 34-41.

58. Ellingworth, *Hebrews,* 32; Ben Witherington III, "The Influence of Galatians on Hebrews," *NTS* 37 (1991): 151.

of the obsolescence of Torah that it is hard to see how he could have made his sermon any more offensive by adding the destruction of the "copy" and "shadow" to his generally unappreciative assessment of the OT cult! While neither the case for nor the objections to a pre-70 date are decisive, Hebrews reads more naturally in a pre-70 setting.[59]

We have already noted that locating the author and audience geographically is even more problematic. The only internal evidence comes from the greeting sent by "those from Italy" (13:24), taken by some scholars to be an indication that the author is sending greetings back to Rome from those now separated from their sisters and brothers.[60] It is equally possible that the author is sending greetings from his Italian compatriots while writing to a church located outside of Italy.[61] Some connection with Rome is favored by the early use of the letter there by Clement, but the correlations between Hebrews and 1 Peter (written from Rome to churches throughout Asia Minor) do not advance, as Harold Attridge suggests, the case that Hebrews was written to Rome.[62] Strangely, none of the added subscriptions claims that the letter was written to Christians at Rome, but they frequently claim that it was sent from Rome or Italy to some other destination.[63] A destination in Palestine is often advanced on the assumptions that the addressees must be a house church exclusively of Jewish Christians, which would tend to be found mainly in Palestine, and that the author writes as if the audience has firsthand knowledge of (and attachment to) the temple cult. The author's purely textual interaction with the cult (i.e., his reliance entirely on LXX descriptions of the tabernacle and its rites) renders the

---

59. A more thorough review of this insoluble question may be found in Spicq, *L'Épître aux Hébreux*, 1:253-61; see also Attridge (*Hebrews*, 6-9), who very judiciously refuses to narrow the range of composition down from 60-100 A.D. Lane (*Hebrews 1–8*, lxii-lxvi), building on the hypothesis of a Roman destination rather than Roman origin for the sermon, narrows down the range to some time between 49 A.D. (when the Edict of Claudius would have led to the expulsion of Jewish Christians, as of all Jews, with their consequent loss of property) and 64 A.D. (when Christians were certainly subject to "resisting to the point of blood," Heb. 12:4). Attractive as Lane's hypothesis is, the sheer multiplication of probabilities and possibilities makes the whole merely that — an attractive hypothesis.

60. Thus Lane, *Hebrews 1–8*, lviii; Pfitzner, *Hebrews*, 30.

61. Attridge (*Hebrews*, 410 n. 79) provides an impressive list of places where the expression is used idiomatically to indicate place of origin (rather than to indicate separation from their home).

62. Attridge, *Hebrews*, 10. The situation addressed by 1 Peter is not the situation of Roman Christianity, but rather the situation of Christians in several provinces in what is now Turkey. If the situation addressed by Hebrews is similar to that addressed by 1 Peter, and I agree that it is strikingly similar, it would be more likely that a Christian teacher in Rome is writing to a church somewhere in a province for which he feels a special pastoral responsibility.

63. Thus manuscripts A, P, 1739, 1881, 81 (but to Jerusalem!), 104, and 0285.

latter "indication" irrelevant, and we have already explored how the former assumption is unwarranted. Some connection with Roman Christianity remains likely, but quite possibly on the part of the author rather than the recipients. Even the early use by Clement, however, is not conclusive for such a connection given the mobility of early Christians, who could copy and share such poignant and helpful texts as Hebrews with sister churches around the Mediterranean.[64]

While it does seem likely that the author addresses a particular Christian community whose circumstances are personally known to him,[65] and whom he plans to visit in person as soon as he can, attempts to limit this audience further to a particular house church among several or to a small group of teachers are unwarranted. Andrew Trotter, reading Hebrews 5:11-14, finds it "hard to believe that the author would address an entire community as those who ought to be teachers; by definition the office of teacher necessitates a much larger group to be taught."[66] This is a particularly insecure passage from which to reconstruct the condition or situation of the hearers since it constitutes an appeal to an emotion (see commentary). More troublesome, however, is the assumption by Trotter that the author refers to an "office" rather than the role of teacher. Hebrews calls the hearers to be mature in their commitment to the Christian group — not acting as children who need to be led but as adults who take responsibility for one another.

The author seeks to nurture a community where each member reinforces the commitment of the other members, "watching out" for those whose grasp on the Christian hope begins to slip (3:12-14; 12:15), "encouraging" one's fellow members to prepare for "the approaching Day" (10:24-25). Members of minority cultures need to offset the messages received from outside the group with reminders that the sect knows the "true" way to please God. Thus, the author's address becomes less "hard to believe." It is necessary for all members of the sect to continue to "teach" one another through reminder, exhortation, and censure, and thus to form a strong "plausibility structure"[67] in a society unsupportive of the Christian enterprise. Hebrews 5:11-14 thus belongs to the author's socio-religious strategy. It does not provide evidence that the author

---

64. For more detailed discussion of the arguments for and against various destinations, the interested reader may consult Spicq, *L'Épître aux Hébreux*, 1:261-65; Bruce, *Hebrews*, 10-14; Attridge, *Hebrews*, 10-11 (his footnotes are a valuable guide to the wider conversation about this question).

65. Thus, rightly, Ellingworth (*Hebrews*, 26), if by "part of a wider Christian community" he means the Church as a whole.

66. Trotter, *Interpreting Hebrews*, 31.

67. P. L. Berger (*The Sacred Canopy: Elements of a Sociological Theory of Religion* [Garden City, NY: Doubleday, 1967], 45-48) introduces the term "plausibility structure" to describe the relationship between holding onto a set of beliefs oneself and having a body of significant others who share those beliefs, the latter being a requirement for the former.

addresses a circle of "teachers" who are falling down on the job, except as this applies to the failure of the community as a whole to act as "teachers" for one another, especially those who are losing sight of the group's vision.[68]

The Author

Identity

The author left his work completely anonymous, with only a passing reference to Timothy in the closing greetings (13:23). Scholars from the first centuries on, however, have not been reticent in proposing his identity. Alexandrian Christianity attributed the work to Paul quite early (the 2nd-century manuscript P46 includes it after Romans among the Pauline epistles). The style of Hebrews stands so far apart from the Pauline letters, however, that the Alexandrian fathers Origen and Clement attributed the actual writing to an associate of Paul, whether as an original composition that includes the thoughts of the apostle or as a translation of a Hebrew letter of Paul into Greek.[69]

Pauline authorship was not the view of the Western churches. Tertullian named Barnabas as the author, and Irenaeus and Hippolytus regarded it as non-Pauline. Only after Jerome and Augustine championed the cause of Pauline authorship did that view take hold in the West. Even these scholars, however, voiced their reservations about authorship. Jerome on one occasion calls it irrelevant, given the prestige the text enjoyed in many churches, and Augustine likewise is more sure of Hebrews' acceptance as a core text of Christianity than of the identity of the author.[70] Advocacy of the book's connection with Paul was subservient to their "feeling" that Hebrews deserved to be recognized as canonical.

Pauline authorship is probably the least likely solution to the question. External evidence actually favors non-Pauline authorship, and internal evidence

---

68. Other views, such as the notion that Hebrews addresses a Jewish-Christian house church in Rome, or a house church of "Hebrew Christians" in Palestine (P. Hughes, *Hebrews*, 18-19), are inextricably bound up with the assumption that this letter is more meaningful to Jewish than Gentile Christians (see discussion above).

69. The hypothesis that this letter was originally written in Hebrew fails to take into account the author's use of the LXX (Greek) version of the OT, specifically grounding essential points of his argument on precisely those words or phrases where the LXX departs from the Hebrew text. As John Calvin rightly pointed out, moreover, the wordplay on "testament/covenant" would not have been possible in the Hebrew language (*Commentaries on the Epistle of Paul to the Hebrews* [Grand Rapids: Eerdmans, 1948], xxvii).

70. See Bruce, *Hebrews*, 17.

does nothing to overturn that view. Most noticeably, the style and syntax of the Greek is far and away superior to anything found elsewhere in the Pauline corpus (both letters of undisputed and disputed Pauline authorship). To suggest that Paul was simply writing in a different style, as if preaching in a synagogue, is a desperate attempt to hold onto Pauline authorship.[71] Why would he reserve his best for this one document and not give a hint anywhere else that he was such an artist with syntax and vocabulary, such a master of ornament? Considerations of content also point away from Paul. While the author of Hebrews argues that Torah is an obsolete predecessor to the new covenant, holds up faith as a central value, and sees Abraham and Jesus as examples for the Christian to follow, he treats all of these topics differently from Paul in his known letters. The thickness of Platonic concepts, interest in cult, and exposition of Jesus' work in terms of priesthood — all make this letter stand out from the Pauline corpus.

Many suggestions for authorship have arisen. The earliest candidate was Barnabas, suggested by Tertullian (*De pudic.* 20). Barnabas was a member of the tribe of Levi (Acts 4:36) and a co-worker of Paul for some time, but we know nothing else about Barnabas that would establish him as the author. Apollos is a popular choice. He enjoyed a reputation for eloquence, even rhetorical training (he was "an eloquent man," ἀνὴρ λόγιος, Acts 18:24); he was well schooled in the OT and able to dispute with non-Christian Jews based on the texts (Acts 18:24, 28). His connection with Alexandria made him an especially popular candidate during the time when the connections between Hebrews and Philo were thought to be foundational.[72] He also was a part of the Pauline mission (at least, he had connections with Prisca and Aquila, and Paul was kept informed of his whereabouts), although clearly a person with a mind of his own, which would explain the points of contact with Paul as well as his independent development of shared motifs. While the profile fits in general, the case remains undemonstrable. Other candidates from the Pauline circle have also been proposed, including Prisca, Luke, Silas, Epaphras, and Aristion. No convincing case

---

71. Such an attempt is usually tied to the presupposition that apostolic authorship is a viable prerequisite for keeping a book in the NT canon (as if anyone would stop publishing Bibles with 2 Peter if its pseudonymity could be conclusively demonstrated!). The criterion of apostolicity, however, called for connection with an apostolic witness, not actual authorship by an apostle, and Hebrews certainly meets that criterion (whether the author should prove to be, in the last analysis, Apollos or Silas or Prisca or any of Paul's associates).

72. The Philonism of the author of Hebrews was championed by Spicq (*L'Épître aux Hébreux*, 39-91) but has been overturned by the work of G. A. Williamson (*Philo and the Epistle to the Hebrews* [ALGHJ 4; Leiden: Brill, 1970]), who demonstrated that the differences in the way the two authors interpret the OT are far greater than any similarities, and L. D. Hurst (*The Epistle to the Hebrews: Its Background of Thought* [SNTSMS 65; Cambridge: Cambridge University Press, 1990]), who rightly emphasizes the eschatological and apocalyptic elements of Hebrews as primary.

can be made for any candidate, however,[73] and Origen's final statement on the question of authorship remains the wisest of all — "But who wrote the epistle? God knows the truth" (preserved in Eusebius *Hist. eccl.* 6.25.14).[74]

While we lack a name for our author, we do not lack a personality. We may also inquire into the nature of his relationship with the community he addressees and the authority in which he grounds his "word of exhortation" (13:22). The author does not count himself as a witness to the Lord Jesus, but rather as one who has himself been evangelized by the apostolic founders (2:3). Neither does he appear to be a leader from within the community to which he writes (13:7, 17, 24). He has, however, been in contact with the community before, as he hopes to be "restored" to them (13:19). On the one hand, he makes extensive use of associative language, referring to their common experience of Christ's activity in the believers' lives, and calling the addressees "partners in Christ" (3:14) or "partners in a heavenly calling" (3:1), as well as "brothers and sisters" (3:1, 12; 10:19; 13:22). He also includes himself through his use of hortatory subjunctives (2:1, 3; 4:11, 16; 6:1; 7:19; 10:19-24; 12:1; 13:13). On the other hand, the author considers himself to have sufficient authority to point out what is amiss in the community, even to berate them for not doing better, and to expect that his imperatives will be followed.

He does not exercise charismatic authority, as John the Seer did in the churches of Asia Minor. That is to say, he does not give his message legitimacy through appeals to visions or revelations or special proximity to divine power (although he does remind the hearers of their original reception of the gospel amid such charismatic phenomena, 2:3-4; 6:4-5). He does not claim authority on the basis of being a community founder, as does Paul, who can call himself the "father" of those he addresses. Charisma, or extraordinary access to the sacred, is now located in the community. For the author, the exhortation "Let us approach the throne of grace with boldness" (4:16; cf. 10:22) corresponds to the exhortation not to neglect to meet together (10:25), for the gathered congregation is the place of access to God.[75] The process of "primary institutional-

---

73. The author's use of a masculine ending for the self-referential participle διη-γούμενον (11:32) would rule out Prisca or another female author. First, it could hardly be a "mistake," given the author's command of the Greek language; second, there would be no reason for a female teacher to hide her gender behind the guise of masculinity, given the openness to female leadership in the early Church; third, the author appears to expect that the audience would have personal knowledge of his identity (see, e.g., 13:18-24), and thus a disguise would not have worked anyway.

74. For readers interested in reviewing the detective work that has produced a horde of suspects but no conviction, see Spicq, *L'Épître aux Hébreux*, 1:197-219; Bruce, *Hebrews*, 14-20; Attridge, *Hebrews*, 1-5.

75. David R. Worley, Jr., "God's Faithfulness to Promise: The Hortatory Use of Commissive Language in Hebrews" (Ph.D. diss., Yale University, 1981), 55.

ization," in which the charisma of the founding leader "is . . . diffused into the group, its customs, rituals, doctrine, verbal tradition, ethos," and in which the community begins to regard itself as an anticipation or prototype of the new society or kingdom to come,[76] has taken place by the time the author writes. It appears that the author works in the time of "secondary institutionalization," in which the founder's staff works "at preserving the original group and fulfilling its mission, and consequently their authority is of necessity traditional and rational and can by no means be purely charismatic, resting in themselves only."[77]

The authority of the author of Hebrews is not charismatic, but rather is based on the "prior tradition or *ratio*" of the converts, namely, the word "declared at first by the Lord and attested to us by those who heard him" (2:3) together with the tradition passed on through the socialization process and contained in the Jewish Scriptures. The author seeks to maintain the community's place within the tradition. The nature of the argumentation from the Hebrew Scriptures and the prior tradition of their Christocentric interpretation (e.g., the application of Psalms 2 and 110 to the person and significance of Jesus) point also to the traditional-rational nature of the author's legitimation.

As a final piece in this puzzle, one may look to the indications in 6:11 and 13:18 that the author is part of a larger circle. In these verses a "we" element appears to be distinguished from the "you" element, indicating a group around the author as well as a community of recipients. The reference to Timothy in 13:23, far from being a later addition in an attempt to bring this letter into the Pauline canon, may show that the author, like Timothy or Titus, was part of the staff of an apostolic founder (in this case, Paul), evangelized by the apostle and now carrying on the mission of the departed apostle (whether he moved on to new mission grounds or died). The connection with Timothy, as well as the clear points of contact with known Pauline letters,[78] confirms that the author comes from that circle within early Christianity. The author belongs already to a later stage of institutionalization — primary institutionalization has been achieved, and now the members of the staff exercise a ministry of teaching and exhorting in an effort to maintain the communities founded by the apostolic leader (who, in the case of early Christianity, was also bound to the tradition). While not part of the local leadership of the congregations, they nevertheless exercise traditional-rational authority over the apostle's former mission field

---

76. Bengt Holmberg, *Paul and Power* (Philadelphia: Fortress, 1978), 145, 148.

77. Ibid., 178.

78. Witherington has conducted a close examination of the points of contact between Galatians and Hebrews ("Influence," 146-52), demonstrating how Pauline thought provides a primary formative matrix for the theology, OT interpretation, and even choice of diction of the author of Hebrews.

and seek to preserve the work accomplished by the member of the senior staff (the apostle) who took them into his service. The author desires to return to the community to visit them and asks them to pray that he may be able to do so more quickly (13:19, 23) and in the company of Timothy (13:23). What delays the author or necessitates the prayers of his audience is unknown — he might be imprisoned, but might equally well be caught up in the affairs of another congregation in need of guidance or encouragement.

Worldview

The author's presentation of the reality in which he and his audience live is very much the cosmos of apocalypticism.[79] Reality is divided into two distinct realms. First, the author speaks of the hearers' (and his own) actions in this world, the visible, material realm of everyday experience (e.g., 2:3-4; 10:32-34; 13:18-19, 23). The Son entered this realm at a precise time, and acted within it "for a little while" (2:9). The visible realm consists of the earth and the "heavens." We must distinguish carefully here between the two uses to which the author puts the term "heaven." There are, on the one hand, the "heavens" (always plural) that are part of the changing, temporary creation:

> Lord, you founded the earth from the beginning, and the heavens are the works of your hands. These will be destroyed, but you will abide, and all will grow old like a garment, and you will roll them up like a scroll and like a garment they will be changed. But You are the same and your years never run out. (1:10-12)[80]

Such an assessment of the durability of the visible world anticipates the author's eschatological expectations set forth in 12:26-28, the "rolling up" and

---

79. These apocalyptic dimensions are so deeply woven into the fabric of the argument that it seems impossible to regard them merely as an accommodation to the views of the audience that the author shored up with occasional images drawn from his alleged "Alexandrian" cosmology (a position advanced by George W. MacRae, "Heavenly Temple and Eschatology in the Letter to the Hebrews," *Semeia* 12 [1978]: 179-99, especially 190-191).

80. The fact that this psalm text is quoted in the context of developing a Christology in chapter 1 rather than a cosmology or an eschatology does not render it irrelevant for these closely connected topics (*pace* L. D. Hurst, "Eschatology and 'Platonism' in the Epistle to the Hebrews," *SBLSP* 23 [1984]: 41-74, 73). The author desires that the addressees regard both Jesus and the invisible realm as the places or sources of stability, and the visible realm as the place of limited, temporary, inferior, shakable things. Christology, eschatology, and cosmology all together call the hearers away from setting their hearts on the things of this world and toward fixing their desires wholly on the things of the "coming world" (2:5) that is also the divine realm.

throwing away of the visible, temporal cosmos at some point in the (near) future, after which the invisible and unshakable kingdom that the believers are inheriting will remain.

Beyond the visible "earth" and "heavens" stands another realm that is superior, even if now it is unseen. This is the realm where God dwells, where God's full and unmediated presence is enjoyed by the angelic hosts and the glorified Christ. The author has this realm in mind when he speaks of "heaven itself" (Heb. 9:24), the place Jesus entered after he "passed through the *heavens*" (Heb. 4:14) and from which vantage point he stands "exalted above the *heavens*" (Heb. 7:26). The author is not considering the visible sky (the "heavens") as part of this superior realm. Rather, "heaven itself" is somewhere beyond what can be seen: the "vertical" dimension is, moreover, an expression of the worth of that realm "beyond" (in which "higher" becomes synonymous with "better," just as we speak of moving "up" in the world). This better realm is not "in the sky" but beyond "this creation," namely the "heavens and the earth" (Gen. 1:1) that are temporary and slated for an end.

In keeping with several distinct strains of Jewish thought, the author of Hebrews conceives of this realm of God in terms of the architecture of the tabernacle.[81] The author differs from Philo and Josephus on this point, however, for the "real" temple of God is not the universe of this creation, with earth and sea as the outer courts and the sky as the inner court.[82] The "true tent" is "not of this creation" (Heb. 9:11), and none of the chambers of the "greater and more perfect tent" (Heb. 9:11) are to be identified with any part of "this creation."[83]

"Heaven itself" is the eternal and abiding realm, "God's country," the place where God has always been and where God's presence is known in its fullness and not in any dim reflection. It is not a realm that will come into being only at the end, but it is the only realm that remains past "the end" as apocalyptists describe it. It is the realm of God's abode from before the creation of the visible, material cosmos. It is the realm where the Son was adored by angels before and after his incarnation. It is the οἰκουμένη of 1:6, which is not the sphere of visible, temporal activity but the realm where the Son is worshiped by angelic hosts (see commen-

---

81. See *1 Enoch* 90:28-29; *Testament of Levi* 5.

82. Thus Josephus *Ant.* 3.123, 180-81; Philo *Vit. Mos.* 2.88; *Spec. Leg.* 1.66; these and other texts are discussed at length in Jean Daniélou, "La symbolisme du temple de Jérusalem chez Philon et Josèphe," in *Le symbolisme cosmique des monuments religieux* (Rome: Instituto Italiano per il Medio ed Estremo Oriente, 1957), 83-90.

83. On this point I thus differ with MacRae ("Heavenly Temple," 187), who understands the author "unequivocally to make use of the Hellenistic concept of the temple-structured universe." The passage of Jesus "from earth to heaven" is only parallel with his "entrance through the veil into the Holy of Holies" if we understand "heaven" here quite differently from the "heavens," or "skies."

tary on 1:6). This divine realm is also, as the author himself clarifies, the "coming realm" (οἰκουμένη μέλλουσα, 2:5). This is another important clue to the author's eschatology: the realm to which the Son returns to the adulation of the angelic hosts is also the realm that is, from our vantage point, "coming."

The realm beyond "this creation" is, finally, the destiny of the "many sons and daughters" who follow Jesus, their pioneer on their eschatological pilgrimage. It is there, in God's realm, that the believers will find their "better and lasting possessions" (Heb. 10:34), their "better" because "heavenly" homeland (Heb. 11:16), and the "unshakable kingdom" (Heb. 12:28) in which is their "abiding" city (Heb. 13:13-14). That God could be said to have "prepared" a city for the faithful in this realm suggests that there are still "created things" in this realm (like the beings who, apart from the Son, populate that realm), but the crucial point is that none of these promised benefits is "of this creation," of a temporary and therefore inferior kind.[84] It is the author's elevation of "abiding" and "lasting" as terms of value in contrast to "something that ends" that most suggests the impropriety of speaking of any "interim" kingdom (something transient by definition) in connection with the eschatology of this letter.

The author's eschatological expectations (namely, the removal of the visible creation and the persistence of the divine realm) introduce assessments of value into his cosmology that will be crucial to the success of the author's strategy. That which belongs to the other realm, the realm of the Son's preincarnate and post-ascension existence, is "better," and everything that belongs to that realm is valued as "better" than its counterpart in this realm of everyday experience. Thus the author contrasts the possessions lost by the converts as a result of their association with Jesus with the "better and lasting" possessions they have in the realm beyond (10:34); Abraham and the patriarchs were looking not for a temporal homeland but for a "better homeland, that is, a heavenly one" (11:16).[85] All material creation is of limited value since it is of limited duration. The appurtenances of the realm beyond are "better" precisely because they are "lasting" or "abiding," as opposed to temporary and, indeed, subject to removal.

The penultimate character of the earth and the heavens — and all that pertain to them — becomes a recurring theme throughout Hebrews, bolstering the author's deliberative cause at every point (primarily in terms of how it defines the topics of "advantage" and "relative expediency"). The honor, wealth, and sense of having a home in this world, all of which was lost by the addressees

---

84. Hurst ("Eschatology and 'Platonism,'" 72) is right to stress that the author does not oppose created to uncreated things, as would Plato, but rather two orders of created things — that which belongs to "this creation" and that which is "not of this creation" (Heb. 9:11) but rather of that better creation which is God's realm, "heaven itself."

85. Access to these "better" goods is, of course, inseparable from the "better" covenant, mediator, sacrifice, and hope that have come in Jesus.

as the price of their continued adherence to Jesus and Jesus' household, pale in comparison with the honor, possessions, and enfranchisement that the believers who persevere will receive in the realm beyond (2:10; 10:34; 13:14). The addressees will therefore be urged to invest only in the eternal possessions (10:34; 11:13-16; 12:26-28; 13:13-14) and to consider worldly goods and security ultimately to be a bad and foolish investment (11:24-26; 12:16-17). Viewed another way, continued commitment to the group (even at the cost of ongoing deprivation of this world's goods, security, and honor) will be urged on the basis of the belief that the visible world is of secondary value to the presently invisible world, in which the believers are to set their hopes and ambitions.

It has been impossible to speak of the spatial elements of the author's cosmology in isolation from certain temporal elements, since the latter do to a great degree define the former. These realms are not static but rather are involved in a dynamic process through time — a feature that sharply distinguishes the author's thought from Platonic thought. The coming, death, resurrection, and ascension of Jesus are in Hebrews, as elsewhere in the New Testament, an event in time that has signaled the beginning of the "end" of this realm and all its evil. The message of Jesus and about Jesus is an eschatological one, coming "in these last days" (1:2). One can recognize its eschatological character in one sense from its relationship to the whole of sacred history and ritual practice. The death of Jesus on the cross and his subsequent entrance into the divine realm "to appear before God on our behalf" (9:24) accomplished a task that centuries of animal sacrifices prescribed by Torah could only prefigure. His death for others made possible the consummation of the journey that the people of God had been on throughout the epic of biblical (and intertestamental) history.

From the perspective of the author of Hebrews, then, the last days have come and the end time has been initiated. With the session of Jesus at the right hand of God, the preparatory work for the end has been accomplished. "Yet a little while," and Jesus will come a second time for the deliverance (the "salvation") of those who eagerly wait for him (9:28; see 10:37-38). The eschatological dimension of salvation is consistently underscored in Hebrews.[86] The "Day,"

---

86. The use of the term "salvation" in 1:14, 2:3, and 9:28 clearly has a future, eschatological orientation. 6:9 posits that the believers will have "better things, things pertaining to salvation, in store for them" (in contrast to "burning" in 6:8), and so falls easily into this same forward-looking vision. The uses of the term in 2:10 and 5:9 are ambiguous when taken in and by themselves, but readily lend themselves to the same eschatological orientation when read in the context of the other passages. Even the appearance of the term in 11:7, where Noah's trust in "things yet unseen" results in obedient action "unto the salvation of his household," highlights this future aspect of deliverance, for "salvation" came not to Noah when he believed God's warning, nor when he began to build the ark, but after he persisted, completed the task, and boarded it with his family.

3which can be no other than the "Day of the Lord," is drawing nearer (10:25). It will be a day of judgment and destruction for God's enemies (10:26-31), who are also the Son's enemies (1:13; 10:13), but of deliverance for those who have kept faith with Jesus in the midst of the pressures of this realm (9:28). It is the theme of "receiving the reward" that also links this Day with the anticipated dissolution of the material, visible cosmos and the revelation of the divine realm, the locale of the believers' "unshakable kingdom" (12:26-28).

For the author of Hebrews, the kingdom of God already exists beyond the material and visible creation, and will simply "remain" after the removal of the temporary, secondary created order. Being part of the Christian community (and remaining a part) is vitally important for survival itself, which is perhaps one reason the author conceives of "salvation" as that which the believer is "about to inherit" (1:14), as the gift that comes with Christ's second "appearing" (9:28): deliverance from the material world that is slated for dissolution and entrance into the abiding realm that alone survives the "shaking"[87]. At this eschatological shaking, the visible creation that stands as a barrier between the believers and their better, abiding, heavenly homeland — the presence of God in the unshakable heaven — will be removed. They will then enter into their promised, eternal inheritance, the "unshakable kingdom" that they are receiving.

The author will remind the addressees at length of these elements of the Christian worldview, which together provide the ideology necessary to sustain

---

87. Stedman's presentation of the eschatology of Hebrews is fundamentally flawed in this regard. He speaks repeatedly about the believers awaiting the appearance of the city of God on earth, and is very specific about the location of this city coming *on earth* (*Hebrews*, 14, 37, 123, 133, 144). He is committed to reading "the coming world" (2:5) and "the unshakable kingdom" as a terrestrial millennial kingdom. Aside from the fact that Rev. 20:4-6 gives no sure indication that this reign of the martyrs would take place "on earth" as opposed to the heavenly realm, we have already seen how the author of Hebrews finds the "material and earthly" to be less reliable, since temporary, than otherworldly realities (i.e., the city God has prepared in the abiding realm).

Another argument advanced by Stedman in favor of reading the millennium into Hebrews is worth discussing as an example of fallacious exegesis. He adduces Eph. 2:7 (*Hebrews*, 37), which speaks of "coming ages," as proof that "at least two more ages lie ahead." Following a popular eschatological scheme, he proceeds to enumerate these as the restored Davidic monarchy on earth (thus making room for the "millennial kingdom") and then the new earth and heavens. The problem, of course, is that the plural of "ages" is frequently interchangeable with the singular. If we were to turn to Luke 18:10 or Mark 10:30, we could match proof text with proof text and say, "But Jesus speaks of only one coming age — 'in the age to come [my followers will receive] eternal life.'" Even Eph. 1:21 contrasts "this age" with "the *one* that is coming," so that it cannot be said on the basis of Eph. 2:7 that two ages are yet to come. That is turning a blind eye to the complexities of the texts themselves for the sake of rigid schematization.

commitment to the group and its confession. The amount of exposition in Hebrews should not lead us to think of the text as an abstract theological tract. The author reinforces beliefs and "ideas" in order to reposition how the addressees think about what would be truly advantageous for them. Commitment to the group wanes as the believer thinks more about temporal losses and temporal expedience. The author therefore spends much time bringing the addressees back to considering their plight in light of eternity as well as in light of the history of God's interaction with humanity.

Use of the Old Testament

The author of Hebrews was clearly a master of OT content and interpretation. The depth and extent of oral-scribal intertexture between this text and the Jewish Scriptures is impressive indeed. For the author, these Scriptures provided the body of authoritative texts in which the worldview and ethos of the community must be grounded. They were not the relics of a Semitic people's tribal and national history, but rather "the oracles of God" (5:12), the God who "spoke to the fathers in the prophets" (1:1). While the revelation of God was "piecemeal and diverse" in those Scriptures, all the pieces came together when viewed in light of the "Son." The meaning of the OT for the author was its testimony to the achievement and significance of Jesus, as well as its guidance for the community, which was responding to God's promises in the Son. Thus the author can freely place verses from the Psalms or Isaiah on the lips of Jesus to find their meaning, or refer them to Jesus, or address them to Jesus (all these techniques are displayed in 1:5–2:13). The author can reconstruct the unseen work of Jesus now in the divine realm based on his conviction that the OT description of the levitical cult provides the shadow of Jesus' more effective priestly service. The Scriptures are read thus in a thoroughly Christocentric manner. They are also read in an ethical manner, providing examples of honorable and faithful response to God for the Christians to imitate (11:1-40) as well as admonitory paradigms of dishonorable, disobedient, or foolish responses to God's promises, which the Christians must not replicate (3:7–4:11; 12:16-17).

The author's OT, however, is not the same text that stands behind the Jewish Scriptures read in synagogues today or printed as the OT in Catholic or Protestant Bibles. These are translations of the MT, an edition of the Scriptures in Hebrew. The author of Hebrews uses a Greek translation of those Scriptures, which closely resembles what has come to be called the Septuagint.[88] Jews living

---

88. There were, of course, a variety of Greek translations available in the centuries before and after the turn of the era, so that speaking of the LXX *tout court* is something of a simplification.

outside of Palestine became, over the generations, alienated from their ancestral language, Hebrew. They required their sacred texts to be translated into the
language that they had come to accept as their own, namely, Greek. The process
of translation appears to have begun around 250 B.C. — first the Torah, then
the prophets and other writings.

Recognizing that the author of Hebrews used an LXX version is significant, since the LXX frequently differs from the MT.[89] Thus if one were to compare the citation of Psalm 40 in Hebrews 10:5-7 with Psalm 40:6-8 in the OT of
most printed Bibles, one would be immediately struck by the differences. The
MT reads "sacrifice and offering you have not desired, but ears you have dug for
me" (Ps 40:6), whereas Hebrews (following the LXX) reads "sacrifice and offering you did not desire, but you prepared a body for me" (Heb. 10:5; LXX Ps.
39:7).[90] The MT clearly speaks of "ears" to emphasize "hearing" the Torah and
doing it as the work that pleases God (rather than ritual acts for sins against Torah and the like). The LXX translator probably understood the psalm in the
same way, but found the expression about "digging ears" to be distasteful, and
so substituted "a body," still to live out the requirements of Torah. The LXX version, however, opens up the psalm to a Christological interpretation, which
would be impossible from the MT. Now Christ becomes the speaker of the
psalm and receives a body from God with which to effect the perfect sacrifice,
which replaces all the ineffective rituals of the levitical cult. Throughout the
commentary we will note these differences and how the author's reading of
Christ in the OT is affected.

Available codices of the LXX contain numerous books not included in the
Jewish canon of the OT, nor, as a consequence, in Protestant Bibles. While it is
unlikely that the author of Hebrews enjoyed the benefit of an LXX codex (it is
virtually certain that the Scriptures were written on scrolls as separate books), it
is likely that the inclusion of the Apocrypha in later LXX codices reflects the
importance of these books for Diaspora Jews and, by extension, the Christian
churches that inherited not the Hebrew but the Greek Scriptures as their OT.
The author of Hebrews certainly read books like the Wisdom of Solomon and
either 2 Maccabees or 4 Maccabees, applying the same Christocentric and ethical principles in interpreting their significance as he applied to the books that
became the official Jewish canon. For example, Wisdom of Solomon has left its
mark on the author's understanding of Jesus' preincarnate life (see commentary on 1:2-3), and the martyrs celebrated in 2 and 4 Maccabees shape his ethi-

---

89. Frequently the differences reflect the ideology or interpretative voice of the translator, but on occasion the LXX is held by OT textual critics to contain the more original reading than the MT.

90. Because the LXX joins Psalms 9 and 10 into a single hymn, the numbering of the
rest of the book is off until Psalm 148 (Psalm 147 being split into two hymns in the LXX).

cal instruction (these are the faithful who "were tortured, refusing to accept release, in order that they might obtain a better resurrection," 11:35).

Finally, the author incorporates a wide variety of exegetical techniques into his interpretation of OT texts.[91] In addition to typology (seen largely in the exposition of facets of the levitical cult to construct a picture of the heavenly cult) and homiletical midrash (seen, e.g., in the admonitory handling of the story of Num. 14 in Heb. 3:7–4:11), the author uses the Scriptures to reinforce his argument, exhortations, and sometimes even emotional effect (thus 10:30, 37-39). He draws out the implications of OT texts (frequently focusing on the literal meaning of a key word like "new" in Heb. 8:8-13 or "yet once more" in Heb. 12:26-27) to advance his argument and employs several exegetical "rules" found in the legal interpretations of the rabbis. Hillel is credited with developing seven principles for applying the legal material of the Torah to situations not covered in the Torah. Of these seven, two are very important for Hebrews.

The first is called, in Hebrew, *qal wahomer*, meaning "light and heavy." This principle states that if something applies in a lesser case, it will apply in a greater case as well. The Torah prescribes that, if one sees one's neighbor's donkey or ox straying, one should return it to the neighbor or keep it safe until the neighbor comes looking for it, or, if one sees it injured in the road, one should help it get back up on its feet (Deut. 22:1-4). The Torah says nothing at this point, however, about what to do if one sees a neighbor's child straying lost or injured on the roadside. By the principle of *qal wahomer*, it would readily be inferred that the same responsibilities were due to the child as to the animals, since a child was of much more value than an animal. This is not, of course, a strictly Jewish principle of interpretation. The argument "from the lesser to the greater" was a mainstay of Greco-Roman argumentation as well *(a minore ad maius).* The author of Hebrews makes frequent use of this principle in his exhortation (see 2:2-4; 9:13-14; 10:28-29; 12:25). In each case, the OT provides the basis for the "lesser" premise, and the message or work of the Son provides the "greater" case.

The second rule is *gezera shawa*, or "verbal analogy," which seeks to clarify the meaning or applicability of one text through a reference to a second text that shares a common, relevant word with the first text. Hebrews employs this technique at 4:1-11, as the author attempts to define what "God's rest" actually signifies in Psalm 95:11. In that passage, both "rest" and "works" remind him of the Creation account, and so he goes to Genesis 2:2 as a means of proving that

---

91. For a more complete treatment of the author's use of Jewish interpretative techniques, see Lane, *Hebrews 1–8*, cxix-cxxiv; Spicq, *L'Épître aux Hébreux*, 1:330-50; Herbert W. Bateman IV, *Early Jewish Hermeneutics and Hebrews 1:5-13* (New York: Peter Lang, 1997), esp. 9-120.

God's rest was not merely the land of Canaan but some primeval creation of God. *Gezera shawa* is also applied in Hebrews 5:5-6, where two citations from the Psalms are linked by the word "you": the first text has already been shown to apply to Jesus ("you are my Son," Ps. 2:7), and so clarifies the referent of the pronoun in Psalm 110:4, "you are a priest forever," to be Jesus as well.

Expertise in Rhetoric

Not only was the author a gifted interpreter of the Scriptures, but he was also a gifted orator, an expert in rhetoric and style. Harold Attridge writes that "the body of [Hebrews], which the epistolary postscript styles a 'word of exhortation' (λόγος τῆς παρακλήσεως), is generally recognized to be a product of rhetorical art."[92] Indeed, Hebrews has been singled out among the NT documents as "the earliest example of Christian artistic literature."[93] The question is not whether the author received formal training in rhetoric, although he would have the best claim to such education among NT authors.[94] Even if he had only the informal training available to all who heard speeches in the marketplaces, synagogues, and theaters, it is clear that he paid sharp attention to the art of persuasion behind such performances. Both at the level of stylistic ornament and persuasive argument, this author shows himself fully equipped in the art of persuasion.[95]

Like many ancient texts, Hebrews appears to have been written with a

---

92. Attridge, *Hebrews*, 14.

93. A. Deissmann, *Light from the Ancient East*, trans. L. R. M. Strachan (New York: Doran, 1927), 244.

94. Lane (*Hebrews 1–8*, l-li) finds the rhetorical ornamentation and careful, studied appeals to logic and emotion in the sermon to be positive proof of the author's formal training in rhetoric. He posits that the author enjoyed a primary and secondary education comparable to Philo's own.

95. Rhetorical critics rarely desire to prove or need to claim "training in and conscious use of the ancient rhetorical rules" on the part of the NT author, as a recent critic of rhetorical analysis seems to suggest (Jeffrey A. D. Weima, "What Has Aristotle to Do with Paul?" *CTJ* 32 [1997]: 458-68, 463). Such matters are, essentially, irrelevant. The question is not whether a NT author received a degree in rhetoric but whether he uses rhetoric and whether or not the persuasive strategies of his text can be illumined (and the impact on the hearers assessed) through further study of those strategies in the ancient textbooks. When we find Paul, or the author of Hebrews, or Peter employing inductive and deductive forms of argument, seeks to arouse certain strategic emotions on the part of the hearers, or defends his own credibility (or attacks the credibility of rival teachers), then we are looking at strategies of argumentation that are the subjects of the rhetorical handbooks. The explicit and systematic discussion of these strategies in the latter illumine when and how they appear in the NT documents.

view to oral delivery.[96] Given that spiritual leaders of the early Church read letters in a liturgical setting, this makes perfect sense.[97] William Lane has brought
together a number of indications from within the text that Hebrews is self-
consciously an oration, that is, a text for oral rather than visual communication.[98] The author uses verbs of speaking when referring to his communication
(2:5; 6:9; 8:1; 9:5; 11:32); he also voices his concern for the addressees' attentive
hearing (not reading) of the message (5:11). Awareness of the orality of Hebrews has opened the door for scholars to examine its use of many of the devices employed by orators, whose goal was not only to create an argument but
to deliver it "in such a way as to *sound* persuasive to [their] audience."[99]

---

96. In the epilogue of 2 Maccabees, for example, the epitomator reveals the assumption that his work would be read aloud: "For just as . . . wine mixed with water is sweet and
delicious and enhances one's enjoyment, so also the style of the story delights the ears of
those who read the work" (15:39, NRSV).

97. Compare Rev. 1:3, NRSV: "Blessed is the one who reads aloud the words of this
prophecy, and blessed are those who hear."

98. Lane, *Hebrews 1–8*, lxxiv-lxxv.

99. Michael R. Cosby, *The Rhetorical Composition and Function of Hebrews 11* (Macon,
GA: Mercer University Press, 1988), 4. Both Cosby and G. H. Guthrie (*The Structure of Hebrews: A Text-Linguistic Approach* [Leiden: Brill, 1994], 146) affirm the oral character of Hebrews and take this into careful account in their respective analyses. In light of these observations, it is surprising to read criticisms of rhetorical analysis such as one finds in Weima
("What Has Aristotle to Do with Paul?" 463): "There is a fundamental problem in mixing the
genre of a speech (oral discourse) with that of a letter (written discourse). If one takes seriously the fact that Paul wrote letters, then the most important source for understanding
Paul's letters must naturally be the letter-writing practices of his day, not the rules for oral
discourse." The distinction between oral and written discourse, letters and speeches, is by no
means as clear-cut as Weima pretends. Many specimens of "written discourse" exist that are
merely literary speeches (e.g., 4 Maccabees, many of the "orations" of Lucian, Demosthenes,
or Dio), and 2 Maccabees, Hebrews, and Revelation presume that the audience will "hear"
rather than "see" the words of the text. If, therefore, Weima had taken seriously the orality of
ancient texts like Paul's letters or Hebrews or Revelation, then he would not conceptualize
writing and rhetoric as so thoroughly incompatible. Ancient handbooks on letter writing are
useful in terms of asking whether or not, say, 2 Corinthians will be heard as a "letter of consolation," but 2 Corinthians does far more than any letter of consolation. It also seeks to persuade, and insofar as it seeks to elicit some kind of response from the audience it belongs to
the art of rhetoric to assist the modern interpreter in sorting out what Paul's goals are and
what strategies he employs to achieve them. One of the benefits of a socio-rhetorical approach, it might be said, would be to view epistolography and rhetoric as complementary
rather than competing backgrounds (Weima's term, "source," is inappropriate) against which
different aspects of the text are illuminated or highlighted. With regard to the Epistle to the
Hebrews, however, the rhetorical quality of the text is especially pronounced given the sono-
rous and oratorical exordium without any of the preliminaries of an epistolary prescript
such as one finds in other NT texts from the second half of the canon. It is only the addition
of an epistolary postscript that makes the title "Epistle" at all appropriate to Hebrews, rather

The author uses a wide variety of the embellishments, ornaments, and forms of argument recommended or listed by the ancient rhetorical theorists, pointing to his rhetorical artistry and acuity. Taking merely the opening verses, one sees at once numerous skillfully employed rhetorical techniques already at work:

> In many and various ways God spoke of old to our fathers by the prophets; but in these last days he has spoken to us by a Son, whom he appointed the heir of all things, through whom also he created the world. He reflects the glory of God and bears the very stamp of his nature, upholding the universe by his word of power. (Πολυμερῶς καὶ πολυτρόπως πάλαι ὁ θεὸς λαλήσας τοῖς πατράσιν ἐν τοῖς προφήταις ἐπ' ἐσχάτου τῶν ἡμερῶν τούτων ἐλάλησεν ἡμῖν ἐν υἱῷ, ὃν ἔθηκεν κληρονόμον πάντων, δι' οὗ καὶ ἐποίησεν τοὺς αἰῶνας. ὃς ὢν ἀπαύγασμα τῆς δόξης καὶ χαρακτὴρ τῆς ὑποστάσεως αὐτοῦ, φέρων τε τὰ πάντα τῷ ῥήματι τῆς δυνάμεως αὐτοῦ.)

The Greek reveals the author's use of extended alliteration in the repeated sounding of the phoneme |p| (five times in one clause).[100] Similarly, one finds a repeated cadence between the two parallel clauses of 1:3a: -στάσεως αὐτοῦ and -νάμεως αὐτοῦ.[101] The two phrases ὃς ὢν . . . τῆς ὑποστάσεως αὐτοῦ and φέρων . . . τῆς δυνάμεως αὐτοῦ exhibit homoeoptaton (similar sounds at the endings of words or phrases) with words at the beginning and ending of each phrase. Hebrews 1:1-2a shows perfect parallelism of the constituent clauses, developed by means of a complex antithesis (contrasts): "of old" stands in contrast with "in these last days"; "to the ancestors" stands in contrast with "to us"; "through the prophets" stands in contrast with "through a son."[102] Verse 4 contains an example of hyperbaton (ὄνομα is in a syntactically unexpected position) and brachylogy, or elliptical expression (παρ' αὐτοὺς stands for παρ' ὀνομάτων αὐτῶν). Hebrews begins in what might be termed the "grand style" but frequently moves back and forth from grand to middle to plain styles, sometimes forming sonorous and embellished sentences and sometimes speaking in terse, concise maxims.[103] Thus the author varies the style and sentence length in ways

---

than simply "Sermon to the Hebrews" or "Oration to the Hebrews" (see above for discussions of the appropriateness of the designation of the audience as "Hebrews").

100. Attridge cites 2:1-4; 4:16; 10:11, 34; 11:17; and 12:21 as other prominent examples of alliteration (*Hebrews*, 20 n. 157).

101. See Attridge, *Hebrews*, 20 nn. 145-47 for this and other indices of attention to rhythm in the author's prose composition. Aristotle advises (*Rh.* 3.8.1, 3): "The form of diction should be neither metrical nor without rhythm. . . . Wherefore prose must be rhythmical, but not metrical."

102. Calvin (*Hebrews*, 1) opens his commentary with a discussion of the careful rhetorical construction of this central proposition.

103. Attridge, *Hebrews*, 20.

that classical rhetorical theorists deemed necessary for effective composition and impact.

In addition to judicious use of alliteration, Hebrews provides the most extended example of anaphora in the NT. Both Michael Cosby and George A. Kennedy note the prominence of this rhetorical feature in chapter 11 with its repetition of πίστει.[104] Harold Attridge has further identified several occurrences of assonance, asyndeton, brachylogy, chiasm, ellipse, hendiadys, hyperbaton, isocolon, litotes, and paronomasia.[105] The author also employs a wide range of metaphors, all from areas of life commonly selected for such illustrative purposes: education, agriculture, seafaring, law, athletics, and the cultus.[106]

The author also employs forms of argumentation that can be analyzed in terms of classical rhetorical theory. The sections of exposition abound in syllogistic and enthymematic arguments (e.g., 7:4-10); arguments "from lesser to greater" are observable throughout the oration (e.g., 2:1-4; 10:26-31); appeals to common rhetorical "topics" such as the just, expedient, honorable, feasible, praiseworthy, and the like abound; examples and analogies are skillfully selected and crafted to furnish inductive proofs in support of the author's exhortations; the author arouses emotions like fear, confidence, shame, and emulation in his audience to lead them to accept his proposals more readily. His use of the LXX as authoritative witness throughout the oration sets him apart from other Greco-Roman orators in terms of his choice of "scriptures," but he is like Greco-Roman orators in the way he employs those scriptures in his proofs.[107] Aristotle saw orators using Homer and Hesiod in much the same way as the author of Hebrews uses the canon of church and synagogue. The rhetorical device of *synkrisis*, or "comparison," figures prominently throughout the argumentation of Hebrews (e.g., the comparison of Jesus with Moses in 3:1-6 or with the levitical priesthood in 7:1–10:18). These kernels of argumentation and discrete rhetorical units are further linked together throughout the oration by means of connecting particles and phrases such as διό, τοιγαροῦν, διὰ τοῦτο and οὖν, as

---

104. Cosby, *Rhetorical Composition*, 3; George A. Kennedy, *New Testament Interpretation through Rhetorical Criticism* (Chapel Hill, NC: University of North Carolina Press, 1984), 156.

105. Attridge, *Hebrews*, 20-21; cf. also Spicq, *L'Épître aux Hébreux*, 1:331-36. All of these rhetorical figures are discussed in book 4 of the *Rhetorica ad Herennium*. It will not be the aim of this commentary to point out the verbal ornamentation employed by the author, save on rare occasions. Attridge and Spicq have done an exceptional job searching out these embellishments, and the interested reader can peruse their work. For an excellent introduction to these rhetorical devices and samples of how they are used in Hebrews, see Trotter, *Interpreting Hebrews*, 163-80.

106. Attridge (*Hebrews*, 21) provides several examples in each of these areas.

107. Cf. T. H. Olbricht, "Hebrews as Amplification," in *Rhetoric and the New Testament*, ed. S. E. Porter and T. H. Olbricht (JSNTSS 90; Sheffield: Sheffield Academic Press, 1993), 382-83.

well as through frequent use of the device of *inclusio*,[108] foreshadowing of themes (e.g., the introduction of Jesus as high priest in 2:17 and 3:1 before arriving at 4:14-16, which initiates the first actual discussion of Jesus' priesthood), summary statements (once explicitly in 8:1: Κεφάλαιον δὲ . . .), and transitional techniques involving linking words and key terms.[109] Moreover, the author of Hebrews forms discrete units that are identifiable as standard rhetorical forms. One finds in chapter 11 a complete encomium on "faith." Burton Mack has argued that 12:5-17 exhibits the characteristic form of elaboration on a theme, found in the *progymnasmata*, the elementary exercises undertaken before advanced schooling in rhetoric.[110] The question of whether or not Hebrews is a carefully crafted piece of rhetoric is answered roundly in the affirmative given this "overabundance" of "structural indices."[111]

The author of Hebrews, in sum, is a member of the Pauline mission whose task it is to nurture and preserve the work started by the apostolic leader. He exercises authority based on his expertise in, and fidelity to, the tradition of the Christian culture, namely, the Jewish Scriptures and the message of Jesus. To encourage the addressees to remain firmly committed to the Christian group and its hope, he brings the resources of the authoritative scriptures of the sect and the full spectrum of rhetorical tactics to bear on the task of reaffirming the worldview of the Christian culture as the context in which to deliberate wisely about what course of action will be advantageous for the hearers and what values will lead to lasting honor.

The Rhetorical Goal and Socio-Rhetorical Strategy of Hebrews

Ancient Rhetoric and New Testament Interpretation

Rhetorical analysis offers a wealth of insights into the way in which a NT text sought to persuade its hearers to take a particular course of action. Since rhetorical analysis will play a large part in this commentary, a concise introduction to its concepts and terminology is in order here.[112] The principal sourcebooks

---

108. Compare Guthrie, *Structure of Hebrews*, 76-89.

109. Ibid., 94-111.

110. B. L. Mack, *Rhetoric and the New Testament* (Minneapolis: Augsburg Fortress, 1990), 77-78.

111. Attridge, *Hebrews*, 16.

112. For more detailed introductions to rhetorical analysis of NT texts, see Mack, *Rhetoric and the New Testament*; Kennedy, *New Testament Interpretation*; Duane F. Watson, *Invention, Arrangement, and Style: Rhetorical Criticism of Jude and 2 Peter* (SBLDS 104; Atlanta: Scholars Press, 1988).

on rhetoric in the Greek, Hellenistic, and Roman periods are Aristotle's *Art of Rhetoric*, Anaximenes' *Rhetorica ad Alexandrum* (wrongly attributed to Aristotle), the *Rhetorica ad Herennium* (wrongly attributed to Cicero), Cicero's *On Invention, On the Orator, Partitions of Oratory, Brutus, The Orator,* and *Topics*, and Quintilian's *Institutio Oratoria*. These books are, for the most part, systematizations of what goes into effective oratory, from the creation of possible arguments or topics to the delivery of the final speech. The handbooks tell us much about how orators and leaders would persuade their audiences to take a particular course of action, to embody a certain value, or to render a certain verdict. They tell us how these community leaders would appeal to the mind, the emotions, and the trust of the audience. By studying classical rhetoric, we can become adept at discerning when a NT author is trying to arouse a certain emotion in his hearers, and to what end. We can analyze the logical argument of a passage. We can see how the author is trying to affirm his own credibility while seeking to undermine the credibility of any rival leaders who are urging a different course of action. Because these rhetorical handbooks reflect the practices current in the period in which the NT was composed, they help us know what to look for in the NT texts as we consider how the author was orchestrating argument and exhortation to produce a faithful response.

1. The Three Genres of Oratory

Oratory grew out of the practical needs of the Greek city and its institutions, mainly the council chamber, law court, and public forum. The enrolled citizens would gather in the council chamber to determine what course of action the city should take to meet some particular need. Inevitably there would be a variety of courses from which to choose, and citizens would speak up in favor of one or another, weighing its advantages and disadvantages, comparing it with other available courses. This was the natural home of deliberative rhetoric, speeches that sought to promote or dissuade a certain course of action. Those in favor of one course would seek to show that it was just and right (in keeping with the culture's core values, like courage, prudence, justice, or generosity), expedient (tending to preserve existing goods, gain other advantages, ward off ills, avoid disadvantages), feasible (the resources to undertake the course being available), honorable (embodying virtues, tending toward the praiseworthy), and the like.[113] Frequently the speaker would employ topics of amplification, showing that the course he favored would be more noble, more just, or more expedient than others. The opposite topics would be used to dissuade the assembly from a certain course of action.

---

113. For a full and useful discussion of these topics, see *Rhet. Alex.* 1421b21-1423a12; *Rhet. Her.* 3.2.2–3.4.9.

People living together under a body of laws never do so flawlessly, hence the need for the law court. Here, jurors would gather to assess the guilt or innocence of those accused of wrongdoing. This was the home of forensic (or judicial) rhetoric, in which the orators (a defender and an accuser) would attempt to affix blame or establish innocence concerning some action that had happened in the past. Oaths, witnesses, material proofs, and probabilities were the chief tools in reconstructing that past event and assigning guilt.

Finally, the citizenry and noncitizens frequently gathered for special occasions in the public forum. Typically, this was to commemorate the life or lives of the honored dead, and so centered on the recital of the dead person's virtues and achievements. This was the birthplace of epideictic rhetoric, speeches that praised the virtuous and censured the vicious, and that, in so doing, reminded the gathered audience of those values that sustained their culture and society. Praise of the departed aroused emulation in the audience, stirring them up to desire the same honor by embodying the same virtues exhibited in the subject of the speech.[114] Topics of a funeral oration included the facts of the person's life (native city, parentage or ancestry, education, friends, wealth, power, offices held, citizenship, kind of death), physical excellence (strength, beauty, health), and moral excellence (virtues possessed; praiseworthy habits, actions, or achievements that manifest interior virtues; attitude in performing those actions).

While the three basic genres of oratory developed in these everyday settings, they did not remain limited to those settings. Deliberative topics would be of use wherever some group needed to make a decision about a future course of action. It was a small step to move from the assembly in the council chamber to the assembly in the synagogue, the church, or any other voluntary association. Paul's letter to the Galatian Christians provides an excellent example of deliberative topics being used to advise an "assembly" with regard to a future course of action (there, dissuasion from undergoing circumcision). Forensic rhetoric could be employed outside the setting of a legal court wherever issues

---

114. In Thucydides' *History,* Pericles gives a eulogy for the fallen Athenian soldiers, at the end of which he fosters the hearers' feeling of emulation by direct exhortation and application: "We who remain behind may hope to be spared their fate, but must resolve to keep the same daring spirit against the foe" (2.43); "It is for you to try to be like them. Make up your minds that happiness depends on being free, and freedom depends on being courageous" (2.44). Similarly, the author of 4 Maccabees aimed at inspiring the feeling of emulation among his auditors and sought to lead them into the resolve to "keep the same daring spirit," drawing them in by the hope of honor and praiseworthy remembrance and by their own sense of honor. Dio Chrysostom closes his eulogy for the boxer, Melancomas, with an exhortation to the audience to show the same commitment to courage and endurance in their respective fields of life (*Or.* 29.21). All these bear witness to the primary goal of such addresses, namely the reinforcement of cultural values.

of blame or innocence were involved. Thus we find forensic topics prominently displayed in 2 Corinthians 1 and 2, where Paul first has to answer "charges" about his sincerity and truthfulness and prove that he did not injure the believers before he can move forward in his attempts to teach the Corinthians about the implications of the gospel for the reliability of flashy appearances.[115] Epideictic rhetoric moved beyond the public forum very early, for praise or censure of a living individual was already an essential element of legal speeches and deliberative speeches by Aristotle's time. Prosecutors would frequently engage in censure of the defendant and his defender in order to undermine their credibility, and orators in the council chamber would frequently praise those figures who pursued a course of action similar to the one they were promoting.

This observation brings us to an important point. Already Aristotle had recognized that a speech was rarely a pure example of a single genre.[116] A deliberative speech, for example, could employ both epideictic and forensic topics along the way. The task of a nuanced rhetorical analysis is not merely to decide that a speech is deliberative, but to discern the ways in which epideictic and forensic topics, if present, support the overarching deliberative goal.

2. The Five Stages of Speech-Making

The task of composing and delivering a speech involved five basic steps — invention, arrangement, style, memory, and delivery. An orator would begin the task by considering all the possible avenues of advancing his case, laying out the proofs and appeals he had at his disposal. He would consider what prejudices and arguments existed against him or his case, and how to answer these obstructions. This was the task of invention.[117] He would then consider how best to arrange the ma-

---

115. For a discussion of a complex rhetorical situation leading to a complex exordium, see D. A. deSilva, "Meeting the Exigency of a Complex Rhetorical Situation: Paul's Strategy in 2 Corinthians 1 through 7," *Andrews University Seminary Studies* 34 (1996): 5-22.

116. *Rh.* 1.3.5: "The end [goal] of the deliberative speaker is the expedient or harmful; for he who exhorts recommends a course of action as better, and he who dissuades advises against it as worse; *all other considerations, such as justice and injustice, honour and disgrace, are included as accessory in reference to this*" (emphasis mine). See also *Rhet. Alex.* 1427b31-35: "In their practical application they overlap"; *Rhet. Her.* 3.8.15: "And if epideictic is only seldom employed by itself independently, still in judicial and deliberative causes extensive sections are often devoted to praise and censure." A similar phenomenon appears in the discussions of types or categories of letters in the ancient theorists of epistolography. Pseudo-Libanius, for example, provides forty-one kinds of letters, the last of which is simply called "mixed," indicating that the composer writes with several goals for the same letter (*Epistolary Styles,* 46, 92; text, translation, and introduction in A. J. Malherbe, "Ancient Epistolary Theorists," *Ohio Journal of Religious Studies* 5 [1977]: 3-77).

117. Most of Aristotle's *Rhetoric* is devoted to this aspect of the oratorical process (1.4–2.26).

terial to make the strongest impression on the hearers. As a general rule, prejudice against the speaker and his case had to be removed up front, prejudice against opponents aroused at the end of a speech. The strongest proofs were made at the beginning and ending of the argument, so as to make a strong first impression and leave a strong impression behind (*Rhet. Her.* 3.10.18). The orator would then give attention to stylistic considerations — when to use the grand style, suitable for rousing attention and emotion, when to use the plain style, suited to rational argumentation, where to use ornaments and figures of diction to "dress up" the way the speech falls upon the ears of the hearers. Once the text of the speech was set, the orator would memorize the speech and go on to consider how best to use his physical presence and gestures in the delivery of the speech.

Since we have only the texts themselves, the stages of memory and delivery are not very helpful for NT interpretation. It is not likely that the reader memorized the letter before sharing its contents, so "memory" simply would not apply. It is worth pondering that the emissary may have been coached in how to deliver the contents to the assembled community, or took thought himself how to make the reading of the letter most effective through varying the tone of his voice, use of physical gestures, and the like, but such matters are irretrievable for us. This means that invention, arrangement, and style are the provinces of most rhetorical-critical studies, and of these the material in the rhetorical handbooks treating the first two is the most helpful in getting at the meaning of a text.

3. Invention: The Three Kinds of Proof

Classical orators understood that people were not persuaded by appeals to the mind alone. They would be influenced by their emotions as well as their assessment of the speaker. Thus rhetorical handbooks routinely refer to three kinds of appeal or proof, which must be woven together into the successful speech — the appeal to logos (the reason of the hearer), pathos (the emotions of the hearer), and ethos (the hearer's perception of the speaker).

While Aristotle says very little about how to make appeals to ethos, he nevertheless calls it the most important form of proof (*Rh.* 1.2.4). A speaker must show himself to be virtuous, expert, and benevolently disposed to the hearers.[118] The combination of these qualities made the speaker credible and

---

118. See Aristotle *Rh.* 2.1.3: "It makes a great difference with regard to producing conviction — especially in demonstrative . . . oratory — that the speaker should show himself to be possessed of certain qualities and that his hearers should think that he is disposed in a certain way towards them; and further, that they themselves should be disposed in a certain way towards him"; *Rh.* 2.1.5: "For the orator to produce conviction three qualities are necessary. . . . These qualities are good sense, virtue, and goodwill (φρόνησις, ἀρετή, εὔνοια)."

disposed the audience to trust and follow him. If prejudice against the speaker exists, this must be eliminated before the speaker can get to the subject matter of his speech.[119] The audience must never be alienated from the speaker — if he blames them harshly he must quickly palliate them so as to assure them of his goodwill toward them. However, it is advantageous to a speaker to cast doubt on the sincerity, reliability, and goodwill of opposing speakers.

Aristotle recognized that people make different decisions when they are angry, calm, afraid, or confident, and that orators frequently used the arousal of particular emotions in the hearers to their advantage (*Rh.* 2.1.2, 4, 8). If an orator wanted to produce a verdict of guilt, he would seek to rouse indignation or anger against the defendant; if he wished to persuade the audience to take a certain course of action, he would perhaps strive to make them feel confident that they could achieve the goal, or afraid or ashamed not to try; and so forth. Aristotle very helpfully gives a long list of topics and situations that arouse eleven different emotions, helping the modern reader to learn sensitivity to this aspect of oratory and to detect where an author may be trying to make his audience feel pity, fear, confidence, emulation, and the like (*Rh.* 2.2–2.11).

Finally, there is the appeal to the reason or mind of the hearer. An orator will tend to establish his case by both deductive and inductive means. Deductive proofs include the syllogism and the enthymeme, which resembles two parts of a syllogism. The orator's aim is to lead the hearer to certain conclusions from established premises (facts that the audience would take for granted and not question) (see Aristotle *Rh.* 2.22; *Rhet. Alex.* 1430a27-34). Syllogisms involve at least two premises and a conclusion, for example:

> All patrons deserve gratitude;
> Erastus has benefited our community;
> Therefore, we must honor Erastus.

An enthymeme typically presupposes a syllogism, but does not rehearse the whole syllogism since the orator will assume that the audience can supply the missing premise: "We ought to honor Erastus, for he has benefited our community," or "Let us honor Erastus, for all patrons deserve gratitude." Aristotle preferred the form of the enthymeme as less pedantic and more effective in persuading. Enthymemes are built around a variety of topics like the possible and impossible, opposites or contraries, the lesser and the greater, projected consequences of an action, analogy, cause and effect, and the like.[120] The topics special to each genre of oratory also provide the raw material of

---

119. See especially *Rhet. Her.* 1.9 on the elimination of prejudice through the "subtle approach."

120. Aristotle provides a host of examples of such topics in *Rh.* 2.18-19, 23-26.

enthymemes (e.g., topics of what is just, expedient, feasible, and the like for a deliberative speech). The example given above employs a topic of justice (the gratitude due benefactors).

Inductive proofs allow the audience to draw the conclusion through consideration of an example (which can be a historical precedent or fictional story) or analogy (Aristotle *Rh.* 2.20; *Rhet. Alex.* 1429a25-28). An orator who wishes to persuade his city to declare war may tell the story of those who, in similar circumstances, forestalled disaster and achieved greatness by taking the initiative in military conflict. Recalling historical precedents was especially effective, since the audience could "see" the outcome of the course they were contemplating (see Aristotle *Rh.* 1.9.40; *Rhet. Alex.* 1428b12-17, 1429a25-28; Quintilian *Inst.* 3.8.36). Dio Chrysostom, in urging his fellow citizens not to parade their quarrels with one another when the new governor first arrived in their province, used analogies drawn from the animal world to support his case (the harmony shown by bees, *Or.* 48.15-16). The author of Hebrews uses many examples and a few analogies (see 3:7–4:11; 6:7-8; 12:2, 16-17) to support his case.

Maxims, legal precedents, and authoritative texts also furnish the raw material of appeals to logos. Maxims or proverbs are statements of common knowledge or opinion, and thus they are likely to add credibility to the conclusions based on them (Aristotle, *Rh.* 2.21; *Rhet. Alex.* 1430a40-1430b7). Similarly, authoritative texts (like Homer and Hesiod for a non-Christian, or the LXX for Christians and Diaspora Jews) lie at the core of group identity and lend their authority freely to the points derived from them. The respect accorded the ancient text bleeds over into the new text.

4. Arrangement: The Outline of a Classical Speech

The typical deliberative or forensic oration consisted of four (following Aristotle) or five (following the Roman rhetoricians) sections, each of which had a particular set of functions.[121] The speech would open with an exordium, the goal of which would be to provide the theme of the speech while also establishing the credibility and authority of the speaker (Aristotle *Rh.* 3.14). The opening should render the hearers "receptive, well-disposed, and attentive" (*Rhet. Her.* 1.4.7). If prejudice existed against the speaker, the exordium could become rather complex as this prejudice would first need to be dismantled. Particularly in forensic speeches this introduction would be followed by a *narratio*, a narration of the events under dispute, which puts the defendant in the most favorable light (if one is the defender) or the most unfavorable light (if one is the ac-

---

121. Eulogies and encomia (epideictic speeches) followed a different outline: external advantages, physical qualities, and moral qualities typically would be handled in turn, although a fair amount of freedom could be expected in the arrangement.

cuser). The narration is not merely a "statement of facts" but a strategically shaped and colored rehearsal of events. After this, one arrives at the proposition, the main point to be demonstrated. The fourth section is the *probatio,* in which were arrayed the proofs at the orator's disposal, generally with the strongest proofs up front and at the end, so as to gain assent early on and leave the hearers with a strong impression. The orator would close with a *peroratio,* in which the main points could be summarized, the concluding exhortation made, appeals to emotion (particularly in legal cases) played heavily, and parting shots taken at the opposing speakers and their cases (Aristotle *Rh.* 3.19).

It is precisely at this point that the rhetorical critics of the NT have come most frequently and most justifiably under fire.[122] Galatians fits this pattern exceptionally well,[123] but other NT texts are resistant to being divided neatly into the four or five parts of the Greco-Roman speech.[124] Thus, it seems more prudent to use the rhetorical handbooks only as strictly or as loosely as the text under investigation suggests, rather than insist on squeezing the text into a mold in which it may not fit. The NT author may have a different plan for achieving the same ends, and the heuristic, rather than normative, quality of the rhetorical handbooks should never be compromised. Hebrews certainly defies division into exordium, *narratio, propositio, probatio,* and *peroratio.* Nevertheless, the classical discussions of what exordia are expected to accomplish help us understand what the author is doing in Hebrews 1:1–2:4. Hebrews 13:1-25, similarly, accomplishes some of the typical functions of perorations. The aim of employing our firsthand knowledge of classical rhetoric is always to lay bare the persuasive techniques and strategies of the author, never to force his text to wear false or misleading labels for the sake of preserving some "textbook" scheme.

Rhetorical Goal and Rhetorical Genre

The attempt to determine whether a NT text is "deliberative," "forensic," or "epideictic" is more than the quest for a label. Rather, it represents an attempt

---

122. See, for example, Gordon Fee's criticism (*Philippians* [NICNT; Grand Rapids: Eerdmans, 1997], 15-16 nn. 41-42) of the cogent but irreconcilable attempts to analyze Philippians according to this five-part scheme by Duane Watson ("A Rhetorical Analysis of Philippians and Its Implications for the Unity Question," *NovT* 30 [1988]: 57-88) and L. Gregory Bloomquist (*The Function of Suffering in Philippians* [JSNTSS 78; Sheffield: Sheffield Academic Press, 1993], 84-96, 119-38).

123. See H. D. Betz, *Galatians* (Hermeneia; Philadelphia: Fortress, 1979).

124. Ben Witherington III (*Conflict and Community in Corinth: A Socio-Rhetorical Commentary on 1 and 2 Corinthians* [Grand Rapids: Eerdmans, 1995]) avoids this pitfall by recognizing that a single letter can contain several discrete arguments, each with their own proposition and proofs.

to discern the fundamental issue in the situation addressed by the text and the principal goal of the author for the people in that situation. It is a way of focusing on what the author wants to accomplish through the text, and it provides a focal point for the exposition of the whole — we can keep returning to that fundamental goal, asking how each passage contributes to moving the hearers closer to responding as the author desires.

Early attempts to fit Hebrews into the form of a forensic (judicial) speech[125] gave way to the long-standing and as yet unresolved debate concerning whether Hebrews is epideictic or deliberative. The author calls his own work a λόγος τῆς παρακλήσεως (13:22), which Harold Attridge takes as an indication of its epideictic character, a sermon "celebrating the significance of Christ and inculcating values that his followers ought to share."[126] While the phrase "word of encouragement" is more suggestive of deliberation, epideictic oratory includes a strong element of inculcating values, virtues, and commitment to a certain way of life. Thomas Olbricht has also proposed that the epideictic genre dominates Hebrews, and has outlined its structure according to the plan of a Hellenistic funeral oration.[127]

Walter G. Übelacker, Barnabas Lindars, and others, however, advance strong cases for regarding Hebrews as a deliberative speech.[128] These emphasize the prominent place given to exhortation in the letter (2:1-4; 3:1, 7-13; 4:1, 11, 14-16; 6:1-3; 10:19-39; 12:1–13:19), which suggests that the author is mainly concerned with urging the community to take a particular course of action. The passages of sustained argumentation serve the purpose of leading the addressees to heed the imperatives and cohortatives, which appear in groups of varying lengths clustered at the end of these arguments.[129]

The problem of the genre of Hebrews arises from the nearly balanced sections of encomiastic exposition and exhortations, a feature that must be dealt with by any attempt to outline the structure and argument. The expository sections of Hebrews move largely within the sphere of *synkrisis*, "comparison," a de-

---

125. E.g., the work of F. von Soden, T. Haering, and H. Windisch, summarized in Lane, *Hebrews,* lxxvii.

126. Attridge, *Hebrews,* 14.

127. Olbricht, "Hebrews as Amplification," 378.

128. Walter G. Übelacker, *Der Hebräerbrief als Appel* (Stockholm: Almqvist & Wiksell, 1989), 214-29, who even analyzes the whole according to the pattern found in Aristotle, *Rh.* 3.13-19; Barnabas Lindars, "The Rhetorical Structure of Hebrews," *NTS* 35 (1989): 382-406; C. P. Anderson, *The Setting of the Epistle to the Hebrews* (Ph.D. dissertation, Columbia University, 1969) 201, 202; T. E. Schmidt, "Moral Lethargy and the Epistle to the Hebrews," *WTJ* 54 (1992): 169; Worley especially stresses the importance of the author's own designation of the work as a λόγος τῆς παρακλήσεως ("God's Faithfulness to Promise," 52).

129. Lane, *Hebrews 1–8,* xcix-c.

vice usually associated with encomia.[130] Hebrews thus gives the impression of being an epideictic speech in praise of Jesus' singular achievements. Nevertheless, Hebrews is punctuated throughout by well-developed exhortations. These are connected, moreover, by inferential particles such as διό and οὖν to the expositional sections that precede them, suggesting that each exposition serves to set up the following exhortation. We must conclude, therefore, that Hebrews, like many orations, utilizes elements of both epideictic and deliberative oratory. The question remains as to which genre represents the author's primary concern and which is ancillary to that goal. A closer look at the topics employed in this text may help lead to a more secure assessment of the rhetorical goal of Hebrews.

1. Hebrews as Deliberative Rhetoric

The *Rhetorica ad Herennium* defines a deliberative speech as "the kind in which the question concerns a choice between two courses of action, or of the kind in which a choice among several is considered" (3.2.2). Hebrews nurtures the sense of a deliberative environment by referring frequently to two contrasting courses of action open to the hearers. Furthermore, the focus of deliberative proofs is on the consequences that follow the possible courses (*Rhet. Her.* 3.17.4): Hebrews lays great stress on the beneficial consequences of one course and the detrimental consequences of the alternative course. Part of the rhetorical strategy is to present in the most negative terms (such as "apostasy," "trampling on God's Son," and the like) the course of seeking peace with society, and thus of compromising one's commitment to the distinctive values of the group.

The addressees are urged to "pay attention" to the message they have received rather than "drift" off. "Neglecting" the deliverance that God has prepared would result in divine punishment (2:1-4; 12:25). They will retain the advantages of being "God's house" and "Christ's partners" if they maintain their commitment to the Christian group (3:6, 14). "Turning away from the living God," showing "distrust" toward God, results in the forfeiture of the deliverance and eternal benefits God has prepared (3:12; 4:1). They are urged to "strive earnestly to enter" God's rest rather than fall short, imitating the negative paradigm of the wilderness generation (4:11; 12:15). Rather, they are to imitate those who persevere in trust and inherit what is promised (6:11), to hold onto their confession (4:14; 10:23), to draw near to God's throne for the resources to persevere (4:16; 10:22). They are exhorted to press on to the end of that journey, which began with their elementary instruction in the faith (6:1), because the contrary course results in permanent exclusion from God's favor (6:4-8). They are not to forsake the assem-

---

130. Thus Aristotle (*Rh.* 1.9.38) advises concerning how to develop the praise of one's subject: "And you must compare him with illustrious personages, for it affords ground for amplification and is noble, if he can be proved better than men of worth."

bly of believers (10:25), for "shrinking back" from the contest with the unbelieving society (10:37-39) results in God's displeasure and, ultimately, their destruction. Thinking so little of God's benefits that one renounces them for the sake of peace with the world leads not to safety but to the gravest danger (10:26-31). Those who follow such a course are like Esau, who also was permitted no second chance to make the right choice, but had to live with his loss and disgrace (12:16-17). Retaining their bold commitment to God's promises, however, results in reward and preservation (10:35, 39). The hearers are urged to show gratitude for the eternal benefits they are receiving (the unshakable kingdom, 12:28, which will be their permanent and lasting homeland and city), to show courage in their race for the greater prize (12:1), and to endure society's hostility as a sign of God's adoption (12:5-11) and as a fitting recompense for the one who endured such hostility and reproach on their behalf (13:11-14). When all the consequences are weighed, the course for the wise to pursue is to keep investing themselves in the worship of God through Jesus and in the nurturing of the community of God's many sons and daughters (13:1-3, 15-16).

There is, therefore, a strong element in Hebrews of dissuasion from one course of action (hiding or renouncing one's connections with the Christian group) and persuasion to maintain the course of action begun at conversion. The author minimizes the advantages and maximizes the disadvantages of pulling away from the group and its confession, and maximizes the advantages and minimizes the disadvantages of remaining firm in one's commitment and continuing to invest oneself in the group.

Moreover, Hebrews is replete with topics typically associated with deliberation in the rhetorical handbooks. The aim of the one who seeks to persuade hearers to take a certain course must endeavor to show that the course is just and virtuous, feasible, honorable, and advantageous. It must be shown that it results in the preservation or advancement of the honor and security of those who will undertake such a course. Those who dissuade, however, must show that a course of action is unjust (or contrary to some other virtue, like foolish or cowardly), dishonorable, and inexpedient — in short, leading to disgrace and danger for those who undertake it.

Justice in the ancient world meant honoring one's obligations, giving to each person what was due him or her. The *Rhetorica ad Herennium* very helpfully rounds out what acting justly entailed, and thus it assists us in detecting topics of justice in texts:[131]

---

131. This is supplemented by *Rhet. Alex.* 1421b37-1422a2: "What is just is the unwritten custom of the whole or the greater part of mankind, distinguishing honourable actions from base ones. The former are to honour one's parents, do good to one's friends and repay favours to one's benefactors; for these and similar rules are not enjoined on men by written laws but are observed by unwritten customs and universal practice."

> We shall be using the topics of Justice . . . if we show that it is proper to repay
> the well-deserving with gratitude; . . . if we urge that faith *(fidem)* ought zeal-
> ously to be kept; . . . if we contend that alliances and friendships should scru-
> pulously be honored; if we make it clear that the duty imposed by nature to-
> wards parents, gods, and the fatherland *(in parentes, deos, patriam)* must be
> religiously observed; if we maintain that ties of hospitality, clientage, kinship,
> and relationship by marriage must inviolably be cherished; if we show that
> neither reward nor favour nor peril nor animosity ought to lead us astray
> from the right path. . . . By their contraries we shall demonstrate that an ac-
> tion is unjust. (*Rhet. Her.* 3.3.4)

The author of Hebrews employs many subtopics of justice as he urges continued commitment to the Christian enterprise. He instructs the members of the
community to maintain the obligations of kinship toward one another (13:1, 3)
— obligations that they assumed when they became part of the "household of
God" (10:21; cf. 3:6). Similarly, he urges the continued fulfillment of the obligations of hospitality (13:2) and the marital covenant (13:4). The primary obligation that must be maintained, however, is that of clientage. Jesus has been presented as the believers' patron (2:9-18), who has given them, among other
noteworthy gifts, access to God as their personal Patron (4:14-16; 10:19-21). It
would be unjust to show disloyalty, dishonoring this selfless benefactor and
spurning his gifts — an injustice not without severe consequences for the addressees (6:4-8; 10:24-31). He urges rather that steadfastness and gratitude be
preserved toward the community's Benefactor (10:23; 12:28), that the alliance
formed at conversion be preserved to the end unblemished.

Hebrews also favors topics of courage, which the *Rhetorica ad Herennium*
(3.3.5) describes in this way:

> When we invoke as motive for a course of action steadfastness in Courage, we
> shall make it clear that . . . from an honorable act no peril or toil, however
> great, should divert us; death ought to be preferred to disgrace; no pain
> should force abandonment of duty; . . . for country *(patria)*, for parents,
> guest-friends, intimates, and for the things justice commands us to respect, it
> behooves us to brave any peril and endure any toil.

Since perils do indeed await the one who remains loyal to the One God and Jesus, the author uses topics of courage to urge them not to allow the threats of
temporary hardship and pain to divert them from the honorable course. They
are not to be cowards who shrink back from the contest. Just as their benefactor
did not shrink back from shame and pain on their behalf (12:1-3), they are to
persevere in loyalty (10:36-39), just as they had done in the past (10:32-35).
They are to match his loyalty and courage with their own (13:12-14) and endure temporary hardships, which lead to honor (12:5-11). Jesus is not only an

example of faith, but also of courage, enduring hardship for the sake of a noble goal (2:9, 14-15; 12:2).

Honor is an essential component of deliberations, insofar as the audience seeks to preserve the honor and reputation it currently enjoys and augment them if at all possible. A course of action that would injure their honor would be rejected outright.[132] Turning away (even drifting away) from Christ and his people leads to the disgrace of punishment (2:1-4; 10:26-31), the physical enactment of a negative assessment of one's worth and virtue. Such a person will be remembered as kin to Esau, who earned a lasting dishonorable remembrance for his foolish choice (12:16-17) and became a byword for poor judgment. Remaining firm in one's trust and loyalty, however, means that one retains the honor of being claimed by God as a son or daughter (2:10; 12:5-11) and part of God's household (3:6), of being in partnership with the exalted Son (2:11-13; 3:14), arriving at the "glory" (2:10) to which he leads his many sisters and brothers. Ultimately it leads to enfranchisement in the lasting city, which God himself has founded (11:13-16; 13:13-14). Citizenship in that city is more noble than citizenship in any earthly, temporary city.

The *Rhetorica ad Alexandrum* defines expediency as "the preservation of existing good things, or the acquisition of goods that we do not possess, or the rejection of existing evils, or the prevention of harmful things expected to occur" (1422a4-7). The author of Hebrews, again, has made extensive use of such considerations. Maintaining solidarity with fellow Christians, one retains the good of being part of God's household, sharing in the honor and enjoying the protection and help of the head of that household (3:6; 4:14-16). The person who trusts God's promises and lives accordingly as a grateful, obedient, and loyal client will attain the eternal goods promised — "eternal salvation" (5:9), survival of the eschatological "shaking," and entrance into God's rest, the heavenly city and homeland (4:2, 6, 11; 12:28; 13:14), where one will enjoy the honor of being God's child and sharing God's virtuous character (2:10; 12:5-11). Continued investment in one another and the Christian hope is the way to preserve the "better and lasting possessions" (10:34) as well as to receive the promised reward (10:35-36). Choosing reconciliation with one's non-Christian neighbors over remaining loyal to the divine Patron, however, is presented as an extremely inexpedient course of action. The one who takes that path loses the benefit of face-to-face access with God as one's personal patron and the prestige of being part of God's household and family. Not only is such a person deprived of the hope of recovering those goods once lost (6:4-8), but he or she also loses any hope for attaining

---

132. Thus *Rhet. Her.* 3.5.8-9. For fuller discussion of the role of considerations on honor in oratory, see deSilva, *Despising Shame,* 37-79; idem, "Investigating Honor Discourse: Guidelines from Classical Rhetoricians," *SBLSP 36* (1997): 491-525.

the goods that had been promised for the future — deliverance at the day of judgment, reception into the unshakable kingdom after the cosmic cataclysm, and entrance into God's rest, the heavenly homeland, and into the real presence of God. In addition to the loss of goods currently enjoyed, "shrinking back" will bring down upon the head of the disloyal the greatest evil — exclusion from God's favor (6:4-8), the experience of God's wrath (3:17), punishment worse than death (2:1-4; 10:26-31), and "destruction" (10:39).

Another prominent topic in deliberation is security — Will a certain course of action expose the doers to risks and harm, or will it insulate them from loss and harm? Will it make their lives more secure, or more liable to peril? Since these topics overlap somewhat, it can probably be discerned from the foregoing discussion how the author of Hebrews employs this topic. As long as the addressees remain loyal, trusting clients, they have the security that a divine ally and patron provides; if they choose a course of action that dishonors and provokes this ally, they expose themselves to grave peril. As the ensuing commentary will demonstrate, the author's skillful use of appeals to the emotions of fear and confidence especially underscore his use of these topics.

Remaining committed to the Christian minority culture meant continued struggle against the tide of society. It is important, therefore, that the author stress that this course of action would be feasible. To this end, he points repeatedly to the help and resources at the disposal of the believers, the assistance that is theirs for the asking (2:16, 18; 4:14-16; 13:5-6, 20-21). Both the Son and God stand ready to provide "timely help." Moreover, the author emphasizes that the larger part of their work has already been accomplished — what is needed now is not more massive investment but merely endurance for "yet a little while" (10:35-37). A host of examples stand near at hand to show that the contest can be endured, and the example of Jesus, who endured far more than the audience has been called on to endure, especially assures the hearers that they can persevere (12:3-4).

More detailed discussion of how the author employs these and other deliberative topics will follow in the commentary, but the above observations should suffice to show that the author of Hebrews is intent on supporting commitment to the group as the virtuous, safe, noble, expedient course and defection or drifting off as unjust, cowardly, disgraceful, dangerous, and inexpedient courses — that is to say, he gives considerable space and emphasis to deliberative topics.

2. Epideictic Topics in Hebrews

While Hebrews closely resembles a deliberative speech with its clear delineation of two courses of action, its projections of the consequences of each course, and its utilization of special, deliberative topics, this sermon also employs numerous epideictic topics from beginning to end. While Thomas Olbricht has pushed the case for reading Hebrews as a funeral oration beyond what the text will bear, he is nevertheless correct to notice that the author has woven in many topics from such a context into his expositions of Jesus' achievement and person.

The funeral oration praised notable aspects of the subject's life (nobility of birth, illustrious ancestors, education, fame, offices, wealth, and death), the person's physical excellences (strength, beauty, health), and his or her moral qualities (virtues like courage, prudence, justice, temperance, nobility, and magnanimity), especially as these were manifested in actions that were beneficial to others and were performed in a timely manner, at great cost to oneself, efficiently, alone, and the like.[133]

The author of Hebrews will include many of these topics in his presentation of Jesus. The descent of Jesus, the Son, is set forth in 1:1-14, which marks his honorable and noble birth. Melchizedek also functions in some ways as Christ's ancestor, so that praise of Melchizedek underscores the honor of his successor in the priesthood. Jesus' education and its noble fruits are mentioned in 5:7-10. Notice of the office of high priest held by Jesus and his session at God's right hand completes the catalog of these notable aspects. Jesus' physical advantages are evident in his "indestructible life" (7:16). More space is given to his moral excellence. His virtues include piety (5:7), holiness, and blamelessness (7:28). He faced every temptation, yet remained steadfast in virtue and sinlessness (4:15). Committed to do God's will, Jesus embodied the value of obedience and piety (5:8; 10:4-6). His death is especially the focal point for the display of virtue, for he approached it courageously (2:14-15; 12:2) in order to bring benefit to others (freedom from slavery and from fear of death). His death on behalf of everyone (2:9) was both noble and happy. The "great cost to himself" is emphasized in 2:14 and 12:3-4, which speak of his endurance of hostility and death, as well as throughout 9:11–10:18, which speaks of his offering up of his own life for the sake of others. Altruistic motives for his actions come to the fore in his commitment to rescue the enslaved and help the "descendants of Abraham" (2:15-18).

Jesus has used his natural advantages — his relationship with God and his endless life — to bring benefit to others. He is the "source of eternal deliverance" (5:9) for those who obey him, giving the gift of open access to God and the resources God can provide (4:14-16) by interceding continually for those

---

133. The most complete discussions of this rhetorical form can be found in *Rhet. Her.* 3.6-7; *Rhet. Alex.* 1440b5-1441a13; Quintilian *Inst.*3.7.7-28. Theon includes a discussion of this form in his *Progymnasmata,* helpfully summarized in H. I. Marrou, *A History of Education in Antiquity* (New York: Mentor, 1956), 272-73.

who come to God through him (7:25). Moreover, Jesus has accomplished what no other had done previously (10:11-12): cleansing the consciences of the worshipers so that they could enter God's presence (9:11-14; 10:19-22) and effecting the removal of sins (10:1-18). While the levitical priests vainly attempted this *en masse*, Jesus accomplished it alone with an efficient, single act. The use made of comparison, or *synkrisis*, also belongs to the genre of the eulogy. The comparisons of Jesus and the angels, Moses, and levitical priests — all of which serve to underscore the greater status or accomplishments of Jesus — belong to an epideictic mode of discourse.[134] From the material in Hebrews, therefore, one could construct a rather complete eulogy of Jesus. Hebrews as it stands, however, cannot be reduced to a eulogy.

The question is not whether Hebrews has elements of deliberative and epideictic oratory,[135] but rather how the elements work together within this text. It is difficult to construe the deliberative elements as subordinate to the epideictic. In a typical epideictic speech, there may be some concluding exhortations to imitate the subject, or even to take up the way of life therein praised.[136] There is not, however, the extended consideration of the relative expedience, or the consequences, of espousing or not espousing those virtues or that way of life. There is no bolstering of the argument through frequent recourse to topics of justice, feasibility, safety, and the like. In Hebrews the epideictic topics serve the deliberative topics, motivating the audience to pursue the course promoted and to avoid the alternative course. We will look at only a few examples here, saving the full discussion for the appropriate passages in the commentary.

The opening of the sermon is dominated by what could be called epideictic topics. The amplification of the honor and status of the Son, particularly through the comparison *(synkrisis)* of the Son with the angels (1:5-14), clearly moves in epideictic modes. What does the author do with this comparison, however? How does it function in the broader argument? The author moves to an exhortation in the form of a lesser-to-greater argument (2:1-4): neglecting the salvation announced in the gospel is a dangerous course of action, resulting in punishment greater than that which attended the violation of the message announced through angels (i.e.,Torah). Hebrews 1:5-14 provides

---

134. Comparison of the subject of a eulogy with his or her peers, or with figures of renown, in order to demonstrate the subject's superiority in some regard was recommended in Aristotle *Rh.* 1.9.38-39; *Rhet. Alex.* 1441a27-28.

135. It appears to have no real connections with forensic rhetoric. Even the discussions of culpability and punishment in 2:1-4 or 10:26-31 concern the consequences that would follow upon a course of action yet to be taken, and so fall within the realm of deliberative oratory.

136. See Epictetus *Diss.* 3.22 on the way of life espoused by the Cynic or 4 Maccabees on the advantages of the Jewish way of life.

the unstated premise in the enthymeme of 2:2-3 by demonstrating the superiority of one messenger over the others. Just as Jesus' honor is greater than that of angels, affronts to his honor (in the form of thinking lightly of the deliverance he won) will be punished proportionately more severely. In 1:1–2:4, then, epideictic topics are used to serve a hortatory goal.

The author's comparison of Jesus' mediation and priestly work with that of the descendants of Levi is not undertaken merely to demonstrate Jesus' superior accomplishment, as in a funeral oration. Rather, it serves as an extended development of a topic of amplification, magnifying the value of the access to God made possible by Jesus — an access never before available to God's covenant people. The incomparable value of Jesus' gift of access to God is used by the author to motivate the hearers to preserve that advantage (10:18-25), as well as to heighten the folly and danger of renouncing such an advantage, which was won for the clients at such a cost to the Mediator (10:26-31; 12:16-17). The author's extensive consideration of the unparalleled goods provided by Jesus and available to those who "approach God through him" (7:25) lends weight to the appeals not to choose any course of action that would lead to the loss of those goods. Dwelling on the magnitude of Jesus' benefactions and the noble and selfless spirit in which he secured them for the addressees heightens the appeals to topics of the just (the appropriateness of remaining loyal clients) and the unjust (the baseness of showing ingratitude or dishonoring such a noble patron).

Finally, we should consider what is perhaps the most well-known part of Hebrews, namely, the encomium on faith in 11:1–12:3. It begins with a definition of the virtue and then celebrates in laudatory fashion those noble figures who embodied faith and who, through faith, made wise choices with regard to short-lived versus lasting goods and who showed courage and temperance. This encomium, however, serves to support the author's exhortations to "hold fast" and remain committed to the Christian confession and hope throughout the sermon. As an encomium, it shows that the path of trust and loyalty is an honorable path, for those who walked it before the hearers have been remembered across centuries for their commitment to God and God's reward. As a series of examples, however, it also speaks closely to the situation of the hearers, who need to discern from contemplation of past examples what course will be advantageous for their future. The esteem in which Abraham, Moses, and the martyrs are held within the Jewish and Christian culture, not to mention the conviction that they enjoy God's "attestation," affirms that their choices resulted in lasting honor, even though they entailed temporary disgrace. Jesus himself provides the capstone to this list since by the path of hardship and ultimate disgrace (the cross) he came to the highest place in the cosmos, the right hand of God. This list of examples, therefore, encourages the addressees in their deliberations to consider that the temporary disgrace that is the cost of discipleship will result in eternal honor.[137] It helps them to chose against defection now and to see in a different, less threatening light the social pressures that might move them to defect in the future.

3. Conclusion

It is clear that the author of Hebrews envisions two opposing courses of action that lay before his hearers. They may choose to remain committed to the Christian confession and hope (and thus to one another and to Christ), or they may "turn away from the living God." Much of Hebrews is calculated to heighten the advantages that accompany, and the positive consequences that follow, the first course of action and the disastrous consequences that would follow the second course. The author's comparisons of Jesus with the other mediators sanctioned by the authoritative tradition (the OT) ultimately serve to magnify the goods and the advantages that the believers now enjoy, and thus to magnify the folly of relinquishing those goods and advantages by "shrinking back," "drifting off," or "falling short." The author's amplification of Jesus' benefactions for the community (indeed all humanity) heighten the topics of the just and the unjust employed throughout the sermon. Such amplification persuades the audience to remain loyal, obedient clients and dissuades them from the alternative course, which would return insult for such favors. The author's celebration of Jesus' exalted status heightens the dangerous consequences of finding oneself alienated from, even inimical to, such a powerful person on the day of reckoning. Laudatory treatment of those who have previously pursued the path of firmness encourages the audience to pursue that path in the future. Hebrews can thus be analyzed as a deliberative speech that uses epideictic topics extensively to amplify the significance of making the right choice between remaining firm and turning away, between pursuing friendship with God and friendship with one's unbelieving neighbors.

Nevertheless, Hebrews surely does not address a whole assembly that is contemplating falling away. Many in the congregation are no doubt as committed to the confession and hope as the author himself, and indeed his strategy depends on having a solid core of believers who will encourage the wavering, warn those who are being deceived by sin, and assist those who are in danger of stopping short of the prize. Hebrews will function to ground such

---

137. Aristotle (*Rh.* 1.9.35-36) writes that "praise and counsels have a common aspect; for what you might suggest in counselling becomes encomium by a change in the phrase. . . . Accordingly, if you desire to praise, look what you would suggest; if you desire to suggest, look what you would praise." This gives us some insight into how positive, praiseworthy examples and negative, censurable paradigms would function in a deliberative speech, providing historical examples that support the recommendations being made by the speaker.

hearers in the values they already hold, even while it seeks to dissuade the wavering from choosing a disadvantageous course of action. Ultimately, the condition of each individual hearer will determine whether Hebrews will achieve the goals of epideictic or deliberative rhetoric. Confusion about its genre results from the rather general nature of the two courses it contemplates, and from the nature of the speech itself. It resembles the sort of speech one would hear on the eve of a great battle, in the midst or at the end of a long campaign. Some of the hearers are ready for the fight, and so the speech reinforces the commitment with which they come to the field. Some have lost their initial vision and zeal for the fight and need encouragement to reinvest themselves in the endeavor. Some need to be kept from running off the field during the night. For the first group, Hebrews will function more like an epideictic speech — the deliberations are purely academic. For the second two groups, the question of whether or not to continue investing themselves in a particular course of action is real, and thus the book's discussions of the ramifications of each choice are real.

William Lane shows proper restraint in affirming that "Hebrews cannot be forced into the mold of a classical speech. . . . Rhetorical devices are clearly discernible in Hebrews, but the presence of an identifiable rhetorical structure is less evident."[138] This is not to deny our earlier observation that Hebrews exhibits great artistry in weaving together its discrete units into a coherent and persuasive whole: rather, the pattern for that whole is not to be sought through wooden application of the usual patterns of arrangement found in rhetorical handbooks. Indeed, the overall pattern is more suggestive of the so-called homily form — a genre suggested by the author's own designation of the work as a λόγος τῆς παρακλήσεως.[139] This term also appears in Acts 13:15, providing a term for the usual synagogue homily, of which Paul's speech in 13:16-41 is presumably a truncated example.[140] Hebrews' frequent alternation between argument from Scripture (as authoritative text, and bearer of "first level rhetorical

---

138. Lane, *Hebrews 1–8*, lxxix; cf. Guthrie, *Structure of Hebrews*, 32.

139. While the author has closed his communication with the elements that were becoming standard parts of the epistolary postscripts of Christian missives, Hebrews strikingly lacks the epistolary prescript, offering instead an artistically crafted, rhetorically embellished opening sentence that gives every indication of being more the script for an oration than the beginning of an "epistle." It is thus the most openly and clearly "rhetorical" of the NT letters and, not surprisingly, very congenial to rhetorical analysis.

140. See Lane, *Hebrews 1–8*, lxx-lxxiv for a discussion of research on this form. H. Thyen executes an in-depth analysis of Hebrews as a λόγος τῆς παρακλήσεως, taken as a technical term for the Jewish-Hellenistic homily, in his *Der Stil der jüdische-hellenistichen Homilie* (FRLANT 47; Göttingen: Vandenhoeck & Ruprecht, 1955). Witherington ("Influence," 147) also suggests that it might be preferable to construe this text as the "Homily to the Hebrews" rather than as an epistle, strictly speaking.

power"[141]) and application appears to reflect a macrostructure more in keeping
with the text-centered synagogue oration. While arrangement appears to be derived largely from the form of the homily, its argumentative elements and strategies are largely informed by classical Greco-Roman rhetorical practice.

The Socio-Rhetorical Strategy of Hebrews — An Overview

The preceding discussion of deliberative and epideictic topics in Hebrews has
already begun to lay out the strategy of this sermon from a strictly rhetorical
point of view. There a number of key components of this author's strategy,
however, that we would do well to bear in mind as we move through the text in
a more detailed manner. This involves pushing beyond the rhetorical strategy
to the ideological and social strategies employed by the author to accomplish
his goals for the community addressed.

1. Repositioning the Deliberations

Some of the addressees have begun to consider the cost of discipleship too great
in terms of what they have lost in status, acceptance, and wealth in society.
Their focus has moved from their hope and their relationship with God to the
hostility and disapproval of their unbelieving neighbors. An essential element
in the author's strategy is to reorient those wavering Christians to their Christian commitment. From the opening paragraph through the concluding exhortations, he calls their attention to the Son and to the significance of the response they have made to him. He draws out the beneficence of the Son toward
the addressees, who have enjoyed many gifts and advantages through him (see
below); he also draws out the eschatological role of the Son, whose enemies will
be subjugated beneath his feet (1:13; 10:13) but whose loyal friends will receive
"salvation" and "reward" at his coming (1:14; 9:28; 10:36). The main questions
facing the addressees as the author repositions the deliberations are, How will
they respond to the Son, and how will they encounter him at his appearing? Everything in the sermon leads the addressees to see losing the promised reward
and incurring God's wrath as the "real" dangers facing them (see especially 2:1-
4; 4:1-13; 6:4-8; 10:26-31; 12:16-17, 25), not the ongoing loss of temporal prestige and goods.

Part of this reorientation involves the reinforcement of the Christian culture's definition of "happiness" and "advantage." The author wants the wavering to begin to think in terms of the "eternal" again rather than the "temporal,"
just as they had in the earlier days of their Christian experience when they "ac-

---

141. Olbricht, "Hebrews as Amplification," 382.

cepted with joy the plundering of their property," knowing that they had "better and lasting possessions" (10:34). He seeks to raise the "reality" of the Christian hope above the everyday "reality" of the discouraging perception of having lost important goods like honor and wealth. Aristotle wrote that the aim of deliberation is happiness — how to preserve happiness and its component parts from loss and make their enjoyment more secure (*Rh.* 1.5.1-2). These components of happiness include noble birth, numerous and good friends, wealth, health, a good reputation, honor, and virtue (*Rh.* 1.5.4), in short, many of the things that were put in jeopardy and in fact lost as a result of joining the Christian movement (Heb. 10:32-34; see also the testimony of 1 Pet. 3:13-17; 4:1-4, 13-16; 1 Thess. 2:14-16).

With their eyes drifting toward their temporal losses and losing sight of the greater goods for which they accepted these losses, the wavering believers might well be tempted to seek to regain their happiness through yielding to their unbelieving neighbors' correction, "coming back to their senses," as it were. For this reason, the author takes great pains to redefine their real happiness as consisting in the eternal, lasting goods that belong to the Christian hope. Remaining connected to the community gives them "noble birth" as children of God as well as virtuous friends in the person of Christ and one another. They have honor as members of God's household (3:6; 10:21), and they look forward to greater honor in their heavenly homeland, the lasting city wherein they hold their citizenship (2:10; 11:13-16; 13:14). The wealth of this world is of secondary value since the material creation is destined for dissolution (12:26-28), but the believers have been promised "lasting possessions" that are "better" by virtue of their existence in the unshakable realm, in the "better" homeland of heaven (in the sense of the presently invisible realm) that will "endure" the eschatological shaking. The examples of Moses and Esau reinforce the author's strategy here. Moses renounced the wealth of Egypt and the honor and status of being heir to Pharaoh's throne for the sake of the reward promised to those who remain attached to the "people of God" (11:24-26). To choose temporary "happiness" over eternal happiness, even though the latter requires some hardship now, is to show oneself as foolish as Esau, who exchanged the double portion of the firstborn's inheritance for a bowl of soup.

2. Responding to the Divine Benefactor

The author of Hebrews makes extensive use of the social code of reciprocity, the mutual expectations and obligations of patrons and clients, in his sermon. This institution was a mainstay of first-century life: the giving and receiving of benefactions was "the practice that constitutes the chief bond of human society" (Seneca *Ben.* 1.4.2). This ethos, well established around the Mediterranean in both Jewish and Greco-Roman cultures, survives only in the most diluted form in most English-speaking countries. Therefore, some introduction to this cultural background is essential for the modern reader's appreciation of the socio-rhetorical strategy of Hebrews.[142]

In a world in which wealth and property were concentrated into the hands of a very small percentage of the population, the majority of people often found themselves in need of assistance in one form or another, and therefore they had to seek the patronage of someone who was better placed in the world than they. Patrons might be asked to provide money, grain, employment, or land; the better-connected persons could be sought out as patrons for the opportunities they would give for professional or social advancement. These latter benefactions were frequently sought from, or offered by, governing officials.[143] Sometimes the most important gift a patron could give was access to another patron.[144] One who received a benefit became a client to the patron, accepting the obligation to publicize the favor and his or her gratitude for it, thus contributing to the patron's reputation.[145] The client also accepted the obligation of

---

142. For more detailed resources on patronage in the ancient world, the reader should consult Seneca On Benefits (De beneficiis) in its entirety, as well as Dio Chrysostom's Thirty-first Oration. Essential works in this area include R. P. Saller, *Personal Patronage under the Early Empire* (Cambridge: Cambridge University Press, 1982); F. W. Danker, *Benefactor: Epigraphic Study of a Graeco-Roman and New Testament Semantic Field* (St. Louis, MO: Clayton Publishing House, 1982). Briefer secondary resources can be found in John H. Elliott, "Patronage and Clientism in Early Christian Society," *Forum* 3 (1987): 39-48; deSilva, *Despising Shame*, 226-44, 272-75; idem, *4 Maccabees* (Guides to Apocrypha and Pseudepigrapha; Sheffield: Sheffield Academic Press, 1998), 127-33. Some NT texts, outside of Hebrews, in which patron-client or friendship (as it is called between social equals) scripts are particularly prominent include Luke 7:1-10; Gal. 2:21; 5:1-4; and Philemon. For those readers wishing to find exercises in sharpening their awareness of this background, these are useful places to begin.

143. Pliny was frequently approached by people in the province of Bithynia for the favor of advancement at the imperial court of Trajan or some other form of social improvement like citizenship (see his *Letters*, book 10). In 4 Maccabees, King Antiochus IV tempts young Jews to defect from the Jewish way of life and embrace the Greek way of life by offering to become the personal patron of those who yield (8.3-7).

144. The term "mediator" applies to such a person, for what the person supplies to his client is a connection to some other patron who would otherwise be inaccessible to the client. Priests were viewed as such "mediators" in the ancient world, for they provided access to God or the gods and maintained that relationship on behalf of the people. The term "broker" has been introduced into the literature by Jeremy Boissevain (*Friends of Friends: Networks, Manipulators, and Coalitions* [New York: St. Martin's, 1974]) for persons whose principal benefaction is access to another person's favors.

145. Seneca *Ben.* 2.22.1; 2.24.2. Aristotle (*Eth. Nic.* 8.13.2 [1163b1-5]) captures the essence of this exchange: "Both parties should receive a larger share from the friendship, but not a larger share of the same thing: the superior should receive the larger share of honour, the needy one the larger share of profit; for honour is the due reward of virtue and benefi-

loyalty to his patron and could be called upon to perform services for the patron, thus contributing to the patron's power.

The reception of a gift and the acceptance of the obligation of gratitude are inseparable (see Seneca *Ben.* 2.25.3; 5.11.5; Ps. 116:12-19). A repeated theme in Seneca and Dio is that the social order works only as long as people honor their reciprocal obligations to one another. Greco-Roman mythology uses the image of the three Graces dancing hand-in-hand in a circle to depict this concept:

> There is one for bestowing a benefit, one for receiving it, and a third for returning it. . . . Why do the sisters hand in hand dance in a ring that returns upon itself? For the reason that a benefit passing in its course from hand to hand returns nevertheless to the giver; the beauty of the whole is destroyed if the course is anywhere broken, and it has most beauty if it is continuous and maintains an uninterrupted succession. (Seneca *Ben.* 1.3.2-3)

The terms "grace" (χάρις) and "faith" (πίστις), now associated mainly with theology and religious contexts, were actually key terms in discussions of the roles and obligations of patrons and clients. Grace had three distinct meanings within this social context. It could refer to the benefactor's favorable disposition toward the petitioner (cf. Aristotle *Rh.* 2.7.2), the actual benefit conferred (cf. 2 Cor. 8:19), or the client's gratitude, the necessary and appropriate return for favor shown (cf. Heb. 12:28). A person who received "grace" in the form of a patron's favor and gifts knew also that "grace" must be returned. Reciprocity was central to this society. Gratitude involved a client's acting in such a way as to enhance the patron's honor and avoiding any course of action that would bring the patron into dishonor. The client also had to display intense personal loyalty to the patron, even if that loyalty should lead one to lose one's home, physical well-being, wealth, or reputation.[146] This was a sacred obligation, and the client who failed to show gratitude appropriately committed an act of injustice akin to sacrilege (thus Dio *Or.* 31.37; Seneca *Ben.* 1.4.4). The greater the benefit bestowed, the greater should be the response of gratitude.

---

cence (τῆς μὲν γὰρ ἀρετῆς καὶ τῆς εὐεργεσίας ἡ τιμὴ γέρας), while need obtains the aid it requires in pecuniary gain." People of similar social standing would also engage in reciprocity, but as "friends," exchanging goods and services of like value. Loyalty among friends was, of course, still essential.

146. Seneca captures this poignantly (*Ep. Mor.* 81.27): "No man can be grateful unless he has learned to scorn the things which drive the common herd to distraction; if you wish to make a return for a favour, you must be willing to go into exile, or to pour forth your blood, or to undergo poverty, or . . . even to let your very innocence be stained and exposed to shameful slanders." For more on the components of gratitude, see Danker, *Benefactor*, 436-86.

"Faith" and its related words also receive specific meanings within the context of the patron-client relationship. To place "faith" in a patron is to trust him or her to be able and willing to provide what he or she has promised. It means, in effect, to entrust one's cause or future to a patron (cf. Dio *Or.* 73 and 74; 4 Macc. 8:5-7), to give oneself over into his or her care. "Faith" also represents the response of loyalty on the part of the client. Having received benefits from a patron, the client must demonstrate loyalty toward the patron. In this context, then, "faith" speaks to the firmness, reliability, and faithfulness of both parties in the patron-client relationship.

In order to give expression to supernatural or unseen realities, people in the ancient world used the language of everyday realities. The relationship between human and divine beings, cosmic inferiors and superiors as it were, was expressed in terms of the closest analogy in the world of social interaction, namely, patronage. We thus find discussion of "patron deities" by individuals and groups. The author of Hebrews, like Philo, Epictetus, or the author of 4 Maccabees, shares this strategy for conceptualizing God's relationship to humanity and the obligations of piety (see, e.g., Epictetus *Diss.* 4.1.91-98; 4 Macc. 12:11-13; 13:13; 16:18-22; Philo *Vita Mos.* 2.256).

The author presents Jesus as one who "lays hold of (ἐπιλαμβάνεται) the descendants of Abraham" (2:16) and comes "to the aid (βοηθῆσαι) of those who are tempted" (2:18). Both terms are used to speak of the actions of benefactors. Christians are to look to Jesus to supply what is wanting in their own resources, which places him in the role of the patron, who provided assistance in many forms to clients. Christians, indeed, have been brought into God's household (3:6) through their clientage to the Son and are thus under God's protection and provision. The author discusses Christ's death in terms of the numerous benefits this selfless act brings to those committed to Jesus. Jesus gave his life on behalf of all (2:9), freeing those who "all their lives were subject to slavery because of their fear of death" (2:14-15).

The author emphasizes as Christ's greatest benefit for his clients, however, the gift of access to God, which Christ's death as a purificatory sacrifice has made possible. He is the broker, the mediator (μεσίτης, 8:6; 9:15; 12:24), who secures favor from God on behalf of those who have committed themselves to Jesus as dependent clients. As Son, Jesus stands closest in relationship to God and is thus a more effective broker of God's favor than even God's trusted and faithful servants (the angels or Moses, 1:5-14; 3:2-5). In the ancient world, the close relatives of the emperor, especially his sons, were sought after as mediators of the emperor's favor: their close, familial relationship to the patron gave great hope of success to suitors. The lengthy comparison of Jesus' mediation with that of the levitical priests, the only other mediators of God's favor sanctioned by Scripture, serves to highlight the unparalleled access to God that has now been granted through Jesus' efficacious removal of sins, those affronts against God that defiled the conscience and prevented humans from standing in the presence of the Holy God in expectation of anything but annihilation.

Apart from the Son, one only had recourse to the ineffective priests established by the Law; now the Son's loyal clients can enjoy unrestricted access to God. Having passed into the true sanctuary of heaven, Jesus does not leave his clients waiting outside without direct access to God. Rather, he opens up the way for believers to know and approach God as Benefactor and Patron. Jesus has entered "as a forerunner for us" (6:20): the Christian pilgrimage ends as we enter the rest of the city of God, the heavenly homeland (11:14; 13:14). Such final access, however, follows upon the access that can be enjoyed now in this life (4:14-16; 10:19-22). The community has access to all the resources it would need for endurance in faith so that it may receive the benefactions promised for the future, to be awarded before God's court at the end of the age (deliverance, 1:14; 9:28; a place in the heavenly, better city and homeland, 11:13-16; 13:14). Believers may draw near to God and expect to "receive mercy and find favor for timely help" (4:16).

The author dwells at length on the generosity of the Son, who spared not even his own life to bring believers to God's favor and promises and granted to believers unparalleled benefactions, in order to motivate gratitude and to dissuade the hearers from any course of action that slighted or affronted such noble and powerful patrons.From the author's perspective, the believer who wavers in commitment, who considers that friendship with God might no longer be worth what it costs in terms of enmity with the world, has lost sight of the value of these benefits provided by Jesus and thinks too lightly of the benefactions God has promised to provide in the future to his trusting clients. Even to think this way would be an insult to one's benefactor and a violation of the cardinal virtue of gratitude. To go further, however, and act in such a way as brings public dishonor upon a patron who has in every way acted nobly and generously should be an unthinkable course of action. Such rank ingratitude would surely provoke the wrath and punishment of the injured patron, who has ultimate authority and power to inflict such deserved punishment. Hiding or renouncing one's commitment to Christ and the "people of God," the author avers, would amount to such an affront, and this line of thought lies especially behind the stern warnings of 6:4-8 and 10:26-31. The addressees are warned not to repeat the error of the Exodus generation, who thought their patron incapable of providing what he promised and disobeyed the command to take possession of Canaan (Num. 14; Heb. 3:7–4:11). Distrust, disobedience, disloyalty, and disrespect toward God and God's Son — these are the things that the addressees are to fear, and not the hostility of human beings (13:5-6).

The warnings and exhortations in Hebrews, then, center on moving the hearers to continue to respond properly to Jesus by continuing to be loyal to

him and obedient from a grateful heart. They are called upon to "show gratitude" (12:28), preserving piety and worshiping God, offering to God the sacrifices of praise (the acknowledgment of God's benefits and augmentation of
God's reputation) and mutual care and sharing (13:15-16) as the acceptable return for the benefits they have received and still hope to receive. They are especially exhorted to "trust," to believe that God is indeed the rewarder of those
who seek him (11:6), and never to seek temporary benefits (such as acceptance
by their neighbors) at the cost of eternal benefits (12:15-17).

3. Insulating the Community from Society's Pressure

Honor and shaming are the primary tools of social control in the ancient
world. A society upholds the values necessary to its well-being by rewarding
with greater degrees of honor those who embody those values in proportionately greater degrees. Because a social group is maintained by individuals behaving in the group's interests, such individuals are valuable. Honor is the expression of that value. Because individuals are raised to seek honor, they are the
more likely to embody those behaviors that the group values and rewards. Dishonoring or shaming represents a group's disapproval of a member based on
his or her lack of conformity with those values deemed essential for the group's
continued existence. The concept of the honorable and disgraceful are given
content and meaning only within a specific culture in a specific period.[147] One
has self-respect on the basis of one's perception of how fully he or she has embodied the culture's ideals; that individual has honor on the basis of the society's recognition of that person's conformity with essential values.[148]

    Different groups within a given location, however, have different and dis-
tinctive values. Frequently, some core values will be incompatible: what would
be considered virtuous and honorable in one group would be censured as
shameful in another group. Jews found themselves in this sort of environment

---

147. Compare Pitt-Rivers, "Honour and Social Status," 38; Bruce J. Malina, *The New
Testament World* (Louisville, KY: Westminster/John Knox, 1993), 53-54. This culture-specific
definition of honor points to the function of honor as a sort of "meta-value," a social value
that reinforces cultural values.

148. This seems to me to be a more precise formulation of the relationship of self-
worth and publicly acknowledged honor than, say, the equation that one finds in B. Malina
and J. H. Neyrey ("Honor and Shame in Luke-Acts: Pivotal Values in the Mediterranean
World," in Neyrey, *The Social World of Luke-Acts*, 25-26), which gives no place to self-
respect apart from the affirmation of others. Bernard Williams has pointed out the value
of self-respect in Greek tragedy (*Shame and Necessity* [Berkeley: University of California
Press, 1993], 81-91), a value echoed by Epictetus in his promotion of the value of self-
respect (living in accordance with nature) rather than recognition based on possession of
external goods.

with the rise of the Greek and Hellenistic kingdoms, a situation that persisted after the rise of the Roman empire. Within Jewish culture, strict observance of the covenant stipulations of Torah was regarded as a mark of honor and value. In the eyes of Greeks and Romans, however, rejection of every deity but one's own, refusal to eat certain foods, refusal to work or fight on certain days (i.e., the sabbath), and the tendency to remain in close-knit communities so that purity and kosher rules could be observed all seemed contrary to the values of piety toward all the gods, solidarity with one's fellow citizens, and the like. Jewish customs were frequently the subject of ridicule, and Jews found themselves the target for sporadic violence and abuse.

In such a situation, it becomes important to decide whose opinion and approval really counts.[149] If a first-century Jew looks only to devout Jews for affirmation of self-worth, he or she will embody the values of devout Jews to attain that affirmation; if a Jew, however, looks to members of the Greek or Roman dominant culture for affirmation, he or she may be tempted to embody the values of the Greek or Roman elite. Where Jewish behaviors conflict with behaviors approved by the Greek or Roman elite, Jews may abandon those behaviors. For Jewish culture to survive, then, it became essential to exclude unsympathetic Gentiles from the "court of reputation" — that circle of significant others whose approval or disapproval matters. The devout Jew looked to God and those who were similarly committed to observe Torah for approval.

If one seeks status in the eyes of the larger society, one will seek to maintain the values and fulfill the expectations of the dominant or majority culture. Members of minority cultures, such as philosophical schools and voluntary associations like the early Christian community, and ethnic subcultures such as Judaism need to redefine the constituency of their "courts of reputation" in order to remain committed to the distinctive values and pursuits of the minority culture. The "court of reputation" must be limited to group members, who will support the group values in their grants of honor and censure.[150] Frequently the minority status of the group will be offset by including some suprasocial entity like God or Nature within this body of significant others. The opinion of one's fellow group members is thus anchored in and legitimated by a "higher" court of reputation, whose judgments are of greater importance and more lasting consequence than the opinion of the disapproving majority or the domi-

---

149. For a more detailed discussion of the dynamics of honor, defining one's "court of reputation," and the preservation of minority cultures, see deSilva, "Investigating Honor Discourse," 506-16.

150. One finds this frequently in philosophical texts, wherein the opinion of the many is contrasted unfavorably with the value of the approval of the few or the one who has devoted his or her life to wisdom and virtue (cf. Plato *Cri.* 44C, 46C-47A; Seneca *Constant.* 11.2; 13.2, 5; 16.3; Epictetus *Diss.* 1.29.50-54; 4.5.22; Dio *Or.* 77/78.21, 25).

nant culture.[151] All groups will seek to use honor and disgrace to enforce the values of their particular culture, so each must insulate its members from the "pull" of the opinion of nonmembers.[152]

The presenting problem in Hebrews appears to be that some of the believers have begun to feel the weight of society's shaming techniques, the insults and abuse calculated to bring the Christian deviants back in line with society's values and worldview. While the Christians were able to resist these pressures in the past, continued exposure to them and to a lower ranking of honor have begun to wear down some of the assembly, to the point that an unspecified number have even stopped gathering with the Christian community (10:25). Such people, if they are to remain committed to Christ, need to have their self-respect grounded again in the group's values and definitions of what constitutes "honor," and to be insulated from the shaming strategies of non-Christians.

The author of Hebrews meets this challenge first by presenting as praiseworthy models for imitation those figures that have chosen a lower status in this world for the sake of attaining greater and more lasting honor and advantages. In 10:32–12:2, several such examples emerge. First, the community merits praise from the author for its earlier courage in their "contest with sufferings," for their confidence in God's promise had enabled them to accept and endure insult, physical abuse, imprisonment, and dispossession with joy. Abraham, the most extended exemplar of "faith" in chapter 11, chose to live out his life on earth at the lower social status of "foreigner" and "sojourner," having left behind his citizenship in an earthly city for the sake of being received into the eternal city built by God (11:8-10, 13-16). He, Isaac, and Jacob refused to return to the status and security of their earthly citizenship, remaining firm in their hope and purpose until their deaths (11:15), for which they received the honor of being forever associated with God (11:16). Moses, whom intertestamental traditions placed next in line for the throne of Egypt, heir-apparent to Pharaoh, renounced his heritage in this world for the sake of the reward God promised to give. He chose "mistreatment" in this world over "temporary pleasures," "re-

---

151. Philosophers frequently appeal to a higher court for validation of their ideals: Plato (*Gorg.* 526D-527D) and Epictetus (*Diss.* 1.30.1) speak of living so as to please God, who naturally approves the distinctive way of life taught by these schools. One finds the same strategy in Jewish subcultural literature as well, wherein God's approval and the hope of honor in God's presence uphold strict adherence to Torah in the face of pressure from the dominant culture to assimilate (cf. Sir. 23:18-19; 4 Macc. 17:4-5).

152. See my *Despising Shame*, chapter 3, for a discussion of how several Greco-Roman philosophers and Jewish authors met this challenge. A survey of how honor language is used to maintain commitment to the Christian community in Matthew, John, 1 and 2 Corinthians, 1 and 2 Thessalonians, Hebrews, and Revelation can be found in my *The Hope of Glory: Honor Discourse and New Testament Interpretation* (Collegeville, MN: Liturgical Press, 1999).

proach" over "the treasures of Egypt" (11:24-26), which in the end brought him an honorable remembrance across the centuries as well as an assured place in God's house. Those who were pushed out to the fringes of civilization, who were even tortured and martyred (held up to the extreme disgrace of execution), are also included in this parade of God's honored ones (11:35-38). Indeed, the author claims, the world showed its own lack of worth in the way it treated these noble persons of faith (11:38). Finally, Jesus stands as the example *par excellence* of one who "despised shame," that is, recognized the disapproval and scorn of unbelievers to be worthless, in order to remain obedient to God's purpose, by which path he arrived at the most honored place in the cosmos (12:2). The addressees are thus urged by their own example, and the examples of these heroes of faith, to continue to set no value on the approval or disapproval of outsiders.

Second, the author seeks to make the endurance of the unbelievers' hostility and reproach easier by reinterpreting that experience in a more honorable light. By attaching positive significance to these experiences the author hopes not only to undermine the force of society's attempts at social control but even make these same experiences an occasion for strengthening commitment to the minority culture by turning the experiences of disgrace into tokens of honor and promises of greater reward. The author recasts the believers' experiences of ridicule, trial, loss of status and property, and endurance of continued reproach as God's training or discipline of his adopted children. The community's endurance of society's rejection and censure, in fact, turns out to be the token of God's acceptance and formative discipline (12:5-11), whereby the addressees are fitted to receive their birthright and to enjoy the honor toward which God leads them (2:10). Therefore, what society intends as an experience of disgrace aimed at bringing the deviant back into line with the values of the dominant culture becomes the proof of the believers' adoption into God's family and a powerful encouragement to persevere in their commitments to the minority group. Only those who have shared in discipline (12:8) will also share the rewards as "partners of Christ" (3:14) and "partners in a heavenly calling" (3:1). The believers may even cherish their marginalization and censure by society as the process by which their character is tried and proven, and which guarantees their future honor and vindication.

The author also uses the image of the contest (ἀγών, ἄθλησις) to cast a new, competitive light on the believers' experience of disgrace, physical pain, and loss (10:32).[153] The rhetorical force of this image is to set their endurance

---

153. One finds this image frequently in the writings of philosophers such as Epictetus and Dio, as well as in Jewish minority cultural literature, such as 4 Maccabees and Philo. See the discussions of athletic imagery in N. Clayton Croy, *Endurance in Suffering: Hebrews 12:1-13 in Its Rhetorical, Religious, and Philosophical Context* (SNTSMS 98;

of hardships in the context of competition for an honorable victory. Hebrews 12:1-4 uses this image extensively. The heroes of faith become an "encircling cloud of witnesses" to the addressees' performance in the great relay of faith. These heroes are the spectators from whom the competitors seek honor and esteem. Like those who compete in races, the believers are to "lay aside" everything that might impede their running: they are to set aside "sin" as if it were a clinging garment that restricts their movement toward the prize. Sin — the temptation to yield to society's pressures — is also their antagonist (12:4) in this contest (12:1). Yielding to society's pressures in fact signals a dishonorable defeat in this wrestling match, while steadfast endurance is the path to an honorable victory.

4. Nurturing a Supportive Community

An essential counterpart to the author's attempt to separate the believers from sensitivity toward the evaluation of outsiders is his attempt to strengthen the mutual interaction and reinforcement within the group. He speaks of the believers as "partners" (3:1, 14) who are to look after one another. They must affirm one another in their pursuit of honor from God more effectively than society voices its disapproval.

The author calls them to look out for those who stray, those who succumb to society's pressure to conform: "Take care, brothers and sisters, lest there be in any of you an evil, distrustful heart, leading you to fall away from the living God. But exhort one another every day, as long as it is called 'today,' that none of you may be hardened by the deceitfulness of sin" (3:12-13, RSV). Near the end of his sermon, he adds: "See to it that no one falls short of the gift of God" (12:15, RSV). The author makes each believer aware that he or she must take some responsibility in keeping his or her fellow believers on track. In the face of unbelievers' encouragements to join in the life and values of the Greco-Roman society, Christians are to double their efforts with encouragements of their own, calling back the wavering and reinforcing the values of the group and the rewards of perseverance and loyalty.

The author seeks to make encounters between believers more frequent and more meaningful, to offset the impact of outsiders and hold up behaviors that support the community as honorable and praiseworthy: "let us consider how to stir up one another to love and good works, not neglecting to meet together, as is the habit of some, but encouraging one another, and all the more as you see the Day drawing near" (10:24-25, RSV). The author himself acts as part

---

Cambridge: Cambridge University Press, 1998), 43-70; V. C. Pfitzner, *Paul and the Agon Motif: Traditional Athletic Imagery in the Pauline Literature* (Leiden: Brill, 1967), 23-48; deSilva, *4 Maccabees*, 92-93.

of this alternate court of opinion, censuring the addressees for their waning fervor and lack of zeal (5:11-14) and praising them for their displays of love and service (6:9-10) and for their former demonstration of commitment even at great cost (10:32-34). The community leaders will also function as an important part of this alternate court, ascribing honor to the obedient and committed, rebuking the half-hearted.

Further, this encouragement is to extend to material support and acts of service, so that each helps his or her fellow Christians feel their losses less deeply. The exhortations of chapter 13, far from being unrelated to the purpose of the whole, continue to promote the author's interests in maintaining a strong group culture. He urges that "familial love" (φιλαδελφία, 13:1) continue, so that members of the community will continue to regard fellow believers as kin: as family, one's fellow believers will be the primary source of one's identity and honor and the primary group to whom one owes one's first duty and allegiance. The exhortation to provide hospitality for traveling fellow believers (13:2) links the local Christian community to the broader Christian minority culture. The author urges special solidarity with those whom society has targeted as deviants (13:3; cf. 10:32-34; 11:25): only the group that is willing to support its members under such conditions can maintain the loyalty and trust of its adherents and show that society's court is not, after all, the final adjudicator of worth. Their loyalty to and confession of Christ is thus joined, in the concluding exhortations, to loyalty and support for one another: "Through Jesus, then, let us always offer a sacrifice of praise to God, that is, the fruit of lips that acknowledge his name. Do not neglect to do good and to share, for with such sacrifices God is well pleased" (13:15-16, RSV). The believers themselves are thus invited to exercise a sort of priestly service, appropriate to the access they have to enter the holy of holies, before the very throne of God. This priestly service includes liturgy — praising the Patron through the Mediator — and liturgical service — but in the everyday activity of loving, encouraging, and helping one another.

When believers take an active part in reinforcing for one another the convictions, values, and promises of the group, and when believers look to one another and to their leaders (13:17) for approval rather than to the unbelieving society, it is easier to disregard the many and forceful voices that call the believer back from deviance to normalcy, to a form of life that supports the existing society's values and structure. The believers will thus affirm one another's worth and honor as children of God, partners with Christ, full citizens of the city of God, and heirs of the better and lasting possessions. They can assure one another of the firm basis for their hope in the better covenant, which Jesus has established between God and human beings, and spur one another on to endure the contest and discipline that, though painful for a time, lead to eternal honor and approval before God.

5. The Ritual Journey of Priest and People

Finally, some notice should be taken here of the extensive use of ritual language in Hebrews and the way it reinforces the direction in which the author urges his audience to go. Jesus' execution on the cross is transformed into the sacrifice of a willing victim on behalf of believers. He leaves human society ("the camp"), bearing abuse, disgrace, and hostility. He goes "outside the camp" to a place characterized by both liminality and sacrality. To the eyes of the unbeliever, Jesus dies a shameful death in a place of uncleanness, outside the "lines" of society; in the eyes of God, Jesus' journey outside the margins of the camp is a ritual act of sacred power. Jesus "suffers" outside the camp, his death becoming a purification offering, his blood serving to cleanse the conscience of the worshipers who wish to approach God. After his death, Jesus passes through the visible heavens (i.e., a part of the material creation destined for "shaking," 4:14) in order to arrive in "heaven itself" (i.e., the unshakable realm wherein is God's throne, 9:24). He enters the heavenly sanctuary to cleanse the invisible holy place (9:23), the real throne room of God and not merely its copy in Jerusalem, and "atone for the sins of the people." The blood of Jesus thus removes the pollution of sin from both the conscience of the worshiper and the presence of God, such that no defiling obstacle remains between God and human being. The worshiper may now approach the throne of favor (4:14-16; 10:19-22), assured that the holiness of God will not consume him or her. As the last movement in this ritual, Jesus sits at God's right hand, there being no more need to stand at the heavenly altar. His priestly work is complete (although he still "intercedes" for believers from that advantageous position).

The dramatic "representation" of this heavenly and unrepeatable liturgy will have a profound effect on the addressees. They will be reminded of the holiness that has been conferred on them by the water of baptism and the blood of Jesus (10:22), and of the access to God, which they have been able to enjoy in congregational worship and private prayer. They have been consecrated, perfected in terms of the conscience. Thus, their impulse will be to preserve what is holy from desecration (which comes through the "willful sin" of apostasy, distrust, shrinking back).

The author, however, capitalizes on the fact that Jesus is not merely priest but "forerunner for us." He lays out the course that the believers are called to "run with endurance" (12:1), and it is a course that takes them "outside the camp." The addressees are called to continue in this journey and, out of gratitude to Jesus for his journey "outside the camp" on their behalf, to sacrifice the sense of at-homeness and belonging in human society and enter a place of liminality — to live in between the home they left behind and the kingdom they are in the process of receiving. This liminal state involves both "humiliation and ordeal, but also . . .

sacrality and power."[154] It is a state of "bearing Christ's reproach" (13:13), of persevering in the endurance of society's hostility and shaming techniques. It is also the place wherein God's presence is known, a state of holiness in which the believer can "approach with boldness the throne of God" (4:14) and enjoy "the altar" from which the levitical priests themselves have no right to eat (13:10).[155] The journey out from worldly society into marginality is the "new and living way," which Jesus has opened up and inaugurated. The rest of the believer's life is lived out in this liminal state, in the margins between status in this world and the next. The author urges the addressees to continue to press on in the margins, for the margins of society are pregnant with promise as the threshold over which they, like Jesus, will pass into the unshakable realm, the full presence of God.

Outline

There have been numerous attempts to discern the structure of Hebrews throughout the twentieth century. These investigations have led to widely divergent conclusions that depend on the scholar's choice of criteria for discerning the joints in the sermon, as well as on the author's ability to weave his material together so artfully that no scheme will be able to separate perfectly what he has so closely joined together. Some approaches have emphasized the alternation between exposition and exhortation throughout the sermon.[156] Other approaches have focused on the use of key words or hook words to define blocks of text and indicate transitions from one section to another. Related closely to this is the observation of the author's use of *inclusio,* the repetition of one or more words at the opening and closing of a section as a means of identifying the boundaries of a section or paragraph.[157] Probably the most sophisticated

---

154. Richard P. Nelson, *Raising Up a Faithful Priest* (Louisville, KY: Westminster/John Knox, 1993), 58. Nelson's discussion is profitably influenced by Turner (*Ritual Process,* 94-147), who at length discusses the paradoxical qualities of the liminal period of rituals (subjection to humiliation and loss of status, but at the same time is charged with awareness of the sacred and its power).

155. Thus Lane, *Hebrews 1–8,* 543-44; Pfitzner, *Hebrews,* 199; J. W. Thompson, *The Beginnings of Christian Philosophy: The Epistle to the Hebrews* (CBQMS 13; Washington, DC: Catholic Biblical Association, 1982), 147.

156. F. Büchsel, "Hebräerbrief," in *Religion in Geschichte und Gegenwart,* ed. H. Gunkel and L. Zscharnack, 2nd ed. (Tübingen: J. C. B. Möhr, 1928), 2:1669-73; R. Gyllenberg, "Die Composition des Hebräerbriefs," *Svensk Exegetisk Årsbok* 22-23 (1957-58): 137-47.

157. L. Vaganay, "Le Plan de L'Épître aux Hébreux," *Memorial Lagrange,* ed. L.-H. Vincent (Paris: Gabalda, 1940), 269-77; A. Vanhoye, *La structure littéraire de L'Épître aux Hébreux,* 2nd ed. (Paris: Desclée de Brouwer, 1976).

attempt made to date is George H. Guthrie's text-linguistic analysis, which combines the above approaches with several other criteria gleaned from discourse analysis (e.g., looking for overlapping segments, such that the last verses of one section serve simultaneously as the opening verses of the next segment).[158] Despite the different results gained by these investigations, the criteria selected are, at least, more useful than the more intuitive approaches, which outline Hebrews based on perceived thematic coherence and tend always to privilege exposition over exhortation and to displace the rhetorical priorities developed by the text with theological summaries.[159]

The "Overview" sections at the beginning of each chapter will provide discussions of structure where this has bearing on the discernment of the units of argument or exhortation and the relationship of blocks of text one to another. Here, only a brief outline is provided as a means of orienting the hearer to the flow of the sermon and the author's strategic arrangement of material.

1:1–2:18   First Appeal to heed properly the word of God in the Son
    1:1-4   Thesis: God's final and complete word has been spoken through the Son, who has greater honor even than the angels
    1:5-14   Confirmation of final element of thesis (Jesus is greater than the angels)
    2:1-4   Inferential conclusion based on "lesser to greater" argument, presented in the form of an exhortation (since the lesser message of the lesser beings was strictly enforced, the threat is correspondingly greater for those who disregard the Son's message)
    2:5-18   Argument in support of the exhortation: Attachment to Jesus is the path to a share in his honor as well as the path of gratitude for past benefits and Jesus' ongoing mediation

3:1–4:13   Second Appeal to honor God's word through trust and perseverance
    3:1-6   Argument: Jesus, as Son over God's house, has greater honor than Moses, the servant in God's house
    3:7–4:13   Exhortation: Do not imitate those who rejected God's patronage under the servant, Moses, for we would find ourselves similarly subject to judgment; rather, let us strive to enter the "rest" that remains open to us

---

158. Guthrie, *Structure of Hebrews;* see also my review of this volume in *CBQ* 57 (1995): 395-97.

159. See, for example, the first part of Stedman's outline (*Hebrews,* 16-17): "Greater than the Prophets" (1:1-3); "Greater than the Angels" (1:4–2:18); "Greater than Moses" (3:1-19); "Greater than Joshua" (4:1-13); "Greater than Aaron" (4:14–5:14).

4:14–10:18[160]   Central Exposition — the "long and difficult word"

4:14-16   Exhortation: We have a high priest who has secured and will maintain God's favor toward us, so let us draw near to God for sustaining help

5:1-10   Argument: Jesus' appointment to high priesthood (hence to position of principal broker of God's favor)

5:11–6:20   Digression (a second *captatio benevolentiae*)

> **5:11-14**   Interruption and appeal for attentive and responsive hearing
>
> **6:1-3**   Exhortation to move forward in Christian journey (rather than drift away, 2:1-4)
>
> **6:4-8**   Argument in support of exhortation: those who do not persevere in gratitude and trust show dangerous contempt for God and God's gifts
>
> **6:9-12**   Palliation: You, of course, will continue to invest yourselves in your fellow believers and your common enterprise, so we can be confident of the outcome
>
> **6:13-20**   Argument confirming cause for confidence: God's oath as prop for perseverance in trust

7:1–10:28   Resumption of argument: the Christians' access to God's favor is superior to anything enjoyed previously in the history of God's dealings with humanity, because Jesus' priestly mediation is superior in every way

> **7:1-10**   The founder of Jesus' priestly line (Melchizedek) was of greater dignity than the founder of the levitical line (Abraham)
>
> **7:11-28**   Jesus' qualifications for priesthood are superior (he possesses an indestructible life rather than meeting genealogical requirements; God's oath establishes Jesus as priest in place of those who priesthood was based on an ineffective law; Jesus' sinlessness means that there is one less stumbling block between the Christian's mediator and God than existed between the levitical priests and God)

---

160. An important insight derived from Wolfgang Nauck ("Zum Aufbau des Hebräerbriefes," in *Judentum, Urchristentum, Kirche: Festschrift für Joachim Jeremias*, ed. W. Eltester [BZNW 26; Berlin: Alfred Töpelmann, 1960], 199-206) has been the recognition that 4:14-16 and 10:19-23 form a major *inclusio* around the central expository section of Hebrews (see "Overview" of 4:14–5:10). This observation clarifies the essential building blocks of the sermon (1:1–4:13; 4:14–10:18; 10:19–13:25 — 10:19-23 really functions as an overlapping segment, completing the *inclusio* around the central exposition but also providing the opening to the concluding exhortation) as well as the primary rhetorical goal the author has for the central expository section, namely, to motivate the hearers to accept, or continue to enact, the course of action proposed in 4:14-16 and 10:19-25.

8:1-5   Jesus carries on his mediation in the heavenly sanctuary, in immediate proximity to God

8:6-13   Jesus' mediation stands on a firmer covenant basis, not one already broken by the sins of the people, but one resting on God's avowed will to forgive (with proof from Scripture, Jer. 31:31-34)

9:1-28   The levitical priests could not prepare the worshipers to enter God's presence (symbolized by the earthly holy places), but Christ's single sacrifice has cleansed the conscience of the worshiper for direct access to God's favor; Christ's ascension into the heavenly sanctuary allows him also to cleanse the true tabernacle of the defilement of human sins, erasing their negative testimony from God's memory

10:1-18   proof from Scripture (Ps. 40:6-8): God has set aside the repetitious, ineffective animal sacrifices in favor of Jesus' single offering of himself, which cleanses the worshipers' conscience once and for all

10:19–13:25   Climactic Exhortation to persevere in gratitude for the benefactions bestowed by Jesus and God

10:19-25   Exhortation: since Jesus has opened up a way for us to enter the eternal, divine realm, let us approach confidently, hold fast to our confession, and continue to encourage one another to persevere in mutual love and service

10:26-31   Rationale for accepting exhortation based on consideration of the contrary course: if we spurn this covenant of grace and show contempt for the gifts the Son has gained for us, we will face worse punishment than those who were executed for transgressing the covenant established through Moses

10:32-39   Exhortation: imitate your former endurance and your own past successes in this contest; rather than shrink back, remain constant in trust ("faith")

11:1–12:3   Encomium on faith, developing the portrait of the orientation to the world and God's promise that the author calls the hearers to adopt

12:4-17   Encouragement to endure: the hardship, pain, and loss the hearers endure at society's hands are actually proof of God's love, care, and adoption of them as his children: God is training them for a share in his holiness; press on in faith; do not imitate Esau, who gave up eternal honor and blessedness for temporary relief from hardship

12:18-29   Exhortation to confidence and gratitude: The hearers are coming closer to their eternal, noble destiny, namely, citizenship in the New Jerusalem; drawing back now would be disastrous; rather, show gratitude in its fullest sense for the unshakable kingdom that God is bestowing

13:1-21   Specific exhortations: the enfleshment of gratitude in everyday life

13:22-25   Epistolary Postscript

Bridging the Horizons

Having developed a picture of the situation in which the audience found themselves and how the author of this sermon sought to solidify commitment and nurture a supportive community of faith, how might we expect to apply its challenge to the situations of Christian communities at the turn of the second millennium? Churches in the United States, Canada, and Western Europe tend to live relatively at peace with the society around them. Social pressures of the type described in Hebrews 10:32-34 are rarely brought to bear on Christians living in these areas. The general lack of interest in persecution in the West of those who hold to any particular confession, be it Christian or otherwise, testifies to the degree of secularization that marks these countries. Religion is a matter of individual choice and freedom largely because the society as a whole can continue to function equally well with or without it. Within each religion, adherents may be concerned about deviancy (e.g., critique of Reformed Judaism among Orthodox Jews, or controversies over infant baptism among Christian groups), but the dominant culture remains disinterested and unaffected by such debates. Religion has been pushed out of politics, economics, and most public spheres. If action is ever taken against a religious group, it is never on religious grounds. The FBI did not intervene in the cult at Waco because it opposed the group's deviant exegesis of Scripture or claims about their leader.

Secularization has had some important effects on Western Christianity. A positive effect is that religious persecution is rarely an issue. Unlike believers in many other countries, Christians in the United States, Canada, or Western Europe do not fear being dragged from their beds at night because they were seen attending a worship service the previous Sunday. A negative effect is that believers are not routinely "encouraged" by their setting to reflect on what their relationship with God in Christ is worth to them. They are permitted to have Christ, wealth, status, and safety all at the same time. Consequently, they begin to internalize the secularized worldview that surrounds them daily. "Christianity" is just one aspect of our lives that coexists alongside our business involvements, our political affiliations, and our social connections.

Perhaps even more insidious, we begin to see certain activities as "religious" and others as "political" and react negatively when a religious figure or group appears to cross the threshold into the political. Take, for example, the civil rights movement. This movement tends to be presented as a social and political one, but is it not strange that so many churches and ministers were centers and agents for the growth of this movement? Was it, then, truly political? Were churches "overstepping" their boundaries by getting involved in "politics," where they "had no business"? Or did the movement grow out of the religious vision of the church? Did Father Romero incur his fate by losing sight of the proper involvements of a priest and getting involved in politics, or by following precisely the path along which God and his religion led him?

Before we can hear the full challenge of the gospel, or the particular challenge of this text, we need to become aware of how a secularized worldview has impacted, and drastically narrowed, our perception of what constitutes the realm of activity called "religion." In the first century, religion, politics, economics, and the like were all inextricably intertwined, which begins to explain the phenomenon of "religious" persecution. Even within the NT we see how the "religion" of Christianity involves care for the poor and sharing of possessions (Luke, Hebrews), critique of unjust governmental policy (Revelation), and the undermining of ethnic boundaries and prejudices (Galatians, Romans, Ephesians, and Colossians). The one who would follow Christ must do so in every arena of life, and not merely in what our secularized society defines as the proper sphere of the "religious."

With this in mind, Hebrews offers both challenging insights into the way of discipleship and an arsenal of strategies for nurturing vital communities of faith. One of the important contributions socio-rhetorical analysis can make to the work of the pastor, lay leader, or missionary is to display the strategies used by one pastor to accomplish many of the tasks faced by all religious leaders. We not only can learn ideas about God and the Christian walk from the sermon "to the Hebrews," but discover models and strategies for motivating those believers in our care to pursue their calling with greater investment and earnestness.

First, Hebrews challenges us on the most basic question of our values and priorities. It is generally not the danger of persecution that might lead us to "sell our birthright for a single meal" (12:16), but the fact that we can invest ourselves so much and so freely in other pursuits. We may be tempted to give our first and best efforts to "laying up treasures on earth," or to invest our resources heavily in acquiring "better" and higher-status products to enhance the "quality of life" promoted by media and reinforced by worldly minded neighbors and friends. We may be tempted to withhold precious time from teaching our children in order to get the edge on a promotion at work. We may, like the society around us, push religion to the side, giving whatever time, energy, and resources that remain at the end of everything else to the pursuit of knowing God and learning how to serve God's vision for our church, community, and world.

The author of Hebrews reminds us of the truly "better" possessions — God's friendship, the honor of being brought into God's family, and the welcome that awaits the faithful in the unshakable kingdom — and challenges us to order our steps to reflect the surpassing value of these possessions. This is the essence of "faith" as the author will define it and shape its exemplars in chapter 11. Only when these are the "things that really matter" to us will we live out the walk of discipleship preached by Jesus. This might mean being content with "less" in terms of worldly goods so that one has resources to place at the disposal of sisters or brothers who stand in need of the most basic necessities. It might mean being content to be passed over for a promotion so that one can use the time to train one's own children and the church's youth group in the message of the Scriptures, investing in their coming to a vital faith. One strategy that the author uses to impress his priorities on the audience is keeping Christ in central focus throughout the sermon. He speaks from the first sentence about the significance of Jesus for past, present, and future history, for the past, present, and future lives of the hearers. He reminds the hearers that the greatest crisis they face is not how they fare in their jobs, in the opinion of their neighbors, or in their worldly security, but how they fare in God's estimation. Responding appropriately to Jesus becomes the most important consideration for the hearer to deliberate upon, and church leaders can learn much from this author about how to stimulate the ambition of Christians to respond to Jesus with wholehearted devotion, gratitude, and service.

Second, Hebrews provides us with an understanding of "grace" that is informed by the social system that gave that term meaning for the first hearers. "Grace" is a relationship with mutual obligations and expectations into which we are welcomed. Accepting God's gifts means accepting an obligation to the Giver. While the author's admonitions about the impossibility of restoring the apostate to repentance should not become the basis for some doctrine of an "unpardonable sin," one should leave the study of Hebrews with a greater awareness that the gifts God has provided — the salvation and inclusion into God's family that cost the Son his life — must be appropriately valued. This means that loyalty to God, the Giver, and to Christ, the Broker, must always be faithfully maintained and enacted in the ways God directs, such as in acts of love and service to other members of God's family and in bearing testimony to God's purposes, values, and gifts. One gift that the author of Hebrews especially highlights is access to God's presence, which we are now enabled to enter through the priestly work of Jesus. Prayer and worship are not duties but manifestations of this great gift that cost the Mediator so much. As such, this sermon can challenge believers to engage in prayer and worship not half-heartedly or sporadically, but with an enthusiasm and frequency consonant with their value.

Within the patron-client relationship established between God and Jesus' followers, Hebrews cautions those who have received God's gifts in abundance to take seriously their obligation in light of the dangerous consequences of slighting God or God's gifts. The honor of God and Christ are to be maintained in the believer's every ambition and action. God's wrath and favor are not in fact two separate faces of God, a view espoused by many theologians and lay persons throughout the centuries in the frequent opposition of the God of the OT and the God of Jesus. Rather, God's generosity and judgment are closely integrated. It is precisely where God's favor, benefactions, and promises have been rejected in favor of the deceitful promises of the world and sin — where God's favor and gifts have been so lightly valued that one would choose the temporary pleasures of following the world's way over God's way — that favor is exchanged for wrath. Favor despised gives rise to anger and judgment. This does not limit God's freedom or undermine God's mercy. Rather, it restores the immense value of God's gracious favor, so often taken for granted and held as a cheap and readily available commodity.

Third, Hebrews shows us that we must be very intentional about establishing and preserving Christian community if we are to fulfill our calling to discipleship. People cannot help but be influenced in their thinking, evaluating, and decision making by the opinions of others, and Western society has a way of bombarding its inhabitants with hundreds of messages daily about what it holds to be truly valuable, praiseworthy, and important. Christians may still benefit from taking to heart the exhortations of the author of Hebrews about strengthening their alternative, Christian culture. Believers need to gather frequently with one another, both in the formal settings of worship and informally for support and encouragement in pursuing values that do not always reflect the values of our society. In their interactions with one another, believers are called to hold up as valuable both the ideals that God values and the actions that Jesus commands, discovering and discussing these together in study of the sacred texts, and encouraging one another to seek out ways of living them out. The voices of unbelievers are not likely to support such goals and actions, and indeed often seem to push us in the opposite direction, trying to stir up greed, prejudice, or self-serving attitudes. Only with the strong support of others who are committed to the visions of humanity and community in the Scriptures can believers hope to remain on course toward their eternal homeland.

Christians living at peace with their surrounding society should always bear in mind, moreover, that many sisters and brothers in the family of God live in conditions that resemble those of the original audience much more closely — indeed, frequently resisting "to the point of shedding blood" (12:4), and thus exceeding the tensions faced by the first audience. Hebrews will speak very directly to those who face the loss of property, freedom, and life itself on account of their association with the name of Christ. Even when the price is so high, the sermon reminds us that the friendship of God and the hope of a place in the city of God are of greater value than the friendship of society and one's safety, or even the safety of one's family, in the earthly city. This is the perspective of trust, which believes against all visible evidence that an invisible God and invisible inheritance merit the loss of all visible goods and comforts. The blood of the martyrs bears eloquent witness to the certainty of this hope — the price they were, and are, willing to pay testifies to the value of God's promises and patronage. In the words of Martin Luther, "let goods and kindred go, this mortal life also. The body they may kill; God's truth abideth still. His kingdom is forever."

When the author of Hebrews urges believers to support one another in their commitment to the faith, this challenge takes on new urgency and meaning as Western churches become aware of the needs of sisters and brothers worldwide and as their means to help increases. What an encouragement it would be to the Christians in the Sudan, China, or Nigeria to know the support of churches from across the globe, to the woman who is imprisoned for her faith to know that her children will be cared for by her brothers and sisters in Christ! As we are challenged in so many areas of life to "think globally," let our definition of "church" be one such area, and in that context let us hear the word of Hebrews: "remember those who are in prison, as though you were in prison with them; remember those who are being shamefully treated, as though you were in their skin" (13:3). Christians who can be secure and even prosperous in their own society have a tremendous opportunity, and indeed a responsibility, to discover ways to encourage those who fight a fiercer struggle, to find ways "to do good and to share" (13:16), and thus to fulfill our priestly service through strengthening the faith of our fellow Christians.

As we read about the honor culture that Hebrews addresses, we find that we, too, live in something of an honor culture. While the word "honor" is not frequently used in conversation, we are often drawn into evaluating others and ourselves by profession, salary, possessions, education, networks of influence ("the right crowd"), and the like. Hebrews reminds us that today, as then, society's criteria for evaluating a person's "success" or "worth" differ widely from Christ's criteria. When the author urges his audience to "despise shame," he speaks also to us, who must be willing to "make less of ourselves" in terms of the world's way of valuing in order to live out fully the truth of the gospel. If following Jesus means caring for the homeless or shut-ins rather than networking with the powerful and well connected; if fulfilling the call to discipleship means freeing time to serve others or to seek God's will rather than devote every possible hour to "getting ahead" at work or at school; if responding to God's love means buying less expensive clothes and cars in order to have more to give to others in need of even food and shelter, then we are to "despise shame" and embrace being a little lower on society's ladder of status in order to be honorable persons in the sight of God. It is our confession that it is God's evaluation of our lives and labors that ultimately counts, and it is in light of that court of opinion that we are to weigh our decisions, desires, and dreams. It is also our confession that the reward of following God's way will more than compensate us for what we "lose" in terms of the temporary and empty rewards of this world. Hebrews thus encourages us to follow boldly where Jesus leads, even where this brings us into criticism, reproach, and even rejection by the unbelieving society. Knowing the love and beneficence of God, we are emboldened to embrace marginalization for the sake of Christ, to "bear his reproach," and to continue in love, service, and witness to the better hope that is found in God.

These, then, may provide the broad contours for our exploration of how Hebrews continues to speak a "word on target" for Christian communities and enable church leaders to develop strong communities of faithful and vital disciples. As we proceed through our closer examination of the sermon, we will continue to return to the question of how socio-rhetorical interpretation opens up new insights not only into the meaning of the text (exegesis) but also into the application of the text to new audiences (hermeneutics).

THE COMMENTARY

Responding to God's Word and Work in the Son: 1:1–2:18

Overview

The sermon opens by focusing the hearers' attention on the word spoken by God through the Son, the last and most complete word in the history of God's many and diverse words spoken through the prophets in former times. The significance of this message, and thus of responding to it appropriately, is developed by dwelling on the honor and power of its messenger, first by a discussion of the Son's work from creation to the present (1:2–4), and then by means of a comparison of the Son with the angels. The first chapter begins and ends on distinctly eschatological notes — God's word "in the Son" comes in "these last days" (1:2), and the Son himself now waits for the forthcoming subjugation of all his enemies (1:13) even while others are identified as "those who are about to inherit salvation" (1:14). This dimension is crucial to the author's strategy for confirming the addressees in their commitment to the Christian group, and especially to deterring the wavering from shrinking back in the face of their neighbors' ongoing disapproval. Ultimately, it is at the Son's judgment seat, and not in the opinion of unbelievers, that the decisive evaluation of one's worth takes place.

The author engages in this lengthy amplification of the Son's honor and authority not because of some theological defect among the hearers, but rather because of a defect in commitment to the Christian worldview and community on the part of some. His objective is to heighten the urgency of the exhortation to "pay attention to" this message spoken through the Son, and not to neglect the "deliverance" he provides so as to "drift away" (2:1-4). The author warns that, just as the Son's honor is greater than that of the angels, so the "payback" (μισθαποδοσία) for slighting this messenger by disregarding his message will be greater than the punishment received by those who neglected the requirements of the law of Moses, delivered by angels (cf. Acts 7:53; Gal. 3:19).

Having drawn out the dangerous consequences of not holding to the "word" of the Son, the sermon continues by defining the benefits of responding graciously to this message. Through his death, Jesus has freed them from the bondage of the fear of death and, now exalted at God's right hand, has become the assurance of the believers' honor as well. Through their attachment to him, they have the opportunity to arrive at their God-appointed destination of "glory" (2:10), the fulfillment of the divine plan for humanity as revealed in Psalm 8. The addressees enjoy the honor of being confessed by Jesus as his sisters and brothers (2:11-13), and having the exalted Son as their helper and mediator (2:16-18).

These opening paragraphs reflect the main aspects of the author's pastoral strategy for his congregation. They need to be reminded to "consider Jesus" (3:1), to recall the debt owed the Son for his role in creation, preservation, and redemption, and to respond as grateful recipients not only of his past benefits but also of his promises for the future. Keeping their eyes securely fixed on the Son, they will understand that true advantage lies in remaining attached to him, which gives them honor now as God's family and hope for the revelation of that honor to the world at the Son's visitation. They will also understand that the greatest danger facing them is not their ongoing experience of shame in the eyes, or abuse at the hands, of unbelievers, but rather the punishment of God if, in thinking so little of God's word in the Son, or of the Son's saving work on their behalf, they forget their obligation and their hope and "drift away" from their commitment. The "coming world" is under the Son's jurisdiction (2:5-9), and thus friendship with the Son is the one thing never to be sacrificed for any apparent gain in the present world. For this reason, the Son is thrust into center stage at the very outset, displacing any other considerations that might weigh on the hearers' minds.

Commentary

1:1-4

While the book of Hebrews may not readily lend itself to division according to the five parts of a classical oration, discussions of exordia, or introductions, in rhetorical handbooks do illumine some aspects of the sermon's opening paragraphs. The purpose of an exordium was to gain the attention and goodwill of the hearers, to establish oneself as an expert and honorable speaker (i.e., make initial appeals to ethos),[1] and to introduce the leading ideas that will be developed in the speech itself. The attention that the author gives to the ornamentation and composition of his opening lines (see the discussion of these verses in the introduction) begins to serve the cause of making the hearers "attentive, receptive, and well-disposed" (*Rhet. Her.* 1.4.6-7). It is artistically crafted to delight the ears of the hearers, to assure them that they are hearing the words of a skilled orator (an ἀνὴρ λόγιος). Throughout the sermon the author will continue to remind the hearers of this through his literary artistry.[2]

Hebrews begins by building an extended contrast between God's earlier oracles and God's word in Jesus, setting the message that brought the hearers together into a community of believers (2:3-4) as God's ultimate revelation in a long history of significant revelations. Almost every element in 1:1 has a counterpart (an antithesis) in 1:2a. The revelation "to the fathers and mothers" was "long ago"; the revelation to "us" comes "at the end of these days," a phrase that signals the arrival of the end time.[3] God's former oracles were spoken "through the prophets," God's faithful servants; God's present word is articulated through "a Son." Both the timing of the message and the status of the messenger become significant considerations in the sermon. Response to *this* message will determine one's eschatological (and eternal) destiny. There will be no further calls to repentance or opportunities to give God what is due God, for the time of judgment and reward is imminent (10:25, 37-39). Attachment to *this* messenger assures one of honor and favor as those who are brought into God's own household by the Son himself. Affronting, insulting, or rejecting this messenger means experiencing the full brunt of divine satisfaction, the punishment reserved for those who fail to honor the Son for his benefits to all creation and humanity.

The title "Son" carries a message that Jesus' honor and worth derives from the honor of the father, God himself. In the Greco-Roman world, one's honor or standing depended largely on one's parentage — whether one was born into low or high status. Ben Sira, for example, urged children always to honor their parents, since "a man's honor springs from his father's honor" (Sir. 3:11). Dio Chrysostom, when affronted by the townspeople of Prusa, claims that they owe

---

1. Compared with Galatians and 2 Corinthians, there is a notable absence of attempts by the speaker to dispel prejudice or subtly introduce the issues. There appears to be nothing to discredit the speaker in his audience's eyes. He may well regard his cause as of the "honorable kind" (*Rhet. Her.* 1.3.5), namely, calling for a just response to the divine benefactor.

2. For further discussion of the use of rhetorical ornaments in Hebrews, see Attridge, *Hebrews,* 20-21; Spicq, *L'Épître aux Hébreux,* 1:361-66.

3. The LXX versions of Num. 24:14; Jer. 23:20; 25:19; Dan. 10:14 all use ἐπ᾽ ἐσχάτου τῶν ἡμερῶν for "the future" or especially "the end of the days," the eschatological threshold. Significant, then, is the author's addition of τούτων to this LXX phrase, which identifies the "end time" as having arrived in the recent past.

him the same honor and respect that they paid to his father and grandfather, whom they only rightly revere if they remember to honor the descendant as well (*Or.* 46.3-4). We have also seen above that encomia (eulogies and other commemorative addresses) included praise of the subject's ancestors as a means of establishing the honor of the subject (see *Rhet. Her.* 3.7.13). Dwelling on Jesus' status as "Son" is a reminder that God stands behind the honor of this person, both to reward those who honor the Son and to punish those who think too lightly of the Son.[4] As the author goes on to amplify this point (1:4-6, 8-9, 13; 2:1-4; etc.), he ensures that each of the hearers will understand the significance of maintaining a reverent response to Jesus.

The one element of 1:1 that has no antithesis, no parallel in 1:2, is the opening adverbs ("in many pieces[5] and in many ways"). Although the author does not explicitly state that the word spoken through the Son contrasts with the "piecemeal and diverse" revelations in the OT, he will proceed throughout this sermon to read the OT as if to bring the many pieces and diverse manners of God's earlier words together into one Christocentric reading. He presents the historic oracles of God as small and scattered pieces of a great jigsaw puzzle, which all come together when seen in light of the final revelation in the Son. The person and work of Jesus is the complete picture, as it were, that serves as a guide for the author in his handling of the many pieces contained in the OT (e.g., Pss. 2, 40, 45, 46, 110; Jer. 31).

The remainder of the opening sentence lists the attributes and accomplishments of the Son, laying out the messenger's significance and honor in what is truly the grand scheme.[6] He is "heir of all things," a designation with a

---

4. The author of 2 Peter also understands Jesus' honor to be linked to God's declaration of his relationship to Jesus, "having received honor and repute from God the Father when the voice was conveyed to him by the Supreme Glory: 'this is my Son, my beloved, in whom I am well pleased'" (2 Pet. 1:17).

5. Πολυμερῶς really should be read as "in many parts or pieces." Stedman (*Hebrews*, 21), for example, retains the common but faulty translation "in various times" or "at many times." This word is the adverbial form of an adjective meaning "consisting of many parts or pieces."

6. Scholars have long debated the possibility that 1:3, or possibly 1:2b-3, contains an early Christian hymn about Christ. It is true that the passage resembles other passages that are similarly seen as early hymns woven into the text of a NT letter, the most well-known being Phil. 2:5-11. Lane (*Hebrews 1–8*, 7) points out that the author's precise wording in his allusion to Ps. 110:1 favors the idea that the author is drawing on a liturgical formulation at this point. Everywhere else the author speaks of the Son as sitting ἐκ δεξιῶν "at the right hand" of God (1:13; 8:11; 10:12; 12:2); here the Son sits ἐν δεξιᾷ. While we can affirm, then, that the author draws on liturgical language, we cannot be as certain about the extent of his "quotation" or paraphrasing of a hymn or acclamation, much less reconstruct the original setting of the hypothetical hymn. Lane's cautious conclusion still underscores the fact that the author is articulating the shared faith of the Christian churches rather than trying to

distinctly eschatological tenor. The author certainly knows Psalm 2 (for he will cite it in 1:5), in which the "Son" is invited to ask God for "the nations as an inheritance." The author of Hebrews broadens the scope of the Son's inheritance here, replacing "nations" with "all things."[7] The Son is not merely heir of the nations of this world, but heir and master of the "coming world" (2:5-10). Those who remain "partners" with the Son (3:14) will enjoy a share in that inheritance, but those who disgracefully break off their alliance will be treated as enemies of the Son (1:13; 10:26-27). The honor and authority of the Son both in this age and the next are grounded in his role as agent of creation, for it was "through him" that God "made the ages." He is thus owed a debt of gratitude and honor akin to the debt owed God for the creation and preservation of all things, both in the shakable and unshakable realms, since he acted from the beginning as the mediator (broker) of God's benefactions, of which creation was the most universally recognized.[8]

The author next appropriates themes familiar from wisdom literature to refine his discussion of the Son's relationship to the Father.[9] The sages of ancient Israel praised the wisdom revealed by God, using the technique of personification to give life to the subject of their paeans. Proverbs 8, which celebrates "Lady Wisdom," represents a high-water mark in this regard. The tendency increased during the intertestamental period. Wisdom of Solomon, a highly influential and popular book in diaspora Judaism and the early Church, praised wisdom as God's partner in creation: she was the "fashioner of all things" (Wis. 7:22), "present with God when God made the world" (Wis. 9:9). She is also credited with playing a part in the ongoing governance of the created order: "she renews all things while remaining in herself" (Wis. 7:27), and "orders all things well" (Wis. 8:1). Perhaps most strikingly,

---

teach the hearers something about Christ they do not already know and hold. For further detail, see Attridge, *Hebrews*, 41-42; Lane, *Hebrews 1–8*, 7-8; J. T. Sanders, *The New Testament Christological Hymns: Their Historical Religious Background* (SNTSMS 15; Cambridge: Cambridge University Press, 1971); J. Frankowski, "Early Christian Hymns Recorded in the New Testament: A Reconsideration in Light of the Question of Heb 1,3," *BZ* 27 (1983): 183-94; John P. Meier, "Symmetry and Theology in Heb 1,5-14," *Bib* 66 (1985): 504-33.

7. Lane, *Hebrews 1–8*, 13.

8. See, for example, Aristotle *Eth. Nic.* 8.14.4: "no one could ever render the gods the honor they deserve, and a person is deemed virtuous if he or she pays them all the honor he or she can"; 4 Macc. 13:13, NRSV: "Let us with all our hearts consecrate ourselves to God, who gave us our lives"; 16:18-19, NRSV: "Remember that it is through God that you have had a share in the world and have enjoyed life, and therefore you ought to endure any suffering for the sake of God"; Rev. 4:11, NRSV: "You are worthy, our Lord and God, to receive glory and honor and power, for you created all things."

9. A rich discussion of the development of the figure of wisdom from ancient Israel through the intertestamental into the early Christian period can be found in Ben Witherington III, *Jesus the Sage and the Pilgrimage of Wisdom* (Minneapolis: Fortress, 1994).

she is portrayed as "the reflection of eternal light . . . and the image of God's goodness (ἀπαύγασμα γάρ ἐστιν φωτὸς ἀϊδίου . . . καὶ εἰκὼν τῆς ἀγαθότητος αὐτοῦ, Wis.
7:26). Wisdom was thus envisioned as a mediator between God and creation, and
these expressions give voice to the conviction that God's creation was gracefully ordered and perfectly planned, and indeed that in the contemplation of the "wisdom"
of God's works one had access to a reflection of the Almighty's goodness and perfection.

Such wisdom traditions, however, become the raw material for Christology
in the early Church, which held to the firm conviction that God's mediator had
been given a definite face in the person of Jesus. The details of the preincarnate life
of the Son as agent of creation were filled out by means of this Jewish cultural
knowledge about wisdom. The Son's current function of "bearing all things by
means of his powerful word" (Heb. 1:3) also reflects attributing to the Son the duties formerly attributed to wisdom. The language of "reflection" and "imprint"
used by the author of Hebrews to describe the relationship of the Son to the Father
bears so close a resemblance to the language of Wisdom of Solomon as to suggest
direct influence.

In calling the Son the "reflection" of God's glory, the author draws attention
to the nearness of the Son to the Father such that the honor of the latter is fully reflected by the One who sits nearest to him in the household.[10] Here, and in the notice of being seated at God's right hand (1:3), the author provides a foretaste of a
central theme of the sermon, namely, the proximity of the Son to the fount of favor
and his efficacy as a mediator of God's benefits. In his attempt to discover "who
possessed *gratia*" in the Roman imperial world — that is, who was in a position to
provide access to imperial *beneficia* — Richard P. Saller points first to the imperial
household: "When sons and grandsons existed, they *and their friends* were always
natural candidates for the emperor's beneficence."[11] The close relatives of the emperor, especially his sons, were sought after as mediators of the emperor's favor:
their close, familial relationship to the patron of the empire gave great hope of success. Saller points, for example, to two letters sent by Cornelius Fronto to Marcus
Aurelius, adopted son of the emperor Antoninus, requesting help in securing imperial benefactions for clients.[12] He concludes that "proximity (physical and emotional) was a critical factor in determining the channels through which imperial
beneficia flowed."[13]

Geoffrey Ernest Maurice de Ste. Croix notes that any member of a great
person's extended household could serve as a broker of that person's favor. The

---

10. On "glory" as the visible manifestation of a person's honor, see deSilva, *Despising
Shame,* 213-15.

11. Saller, *Personal Patronage,* 59 (emphasis mine).

12. Fronto, *Ad M. Caes.* 5.34, 37; Saller, *Personal Patronage,* 59.

13. Saller, *Personal Patronage,* 63.

list includes "his friends, who had the ear of the great man; their friends, even, at only one further remove; even the personal slaves of the great man, who often, for the humble client, could procure or withhold audience with the patron — all these satellites shone with various degrees of reflected glory and were well worth courting."[14] His conceptualization of the household of a high-status person as a system within which members of the household shone with different degrees of "reflected honor" is especially intriguing in light of Hebrews, wherein the Son is frequently contrasted with servants of the household of God (e.g., the angels in 1:4-14 and Moses in 3:2-6). As a valued servant in the household, Moses would provide a certain level of access to the Patron of the house, namely, God. The author stresses, however, that the believers have gained the Son as their patron and broker of God's favor: their access to favor (see 4:14-16; 9:14; 10:19-22) is assured by the mediation of the one who stands in such close proximity to God that he bears "the reflected radiance of God's glory" (1:3).

The meaning of the term χαρακτὴρ has been much debated in light of the usage of this term in Philo. Its use in 4 Maccabees 15:4 within the context of a discussion of parenting is also worth noting: "we impress upon the character (χαρακτὴρ) of a small child a wondrous likeness both of mind and of form." The child's character is thus largely a reflection of the parents' character, which impresses itself upon the former like a seal in warm wax. This parallel, while inexact, is suggestive in the context of Hebrews 1:1-4, where the likeness of the Son to the Parent is being described. The notion of a parent imprinting his or her essence and accident (likeness both of mind and of form) upon the child is certainly an apt resonance for the relationship between the Son and God.

A second foretaste of a major theme of the sermon appears in the brief reference to the work of the Son, who, "having made purification for sins, sat down at the right hand of the majesty in the highest places" (1:3). The author shares with a broad spectrum of the early Church the conviction that Jesus' death had significance for the relationship between God and humanity.[15] This recalls for the hearers the debt that they particularly owe the Son, who laid down his own life in order to bring benefit to his clients. This will be developed at length in 2:9-18; 7:11–10:18. The phrase "making purification for sins" seems to answer the lament of Job "Why do you not make forgetfulness of my transgression and purification for my sins?" (τί οὐκ ἐποίησω τῆς ἀνομίας μου λήθην καὶ καθαρισμὸν τῆς ἁμαρτίας μου) (7:21).[16] Whether or not the Job text is in

---

14. G. E. M. de Ste. Croix, "Suffragium: From Vote to Patronage," *British Journal of Sociology* 5 (1954): 41.

15. See Rom. 3:21-25; 8:3, 34; 1 Cor. 5:7; Eph. 5:2; 1 Pet. 1:19; 1 John 2:2; 4:10; Rev. 5:9 (references gathered in Nelson, *Raising Up a Faithful Priest,* 143).

16. The allusion is suggested in the marginal notes of the Nestle-Aland text and taken up by Lane, *Hebrews 1–8,* 15.

our author's mind, it is precisely "forgetfulness of transgression" that will also become a major theme through the incorporation of Jeremiah 31:31-34 in Hebrews 8:7–10:18, alongside the "purification for sins."

The honor that followed this purificatory offering, namely, session at God's right hand, underscores the nobility of Jesus' death.[17] The exaltation of Jesus will be kept clearly in the hearers' view throughout the sermon as a means of underscoring the importance of staying within the sphere of the Son's favor and not acting in any way that will alienate one from the Son's friendship. It also serves to prove an important point about the path to honor in God's sight and the unreliability of the world's estimation of honor. Jesus died, in the eyes of unbelievers, a shameful death, executed as a worthless criminal. The author of Hebrews, however, takes great pains to remind the addressees of the nobility of that death both in terms of the virtues that Jesus exhibited on the way to that death (generosity, piety, and courage, 2:9, 14-15; 5:7; 12:2) and of its noble consequences both for the hearers (2:9-18; 9:14; 10:19-22) and for Jesus himself (2:9; 10:12-13; 12:2).[18]

---

17. See Aristotle *Rh.* 1.9.16 on the reward for an action revealing the nobility or baseness of that action.

18. Various proposals have been made for the meaning of the middle voice of the participle in 1:3b (καθαρισμὸν τῶν ἁμαρτιῶν ποιησάμενος). It may be frequently translated as "having made purification for sins by/in himself" (see Lane, *Hebrews 1–8,* 15), but we must recall that the principal sense of the middle voice was to underscore that advantage or disadvantage accrues to the doer of the action. This option is rarely considered due to our inability to hold notions of altruism and ambition together (see the excellent critique of this conviction in the history of interpretation of Heb. 12:2 found in Croy, *Endurance,* 177-85). While it would be reckless to insist that all true middle voices in Hebrews retain the more classical sense of "to the doer's advantage or benefit," this remains a lively option here for a number of reasons. First, the accrued advantage hinted at by the middle voice is immediately described as session at God's right hand; second, the notion that Christ enacted his sacrificial death with an eye to "the joy set before him" (again, this session at God's right hand) is one possible, and I believe the stronger, reading of 12:2 (see, again, Croy, *Endurance,* 66-67, 175-85); third, the author of Hebrews describes Jesus' death in terms reminiscent of discussions of courage in the Greco-Roman world, in which one endures hardship (including hardships undertaken specifically to bring benefit to others, as courage in battle when defending one's city) for the sake of the noble ends it will achieve, including the honor that accrues to the courageous.

Such a reading would not in any way imply that Jesus did not act in our interest, but merely highlights the awareness that his sacrifice also brought benefit to him, that he was acting in fact as an honorable person. We must remember that beneficence of any kind was a central path to acquiring honor, so that extracting motives for honor from motives for beneficence is not so easy. Neither would reading this participle as a true middle voice detract from the debt we owe Jesus for his self-surrender for us. Seneca (*Ben.* 6.13.1-2) gives us a contemporary perspective on this question: "I am not so unjust as to feel under no obligation to a man who, when he was profitable to me, was also profitable to himself. . . . nay, I am also desirous that a benefit given to me should even be more advantageous to the giver, provided

The real honor of Jesus and his death was not recognized by the world, but it was recognized by God — to the extent that he now occupies the highest place in the Christian cosmos. This becomes a paradigm for the hearers, who are called to see in Jesus the proof that, though their own honor and the nobility of their actions go unrecognized (even reproached) by their neighbors, God will recognize and actualize their honor in the kingdom he has prepared for them.

The discussion of Jesus' exaltation — his taking a seat at the right hand of God[19] — represents an important instance of the early Church's use of the OT as authoritative witness to provide information on events in Jesus' career otherwise without any witnesses. The author of Hebrews so intensely believes the OT to be a witness to Christ that it can be used to speak about his activity before his birth as well as his ministry after his ascension through the heavens (the last event for which the NT texts claim human witnesses). Here it is specifically Psalm 110:1 to which the author alludes, and which he will recite directly in 1:13 (and return to frequently throughout the sermon: 8:1; 10:12; 12:2): "The LORD said to my Lord, 'Sit at my right hand until I make your enemies a footstool for your feet.'" A royal psalm is removed from the context of the installation rites of the (now defunct) Israelite monarchy and applied messianically to the Davidic successor *par excellence*. The exaltation of the Son is the present reality that the addressees should consider. It is the proof of the efficacy of his ministry of mediation and guarantee of God's favor for those who approach God through the Son; it is also pregnant with menace for those who make themselves enemies of the Son, as the full citation of Psalm 110:1 in 1:13 will make evident. For the past, present, and future, the Son is all-important — this is the first and primary fact that the author would impress upon the hearers.

With the declaration that this Son "has become so much better than the angels as the name he has inherited is more distinguished than theirs" (1:4), the author arrives at the point of comparison that he will develop in 1:5-14. The

---

that, when he gave it, he was considering us both, and meant to divide it between himself and me. . . . I am, not merely unjust, I am grateful, if I do not rejoice that, while he has benefitted me, he has also benefitted himself."

A second possibility, however, is even simpler. H. W. Smyth (*Greek Grammar* [Cambridge, MA: Harvard University Press, 1928], §1722) documents a Greek idiom wherein the middle voice of ποιέω plus a verbal noun (a noun that has a cognate verb) substitutes for that cognate, causative verb. Thus "to make war" could be expressed by the verb πολεμέω or by the idiom πόλεμος ποιοῦμαι. Other examples are given by Smyth, leading us to think that the phrase καθαρισμὸν ποιησάμενος merely substitutes for the verb ἐκαθάρισε, "he effected, or brought about, purification."

19. The construction τῆς μεγαλωσύνης ἐν ὑψηλοῖς is formed from the liturgical language of the Psalms. In Ps. 70:21 (LXX), μεγαλωσύνη refers to God's "greatness" and becomes a metonym for God's own self (the quality substituting for the one described). Psalm 112:5 (LXX) speaks of God dwelling ἐν ὑψηλοῖς.

"better" name, of course, is that of "Son," the title that clarifies Jesus' place in God's household and his greater nearness to God than the "ministering spirits" (1:14). The sudden emergence of angels as a prominent topic here appears, at first, most strange. It has given rise to theories, based on unduly imaginative mirror reading, that the author is addressing a congregation stricken by some heretical belief or deviant ritual — either a notion that Christ was merely an angel, or the practice of worshiping angels.[20] As we read on in Hebrews, however, we find no polemical remarks concerning angels that might support either hypothesis.[21] Angels continue to appear as honored messengers of God in comparison with whom the Son's significance can positively be developed. This is in keeping with the rhetorical device of *synkrisis,* or comparison. *Synkrisis* is a feature of epideictic speeches (eulogies mainly), in which the honor of the subject

---

20. Such arguments are advanced in T. W. Manson, "The Problem of the Epistle to the Hebrews," *BJRL* 32 (1949-50): 1-17; Jewett, *Letter to Pilgrims,* 5-7, 20-27; A. J. McNicol, "The Relationship of the Image of the Highest Angel to the High Priest Concept in Hebrews" (Ph.D. diss., Vanderbilt University, 1974), 1-38. Bruce (*Hebrews,* 51) allows this to be a possible reference for the "sorts of strange teaching" against which the author warns in 13:9. Stedman (*Hebrews,* 12) goes so far as to read the Colossian heresy completely into Hebrews: "Their geographical nearness to Ephesus would . . . help explain the references in Hebrews to Sabbath observance, new moon festivals, food restrictions and especially the worship of angels, which are also treated in Colossians." The presence of any of these teachings in Hebrews, however, is highly debatable. The author urges the hearers to strive to enter the sabbath observance of heaven, but never cautions against sabbath observances on earth (unless we assume that every positive injunction in a biblical text must correct a negative practice in the audience, which is, of course, fallacious mirror reading). New moon festivals are never mentioned at all, and restrictions on diet would be an unlikely meaning for the "foods" that might give (false) strength to the heart in 13:9 (which seems more naturally to imply eating rather than abstaining from eating). Nor, as it happens, is there any indication of angel worship breaking out among the hearers of this sermon. If Stedman is right in asserting angel worship in the setting of Hebrews, then 2:1-4 should have read: "Therefore, we must leave off adoration of these lesser beings, sent to serve us who are to receive salvation, and reserve our worship for the one who truly is worthy of such praise. For if the angels are inferior to Jesus, and indeed worship him themselves, ought we not to join in their circle of praise to the Son rather than be distracted by their secondary radiance?" As it stands, however, the comparison of the angels and the Son serves solely and wholly to emphasize the superiority of the message spoken through the Son to that message given through angels, and thus serves the injunction to remain loyal to Jesus and the relationships formed through the gospel proclaimed by him and confirmed by the Father.

21. Thus, correctly, Attridge, *Hebrews,* 51; Lane, *Hebrews 1–8,* 9. Attridge entertains the possibility that the author is pushing against a tendency to assimilate Christology with other available conceptions of an angelic messiah figure. However, this is problematic in light of the absence of direct polemic against such tendencies and the presence of a clear rhetorical purpose for the comparison present in 2:1-4 (in which angels are in no way seen in a negative light).

is amplified or underscored by comparing his characteristics or achievements with other honored figures (see Aristotle *Rh.* 1.9.38-39; *Rhet. Alex.* 1441a27-28). This is a mode of discourse that will figure prominently in Hebrews 3:1-6 and 7:1–10:18.[22] The *synkrisis* will serve an important rhetorical function, but not as polemic and not as a signal that the dominant mode of Hebrews is epideictic. Rather, as we look for some place where the author bases some appeal on this comparison with angels, we find the warning of 2:1-4, a lesser-to-greater argument for which 1:4 and 1:5-14 establish the relationship of angels to Jesus as lesser to greater.[23]

A Closer Look: Angels in Intertestamental Judaism

The conviction that God was surrounded by spirit beings who served his will was part of Israel's religious heritage from the earliest Pentateuchal narratives and Psalms. These beings constituted God's entourage like the courtiers and servants in the hall of a great king, and the functions attributed to them early in Israel's history persisted through the intertestamental period. The angels honor God in worship (Ps. 103:20-21; 148:2; Isa. 6:1-3; Rev. 4:1–5:14) and serve God's purposes in a wide variety of ways — delivering God's messages (Gen. 18:1-22; 22:11-18), enacting judgments and punishment upon transgressors (Gen. 19:1-24; Num. 24:15-17; *1 Enoch* 56:1-8; 2 Macc. 3:25-26; 4 Macc. 4:10-11), protecting God's clients (Exod. 14:19-20; Ps. 91:11; *1 Enoch* 100:5; Tobit), fighting against the enemies of Israel as a celestial army (Ps. 68:17-18; 2 Kgs. 6:15-17; 19:32-36; Zech. 1:7-11; 2 Macc. 15:22-23; 3 Macc. 6:18-21).

Angels become increasingly prominent features of Jewish cosmology throughout the intertestamental period, serving still in the capacity of mediators between God and human beings. They are frequently credited for acts attributed directly to God in the OT. One prominent development is the belief that angels served as the first link in the chain of the mediation of Torah between God and the people (see *Jub.* 1:27-29; 2:1; Gal. 3:19; Acts 7:38, 53), a tradition with which the author, who refers to the Torah as the "word spoken

---

22. In this way, the initial paragraph continues to give foretastes of what is to come in the rest of the speech (see Aristotle *Rh.* 3.14.1). The adjective κρείττων also announces a recurring theme and a major interest of the author. It is used thirteen times in this sermon, with reference either to Christ in comparison with figures or aspects of the Old Covenant (1:4; 7:7, 19, 22; 8:6; 9:23; 11:40; 12:24) or to the benefits that have fallen to the believers' lot as a result of their association with the Son and his mediation (6:9; 10:34; 11:16, 35).

23. It is not helpful to consider 2:1-4 a "pause" in the "christological hymn-sing" (Long, *Hebrews,* 24) or to suggest that the danger against which 2:1-4 warns is the "dangerous territory" that lies "directly ahead in the sermon," specifically in "the narrative of the incarnation, the story of Jesus' anguish and vulnerability" (Long, *Hebrews,* 25). Rather, the argumentative payload of 1:5-14 arrives at its enthymematic target in 2:1-4, and the danger facing the hearers is not the contemplation of Jesus' path to perfection through suffering but the potential unwillingness of some to persevere along the same road in obedience to God's word and trust in God's promises concerning what lies at the end of that road.

through angels" (2:2), is familiar. Visualization of angels and speculation about their significance is augmented by the development of apocalyptic literature. Apocalypses, perhaps thought of mainly in terms of their predictions about the end of time, frequently included tours of the realms ordinarily beyond human access, such as heaven and hell and their inhabitants (cf. *1 Enoch* 17–36; *T. Levi* 2–5; *Apoc. Abr.* 18–29; Rev. 4–5, 12).[24]

Particularly relevant for Hebrews, however, is the growth of the function of angels as mediators. Angels stand closer to the presence of God than human beings. In particular, the archangels are thought to stand in God's very presence (Tob. 12:15; *T. Levi* 3:4-8; Luke 1:19; Rev. 4:5; 8:2), hence they come to be known as "angels of the presence" (*Jub.* 2:2, 18; 1QH 14:13; 1Q28^b 4:25-26). These creatures are well placed to secure God's favor for those clients further removed from God's household. They direct the prayers of the righteous to God (Tob. 12:12; *1 Enoch* 9:1-11; Rev. 8:3-4; implied in Matt. 18:10?), and their priestly functions are augmented as the tendency increases to envision God's abode as a heavenly temple (cf. *1 Enoch* 14; 4Q400). The angels become priests and ministers of the courts of the heavenly temple, of which the ministry of Levi will be a reflection (*Jub.* 30:18; 31:14). The most striking expression of this comes from the *Testament of Levi*. Levi has a vision of the heavens, passing from the lower heavens in which are arrayed angels for the punishment of sinners and angelic armies for the defeat of the demonic forces, into the upper heavens where God dwells. "There with him are the archangels, who serve and offer propitiatory sacrifices to the Lord in behalf of all the sins of ignorance of the righteous ones. They present to the Lord a pleasing odor, a rational and bloodless oblation" (3:5-6).

The author's decision to develop the value of Jesus' mediation through comparison with the angels, therefore, may stand in a direct connection with his use of Moses and the levitical priests for comparisons in 3:1-6 and 7:1–10:18 — all of these figures were believed to stand as mediators of God's favor and intercessors on behalf of God's erring clients. Just as the Son stands closer to God than the faithful servant, Moses, so he also stands in closer proximity to God than even the "angels of the presence." His friendship is more valuable than theirs for gaining the favor of the Divine Patron.

1:5-14

Having posited the theme of his first extended *synkrisis*, the author presents a beautifully crafted tour through OT scriptural witnesses to the exalted status of the Son, particularly with a view to demonstrating his exaltation over the angelic beings (themselves a higher order of creation than human beings, cf. Ps. 8:5-7, cited in Heb. 2:6-8). There is a tendency for commentators, when working through the comparison of the Son and the angels in 1:5-14, to lose sight of

---

24. For further discussion of angels in the OT, NT, and intertestamental literature, see T. H. Gaster, "Angels," *IDB* 1:128-34; H. B. Kuhn, "The Angelology of the Non-Canonical Jewish Apocalypses," *JBL* 67 (1948): 217-32; Carol A. Newsom and Duane F. Watson, "Angels," *ABD* 1:248-55; D. G. Reid, "Angels, Archangels," *Dictionary of Paul and His Letters* (Downers Grove, IL: InterVarsity Press, 1995), 20-23; Christopher Rowland, *The Open Heaven: A Study of Apocalyptic in Judaism and Early Christianity* (New York: Crossroad, 1982).

the main clause of the opening paragraph on which the rest depends — "God spoke to us in a Son" (1:2a).[25] Hebrews 1:2b-14 develops the comparison between the Son and the angels in order to amplify the importance of the message God announced through the Son and in order to set up the lesser-to-greater argument undergirding 2:1-4, a warning specifically urging the hearers to pay proper attention to the word spoken by God through the Son (thus returning to the main point of 1:1-4). The angels serve the purpose of embellishment, of amplification — and even the amplification of the honor of the Son himself serves the purpose of heightening the importance of responding appropriately to the word that God spoke through that Son. The focus on our response to God's word remains a dominant topic (1:1-4; 2:1-4; 3:7-11; 4:12-13; resumed finally in 12:25-29) of which we cannot lose sight.

As there is little evidence for a defective angelic Christology or a practice of angel worship in the sermon, we should not expect these opening verses to be heard as polemic against some position held among the addressees. This would be, incidentally, bad rhetorical form, running the risk of alienating the hearers by "correcting" them too quickly (before trust has been fully established within the speech). Rather, we should expect everyone in the congregation to be nodding with approval at the words being read to them, for the crisis facing the congregation is not the purity of the confession but the purity of each member's commitment to live out that confession, to continue to make choices that reflect that the message brought by the Son and the reward promised the faithful are the most significant factors in their lives. They thus should show the proper respect for the gifts they have received and have been promised. They should be duly impressed with the author's mastery of the oracles of God and his ability to pull together a complete demonstration relying on such quotations from ancient authority. All of 1:1-14, then, is setting the hearers up for the exhortation of 2:1-4, and for the beginning of the author's case that, since they have received knowledge of the truth, they had better live up to that knowledge.

The proof from Scripture is framed by the rhetorical questions in 1:5 and 1:13, which form an *inclusio*, marking the boundaries of the paragraph, as it were:

"For to which of the angels did he ever say"
(Τίνι γὰρ εἶπέν ποτε τῶν ἀγγέλων)

---

25. It is this tendency to get lost in the amplification, by the way, which makes many scholars regard Hebrews as a sample of epideictic rhetoric. It might well be construed as an epideictic exordium, drawn from "the person we are discussing" (*Her.* 3.6.11), but this would be to lose sight of the topic sentence of 1:1-4 and the subordinate relationship of 1:5-14 to 2:1-4.

"But to which of the angels has he ever said"
(πρὸς τίνα δὲ τῶν ἀγγέλων εἴρηκέν ποτε)

Each rhetorical question anticipates a negative answer from the hearers, who are expected to know already that God has said these things "to no angel." The proof moves through three phases (1:5-6; 1:7-12; 1:13-14), the first two making prominent use of antithesis, a rhetorically pleasing and effective form of expression (Aristotle *Rh*. 3.10.5). The proof begins with the recitation of Psalm 2:7 and 1 Samuel 7:14:

> To which of the angels did he ever say, "You are my Son; this day I have begotten you"? And again, "I will be a father to him, and he will be a son to me" (1:5).

The author uses first a royal psalm (a hymn sung at the accession of Israelite kings or celebrating the relationship of the king to the One God) and a pronouncement made to David by God, now applying them to Jesus, the Son. Such a use would not be unusual or unexpected, since Psalm 2 and 2 Samuel 7:14 were already being interpreted as messianic texts, speaking of the eschatological king of David's line rather than of any of the past Davidic monarchs (cf. 4QFlor, which includes both 2 Sam. 7:10-14 and Ps. 2:1). The use of these two texts in particular was widespread in Christian culture. (Psalm 2 is cited or alluded to in Acts 4:25-26; Rev. 2:26; 12:5; 19:15-19; Ps. 2:7 may stand behind the pronouncement at Jesus' baptism in Mark 1:11; 2 Sam. 7:14 is used in 2 Cor. 6:18 and Rev. 21:7, but there its meaning is broadened to include all the faithful as God's children.) The psalm in its original setting demonstrates that the title "Son" (i.e., of God) could be applied to a human being; here it is an indication specifically of the Messiah's elevated status above the "servants" in God's household, in particular the angels (1:7, 14).

The contrast that completes this antithesis follows in 1:6: "but when again he leads the firstborn into the world, he says, 'and let all God's angels bow down to him in homage.'" The title "firstborn" was also applied to the Davidic king in Psalm 89:28, who was exalted above the other kings of the earth, and so may have entered Christological terminology as part of the messianic appropriation of the terminology of the ideology of the Israelite monarchy. Applying the title of "firstborn" to Jesus is also significant in Hebrews as an anticipation of the forthcoming development of the relationship between the destiny of the firstborn and that of the "many sons and daughters" (2:5-10, by means of an exegesis of Ps. 8).

A much-debated question concerns the event to which Hebrews 1:6 refers.[26] Does the author envision this declaration by God happening when the

---

26. See A. Vanhoye, "L'οἰκουμένη dans l'Épître aux Hébreux," *Bib* 45 (1964): 248-53.

Son first enters the sphere of human activity in the incarnation, returns to the world of the angels, or appears a second time on the earth? The use of οἰκουμένη in 2:5, particularly its definition there as the "coming world about which we have been speaking," strongly suggests that the author has in mind the return of Christ to the divine realm after his death and resurrection.[27] That such a world (οἰκουμένη) can be "coming" from the perspective of the author and his audience, but already present for God, his Son, and his angels, is a function of the author's peculiar eschatology, expressed most clearly in 12:26-28. The author anticipates a final "shaking" of the earth and heavens, which will mean the removal of the shakable, impermanent creation (cf. also 1:10-12). The "unshakable kingdom" will remain, however — that is, the unshakable realm that already exists will survive the shaking.

The author's terminology may well have been influenced by the use of the terms γῆ, "earth," and οἰκουμένη, "world," in the Psalms. There are numerous psalms in which the earth is shaken but the οἰκουμένη is unshaken or declared unshakable. Psalm 95:9-10 (LXX), for example, reads: "let all the earth be shaken from before your face (σαλευθήτω ἀπὸ προσώπου αὐτοῦ πᾶσα ἡ γῆ); say among the nations, 'the Lord reigns, for he indeed established the world, which will not be shaken (κατώρθωσεν τὴν οἰκουμένην ἥτις οὐ σαλευθήσεται).'" Psalms 45:5-7; 76:19; 96:4 (LXX) would have reinforced this distinction for the author and his congregation. Although the psalmists are not consistent in their application of their terminology and no doubt considered "earth" and "world" to be synonymous, the author of Hebrews appears to adopt the distinctions present in the passages above to create a differentiation between the created world and the unshakable realm where the Son is enthroned and which the believers will enter at the last "shaking" of the created order.

At the Son's return to the unshakable realm, then, something like a coronation — an enthronement — of the Son takes place. The OT texts become the author's window into this unseen rite, the session of the Son at God's right hand as God's vice-regent. God first acknowledges Jesus as his Son and then commands the heavenly court to do obeisance to God's vice-regent — "let all the angels of God worship him." The referent for the pronoun, of course, has been changed from God to the Son. Such *proskynesis* is a physical representa-

---

27. Attridge (*Hebrews,* 56) reads the adjective "coming" as a qualifier that distinguishes the "world" that is the subject of 2:5-9 from the "world" that appears in 1:6. Such a view hardly takes account, however, of the author's own clues that these two "worlds" are in fact the same, the one "about which [he has] been speaking." His criticism of Vanhoye's attempt to read οἰκουμένη as a technical term in the OT for the realm in which God's kingdom will be realized may be justified, but only insofar as it applies to the "technical" quality of that term. It remains probable that the author of Hebrews, while not relying on the previous establishment of οἰκουμένη as a "technical term," nevertheless uses it to distinguish the divine realm from the created, impermanent realm of human activity.

tion and acknowledgment of the superior honor of the Son to the angels. The author recites Deuteronomy 32:43, but specifically as this Song of Moses is found in the book of Odes, the first "hymnal supplement" in church history.[28] There the phrase "sons of God" has been changed to "angels of God." Clearly the Odes version serves the author's purpose (which involves creating a distinction between sonship and the servanthood of angels) better than the version in Deuteronomy.

Thus far, the author's appeals to the OT underscore his strategy to hold up the Son before the eyes of his audience as the most significant factor to consider as they chart the courses of their everyday lives. Hebrews 1:5-6 places the Son at the center of heavenly activity and interest, both in terms of God's pronouncements and of the angels' obeisance. As the enthronement of the Son continues in 1:7-9 with the praise of the Son's throne and scepter and with his anointing by God, this design to bring the Son into center stage and focus will be further enhanced.

Hebrews 1:7-12 takes a second approach to demonstrating the Son's superiority, focusing on his unchangeableness and his eternity. The angels continue to serve as a foil in 1:7-9, but in 1:10-12 the contrast is broadened to include heaven and earth, the temporality of which contrasts with the eternity of the Son. The author begins with a recitation of Psalm 103:4 (LXX): "and concerning the angels, on the one hand, he says: 'the one making his angels winds and his ministers a flame of fire.'" In the MT, this verse speaks of God's mastery over creation, bending such ethereal and, to humans, hardly controllable forces as wind and fire to serve his bidding. The LXX version appears to most commentators to reverse the subjects and the predicate nominative, suggesting now the mutability of the angels,[29] although this point remains contested by so fine a linguist as Paul Ellingworth.[30] Such a reading would certainly be in keeping with the development of 1:7-12, celebrating the permanence of the reigning Son by drawing attention to the unstable quality even of the ministering angels, whose form is altered to suit God's will. If Ellingworth is correct, however, that the LXX means exactly the same thing as the MT, then the single point of contrast becomes the status of these lofty spirit beings (πνεύματα) as still but messengers and servants (ἀγγέλους . . . καὶ . . . λειτουργοὺς) who serve the exalted Son.

The antithesis is completed in 1:8, when the author turns to what is said, "on the other hand, concerning the Son" with a recitation of Psalm 44:7-8 (LXX): "Your throne, O God, is forever, and the scepter of righteousness is

---

28. See G. L. Cockerill, "Hebrews 1:6: Source and Significance," *BBR* 9 (1999): 51-64.

29. See, for example, Bruce, *Hebrews,* 58-59; Attridge, *Hebrews,* 57-58; Lane, *Hebrews 1–8,* 28-29.

30. *Hebrews,* 120.

the scepter of your kingdom. You loved justice and hated lawlessness: therefore, O God, your God anointed you beyond your peers with the oil of gladness."[31] Angels are spoken of as messengers and servants, but the Son is addressed as sharing the title of God and as participating in the eternal and stable rule of God. The author extends the quotation for two verses, since the reference to the Son's being "anointed above his partners" underscores the Son's elevation above other celestial figures. The Son's elevation is based not merely on filial connections with the Almighty but also on the nobility of the Son, who has exhibited the virtue of wholehearted commitment to justice and abhorrence of vice. The OT thus becomes also a character witness for Jesus, presenting his exaltation as the just reward for his noble character, which God thus acknowledges.[32] The anointing of the Son is another physical sign of his honor status, like the *proskynesis* of the angels and the session at God's right hand. This act completes the imagery of the enthronement ceremony, which has run throughout the opening of the sermon.[33]

Hebrews 1:10-12 presents a third antithesis highlighting the Son's abiding, lasting nature in contrast with the mutability and temporality of created things. Unlike previous antitheses, this one is inherent in the quotation and not the product of the author's construction:

---

31. The translation of this verse is an area of debate on account of the lack of certainty regarding whether or not ὁ θεός functions as a nominative or a vocative, which is a common option in LXX Greek. The alternative reading would be "God is your throne forever," which has the advantage of being perfectly parallel in construction with the second half of the verse, both now being predicate nominative sentences (the extra article before θεός, which is not expected in such a sentence, would be readily explicable since "God" almost always appears with an article). If this translation is correct, the author of Hebrews would be underscoring the fact that the Son's rule is completely embedded in and backed by the rule of God. It is, however, a minority opinion among scholars, who favor a vocative reading for ὁ θεός in Heb. 1:8. Acquiescing to this, I would also suggest then that the second ὁ θεός (the first in 1:9) would be heard as a vocative by the audience.

32. The OT quotation has a profound impact on the hearers' assessment of Jesus' life and ministry, confirming the Christian cultural interpretation of that ministry as committed to the promotion of righteousness (since the reward was honor, the work must have been noble; cf. Aristotle *Rh.* 1.9.16). This would stand counter to both Jewish and Greco-Roman assessments of Jesus. In their eyes, the "reward" of crucifixion proved his life to be base.

33. Jacob P. Milgrom (*Leviticus I–XVI: A New Translation with Introduction and Commentary* [AB 3; Garden City, NY: Doubleday, 1991], 553) captures well the symbolic significance of anointing: "The main role of symbolic anointment in the ancient Near East, aside from its cosmetic, therapeutic, and magical functions, was to ceremonialize an elevation in legal status . . . [e.g.], the inauguration of a king, the ordination of a priest." Compare also Pitt-Rivers, "Honour and Social Status," 25: "We should note the intimate relation between honour and the physical person. The rituals by which honour is formally bestowed involve a ceremony which commonly centres upon the head of the protagonist."

From the beginning, Lord, you laid the foundations of the earth, and the heavens are the works of your hands. These will perish, but you remain; they will all grow old like a garment, and like a scroll you will roll them up, and as a garment they will be changed, but you are the same and your years will not fail. (Heb. 1:10-12)

The author has used an extended but inexact recitation of Psalm 101:26-28 (LXX),[34] which in its original setting would have addressed God but now is taken to address the Son as "Lord." The quality of the material creation, both heaven and earth, is described by means of similes of scrolls being rolled up and garments wearing out and being changed. Such an assessment of the durability of the visible world anticipates the author's eschatological expectations set forth in 12:26-28, the final "rolling up" and throwing away of the visible, temporal cosmos. These verses introduce axiological claims (assessments of value) that will be crucial to the success of the author's strategy. All material creation is of limited value since it is of limited duration. The addressees will therefore be urged to invest only in the eternal possessions (10:34; 11:13-16; 12:26-28; 13:13-14) and to consider worldly goods and security ultimately to be a bad and foolish investment (11:24-26; 12:16-17). Viewed another way, continued commitment to the group (even at the cost of ongoing deprivation of this world's goods, security, and honor) will be urged on the basis of the belief that the visible world is of secondary value to the presently invisible world, in which the believers are to set their hopes and ambitions.

Unlike the earth and heavens, the Son "remains." He was present before the foundations of the material creation were laid, and will abide long after the earth and heavens are rolled up like a scroll or wear out like an old garment. On the one hand, this quotation affirms the significance of the Son, as one who will outlast all that is seen. On the other hand, Hebrews 1:10-12 has significant resonances with discussions of trustworthiness or reliability in the Greco-Roman world. Dio Chrysostom, for example, devotes two orations to the topics of accepting the responsibility of being entrusted with something and the causes for distrusting others (Or. 73 and 74). In his oration on "distrust," he presents the following as the greatest impediment to trust:

What someone has said about Fortune might much rather be said about human beings, namely, that no one knows about any one whether he will remain as he is until the morrow (εἰ μέχρι τῆς αὔριον διαμενεῖ τοιοῦτος). At any rate, men do violate the compacts made with each other and give each other

---

34. ἑλίξεις replaces ἀλλάξεις in the LXX version to provide a more violent and vivid image; the addition of the second ὡς ἱμάτιον "keeps the imagery of clothing prominently in view and serves to stress the frequency and casualness with which the created order is altered" (Lane, Hebrews 1–8, 31).

different advice and, believing one course to be expedient, actually pursue another. (*Or.* 74.21-22)[35]

Topics of trust and distrust are indeed quite central to Hebrews (3:7-19; 6:13-20; 7:20-21, 28; 10:23; 11:1-40; 13:7-9), and so it would be appropriate to consider the impact of 1:10-12 and 13:8 on these issues. The author is making assertions about the constant nature of Jesus, but this will have important ethical ramifications. With Jesus there is none of that variableness that makes people untrustworthy. Jesus will indeed "remain as he is until the morrow" and through all tomorrows (13:8), and thus he can be trusted never to violate his compacts made with his clients and partners (3:14). By advancing the trustworthiness of the Son and of God himself, the author is serving his goal of motivating the addressees to hold fast to their confession of hope — a hope anchored in the efficacy of Jesus as broker (3:6, 14; 6:19-20; 10:23). Moreover, the addressees are being reminded that they cannot place their trust in, or seek to build their sense of security and safety on, anything belonging to this shakable, visible creation. Material wealth and the security or honor that are afforded in this earth are ultimately unreliable, destined not to "remain" constant but rather to be shaken and removed (12:26-28). Only the Son and his promise provide a "sure anchor" (see 6:19-20).

The author rounds out this demonstration from Scripture with a recitation of Psalm 110:1, which has been alluded to in the opening paragraph (1:3) and will remain an important text throughout the sermon: "and to which of the angels has he ever said: 'Sit at my right hand until I set your enemies as a footstool under your feet'?" The relative placement of bodies played an essential role in the enactment of honor and display of relative worth. The author's repeated references to Jesus' session at the right hand of God (1:3; 8:1; 10:12; 12:2) is an important claim about Jesus' significance in the cosmos. In the ancient world, seating order was based on the appraisal of relative worth or honor. The most distinguished people enjoyed the best seats. This is most apparent in court stories, such as Esther, where sitting next to the king is a sign of high ranking, and where all the nobles have their place of sitting established by rank: "After these things King Ahasuerus promoted Haman the Agagite, the son of Hammedatha, and advanced him and set his seat above all the princes who were with him" (3:1, RSV; cf. 1:14).

The instructions concerning taking the lowest seat at a banquet in Luke 14:8-10 bring the court practice into the everyday life of social gatherings:

When you are invited by someone to a wedding banquet, do not sit down at the place of honor, in case someone more distinguished than you has been

---

35. Compare also Dio *Or.* 74.4: "Accordingly, those who wish to live at peace and with some degree of security must beware of fellowship with human beings. For with human beings there is no constancy or truthfulness at all (οὐ γάρ ἐστι παρ' αὐτοῖς βέβαιον οὐθὲν οὐδὲ ἀληθές)."

invited by your host; and the host who invited both of you may come and say to you, "Give this person your place," and then in disgrace you would start to take the lowest place. But when you are invited, go and sit down at the lowest place, so that when your host comes, he may say to you, "Friend, move up higher"; then you will be honored in the presence of all who sit at the table with you. (NRSV)

By applying Psalm 110:1 to Jesus, the author claims for him the place of highest honor in the Jewish-Christian cosmos, namely, a seat at the right hand of God.[36] Lane correctly observes that session at God's right hand "would convey to contemporaries an impression of the Son's royal power and unparalleled glory."[37]

The recitation of Psalm 110:1 goes further here than the allusion in 1:3, which only spoke of session at God's right hand. Now the rest of the story is made explicit, together with the eschatological significance of the Son — he is the eschatological "winner," all of whose enemies are subjected to his reign, indeed, specifically dishonored (see 10:26-29).[38] The author will keep that eschatological horizon clearly in view for his audience, since it introduces the "crisis" with which he wants them to be primarily concerned. As long as their eyes are on this world, commitment to the Christian group may begin to appear disadvantageous. With their eyes on the "day" of the Son's return, they will be more apt to accept and follow the author's plan for survival and even success, which involves continued commitment to the confession and investment in one another and in Christian witness.

While the Son sits in the place of highest honor, the angels remain "ministering spirits" (λειτουργικὰ πνεύματα, 1:14, repeating key terms from 1:7). The author articulates this in the form of a rhetorical question anticipating a positive answer from the hearers ("Are they not all ministering spirits?"), again indicating that the subject matter of 1:5-14 is not being contested by the addressees. Moreover, these angels are sent to serve "on behalf of those who are about to inherit salvation" (1:14). This phrase is significant as it contains the first description of the addressees, the first contours that the author gives to the identity that he wants them to accept as their own self-definition and from which he wants them to live. They should identify themselves as those who "are about to inherit salvation," and their guiding concern should be how to achieve that goal for which they are specially marked, for which they have the help of ministering angels (1:14) and, as they will be reminded later, God himself (4:14-16). "Salvation"

---

36. It is a commonplace to note that "the right side is the side of honour" (W. Grundmann, "Δεξιός," *TDNT*, 2:38).

37. Lane, *Hebrews 1–8*, 16.

38. Being "made a footstool" is an image of forced submission. While the *proskynesis* of the angels also acknowledges the superior status of the Son, the angels lose no honor through that ritual. The contrary enemy who must be subjugated, however, loses honor.

(σωτηρία) is conceived in Hebrews as a future deliverance (1:14; 9:28; 11:7), which resonates well with everyday uses of the term in both Greco-Roman and Jewish documents. It also resonates with 1 Peter 1:5, 9; 2:2 as an understanding of the specific deliverance that has been made available through Jesus. Theological discussions that speak of "losing salvation" in Hebrews, therefore, ignore the specific thought-world of this sermon, for deliverance is not something to be lost but yet to be received at the appearance of Jesus the second time (9:28). Deliverance is specifically the opposite of the degradation of the enemies of the Son, which is expected in Hebrews 1:13. The author will be interested throughout his sermon in highlighting the different destinies of the friends or partners of the Son and those who remain, or become once more, his enemies.

Christians are thus named as beneficiaries of God's favor and deliverance. This "salvation" is a benefaction yet to be conferred, and thus the hearers must remain firm in their hope and trust, remaining "connected" to their patron through loyalty and reverent service. The identity of "heirs of deliverance" is very positive, particularly in light of the alternative. The audience should thus have little trouble accepting this delineation of "who they are." If they do, the author will have achieved an important step toward securing their assent to his exhortations, since all that follows has specifically to do with how to attain that inheritance and how not to exchange a good, lasting inheritance for divine wrath and punishment.

In 1:5-14, then, the author has provided a demonstration from Scripture for his premise in 1:4. The addressees would no doubt agree with him every step of the way, appreciating his exegetical finesse in applying OT texts as well as his rhetorical art in shaping antitheses to establish his point. He has not, however, merely established the premise for his lesser-to-greater argument in 2:1-4. Through this *catena* ("chain") of OT citations he has heightened the hearers' appreciation for the honor of Jesus (1:5-9) as well as the dangerous consequences for failing to acknowledge that honor (1:13). He has reminded them of the transient value of the material and visible creation, such that the only firm ground for hope and trust remains the Son (and not the recovery of material goods or honor in the eyes of the Son's enemies). He has, in every way, established the significance of the Son, such that the consideration that should be moving to the forefront of each hearer's mind will be, "How shall I respond to this Son so as to remain in favor, and not fall into the number of his enemies?" This is precisely the sort of question that the author goes on to answer.

2:1-4

Having laid the foundations for his appeal, the author now draws a logical conclusion (Διὰ τοῦτο) from the premises he set forth in 1:2 and 1:4: "Therefore it

is necessary for us to attend all the more to the things heard, lest we drift away"
(2:1). The skeletal framework for this syllogism is as follows:

> God spoke to us by a Son (1:2)
> The Son is greater than angels (1:4, amplified in 1:5-14)
> Therefore we had better attend to that message, knowing what befell
> those who transgressed the earlier message that God spoke through
> angels (2:1-2).

Hebrews 2:1 may catch the hearer by surprise, possibly because of the expansiveness of the lofty demonstration in 1:5-14. Since the addressees would agree that the Son is superior to the angels, they will have been listening with approval to the foregoing discussion, never dreaming that the point of that discussion was to underscore the importance of their now responding appropriately to the message spoken through the Son. The author's return to "the things heard" (i.e., in the preaching of the gospel, 2:3-4) takes the hearers back to the topic sentence of the first paragraph (1:2) and sets all that has intervened in the service of elevating the importance of heeding that message.

The author has thus devised a clever strategy for drawing the hearers in and getting their attention. Indeed, the author's declaration that it is "all the more necessary for us to pay attention (προσέχειν)" suggests that 2:1-4 is fulfilling a major function typical of exordia, namely, securing the hearers' attentiveness. This particular verb dominates *Rhet. Alex.* 1436b5-18, a discussion of what exordia must achieve. Unlike the typical exordium, however, it is calling for attention not merely to the speech but to the word that God had spoken already to the addressees, of which the speech will be but a reminder. Hebrews 2:1-4 also presents key notes or themes that will resound throughout the book. First, it emphasizes the importance of "hearing" and "responding" to God's word, which is central to 1:1–4:13. Second, it sounds a warning of the dangers that attend neglect of the great deliverance and benefits announced in the good news, which returns in 4:1-11; 6:4-8; 10:26-31; and 12:25-26.

The author's pairing of προσέχειν and παραρυῶμεν suggests a nautical metaphor: keeping one's attention firmly on the word of the Son signifies holding one's course, or even one's anchorage. It is the way to remain constant and secure in the midst of an untrustworthy sea. Failure to remain fixed in that word results in "drifting away," being borne along with the tides and waves, losing one's way.[39] We should note at this point how the author's language is di-

---

39. Παραρυῶμεν is the first instance of the author's use of the prepositional prefix παρα- with verbs denoting movement away from God, sin against God, and the like: 2:1; 3:8, 15, 16; 6:6 (*bis*); 12:12; 13:9 (P. Proulx and L. A. Schökel, "Heb 6,4-6: εἰς μετάνοιαν ἀνασταυροῦντας," *Bib* 56 [1975]: 198; Lane, *Hebrews 1–8,* 142). The author is reinforcing

rected at sustaining commitment to the Christian group. Movement away from this commitment is interpreted as "drifting" — the very movement that the non-Christian neighbors would affirm as "getting back on course." Already this author is at work disarming and countering society's (the Christians' neighbors') agenda for the believers, such as was evidently at work in the shaming techniques recalled in 10:32-34. The "rehabilitation" that the neighbors seek is being presented as a deviation from the right course, even as an affront to God's own self, which will result not in safety but gravest danger when that time of crisis (1:13-14) manifests itself. In that day, there will be "no escape" for those who have thought too lightly of the gospel's promise and the obligations such a promise lays on the clients.

To support this claim, the author presents a lesser-to-greater enthymeme, relying on the momentum he has created in setting forth the greater honor, dignity, and significance of the Son with regard to the angels: "for if the word spoken through angels was secure and every transgression and disobedience received its just deserts, how will we escape, neglecting so great a salvation?" (2:2-3a). The "lesser case" involves infractions against the divine message brought through the angels, namely, the Torah.[40] The OT is replete with stories that affirm the legal validity of the Torah: individual transgressors come to grief, to be sure; the rise and fall in the fortunes of the nation as a whole is also narrated in terms of Israel's attending to, or neglecting, this covenant. Books like 2 and 3 Maccabees bear witness to the extension of this conviction into the intertestamental period. Whether at the hands of God or the hands of human beings acting as God's instruments, the transgressor of the message spoken through angels receives punishment (often extreme, such as exile or death).

What holds true in the lesser case will also hold true in a greater case, so that if God's word spoken through the lesser mediator (the angels) is enforced, then God's word spoken through the greater Mediator (the Son) will certainly be enforced as well, and probably more forcefully (2:3a). "Neglecting such a great salvation" arouses the danger of inescapable punishment since the proper response to great benefits is to remain mindful of them and to continue to respond gratefully toward the giver in reverence, loyalty, and service. Seneca (*Ben.* 3.2.1) writes: "Who is so ungrateful as the man who has so completely excluded and cast from his mind the benefit that ought to have been kept uppermost in his thought and always before him, to have lost all knowledge of it?" This is the dynamic behind the author's response to those hearers who might be tempted to shrink back from

---

even at the level of repetitive patterns the contrast between the courses of approaching God through the Son or falling by the wayside, missing the goal, and the like.

40. The author draws here on Jewish cultural information, specifically the tradition that the Torah was given through angels to Moses. It has entered the heritage of early Christian culture as well (see *Jub.* 1:27-29; 2:1; Gal. 3:19; Acts 7:38, 53).

open commitment to Jesus and the church, since they "forget" the magnitude of what the Son has done for them so as to forget their obligation of gratitude. By going on to remind them at great length throughout the sermon of the amplitude of the gifts that have been given them, he hopes to dispel any thought among them of responding ungratefully and to motivate them to remain openly grateful clients of the Son of God no matter what that loyalty should cost them.

Dwelling on the honor of Christ in 1:1-14, therefore, enhances the severity of the insult offered to Christ when his message and gift are neglected. Inherent in the participle ἀμελήσαντες is the notion of showing contempt for the thing "neglected."[41] Perhaps this semantic relation is best demonstrated in a passage from Epictetus (*Diss.* 4.10.14), in which the philosopher expresses his hope that he will die while occupied with tending his moral faculty, so that he may claim before God: "the faculties which I received from Thee to enable me to understand Thy governance and to follow it, these I have not neglected (τούτων οὐκ ἠμέλησα); I have not dishonoured Thee (οὐ κατῇσχυνά σε) as far as in me lay." Neglect for God's gifts and revelation — thinking other concerns to be more weighty or deserving of attention — means dishonoring God. To show such neglect toward the promise of the gospel, and hence to affront the bearer of that message, would put one in greater danger than those who transgressed the Torah, since the injured honor of the Mediator will be restored through the punishment of the transgressor.

The author has thus arrived at his primary agenda item. He wants his audience to consider holding fast to the message that constituted the community, which gave them their hope of inheritance, as the most necessary thing, the *sine qua non*, of their everyday lives. The exaltation of Jesus has made this agenda "more abundantly necessary." "Drifting away" would be a great loss, since an "inheritance of salvation" is at stake (where lack of deliverance, of course, equals eschatological disaster). "Drifting" would, in fact, be culpable. It is painted not merely as a misfortune but as a blameworthy act. The drifter would be guilty of forgetting the benefits won for him or her by the Son, ignoring his or her obligation to remain mindful of past gifts and future promises, and to live out his or her gratitude. The author has marshaled the deliberative topics of security and expedience to make his presentation of the *sine qua non* more compelling: failing to act so as to show how greatly one values God's promises in the Son brings one into the gravest danger; continuing to set that message at the center of one's life alone provides the means for "preventing harmful things expected to occur" (*Rhet. Alex.* 1422a6-7 on the "expedient"). In addition to appeals to logos, this passage may represent a first appeal to the pathos of fear. The author has created

---

41. Thus Delitzsch (*Hebrews,* 1:97) offers a word indicating contempt as a synonym of "neglect" when commenting on this verse: "how shall we escape . . . if we shall have neglected or despised so great a salvation?"

"an impression of an imminent evil that causes destruction or pain" (Aristotle *Rh.* 2.5.1) specifically through positing the punishment that awaits those who have outraged the Son, "for it is evident that [virtue] always desires satisfaction, when it is affronted, and now it has the power" (*Rh.* 2.5.5). The author wants to make the audience afraid of choosing any course that will lead to such an outcome. Appeals to fear throughout this sermon (see 4:1-13; 6:4-8; 10:26-31; 12:25) will continue to push the wavering to choose the path by which they can in fact escape eschatological punishment.[42]

The author rounds out this admonition by stressing the reliability of the message spoken through the Son, and thus of the promise of deliverance: after it was "first declared through the lord, it was confirmed (ἐβεβαιώθη) for us by those who heard, God bearing witness as well (συνεπιμαρτυροῦντος τοῦ θεοῦ) by means of signs and wonders and diverse marvels and disbursements of Holy Spirit according to his will" (2:3b-4). The author points to the human witnesses of the message of Jesus as the first proof of the gospel's confirmation, but dwells at even greater length on the ecstatic phenomena surrounding the proclamation and reception of the gospel, which the author interprets as God's own testimony alongside the witness of the evangelists.[43] These witnesses leave no room for doubting the word, and, as presented here, greatly surpass the confirmation of the earlier word, which was also "confirmed as valid" (βέβαιος), but not thus established by such an impressive array of proofs (2:2). "Drifting," on the one hand, would now mean spurning a revelation authenticated by God firsthand. "Heeding" the message, on the other hand, is promoted by these reminders of the reliability of that word which was confirmed even by God directly. The Christian confession and hope is thus set forward as a sure anchor (to return to the nautical metaphor) for the hearers, indeed a lifeline into the harbor of the unshakable realm.

The concentration of the rhetorical device of "amplification" in this exordium (1:5-14; 2:1-4 both include topics of amplification) indicates that some of the hearers have been attaching "too little importance to the question" being discussed (Aristotle *Rh.* 3.14.12). Considering 1:1–2:18 from this angle may help to clarify the speech's goals, the articulation of which is the chief function of an exordium (*Rh.* 3.14.6). It is not that the hearers have been thinking "wrong" things about Jesus — it is, rather, that some of them are not thinking

---

42. The author posits neglect of the gospel as leading to a hopeless state with no possibility of escape. The addressees, however, are not yet in that hopeless state; they can, therefore, feel fear at the prospect of falling into such a state, and hence take steps to avoid it (Aristotle *Rh.* 2.5.14).

43. Both the presence of ecstatic phenomena and the interpretation of these phenomena as God's testimony to the validity of the message are common features of accounts concerning the reception of the gospel (see Gal. 3:1-5; 1 Cor. 2:1-5; Mark 16:20).

enough of Jesus, the benefactions he has brought, and the promises that have been made regarding benefits yet to come. The use of amplification throughout serves the author's strategy of elevating the audience's relationship to the divine Patron as the first and foremost consideration that should guide their actions and commitments. Particularly for the wavering, this should replace the other considerations that have begun to erode their wholehearted commitment to their fellow believers and the hope that binds them together into one family.

2:5-9

Having raised the hearers' awareness of the necessity of continuing to heed and to respond becomingly toward the Son and the message he brought, the author continues to dwell on the significance of the Son, particularly for the "coming world": "for it was not to angels that he subjected the coming world, concerning which we are speaking" (2:5). To whom are all things subjected, if not to angels? The hearers will have been led by the previous discussion of the Son's enthronement, the *proskynesis* of the angels, and most especially the application of Psalm 110:1 to the Son (expressing the expectation that his enemies will be put "under his feet") to think that the author has this Son in mind still. This verse thus continues to support the force of 2:1-4, for which it is offered explicitly as a rationale (signaled by the use of γάρ): if the coming world is subjected to the Son (as the Christological reading of Psalm 8 will maintain), those who would enter it must behave becomingly toward the Son and certainly not slight him.

The author introduces Psalm 8:5-7 (LXX) as a witness that will testify concerning the identity of the one to whom this "coming world" is subject. This passage is linked with Psalm 110:1 by the shared expression ὑπο- . . . τῶν ποδῶν αὐτοῦ.[44] While not precisely an example of *gezera shawa*, this shared pattern does suggest why the author would choose to develop the theme of the first text through contemplation of the second:[45]

> What is a man, that you are mindful of him,
>   or the son of man, that you watch over him?[46]

---

44. Thus Pfitzner, *Hebrews*, 61.

45. Psalm 8:7 is also prominent in 1 Cor. 15:23-28, first being recontextualized in Paul's exposition of eschatological events (15:25) and then being recited directly (15:27) and further expounded. There the text is also applied to Christ's exaltation above every power and authority (save God) and to the ongoing subjugation of the enemies of God and God's people until the last enemy, death, is itself subjected.

46. I have retained gender-specific language here in order to preserve the flexibility of the Greek, which allowed the author to move so freely from general humanity to one man, Jesus, as the referent of this text.

You have lowered him a short space below the angels,
> you have crowned him with glory and honor,
> you have subjected all things under his feet.

Hebrews 2:5-8a is thus a recitation of Psalm 8:5-7 (LXX), which in its original context speaks with awe and wonder at God's care for humanity and the great honor God has bestowed on human beings, entrusting them with the care of creation. The author of Hebrews, however, has omitted one line from the verses he quotes: "you have set him over the works of your hands." This omission points to the author's desire to elevate a Christological reading over a general, anthropological one.[47]

The author moves directly from quotation to commentary, focusing on the scope of the "subjection" envisaged: "In subjecting all things he left nothing free from subjection to him: but now we do not yet see all things subjected to him" (2:8). Repetition of ὑποτάσσω and related forms (ὑπέταξεν, 2:5; ὑπέταξας; ὑποτάξαι; ἀνυπότακτον; ὑποτεταγμένα, 2:8, to which we may add ὑποκάτω, 2:8, which employs the same prepositional prefix and the same consonantal sounds) underscores the completeness of the subjection envisaged.[48] The author has not yet, however, specified the identity of the "him" in this quotation. As we will explore below, he may be sustaining the suspense or the ambiguity purposefully.

Although "we" do not yet see the psalm's declaration as reality, the author will go on to tell the hearers what they can see: "but we see the one who was made lower than the angels for a little while, namely Jesus, crowned with glory and honor in order that he might taste death on behalf of all by the favor of God" (2:9). This verse recontextualizes the psalm in the interpretative context of Jesus' career, and the choice of LXX over MT significantly opens up this possibility. The MT is clear that the subject of the psalm is made "a little bit" lower than the angels, that is, fixed at a lower rung on the ladder of creation. The LXX, however, uses a more ambiguous expression (βραχύ τι), which can indicate either "a little bit" or "a little while" (an ambiguity difficult to capture in English, but "a short space" may suffice). As the author now reads the psalm, the latter possibility is preferred: Jesus is the one who was "made lower than the angels

---

47. Another interesting aspect of the author's interpretation of the psalm is that it applies not to the present age (as the psalm most assuredly did for its pre-Christian readers), but to the next age (or the coming world, in the author's terminology). The underlying logic of his hermeneutic may run thus: universal subjection is not yet an observable reality, but no word of Scripture proves ultimately invalid; if it is not true for this age, it will be true for the coming age.

48. This is a fine example of the device of "transplacement" or "paronomasia" (pun), something that would be especially delightful to the ears of those accustomed to an inflected language like Greek.

for a short while" during his incarnation, when he obediently accepted the "body" prepared for him by God as the vehicle by which he could fulfill God's will (10:4-10). After this humiliation came his exaltation — his anointing and enthronement (1:5-9), which left him "crowned with glory and honor." "We do not yet see all things subjected to him," but it is a firm conviction of the Christian hope that this also will be fulfilled, as indeed Psalm 110:1 (cited in Heb. 1:13; 10:13) leads the audience to anticipate for the future.

We mentioned above that the author might be attempting to foster a double reading of this psalm. In the explicated reading, of course, it is Jesus to whom the coming world is made subject; a second reading may point to the hearers as those who will share in the dominion over the coming world. Hebrews 1:14 may begin to suggest to the hearers this second reading, for there the hearers are brought into the comparison of the Son and the angels. The people of God are also the objects of angelic service, in addition to the Son. The historical reading of the psalm would also suggest a "general" application to humanity, and, significantly, there is nothing to subvert this expected reading until 2:9. The hearers may hear the psalm first in its general sense, and then have their reading given a specific application to the one man Jesus Christ. Hebrews 2:8b-9 would then suggest that the psalm, as an oracle concerning God's purpose for God's clients, has begun to find its fulfillment in Jesus, and the "not yet" looks forward to complete fulfillment in the future first when Jesus will have complete dominion over the coming age, but finally when all "those who are about to inherit salvation" share in the honor of the Son. Since the author of Hebrews will immediately go on to declare that God's plan involves "leading many sons and daughters to glory" (2:10, returning to the key word δόξα, which appears prominently in 2:7, 9), the general reading would continue to find support. As the locus for the fulfillment of Psalm 8, then, Jesus acts (as often throughout the sermon) as the pioneer for those in his household.[49]

The reason for, and result of, the Son's incarnation and exaltation is that he might taste death on behalf of everyone by God's grace (ὅπως χάριτι θεοῦ ὑπὲρ παντὸς γεύσηται θανάτου, 2:9). This is the point that the author interjects into his interpretation of the psalm (it is not connected to anything in the psalm text itself), and that he will go on to develop in 2:10-18 — the solidarity of the Son with the many sons and daughters in his incarnation (his abasement beneath the angels for a short time), and in his experience of suffering, testing, and death on their behalf. Much of the sermon will treat the death of Jesus, de-

---

49. This point is well made by Danker, *Benefactor*, 418-19. For an excellent discussion of the relationship of the exaltation of the Son to the destiny of the many sons and daughters, see L. D. Hurst, "The Christology of Hebrews 1 and 2," in L. D. Hurst and N. T. Wright, *The Glory of Christ in the New Testament: Studies in Christology* (Oxford: Clarendon, 1987), 151-64.

picting it as a noble death insofar as it brought benefit to others[50] and led to honor for himself.[51] Since Jesus' humiliation and experience of death were "on behalf of all," they were noble acts, and all the more so for being "at great cost to himself."[52] The author will continue to remind the hearers of this cost ("perfected through sufferings," 2:10; being tested so as to be equipped to help those who are tested, 2:18; the lengthy central discourse on the benefits of Jesus' death, 9:11–10:18; the cross and hostility from sinners, 12:2-3) not merely to amplify the nobility and courage[53] of Jesus' death but to amplify the obligation that such a generous patron lays on the recipients of gifts that cost so dearly.

Contemplation throughout the sermon of how the exalted Son (1:1-14) has used his "exterior advantages," another central topic of the encomium (*Rhet. Her.* 3.7.13; Quintilian *Inst.* 3.7.13), should serve the aim of stimulating a sense of gratitude and motivating a proper response. Jesus uses his exterior excellences (noble birth, strength) to bring the believers into contact with God as a patron (4:14–5:10; 7:1–10:18), to rescue them from slavery to the fear of death (2:14-15), and to lead them to share in his glory (2:10). In short, he uses his advantages in every way to help those who lack his advantages. His "attitude in the exercise of his [very great] prerogatives" has been that of generosity and beneficence (*Rhet. Her.* 3.7.14). All these discussions of Christ's benefits, beginning in earnest here at 2:9, should stimulate gratitude and make disloyalty on the part of the addressees seem all the more vicious and unthinkable. The crowning of Jesus with glory and honor thus becomes the public recognition of a benefactor.[54]

In 2:5-9, the author again refuses to let the addressees "see" anything besides Jesus, now as the focus for the fulfillment of God's vision for humanity as revealed in Psalm 8:5-7 (LXX). Jesus is the sole tether connecting the addressees to God's inheritance for them, a point that will be developed in 2:10 and 6:19-20. He uses the language of the psalm to affirm the Christian ideological read-

---

50. The eulogy or encomium included some discussion of the kind of death that the subject died and the consequences of that death (*Rhet. Her.* 3.7.14). A noble death was the honorable crown at the end of a noble life.

51. Thus a "happy death," one of the "exterior excellences" that Theon prescribed for treatment in an encomium.

52. Aristotle *Rh.* 1.9.16-17, 19; Quintilian *Inst.* 3.7.16. Theon prescribes that the "Spiritual Excellences" of the subject of an encomium be developed through discussion of the actions that resulted from the subject's virtue. Actions that were "altruistic," "in the public interest," and performed "at great cost" to the subject of the speech were especially indicative of nobility.

53. Courage is the endurance of fearsome things for the sake of what is noble (Aristotle *Eth. Nic.* 1115b12): topics of courage will be applied to Jesus' death as well as invoked to motivate the hearers to endure temporary hardship and privation for the sake of the honor that lies before them in God's realm.

54. Danker, *Benefactor,* 419 and n. 10.

ing of Jesus' death, countering dominant-cultural evaluations of the group's leader and founder and hence of the group members themselves. Being "crowned with glory and honor" as a result of the endurance of death contrasts with being "memorialized with lasting disgrace," the intended effect of crucifixion which was realized, for example, in Tacitus' memory of Jesus (*Ann.* 15.44).[55] Further, the author provides an interpretation of the crucifixion as an act of beneficence, indeed as God's beneficent provision for bringing the addressees to their inheritance, which will be defined as "glory," borrowing a term from the psalm (2:10), thus beginning to appeal in earnest to the addressees' sense of debt and gratitude as part of his strategy for maintaining commitment to such a patron and to his household, the church.

2:10-18

The "grace of God" manifest in the humiliation, death, and exaltation of Jesus is explicated in the paragraph that follows. The γὰρ in 2:10 alerts us that the new developments in the author's sermon are meant in the first place to elucidate 2:8-9:

> For it was fitting for him, on whose account and through whom all things exist, to bring the pioneer of the salvation of those many sons and daughters whom he leads to glory to the end of his journey through sufferings. For the sanctifier and those being sanctified all derive from one, for which cause he is not ashamed to acknowledge them as brothers and sisters. (2:10-11)[56]

---

55. "Nero . . . punished with every refinement the notoriously depraved Christians (as they were popularly called). Their originator, Christ, had been executed in Tiberius' reign by the governor of Judaea, Pontius Pilate. But in spite of this temporary setback the deadly superstition had broken out afresh, not only in Judaea (where the mischief had started) but even in Rome" (Tacitus *Ann.* 15.44). The fate of the founder enables Tacitus to regard the beginning of the movement as "mischief," an assessment that continues to reinforce the view of Christians as a whole as a base, depraved, suspect movement.

56. Ἔπρεπεν γὰρ αὐτῷ, δι' ὃν τὰ πάντα καὶ δι' οὗ τὰ πάντα, πολλοὺς υἱοὺς εἰς δόξαν ἀγαγόντα τὸν ἀρχηγὸν τῆς σωτηρίας αὐτῶν διὰ παθημάτων τελειῶσαι. A much debated issue in the translation of this verse concerns the participle ἀγαγόντα — does this speak of God's action or Jesus' action? Attridge (*Hebrews,* 82 and n. 42) and Lane (*Hebrews 1–8,* 55-56) believe, based on their grammatical analysis, that it must refer to God. Neither demonstrates, however, that the grammar necessitates, or even makes more probable, an identification of God as the subject of the participle. Lane suggests that there would need to be a τὸν before πολλοὺς υἱοὺς to link the participle ἀγαγόντα with ἀρχηγὸν. Article-modifier-article-noun, however, is not a pattern of attributive position (article-noun-article-modifier, or article-modifier-noun would qualify), and thus the addition of an article at this point would not accomplish what Lane hopes. In its present form, however, it does stand in predicate position,

The author will attempt to explain the strange path of this pioneer (through suffering to glory) in 2:10-18 using the topic of the "suitable" or "fitting." Only by such a path could Jesus become a merciful and capable high priest (2:17-18), and only thus could Jesus take on our most fearsome enemies (death, the devil, 2:14-15).

The description of God as the one "on whose account and through whose agency all things exist" recites a familiar expression from Stoic thought.[57] While, on the one hand, it serves as a reminder of the universal debt of gratitude owed to this God — the obligation not to be shirked for any cause[58] — it also embeds the first rationale for the "fittingness" of this undertaking. Frederick Danker makes the insightful observation that, "conscious of the role of God as Benefactor, the writer . . . states that in conformity with God's initial creative deed it was appropriate for him, when he 'brought many sons to glory, to perfect through sufferings the one who was responsible for rescuing them.'"[59] God as Creator acknowledges his ongoing responsibility for everyone and takes measures to secure their welfare "through the gift of a benefactor [Jesus] who is endangered to the uttermost."[60] This is an important insight into how Jesus' tasting of death on behalf of humanity occurred "by the favor of God" (2:9), setting Jesus' beneficence in the context of God's provisions for his creation.

The phrase "leading many sons and daughters to glory," which posits the future benefaction to be bestowed on the faithful clients, reintroduces the au-

---

and thus would make perfectly good grammatical sense as an adverbial participle, speaking of the attendant circumstances (or some other adverbial function) in which the "pioneer" was involved as he was being perfected. Attridge suggests that the accusative participle still modifies the dative pronoun (in Ἔπρεπεν γὰρ αὐτῷ), the former being assimilated to the case typically representing the subject of an infinitive. The problem here, however, is that no such accusative subject is needed with Ἔπρεπεν. LSJ and BAGD both lead us to expect this verb to appear with a personal dative and an infinitive, "it was fitting for so-and-so to do such-and-such." On the basis of grammar, therefore, the participle is more likely to be heard as an adverbial participle dependent on "pioneer," with which it agrees in gender, number, and case and with which it is linked by predicate position. The difficulty of translating this so as to preserve the placement of the referent ("many sons and daughters") in the adverbial clause and the mere pronoun ("their salvation") in the main clause is a massive problem for English (hence the freedom taken in the translation above), but would not be a problem for the Greek listener.

57. Attridge (*Hebrews*, 82) refers to Ps-Aristotle *De mundo* 397b; Marcus Aurelius *Med.* 4.23; Aelius Aristides *Or.* 45.14. This expression also enters Christian discourse in Rom. 11:36.

58. In 4 Macc. 13:13; 16:18-19 the brothers and their mother incite one another to hold firm against the compulsion of the tyrant on account of this debt owed God as creator and giver of life.

59. *Benefactor*, 358.

60. Ibid., 429 n. 11.

thor's ideological construction of the hearers' destiny, providing another angle on 1:14. The hearers are led to think of themselves in terms of this new identity given to them through their attachment to the group, and again to see the whole of their lives primarily as a process aimed at entering "glory" (= "inheriting salvation," 1:14). The addressees are led to see leaving the group as missing out on the high and honorable destiny that awaits them — as in fact a path to loss rather than recovery. Such images of being led to an inheritance of glory (the Promised Land, as it were) will set up the author's use of the wilderness generation as a negative paradigm. As noted above, the expression grows out of the author's double reading of Psalm 8 (recalling that psalm and its exposition through the repetition of the term "glory," 2:7, 9, 10) and now confirms this double reading. As "founder of their salvation,"[61] Jesus fulfills the psalm first and is in the process of bringing the psalm to its complete fulfillment for all the "human children."[62] That God brings this deliverer to the end of his course, or the completion of his work of deliverance, "through sufferings" looks back to 2:9 first and foremost. Jesus made it to the goal described by the psalm (crowning with glory and honor) through the path of suffering (the known facts of Jesus' life). But why should suffering be a "fitting" path for Jesus?

The first reason adduced to explain this suitability is the common origin of the Son and the many sons and daughters in God: "for the sanctifier and those being sanctified all derive from one" (ἐξ ἑνὸς πάντες). This elliptical phrase echoes yet another Stoic idea, namely, the common descent of all humanity from God.[63] The maximlike quality of this phrase suggests that the author expects his addressees to be familiar with the concept and to accept it as a basic truism. Suffering as the path to perfection is fitting for the Son, the champion or pioneer, because it is the path that lies ahead of the many sons and daughters. It was therefore suitable for the Son to share fully, and triumph, in the human condition of frailty, vulnerability, and mortality in which all the sons and daughters share. This rationale remains implicit here in the mention of common origin but will be developed further in 2:16-18.

---

61. The term ἀρχηγὸς is a common designation for leaders, inventors, and originators (thus Attridge, *Hebrews*, 88 n. 104; N. C. Croy, "A Note on Hebrews 12:2," *JBL* 114 [1995]: 117-19; G. Delling, *TDNT* 1:487-88). The whole expression, τὸν ἀρχηγὸν τῆς σωτηρίας αὐτῶν, also resonates with terminology for patrons. Seneca, for example, describes a benefactor as *salutis auctore*, the "author of salvation" (*Ben.* 4.11.3).

62. The author of 2 Thessalonians similarly posits the honor enjoyed by Jesus as the future prize of the believers as well: "For this purpose he called you through our proclamation of the good news, so that you may obtain the glory of our Lord Jesus Christ" (2:14).

63. Compare Seneca *Ben.* 3.28.1-2: "We all spring from the same source, have the same origin *(Eadem omnibus principia eademque origo)*. . . . Heaven is the one parent of us all *(Unus omnium parens mundus est);* also Acts 17:28: "we are all his offspring" (a quotation of the Stoic Aratus); Epictetus *Diss.* 1.9.1-6.

Naming Jesus as ὁ ἁγιάζων applies an LXX designation for God (e.g., Exod. 31:13) to the Son, who "sanctifies the people" (Heb. 13:12). The author thus subtly indicates the manner in which Jesus' death will provide benefit to his followers, a topic that will become more prominent later in the sermon. Describing the group that benefits from Jesus' work as "those who are being sanctified" leads the addressees to choose to identify themselves with this group (as "sanctification" is a positive value). Forms of ἁγιάζω will appear again at 9:13; 10:10, 14, 29; 13:12, creating, together with nouns based on the same root, an identity and a vision for the audience: the addressees have been sanctified (10:10, 29), are being sanctified (2:10; 10:14), are told to pursue sanctification (12:14), and are assured that their endurance of discipline now will result in sharing God's holiness (12:10) as its end result. A similar tension between present and future state appears in 4:1-11 with regard to "entering the rest" of God: in 4:3 the addressees are identified as "we who are entering," while in 4:11 they are urged to "strive earnestly to enter."

The demonstration of the solidarity of the Son with the many children — and thus the hope of honor that awaits the many siblings of such an exalted Son — begins at this point of common ancestry. Moreover, because of this common origin, Jesus is not ashamed (οὐκ ἐπαισχύνεται) to call the addressees his brothers and sisters. The author is creating a sense of the esteem in which Jesus, the exalted Son, holds the believers. He does not fear that association with them, owning them as his own family, will bring disgrace upon him. This indicates that Jesus' beneficence toward the hearers is accompanied by Jesus' estimation of them as people of worth, judging them to be suitable beneficiaries and reliable clients who will not disappoint or bring shame upon him.[64] This is not to suggest that Christ died for us because we "deserved" it, but the fact that Christ died on our behalf does indicate the value that he attaches to us. That Jesus esteems the believers highly enough to associate with them as sisters and brothers would restore the hearers' shaken sense of their own honor (assailed so thoroughly by their unbelieving neighbors) as well as deepen their sense of gratitude and obligation to the Son who has treated them with honor beyond their deserving.

Hebrews 2:12–2:13b supply three verses from the OT as "proof" that the Son has made this confession. The way in which the author puts OT words on Jesus' lips to make his point is striking, using the scriptural texts as a living "witness" in the court, as it were. This has some important implications for his

---

64. That the addressees might be moved by thinking that Jesus' assistance is a token of the esteem in which he holds them is suggested by Seneca: "A gift is not a benefit if the best part of it is lacking — the fact that it was given as a mark of esteem" (*Ben.* 1.15.6); "the motive of my action must be the interest of the one for whom the benefit is destined, that I should deem him worthy of it" (4.29.3).

view of the Scriptures: since the final word was spoken through the Son, the earlier words can frequently find their "true" meaning when spoken by him as well. The first verse recites Psalm 21:23 (LXX; MT 22:23) as direct speech by Jesus: "I will announce your name to my brothers and sisters; in the midst of the assembly I will praise you." The Christocentric reading of this psalm is familiar from the Synoptic passion narratives, in which one also finds the words of the psalm being spoken by Jesus (Mark 15:34; Matt. 27:46). Reading the remainder of this hymn as Jesus' own enables the author to find a clear confession of those who hear Jesus' proclamation of God's "name" as Jesus' family.[65]

The meaning of the second OT text (Heb. 2:13a) is more problematic: "I will be confident in him." This is most frequently read as Jesus' confession of trust in God, which shows his solidarity with human beings in utter dependence on God for vindication and his commitment to that essential posture of faith in God.[66] This certainly has merit and preserves the sense of the text in its original context, where God is the object of this trust. The author has, however, deliberately separated Isaiah 8:17 from 8:18 in his presentation, which seems to indicate that he wants the two verses to make two distinct points.[67] We should recall, moreover, that this verse is now being offered as proof that Christ is not ashamed to associate himself closely with those whom he receives into his protection (2:11). I would suggest, therefore, that the author would have the believer see himself or herself as the object of Jesus' declared trust.

The danger to Jesus' honor in associating himself with human beings is that they might fail to prove just and reliable in regard to their obligations to the Son. Dio, for example, recognized that fearing the unreliability of others was a cause for being reluctant to associate with certain people (*Or.* 74.4). Particularly between friends or patrons and clients, the patron had only the "good faith" of the client as assurance that his generosity would not prove unfruitful, and that the recipient would honor the bond that was created by the gift.[68] An ungrateful client brought shame to the patron, for which he or she would seek satisfaction if possible. Jesus, however, refuses to recognize association with the believers as a potential source of disgrace to himself — he is confident that they will not act so as to put him to shame through their lack of reliability or, worse, through open affronts to one who has been so generous and unsparing.[69] This would resonate

---

65. Perhaps the author was familiar with Jesus' own construction of a fictive kinship group based on obedience to the word of God (Mark 3:31-35; Matt. 12:46-50).

66. Thus Attridge, *Hebrews*, 91; Lane, *Hebrews 1–8*, 60; Ellingworth, *Hebrews*, 169; P. Hughes, *Hebrews*, 108-9.

67. Attridge, *Hebrews*, 90.

68. Seneca, *Ben.* 3.14.2: "no law will restore you to your original estate — look only to the good faith *(fidem)* of the recipient."

69. The terms used by the author ("being confident," πεποιθὼς, and "become ashamed," ἐπαισχύνεται) frequently appear as antonyms in the LXX. Those who "trust" or

well with the admonition forcefully expressed elsewhere in the sermon against bringing dishonor to the Son through violating that bond, acting disloyally, and showing contempt for the gifts and giver (cf. 6:4-6; 10:29): such a course would be to violate the trust and confidence that Jesus invested in the addressees.

The final quotation, a recitation of Isaiah 8:18, parallels the first as a confession of solidarity between the Son and God's many children: "Behold, [here am] I and the children God gave to me." While 2:10-13 have been offered as an explanation for the "suitability" of the path walked by the Son, they have also presented an important reaffirmation of the addressees' sense of their own honor, as this would be constructed within the Christian group. Discussion of the hearers' descent from God, and their relationship to the Son as brothers and sisters, speaks to the topic of their own "noble birth."[70] The author is here developing an element of the Christian's "happiness" (Aristotle *Rh.* 1.5) as this is defined within the context of the Christian worldview. Remembering that they enjoy the honor of being Christ's siblings and God's children should help them endure their loss of lesser honor (see also 12:5-11). Christ's exaltation, celebrated at length in 1:1-14 and 2:5-9, becomes a source of honor for the addressees as well, since the "advance of one member of a . . . family would advantage all his kindred."[71] While they must still look forward to the manifestation of the honor that is theirs, they are assured that, as they remain connected with the Son, their honor remains intact.

---

are "confident" in idols, cities, or the strength of the pharaoh end up "shamed" (αἰσχύνην ὀφειλήσουσιν οἱ ἐπὶ πόλεσιν καὶ χρήμασιν πεποιθότες, Job 6:20; ἔσται γὰρ ὑμῖν ἡ σκέπη Φαραω εἰς αἰσχύνην καὶ τοῖς πεποιθόσιν ἐπ' Αἴγυπτον ὄνειδος, Isa. 30:3; αἰσχύνθητε αἰσχύνῃ οἱ πεποιθότες ἐπὶ τοῖς γλυπτοῖς, 42:17); those who trust in God do not come to shame (οὐκ ἔστιν αἰσχύνη τοῖς πεποιθόσιν ἐπὶ σοί, Dan. 3:40 [LXX]). This would tend to lead the hearer to read Heb. 2:13 as a declaration of confidence in the believers (Heb. 2:13a), the same group from whom the speaker, Christ, expects no disgrace (2:11).

70. This concept resonates strongly with Stoic discourse. Epictetus (*Diss* 1.3.1, 4), for example, promotes awareness of one's kinship with the divine as the true and most secure basis for self-respect, which consequently frees one from such heavy reliance on the nonphilosopher (the society-at-large) for recognition of one's worth and confirmation of self-respect: "If a man could only subscribe heart and soul, as he ought, to this doctrine, that we are all primarily begotten of God, and that God is the father of men as well as of gods, I think that he will entertain no ignoble or mean thought about himself. . . . Since, then, it is inevitable that every man, whoever he be, should deal with each thing according to the opinion which he forms about it, these few, who think that by their birth they are called to fidelity, to self-respect, and to unerring judgement in the use of external impressions, cherish no mean or ignoble thoughts about themselves, whereas the multitude do quite the opposite." Awareness of this kinship with God, Epictetus argues (*Diss.* 1.13.3), transcends the false distinctions and inequalities created by human society.

71. J. D. M. Derrett, *Jesus' Audience: The Social and Psychological Environment in which He Worked* (New York: Seabury, 1973), 38.

Picking up on the word "children" from his last OT quotation, the author moves forward to the heart of the rationale behind the Son's subjection to suffering and death: "since, therefore, the children have flesh and blood in common, he himself also fully shared the same things in order that, through death, he might destroy the one holding the power of death, namely, the Slanderer, and bring release to those who were liable to slavery all their lives by means of the fear of death" (2:14-15). Since the many children were subject to mortality, the Son also became subject to mortality in order to confront and defeat, through his own death, the devil who had used death as a tool for enslaving the human race. People in the ancient world held that "freedom is the greatest of blessings, while slavery is the most shameful and wretched (αἴσχιστον καὶ δυστυχέστατον) of states" (Dio Or. 14.1), so that liberation from slavery would be considered a great benefit — indeed, a benefit of the highest order.[72] Jesus' own death is ennobled, and the obligation of the hearers to remain loyal clients magnified, by the greatness of the gift and the extent of the cost incurred by their benefactor.[73]

While this passage resonates with the traditions of the apocalyptic victory of the Messiah over demonic forces,[74] it echoes philosophical discourse on liberation from the fear of death even more closely. "Fear of death" as an obstacle to commitment to what is right is a frequent topic of philosophical literature, and certainly may be relevant here — not because of a renewed persecution,[75] but as the extreme that should make every lesser hardship all the more bearable. Jesus is presented in terms reminiscent of the portrayal of Socrates in Seneca (*Ep.* 24.4):

---

72. Seneca *Ben.* 1.11.2: "Of the benefits that are necessary, some, those without which we are not able to live, have the first place, others, those without which we ought not to live, the second, and still others, those without which we are not willing to live, the third. The first are of this stamp — to be snatched from the hands of the enemy, from the wrath of a tyrant. . . . for the thought of the greatness of the ills from which they have been freed will linger in men's minds, and their earlier fear will enhance the value of our service."

73. Hearers would be familiar with the gratitude and respect earned by those who delivered their people, or some city, from an oppressive regime (cf. Danker, *Benefactor,* 393-94, 397-98).

74. See Attridge, *Hebrews,* 93 n. 153 for comparative texts.

75. Lane (*Hebrews 1–8,* 54, 61) takes "liberation from the fear of death" as a reflection of the immediate needs of the addressees' situation, namely, that they face an imminent persecution that is the cause of their wavering and potential apostasy. The suggestion that the addressees are about to face bloody persecution rests, however, on a questionable reading of 12:4, and the author's own language throughout the sermon suggests more a drifting, a wavering, a lack of perseverance, than a flight from upcoming hostility. It is preferable, therefore, to read Jesus' liberation of the believers "from the fear of death" as an appeal to a common philosophical topos by which the author stresses that believers, like Stoics or other philosophical devotees, should not be guided by any external threat or compulsion, but rather are free to remain constant in the virtuous course of action (here, loyalty to God and Jesus in the face of society's shame and abuse).

"Socrates in prison ... declined to flee when certain persons gave him the opportunity ... in order to free humankind from the fear of two most grievous things, death and imprisonment."[76] Just as freedom from this fear enabled the philosopher to maintain his virtue intact in the face of any external compulsion, so, the author avers, Jesus has enabled the audience to maintain their virtuous response to God and arrive at the honor promised them no matter what deviancy-control techniques society might use to hinder them. Having been confirmed in the knowledge that death was but the portal to eternal honor in the unshakable realm for Jesus, the addressees should no longer be subject to the fear of death (or any lesser compulsion their neighbors might employ) themselves.

Jesus' interest in these actions is succinctly summarized:

> For he does not take hold of angels, but he takes hold of Abraham's seed — whence he was obliged to be made like his sisters and brothers in every way, in order that he might be a merciful and faithful high priest in matters pertaining to God unto the expiation of the sins of the people. For in what he himself experienced, being tested, he is able to help those who are being tested. (2:16-18)

Hebrews 2:16, 18 appears to involve an extended recontextualization of Isaiah 41:8-10: "Seed of Abraham whom I loved, of whom I took hold. . . . I am your God who helped you."[77] The effect of the recontextualization is to ascribe to the relationship between Jesus and the many sons and daughters the relationship celebrated between God and Israel. Divorcing the epithet "children of Abraham" from its ethnic moorings and applying it to the Christian community is widespread in Christian discourse (e.g., Gal. 3:29).[78] This becomes a useful term by which to link the actions of Christ with the promises given to Abraham, suggesting that God's fidelity to that promise (cf. Heb. 6:13-18) stands now behind the new covenant and that the Christians are indeed the legitimate heirs of God's promises.[79]

---

76. Lucian, commenting on the motives of the wandering sophist Peregrinus, comes to the final scene in the life of this pseudo-philosopher, his self-immolation (*Peregr.* 23): "He [Peregrinus] alleges that he is doing it . . . that he may teach them to despise death (θανάτου καταφρονεῖν) and endure what is fearsome" (cf. also *Peregr.* 33). Seneca also recasts Hercules' feats in these terms (*Hercules furens* 858-92, cited by Fred B. Craddock, "Letter to the Hebrews," in *The New Interpreter's Bible*, vol. 12, ed. Leander Keck et al. [Nashville: Abingdon, 1998], 66). Such concerns appear not to be limited to Mediterranean society. Douglas (*Purity*, 178), for example, comments on the suicide of the Dinka elder in similar terms: "His own willing death, ritually framed by the grave itself, is a communal victory for all his people. By confronting death and grasping it firmly he has said something to his people about the nature of life."

77. This recontextualization is well analyzed in Lane, *Hebrews 1–8*, 63-64.

78. See Attridge, *Hebrews*, 94 n. 179.

79. See Heb. 6:12; Gal. 3:8-9, 29; 4:29-31; Rom. 4:1-25; Luke 1:55; Attridge, *Hebrews*, 94.

In doing battle with the enemies of humankind, the Son "lays hold of" these heirs of the promises. The verb ἐπιλαμβάνεται has strong overtones of helping and assisting. It is used by Ben Sira's translator to express wisdom's care for her devotees: "Wisdom exalts her children and lays hold of those seeking her" (Sir. 4:11). It will appear again in Hebrews 8:9 (as part of the quotation from Jer. 31:31-34) to describe the action of God on behalf of the exodus generation in bringing them out of Egypt. "Laying hold" here speaks of Jesus' role as rescuer, deliverer, and protector of his clients in the new exodus from the shakable realm and entrance into the "rest" of God. As such, it is also a reminder of the patron-client relationship that has been established between the hearers and the Son.[80]

Laying hold of mortals and effecting their deliverance "obliged" the Son to be made like those whom he sought to rescue and help. This necessity explains why "it was fitting" (2:10) for the Son to enter glory only through suffering. It was by this means that God could make Jesus the most effective and sensitive helper and broker of God's favor that he could be. Once again, this will impress upon the hearers that everything Jesus endured, he endured for their sake — both to bring them the benefits already conferred (freedom from bondage to the fear of death, access to God's favor, and the like) and to fit himself to be their sympathetic patron and helper each day of their journey until at last they enter the promised goal. Jesus' brokerage will be articulated in cultic terms — he is the *pontifex,* the bridge builder, between humans and God. The language used by the author appears at this point to be drawn from 1 Samuel 2:35, in which God promises that he will "raise up a faithful priest . . . and build for him a faithful house (καὶ ἀναστήσω ἐμαυτῷ ἱερέα πιστόν . . . καὶ οἰκοδομήσω αὐτῷ οἶκον πιστόν). That this text lies at the back of the author's mind may be supported further by the immediate move from delineating Jesus as this "faithful high priest" to the discussion of the "house" and God as "the builder" in 3:1-6, a passage in which "faithful" also remains a prominent word.

Since Jesus' mediation is between God and human beings, the author will explore that mediation in terms of priesthood and sacrifice, the usual means of mediation between the human and divine. Hence Jesus secures divine favor for his clients through "atoning for the sins of the people" (cf. 9:11–10:18; 13:12). A principal title for Jesus besides "Son" will be "high priest" throughout the remainder of the sermon. The early use and repetition of this term (ἀρχιερεὺς, 2:17; 3:1; 4:14, 15; 5:1, 5) prepares the hearers to accept it as a suitable replace-

---

80. The author mentions "angels" again in 2:16 merely for the sake of creating a balanced antithesis (not angels, but Abraham's seed); it is decorative, an addition that "superficially unites the two chapters" (Attridge, *Hebrews,* 94; so also Lane, *Hebrews 1–8,* 63).

ment for the simpler form ἱερεὺς in Psalm 110:4 (see how the author revises this verse in 5:10; 6:20), on which the author will depend so much.[81]

Hebrews 2:18 explicates further how the Son's suffering relates to his ability as a benefactor. It is through his own experience of temptation and suffering that he is able to come to the aid of the many children who experience temptation. He has gone further in the endurance of testing and hardship than any of the addressees will be called to travel, and so they will never find themselves at a place where Jesus will not be sympathetic to their plight, will not know from personal experience the discomfort their needs create. Rather, he stands ready to provide them with the resources they need to resist their particular temptations (e.g., to shrink away from open confession and association with the church) — he knows what needs to be done to equip them, since he has had to face those temptations himself.

Seneca wrote (*Ben.* 1.12.1) that "even the ungrateful have their memory aroused when they encounter the gift itself, when it is actually before their eyes." In 2:10-18, the author reminds the hearers at some length about Jesus' benefits, amplifying the nobility of Christ's actions with topics familiar from the praise of service in the public interest at great cost to the Benefactor. The effect on the hearers should include the arousal of feelings of gratitude[82] toward Christ for these numerous benefits and for the generous spirit with which Jesus took up their cause (2:16), brought them deliverance from a wretched state (2:14-15), and leads them still to a more honorable state (2:10), all the while standing ready to "help" them (2:18). This is effected by the author's dwelling on how Jesus used his "external advantages," namely, all to the benefit of the hearers (*Rhet. Her.* 3.7.13). These topics will be further developed in 4:14-16; 7:11–10:25.

The author's argument from what is "fitting" or "suitable" is a truly ingenious response to the situation he addresses. He appears at the outset to be making sense of the shape of Christ's career, but he is actually showing the hearers how God had shaped Christ's career specifically to equip him (2:16-18) to help them make it to. God's goal for them ("glory," 2:10). The author appeals to the topic of feasibility here for the first time, pointing to the resources that are available to ensure that the hearers can complete the task they have started (namely, the ongoing aid of the Son, their personal patron). They have little excuse to "drift" away but every reason to feel confident as

---

81. It will continue to be prominent, mainly in the contrast between the One High Priest and the many high priests: 7:26-28; 8:1, 3; 9:7, 11, 25; 13:1.

82. In his discussion of how to appeal to the emotion of "favor" or "gratitude," Aristotle says that "the [feeling of] favour will be great if the recipient is in pressing need, or if the service or the times and circumstances are important or difficult, or if the benefactor is the only one, or the first who has rendered it, or has done so in the highest degree" (*Rh.* 2.7.2).

they proceed in their Christian journey.[83] God's investment and the Son's investment in them should motivate perseverance. Moreover, their experience of suffering ("testing") is foreseen by God and prepared for in the Son's own endurance. It is not unexpected; it should not be disconfirming to the hearers (i.e., a message that they are not, in fact, favored by God, that they have been deceiving themselves). Even if the hearers are getting more than they bargained for as a result of joining and remaining with the Christian minority group, they did not get more than God foresaw nor more than Christ prepared himself for to help them in their trials. Even this notion of "testing" is an ideological interpretation of the experience of deprivation, hostility, and the like. What outsiders view as correction, even punishment, the author depicts as an occasion for the hearers to "prove themselves." The abuse or reproach is not meaningful censure (i.e., an accurate reflection of their worth) but a test laid before the hearers, in which "passing grades" are assigned to those who endure rather than succumb.

A Closer Look: Priestly Messiahs in the Intertestamental Period

The Christology of Hebrews is distinctive in its emphasis on Jesus as heavenly high priest. Attributing priestly functions and status to a Messiah figure, however, was not without precedent. Descriptions of God's agents of end-time deliverance were patterned after those figures who played prominent roles in Israel's past history and ideology, such as the prophet (beginning with the "prophet like Moses," Deut. 18:18) and especially the king of David's line. Messianic hopes during the intertestamental period, however, did not neglect the important figure of the priest, who stood between God and Israel as a channel for God's favor and forgiveness. The high priest became increasingly important for the Jewish people during the Persian, Greek, and Ptolemaic periods, in which there was no Jewish king. The high priest acted both as spiritual leader and as local governor. During the reign of Antiochus IV (175-164 B.C.), the Seleucid monarch, the office of the high priesthood was thrown into disarray. The office was treated by the monarch as his prize to award to the highest bidder, such that the office even passed from the Zadokite line to priests of nondistinguished heritage. As local governor of Judea, the high priests also made policy. Several high priests were radical advocates of Hellenism, such that the local population would witness not only the buying and selling of the office but also the use of the office to replace Torah itself with the constitution of a Greek city (see 2 Macc. 3:1–4:25 for a window into this sordid period). After Torah observance was outlawed and repressive measures taken to suppress Jewish practices in the new Greek city, the family of Judas Maccabaeus (the Hasmonean family) led a successful revolt against the Seleucid kings,

---

83. The emphasis in 2:16-18 on the availability of help in time of duress (a topic that will be revisited in 4:14-16) indicates that these verses may arouse the emotion of confidence among the addressees, for this is a main ingredient of appeals to this pathos (see Aristotle *Rh.* 2.5.17, 21).

with the result that the Torah was restored in the land. Jonathan, a brother of Judas, was appointed high priest, an office that remained in this family of king-priests for another 100 years.

It was against this backdrop that messages about God's eschatological restoration of the priesthood began to circulate. That office, which had suffered such dishonor, would one day be gloriously purified and restored by God. Dissatisfaction with the Hasmoneans' decision to consolidate both kingly and priestly offices in one person led to the development of the hope for a "Messiah of Aaron and Messiah of Israel" at Qumran, the expectation that God would restore the monarchy to David and the priesthood to Zadok (and the Hasmoneans were of neither house).[84] Messianic expectation at Qumran was, of course, not uniform during the life of the sect, such that one finds now evidence of one, sometimes two, sometimes even three end-time agents of God's deliverance and governance in the restored Israel. Of interest to us here, however, is the role of an eschatological priest in these schemes:

> He will atone for all the sins of his generation and will be sent to all the sons of his [peo]ple. His word is like a word of heaven, and his teaching is according to the will of God. His eternal sun will shine, and his fire will spring forth to all the ends of the earth, and will shine over darkness. The darkness will pass away [fr]om the earth, and deep darkness from the dry land.[85]

The inhabitants of the settlement at Qumran, then, looked forward to a priestly leader whose offerings would be acceptable to God and whose teachings would be in line with God's Law.

The *Testaments of the Twelve Patriarchs* also bears witness to the expectation of a priestly Messiah, and he is described there in even more impressive terms. The question of the origin and date of the *Testaments*, however, is rather problematic. While there is a general consensus that the work is Jewish in origin,[86] there is equal consensus that early Christians performed free and extensive editing of the document to conform it more closely with Christian belief in Jesus as the Messiah of which it speaks (even though the *Testaments* appears to speak of two messiahs, one from Levi and one from Judah).[87] The original, Jewish strata may date anywhere from 100 B.C. to 50 A.D. In the *Testament of Levi*, a series of predictions (concerning the history of Israel from Levi through the corruption of the priesthood during the Hellenization crisis mentioned above) climaxes in the appearance of this priest:

> When vengeance will have come upon them from the Lord, the priesthood will lapse. And then the Lord will raise up a new priest to whom all the words of the Lord will be re-

---

84. See 1QS 9:11; 1QSa 2:20. See J. J. Collins, *The Scepter and the Star: The Messiahs of the Dead Sea Scrolls and Other Ancient Literature* (Garden City, NY: Doubleday, 1995) for a truly insightful survey of the messianism of the Dead Sea Scrolls and other intertestamental Jewish literature.

85. *4Q541,* translated by Geza Vermes (*The Complete Dead Sea Scrolls in English* [Harmondsworth/New York: Allen Lane/Penguin, 1997], 527).

86. Thus H. C. Kee, "Testaments of the Twelve Patriarchs," *OTP* 1:775-81; J. J. Collins, *Scepter,* 89; Attridge, *Hebrews,* 98; versus Marinus de Jonge, *The Testaments of the Twelve Patriarchs: A Study of their Text, Composition, and Origin* (Leiden: Brill, 1953).

87. Attridge, *Hebrews,* 98.

vealed. . . . This one will shine forth like the sun in the earth; he shall take away all darkness from under heaven. . . . From the temple of glory sanctification will come upon him,
with a fatherly voice, as from Abraham to Isaac. And the glory of the Most High shall
burst forth upon him. And the spirit of understanding and sanctification shall rest upon
him. . . . And there shall be no successor for him from generation to generation forever. . . . In his priesthood, sin shall cease and lawless men shall rest from their evil deeds,
and righteous men shall find rest in him. And he shall open the gates of paradise; he shall
remove the sword that has threatened since Adam, and he will grant to the saints to eat of
the tree of life. The spirit of holiness shall be upon them. And Beliar shall be bound by
him. (*T. Levi* 18:1, 2, 4, 6-12)[88]

Connections with the priestly Christology of Hebrews abound. Noteworthy is the expectation that God appoints this priest directly, that he will be a reliable mediator of God's
word, that God will regard him in some sense as a son. Most notably, the expectation that
this priest will have "no successor" resonates with the author of Hebrews' frequent reminders that Jesus is high priest "forever." The priestly Messiah of the *Testament* will cause
sin to cease (i.e., no new sins will be committed); Jesus removes sins (i.e., the defilement of
the conscience caused by former sins). The parallel is not exact, but the shared interest in
dealing decisively with sin is noteworthy, as is the affirmation that this priest opens up the
way to "rest." Finally, the priestly Messiah, like Jesus, champions the cause of his dependents against the devil, here called Beliar.

These models, however, do not yet suggest a heavenly high priest in the "true" sanctuary. The closest parallel to this concept in Jewish thought appears to be the "angels of the
presence" who serve as priests, interceding for the righteous before God's throne (see "A
Closer Look: Angels," 93-94 above). Harold Attridge suggests that the selection of a leading
angel as high priest would have been a "natural extension" of the idea of an angelic priesthood, which provides an immediate background for replacing such an angel with the Son
as high priest in heaven.[89] Moreover, the intercessory function of the priestly Messiah is
muted, if present at all, in non-Christian Jewish expressions of this hope, and the idea of
his self-sacrifice as a purification for sins is uniquely Christian, determined by the known
data of Jesus' death. Thus while several strains of Jewish thought contribute to the expectation of an eschatological priest or high priest, the form that such a priest takes in Hebrews is deeply informed by the development of Christ's intercessory and atoning ministry in Christian culture.[90]

Summary

Whether a particular hearer is already committed to the Son for the long haul
or wavering in his or her conviction that this association is truly advantageous,

---

88. Translation by Kee ("Testaments," 794-95), who brackets none of the above as
Christian interpolation.

89. *Hebrews*, 100 and n. 240.

90. For Jesus' intercessory role, see most notably Rom. 8:34 and 1 John 2:1; for Jesus'
death as atoning sacrifice, see Rom. 3:25; Eph. 5:2; 1 John 2:2; 1 Pet. 1:2; 2:24; 3:18; Rev. 5:6, 9.

the author calls all of them to look long and hard at this Son. As agent of the creation and preservation of all things, he commands the gratitude of all. As heir of all things whose enemies will at the last be thrown down at his feet, the Son's friendship is the most valuable commodity. His most exalted status guarantees their own honor, both now as members of his family and into eternity as they come into their full inheritance. His beneficence, manifested at such great cost to himself, commands their gratitude and loyalty. The trust with which he welcomes them into his household and family demands that they not show themselves unreliable, betraying his confidence and generosity. The amplification of that same honor possessed by Jesus, which assures the believer of his or her own honor, also serves to caution the hearers against thinking that any act that dishonors Christ is advantageous. Eternal reward or inescapable punishment — these two outcomes depend wholly on whether or not one has preserved honorably the patron-client bond, which the Son graciously initiated and into which he welcomed the believers.

The hearers have been freed by this Son from the fear of death itself and certainly of any lesser evil. In the Son they have the resources to exhibit the freedom of the philosophers, who remain committed to the virtuous course of action in the face of any tyrant's coercive measure. They, too, have every reason to remain steadfast in the face of their neighbors' attempts to subvert their commitment. Most particularly, they have the ongoing assistance of the Son of God, who will equip them to endure and overcome any temptation if they will but rely on their Patron, trusting his ability to help them.

Bridging the Horizons

Hebrews 1:1–2:4 confronts us as powerfully and directly as it did its first audience. As many as have heard the word spoken through the Son, whatever their circumstances or particular challenges, here come face to face with the necessity of giving that message its due attention, the necessity of appreciating the significance of this message and giving it its due weight in one's life. That weight is augmented by the honor of the apostle of this confession, Jesus, and the critical nature of the time in which it speaks, namely, the "last days." We are reminded of Jesus' position in the cosmos, exalted to God's right hand and the object of celestial homage, so that, as we draw close to Jesus as "friend," we will not lose sight of the honor due this friend. How do we give Jesus the honor that is his due? The author of Hebrews is very clear on this point. It is by giving due attention in our lives to the word he spoke and the deliverance he announced.

For some of the original hearers of this sermon, "neglect" of this salvation might manifest itself in "running for the exit" of the church so as to escape the losses and tensions that being a Christian entailed. Christians who now face marginalization or worse for their association with Jesus will certainly resonate with the challenge facing that original audience. The author's use of a wide variety of images to describe movement away from God's call, however, allows him to speak to a wide variety of audiences across the centuries. Some might find themselves contemplating the renunciation of their faith, hence "turning away"; others might simply find themselves nodding off in their pews, slowing down in their fervor, or becoming absorbed in worldly pursuits, hence "drifting away," "wandering," or being "deceived by sin's guile." Whatever situations match our own, the opening of Hebrews sounds a clarion call to remember the significance of the word we have received, to watch out lest we think not wrong things about Jesus, but too little of Jesus, his way, and his gifts. Hebrews shakes us especially out of our piecemeal and compartmentalized sense of life, with business, family, politics, social action, and religion all in their proper places with their proper boundaries. It presses us to focus our whole being on one thing — and on everything else in light of that one thing. For most hearers of Hebrews today, the issue will not be staying with or leaving the church,[91] but the level of one's investment in the work of the church and the call of God.

The collect for the fifth Sunday in Lent in the *Book of Common Prayer* asks: "Grant your people grace to love what you command and desire what you promise; that, among the swift and varied changes of the world, our hearts may surely there be fixed where true joys are to be found." So also the author of Hebrews urges each new audience to focus its desires on God and God's favor, so that believers will set their priorities and invest their time, resources, and energies accordingly. To "neglect so great a salvation" for the sake of attending to lesser goods would be to show less regard for God and the Son than is their due. If this leads the individual believer into places where he or she experiences the scorn or even hostility of those who are not so committed to the word of the Son, he or she will have the help of fellow believers and God's own self as resources for the contest. The author's reminders of eschatological judgment, when "rewards" both good and bad will be paid and the Son's enemies disgracefully subjected to him whom they refused, still focus our attention on the one whose estimation of us should be our first concern. Epictetus, the Stoic philosopher, desired to live so as to stand before God and say that he had not neglected God's provisions for living in line with God's values and had "not dis-

---

91. We are not concerned here with commitment to a particular church over against other churches, but with commitment to some church as a manifestation of the universal Church — the rhetoric of Hebrews ought not to be employed in the service of cajoling individuals to stay with, say, First United Methodist Church, as opposed to seeking a different venue of worship and service at St. Matthew's Episcopal Church.

honored Thee as far as in me lay" (*Diss.* 4.10.14). The author of Hebrews urgently presses us to make a similar resolution.

Alongside this primary interest, Hebrews 1:1–2:4 invites reflection on a number of other points. First, the author makes the striking affirmation that the Son is the "reflection" and "exact impression" of God. Humankind's search for the nature of God predates history. While "no one has ever seen God" (to borrow from John 1:18), at least two early Christian texts (Heb. 1:1-3; John 14:1-6) affirm that to see Jesus is in fact to see God. The prologue of Hebrews is, then, not just about who Jesus is but also about who God is and how we can know God. Stoics as well as Hellenistic Jews believed that God could be known through contemplation of creation (cf. Wis. 13:1-9); for the author of the Wisdom of Solomon, contemplation of wisdom led to an understanding of the nature and mind of God (Wis. 7:25-27; 9:16-18). The conviction of the church is that God's character and values are known in the man Jesus of Nazareth. This takes us to the Gospels with a renewed interest — to learn from the evangelists' shaping of Jesus traditions and sayings what it means to "love righteousness and hate lawlessness" (Heb. 1:9), to embody those values that God certified as his own in the resurrection and exaltation of his representative. In Jesus' critique of the uncharitable, in his concern for the outcast, in his rehabilitation of the penitent, in his mingling with the poor and sick, we see the heart and mind of God.

The author poses a contrast between the Son and the material creation that also begins to reorient our values in an essential manner. The world is a temporary reality, from the perspective both of apocalypticism, which posits the passing away of this creation, and of personal eschatology, which affirms that our time in this world is limited. Investing our lives in the gathering of wealth, or the increase of reputation, or anything that dies with us or with this world amounts to a poor investment in the eyes of faith — like Esau, such people sell their birthright for short-lived satisfaction. The author of Hebrews is not, however, just speaking about the destiny of the Son versus that of creation, but of the essential reliability of the Son vis-à-vis the visible world. The Son remains. He is the one constant, the one certainty upon which to build a secure life. The visible world is subject to change and to being shaken. We should perceive in the volatility of global markets and political arrangements, the ease with which uneasy peace erupts into conflict, and the subjection of human experience to crime and natural disaster, the signs of the basic instability and unreliability of all worldly things. Hebrews invites us to look long and hard at this reality and to understand that it is the friendship of Jesus and the pursuit of works that will bring one honor in God's sight and that, perhaps ironically, alone provide security even in this visible world. Again we return to the importance of responding faithfully to the word spoken by the Son — "all those who hear these words of mine and do them will be likened to a prudent person, who built his house upon rock" (Matt. 7:24).

Hebrews 2:5-18 also speaks rather directly to the condition of the believer in every age. It speaks of our value, seen both in Jesus' confession of us as his own family and in the cost he was willing to pay to bring us benefit. His association with us and his death on our behalf tell us what we are really worth in his sight.[92] The passage also speaks, however, of our obligation to prove trustworthy in our relationship with Jesus and to avoid dishonoring the one who has taken us into association with him, who underwent so much to benefit us. Jesus' expectation that he will not be put to shame by us, that he can be "confident" in us, can be used to nurture our own sense of responsibility toward Jesus, which in turn becomes an inner motivator to honor him with our lives, loyalty, and service. This passage assures us of help in temptation or times of trial. Jesus did not shy away from the hard experiences of being human and now, having undergone them, stands ready and willing to help us in our trials. This should embolden us not to shy away from any hardship, self-denial, or suffering that might be encountered in our service to God or our struggle against sin. As we grow in our awareness of Jesus' help in our trials, we may be enabled to look openly at the suffering of others rather than push such suffering to the back of our consciousness, whether the suffering of those in nursing homes and care facilities, of those in the inner cities, of the rural poor, or the hungry and persecuted in foreign lands. Frequently we do not allow ourselves to look at suffering, feeling overwhelmed and powerless in the face of it. Not only may the Son help us in our suffering, but he may manifest his help through us in the support of others in their suffering (see 2 Cor. 1:3-7).

Perhaps most poignantly, Hebrews 2:5-18 speaks of our freedom from the bondage that ensues from the fear of death. To appreciate properly the deliverance won for us by Jesus, we need to grapple with the nature of the bondage endured apart from his rescue. The power of the "fear of death" to enslave a person has long been recognized. One of the fundamental goals of Epicurus was to free people from fear of death; Socrates' choice of death over flight from prison was held by Seneca, at least, to be a purposeful demonstration that death is not to be feared; and Peregrinus, even if a charlatan (or literary fiction), still performed self-immolation to free others from "the fear of death." Particularly the Stoics sought to affirm that death (like loss of property, family, or reputation) was not something to be feared in order to embolden people to endure any loss other than their commitment to virtue. Being unafraid of death meant freedom

---

92. Commitment to the belief that human beings do not deserve salvation but receive it as an unmerited gift ought not to obscure the more positive side of our confession, namely, the value that God places on us, merited or not. If the Son thought us worth dying for, this gives us a clear sense of our value to God.

in the face of any coercive measure that might be brought to bear on the philosopher to subvert his or her dedication to virtue. In a sense, fear of death continues to enslave us in the modern age by making us timid in the face of injustice. How often has violence, oppression, or injustice not been opposed because those who stood by watching feared some reprisal, whether death or one of its symbolic manifestations (abuse, reproach or censure, imprisonment, shunning, or loss of employment)? Whether we fear the little death of belittlement or the full measure of death itself, we frequently do not expose ourselves by standing up for God's values and vision.

Consciousness of death can pervert the human psyche in other ways as well. The author of the Wisdom of Solomon recognized that fear of death could essentially turn a person's attentions to the pleasures that are to be found in this life alone. For the ancient author, this led to the loss of moral restraints on the pursuit of pleasurable things, such that the "righteous person" becomes the victim of persecution as an annoying reminder of the hope the worldly person rejects (Wis. 1:16–2:24). Perhaps it is still the fear of death that drives us today to try to build up visible, worldly defenses against our own mortality, to find ways to affirm our significance in the face of our eventual decay. Whether this takes the form of finer homes and possessions, power or control issues (whether within family relationships, business arrangements, or government), the production of other monuments to our existence (even the writing of commentaries), obsession with appearance (painting our faces and hair so as to disguise the onslaught of age), or an overemphasis on the "little things" as a defense against facing the larger issues of life's meaning, the fear of death can trammel us up in trivial and empty pursuits. Ernest Becker, siding with an impressive cadre of psychologists, writes that the "terror of death" — what William James called the "worm at the core" of human pretensions to happiness[93] — was the basic datum of our psyche.[94] How well or poorly we repress this fear, transfer it, and affirm our lasting significance in the face of it marks the difference between the balanced person and the neurotic or psychotic personality.

Reflection on how the "fear of death" manifests itself in our obsessions, our ambitions, our patterns of relationship may indeed prove a fruitful avenue for discovering the freedom that Jesus has won at such cost to himself. Since the church has the unique resource of knowing the one who rescues us from this great instrument of the devil's oppression, it can boldly help its members and others uncover this fear and its symptoms. How does Christ free us? The death of Jesus was interpreted by the author of Hebrews as a contest in which Jesus took on the most fearsome adversaries of humanity — death and the devil.

---

93. William James, *The Varieties of Religious Experience: A Study in Human Nature* (New York: Mentor, 1958), 121.

94. Ernest Becker, *The Denial of Death* (New York: The Free Press, 1973), 11-24.

Marching intentionally into their realm by way of the cross, he robbed them of their power in much the same way as Socrates, showing that both can be met courageously, even intentionally. That the church's confession of Jesus does not end there, however, is significant. The resurrection and exaltation of Jesus prove that not only can death be looked full in the face, but also that death can be "survived." For those who please God, death is not the "end" of the journey. While it is correct to note that many mystery cults involve a dying and rising hero, one who travels to the abode of the dead and returns, the early Church stood out from the rest insofar as it claimed not some hero of the mythic past but a hero of recent history. The emphasis on juridical proofs at the heart of the kerygma — the testimony of "witnesses" to Jesus' triumph over death (not to mention the interpretation of charismatic phenomena as God's own testimony from the witness stand) — set Christianity apart from its contemporaries. What, then, becomes the human project if death is not the be-all and end-all of our existence, if, in fact, it is not for this material creation that we are ultimately destined? On the one hand, there lurks the danger of nurturing an other-worldly mentality that withdraws from meaningful involvement in the course of human society. On the other hand, if we hold our transcendence of death together with God's call to "love righteousness and hate lawlessness," we are greatly empowered to strive for God's values and vision even in the face of great personal loss and opposition. Such an orientation to the world also throws us a lifeline by which we may be pulled out from the entangling snares of our own "defense-against-death" pursuits, freeing us to serve a different, God-centered agenda.

Finally, the author provides assurance concerning what our end will be. In the exaltation of the Son, we see the destiny of the Son's many siblings. Even if the path of true discipleship leads us to places of loss, opposition, and reproach, even as it did for the pioneer, Jesus, our hope, and that of all Christians, is that obedience to God's word leads at last to "glory," to the enjoyment of the fullness of God's presence in the unshakable realm. Those whose hope is set on that end find it to be a sure anchorage even in this present, shakable realm.

The Inexpediency of Distrust: 3:1–4:13

Overview

The movement of Hebrews 3:1–4:13 reinforces the central points of 1:1–2:18. First, the author calls the hearers to set Jesus before their mind's eye, just where he has placed Jesus from the opening of the sermon. The author engages in a comparison of Jesus with Moses, affirming the superiority of the former based on his position in God's household. Even though Moses, like the angels (see 1:4-14), was faithful, and even though he was a great figure, he was but a servant in the house of God. Jesus, however, was a faithful Son, and attachment to God through the Son promises greater honor and more certain access to God's favor and help than a servant could provide. As in the first section of the sermon, epideictic topics (the elevation of Jesus through comparison with another illustrious person) serve deliberative topics (the advantage of remaining connected with such a great figure as Jesus, so well placed in God's household, and the disadvantages that would follow any affront to Jesus through neglect and disobedience). Second, the author underscores the importance of responding faithfully to God's voice (see 2:1-4), which is here developed through a lengthy examination of the failure of the wilderness generation to respond to God's word of promise appropriately. This author addresses the audience with promise, just as God encountered the Exodus generation with promise. The author urges them to respond with trust and with a commitment to hold fast to the hope the word of God has engendered among them. In doing so, they might cross the threshold into God's "rest" (the unshakable realm, the heavenly homeland), which the wilderness generation had failed to do.

This ambition, the author hopes, will replace any others that may be taking root again in the hearers' hearts. To reinforce his point, the author concludes this section with a powerful and dreadful image of facing God's judgment. If the hearers keep their hearts from wandering, from distrust, and from being taken in by the guile of sin, they will be able to stand before God's scrutiny; if they harbor base motives, waver in their trust, or doubt the value or validity of God's promises, the word of God like a two-edged sword hovers above their exposed necks, waiting for the Judge to pronounce sentence on them (4:12-13; cf. 2:2).

Commentary

3:1-6

Having dwelt at length on Jesus' use of his advantages to bring benefit to the hearers, the author resumes direct exhortation: "wherefore, holy sisters and brothers, partners in a heavenly calling, consider the apostle and high priest of our confession — Jesus, who was faithful to the one who appointed him even as Moses in his house" (3:1-2). The author begins with a string of terms by which he reaffirms a certain identity and self-designation for the addressees. His choice of terms is suggestive for the kind of community and group boundaries he is striving to nurture. "Holy sisters and brothers" combines two key terms of 2:11-13: the hearers are both made holy and made kin through Jesus' sacrifice and Jesus' confession of them as his family. The author had already introduced kinship language by calling the hearers heirs and "sons and daughters" (1:14; 2:10), and he will further enhance this image through the designation of the audience as God's "household" (οἶκός, cf. 3:6; 10:21), a term that will dominate 3:2-6 (five occurrences).

Understanding the church as a fictive kinship group — those whose birth into God's family gave them a new status, new kin, and hope of a new inheritance — was widespread in the early Christian movement. The ethos of kinship obligations became a great resource for affirming the status of Christians and for mobilizing aid within the Christian group, and the author of Hebrews uses this image prominently in his delineation of the audience's identity. They are a family of which God is the head, over which the Son serves as a faithful high priest (and senior brother). The hearers are all children of one parent and have thus become sisters and brothers one to another. This is the identity from which they are to understand their obligations to one another ("brotherly love," the strongest bond of affection and mutual obligation; cf. 13:1-3), their endurance of hostility from non-Christians (God's parental, formative discipline; 12:5-11), and their hope (an eternal inheritance, a share in the Son's honor; 1:14; 2:10; 3:14; 9:15). For the present, being joined to God's household gives them their honor (as siblings of the Son and children of the One God) and their security (their place in God's favor as members of God's household, 3:1-6; 4:14-16; 10:19-22). He seeks to move them to see themselves "at home" with God and one another and in no need of the home, honor, hope, and security they left behind when they converted to membership in this group.

The "holiness" of the believers will become a central topic in 9:11–10:25, as the author reminds the hearers of the process of their being made fit to stand in God's presence. Being made "holy" opened up the addressees to the great privilege of direct access to God, such as had not been enjoyed before in the history of God's dealings with his people. Having been effected at so great a cost, and by so unique and unrepeatable a process, the holiness of the believers must be preserved at all costs. They cannot afford to "defile" their consciences willfully by turning away from Jesus for the sake of peace with their neighbors; rather, they are challenged to show their appreciation for this gift of consecration by making frequent and uninterrupted use of the privileges that it has opened up for them (4:14-16; 10:19-25). "Holiness" is thus used by the author to sustain commitment to the group as well as to motivate the mutually reinforcing activities of assembling together (to remind one another of the group's values and hope) and helping one another (10:23-25; 13:15-16).

"Partners in a heavenly calling" reinforces the first two designations of the hearers' destiny (1:14; 2:10). The author continues to direct their interests and ambitions beyond earthly well-being, drawing them in now as partners in this enterprise of assisting one another to attain that destiny which God has prepared for them all. Aristotle described partners as people who desire the same things without being in competition for them (*Rh.* 2.4.22). The addressees are invited to consider themselves as partners in a joint venture, who will be given responsibility to assist one another along the way, to keep one another on track, as it were, so as to make sure that no one falls short of the goal of this calling. The image of being partners responding to God's "call" lends itself especially to exhortations to perseverance and endurance in pursuit of that goal.[1]

The author urges the hearers to "consider Jesus," to hold him before their eyes. This exhortation makes explicit what the author has already accomplished in the first two chapters of his sermon, in which he has held Jesus before their eyes as the Son who, being the most significant figure in the history of God's revelation and in the future of God's eschatological acts, made himself their patron and helper. It is Jesus whom the author insists must be in their eyes as they contemplate what course their lives will take (particularly

---

1. Attridge (*Hebrews,* 107) helpfully distinguishes between being "called" to enter the heavenly realm and being guaranteed entrance. Such a distinction is both useful and correct in light of the many exhortations and warnings in Hebrews to continue to invest themselves fully in this enterprise so as not to miss out on the prize that awaits.

for those who are deliberating about continued commitment). Calling Jesus an "apostle" may appear strange in light of the fact that this term is usually reserved for the witnesses of the resurrected Lord who went out to preach the gospel. The author, however, presents Jesus from the outset as the messenger of God's ultimate word. It was the Son who brought the message and the promises to which the hearers have responded (1:2; 2:3), and who is therefore the preeminent apostle, the one "sent" from God. Jesus is also "high priest" in that he represents us to God and maintains the relationship formed with God through him (2:17; 5:1; 7:25). The two terms capture Jesus' involvement as "mediator" or "broker," as the one who brings God's message to us and represents our needs to God.

Jesus has just been described as a "faithful high priest" (2:17), a term that recalls God's declaration to Eli, in the wake of the faithlessness and disobedience of Eli and his sons, that God "will raise up for myself a faithful priest who will do everything that is in my heart and in my soul" (1 Sam. 2:35 [LXX]). While the author will not appeal to this text explicitly in the expositions to follow, it does appear to resonate at a deeper level with the sermon. Jesus will be presented as that priest who does indeed do God's will, effecting what centuries of sacrifices could not (10:1-14). God went on to declare concerning this "faithful priest": "I will build for him a faithful house" (1 Sam. 2:35 [LXX]; MT reads "enduring house"). The purpose of the sermon is, in fact, to confirm the hearers in this faithfulness toward Jesus, this firmness with regard to trust in God's promises. The response of "faith" dominates the concluding exhortation (10:37–12:2; 13:7-9). The author's decision to dwell on "faithfulness" as a positive term of value and source of honor (for both Moses and Jesus) in 3:1-6 can be no accident when the fidelity of some believers is precisely the matter at issue.

Rather than turning to 1 Samuel 2:35, however, the author moves into a comparison of Jesus with another figure whose "faithfulness" was celebrated in Scripture, namely, "my servant Moses," who was attested by God himself to be "faithful in all my household" (Num. 12:7 [LXX]). As in the comparison between the Son and the angels in 1:5-14, so here the author chooses a highly revered figure by which to demonstrate the greater nobility and honor of the Son. That is, the author employs the rhetorical device of *synkrisis* a second time.[2] The comparison with Moses, like that with the angels and the levitical priest-

---

2. Aristotle (*Rh.* 1.9.38-39) instructs the would-be orator to include comparison as an essential feature of an epideictic oration: "And you must compare him with illustrious personages, for it affords ground for amplification and is noble, if he can be proved better than men of worth. Amplification is with good reason ranked as one of the forms of praise, since it consists in superiority, and superiority is one of the things that are noble." Seneca (*Ep.* 43.2) likewise points to the importance of comparison as a means of appraising the greatness of any one individual: "Any point which rises above adjacent points is great, at the spot where it rises. For greatness is not absolute; comparison increases it or lessens it."

hood, does not suggest a polemical purpose. Indeed, there are strong indications to the contrary. Otto Michel notes with regard to the comparison of Jesus and Moses that

> Hebrews might have highlighted Moses' unfaithfulness or his murmuring against God (Num 20:12): the faithfulness of Moses adds to the bargain. Hebrews also refrains from speaking as 2 Cor 3:7ff concerning the fading nature of Moses' δόξα (Ex 34:33ff.) as opposed to the abiding δόξα of Christ.[3]

The author does not denigrate Moses in any way but rather builds his comparison on a shared high regard for Moses. Christ's superiority to Moses aims not at disqualifying the latter as a servant within God's house but rather at enhancing the honor of the former as Son over God's house (3:5).[4]

Why should the author choose Moses for the object of comparison? Aristotle advises that the speaker should choose "great" figures for the comparison, so as to demonstrate the worth and significance of the figure one is praising. One could hardly find a more revered figure in Jewish tradition, which became the inheritance of the church, than Moses. A sampling of Hellenistic Jewish texts provides an overview of the esteem that Moses enjoyed. Sirach's hymn in praise of the Jewish heroes includes this portrayal of Moses:

> From his descendants the Lord brought forth a man of mercy, who found favor in the sight of all flesh and was beloved by God and humanity, Moses, whose memory is blessed. He made him equal in glory to the holy ones (ὠμοίωσεν αὐτὸν δόξῃ ἁγίων), and made him great in the fears of his enemies. By his words he caused signs to cease; the Lord glorified him in the presence of kings. He gave him commands for his people, and showed him part of his glory. (45:1-3; RSV with modifications)

The exaltation of Moses in the presence of kings and above the "holy ones" raises this servant of God to a high station in God's court.[5] Josephus (*Ant.* 3.38) speaks of Moses as "the one honored by God (ὁ ὑπὸ τοῦ θεοῦ τετιμημένος)." The author of Hebrews himself speaks of Moses as "faithful" or "reliable" (πιστός) with regard to his service in God's house (3:2, 5), for which he was indeed held in honor.

---

3. Otto Michel, *Der Brief an die Hebräer,* 12th ed. (MeyerK 13; Göttingen: Vandenhoeck & Ruprecht, 1980), 96-97.

4. Attridge (*Hebrews,* 105), observing that "in encomia generally, the comparison serves not so much to denigrate the comparable figure as to exalt the subject of the discourse," correctly surmises that the author's "contrast between Christ and Moses derives at least part of its force from the high regard in which Moses was held in the first century."

5. See also *1 Enoch* 90:36-38, where Moses is transformed from a human being into an angelic one (symbolically, a sheep like the rest of the flock turned into a human being).

Moses' special honor, however, derives specifically from his status as mediator or broker of God's revelation, forgiveness, and favor.[6] Indeed, the point of Numbers 12:6-8 (the verse that Heb. 3:2-6 continues to recontextualize and recite) is the distinction between Moses as prophet of God and every other prophet who would come after Moses. To the latter, God will speak in dreams or visions, and not "mouth to mouth, in sight and not through enigmas," as God had with Moses. Moses thus had the most direct access to God of any OT prophet, for "he saw the glory of the Lord" (Num. 12:8 [LXX]; see Heb. 11:27). How do the Scriptures portray Moses using this access? Moses does not merely receive messages from God for the people but stands in God's presence throughout his ministry to intercede on behalf of Israel when it provokes God, or to acquire the necessary help or resources for the people during their wanderings (see, most notably, Exod. 32:7-14, 30-34; Num. 14:17-20). It is precisely Moses' activity and success as a mediator — a broker of God's favors — that will be commemorated in Jewish tradition. In the *Testament of Moses,* for example, which probably dates from the first century A.D. in its present form but which contains substantial materials from older strata, Joshua fears that the enemies of Israel will attack the people after Moses' death, reasoning to themselves that

> there is now no advocate for them who will bear messages to the Lord on their behalf in the way that Moses was the great messenger. He, in every hour both day and night, had his knees fixed to the earth, praying and looking steadfastly toward him who governs the whole earth with mercy and justice, reminding the Lord of the ancestral covenant and the resolute oath. (11:17)[7]

Moses' efficacy as mediator extends, according to Pseudo-Philo's *Biblical Antiquities* (19.11), even beyond his death, for God sets the staff of Moses before God's throne as a perpetual reminder of Moses' prayers on behalf of the people. Whenever God was provoked to destroy Israel for their sin, he said that he would look at Moses' staff and relent. The comparison of Jesus with Moses,

---

6. While Moses was indeed remembered occasionally as filling a priestly function, for example, in Ps. 99:6, which celebrates his priestly function ("Moses and Aaron were among his priests"), Milgrom (*Leviticus I–XVI,* 555-58) carefully reveals how the priestly function of Moses is downplayed in the Pentateuch and in later rabbinic tradition. He officiates over the consecration of Aaron and his sons by default: "it was Moses alone to whom the proper sacrificial procedure was revealed (Lev. 1-7), he would have been the only person sufficiently qualified both to impart the divine instructions to Aaron and his sons and to demonstrate the proper procedures by his personal example (*Sipra,* Millu'im Saw 14)" (ibid., 556). At stake here, however, is not Moses' involvement in the rituals of the tabernacle, but his ongoing intercession for the people and his role in securing God's favor "for timely help."

7. Translated by J. Priest, "Testament of Moses," *OTP* 1:919-34.

therefore, is a comparison between those who have functioned as brokers of divine favor, and it is precisely on this point that the author's claim for Jesus' superiority makes a meaningful statement.

Jesus and Moses are not contrasted with respect to the quality of their fidelity to God. Each was "faithful to the one who appointed him,"[8] and both were "reliable" and "trustworthy." The author asserts, however, that Jesus occupies a more elevated position in the household of God. This is not a claim that the author is asking the addressees to evaluate. Rather, the evaluation has already been made (presumably by God), as the exaltation of the Son in chapter 1 shows. An analogy with building is introduced to illustrate the claim being made: "this man has been thought worthy of greater honor than Moses in the same degree that the builder of a house has greater honor than the house: for every house is built by someone, and the builder of all things is God" (3:3-4). The convoluted logic of these verses is difficult to untangle, but it will be easier to follow if we bear in mind that "house" can refer to a physical structure or to an extended family ("household") and "builder" can refer to the craftsperson who assembles the physical structure or to the person who "establishes" a household and gives it distinction (as God established the house of David or the house of Samuel, where the LXX also uses a word for "build"). Hebrews 3:3, then, aligns Jesus with the founder of a house and aligns Moses with the house that is being founded. Jesus is involved in "building" the house and thus deserves greater honor than those who merely belong to the household (however faithful they are).

Hebrews 3:4 introduces a "probability" (*Rhet. Alex.* 1428a27-28, 32-35) that the author expects the audience to accept as a truism: every house is built by someone, since every effect must have a cause. The point of introducing God as the "builder of all things" is twofold. First, it continues to establish the proportion begun by the analogy of 3:3: Jesus:Moses :: builder:house :: God:universe.[9] This extended proportion works because 1:1-14 has already shown how deeply embedded in God's honor is Jesus' own honor. The first purpose, then, is to continue to underscore the significance of Jesus, this time in comparison with the significant figure of Moses. Second, 3:4 identifies explicitly the founder of the house that is being built — the household that contains not only Moses but the addressees themselves (3:6). Moses was introduced in 3:2 as "faithful in his house," but the referent of the pronoun "his" was left vague. This would no longer be vague after 3:4, which clarified God as the ultimate head and founder of this household.

---

8. τῷ ποιήσαντι αὐτὸν appears in Ps. 149:2 (LXX) and Isa. 17:7 as a circumlocution for God. The verb, which can mean "to make," here means "to appoint" (Lane, *Hebrews 1–8*, 76; Attridge, *Hebrews*, 108 n. 50, citing 1 Sam. 12:6 [LXX] and Mark 3:14 as clear instances where the verb denotes "selection" for special service rather than "creation."

9. Lane, *Hebrews 1–8*, 77.

The author comes to the central point of his comparison in 3:5-6a, using once again the device of antithesis: "and Moses was faithful in all his house as a servant for a witness to the things that would be spoken, but Christ as a Son over his house." The author had purposefully positioned his comparison to arrive at this key point only after the analogies in 3:3-4 were developed, for he refrained from including the phrase "as a servant" from Numbers 12:7 when he first introduced Moses as "faithful in his house" at 3:2, saving it for the second and fuller recitation of Numbers 12:7. The distinction between a servant and a son recalls the comparison with the angels in 1:5-14, who also were designated "servants" (1:7, 14). If Moses knew God face-to-face and had access to the very presence of God such that he could see God, he still enjoyed the access of a servant. The access enjoyed by a Son would be greater, and the mediation of a Son, whose proximity to the head of the household was so much greater, who shone with the reflection of the honor of the head of the household since he stood so close to the Father, would be more effective and sure than that even of a faithful servant (see discussion on Heb. 1:3).

The author's choice of subjects for comparison with Jesus appear to have a dual internal logic. On the one hand, the angels, Moses, and, of course, the levitical priests are all known in the intertestamental period for their mediatorial functions. Each works (or had historically worked) in some way to secure and maintain God's favor. By comparing Jesus with each in turn, the author is able to impress upon the hearers that human beings have never enjoyed the help of a more able mediator, nor ever been granted access to God more open and direct than that which the Son provides. On the other hand, the author is following a sort of chain of revelation of the earlier "word" of God, the Torah, entrusted to the angels (2:2), who gave it to Moses, who delivered it to the priests to execute. The earlier message remains an important foil for amplifying both the promise of heeding and the peril of neglecting the final "word" of God in the Son.

All these topics of amplification, however, are consistently brought to bear on the audience's response. The author seeks to underscore the significance of the Son and the word brought by the Son so as to heighten the importance of this Son and his word of promise for his addressees. Thus Moses himself becomes faithful "as a witness to the things that would be spoken," namely, this ultimate revelation (a gloss by the author on Num. 12:7 adduced to affirm the superiority of the gospel to previous "words" and the privileges and penalties attached to previous words from God).[10] If the addressees continue to value this word, they have the opportunity to retain their place within God's household: "we are that house, if we hold firm the boldness and the boast of hope" (3:6b).

---

10. In this regard, 3:1-6 functions in relation to 10:26-31 as 1:4-14 did in relation to 2:1-4: in both "expository" sections the groundwork is laid for a "lesser to greater" argument in a subsequent exhortation.

This returns to one theme developed in 2:10-18, namely, the noble birth of the many sons and daughters as children of God. Being embedded in the household of God (cf. 10:21) means that they share God's honor and enjoy God's protection and patronage as head of the household through the intercession of the Son (not merely of a servant, however faithful). This is a positive good that it would be expedient to preserve. Perseverance in the Christian group, moreover, is being positively interpreted as remaining attached to God's family. If the hearers continue to accept these claims, they will regard it as essential to their own self-worth to continue in the fellowship of believers.

"Boldness" (παρρησία) is a term familiar from discussions in Greek political works of the democratic ideal of free speech ideally enjoyed by citizens of Greek cities. It is the mark of the "free" person rather than the slave. This positive value is given specificity by the author of Hebrews as the sermon unfolds. It will appear again in 4:16 and 10:19, both times in the context of an exhortation to the hearers to take advantage of the "boldness" Jesus has given them in their relationship to God. It denotes specifically boldness or confidence to enter God's very presence, notably in the context of Christian fellowship (10:19-25 will emphasize this). The fourth occurrence of the word appears in 10:35, after the author has praised the addressees for their former endurance of society's deviancy-control techniques. Not reproach, not abuse, not plunder, not imprisonment could enslave their spirits and compel them to give up their hope in those earlier days (10:32-34). Now the author calls them not to "throw away their boldness, which has great reward." There, the term appears to denote the addressees' openness with regard to their commitment to God, the Son, and the promises and obligations associated with the gospel. They are not to let their neighbors, in effect, bully them (like tyrants, the stereotypical enemies of democracy and, especially, free speech) into muting or hiding or dissolving their associations with their fellow believers and the message that made them part of God's family.[11]

The addressees are urged also to hold onto the "boast" (καύχημα) that derives from their hope. A "boast" is a claim that a person makes to honor or precedence. It is a characteristic term of the Corinthian correspondence, in which Paul lays out at great length what constitutes appropriate and inappropriate claims to honor (i.e., what truly establishes one's honor within the Christian community).[12] The claim to honor that is theirs as God's family, as Jesus' own sisters and

---

11. Lane (*Hebrews 1–8*, 79) and Attridge (*Hebrews*, 112) agree that the term has connotations in Hebrews both of confidence before God in prayer (Attridge refers to Philo *Rer. Div. Her.* 5, 21; 1 John 3:21) and of boldness in public testimony to the Christian hope (Attridge again refers to Heb. 10:35; Wis. 5:1; Acts 2:29; 4:13, 29, 31; Mark 8:32).

12. See D. A. deSilva, "Let the One who Claims Honor Establish that Claim in the Lord: Honor Discourse in the Corinthian Correspondence," *BTB* 28 (1998): 64-67.

brothers, as those who have been made holy so as to stand in the very presence of God (and the many claims to honor that the author will continue to develop throughout the sermon) is not to be compromised in the face of society's attempts to deny that claim and inflict disgrace upon them. The honor that God has prepared for them in the unshakable kingdom is too great to be relinquished for the sake of the approval of sinners. Their claim to honor, however, is qualified as "belonging to hope," a term that will be significantly developed in 6:11, 18; 7:19. This "hope" is all that they possess of their future honor and homeland, but it is the very essence of those good things (cf. 3:14; 11:1). The author wants the addressees firmly to believe that, as long as they hold onto their hope, their claim to honor is secure regardless of the efforts of their neighbors.[13] In this way, they will be insulated from the dominant culture's attempts to "reform" them.

Hebrews 3:1-6 prepares naturally for the exhortations based on the negative example of the wilderness generation, those who enjoyed the benefits of Moses' revelation and mediation, which dominates 3:7–4:13. The people of that generation did not hold onto their confidence and hope and thereby lost irrevocably God's promises and the gift of a homeland. The recitation of Psalm 95:7-11 will heighten the hearers' sense of the urgency behind the author's call to hold onto the boldness and claim to honor that come from the Christian hope. "Today" that must be their primary agenda — as long as it is called "today."

3:7-19

Since the "apostle . . . of our confession" (3:1) occupies so honorable and significant a position over God's household, the addressees must attend to that apos-

---

13. Stedman (*Hebrews*, 50) is troubled about how to reconcile the word of Hebrews with the doctrine of eternal security: "This *if* [in 3:6] has troubled many people for it seems to imply that being a member of Christ's house can be lost after it is gained by wavering in our courage or hope." This leads him to read "if we hold onto our courage and the hope of which we boast" as descriptive rather than conditional (ibid., 54), meaning that, while there will be times of weak faith and struggle, the Christian will generally be characterized by courage and hope. Stedman's misstep here, even if it is motivated by pastoral concern for those who fear "losing salvation" during periods of doubt or dry spells in prayer life, is that inner feelings are not the subject of 3:6. The author of Hebrews is not concerned with subjective, negative feelings but the betrayal of a relationship. Whatever our feelings, we are not to break faith with God or the Son who brought us to God. Whatever our feelings, we are to exercise boldness in our open association with the Christian community and the word of Jesus and to regard our honor as deriving only from our place in God's family and our share in Christ's honor. There is no warrant, therefore, to weaken the condition to the status of description: the author is vitally concerned that all his hearers remain steadfast in their commitment to God rather than hide their confession and seek means of avoiding the shame heaped upon them by their non-Christian neighbors.

tle's word all the more carefully and reverently. Thus the author returns in 3:7–4:13 to the theme of "hearing" God's voice and the urgency of responding appropriately (cf. 1:1-2; 2:1-4). The author wishes to demonstrate that distrust — hearing God's promises and assurances, and then insulting God by not trusting them — is the essential danger to be avoided. Since Jesus was both faithful to God (hence a model for the believers' own commitment) and reliable (hence worthy of the believers' trust), they would indeed be in greater danger than those who distrusted God's promises on the basis of Moses' mediation.

The example of the wilderness generation is introduced as an inductive proof by means of which the author hopes to demonstrate the reality and gravity of the danger of thinking too lightly of God's promises and not remaining firm in one's trust in God to provide what God promised. Examples from historical precedents were especially valued by orators in deliberative situations, in which the goal was to convince the hearers that a certain course of action would entail certain consequences (whether positive or negative, depending on whether or not one's goal was to promote the course of action or dissuade the hearers from taking such a course). How could one convince people concerning events yet to happen? The "quickest method of securing assent" was to point the audience to historical parallels, for which the consequences are now a matter of record (Quintilian *Inst.* 3.8.36). According to Aristotle, the future is held to resemble the past — that is, there is a certain continuity in the fabric of human history such that "similar results" are expected naturally to "arise from similar causes" (*Rh.* 1.4.9; see also 2.20.8). Establishing an analogy between a situation in which the outcome is not yet known and a situation in which the outcome is already known enables the orator convincingly to "predict outcomes," for "it is by examination of the past that we divine and judge the future" (*Rh.* 1.9.40).[14]

The author is therefore on strong ground when he turns the attention of his hearers to the experience of the wilderness generation as they stood at the threshold of the Promised Land. The outcome is recorded in an authoritative source and, indeed, is well known through the liturgical recitation of Psalm 95. The wilderness generation's decision not to trust God's word and act accordingly makes them a perpetual example of failure — their remembrance is forever marred by their folly. The hearers will be moved to avoid taking the same course of action

---

14. *Rhetorica ad Alexandrum* gives similar advice about persuasion through historical examples: "in exhortations and dissuasions it has to be proved about the matter under consideration that the line of action which we are urging or opposing itself has the effect that we assert it has; or if not, that actions resembling this line of action generally or invariably turn out in the way we assert" (1428b12-17). Examples should be used "in order that your audience may be more ready to believe your statements when they realize that another action resembling the one you allege has been committed in the way in which you say that it occurred" (1429a25-28).

both to avoid the lasting disgrace attached to it in the past and to avoid the wretched consequences of being forever excluded from the promise.

The author chooses to approach this historical example not directly through the narrative of Numbers 14 (although recitations and recontextualizations from Numbers 14 will certainly occur throughout 3:12-19), but rather through the second half of Psalm 95. As part of the Psalter, the hymnal of both synagogue and early Church, the text would have been quite familiar. More relevant, however, is the fact that the psalm itself very succinctly summarizes the Numbers 14 incident (see discussion below) and derives a moral exhortation from it, calling each new generation of hearers not to repeat the error of the wilderness generation. It speaks with a sense of urgency that the author clearly found helpful for advancing his own agenda for the audience: it makes "today" an opportunity to respond to God's voice (resonating strongly with 1:1-4; 2:1-4) or to suffer a self-destructive hardening of the heart. The recitation of the psalm, therefore, serves to amplify the danger or crisis of which the author wants the hearers to be aware. If hearing God's message of deliverance does not produce the response of trust and loyalty, there will be a provoking of God's anger with disastrous and irrevocable consequences.

The MT version of the psalm directs the reader to the complaints of the wilderness generation over the lack of water at Massah and Meribah (Exod. 17:1-7; Num. 20:2-13), while also alluding to the oath made by God (Num. 14:21-23) in the wake of the rebellion. Once again, the departures of the LXX from the MT are significant for the author's use of the text. The Hebrew place names Meribah and Massah have been translated as "provocation" and "testing,"[15] such that the geographical references are removed and the whole passage now refers to the single episode contained in Numbers 14, namely, the people's refusal to take the land as God commanded on account of their fear of the inhabitants.[16]

---

15. Whatever the devotional value of contemplating Exod. 17:1-7 at this point (see Stedman, *Hebrews*, 51), the preacher or teacher should be aware that the LXX version has completely obscured this connection, and that it is unlikely that the author or hearers would have called Exod. 17:1-7 to mind as this psalm was read in Greek.

16. The author introduces one striking change in the recitation of Psalm 95: the author adds the word "therefore" before "I was angry" in order to link the period of forty years with the experience of seeing God's works. The MT and LXX both read more naturally with the "forty years" linked to the experience of God's anger (which is explicit in Num. 14:34). The author will revert to this position later in the exposition (3:17). Lane (*Hebrews 1–8*, 88-89; also Attridge, *Hebrews*, 120 n. 95; Otfried Hofius, *Katapausis: Die Vorstellung vom endzeitlichen Ruheort im Hebräerbrief* [Wissenschaftliche Untersuchungen zum Neuen Testament 11; Tübingen: Mohr, 1970], 129-30) convincingly defends this as a sign that the author is aware of two different OT traditions that speak of (the same) forty years as a period of God's gracious provision and a period of experiencing God's punishment. The author high-

That Numbers 14, and not merely Psalm 95, undergirds the author's exhortation from example can be demonstrated by the recitations and recontextualizations of material found in the former but not in the latter text. Most telling is the mention of those "whose corpses fell in the desert" (ὧν τὰ κῶλα ἔπεσεν ἐν τῇ ἐρήμῳ, 3:17), a direct reference to Numbers 14:29: "your dead bodies shall fall in this wilderness (ἐν τῇ ἐρήμῳ ταύτῃ πεσεῖται τὰ κῶλα ὑμῶν)."[17] The introduction of the language of "sin" (3:13), and specifically the identification of the fallen corpses as belonging to "those who sinned" (3:17), also recalls Numbers 14:34, which gives "sin" a prominent role in their downfall: "According to the number of the days in which you spied out the land, forty days, for every day a year, you shall bear your sin (λήμψεσθε τὰς ἁμαρτίας ὑμῶν), forty years, and you shall know the fierceness of my anger." Moreover, the author's injunction to "watch out" for the danger of "turning away from the living God" (ἐν τῷ ἀποστῆναι ἀπὸ θεοῦ, 3:12) recalls the plea of Joshua and Caleb in Numbers 14:9: "do not become apostates from the Lord" (ἀπὸ τοῦ κυρίου μὴ ἀποστάται γίνεσθε). Finally, the author cites as the two key errors of the wilderness generation distrust and disobedience: "they were not able to enter on account of distrust" (δι᾽ ἀπιστίαν, 3:19); "they did not enter on account of disobedience" (δι᾽ ἀπείθειαν, 4:6; see 4:11). These are also presented as fatal flaws in Numbers 14: God's anger is provoked by the people's lack of trust ("how long will they not trust me," οὐ πιστεύουσίν μοι, 14:11); the Hebrews failed in their attempt to take the land after their rebellion because they had disobeyed God (ἀπειθοῦντες κυρίῳ, 14:43).

What, then, was the nature of this event that stands behind Hebrews 3:7–4:11, and what would the author have his hearers learn from this historical precedent? The people following Moses experienced God's liberation from slavery and deliverance from the oppressor, receiving also the promise of a good land to call their own possession. Arriving at the threshold of that land after forty days of traveling through the desert, experiencing God's care and protection all along the way, they sent twelve spies into the land. Ten return with an alarming report concerning the size and strength of the current inhabitants, thinking them too formidable an enemy to engage (Num. 13:31-35). Joshua and Caleb, however, speak of the goodness of that land and assure the congregation of God's ability to bring the people in (Num. 14:6-8). Because the con-

---

lights in 3:9-10 the extent of time that the wilderness generation witnessed God's faithful provision in order to underscore the inappropriateness of showing distrust toward this God.

17. Possibly the author also has in mind Num. 14:31-32, where this phrase is repeated in connection with the people's low evaluation of the prize they were abandoning: "But your little ones, who you said would become a prey, I will bring in, and they shall inherit the land which you have rejected (καὶ κληρονομήσουσιν τὴν γῆν ἣν ὑμεῖς ἀπέστητε ἀπ᾽ αὐτῆς). But as for you, your dead bodies shall fall in this wilderness (καὶ τὰ κῶλα ὑμῶν πεσεῖται ἐν τῇ ἐρήμῳ ταύτῃ)."

gregation accepts the majority report, the day of their inheritance became the "day of testing" (τὴν ἡμέραν τοῦ πειρασμοῦ), in which the people manifested finally and fatally their distrust in their patron's ability to provide.

It is this distrust that the author will elevate first in his exhortation. The term ἀπιστία forms an *inclusio* uniting 3:12-19 and giving that section a specific focus (3:12 warns against distrust; 3:19 established the consequences of distrust from Num. 14). The term is often translated as "unbelief" (cf. NASV; NRSV), but the word group sharing the root πιστ- belongs to the sphere of patronage, friendship, and reciprocity. Dio of Prusa, for example, delivers an oration on ἀπιστία (*Or.* 74) in which he recommends distrust of other people as a path to safety in human affairs. Because human beings cannot be counted upon to fulfill their obligations and agreements, the way to peace lies in minimizing one's entanglements with other people. The companion oration, περὶ πίστεως (*Or.* 73), speaks of the burdens of being entrusted with some charge or responsibility. Frederick Danker catalogues several inscriptions in which πίστις refers to "that which is entrusted," such that "faith is required by the one who awaits fulfillment of the obligation that has been accepted by another."[18] In common Greek usage, then, πίστις refers both to the responsibility accepted by another to discharge some duty or provide some service and the trust placed in that person by the one who awaits the fulfillment of the obligation. Πιστός, the adjectival form, describes the person who may be relied upon to carry out the obligation, who is "trustworthy." Ἀπιστία may signify either the untrustworthiness of a base person or the feeling that ascribed unreliability to another, such that one neither entrusts the other with something nor trusts the other to fulfill an obligation.

The situation of the wilderness generation falls within the sphere of patronage, promises, and fulfillment of obligations. God had undertaken an obligation on behalf of the people, namely, to bring them into the land he would give them as an inheritance, and he had provided many proofs of reliability (Num. 14:11, 22; Ps. 95:9; καὶ εἶδον τὰ ἔργα μου, 3:9). In light of the spies' report concerning the strength of the native inhabitants of the land, however, the people wavered in their trust, that is, doubted whether or not God would be able to fulfill his obligation. Indeed, they ascribe to their patron the base motive of treachery, suggesting that he intended to bring them to the threshold of the Promised Land merely to let them die (Num. 14:3). They abandon the prospects of the promise being fulfilled by setting in motion a plan to return to Egypt (Num. 14:4), thus negating all the benefits God had already given them. They completely deny the validity of God's promise as they exclaim: "our children will become a prey" (Num. 14:3, 31). Such distrust is interpreted by God as a denial of his reliability and ability to provide, which is nothing less than a

---

18. Danker, *Benefactor*, 352-53.

challenge to the benefactor, all the more inappropriate given the number of tests God had allowed in order to stimulate trust (πίστις).[19]

Distrust derives from a value judgment, specifically a low estimation of the honor and ability of the person whom one distrusts.[20] It is the proper response to persons of a vicious or questionable character. As such, the wilderness generation's response of not trusting God enacts a negative value judgment on God and insults their patron, who alone is truly "good." The Numbers narrative explicitly links distrust and the provocation that arises from contempt: "How long will this people despise me? And how long will they not believe in me (ἕως τίνος παροξύνει με ὁ λαὸς οὗτος καὶ ἕως τίνος οὐ πιστεύουσίν μοι), in spite of all the signs which I have wrought among them?" (14:11). The verb παροξύνω, often translated as "to urge, prick or spur on," or "to provoke, irritate, excite" (LSJ), carries definite connotations of contempt, such that the provocation would spring from the understanding that one has been slighted or insulted.[21] Thus, when the wilderness generation is said to have provoked God (Num. 14:11), the source of this provocation is the people's choice of a course of action that displayed contempt for God. Insofar as they withdrew their trust from their benefactor, they declared God to be unreliable and unable to fulfill the obligation he had assumed in their behalf, repaying him with flagrant contempt.

What led the wilderness generation to take such an unjust course of action? They feared the hostility and strength of the Canaanites more than they trusted God. Joshua, while not disputing the facts of the majority report, nevertheless urges confidence in God's favor: "do not become rebels against the Lord (ἀλλὰ ἀπὸ τοῦ κυρίου μὴ ἀποστάται γίνεσθε·); and do not fear the people of the land (ὑμεῖς δὲ μὴ φοβηθῆτε τὸν λαὸν τῆς γῆς), for they are bread for us; their protection is removed from them, and the LORD is with us; do not fear them" (Num. 14:9). The people, however, do turn away from God (ἀποστῆναι), enacting their lack of honor for their patron.

God responds with "wrath" or "anger" toward those who have been dis-

---

19. Distrust and challenging God are linked also in Wis. 1:2, RSV: "God is found by those who do not put him to the test, and manifests himself to those who do not distrust him (ὅτι εὑρίσκεται τοῖς μὴ πειράζουσιν αὐτὸν ἐμφανίζεται δὲ τοῖς μὴ ἀπιστοῦσιν αὐτῷ)."

20. Ps-Isocrates (*Ad Dem.* 22), for example, advises his young friend: "Consider that you owe it to yourself no less to mistrust bad men than to put your trust in the good (προσήκειν ἡγοῦ τοῖς πονηροῖς ἀπιστεῖν, ὥσπερ τοῖς χρηστοῖς πιστεύειν)."

21. This is made clear by the tendency of the LXX translators to use this verb in synonymous parallelism with the verbs ὀνειδιεῖ and ὠνείδισεν in Ps. 73:10, 18 (LXX). Also telling is the use of the verb to express the effect of Israel's idolatry upon the one true God. In Isa. 65:1-7, God's appeal to the Israelites is continually rejected while the people reach out to idols. Their spurning of God and adoration of other objects of worship, which amount to insults against God, constitute a provocation of God.

obedient, who have trampled the promise, and who have faltered in their trust. Anger, according to Aristotle (*Rh.* 2.2.1), is aroused in response to a violation of the honor to which one believes oneself entitled: "Let us then define anger (ὀργή) as a longing, accompanied by pain, for a real or apparent revenge for a real or apparent slight."[22] Among the various situations in which slighting causes anger, he explicitly mentions that people "are angry at slights from those by whom they think they have a right to expect to be well treated; such are those on whom they have conferred or are conferring benefits (εὖ πεποίηκεν ἢ ποιεῖ) . . . and all those whom they desire, or did desire, to benefit" (*Rh.* 2.2.8). This describes the situation in Numbers 14. From the opening of the story in Exodus, God has acted so as to bring the people from a wretched into an enviable state, leading them from slavery to a land for their own possession. Those whom he desired to benefit, however, returned insult for favor, slighting God through their distrust of God's goodwill and ability. In response to the challenges or tests with which the wilderness generation affronted God, the psalmist declares in God's voice (3:10): "Therefore I was angry (προσώχθισα) with that generation" (cf. Num. 14:34 [LXX]).

The result of God's wrath is the people's loss of access to the promised benefit. It is specifically out of God's anger that God swears the oath that excludes the rebellious generation from the Promised Land (3:11): "As I swore in my wrath, 'They shall not enter my rest.'" The author of Hebrews ascribes this loss explicitly to disobedience and distrust (3:18-19): "And to whom did he swear that they should never enter his rest, but to those who were disobedient (τοῖς ἀπειθήσασιν)? So we see that they were unable to enter because of unbelief (δι' ἀπιστίαν)." The impossibility of a return to favor, that is, to the hope of acquiring the benefits that were once spurned, figures prominently in Hebrews. Esau is permanently barred from his birthright once he trades it away (12:17), and the believers themselves are faced with the threat that, once they turn away from Christ and bring him dishonor, there is no repentance, no sacrifice, that can restore their standing in God's favor (6:6; 10:26). The author does not mention explicitly the irrevocability of the loss of the wilderness generation. The finality of their rejection and the fulfillment of God's oath not to allow them to enter, however, are captured succinctly in the author's recontextualization of Numbers 14:29: "And with whom was he provoked for forty years? Was it not with those who sinned, whose bodies fell in the desert?" (3:17). The reminder of their death "in the desert" recalls their failure to reverse their divinely decreed fate (4:6).

The fate of the wilderness generation, therefore, demonstrates that showing distrust toward God (and acting as if God's promises are unreliable or not

---

22. Thus Malina and Neyrey ("Honor and Shame," 46) are correct to include "nouns such as vengeance, wrath, anger" among "perceptions of being challenged or shamed."

worth the cost of attaining) leads to a bad end. Such a course is proven inexpedient both in the goods that are lost (the promised benefactions) and in the evils that are gained (exchanging God's favor and protection for God's anger). It is an unjust course, as it dishonors the patron one should honor and serve. It is also, ultimately, a dangerous course since it leads to the experience of God's anger and the penalties God would deem fit to inflict. Allowing the fear of God rather than of human beings to determine one's course of action, however formidable the threats of humans appear, is shown to be the advantageous course. How does the author hope recollection of this failure will affect his audience?

Key to the success of a proof from historical precedent is establishing that precedent as an analogous situation. The author must be certain that the addressees will be able to see their situation mirrored in that of the wilderness generation before its fateful choice. He will point out two prominent similarities in 4:1-2. First, both the wilderness generation and the audience "had good news announced to them," in which God's beneficent will was made known and promises were made. Second, the "promise to enter [God's] rest" stands before the current addressees just as it had stood before the wilderness generation. The analogy extends further, however. The addressees had also experienced God's gracious provision, beginning with deliverance from their own slavery (enforced by the fear of death, 2:14-15); they, too, had "seen God's works" (3:9), now in the form of the "signs and wonders and diverse miracles and disbursements of the Holy Spirit," by means of which God confirmed the "good news" announced through Jesus (2:3-4; cf. 6:4-5). They, too, stand at the very threshold of their inheritance, having need only to endure "yet a very little while" before the time of reward (10:35-39). Indeed, the author can speak of them as being in the process of "entering" that rest (4:3), choosing to use the present rather than the future tense.

As the author portrays their situation, they are said to face the same challenges as the wilderness generation. Around them are unbelievers, dauntingly empowered with the weapons of reproach, physical abuse, dispossession, and possibly even manipulation of the judicial and prison systems. Some of their number have already begun to shrink back in the face of these enemies, fearing human hostility and thinking it a weightier consideration than God's promise. They need to be reminded that God's patronage enables fearlessness in the face of human opposition (13:5-6), but also that God's promise demands faithfulness and firmness.

Certain, then, that his audience will see their own situation in the mirror of Numbers 14, the author uses the text of Psalm 95 to announce the clear and present danger to attaining what the author has been promoting as the single item that should occupy the addressees' minds — inheriting salvation and being led to glory (1:14; 2:10): "I swore in my anger, 'they shall not enter my rest'" (3:11). The psalm seeks to impress upon its hearers the urgency of maintaining an appropriate response to the word of God, and the author goes on to use language from the psalm to apply this admonition to his congregation. Specifically, he recontextualizes the words "heart," "harden," and "today" from the psalm in the exhortation that follows: "watch out, sisters and brothers, lest there be in any one of you a base heart of distrust in turning away from the living God, but encourage one another every day — as long as it is called 'today' — in order that none of you be hardened by the guile of sin" (3:12-13).

The author wants the hearers to see that the greatest danger facing them is not continued hostility from their neighbors or deprivation of worldly goods and honor, but rather the "deceitfulness of sin," which threatens to "harden" their hearts, and the encroachment of "distrust," which might turn them away from the living God.[23] They would then end up excluded from the promised "glory," "deliverance," and now "rest." The example of the wilderness generation in fact proves that this weakening of firmness with regard to God's promises, and not the assaults of human beings, is the real danger that must be overcome. The word "heart" emerges as an important term in 3:7–4:13. The heart may show a person to be wicked (hence dishonorable) both through failing to trust the reliable God and through acting faithlessly with regard to one's obligations to honor and remain committed to the divine Patron. Either sense of ἀπιστία, or both, may be active here. The heart has the potential to wander or to be hardened (i.e., become unable to respond to God's saving word, leaving it beyond rescue or help; 3:8, 10, 15; 4:7). Finally, the heart is the object of God's scrutiny (4:12). It is therefore vital to guard it from distrust and instability (cf. 13:9) and to keep it from wandering (specifically, wandering from firm trust in God and commitment to attaining what God promises). In ancient thought the heart was the seat of thought, will, affections, and core personality.[24] The heart represented the essence and central drives of the individual. The author is thus urging the addressees to center themselves once more on God's promises, to make these the core of their own identity and agenda, and to remain firmly fixed in the sphere of God's favor, neither wavering to the right or the left in the face of the pressures from outside the group.[25]

---

23. Depicting the decision to mute one's association with the church (10:24) as "turning away from the living God" reveals ideological texture at work. The author presents such a course in the most fearsome and absolute manner possible, so as to make it appear all the less appealing to those who might contemplate it.

24. Robbins, *Exploring*, 30-31.

25. The heart returns to prominence later in the sermon. The Jeremiah quotation (8:10; 10:10) speaks of the New Covenant, including a provision for the heart to be clean, constant, and stable in God's ways. Hebrews 10:22 encourages the addressees to draw near to God with "a true heart," which is "full of trust." This contrasts with the "base heart of distrust" in 3:12. Finally, 13:9 speaks of the grace relationship with God through Jesus that enables the heart to be stable and constant. Trust in God is thus the remedy to being susceptible to wandering (3:10) or to sin's guile (3:13).

Such pressure, ultimately, is interpreted here as "sin's deceitfulness" (3:13). Those voices that suggest that temporal goods are worth preserving or recovering at the expense of God's promises, or that erode one's conviction that God's promises are real, reliable, and worth any investment to retain, are neutralized with this effective label. The believer's task, in light of this revelation, is clear: sin must be resisted. The label "sin" makes the messages of one's neighbors easier to reject and resist as something disadvantageous and dishonorable. Numbers 14 had also spoken of "sin," which there specifically involved distrust toward God's promises and failure to walk in line with those promises (which should have resulted in an immediate attack on the Canaanites at Joshua and Caleb's urging). This illumines the meaning of "sin" in Hebrews, where the fundamental issue appears again to be unwavering commitment to God's promise and people (cf. the meaning of sin in 11:24-26). "Sin" is a rejection of one's obligations to such a patron and the household into which one has been welcomed.

The author invites the addressees to participate in helping one another overcome this danger by exhorting one another "every day, as long as it is called 'today.'" The psalm allows for the author to heighten the urgency of how one will respond to the word "today" by calling attention to the Christian cultural knowledge that there are a limited number of "todays" left before God tears into the fabric of human history to execute judgment and bestow rewards (cf. 10:25, 37-39; 12:26-28).[26] The author urges his audience to continue to reinforce for one another the redefinition of what is truly disadvantageous and advantageous — "truly," as the author has laid out the dangers and desiderata of their situation. The author understands the importance of what sociologist Peter Berger has called a "plausibility structure," the social base that makes a particular worldview tenable for any particular individual within that group.[27] Sustaining beliefs, values, and hopes requires social reinforcement, particularly when other social groups seek to reinforce different beliefs and values. "Put crudely, if one is to believe what neo-orthodoxy wants one to believe, in the contemporary situation, then one must be rather careful to huddle together closely and continuously with one's fellow believers."[28] *Mutatis mutandis,* the same holds true for the addressees of Hebrews, who may maintain a distinctive view of reality or yield, one-by-one, to the view reinforced by members of the dominant culture. Floyd Filson writes about the author of Hebrews:

---

26. This gloss is highlighted by the author's clever use of *paronomasia,* or "pun": "encourage (παρακαλεῖτε) one another each day (ἡμέραν), as long as 'today' (Σήμερον) it is called (καλεῖται)."

27. Berger, *Sacred Canopy,* 45.

28. Ibid., 164.

He wants them to show solidarity . . . in regular assembling for common worship. . . . He knows they need to keep the bond of Christian brotherhood strong especially in times when hostility from without actively besets them. They need the inner resources that can come only through common worship and mutual encouragement.[29]

Throughout the letter, the author of Hebrews expresses his desire that the community work hard to reinforce the commitment and behavior of its individual members. Hebrews 3:12-13 is the first of many exhortations promoting this agenda (see further 4:1, 11; 10:24-25; 12:15-16; 13:1-3). The members of the community are collectively to take responsibility for the encouragement of each individual, to be accountable to and for one another, in order that no individual should begin to become detached from the group, that is, cease to regard the community as the body of his or her significant others, whose approval means life and self-respect. This will provide the necessary social reinforcement that will keep the individual's heart from "wandering" or being "hardened" to the message of the Christian group through listening too intently to the messages from outside. By means of these exhortations, the author seeks to delegate to each member the task of reminding the sisters and brothers of their hope, their honor in Christ, the irrelevance of society's approval or censure, and the promise of honor before God for those who persevere, which he began in his sermon.

Such mutual encouragement in the struggle against the forces that would conspire to rob the believers of their prize is necessitated by the grandeur and excellence of the benefits that have been made available to the congregation: "for we have become Christ's partners, if we hold the first installment of the reality secure until the end" (3:14).[30] The term "partners of Christ" provides an-

---

29. Floyd V. Filson, *Yesterday: A Study of Hebrews in the Light of Chapter 13* (SBT 4; London: SCM, 1967), 69.

30. The translation of the phrase τὴν ἀρχὴν τῆς ὑποστάσεως is difficult, mainly due to the slippery nature of the final word. Here, its connotation of "underlying reality" or "essence" is preferred, and the hearers are being enjoined to hold onto that part of their future possession which is presently available to them, namely, their trust in their patron's promise. Thompson (*Beginnings*, 94) insightfully comments that the ὑπόστασις "refers to the essential reality which 'stands beneath' all appearances" so that the phrase "is a description of the reality on which the existence of the community rests in the same way that Christ is the reality of God (1:3)." To this metaphysical sense, however, we must add a teleological sense, pointing to the relationship between holding on to "trust" in God as the "title deed" to the future enjoyment of this underlying reality, namely, the unshakable kingdom (12:26-28). The meaning is clarified by a comparison with 6:19-20, in which it is the believer's hope that enters the inner sanctum of the heavenly temple "where Christ has entered as a forerunner for us." In the present time, the believers' tether to that heavenly realm is their mooring in the Christian hope, which anchors them in the harbor of their final destination. This will be further explicated in the commentary on 11:1.

other facet for the communal identity of the hearers that the author seeks to craft. It is a term that invites loyalty to Christ (as to one another, 3:1) for the sake of arriving at the goal of the partnership, namely, the entrance of the "many sons and daughters" into their inheritance of deliverance and glory. Contemplation of "partnership" introduces a familiar topos from Greco-Roman discussions of friendship. "Friends" hold possessions in common, and thus have fellowship (κοινωνία): although friends will not actually establish a community of shared goods, they will place their goods at the service and disposal of one another.[31] Thus Christ "shared fully" in the flesh and blood of the addressees (2:14) as an outcome of this partnership. As Christ's friends, the believers have access to the goods and services Christ can provide, notably to his mediation for God's favor. They likewise have honor now through their association with the exalted Son, and they have the hope of sharing in Christ's inheritance when they, too, enter the heavenly realm where Christ "entered as a forerunner" (6:20). "Holding firm" now will lead to the enjoyment of surpassing honor (expressed as "glory," δόξα, in 2:10) in the future. The verse recalls 3:6, in which the believers' honor and access to great resources as God's household was similarly predicated on their continued commitment to the Christian group and its confession. By such means, the author repeatedly affirms the advantages of continuing to invest oneself in the Christian group and the great loss that would follow dissociation from that body.

The author reinforces the impact of the example of the wilderness generation by recalling their story more directly in 3:16-19. He employs the technique of "reasoning by question and answer," giving the answers, however, in the form of rhetorical questions with which he expects the addressees to agree. Since we have explored this story at length already, we will not repeat that treatment here. The pointed questions and responses framed by the author highlight the essential points of the example: provoking God, sinning, disobeying, and showing distrust are the most inexpedient and dangerous courses that those previously welcomed into God's favor could pursue. The addressees should regard such a course not with interest, but with fear (4:1).

4:1-11

The consequences of distrust demonstrated in the episode of Numbers 14 become the basis for an appeal to the emotion of "fear," by which the author seeks

---

31. Compare Luke T. Johnson, *Sharing Possessions: Mandate and Symbol of Faith* (Philadelphia: Fortress, 1981), 117-32 for an excellent discussion of the development of this ideal through the primary sources. Aristotle (*Eth. Nic.* 8-9) provides a helpful overview of friendship in the ancient world.

to heighten the addressees' abhorrence of showing distrust and unreliability toward God their Patron: "Let us be afraid, therefore, lest while a promise to enter his rest remains any one of you should seem to fall short" (4:1). Once again the author suggests that the real danger — the fearsome thing — is not the continued rejection by and opposition of non-Christians, but failing to enter that which God has prepared for those who trust him.[32] The thing for Christians to fear is not the wisdom of continued investment in an enterprise that has brought measurable temporal loss, nor the danger of spending the remaining decades of their lives in unnecessary deprivation. The author wants to reposition the addressees' concern so that they will be more interested in how to avert the danger of "falling short" of what God has set before them than in how to avert the reproaches of their neighbors or how to regain their place in society.

The author makes conspicuous use of the verb "entering" and the specific phrase "entering God's rest" throughout 3:18–4:11. Such thick repetition of this phrase merits display:

"not to enter into his rest"
μὴ εἰσελεύσεσθαι εἰς τὴν κατάπαυσιν αὐτοῦ, 3:18

"They were unable to enter on account of distrust"
οὐκ ἠδυνήθησαν εἰσελθεῖν, 3:19

"While a promise to enter into his rest remains"
καταλειπομένης ἐπαγγελίας εἰσελθεῖν εἰς τὴν κατάπαυσιν αὐτοῦ, 4:1

"For we who trust are entering into rest"
εἰσερχόμεθα γὰρ εἰς [τὴν] κατάπαυσιν οἱ πιστεύσαντες, 4:3

"They shall not enter into my rest"
Εἰ εἰσελεύσονται εἰς τὴν κατάπαυσίν μου, 4:3

"They shall not enter into my rest"
Εἰ εἰσελεύσονται εἰς τὴν κατάπαυσίν μου, 4:5

"It remains for some to enter into it"
ἀπολείπεται τινὰς εἰσελθεῖν εἰς αὐτήν, 4:6

"They did not enter on account of disobedience"
οὐκ εἰσῆλθον δι' ἀπείθειαν, 4:6

---

32. The author assumes here, and will go on to "prove," that the promise to enter into God's rest still remains open — it was not nullified in Num. 14, even though some were excluded from it, and, as we shall see, it was not fulfilled by the generation of Joshua and Caleb.

"For the one who enters into [God's] rest"
ὁ γὰρ εἰσελθὼν εἰς τὴν κατάπαυσιν αὐτοῦ, 4:10

"Let us strive earnestly therefore to enter into that rest"
σπουδάσωμεν οὖν εἰσελθεῖν εἰς ἐκείνην τὴν κατάπαυσιν, 4:11

This is a stunning example of repetitive texture giving thematic coherence to a passage, but even more significantly serving the ideological agenda of an author. Repeating the phrase with slight alterations impresses upon the hearer the importance of the movement expressed, namely entry into God's rest. Arrival or nonarrival marks the difference between success and failure, between noble achievement and the disgrace of falling into the "pattern of disobedience" established by the exodus generation (4:11). This repetitive recontextualization of Psalm 95:11 allows "entering God's rest" to saturate the hearers' minds, replacing any contrary or competing agendas they may have brought to the hearing of this sermon.

Two questions stand at the center of debate about this passage: when do believers "enter" this "rest," and what precisely does the author mean by "rest"? The first question is posed as interpreters observe the apparent discrepancy of tenses within the text. On the one hand, the future aspect of the "rest" is underscored by its character as "promise" ("while a promise to enter God's rest remains," 4:1) that can be missed by the addressees ("lest any of you think to fall short," 4:1). The audience is exhorted to "strive to enter that rest" (4:11), as if the believers have not yet entered it but will in the future. On the other hand, one reads that "we who believe enter that rest" (4:3) and even that "the one who enters his rest ceased from his labors" (4:10).

A number of scholars, emphasizing the use of the present tense "we enter" (εἰσερχόμεθα, 4:3), argue that believers can in some sense enter into this "rest" in the present time.[33] This is occasionally, but mistakenly, bolstered by an interpretation of the "today" of Psalm 95 and the homiletic application of the psalm as a reference to the timing for entering into this "rest."[34] The problem with this argu-

---

33. Both Lane (*Hebrews 1–8,* 99) and Andrew T. Lincoln ("Sabbath, Rest, and Eschatology in the New Testament," in *From Sabbath to Lord's Day,* ed. D. A. Carson [Grand Rapids: Zondervan, 1982],197-220, especially 212) insist that the verb in 4:3 be taken as a "true present," with the result that "believers are already to enjoy the rest referred to in the quotation of Ps 95:11" (Lane, *Hebrews 1–8,* 99). There are other ways, however, in which the present continuous tense can be rendered "truly," although the use of this term of legitimation to defend only one possible reading is interesting to note.

34. So, uncharacteristically, Lincoln, "Sabbath," 212-213: "the time for entry into rest is 'today,' not after death or at the parousia"; " 'There remains' (4:9) is with reference to the rest of the promised land. It is future to *that* time, the time of Joshua (4:8). It is set for a 'certain day "Today" ' (4:7) and 'another day' (4:8), which as we have seen, begins right now." Stanley D. Toussaint, "The Eschatology of the Warning Passages in the Book of Hebrews," *GTJ* 3 (1982):

ment is that it results from a misunderstanding of the meaning of "Today" in the psalm and its exposition. This new "Today" and every "today" ("as long as it is called 'Today,'" 3:13) is the day for responding to God's promise, to God's voice, with trust and obedience. It is the "day" for not hardening one's heart or allowing distrust to turn one's heart away from the prize. "Today" sees the new announcement of the promise and the new opportunity to respond in a salutary way, such as the wilderness generation did not, with the result that one will be allowed to enter God's rest (as the wilderness generation was not).[35] In favor of this position regarding the time of entering is that it attempts to take seriously the immediacy of 4:3, a potentially strategic factor invoked by the author himself at this point by avoiding the use of a future tense verb.

Other students favor the future tense of entering suggested by the context of 4:1-11 over the present tense of 4:3, explaining the latter as "a futuristic present such as one finds in Matt 17:11; John 14:3; and 1 Cor 16:5,"[36] or as "proleptic,"[37] or as looking "from a futuristic vantage point."[38] Strongly in favor of this reading is the parallel it sustains between the audience being addressed and the wilderness generation whose example the audience is admonished not to imitate. They are called to persevere so as to enter the rest that the wilderness generation failed to enter. Also in favor of this view is the clearly future orientation of the immediate, surrounding context (4:1, 11).

Perhaps sensing the strength of both positions, a number of scholars advocate an interpretation that embraces both a present, proleptic enjoyment and a future consummation of this "rest."[39] But neither those who hold "rest" to be entered now (i.e., really, to have been entered and now enjoyed) nor those who

---

67-80, 73), also mistakenly identifies this "Today" with the day of entry into rest, even though he is doing so in the context of a futuristic interpretation: "Heb. 4:8 speaks of another prophetic 'day.' This clearly is a period of time and is explained in 4:9 as the Sabbath rest."

35. Lane (*Hebrews 1–8*, 104-5) says it best: "The prophetic announcement of another day in which the *promise* of entering God's rest would be renewed" (emphasis mine).

36. Toussaint, "Warning Passages," 71.

37. Thomas K. Oberholtzer, "The Kingdom Rest in Hebrews 3:1–4:13," *Bib Sac* 145 (1988): 185-96, especially 192.

38. G. K. Beale, "Eschatology," in *The Dictionary of the Later New Testament and Its Developments*, ed. R. P. Martin and P. H. Davids (Downers Grove: InterVarsity Press, 1997), 334-35. The aorist in Heb. 4:10 ("has rested") is seen then as akin to the "Hebrew prophetic perfect." Scholer (*Proleptic Priests*, 202-3) also strongly argues against identifying current access to God with the "rest" that shall be entered, as well as against the paradox that the "'rest' is entered, but yet will somehow still be entered into."

39. Thus Barrett, "Eschatology," 372: "The 'rest' is and remains a promise, which some of the readers of the Epistle may fail through disobedience to achieve (iv.1) and all are exhorted to strive to enter. The 'rest', precisely because it is God's, is both present and future; men enter it, and must strive to enter it. This is paradoxical, but it is a paradox which Hebrews shares with all primitive Christian eschatology."

put that entrance off to a distant future capture the author's vivid eschatology and rhetorical strategy. It is at this point that some adjudication may be brought to bear on these various positions, beginning with the proponents of this last position. Lincoln writes, for example, concerning "the fact that those who by faith already enter rest (4:3) need at the same time to be exhorted to strive to enter that rest (4:11)."[40] This reflects the tendency to read the present tense of εἰσερχόμεθα more as a perfect tense ("*already* enter," the adverb being supplied interpretatively by Lincoln, expressing a completed state) rather than a progressive action, an "entering" currently in progress.[41] Those who claim to take this verb as a "true present" lean more toward taking it truly as a "perfect." If believers presently occupy the "rest" of which the author speaks, he should have used a perfect tense for "enter" — "we who believe *have entered,* and thus are in, that rest." It is unlikely that the excellent Greek writer who composed Hebrews would be imprecise in his choice of a verb tense.

A better way of interpreting the verb as a "true present" would be to highlight its progressive or continuous aspect, something as integral to the Greek "present" as "time of action." Such a reading allows the verse to impact the hearers with all the immediacy that the author desires, while at the same time not violating the future aspects of entering that rest that are so clearly indicated in the surrounding context. Thus, "we who believe are entering that rest," that is, we are crossing that threshold into the "better" promised land.[42] But we

---

40. "Sabbath," 206.

41. A certain lack of precision in translation at 12:22 also contributes to the sense that the believers are further along than the author claims they are. Consider the following: "This rest has already become a reality for those who believe. . . . the readers can be told that already 'you *have* come to Mount Zion and to the city of the living God'" (Lincoln, "Sabbath," 210; emphasis original); "It can also be said that Christians in their conversion have come to this city" (Barrett, "Eschatology," 376). Both scholars do not recognize the careful distinctions between προσέρχεσθαι, εἰσέρχεσθαι, and the simple ἔρχεσθαι (see especially Scholer, *Proleptic Priests,* passim) observed by the author of Hebrews. Christians can be said "to have come *near*" this city or "to have approached" this city, but it remains for them to "enter" the city. Lincoln and Barrett translate *proselēlythate* as if it were simply *elēlythate:* the author stresses that the addressees "have drawn near," not that they "have come" in the sense of "have arrived."

42. Thus, rightly, Attridge, *Hebrews,* 126: "This verb should not be taken simply as a futuristic present, referring only to the eschaton or to the individual's entry to the divine realm at death, but as a reference to the complex process on which 'believers' are even now engaged, although this process will certainly have an eschatological consummation." Similarly, see Hugh Montefiore, *A Commentary on the Epistle to the Hebrews* (New York: Harper, 1964), 83: "The Greek text means neither that they are certain to enter, nor that they will enter, but that they are already in the process of entering." Both of these authors capture the nuance of the Greek present as well as the rhetorical force of the author's vivid expression, underscoring their current movement through the process of entering toward the end of that threshold experience.

must still "strive earnestly to enter" since wavering on the threshold can still prove disastrous as it had in the past (4:11).

Lincoln comes very close to this insight at one point in his article, but unfortunately does not allow it to refine his interpretation: "In Numbers 14 the wilderness generation are not in the midst of their wanderings but stand on the verge of entry into the promised land, having arrived at the goal of their pilgrimage. It is this that provides the comparison with the New Testament people of God. Both groups stand directly before the fulfillment of God's promise."[43] All of this is quite precise and correct save for the phrase "having arrived at the goal of their pilgrimage." The reader of Number 14, and all the more the reader of Hebrews 3:7-19, understands that to stand on *this* side of the Promised Land is not to have yet arrived. The fact that the wilderness generation does not in fact enter, but falls short of the goal of their pilgrimage, makes this abundantly clear. This is the point of comparison with the addressees of Hebrews. Like the wilderness generation, they stand at the threshold of the goal of their pilgrimage and must now act so as to embody that trust and obedience that does achieve the promised goal.

Strategically, the author of Hebrews consistently places the hearers at the threshold of entering their great reward (see also 10:19-23, 35-39), assuring them of its present *reality,* to be sure, since this is what "trust" or "faith" grasps,[44] but not of its present availability except as the addressees continue to move forward in their commitment to Jesus, forward against society's pressures to desist, forward across that threshold into everlasting honor, enfranchisement, and blessedness. They are moving across the very threshold, and need only move forward to enter, and this is precisely the ideological device the author uses to convince them that moving forward is indeed the best course of action (rather than "shrinking back" and blending in again with the surrounding culture). Thus in the face of the unbelieving society's shaming and deviancy-control techniques, it remains necessary to "strive earnestly to enter that rest" (4:11) rather than fall short at the very threshold.

The second question concerns the nature of this "rest" that is "being entered" and which the addressees "strive to enter." The options are closely related, as might be expected, to the position one takes on the "time" of entering. Thus Stedman, who regards the rest as a present state enjoyed by believers, identifies the "rest" as "the rest of justification and salvation," the rest that ceases to gain salvation by works and accepts it as God's gracious gift.[45]

---

43. Lincoln, "Sabbath," 211.

44. Hence rightly Barrett ("Eschatology, 381), who defines faith as "a present grasp on invisible truth," but not in the way that Barrett and Lincoln develop this observation to turn "present grasp" into "present enjoyment."

45. Stedman, *Hebrews,* 52, 56, 58-59. Although Lincoln does not think this is the

Toussaint lists several expositors who speak of this rest as "the present Christian experience of peace."[46] We have shown above, however, that the author does not conceive of "rest" as something the addressees have entered, but rather something they are currently in the process of entering, and at which they will arrive if they persevere in this process.

One prominent interpretation found among those who favor the view that the "rest" is still something future, something yet to be finally entered and enjoyed, is that the "rest" refers to the millennial kingdom. Walter Kaiser championed this view in a 1973 article. Beginning with an interpretation of the enthronement psalms (including Ps. 95, from which the author of Hebrews derived the terminology of "rest") as announcements of the eschatological reign of God on this earth, he argues that "the writer [of Hebrews] has no more intention of severing the physical and spiritual aspects of this rest than he has of isolating the promise of the geographical land of Canaan from the spiritual and material aspects of the kingdom of God."[47] He goes on to link (one might say by *gezera shawa*) Hebrews 9:15 and 11:9 in an attempt to prove that the "promise of an eternal inheritance" is the same as "the firm possession of the land."[48]

---

meaning of the "rest" in Hebrews, he does draw a similar practical application of Heb. 4:1-11 ("Sabbath," 215): "In fact the Sabbath keeping now demanded is the cessation from reliance on one's own works (Heb 4:9, 10)." This is a blatant introjection of the old "faith" versus "works" dichotomy (one that is itself in need of nuancing in light of the recognition that Paul opposes not "good works" but "works of Torah" in the sense of ethnic-boundary-maintaining marks) into Hebrews. Toussaint ("Warning Passages," 72) insightfully shows the problem with this line of interpretation or application, namely that "resting from reliance on works" or "fleshly strivings" is in view: "The clear implication of the faith-rest view is that God's works were bad! In other words, the viewpoint which takes this passage as referring to the Christian's intimate walk with God and the peace which results from it enjoins the Christian to cease from his law-works, his striving, his fleshly labors, and simply to trust in God. If the parallel is carried out in 4:10, then God's works [the object of comparison] were also carnal and fleshly strivings." The possibility that 4:10 is a veiled reference to Jesus, who alone has "rested from his works" by completing his priestly ministry once-for-all (see 10:11-14), if it could be shown to be a probability, would also work counter to such "faith" versus "works" readings. Oberholtzer ("Kingdom Rest," 193) offers a much better interpretation of the "works" in view in 4:10: "The readers' entrance into rest depends on faithful perseverance (i.e., completed works), for the writer linked God's creation work with that offered to Israel (vv. 3-5). God's rest on the seventh day of creation (Gen 2:2-3) is cited in Heb. 4:4. As Elohim rested after completing His creation works, so this rest is offered to readers of Hebrews who complete their works (4:10). Their entrance into rest is conditioned on faithful endurance (3:6, 12, 14, 19; 4:1, 2, 6, 10-11). The Exodus generation failed to complete their works of obedience and to possess the land, thus forfeiting His rest (4:5-6)."

46. Toussaint, "Warning Passages," 71.

47. Walter C. Kaiser, Jr., "The Promise Theme and the Theology of Rest," *Bib Sac* 130 (1973): 135-50, 146.

48. Kaiser, "Promise Theme," 149.

Because of this focus on the "geographical land" and "firm possession of the land [Canaan]," Kaiser considers the "final realization" of rest to be "that millennial reign of the world's new sabbath."[49]

Stanley Toussaint builds appreciatively on the work of Kaiser in a 1982 article promoting the same reading of "rest" as the millennial, terrestrial kingdom. He finds "three 'rests'" in Hebrews 4:1-11: "First, there is God's cessation from His creation work. This rest will be manifested in the kingdom age when redeemed humankind enters His inheritance. The second rest was Israel's conquest and possession of the promised land under Joshua. This is a picture of the kingdom rest. The third rest is the promised rest which actually is God's rest which comes to man in the millennium."[50] Toussaint accepts Kaiser's reading of the enthronement psalms as "clearly eschatological" and as anticipating "the rule of the Lord on this planet": "the 'rest' of Psalm 95 must therefore anticipate the millennium. . . . Buchanan asserts that the Epistle to the Hebrews is so steeped in the OT that the concept of rest cannot be limited to a spiritual interpretation but must include national and earthly concepts; in fact, he feels that any other interpretation is inconsistent."[51] Since, then, the "rest" of Psalm 95 spoke of inhabiting the land of Canaan, "the promised rest can scarcely be divorced from settlement in the land."[52] Like Kaiser, he appeals to the example of Abraham in Hebrews 11 for corroboration: "What the reward involves is stated more clearly in 10:36. It consists of receiving 'what was promised.' The Greek literally says 'the promise.' The verb used in this verse is used with the promise in 11:13 and 39. This can hardly be accidental. In both of the occurrences in chap. 11 this vocabulary anticipates the millennium. The promise then looks ahead to life in Christ's earthly kingdom."[53]

---

49. Kaiser, "Promise Theme," 149.

50. Toussaint, "Warning Passages," 74.

51. Toussaint, "Warning Passages," 73; the reference is to G. W. Buchanan, *To the Hebrews* (AB; Garden City: Doubleday, 1972), 64-65, 72-73.

52. Toussaint, "Warning Passages," 73. Kaiser and Toussaint both assume that if Ps. 95 speaks of God's rule "on this planet," the author of Hebrews must read the psalm in this way. The author of Hebrews, however, has the benefit of looking back on the revelation of God in Christ, and reading those ancient psalms in light of Jesus' manifestation (hence his Christocentric reading of "royal" Pss. 2 and 110, a reading inaugurated by Jesus himself in Mark 12:36-37). There is a much deeper ideological issue, however, concerning whether or not an NT reading of an OT passage can be "true" without reflecting the "authorial intent" of the OT writer. Hebrews 1:1-2 suggests to me that the Christ-event brings a new order and light to those "many pieces and many manners" of God's earlier revelation.

53. Toussaint, "Warning Passages," 79. Toussaint ("Warning Passages," 74) also appeals to the "idea of a Sabbath day being the millennial age," which he correctly says "is no recent, innovative interpretation. It dates back at least to the Epistle of Barnabas in the early second century." Barrett ("Eschatology," 369-71, 373) had already demonstrated, however, the vital differences between Hebrews and Barnabas on this *sabbatismos* — the two authors are simply

I find this reading to be overly bound to a small piece of this transitory, shakable world. Certain doctrinal systems (notably dispensationalism) insist upon a renewed rest in Canaan/Palestine and even a millennial kingdom of Christ centered in Jerusalem, but this is not a concept invoked by the author of Hebrews, who, rather, calls attention consistently away from any such geographic and nationalistic conception of the believers' destiny. He does not show interest in any inheritance in the material world. First, the author does not himself see "three 'rests'" in his passage. He specifically disallows that the conquest of Canaan merited the label "rest" in his past, contrary-to-fact conditional statement in 4:8 ("If Joshua had given them rest, he [God "speaking through David"] would not have spoken concerning another [rest] after these days").[54] Moreover, the author's location of "God's rest" prior to and beyond human history in the creation story distinguishes this particular "rest" from the many OT references to "God's resting place" in the Temple in Jerusalem or in "the land" of Canaan.[55]

As we have already seen, the author's cosmology and eschatology in the other parts of this sermon do not at any point focus on an interim, terrestrial kingdom. Rather, he calls attention consistently to the divine realm that exists now beyond "this creation" and that shall be opened to the believers at the conclusion of their pilgrimage (namely at the second coming, which the author takes to be "yet a very little while," 10:37). Buchanan's observation concerning the author being "steeped in the OT" is not remotely persuasive: Philo was equally "steeped in the OT," and was also quite content to read it in a nonnationalistic and nonearthly direction. Paul, similarly "steeped in the OT," also looks forward to the passing away of the visible, temporary things, setting his heart wholly on the "unseen," "eternal" things (4:16-18) where the believer shall enjoy the "eternal weight of honor" and

---

worlds apart (no pun intended). Just because the view is old does not mean that the view is that espoused by the author of Hebrews, and Toussaint does nothing at this point to build up the connections that Barrett had dissolved. The "millennial age" is also not the only interpretation of the eschatological "sabbath" in the centuries around the turn of the era, most of which focus more simply on "the age to come," which, taken into a Pauline Christian framework at least, would point to the "new heavens and new earth" rather than the interim kingdom of the millennial sort at the end of "this age." See *Vita Adae* 51.2; *Apoc. Mos.* 43.3 *Gen. R.* 17:5; *Tamid* 7.4. This topic is discussed in Andrew T. Lincoln, "Sabbath, Rest, and Eschatology in the New Testament," pp. 197-220 in D. A. Carson (ed.), *From Sabbath to Lord's Day* (Grand Rapids: Zondervan, 1982), 199-200; Barrett, "Eschatology," 371.

54. Thus Lincoln, "Sabbath, Rest, and Eschatology," 207; Lane, *Hebrews 1–8*, 101; Attridge, *Hebrews*, 130.

55. So Barrett, "Eschatology," 367: "The 'rest' was the rest of the seventh day, the Sabbath; a rest always available since God had prepared it and himself entered upon it, but never in the days before Christ entered by human beings (as the Psalm proves)."

"citizenship in heaven" (Phil. 3:21) accrued through the endurance of temporary suffering. It is possible for the author of Hebrews, therefore, also to be "steeped in the OT" without showing interest in the things of "this planet."

That the author is in fact not looking ahead to a future, temporary kingdom in the land of Palestine emerges rather clearly from his treatment of Abraham and the patriarchs, ironically the example both Toussaint and Kaiser invoke to press for an identification of "promise" and "Palestine." Abraham dwelt in Canaan, the "promised land," as a sojourner precisely because he knew he was looking not for any earthly region as his abiding dwelling place, but rather for the heavenly homeland (11:13-16). The author of Hebrews looks at the way Abraham referred to himself as a stranger and sojourner even after he arrived within the boundaries of Canaan (Gen. 23:4). Abraham did not consider Canaan to be his "home" but was looking for a better homeland, specifically looking beyond an earthly homeland to the heavenly, abiding homeland as the true object of God's promise to him and to his children. The promise to Abraham is being redefined in Hebrews 11:13-16: it is no longer an inheritance in the land of Canaan but an inheritance in the eternal realm.[56] The description of this goal as a "city having foundations, whose architect and builder is God" (11:10) again points away from the earthly Jerusalem, ravaged by Nebuchadnezzar, Antiochus IV, and then by the Roman occupying forces, to the "heavenly Jerusalem," which *2 Baruch* 4.1-7 significantly claims God revealed to Abraham.[57] Within the material realm is "no lasting city," and so the believers, together with Abraham, are looking for the "city that is coming" (Heb. 13:14), and that is not part of this shakable creation. The author thus draws the gaze of Abraham, together with the gaze of the addressees, away from the "land of promise" *qua* Canaan toward the "heavenly country" as the true and final destination of pilgrimage. The patriarchs understood, so the author of Hebrews at least believes, God's promise to be something better than a land in this temporary creation.

Within the articles of both Toussaint and Oberholtzer[58] lie the seeds of a

---

56. This is a crucial point missed by both Kaiser and Toussaint, who effectively import the old content of the promise into the uses of this term in Hebrews without acknowledging how the author of Hebrews has changed and reinterpreted (indeed, magnified) that promise.

57. Of course, Rev. 21 is the most famous Christian text speaking of this heavenly Zion "coming down from heaven." Noteworthy is the fact that, even in Revelation's sequence of events, this city does not appear until the interim, millennial kingdom is finished, the final eschatological battle won, and the present creation replaced by the "new heavens and new earth." That is, the city does not belong to the present, transient age, while the millennium does.

58. T. K. Oberholtzer has also attempted to support a "millennial" reading for this "rest." He prefaces the first article in his five-article series with the following claim: "Walking in obedience to His Word today will result in rewards in the coming millennial rule of Jesus

better interpretation of the meaning of this "rest." At the close of his article, Toussaint quotes Hewitt, without noticing how the quotation actually works against his case: "Hewitt affirms, 'At the second advent of Jesus Christ, just as the material and transitory will disappear and the eternal and permanent will remain, so what is false and vile will be revealed in the fire of God's holiness and those whose characters are such will be consumed by the fire of His judgment.'"[59] Hewitt accurately describes the eschatological vision of Hebrews, but in this vision there is no room for the transient, time-bound, "millennial kingdom." Such a kingdom belongs to this age, not the age to come; it exists at the same time as the "material and transitory" realm before the manifestation of the "eternal and permanent," at least in the chronological scheme of Revelation 20–21.

Similarly, Oberholtzer himself will say: "Though creation will perish like an old garment or rolled-up mantle, the Son will remain; his years do not end (Heb. 1:10-12). These comparisons point to the eschaton, when the final trans-

---

Christ. The book of Hebrews emphasizes the importance of believers living with a view to future service in the Lord's millennial kingdom" (Oberholtzer, "Warning Passages," 83). Oberholtzer limits the scope of the discussion to participation or nonparticipation in the millennial kingdom mainly because questions of "eternal salvation" have to be bracketed somehow from any discussion of the warning passages in Hebrews, lest the doctrine of eternal security (and the conviction that "believing" in Jesus at any one point in one's life settles the question of one's eternal destiny) be jeopardized. This becomes explicit in T. K. Oberholtzer, "The Thorn-Infested Ground in Hebrews 6:4-12," *Bib Sac* 145 (1988): 319-28, especially 326.

After noting correctly that "eternal salvation is not in view in Num. 14 [and] Ps. 95," he makes a problematic leap when he simply assumes (rather than demonstrates) that the same is true for Heb. 3–4. Based on this assumption, he arrives at the thesis statement that will run throughout the five articles like a refrain: "the principle is that disobedience by the people of God may result in temporal judgment and loss of future blessing" (Oberholtzer, "Eschatological Salvation," 188). If we are to bracket entrance into "heaven" or whatever describes the "eternal" state of believers, all that is left to consider as relevant in Hebrews is the millennial kingdom.

With regard to Num. 14 and Ps. 95, "eternal salvation" is not in view simply because otherworldly retribution (either good or ill) is not present in the earlier strata of the OT. Rather, such concepts await the exilic and especially the postexilic periods to be developed. Just because Num. 14 did not speak of the "eternal damnation" of the wilderness generation (nor, we should add, of their "eternal salvation" despite their "temporal judgment"), it does not follow that the author of Hebrews also does not speak of "eternal salvation" or its opposite. Such a move is all the more tenuous in light of the fact that the author of Hebrews consistently looks at the content of OT cult and story as temporal, material, this-worldly figures and types for eternal, heavenly (in the sense of "belonging to the divine realm") realities extant beyond "this creation," that is, for "ultimate" things.

59. Thomas Hewitt, *The Epistle to the Hebrews* (Grand Rapids: Eerdmans, 1960), 204, cited in Toussaint, "Warning Passages," 80.

formation of all things will occur (Isa. 66:22; Heb. 12:26-27; Rev. 6:14; 21:1). The universe, seemingly so permanent and established, will be rolled up, changed, and replaced by new heavens and a new earth." If this is the topic of Hebrews 12:26-27 (and I agree that it is), how can the "unshakable kingdom," which appears only after the removal of the visible cosmos, be the millennial kingdom, which is a transitory, this-worldly, penultimate state of affairs *before* the transformation of the cosmos?

It is, therefore, an unfortunate mistake to import the millennial kingdom into Hebrews as an interpretive device, one that distracts us from how the sermon as a whole leads the addressees to understand the "rest" that lies open before them, that they are in fact in the process of entering, and that they must continue to strive to enter. How the author of Hebrews conceives of "entering that rest," and what that "rest" itself is, would be best discovered by looking at other passages in Hebrews in which "entering" happens, and other descriptions of the destiny of the believers who persevere toward the reception of God's promised benefits. If we follow this path, we find that the "many sons and daughters" are being led to "glory," following the path of Jesus, their "pioneer" (2:10); we find Jesus entering the heavenly holy places specifically as "our forerunner" (6:19-20); we find believers prepared by Jesus' sacrifice and priestly mediation "for the entrance into the holy places" (10:19), being called to "draw near" in the direction of that procession into the better temple that is "not of this creation" (9:11). We find ourselves following Jesus in the "race set before us," a race that ended for him "at the right hand of God" (and, presumably, for us in the same real presence of God; 12:1-2).[60] We find believers "approaching" the place where the heavenly hosts and perfected righteous worship God in festal song, approaching the "city of the living God" (12:21-24), to enter after the eschatological "shaking" of the earth and heavens of this created order.[61]

---

60. It is possible that 4:10-11 also points in the direction of the believers following Jesus into this rest, just as they (we) follow Jesus into glory, into the heavenly tabernacle, and so forth. See commentary on 4:10 below.

61. This approach to the question has been helpfully and correctly taken by Lincoln ("Sabbath"), 209, "The writer of Hebrews views 'rest' as an eschatological resting place with associations with the heavenly promised land, the heavenly Jerusalem, and the heavenly sanctuary," and more completely by Attridge (*Hebrews*, 126-28). Attridge places 4:1-11 in the context of "4:16; 6:1; 10:22; 12:18, where various aspects of the believer's movement into the divine presence are mentioned" and makes the crucial connection between Jesus' trajectory and the addressees' trajectory (if they remain faithful): "It is important to note the correlation between such soteriological themes and the author's christology. The Christians' 'entry into rest' parallels Christ's entry into the divine presence and in fact their entry is made possible by his. . . . It is the process of entry into God's presence, the heavenly homeland (11:16), the unshakeable kingdom (12:28), begun at baptism (10:22) and consummated as a whole eschatologically" (*Hebrews*, 128).

In such a context, "entering the rest" can be no other than entering that divine realm. The rest that God enjoys, which is specifically the rest into which the loyal believer will be inducted, is not the land of Canaan, and it is not certainly Canaan that Jesus entered as a "forerunner for us." God's rest is in the realm beyond "this creation," as is the city and homeland for which, according to Hebrews, the patriarchs themselves were seeking even as they dwelt in the midst of Canaan. Far from invoking, then, the notion of an intermediate, transitory, earthly kingdom of Jesus as part of the believers' reward, the author of Hebrews is concerned throughout with entrance into "glory," into the place "behind the curtain," into the "unshakable kingdom," into the "abiding" and "coming city" that exists beyond any earthly locale like Canaan and that sees the ongoing festal liturgy of angels and the perfected righteous, indeed, into the "holy places." The precise locale of all these destinations, which are really one and the same destination, is defined by Jesus' own itinerary:

> And he leads his children on
> To the place where He has gone.

Entering God's "rest," then, is another image for the goal the author has set before the addressees from the beginning of the sermon. Inheriting "salvation" (1:14) and being led to "glory" (2:10) are conceptual synonyms, and the author will add to this repertoire as the sermon continues — entering "the inner side of the curtain" (6:20), that is, the inner sanctum of the heavenly Temple, arriving at the "better, heavenly homeland" (11:16) and the "city which is to come" (13:14), and receiving the "unshakable kingdom" (12:28) after the material, visible creation is removed. "Rest" is not yet the believers' possession, as if they "have entered" that rest. Rather, the author at the same time affirms that they "are entering" that rest (4:3) and urges them to "strive earnestly to enter that rest" (4:11) rather than fall short at the very threshold.

The addressees have enjoyed the same promise as the wilderness generation, namely, having a message of deliverance[62] proclaimed to them. That word

---

62. The verb εὐαγγελίζω frequently appears in Isaiah, for example, when he is announcing the promise of God's deliverance. The verb and related noun form were also used prominently in Greco-Roman literature to speak of the accession of an emperor or other such "good news." It is therefore unnecessary, indeed misleading, to assume that the word must have a technical meaning for "the proclamation of the Christian message," as Stedman (*Hebrews*, 54, 56-57 and notes; see also 121-22 on Enoch) does. He claims that before Christ people were saved on the basis of their belief in the "redemptive provisions that pointed later to Christ," which is an indefensible stretch grounded in the assumption that εὐαγγελίζω must mean "I preach the gospel about Christ" rather than "I proclaim good news." There is another solution to the statement that the "gospel" was preached to the wilderness generation just as it was to the Christian addressees of Hebrews and to us as well. The gospel fundamentally effects trust in and obedience to God. It is not necessary to demand faith in Jesus for

"did not benefit" the first hearers, and there is a danger that it will not benefit some of these hearers, hence the warning of 4:1. The word of God failed to benefit the wilderness generation because the majority of them were "not joined in faith with those who harkened." Joshua and Caleb were certainly people who "harkened" to, that is, "heard" in a deeper sense, the promise of God. Since the other Hebrews did not take their side and trust in God, they failed to enter the land with these two heroes of faith. Harold Attridge suggests, however, that the author, who identifies the hearers in the next verse as "those who trust," has the addressees in mind in 4:2 as well. That is to say, the wilderness generation failed to enter because they were not united by faith with the present generation of those who had received God's final revelation.[63] The claim in 11:39-40 that the many exemplars of faith from the pre-Christian era arrive at God's goal for his people only together with the church would tend to support this reading. Such a claim, whatever its significance for the metaphysics of God's economy of salvation, has immediate pastoral relevance, particularly for a congregation that has already suffered the loss of some members on account of the deprivation inflicted on the Christians by their host society. Attaining God's promised benefactions depends on "being unified" with the faithful clients of God, a solidarity effected by shared trust in God's word of promise. Remaining connected with the "people of God" is the prerequisite to receiving deliverance and the eternal inheritance (see the example of Moses in 11:24-26).

Hebrews 4:3 reinforces the centrality of "trust" as the quality that allows one to enter into the rest God has prepared, in opposition to the distrust manifested by the wilderness generation (3:12, 19) and which some of the addressees are in danger of showing. Those wavering in their commitment to God's promises out of concern for their neighbors' friendship may yet find themselves excluded from God's city because they "were not joined by trust with those who harkened" to God's word. At two crucial junctures (4:3; 10:39) the author identifies the hearers, together with himself, as "those who trust," or those who are "of trust." He wants the audience to set this virtue as the centrally defining value of their character since it is "trust" in the value and certainty of God's

---

those who came before the Son's incarnation. Indeed, simple trust and obedience were what the wilderness generation lacked, and simple trust and obedience are the virtues commended in the exemplars of faith in chapter 11. To go beyond this, as Stedman does, and insist that for their salvation they required a particular understanding of the proleptic nature of the things God was revealing seems a strange and perverse form of justification by gnosis. It goes well beyond the meaning of our author, as well as Paul's meaning in Gal. 3:8. When Abraham has the gospel preached to him in advance, the content of that gospel is given explicitly as "in thee all nations (i.e., the Gentiles as well as the Jews) shall be blessed." Stedman produces a level of required knowledge about God's future workings that simply goes beyond what Hebrews and Paul attribute to those who are "saved by faith" before the incarnation.

63. Attridge, *Hebrews*, 125-26.

promised gifts that will enable them to persevere in their commitment to Jesus (and thus to one another) rather than to "shrink back" from the implications of that commitment (10:37-39).

A rather difficult argument from Scripture follows, in which the author seeks to demonstrate that there does in fact "remain a . . . rest for the people of God" (4:9), providing a proof of the "reality" of their hope (3:14) and this promise from authoritative texts. "Rest" had in fact been identified with the land of Canaan in the Pentateuch. Deuteronomy 12:9-10 (LXX) reads: "you have not up till now come into the rest and into the inheritance which the Lord your God is giving you. And you will cross the Jordan and inhabit the land . . . and he will give you rest from all your enemies around you." The author will "prove," however, that this is not the ultimate "rest" for God's people. Psalm 95 describes this "rest" specifically as "God's" rest, leading the author to consider where God does in fact "rest." He uses the technique that would come to be named *gezera shawa* in rabbinic sources.[64] Psalm 95:9, 11 had used both the terms "works" and "rest" in close proximity, which takes the author to Genesis 2:2, when God rested after "his works were brought into being from the foundation of the cosmos" (4:3).

The logic of 4:3 requires a more minute examination, since the rest of the argument grows from this verse. The author claims that the addressees, who exhibit trust, are in fact the ones who are entering God's rest. Psalm 95:11 is quoted again as a proof of this claim: "as he says, 'as I swore in my wrath, "they [i.e., the wilderness generation] shall not enter my rest."'" The fact that God could say this, "despite the fact that his works had come into being from the time of the founding of the cosmos," will be the salient point. When did God rest? "He speaks somewhere concerning the seventh day thus: 'And God rested in the seventh day from all his works'" (4:4).[65] God's rest is not merely one of the works of creation but is rather specifically distinguished from created works by the author.[66] The fact that God can say through David that "they will not enter my rest" at a point in time so far removed from the "foundation of the world" suggests to the author that God's rest was not merely experienced on the seventh day of creation, but remains open for God's people to enter. If it remained open for the wilderness generation to enter — and the author assumes that it did, because they were excluded

---

64. Attridge (ibid., 129) points out that exegesis of one text by appealing to other texts sharing key terms was not exclusively a rabbinic procedure and was used already by Philo of Alexandria. This, together with the observation made earlier that *qal wahomer* represents the same mode of argumentation known in Roman argument as *a minore ad maius* and practiced by Greek and Latin orators alike, should guard against overstating "rabbinic" influences on this author.

65. The verbal connection between Psalm 95 and Gen. 2:2 is only possible based on the LXX text, where the words for "rest" in both texts are formed from the same root.

66. Thus, rightly, Lane, *Hebrews 1–8*, 99.

from it[67] — then it remains open for his audience to enter. Since this possibility remains, and those who first received the good news failed to enter because of disobedience, God appoints a new day, the "today" of the psalm, which extends the invitation to future generations of hearers.

This "today" raises a second point. The "rest" referred to by the psalm cannot refer merely to Canaan, the land that the people eventually entered under Joshua, since David speaks about the possibility of entering the rest after "so much time" (4:7). The author latches onto this chronological argument[68] as a means of refuting a more "natural" reading that the "rest" is Canaan (cf. Deut. 12:9-10). The fact that David speaks again of that "rest" long after Joshua had led the people into the land of Canaan acts as a "token" (*Rhet. Alex.* 1430a14-16), a fact that disproves the contrary argument.[69] The success of this argument depends, of course, on the success of 4:4-6, which seeks to establish that Psalm 95:11 necessarily implies that the "rest" remains open to the hearers and that the "today" announces an invitation to enter the eternal rest of God, which the wilderness generation missed (in addition to losing Canaan).

The author regards his case as proven as he announces in 4:9-10 that God's "sabbath observance" still remains open for God's people. In light of the introduction of Genesis 2:2, a text that becomes one prominent rationale for the Jewish observance of the sabbath (Exod. 20:9-11), the author gives "rest" the new name of "sabbath observance." The sabbath had been regarded as a type of the eschatological "rest," which would come after God's rule was established on earth but before the new creation. It was a symbol of the resurrection at the end of time (*Adam and Eve* 51.2-3) and also the millennial kingdom (*Barn.* 15.3-8).[70]

Paul Ellingworth cautions the reader, however, against assuming that the author of Hebrews is interested in such traditions, given his absolute silence on the question of the timing or order of eschatological events at this point.[71] Essentially in agreement with this point, William Lane reads the author's appeal to Genesis 2:2 as an affirmation "that the promised rest does not refer in the first instance to some future reality prepared for humanity, but has primary ref-

---

67. This is a topic of the "possible," which says that if one possibility of a pair of opposites exists, the other in the pair also exists (Aristotle *Rh.* 2.19.1): if it was possible for them to be excluded from the rest, it must have been possible for them to have entered the rest.

68. Spicq, *L'Épître aux Hébreux*, 1:365.

69. Ellingworth (*Hebrews*, 247) reads the appeal to Gen. 2:2 as essentially demonstrating the same fact — since this "rest" existed from creation itself, it cannot be simply identified with the land of Canaan.

70. *Barn.* 15 reads the six days of creation as a prophecy that after six thousand years of history the seventh millennium of Christ's kingdom would come; following that seventh millennium would come the first "day" of the new creation, which explains, in part, why Christians worship on the first day of the week (which he calls the "eighth" day of the week).

erence to God's own repose, which precedes and stands outside human history."[72] This accords with the observation that God's rest is to be distinguished from "works" of creation (4:3-4), and as somehow separate from these works. God's rest is none other than the unshakable kingdom, the divine realm where even now festal liturgies are performed by angels and the "spirits of the righteous made perfect" (12:22-24).[73] This rest already exists in the heavenly realm and only awaits the removal of the shakable, visible realm for it to become the present reality for the hearers as well. From their perspective (contra Lane) it remains a "future" experience, but for God and the inhabitants of the divine realm it is a present reality.

The next verse poses some intriguing exegetical problems. Hebrews 4:10 describes this "sabbath" with language that recontextualizes both Genesis 2:2 and Psalm 95:11: "for the one who enters into God's rest has himself rested from his works just as God [rested] from his own works" (4:10). In the history of interpretation, there are two principal ways of reading this verse. First, it describes in general terms the believer who experiences rest from his or her labors after entering God's rest. An obstacle to this would seem to be the aorist tense of the verb "rest." Since the hearers are being urged in the reader's next breath to "strive zealously to enter that rest" and not fall short of it like the Exodus generation, it would appear strange to use an aorist rather than a present or future tense: "the one who enters into God's rest *will* have rest from his or her labors." Paul Ellingworth, however, draws attention to the use of the aorist in "gnomic" sentences, that is to say, general proverbs or maximlike sayings. Hebrews 4:10 would certainly qualify as such a general truism (in form, at least). The tense of the verb would also be explicable if the author had a certain body of people in mind, for the author later voices the conviction that those who have been just toward God (i.e., responded to God's promises and commands as trusting and obedient clients) are already present to enjoy the liturgy around God's throne (12:22-24). Those "spirits of the perfected righteous" whom the hearer meets later at "Mount Zion" have themselves "rested" from their labors and entered the rest of God, namely, the abiding city, "heavenly Jerusalem, the city of the living God."

A second way to read the verse, however, is as a specific reference to Jesus.[74] The force of 4:9-10 would then be to affirm the possibility of enjoying this "sabbath observance" for God's people by pointing to the completed work

---

71. *Hebrews*, 249.

72. *Hebrews 1–8*, 99.

73. In light of Heb. 12:22-24, which presents what appears to be a present phenomenon to which the believer has "drawn near" in the local assembling of the church, I would be thus inclined to agree with Attridge (*Hebrews*, 131) when he insists on this rest as festive worship rather than mere inactivity.

74. See L. Sabourin, *Priesthood: A Comparative Study* (Leiden: Brill, 1973), 204; Vanhoye, *Structure*, 99-100.

of Jesus, which makes observance possible. This interpretation would give a foretaste of a topic that shall occupy 9:11–10:18 and would give the γὰρ its full force (something too often neglected) as a particle presenting a rationale for what precedes, thus completing an enthymeme — this sabbatical remains for God's people because the one who entered the divine realm has finished the work of consecrating his sisters and brothers for entrance themselves into that sacred observance. Would the larger context of the sermon support such a reading? Jesus has already been presented as the one who has arrived at the glory to which the many children are still being led. Later in the sermon, the author will speak of Jesus again as having arrived in that space which the believers would eventually occupy — specifically the inner chamber of the heavenly temple, naming Christ the "forerunner" for the hearers (6:19-20; his "entering" into the heavenly, abiding realm reappears in 9:12, 24-25). The fact that Jesus has ceased from his priestly labors is a climactic moment in the argument of 9:11–10:14. In contrast to the priests who stand about ministering and offering frequent sacrifices, Jesus "having offered one sacrifice for sins sat down forever at the right hand of God," waiting for the consummation (10:11-13). In this reading, then, the aorist tense as reference to past action takes on full significance (and the emphatic pronoun makes more sense as the author's way of highlighting the completion specifically of the work of the one man, Jesus). The strongest objection to such a reading is the author's elusiveness in naming this "one" as Jesus.[75] Nevertheless, the author has given the hearers sufficient information to read this verse plausibly as a reference to Jesus, their pioneer and enabler, and will continue to confirm such a reading as the sermon develops.

The hearers are then urged in 4:11 to strive to enter that same rest which Jesus had entered as a forerunner on their behalf (6:19-20), to press on to take hold of that "glory" into which the Son is leading them. The author thus returns to promoting directly what he hopes will become the overarching agenda for the hearers' lives — "striving to enter that rest." Investigation of ideological texture invites us to consider the "real world" references behind religious language. What does such "striving" actually look like in "real life"? After all, "entering that rest" lies beyond earthly experience. What is the author actually urging as he sets "striving to enter that rest" at the top of the day's agenda, as long as it is called "today"? He appears to urge his hearers to look out for their fellow believers, assisting one another to keep their eyes on the prize of trust and faithfulness so that "no one fall by the same pattern of disobedience." That is, they should engage in a campaign of ongoing mutual encouragement so that no brother's or sister's commitment is eroded by the persistent shame, loss, and hostility shown against the Christians. It involves continuing to identify with

---

75. Ellingworth, *Hebrews,* 257. Attridge (*Hebrews,* 131-32) is open to the possibility of a Christocentric reading.

the "people of God" through worship (10:25) and acts of love and service, especially to those members of the household of God who have been most marginalized by their non-Christian neighbors (6:9-10; 13:3). Striving to enter that rest, then, means an ongoing investment in maintaining the minority culture and the individual commitment of that group's members.

"Pattern" or "example of disobedience" introduces the element of shame to "failing to enter." Hebrews 3:12–4:11 has established that failing to attain God's promises points to a lack of virtue on the part of those who fail. A repetitive pattern has made two vices in particular stand out in this exhortation:

"They were unable to enter on account of distrust"
(οὐκ ἠδυνήθησαν εἰσελθεῖν δι᾽ ἀπιστίαν, 3:19)

"They did not enter on account of disobedience"
(εἰσῆλθον δι᾽ ἀπείθειαν, 4:6)

The wilderness generation did not show God the proper trust and obedience, which is certainly his due. In responding to God so basely, they became a pattern of censurable behavior rather than an example of praiseworthy behavior to be emulated. That is to say, they gained a disgraceful memory rather than an honorable one, such as continues to be enjoyed by those who exhibited trust and steadfastness toward God (11:1–12:2). It would therefore be a mark of shame for the hearers to fail to enter into God's rest, since it would reveal their own distrust and disobedience (motivated by the lack of two cardinal virtues, courage and justice). The author hopes that, by arousing shame especially in the hearts of the wavering,[76] they will be all the more motivated to remain committed to God's promise.

4:12-13

The exhortation from the negative example of the wilderness generation closes with a return to the contemplation of the power and significance of the word of God. It is a fitting, powerful conclusion to the first phase of this letter. All the while the audience's focus has been drawn back to the Son and to the God who speaks through the Son. Now once more the divine court of reputation is impressed upon the minds of the hearers as the ultimate, indeed, the sole, court of reputation with which they should be concerned. It is before the all-penetrating

---

76. Acts of vice, according to Aristotle (*Rh.* 2.6.3-4), should make one feel ashamed; it is very likely, therefore, that the author is incorporating an appeal to this emotion here as he warns the hearers against a course that exhibits cowardice (in the face of human foes, when one enjoys divine aid) and injustice (treating God's promises of protection and patronage lightly).

eyes of God that they are to live and make their decisions, and it is to God to whom they must "give account." As they deliberate, then, they again are reminded of the One who examines their motives and decisions, to whom they will have to explain their distrust and disobedience should they choose that most dangerous path:

> For the word of God is living and active, sharper than every double-edged sword, cleanly cleaving soul from spirit, joint from marrow, and discerning the thoughts and intentions of the heart. No creature is hidden before him, but all are naked with their throats laid bare to the eyes of him (γυμνὰ καὶ τετραχηλισμένα τοῖς ὀφθαλμοῖς αὐτοῦ) with whom is our account.

While this is often excerpted to serve as a doctrine of Scripture, in its present context it constitutes a final and climactic warning, providing the ultimate rationale (again, γὰρ connects this paragraph with the preceding verse) for accepting the author's proposal that "striving to enter God's rest" should occupy the first place in the hearers' minds and lives. The image is crafted to arouse the emotion of fear by creating an impression of imminent harm (Aristotle *Rh.* 2.5.1-2) about to befall those unprepared to give an acceptable account. It describes the "word of God," which encounters the hearers and to which they must respond obediently (1:1-4; 2:1-4; and, now, 3:7-11), as a fearsome force. The author uses a metaphor of comparison to capture the nature of this word: it is sharper than every two-edged sword and just as able to cut through our poor flesh (for by God's word, armies or crowds of people have fallen). The author employs the technique of vividness (Aristotle *Rh.* 3.11.2), giving to the inanimate "word" the animate qualities of being "living, active,"[77] and "discerning." God's word discerns the thoughts and intentions of the heart. Nothing is hidden; all is laid bare before God.

The image created by these verses is that of a defendant being hauled before a judge, whose eyes can penetrate into the depths of the soul, and therefore the guilt, of this defendant. The antithesis of 4:13a emphasizes the addressees' vulnerability before God's all-piercing scrutiny.[78] The author thus seeks to remove one

---

77. In so doing, our author follows the tradition of Wis. 18:15-16, which presents the word of God as a powerful and stern warrior wreaking havoc on his enemies. Revelation portrays the glorified Christ as having such a two-edged sword, representing the force of his word issuing from his mouth (1:16; 2:12; 19:15).

78. Hebrews resonates with both Greco-Roman and Jewish cultural knowledge about the complete exposure of human beings to God's scrutiny. *1 Enoch* 9:5 bears a particularly striking resemblance to Heb. 4:13: "all things are clear and unveiled before you" (πάντα ἐνώπιόν σου φανερὰ καὶ ἀκάλυπτα); see also Ps. 139:1-4, 11-16, 23-24. Attridge (*Hebrews*, 136 n. 48) points to Seneca *Ep.* 83.1-2; Epictetus *Diss.* 2.14.11; Marcus Aurelius *Med.* 12.2 for parallels in Stoic thought.

of the motives listed by Aristotle as incentives for wrongdoing, namely, thinking that an act will remain hidden or unpunished (*Rh.* 1.12.1). Moreover, the term τετραχηλισμένα, usually translated "laid bare" or "exposed," refers more fully to the condemned criminal whose throat is exposed to the executioner's blade. The author places the addressees before God naked with the throat pulled back (i.e., awaiting the stroke delivered by the word that is sharper than any two-edged sword) to reinforce his contention that distrust and disobedience toward God are really the greatest dangers facing the audience, and not the temporal concerns that have convinced a few that drawing back is advantageous. Hebrews 4:12-13 supports the author's exhortation to respond appropriately to God's word so that one's account will result in approval rather than judgment.

The author strategically juxtaposes this fearsome image of the danger of refusing God's benefits and falling under the condemnation of God as judge to an exhortation that appeals to the emotion of confidence and topics of safety, focusing on the favor obtained by Jesus the high priest (4:14-16). In effect, the author sets an image of God the Judge in 4:12-13 beside an image of God the Patron in 4:16. All that separates these two images, and all that enables one to stand before God as patron rather than as judge, is the brokerage, or mediation, of Jesus. To lose this mediation through falling away would be to lose access to God's throne as locus of favor and to gain access once more to God's throne as site of judgment and execution.

A Closer Look: The Divine Other and Sustaining Minority Cultural Values

When the majority of one's neighbors are dedicated to values different from one's own, and may even regard one's ambitions and priorities as foolish, one must either surrender one's values or find some way to offset the force of the majority's opinion. Many minority cultures in the Greco-Roman world accomplished this by focusing their adherents on the opinion and approval of God. Each of these groups believed that their values were in fact in line with what God valued, and that their priorities reflected God's priorities. Commitment to the values of a particular group, then, could be enhanced by affirming that those who fulfilled those values pleased God, while the majority of humanity, unaware of what God truly valued in God's creatures, lived out their whole lives displeasing God and pursuing what God hated or regarded as empty. If representatives of that majority culture would, from time to time, reproach the group members for their commitment to different values, the group members or their leaders could sustain commitment by saying, in effect, "The opinion of the uninitiated matters nothing. Remember the One whom you must please, whose approval matters for eternity."

God becomes the most important judge of one's honor or lack of honor since only his knowledge is complete and only his sanction matters beyond this life. Greco-Roman philosophers frequently appealed to this divine court as the ultimate sanction of the behavior and goals promoted by the particular philosophy, and the lever by which society's sanctions could be moved aside. Plato (*Gorg.* 526D-27A), for example, pits this conviction against Callicles' (the spokesperson for Greek society in this dialogue) assertion that failure to excel in rhetoric so as to be unable to defend oneself, one's friends, and one's kin in the law courts is a great disgrace and puts one in danger of grave dishonor:

> I consider how I shall present my soul whole and undefiled before the judge in that day. Renouncing the honours at which the world aims, I desire only to know the truth, and to live as well as I can, and, when I die, to die as well as I can. And, to the utmost of my power, I exhort all other men to do the same. And, in return for your exhortation of me, I exhort you also to take part in the great combat, which is the combat of life, and greater than every other earthly conflict. And I retort your reproach of me, and say that you will not be able to help yourself when the day of trial and judgement, of which I was speaking, comes upon you; you will go before the judge, the son of Aegina, and, when he has got you in his grip and is carrying you off, you will gape and your head will swim around, just as mine would in the courts of this world, and very likely someone will shamefully box you on the ears, and put upon you any sort of insult.

The verdict of a human court, whether the court of law or court of opinion, is not a matter of concern to Socrates (the speaker above), such that he should shape his life and mold his actions with a view to gaining its approval. Rather, he sets before Callicles a portrait of the court whose verdict and opinion does govern his life — the court of God. Indeed, the only disgrace that counts for him is the threat of disgrace before that court of reputation, and those who live with a view to human courts may find themselves in great danger before the divine court. For Plato's Socrates, honor before the divine court, which is eternal, is of greater value than honor before the human court of opinion, such that the latter is profitably renounced in order to concentrate undistractedly on how to attain the former.

The late first-century Stoic philosopher Epictetus (*Diss.* 1.30.1) advised his audience: "When you come into the presence of some prominent man, remember that Another looks from above on what is taking place, and that you must please Him rather than this man." The philosopher would be kept from violating his way of life for the sake of catering to the whims and expectations of the uninitiated by reminders such as this. Indeed, the omnipresence of God, and thus of God's constant watching of the individual, became a useful support for the promotion of complete integrity in life:

> It is within yourself that you bear Him, and do not perceive that you are defiling Him with impure thoughts and filthy actions. Yet in the presence of even an image of God you would not dare to do anything of the things you are now doing. But when God Himself is present within you, seeing and hearing everything, are you not ashamed to be thinking and doing such things as these, O insensible of your own nature, and object of God's wrath! (Epictetus *Diss.* 2.8.13-14)

Belief in a personal God who was involved in human affairs and would one day rise up in judgment of humankind allowed Jews and Christians alike to regard God as a significant other whose approval or disapproval could be earned and experienced. The recognition of God would be sufficient to assure the individual devotee to esteem herself or himself as a person of worth regardless of society's evaluation. The openness of all parts of a person's life to divine scrutiny is a familiar part of the Jewish tradition, perhaps reaching its highest expression in Psalm 139, which speaks of the impossibility of distance or darkness obscuring the sight of God, who sees his creatures even in their mothers' wombs. The wisdom tradition frequently returns to the topic of God's scrutiny: "the ways of a person are before the eyes of God, and God looks into all his or her paths" (Prov. 5:21).[79] One might be tempted to violate the norm of Torah if it were only a matter of escaping the notice and censure of the human court of opinion. However, God's ubiquitous witness to the deeds of human beings, and his announced intention to hold human beings accountable, makes this rather more dangerous.

So important was approval before God's court that a pious Jew might endure even the most severe degradation and abuse at the hands of human beings rather than win human approval at the cost of God's approval. The author of 2 Maccabees, for example, portrays the martyr Eleazar as regarding disgrace and pain before Antiochus's court of no consequence when set against dishonor and punishment before God's court: "Even if for the present I would avoid the punishment of mortals, yet whether I live or die I shall not escape the hands of the Almighty" (2 Macc. 6:26, RSV). Similarly, the author of 4 Maccabees sets "honor before God" (17:5) as the prize of those who endured tortures rather than violate the norms of the Jewish subculture, who had more regard for the wrath of God than the wrath of a human king (13:14-15).

Christian authors, sharing in this minority cultural rhetoric, also emphasize the importance of seeking God's approval, and use this goal as a motivator to preserve the values of the Christian culture. Paul, for example, stresses that he seeks to please (i.e., gain the approval of) God and not human beings (1 Thess. 2:4; Gal. 1:10). Not only the apostle and his team but every true follower of God's law acts so as to receive praise from God, not from other people (Rom. 2:29): "therefore we are ambitious, whether at home or away, to be pleasing to him, for it is necessary that we all appear before the judgment seat of Christ in order that each may be rewarded for the deeds done in the body, whether good or base" (2 Cor. 5:9-10). As that day of reward or censure becomes the focal point for the Christian, that person is more and more likely to seek to embody the norms of the group regardless of society's affirmation or disapproval.

The author of Hebrews shares this aspect of the common Jewish and Christian worldview, namely, that God is the final judge in whose sight one lives and with whose evaluation one must be ultimately concerned. This is grounded for the author of Hebrews not only in the future prospect of God's judgment of the world, but in the manifestation of Jesus as Son and Savior. Jesus' resurrection and exaltation proclaims not only the radical difference between God's evaluation and the world's, but also the ability of God's verdict to overturn the verdict of the lower court. Jesus, utterly humiliated in the estimation of the world by his shameful death on the cross (12:2), has been thought worthy by God of the highest honor. Jesus is thus named the "Son" of God (1:1-3), appointed by God to the dignity of "high priest after the order of Melchizedek" (5:4-6), and seated at the place of highest honor, at God's right hand (1:3), whence he awaits the subjection of all things (including his enemies, 1:13) under his feet (2:6-9). God's authority to overturn the verdict of society and power to enforce God's own evaluations of

---

79. See also Sir. 23:18-19 (RSV): "A man who breaks his marriage vows says to himself, 'Who sees me? Darkness surrounds me, . . . and no one sees me. Why should I fear? The Most High will not take notice of my sins.' His fear is confined to the eyes of human beings, and he does not realize that the eyes of the Lord are ten thousand times brighter than the sun; they look upon all the ways of human beings, and perceive even the hidden places"; "their ways are always before him, they will not be hidden from his eyes" (Sir. 17:15).

honor and disgrace elevate the divine opinion above all human courts of reputation (although, certainly, the believing community reflects the opinion of God and provides the visible counterpart to the divine court). Free from the limitations of physical beings, God becomes the sole significant other whose sight extends beyond the reach of human eyes. Distinctions between private and public are meaningless before the all-seeing eye of the creator (4:12-13), whose sight penetrates the deepest recesses of a person and holds all accountable. This same all-seeing God will not "forget" the deeds of which he approves, such as acts of love and mutual service within the community (6:9-10). The one who seeks God's approval will be reminded that this is one sure path to receive a positive evaluation of one's honor by God.

The author keeps God's approval in the forefront of his exhortation. When he asserts that it is necessary to trust God (11:6) in order to please him, he assumes that "pleasing God" is a goal firmly in place. Pleasing God appears again in 12:28 and 13:16 as the author commends reverent worship and, once again, sharing and mutual service as the way of life that receives God's approval. He closes the letter by commending the addressees to God in the hope that God will approve of them:

> Now may the God of peace who brought again from the dead our Lord Jesus, the great shepherd of the sheep, by the blood of the eternal covenant, equip you with everything good that you may do his will, working in you that which is pleasing in his sight, through Jesus Christ. (13:20-21)

Finally, the references in Hebrews to the last judgment, when God will make known the divine evaluation of all people and actions, call the audience's attention to the ultimate importance of God as significant other. The author urges his hearers to increase their work of mutual encouragement and good works — the works that please God and bring honor before the divine court — in light of the approach of the Great Assize, which is not depicted as remote but as an ever-nearer event on the horizon: "Let us consider how to stir up one another to love and good works, not neglecting to meet together, as is the habit of some, but encouraging one another, and all the more as you see the Day drawing near" (10:24-25, RSV). That day will be a day of reward and salvation (9:28) for those who have lived in the light of God's judgment and have sought to be pleasing to him. It will be a day in which, to borrow words from Paul, "each person will receive his or her commendation from God" (1 Cor. 4:5); it will also be a day of disgrace for those who are evaluated by God as worthy of punishment (cf. 10:29; 10:30-31) for their transgression of the norms and standards that God has established. From the author's point of view, fear of God's censure must outweigh fear of human society's censure since the effects of the former are so much greater and lasting. The image of divine judgment remains, thereby, a most powerful tool for strengthening commitment to group values over against society's values when these are in conflict.

Summary

The author dwells at some length on the failure of the wilderness generation in 3:7–4:11 because he wants the hearers to see themselves in a fully analogous situation. In effect, the exegesis and application of Psalm 95:7-11 serves to create a highly charged view of their own situation, a view that in itself invites continued investment in the minority culture. The audience has received promises of entering God's rest (4:2; as the sermon continues, the images of the better country, homeland, heavenly city, the inner sanctum of the heavenly tabernacle will also be applied to that "undiscovered country"). They, like the wilderness generation, are in the process of entering, are ready to take possession. The author places them at the same threshold moment in which the wilderness generation found themselves, but at which point the latter failed, to their irreversible disadvantage and lasting disgrace. Having the benefit of their example, that is, knowing now just how dangerous and how great a threat to honor and security both distrust and disobedience are, the addressees should be able to face their threshold moment successfully, to make the correct choice of moving forward in obedience and trust rather than quaking at the exaggerated force of the hostile sinners, who stand between them and God's rest and seek to divert them from attaining their inheritance and glory.

By making the choice to hold firm to their present grasp on God's promised gifts, the addressees can remain part of his house (3:6), enjoying the honor now that comes from being embedded in the head of that household, namely God, and enjoying the access to the help and favor that his own Son assures for his clients. They can remain "Christ's partners" (3:14), with the hope before them of sharing in the exaltation of the firstborn when they arrive at the promised "rest," "glory" itself. If such positive incentives are insufficient, the author is not reticent to remind the hearers of the dire consequences of refusing to remain loyal to the bond that the Son has formed between them and God at such cost to himself. How will they explain, as they give their account to the all-discerning God, their failure to persevere, when God himself stood ready to supply any assistance or support that they needed for their contest?

Bridging the Horizons

The author of Hebrews presents certain conditions for remaining part of God's household or partners with Christ (3:6, 14). While, on the one hand, this might contradict certain theologies that stress the absolute lack of conditions involved in our salvation, we should not, for the sake of such theological convictions, blunt the edge of these verses, which can certainly assist the believer to remain focused on Christ and his promises.[80] If we are to avoid "drifting away" (2:1),

---

80. The question of "eternal security" and the message of Hebrews will be discussed in the commentary on chapter 6, at the celebrated "problem passage" of 6:4-8.

then we must indeed "hold onto" (3:6, 14) something that will allow us to maintain a sure course or to keep our place at anchor in a strong tide. The preacher suggests that our "boldness," "the boast of hope," and the "first element of the reality" that faith expects form a threefold cord by which we are tethered to our eternal port. He urges us to continue to exercise confidence before God in prayer and in worship (cf. 4:14-16; 10:19-25), those liturgical and ritual acts that remind us where our true center is, and before other people as we tell others what God in Christ has done for us. Many believers are reticent to speak of the traces of God's hand in their lives, but in each one of them God has written a testimony to his goodness, reality, and dependability. This testimony is written not only for our benefit but for the encouragement of our fellow believers, and we would do well to nurture an atmosphere that encourages reflection on, and sharing of, those traces of God's favor in our midst. As we speak of God's help or guidance, his gifts become more of a reality not only to ourselves but to our conversation partners. In a culture that is heavily prejudiced against the intervention of God and the supernatural generally, such testimony becomes all the more essential to nourish trust and hope.

Holding onto our "boast," our claim to honor and basis for self-esteem, is equally vital. There are many arenas in which we may claim honor and accomplishment, but only if we hold onto the claim that derives from and is defined by our Christian hope will we remain on course in the way of discipleship. If we allow ourselves to be drawn into grounding our self-respect in, and asking for acknowledgment of our worth based on, possessions, finances, or any other worldly criteria, we will drift into double-mindedness and be hobbled in our efforts to walk after Christ. Finally, we have in our possession now the down payment or first installment of our future inheritance, and we are challenged to hold this secure until the end. Jesus expressed this situation using the imagery of seeds in different kinds of soil: in some soils the seed was nurtured until the end so that it bore great fruit, but in others the seed was choked out. The "installment" was not guarded against the onslaught of rival pursuits or ambitions. This "installment" or surety can take many forms: Heb 6:4-6 appears to present a variety of ways in which God can confirm the believer in his or her hope. The essential point is to value these experiences of God's power, presence, or voice so that they do not drift from our memories, and so that their impact does not fade over time.

As we read the Scriptures, listen in prayer, participate in worship, or converse with fellow seekers of God, God's voice speaks inwardly to us. The example of the wilderness generation and the call of the psalm elevate for us the importance of listening for that voice and, when it encounters us, valuing, trusting, and building on that word. The human "heart" — the core of our personality, the seat of our desires and will — is prone to several forces that threaten to undermine the call of God in our lives. We may distrust God's word and question the reality or value of God's promises given the availability of other promises from sources that often seen more real and accessible; we may wander in our hearts and be pulled off course to pursue other aims and desires; and we may be taken in by the "guile of sin," that is, lulled into thinking that this world and its pleasures and treasures are really what we ought to be striving for.

The preacher recognized that we will need the assistance of one another in order for our hearts to be "surely fixed where true joys are to be found" and in order for us to keep "striving to enter God's rest," which should be the overarching goal of our lives. We are urged to discover ways in which to keep one another's eyes firmly focused on our pioneer, Jesus, and our goal to walk as he walked and enter the rest he has entered. The cultural lie that "religion is a private matter" must be renounced in favor of honesty between sisters and brothers in Christ. For this to happen, of course, church leaders will need to nurture communities of healing rather than of judging and to teach congregations about the sanctity of knowledge shared among believers and the importance of not using such information wrongly. Wesley's "class meetings" were an admirable experiment in this vein. They brought together small bands of committed believers who helped one another remain true to the commitments they had set for themselves and encouraged one another to love what God commanded and to desire what God promised above all temporal distractions and criticism. The emergence of small group ministries in many churches, or "accountability groups" formed in conjunction with parachurch ministries, in many ways provides precisely the sort of support, focus, and assistance that the author of Hebrews sets before us as a necessity for completing our race. In addition to the formation of cell groups of the Christian family, the smaller cell group of one's own natural family can become a great resource for growth in discipleship. Parents and children frequently have the privilege of living under one roof for eighteen years, with, one hopes, frequent contact thereafter. If mutual nurture in the reading of Scriptures, in prayer, and in honest conversation about the relationship of this "faith" to the everyday concerns of life at every stage can become an intentional part of the rhythm of a family's week, God's natural provision for discipleship would be well used.[81]

---

81. The ancient Israelites certainly appreciated the role of parents as primary teachers of the faith and of its application to daily life. What is arguably the core text of Judaism, the *Shema,* commands the hearers to "recite [God's commandments] to your children and talk about them when you are at home and when you are away, when you lie down and when you rise" (Deut. 6:7, NRSV). 4 Maccabees, written during the first century A.D., tells of the commitment to God and Torah shown by seven young brothers, who endured torture to the point of death rather than give up their place in God's favor and their hope for a welcome in God's kingdom. The source of such grounding in the faith was none other than the education given them by their parents (see 4 Macc. 18:9b-19).

Finally, the preacher would remind us of the one to whom, ultimately, we are accountable. Using the image of the word of God as a two-edged sword, he reminds us that it does indeed "cut both ways." It is a word of promise to the trusting and persevering; it is a pronouncement of judgment to those who do not trust God or who choose the lesser promises of the world and sin over God's benefactions. Hebrews 4:12-13 can provide a word of liberation to believers, for in drawing their attention to the God to whom alone they must render an account, the text also proclaims their liberty from all other pretenders to the throne of the Judge. Not the standards or expectations of parents and secular peers, not the prejudices we are taught from birth, not the standards of living promoted in advertisements and shopping malls (those modern Meccas), but God's values and vision alone claim our allegiance. Again this can assist us to keep our focus as we seek to order our thoughts, our steps, and our ambitions so as to be found pleasing to him, "with whom is our account."

Jesus, Our Guarantor of God's Favor: 4:14–5:10

Overview

Having raised the stark image of standing completely vulnerable before God's all-piercing word and all-seeing eye, the author turns immediately to an exhortation to hold onto the favor of God that Jesus the mediator *par excellence* has made available. The addressees should regard the friendship of Jesus and the access to God's help he provides as all the more desirable, even essential, after the warnings and images of 3:7–4:13. As long as the hearers "hold fast the confession," that is, the Christian view of reality and the hopes and values it articulates, they enjoy the mediation of a sympathetic yet completely effective high priest in heaven (thus returning in earnest to the theme announced in 2:17-18). Whatever trials they find themselves in, they are assured that God will be favorably disposed to provide them with the "favor for timely help" (4:16) that will enable them to persevere unto their goal.

This exhortation provides an introduction to the central topic of the sermon, namely, the quality and effectiveness of Jesus' mediation. The author signals the limits of this central section by crafting an impressively rich *inclusio* between 4:14-16 and 10:19-23, underscoring also the importance of these exhortations in the program of the author for his audience. The correspondences, laid out to show verbal correspondences in the Greek, are as follows:[1]

---

1. See Nauck, "Zum Aufbau des Hebräerbriefes," 200-203; Guthrie, *Structure of Hebrews*, 79-80.

4:14-16	10:19-23
Having, therefore, a great high priest	Having, therefore, . . . a great priest
Jesus	[through the blood of] Jesus
[the Son] of God	[the house] of God
let us hold onto the confession	let us hold onto the confession
let us draw near	Let us draw near
with boldness	[since we have] boldness

Within these verbal brackets stands the "long and difficult word" (5:11) about the heavenly rites performed by the "great high priest" and the significance of these rites for "those who approach God through him" (7:25). Since Jesus' priestly ministry is the basis of the Christian's standing before God as well as the inauguration of the new covenant, the author will give much attention and space to developing what that ministry looks like and how it surpasses all previous channels of access to God. This central exposition is essentially an amplification of the value of Jesus' mediation, which serves the purpose of making the hearers aware of how specially favored they are and how unthinkable it would be to give up such advantages for the sake of temporary gain or release from temporary hardships. The magnitude of the gift Jesus provides makes the injustice and cowardice of defection from the Christian community (or merely the hiding of one's bold association with this group and its hope) all the more pronounced and disgraceful.

The exposition that begins in 5:1-10, which announces the topic of a "high priest after the order of Melchizedek," might well have led directly to 7:1-28, where that topic is specifically developed. 5:11–6:20, however, will interrupt this development for the sake of tilling the soil of the addressees' hearts, preparing them to "hear" the argument of 7:1–10:18 more attentively and advantageously and to respond as the author would like.

Commentary

4:14-16

Jesus appears now a second time as "high priest," the title that closed the first section of the sermon (2:17) and opened the second section (3:1). The author will now begin to treat directly the advantages that have come upon the addressees as a result of Jesus' priestly ministry and to draw out the implications of what it should mean to "consider" Jesus, the "high priest of our confession" (3:1). Acts 1:9-11 tells of Jesus' ascension into heaven after his resurrection and appearances to the disciples (see also Mark 16:19; 1 Tim. 3:16). This conviction is affirmed by the Christological reading of Psalm 110:1. The author of Hebrews also knows of the ascension of Jesus, describing it as his passing "through the heavens" (4:14). Indeed, in this author's cosmology, Jesus passes through the material, visible heavens to enter the divine, unshakable realm of God's real presence.[2] He passes into this space, however, not merely as a Son but also as a high priest.[3] That is, he stands before God as a mediator on behalf of human beings (see 5:1; 7:25; 9:24). Naming this mediator not merely as Jesus but as "Jesus, the Son of God," the author reminds the addressees of Christ's proximity to God in the household of God, and thus of the better chance he has of gaining favor for his clients.

Jesus' chief gift is that he affords access to God. He is the broker, or mediator (μεσίτης, 8:6; 9:15; 12:24), who secures favor from God on behalf of those who have committed themselves to Jesus as client dependents, who "approach God through him" (7:25).[4] Jesus provides the second-order resource of access to God as μισθαποδότης, "rewarder," allowing his clients, formerly separated from God by their sins, to approach him as their patron rather than as the judge of those who have affronted him through disobedience (cf. 4:12-13; 10:30-31). Access to God as patron and protector was a familiar topos of philosophical literature. Epictetus (*Diss.* 4.1.91-98), for example, speaks of the search for the best patron under whose aegis to travel through life — one who could provide security against all assaults and in whom one could rely utterly not only for today but also for tomorrow. His search leads finally and only to God: "Thus [the searcher] reflects and comes to the thought that, if he attach himself to God, he will pass through the world in safety." Christianity, to use the expression of Barbara Levick, "gave access . . . through an incorruptible intermediary, to a reliable authority," an important offering indeed in a patronal society.[5]

The next verse employs antithesis to emphasize Jesus' sympathy for those he seeks to help: "for we have not a high priest who is unable to sympathize with our weaknesses, but one who has been similarly tested in every way apart from

---

2. οὐρανοί refers to a part of the visible creation at 1:10; 4:14; 7:26; 11:12; 12:26; the singular form appears to refer specifically to the invisible, divine realm at 8:1; 9:23, 24; 12:23; 12:25(?). For further discussion of this author's cosmology and related cosmologies in the intertestamental and NT periods, see D. A. deSilva, "Heaven, New Heavens," in R. P. Martin and P. H. Davids, *Dictionary of the Later New Testament and Its Developments* (Downers Grove, IL: InterVarsity Press, 1997), 439-43.

3. The author will develop the significance of this piece of the kerygma at length in 8:1-5; 9:11–10:14.

4. The basic meaning of μεσίτης as "one who establishes a relation which would not otherwise exist" (A. Oepke, "μεσίτης," *TDNT* 4:601) demonstrates the suitability of this term as a Greek equivalent of what Boissevain called a "broker" in patron-client relations.

5. B. Levick, *The Government of the Roman Empire: A Sourcebook* (London: Croom–Helm, 1985), 151.

sin" (4:15). This is a point the author will continue to refine as the sermon continues. It is important for his characterization of Jesus as mediator to emphasize first
that Jesus regards the addressees with sympathy and a gentle disposition, for he
twice claims that Jesus has shared their experience of testing fully (2:18; 4:15) and
so identifies himself with their plight. However, it is equally vital for the author to
stress that, in all Jesus' experience of testing, he remained without sin. The basis
for Jesus' sympathy is not the same "liability to weakness" that is the basis for the
sympathy of the high priest who serves at the earthly tabernacle (5:2; 7:28). The
high priest's weakness actually indicates an obstacle that stands between the
earthly mediator and God and must be removed before the priest can even function as a mediator on behalf of the people (5:3; 7:27). Jesus, however, is perfectly
suited as a broker between humans, for whom he has complete sympathy (and
hence greater willingness and eagerness to help), and God, with whom he remains in an unblemished relationship at all times.

Because of the mediation of Jesus, the author can urge the addressees to
approach God in the expectation of favor: "Let us therefore with boldness draw
near the throne of favor (χάριτος) in order that we may receive mercy and find
favor (χάρις) for timely help" (4:16). The relationship between God and the addressees is defined as "favor" (χάρις), which is a term of central importance for
discourse about patronage in the Jewish and Greco-Roman environments of
early Christianity (see introduction), as well as a prominent term in Hebrews
itself.[6] The throne of God has become a source of "favors" (i.e., the resources
that will provide "timely help") due to the "favorable disposition" toward the
addressees of the One who sits upon it. Jesus' gift of access to God affords the
community access to resources for endurance in faith so that they may receive
the benefactions promised for the future, to be awarded before God's court at
the end of the age. God's assistance is, of course, a great good, not to be sacrificed for any temporal good (recall Epictetus on the value of a divine patron).
The author highlights the value of God's help by calling it "timely." God knows
when and how to intervene on behalf of his clients; when their need is great,
God will not hold himself or his favor from them. Seneca (Ben. 4.4.2) writes
that people are especially "conscious of [divine] benefits that sometimes are
presented unasked, sometimes are granted in answer to prayer — great and
timely gifts, which by their coming remove grave menaces."[7] In the author's

---

6. The term χάρις appears in 2:9; 4:16 (bis); 10:29; 12:15, 28; 13:9, 25. All of these occurrences fit very naturally into patronage roles and scripts, whether as God's favor toward
us (2:9; 4:16; 10:29; 13:25), the gift in view (12:15), or the grateful response of the recipients
of a gift (12:28). The precise sense of χάρις in 13:9 remains ambiguous, pointing perhaps intentionally to the whole patron-client relationship formed between God and the believers
rather than any one of its three aspects in particular.

7. See also Aristotle Rh. 1.7.35, which lists as a greater good that which is available in
greater need.

construction of reality, God's help would constitute the greatest of advantages, particularly in light of the menaces looming on the eschatological horizon (the judgment of God's enemies and the shaking of the visible creation).

These verses are calculated to have a profound effect on the hearers. First, they should arouse the emotion of confidence, based on the availability of divine aid. The author puts this emotion in the service of helping the addressees endure "the hostility of sinners." Aristotle (*Rh.* 2.5.16) defines confidence as "the contrary of fear and that which gives confidence of that which causes fear, so that the hope of what is salutary is accompanied by an impression that it is quite near at hand, while the things to be feared are either non-existent or far off." Specifically, signs of the friendship of the gods engender confidence (*Rh.* 2.5.21). Through Jesus, the believers are brought into the presence of God, near to the One who has the will and power to provide help.[8] Thus the believer has become a client of God, and may say with the psalmist:

> The Lord is my light and my salvation; whom shall I fear? The Lord is the stronghold of my life; of whom shall I be afraid? . . . Though a host encamp against me, my heart shall not fear; though war arise against me, yet I will be confident. (Ps. 27:1, 3 [RSV]; see Heb. 13:5-6)

Second, in emphasizing this benefit won by Christ for his clients, the author has moved into the topic of security, according to the author of the *Rhetorica ad Herennium* the second major component of "advantage" and goal of deliberative oratory (together with honor).[9] The allegiance of the addressees to Christ gives them access to the resources that will help them in the face of the exigencies of their life as Christians in society. This, the author hopes, will make his recommended course of action seem all the more feasible, since the resources are there to help the addressees complete the journey they had begun at their conversion. Hebrews 5:9; 6:10; 13:5-6 will continue to promote confidence in order to lead the hearers to persevere in this course of action, and the central discourse of 7:11–10:25 is replete with topics of confidence (the availability of help, the greater advantages enjoyed by the addressees than anyone outside the group or prior to the Christian era, the nearness of salutary things).[10]

---

8. Compare Aristotle *Rh.* 2.5.17: People may be made to feel confident "if remedies are possible, if there are means of help, either great or numerous, or both."

9. *Rhet. Her.* 3.2.3: "Advantage in political deliberation has two aspects: Security and Honour (*tutam, honestam*). To consider Security is to provide some plan or other for ensuring the avoidance of a present or imminent danger."

10. The arousal of gratitude is also a likely effect of 4:14-16, but especially as the cumulative effect of 4:14–10:25. The author amplifies the favor that Jesus provides according to recognizable topics from Aristotle (*Rh.* 2.7.2) — a favor is greater if the recipients are in

Aristotle's observation that confidence and fear are opposite emotions takes one to an important component of the author's strategy, seen in minuscule at 4:12-16. Hebrews 4:12-13 was crafted to arouse fear (an emotion also aroused in 4:1-2, although for a different reason). The author has presented two possibilities for the way the audience will encounter God. They may have the Son as mediator and helper along the way to attaining the promised benefac-- tions (4:14-16), or they may have God as judge and executioner, excluding the faithless from the promised benefactions (4:12-13).[11] Emotions are aroused by orators specifically to make the hearers more prone to decide in favor of the course promoted (or, in legal cases, the party represented) by the speaker. The way the author is laying out the options for the audience, the decision to remain firmly committed to one another and to God is the path that will make them feel confident, while leaving the group, undervaluing the gifts and promises mediated through Jesus, and thus displaying ingratitude toward their benefactor is the path that will make them feel afraid.

In light, then, of the patron-client relationship that Jesus has established and maintains between God and believers, the addressees are urged to "hold fast the confession" (4:14) that makes their access to God's favor possible. Holding onto their confession is presented as the expedient course since it makes possible their relationship and right of access to God's patronage. Such a course preserves an existing "good." The "difficult and lengthy word" of 7:1–10:18 will amplify the value of this good and discuss the unparalleled quality of this access to God gained for us by the Son; 6:4-8 and 10:26-31 will amplify the evil that will be experienced should the alternative course (shrinking back, turning away, etc.) be adopted. These topics of amplification, showing the magnitude of the benefit now enjoyed and of the harm that would accrue should the response of loyalty and endurance not be maintained, strongly support the author's exhortations to choose (or maintain) one course of action over another.

---

greater need, or if the benefactor is the first or only one to provide the needed help, or has done so in the highest degree. All these topics emerge in Hebrews. Moreover, Jesus has given the kind of gift that needs no supplement, unlike the access to God provided under the levitical priesthood, which needs endless supplements (and which is of an inferior, restricted quality to begin with). Such a gift as Jesus gave, according to Seneca (*Ben.* 3.35.5), constitutes a superior one. The many discourses on Jesus' benefits and brokerage, then, feed the challenge to "show gratitude" (12:28) and avoid making a response that shows ingratitude (6:4-8; 10:26-31).

11. The author will frequently take up throughout the remainder of the sermon appeals to the emotions of fear and confidence, discussions of the dreadful consequences of abandoning the Christian group, and the positive outcome of holding onto the confession (see 6:4-12; 10:19-31; 12:18-24), all as a sort of therapy of contraries calculated to lead the hearers to choose steadfastness in their commitment to God and their sisters and brothers as the only advantageous path.

The content of this "confession" is left unspecified, but it would not be necessary to overload it with any specific doctrinal requirements so highly favored in many Protestant denominations today. Rather, the term suggests that the addressees need to "hold onto" the basic counterdefinitions of reality that are articulated in the Christian gospel and undergird commitment to that movement. This is essentially the same posture promoted earlier in 3:6, 14, where the audience was exhorted to hold onto their boldness, the claim to honor that their hope provided, and the firstfruits of their eternal inheritance. Here they are told that they "have" a great high priest. Thanks to their partnership with the Son, they enjoy his brokerage before God (cf. 5:1 for brokerage expressed in priestly terms) and have access to divine help and God's resources to sustain them and meet their needs along the way to attaining their inheritance. The author wants them to continue to value these spiritual resources more than the material or temporal resources that they continue to do without, in order that they might not jeopardize what they "have" in Christ for what they might want in this temporary world.[12]

The addressees are urged both to "hold on" and to "draw near" (προσερχώμεθα, 4:16) to God. This second action is prominent in Hebrews (7:25; 10:22; 11:6; 12:18, 22) as a suitable foil for "shrinking back" or "turning away" (3:12; 6:6; 10:38-39). The author's choice of words here reveals his ideological strategy at work. Joining the Christian movement has not pushed believers out to the margins but rather has brought them closer to the divine center of the universe. There is a certain centripetal force to the language. Gathering with one's fellow believers and holding onto the Christian confession means moving to the center — "drawing near"[13] — while movement back to the bosom of society is actually "shrinking back" or "turning away" from the center. This image reinforces the linear model that the author uses to orient the audience to life in this world, which casts leaving the group to rejoin one's neighbors as "falling short" of, or "failing to enter," the goal prepared for them by God (hence failure rather than recovery). Rather than succumb to the centrifugal forces that would rip the hearers away from the divine center and their eternal inheritance, they are to come before God to exercise "boldness" (παρρησία) in making their needs known to the one who is both favorably disposed to help and supremely

---

12. The author's reminders of judgment and eschatological crisis heighten the value of having such a well-placed ally and helper.

13. The term is frequently used within the LXX in cultic contexts, where worshippers or priests "approach" God. Attridge (*Hebrews,* 141 nn. 56, 57), for example, refers to Exod. 16:9; 34:32; Lev. 9:5; Num. 10:3-4 where the verb is used for the drawing near of worshippers, and to Lev. 9:7; 21:17, 21; 22:3; Num. 18:3 where it is used to speak of the approach of priests as they drawn near to perform their duties. A much fuller study of this term can be found in J. M. Scholer, *Proleptic Priests: Priesthood in the Epistle to the Hebrews* (JSNTSS 49; Sheffield: Sheffield Academic Press, 1991), 91-149.

able to assist. There before God's throne, accessed through the fellowship of the believers (see 10:19-25), they will find the "timely help" to meet the challenges they face and triumph in their contest against sin and sinners (12:1-4), rather than fall or retreat before those pressures.

5:1-10

The sermon moves at last into a deeper exploration of Jesus' appointment to the high priesthood and his ongoing exercise of that office. Exegesis of Scripture, analogy, and constructive argumentation become the "evidence for things unseen," namely, the Broker in the invisible realm and his work. As the author moves into his description of Jesus' priesthood, and even into the details of the rites he performed beyond human sight, he impresses the reality of this priesthood more deeply into the consciousness of the audience.

The discussion begins in 5:1 with a definition of the role and qualities of a priest based on a general reference to the function and office of priest known from the Pentateuch. Calling Jesus the "high priest of our confession" (3:1; cf. 2:17; 4:14; and 6:20) attributes to Jesus a great honor in addition to describing his activity within the heavenly sanctuary. In terms of epideictic topics, the author is here treating Jesus' "external advantages," specifically his "titles to fame" or "forms of power." Jesus' honor derives, however, not only from holding such a title or office but from his beneficent use of his power on behalf of his clients (4:14-16; 5:8-10). The office of high priest was still held in deep regard during the first century A.D., even after the corruption that had eroded the office during the Maccabean period. Josephus (*J.W.* 4.164) calls the title of high priest the "most honored of revered names." Elsewhere (*J.W.* 4.149) he refers to the office as "the highest dignity." Similarly, Philo of Alexandria, far removed from the actual temple cult in Jerusalem, refers to the priesthood as an honor (see *Vita Mos.* 2.142), even going so far as to claim that "the law [i.e., Torah] invests the priests with the dignity and honor that belongs to kings" (*Spec. Leg.* 1.142).

The definition provided by the author of Hebrews, particularly when seen against the background of patron-client relations, makes clear why the high priest would be held in such high esteem and would be accorded the honors that belong to the greatest of benefactors (monarchs). "Every high priest, being taken from among human beings, is appointed on behalf of human beings with reference to what concerns God[14] in order that he might offer gifts and sacrifices for sins" (5:1). This definition casts priests in the role of brokers between human beings and God — a role that applies equally well to pagan

---

14. Ellingworth (*Hebrews,* 188) thus negotiates the translation of the adverbial phrase τὰ πρὸς τὸν θεόν.

priests (the Latin word for priest, *pontifex,* means "bridge maker") as Jewish priests. The "broker" or "mediator" provides, for his or her clients, access to the goods and services of other benefactors (who may be the broker's own patrons or friends). The high priest served as a broker of the benefits of God, the patron *sans pareil.* Standing before God on behalf of his fellow human beings, the high priest offers gifts and sacrifices as satisfaction for the affronts to the authority of God (the sins committed contrary to God's commands),[15] thus maintaining the benefactor's favorable disposition (χάρις) and sustaining the nation's confidence in the hope that God would continue to show beneficence in his dealings with the people. The very institution of priesthood makes lay people clients of priests since they depend on priests for their access to divine benefits.

The need for such mediation is grounded in ancient concepts of holiness, which entailed both a wonder at and a dread of the "holy." Holy places, frequented by holy beings, were full of power. The uninstructed — or worse, the profane or even unclean — could not safely approach such power and channel it into beneficent directions. The potential for danger was great, as the "holy" might "break out" against the unclean or the unsanctified person who came too close. Nevertheless, humanity needed to have access to the holy, to have the help that its power could provide. Thus arose the perceived need for priests, those who could keep themselves in a state of cleanness, who were themselves set apart to be "holy," and who were instructed in the proper procedures for approaching the Holy One on behalf of the people. Holiness "was a burden on the priests, but it was also an important social privilege. . . . It was their holiness that permitted priests to approach the sanctuary, and this was the key to their exclusive social status. Thus the culture map that priests taught and enforced in turn provided them with their position in society," a position that commanded the respect and gratitude of all others on account of the value of the benefit the priest provided.[16] We who live

---

15. Hebrews 5:1b refers to the cultic provisions for atonement for unintentional sins against the law (found, for example, in Lev. 4:2, 13-14, 22-23, 27-28; 5:14-19; Num. 15:22-31). These sins stand apart from willful sins (cf. Heb. 10:26; Lane, *Hebrews 1–8,* 117; Attridge, *Hebrews,* 144) and sins "committed with a high hand" (Num. 15:30-31), for which there are no provisions for sacrifice. (This distinction was eventually eased within Judaism by rabbinic developments of the doctrine of repentance as a procedure by which willful or intentional sins became unintentional ones, based on the precedent recorded in Lev. 5:20-26//Num. 5:6-8; see Milgrom, *Leviticus I–XVI,* 373-78.) Ellingworth (*Hebrews,* 274-75) convincingly argues that the author of Hebrews is not postulating two different classes of offering in the phrase δῶρά τε καὶ θυσίας ὑπὲρ ἁμαρτιῶν, but is rather treating "gifts" and "sacrifices" somewhat synonymously as aspects of the cultic provisions for covering sins.

16. Nelson, *Raising Up a Faithful Priest,* 30. For further discussion of priests as brokers/mediators, see ibid., 85-88, 107, 144. Nelson's discussion of the purity map of Israel and the logic of sacrifice is also indispensable to a proper appreciation of the dynamics of the tabernacle and temple cult, as well as the argument of Hebrews (ibid., 17-38, 55-82).

centuries after the Protestant Reformation questioned the need for any mediator save one, and especially those who live in the Western world where the "holy" tends to be perceived as more harmless than menacing, will need to work hard to appreciate the incredible breakthrough that the author of Hebrews will proclaim in his central discourse.

High priests in general are, so the author avers, sympathetic and patient toward the "wayward and ignorant" (5:2). This is not a quality possessed by Jesus only (2:17), but common to all who serve as mediators between God and humanity. The point of contrast, however, is in the source of this sympathy, which, for the typical priest, is his own weakness where sin is concerned. Like those on whose behalf he acts as broker, he also has the obstacle of sin standing between him and God, and thus he must offer sin offerings for himself as well (5:3). The author has in mind particularly the cultic provisions for the high priest's atonement for his own sins, which he must undertake before he can mediate on behalf of the people (see, notably, Lev. 9:7-14; 16:6-17). This contrasts unfavorably with Jesus, who is able to deal sympathetically with his clients yet had not himself drifted into sins against God (4:15; the author will develop this more fully and directly in 7:26-28 and remind the hearers of the earthly priests' weakness again in 9:7). The author regards the fact that the levitical priests had to atone for their own sins as a serious flaw in their mediation: they, too, have obstacles in their relationship with the holy God. The mediator of the New Covenant, however, is a more effective broker not only on account of his proximity to God in space and familial relationship, but also on account of the absence of any affront to God in his own life.

Another "given" within the institution of priesthood is that individuals may not volunteer their services or select themselves for the honored office. Rather, they must be legitimately appointed by God (or through such procedures as God set in motion, such as hereditary accession to the office).[17] Just as Aaron was "called by God" to serve in the capacity of mediator (a reference to the tradition contained in Exod. 28:1; Num. 17:1-11; 18:1-8), so every legitimate priest must be able to demonstrate his divine appointment. Whence, then, comes Jesus' appointment? The author appeals to Psalm 110 as a witness to the fact that Jesus did not usurp this privilege for himself, thus making a false claim to an honor not his own ("Christ did not glorify himself," 5:5). Rather, he was given this honor by the command of God just as Aaron had formerly received divine legitimation for his priesthood.

The author achieves this through something resembling an application of

---

17. This premise was sorely tested during the Hasmonean dynasty, when the ruler also served as high priest even though he was only of a priestly rather than a high-priestly family. Protest against this arrangement is widely attested in the Qumran texts as well as the Psalms of Solomon (see Collins, *Scepter and the Star,* for an excellent discussion).

gezera shawa. A second recitation of Psalm 2:7 (see Heb. 1:5) prepares the way by reminding the hearers of the exegetical principle that the psalms are to be read as pertaining in some way to Jesus. Just as Psalm 2:7 addresses Jesus directly — "*you are my Son; today I have begotten you*" — so also Psalm 110 can be read as addressing Jesus directly. The author has already used Psalm 110:1 as an address to Christ (at 1:13), so the audience is prepared to accept Psalm 110:4 as addressing Christ as well — "*you* are a priest forever after the order of Melchizedek."[18] The two recitations are held together by the pronoun "you" (σύ) and the formulation of predicating some title or quality of this "you." Obviously, the success of this demonstration depends on a mutual acceptance between author and audience of the Christocentric reading of the OT, but the author gives no indications in his sermon that such an expectation would be ill-founded.

In a natural sense, the phrase "priest forever" refers to the fact of ordination as effecting "an irreversible transfer into priestly office." Consecration to the priesthood was a "status-elevation ritual" that "brings about an irreversible change in role," like the transition from childhood to adulthood at puberty or the coronation of a monarch.[19] The author of Hebrews, however, will exploit this "forever" in a different sense, namely, as a reference to the "indestructible life" of the Mediator who "always lives to make intercession" for those who approach God through him (7:16, 25).

Having (re)affirmed the existence of this high priesthood of Jesus through the legitimating power of the OT, the author now goes on to paint a portrait of the piety of this priest, connecting Jesus' mediation in the heavenly sanctuary with his life of prayer and obedience "in the days of his flesh" (5:7): Jesus offered "prayers and petitions with loud cries and tears to the one who was able to rescue him from death, being heard on account of his piety" (5:7). There is a strong temptation to identify this description with the account of Jesus in the Garden of Gethsemane as recounted in the Synoptic Gospels (Matt. 26:36-46; Mark 14:32-42; Luke 22:40-46),[20] but there are indi-

---

18. Ps. 110:4 introduces vocabulary and phraseology that will remain prominent through chapter 7 as the author repeatedly recontextualizes this text: "priest forever" (ἱερεὺς εἰς τὸν αἰῶνα) appears at 5:6; 6:20; 7:17, 21; "forever" (εἰς τὸν αἰῶνα) appears alone at 7:24, 28; 13:8; and "according to the order of Melchizedek" (κατὰ τὴν τάξιν Μελχισέδεκ) appears at 5:6, 10; 6:20; 7:11, 17 (7:15 substitutes "likeness" for "order"). In effect, 5:1-10; 7:1-28 are a working out of the implications of the claim that Ps. 110:4 provides information about the significance of Jesus.

19. Nelson, *Raising Up a Faithful Priest,* 56.

20. As does Stedman (*Hebrews,* 64-65), without any awareness of the difficulties involved, and P. Hughes (*Hebrews,* 182-85), whose claim that "the occasion intended is beyond doubt that of Christ's agony in the Garden of Gethsemane" does little justice to the serious "doubts" raised by scholars such as Lane (*Hebrews 1–8,* 119-20), Attridge (*Hebrews,* 148-50), and Pfitzner (*Hebrews,* 92-93).

cations that such a link to the story of those three Gospels is to be resisted. We might question whether or not the description of God in Hebrews 7 as the "one able to save from death" is best read as also the content of Jesus' prayer (e.g., "Save me from death, O God") in precisely the sense this was portrayed in Gethsemane.[21] If it is, then it is difficult to understand in what sense Jesus' prayer was "heard" (unless it was heard and ignored). On the one hand, the description of God as the one who can save from death may simply call attention to this power of God rather than the content of Jesus' prayer (for anyone who prays to God prays to "the one who is able to save from death" regardless of their specific petitions). On the other hand, if the author means for the hearers to infer the content of Jesus' prayer, then we must hear it as a petition to be delivered "out of death," i.e., on the other side of death, since he was in fact "heard" (which carries strong implications of the prayer being granted). The author's choice of preposition (ἐκ instead of ἀπό) would reinforce this reading. In this case, the prayer would still be a far cry from what we hear in Gethsemane.[22]

It may surprise us to discover that there are other traditions with which Hebrews 5:7 bears a far more striking resemblance than the Gethsemane tradition — traditions not about Jesus per se but about the prayers of the pious. Jesus offers "prayers and petitions" (δεήσεις τε καὶ ἱκετηρίας) with loud cries and tears (μετὰ κραυγῆς ἰσχυρᾶς καὶ δακρύων). The author of 2 Maccabees says that the people of Judea, faced with the siege of Lysias under Antiochus IV, "were praying with lamentations and tears" (μετὰ ὀδυρμῶν καὶ δακρύων ἱκέτευον, 2 Macc. 11:6). 3 Maccabees repeatedly includes these elements in descriptions of prayers. When the temple was threatened with desecration, the priests "pray to the supreme God . . . with both cries and tears" (δεομένων . . . κραυγῆς τε μετὰ δακρύων, 3 Macc. 1:16). The Jews of Egypt, herded into the hippodrome to await their execution, "cried out with tears, praying" (μετὰ δακρύων ἐπεκαλέσαντο δεόμενοι, 5:7); a second time they make

---

21. For Bart Ehrman (*The New Testament: A Historical Introduction* [Oxford: Oxford University Press, 1997], 356), for example, 5:7 "indicates that Jesus went to his death with 'loud cries and tears', beseeching God to save him from death."

22. Hebrews stresses rather Jesus' unflinching commitment to performing God's will. This is made even sharper by his application of Ps. 40 to the lips of Jesus in Heb. 10:5-10. There are a number of additional elements in Heb. 5:7-8 that do not appear directly to recall the Gethsemane accounts: for example, the "tears" that go unmentioned in all three Synoptics. Further, the "loud cry" seems more directly resonant with the exclamation of Jesus from the cross, for none of the Synoptic accounts describes the prayer, however fervent, as executed with "loud cries."

23. See Attridge, *Hebrews*, 151 nn. 172-73 for these and other references, particularly in the writings of Philo. Also helpful is H. W. Attridge, "'Heard Because of His Reverence' (Heb 5:7)," *JBL* 98 (1979): 90-93.

"tearful petition, . . . praying" (πολύδακρυν ἱκετείαν . . . ἐδέοντο, 5:25).[23] This suggests that the author of Hebrews is drawing on cultural resonances with other depictions of the fervent and emotive prayers of the pious rather than making a specific reference to the Gethsemane tradition within the Christian culture. His goal is to display Jesus' piety, an essential qualification for the high priesthood, which God confirmed through hearing Jesus' prayer.[24] This is also a goal of the remainder of the passage, which focuses on Jesus' "education" (a topic of encomia in general, even though the specific curriculum of Jesus' education — suffering — was not the norm) and the virtuous fruit his education bore, namely, "obedience" toward God.

Many translations obscure the syntax of 5:7-10 by forming two or more separate sentences. This has the effect of casting too much weight on the material in 5:7, as though this provided an independent and therefore equally significant piece of information about Jesus' "earthly existence." The spine of 5:7-10, however, is "who . . . learned obedience from the things he suffered [experienced] and became the source of eternal salvation to all who obey him." The remainder contains participial clauses, which qualify these main verbs ("learned" and "became").[25] This suggests that the material about Jesus' prayers and piety describes the attendant circumstances (or some similar adverbial function) of Jesus' "learning" obedience from the things he suffered.[26] The author presents Jesus as one who encountered hostility and eventually the most extreme form of marginalization (execution) entrusting his life, spirit, and honor to God rather than turning away from the opposition that obedience to God brought. "In the days of his flesh," Jesus availed himself of prayer and the access it brings to God's throne of favor, finding in that experience the ability to endure the slings and arrows of his opponents. In effect, Jesus provides a model here for what the audience is being called to do (cf. 4:14-16). The implicit appeal to emulation here will be made explicit in 12:2-3.

As we consider 5:8-9 within the context of the whole sermon, we find this mimetic chain being fortified. The Son, Jesus, learned obedience through what

---

24. That God "hears" (i.e., answers) the prayers of the righteous but not the prayers of the impious and irreverent appears to be an assumption undergirding, for example, John 9:31-33. Effective prayer appears to have functioned as proof of character in at least some circles. In affirming that Jesus displayed piety, the author of Hebrews was already in strong disagreement with other assessments of Jesus' character, which tended to put him in the categories of blasphemer, deceiver, or sorcerer — in short, anything but "pious" and therefore virtuous (see Luke T. Johnson, *The Real Jesus: The Misguided Quest for the Jesus of History* [San Francisco: HarperCollins, 1995], 112-17 for further discussion).

25. This has been helpfully observed by Ellingworth (*Hebrews*, 284).

26. The experience of rejection, arrest, trial, and execution is certainly in view, but limiting the hostility and rejection Jesus experienced solely to the last week of Jesus' life may be too confining. The author is probably referring to Jesus' entire life as an experience of hostility, reproach, opposition, and rejection.

he suffered;[27] the many sons and daughters must obey this Son in order to be recipients of his benefactions, to enjoy him as the "cause/source of eternal salvation" (5:9);[28] the many sons and daughters also learn this obedience through suffering (12:5-11, hinted at already in 2:18 and 4:15). The author, addressing those who have experienced and continue to experience hardship as a result of their association with the Christian group, wishes to assure them that such hardship is not a sign of the displeasure of the divine. Since the Son himself was subject to the educative discipline of hardships, the "many sons and daughters" should not be surprised at their own endurance of discipline. Like the Son, they also have need to cry out to God with loud supplications and tears, and, like the Son, they will also be heard by God, as 4:14-16 assures them. Thus the pattern of enduring hardship and calling upon the Lord for help is affirmed as the "normal" condition, the "proper" condition, and not a disconfirming one that makes the believers question their commitment to this group. What counts is not avoiding hardships but seeing in those hardships an opportunity to learn obedience (and a deep reliance on God in prayer), which has eternal value (leading to a place in the "rest," "homeland," or "city" prepared by God).

It is difficult to know exactly which action or condition the concessive phrase "although he was a son" (καίπερ ὢν υἱὸς) is explaining. One possible reading would see the concessive clause clarifying what precedes, in this case the reason for Jesus' prayer being "heard" by God.[29] This reading would emphasize that it was Jesus' virtue (piety) rather than his filial connection with God that led to his resurrection. God hears Jesus not because of their special relationship (Jesus' exterior excellence or advantage) but because of Jesus' virtue (an interior excellence that is truly praiseworthy). This could also serve a pastoral goal, assuring the audience that God's vindication of Jesus was the vindication of a pious, trusting, obedient person, and therefore a vindication that any of them could expect and rely upon as well. This is not just a special intervention for a relation.

---

27. With the words ἔμαθεν . . . ἔπαθεν the author has incorporated a celebrated Greek wordplay, appearing, for example, in Aeschylus *Ag.* 177; Herodotus, *Hist.* 1.207; and scores of other places in surviving literature. For further references, see Attridge, *Hebrews,* 152 n. 192; for an in-depth treatment, see Croy, *Endurance,* 139-44.

28. The repetitive texture of "obedience . . . all who obey him" (ὑπακοήν . . . ὑπακούουσιν) forms a meaningful connection: Jesus learned obedience through suffering and received God's reward; the many sons and daughters themselves learn obedience to Jesus as they undergo a curriculum of hardships and themselves receive the Son's reward ("deliverance").

29. Attempts to demonstrate that such a reading is *necessary* on grammatical grounds (see F. Scheidweiler, "ΚΑΙΠΕΡ: nebst einem Exkurs zum Hebräerbrief," *Hermes* 83 [1955]: 220-30) have been rightfully challenged and overthrown in more recent studies (Attridge, *Hebrews,* 152; Lane, *Hebrews 1–8,* 110 n. "w"); one is left to choose between two grammatical possibilities on some other grounds.

The majority of commentators and translators, however, take the clause with the material that follows — "although he was a Son, he learned obedience from what he suffered." The author of Hebrews is at pains, however, to show that there is nothing contradictory between the status of being "God's child" and the experience of hardships (see again Heb. 12:5-11). The sons and daughters experience discipline and are thus shaped for their exercise of citizenship; it is the lack of such discipline that should worry the believers, not the experience of it! Those commentators favoring this reading, rightly noting the tension with Heb. 12:5-11, insist that "although being a son" (or even "Son though he was")[30] points to the unique quality of *this* Son, namely Jesus. Even such a Son, eternally God's Son,[31] was not exempt from the common lot of sons and daughters, which is to learn virtue through discipline.[32] This line of argumentation could be strengthened by the observation of the connection between 5:8a and 5:5b, where God addresses Jesus specifically and particularly with the words "you are my son."

The difficulty I have with the second reading is the amount that one must read into "although being a son" to make it consonant with the author's later claim that suffering and belonging to God's family (sonship) are completely compatible (12:5-11). These commentators turn the clause, in effect, into "*even so great a* Son learned obedience from what he suffered," which I believe the author could have expressed more clearly were that his intention. I find it less problematic, therefore, to read the clause as qualifying what precedes. A translation that might capture the relationship of subordinate to independent clauses would be: "who learned obedience through what he suffered, offering prayers and petitions in the days of his flesh to the one who was able to rescue him out from death and being heard on account of his piety (although he was a son)."

The passage concludes with an affirmation of how Jesus has used the "exterior advantages" or "excellences" of the office of high priest: "and having been perfected, he became to all who obey him the cause of eternal deliverance, having been appointed by God a high priest after the order of Melchizedek" (5:9-10). Once again the author links Jesus' "perfecting" (see "A Closer Look" below) with his suffering (see 2:10): Jesus' willing endurance of the latter so as to arrive at a place from which he could bring benefit to the audience should serve further to stimulate their sense of gratitude and obligation toward him, making

---

30. Bruce, *Hebrews*, 130.

31. Ellingworth, *Hebrews*, 293.

32. Thus Lane (*Hebrews 1–8*, 121) writes: "Although Jesus was the eternal Son of God, he entered into a new dimension in the experience of sonship by virtue of his incarnation and sacrificial death." See also Attridge, *Hebrews*, 152; Ellingworth, *Hebrews*, 293; Bruce, *Hebrews*, 130.

those who were wavering less likely to "turn away from," or perhaps "turn against," so generous a benefactor. As high priest, Jesus has the capacity to provide great and important benefits to his clients, to be a cause or source (αἴτιος) of necessary goods and services. The phrase "source of good things" is used elsewhere to describe patrons (e.g., Dio Chrysostom [Or. 31.75], who uses αἴτιος with a genitive as a way of referring to a benefactor: "the authors of greater blessings (μειζόνων ἀγαθῶν αἰτίους)." Here the benefit is specified as a "deliverance" of "eternal" significance, referring to the deliverance of the faithful at the second coming (1:14; 9:28).[33]

The effect of this affirmation is, first, to remind Jesus' clients of their obligation to obey him if they hope to remain recipients of God's favor, especially this forthcoming deliverance. One message derived from the "pattern" of the wilderness generation, the inexpedience of disobedience, is here positively reinforced. Second, it addresses once again the deliberative topic of the expediency and consequences of a particular course of action, articulating the relationship between remaining the loyal and obedient client of the Son and receiving the good of "eternal salvation" (cf. "inheriting salvation" in 1:14). If one dissociates oneself from the "cause," one will also separate oneself from the effect.

Hebrews 5:10 reiterates what 5:5-6 demonstrated, namely, the divine appointment of Jesus to the office of priest. It provides a sort of recapitulation at the close of the section, at once giving closure to 5:1-10 and preparing for 7:1-11, which will look more closely at the founder of this mysterious order. The author here for the first time merges the title of "high priest," which he has repeatedly ascribed to Jesus (2:17; 3:1; 4:14-15; 5:5), into a recitation of the OT text on which he bases his demonstration of Jesus' priesthood, changing "priest" in Psalm 110:4 to "high priest according to the order of Melchizedek."

A Closer Look: "Perfection in Hebrews"

The author's use of the language of "perfection" (τελειόω, τέλειος, τελειότης, and the like) has occasioned a plethora of scholarly works and been the subject of considerable debate

---

33. The only OT text that speaks of "eternal salvation" (σωτηρίας αἰωνίου) is Isa. 45:17 (LXX): "Israel will be saved by the Lord for an eternal salvation (σωτηρίαν αἰώνιον); they will not be ashamed nor dismayed forever." The passage contrasts fate of Israel with the fate of those who manufacture idols, who shall indeed be led off in shame and disgrace (45:16). The author of Hebrews shares the basic conceptual framework of a future intervention of God that will subject those who are not part of God's people to disgrace and punishment but bring an end to the shame and hardship of those who keep God's commands. "Salvation" and "judgment" are thus both viewed as future acts.

in the history of interpretation.[34] This language is applied to Jesus, who is "perfected through sufferings" (2:10), "perfected" so as to become the "source of eternal salvation" (5:9), and "perfected forever" in contrast to the levitical priests who continue to "have weakness" (7:28). Finally, Jesus is himself the "perfecter of faith" (12:2). The author also applies the language of perfection to human beings. The Torah and its priesthood are criticized because they are unable to perfect anything: "the law perfects nothing" (7:19); "gifts and sacrifices are being offered which are unable to perfect the worshiper with regard to the conscience" (9:9); and "the law . . . can never perfect those drawing near by means of the same sacrifices offered year after year" (10:1). Christ, however, "by means of a single sacrifice perfected forever those who are cleansed" (10:14). While the faithful people of God who went before "did not receive the promise . . . in order that they might not be perfected apart from us" (11:40), the author also sees "the spirits of the perfected righteous ones" joining in the angelic liturgy around God and Jesus (12:23). Besides verbal forms, the author employs the adjectival and nominal forms of this root: he calls the audience to act as "perfect" people rather than "infants" (5:11-14) and challenges them to "be borne along to perfection" (6:1). In order to treat these diverse occurrences of the term intelligently, we need to pierce through to the underlying logic of the "perfection" word group, so as to arrive at the "general" use, which holds together the rather varied "specific" uses.[35]

The semantic range of this word group is indeed broad,[36] so much so that the audience of Hebrews would itself need careful clues from the author to understand what any word from this group connotes in a particular setting (we will look for these clues below). Outside the NT, the adjective is used in philosophical texts to refer to those who have attained the goal of the philosophy (whether contemplation of the realm of ideas in Plato, or the realization of every virtue in Stoic authors). It is used frequently in cultic contexts (pagan and Jewish) to express "cleanness" or "wholeness" (e.g., "unblemished," of sacrificial animals). The "perfect" is also that which has arrived at its full excellence, beyond which there is no progress in quality or in kind (thus Aristotle *Metaph.* 4.16 [1021b]); it can also mean "adult" as opposed to "child," for the adult is the "completed" state of the child (or the butterfly of the caterpillar). The adjective is also used to describe the person whose initiation into a mystery cult is completed. The verb form is "factitive":[37] to "make something perfect" or "to complete something" in one of the senses expressed by the adjectival form; to bring something to its proper end or goal (its τέλος).[38] In the LXX, in addition to the more general sense, one also finds the verb being used

---

34. A fine summary of the landmark positions in this history can be found in Peterson, *Hebrews and Perfection*, 1-20; a more recent review of major positions appears in Scholer, *Proleptic Priests*, 185-200.

35. As Scholer (*Proleptic Priests*, 187) maintains, we need an "understanding of the term, whereby a coherence throughout the Epistle is maintained."

36. See the surveys of meaning by G. Delling ("τέλος, τελέω, τελειόω, etc.," *TDNT* 8:49-87), H. Hübner ("τέλειος" and "τελειόω," *Exegetical Dictionary of the New Testament,* ed. H. Balz and G. Schneider [Grand Rapids: Eerdmans, 1993], 3:342-45), and Attridge (*Hebrews,* 82-87).

37. Delling, *TDNT* 8:79; Attridge, *Hebrews,* 82.

38. Perhaps "to perfect" should be preferred since this captures the sense of ending a process, while "to make perfect" connotes imparting a quality. The latter translation is heavily laden with ethical and performance-oriented overtones in our culture, as is rightly noted by Moisés Silva ("Perfection and Eschatology in Hebrews," *WTJ* 39 [1976]: 60). A. A.

prominently in Exodus 29 (cf. Lev. 4:5; 8:33; 16:32) to mean "consecrate" or "ordain" to priest-hood (the expression is idiomatic — "to perfect the hands" — and may be informative for the meaning of "perfecting" in Hebrews). Another specifically religious use of the term, in Philo, expresses the "unmediated vision of God."[39]

It is the formal sense — "to complete," "to bring something to its goal" — that provides the "general" sense capable of including and bringing coherence to the specific senses.[40] Such a conception of "perfecting" or "being perfected" has the additional benefit of allowing one to understand the nominal and adjectival forms (as well as forms of τέλος, the end or final state, 3:14; 6:8, 11; 7:3) as being relevant to the discussion. The τελει-words in Hebrews, then, share in common the sense of bringing something to, or having something arrive at, its appointed end (whether that end be naturally, divinely, or ritually appointed). Many times the term refers to the completion of a process that involves a rite of passage from one state to another, the latter state being defined somehow as "perfected" or "complete" or even "whole." This last meaning is especially appropriate in the context of a symbolic world in which defilement and pollution arise from a state of being incomplete or "not whole" (e.g., imperfect body boundaries): "Wholeness was clean. The integrity of boundaries and the physical completeness of the body were positive notions."[41] Many of the specific uses of "perfection" language fit within this general pattern:

Unfinished State		Perfected State
Child	I	Adult
	rite of passage marks transition	
Profane Layperson	I	Consecrated Priest
	rite of ordination marks transition	
Defiled	I	Cleansed[42]
	rite of atonement marks transition	
Outsider	I	Initiate (mystery cults)
	rites of initiation marks transition	

To this group we may add a cosmological/eschatological use of "perfection" terminology:

Ahern ("The Perfection Concept in the Epistle to the Hebrews," *JBR* 14 [1946]: 164-67) attempted to read this terminology as an articulation of a doctrine of moral development, but, as Delling rightly argues (*TDNT* 8:77), "one does not find [in Hebrews] any understanding of the adjective in terms of a gradual advance of the Christian to moral perfection."

39. Attridge, *Hebrews*, 84 and n. 67.

40. So, rightly, J. Kögel, "Der Begriff 'τελειοῦν' im Hebräerbrief im Zusammenhang mit dem neutestamentlichen Sprachgebrauch," in *Theologische Studien: Martin Kähler zum 6. Januar 1905*, ed. F. Giesebrecht et al. (Leipzig: A. Deichert, 1905), 39; Scholer, *Proleptic Priests*, 191, 195. The "formal" can include the cultic, eschatological, and even the metaphysical and ethical, so that setting the five categories side-by-side (as does Peterson, *Hebrews and Perfection*, 20) is less helpful than setting them within a subordinating relationship of general and specific.

41. Nelson, *Raising Up a Faithful Priest*, 22.

42. This sense is especially important for the author's discussion of the perfecting of the "conscience" in 9:9, 14. Hebrews argues that the Torah-prescribed sacrifices were incapable of effecting precisely this transition.

Resident in earthly realm | Resident in divine realm
eschatological shaking effects transition

While the specific meaning will shift throughout Hebrews depending on the context, the general sense of arriving at one's proper, completed, finished state will remain constant.

Hebrews will help us to understand this concept better as we look at expressions that parallel, and therefore help clarify, "perfection" language. We should investigate how the author himself guides the hearers to understand "perfection" through the use of synonymous expressions, since his own hearers would be at the same loss we are with regard to what the author means by "perfection" without such guidance.

The Perfecting of Christ

In what sense is Jesus perfected? Hebrews speaks only three times about God perfecting Jesus or Jesus being perfected, so we will have to be especially attentive to the author's clues as to the meaning of this expression. I would take it as axiomatic, however, that the perfecting of Christ will be related to the perfecting of believers,[43] since in so many places Christ is the model, forerunner, or example for believers to follow, and particularly since the trajectory Christ followed "through suffering into glory" is the course on which the believers have been set (see 2:10; 6:19-20; 10:19-20).

The perfecting of Jesus first appears in 2:10, where God perfects Jesus, the pioneer (ἀρχηγός, a word that creates a significant contrast with the τελ- root) of the believers' salvation, through sufferings. This juxtaposition of roots signifying "beginning" and "finishing" intimates a major theme of the sermon: many sons and daughters will also arrive at their final state through sufferings, following their leader. "Sufferings" thus constitute events along the path that Jesus followed during his earthly life prior to his being "perfected" ("sufferings" are events along the believers' paths as well). The author has just completed his Christocentric exposition of Psalm 8 at this point, speaking of Jesus being "crowned with glory and honor" after, and specifically on account of, his experience of death. Hebrews 2:10 grows out of this exposition of the psalm (see commentary on 2:10) with its presentation of Jesus as the pioneer in whom the psalm is fulfilled and who leads the many for whom the psalm is yet to be fulfilled. It is likely, therefore, that the audience will hear "perfection" after sufferings as a parallel expression for his exaltation after death.[44] The audience knows that Jesus passed "through sufferings" (taking the preposition in its spatial sense "by way of" rather than its instrumental sense "by means of")[45] on the way to his exaltation, his return to the unshakable, heavenly realm where he now sits enthroned. This marks the completion of his task as well as his personal destiny and di-

---

43. A. Wikgren ("Patterns of Perfection in the Epistle to the Hebrews," *NTS* 6 [1960]: 161) stresses the relationship, indeed the "parallelism," between the perfecting of Jesus and the perfecting of human beings.

44. Thus rightly Silva, "Perfection and Eschatology," 66; Scholer, *Proleptic Priests,* 195-96.

45. Such a sense is reinforced by the context of the preposition, which speaks of a pioneer leading others along a path to a destination — the sense of "motion" that tends to favor a spatial reading of διά (BAGD, 178).

vinely appointed goal: session at God's right hand. The author presents this as a suitable path based on his knowledge that believers must frequently endure hardship in this world. Since believers press on to their divinely appointed final state through sufferings, it was suitable for God to send their pioneer through that path ahead of them. Such an affirmation gives the hearers assurance that their hardships are leading them toward their divinely appointed goal rather than away from it.

It is frequently argued, however, that sufferings actually represent the means by which Jesus is qualified for his office of high priest (especially rendered "merciful"), a point that the author develops especially in 2:14-18.[46] According to this reading, διά is read as indicating instrumentality: "by means of suffering" God formed in Jesus the interior excellences that would enable him to exercise his priesthood. The author clearly goes on to develop the "suitability" of the path of sufferings through which Jesus walked (2:11-18), since by means of it he was fitted with mercy and sympathy for those on whose behalf he would intercede (2:17; 4:15). God may have used sufferings to develop certain qualities in Jesus without using sufferings to "perfect" him per se. This merely makes a terminological distinction, but it is worth considering before asserting that "the vocational understanding" of the term is the "only" one that does justice to the text.[47] Vocational issues are indeed present, but they are not necessarily attached to the term "to perfect."[48]

Hebrews 5:9 is the second passage to speak of the perfecting of Jesus. After we are told that Jesus "learned obedience through what he suffered," the author points to Jesus as "having been perfected," from which vantage point he is able to be a "source of eternal salvation for those who obey him." Being "perfected" is contrasted specifically with the "days of his flesh," in which he learned through suffering. It is in view of his heavenly session and proximity to God (his departure from the earthly realm and return to the divine realm) that he is able to be the source of eternal salvation. "Having been perfected" signals the completion of the rite of passage — the liminal state marked by the endurance of humiliation, suffering, and death[49] — which was the incarnation. Some scholars read 5:8-9 as a vocational process by which Jesus is made fit for the office of high priest (i.e., "perfected"),[50] but the passage is fully comprehensible if we allow "having been perfected" to

---

46. Thus Peterson, *Hebrews and Perfection,* 73: "The vocational understanding of the perfecting of Christ is the only interpretation that allows for all the dimensions in our writer's presentation. Adopting the rendering 'to qualify' or 'to make completely adequate' . . . in 2:10 . . . much of this passage [i.e., 2:11-18] is concerned to explicate the meaning of this concept. . . . The incarnation is necessary that he might become 'a merciful and faithful high priest.'" See also the earlier promotion of this interpretation by A. A. Hoekema, "The Perfection of Christ in Hebrews," *CTJ* 9 (1974): 33-37; Attridge, *Hebrews,* 86-87.

47. Peterson, *Hebrews and Perfection,* 73.

48. The addressees will also be asked to see their own endurance of hardships as "fitting them" for their participation in the city of God, equipping them with "holiness" and the "peaceful fruit of righteousness" (12:5-11). In their case, however, it is even clearer that these hardships are not the means of their being perfected, which is rather effected by the sacrifice of Christ and fully manifested at the eschatological intervention of God.

49. Turner, *Ritual Process,* 100-9; Milgrom, *Leviticus I–XVI,* 566-69.

50. Most of these are careful to distinguish between a vocational and ethical interpretation since the author of Hebrews holds Jesus to have been perpetually without sin, such that "learning obedience" does not imply a time of disobedience (Attridge, *Hebrews,* 86-87;

carry simply its formal sense of "having been brought to the final goal" of that journey described in 5:7-8, namely, having entered the divine realm from which advantageous location he can secure divine benefits for his loyal clients.[51]

The final occurrence of the verb in relation to Jesus is found at 7:28, where "a Son perfected forever" is contrasted to "human beings subject to weakness." The weakness of these priests is specifically their liability to sin (5:2-3; 7:27), but it may also include their liability to death, another prominent obstacle to their mediation (7:23-25). "Perfected" here would most likely be heard as "removal from the sphere of liability to weakness," that is, in his passing through to the heavenly, divine realm. The author of Hebrews regards the earthly priests as slipping in and out of holiness on account of their own sins (and hence as in constant need of purification offerings). If this is the primary point of contrast, then the "eternal perfecting" of the Son would again underscore Jesus' nonliability to weakness, his nonliability to moving back and forth across the barrier of clean/defiled. In both cases, perfection signifies breaking through and existing on the other side of a boundary, whether death or sin, that trips up every other priest. It signifies crossing a threshold that other priests were unable to cross, arriving at a finished state that all other priests fail to achieve.

In sum, the perfecting of Christ signifies chiefly his arrival at his heavenly destiny (as, in one sense, it will also mean for the "many sons and daughters"), while the path through which he passed toward that destiny is certainly seen by the author to fit him for the ministry he performs "on the other side."

The Perfecting of the Believers

The author disrupts his discourse on Jesus' priesthood to present a challenge to the hearers to hear the sermon attentively and respond wisely. In this challenge, the adjectival and nominal forms of the "perfection" word group figure prominently. In 5:11-14, he urges the

---

Hoekema, "Perfection of Christ," 31; Scholer, *Proleptic Priests*, 187-88; Kögel, "Begriff," 41). Scholer (*Proleptic Priests*, 188) perhaps puts it best: "what Christ experienced was not a development of moral character but a full acquaintance with the entire range of human existence and depravity, i.e., his brothers' [and sisters'] very situation."

51. Jesus' induction into his heavenly priesthood has been seen by a number of scholars as his "perfection." This rather straightforward solution to the problem of "perfection" in Hebrews takes the activity of 5:10 ("having been appointed a high priest after the order of Melchizedek") as parallel and epexegetical to the cryptic participle of 5:9 (τελειωθείς). This position is favored by Attridge (*Hebrews*, 87): "Christ's perfecting, as developed in the text, may be understood as a vocational process by which he is made complete or fit for his office. This process involves, not a moral dimension, but an existential one. Through his suffering, Christ becomes the perfect model, who has learned obedience (5:10), and the perfect intercessor, merciful and faithful (2:17). Christ's perfection is consummated in his exaltation, his entry into 'honor and glory', the position where he serves to guarantee his followers' similar perfection." The chief difficulty I have with this line of reasoning is the implicit assumption that the author is interested in describing the "process" of perfection rather than in indicating merely the fact of perfection (arrival at the final state). Lane (*Hebrews 1–8*, 122) favors the sense of "consecration to divine service" (e.g., as priest), the well-attested LXX use of "perfection" terminology.

hearers to be "mature" rather than "immature" in their engagement of their responsibilities toward one another. This is a rather straightforward appeal to the "biological" sense of "perfection," as the "adult" is the completed or final form of the "child" or "infant." In 6:1, the author proposes a course of action, namely, to "be borne along to perfection" (τελειότητα), leaving behind the initial (ἀρχῆς) instruction of Christ. Again the juxtaposition of ἀρχ- and τελ- words is striking. Hebrews 6:4-6 provides a rationale for accepting this injunction to move forward from a consideration of the contrary situation, the impossibility of repentance for those who "fall away." Those who give up now will not be given a second chance to undergo this process. One either remains constant and reaches the goal, the divinely appointed end, of the Christian calling or falls short of the goal (cf. 12:15) by falling away along the path. "Perfection" here carries the sense not merely of "maturity" but of "arriving at the appointed goal." This use parallels the meaning of τέλος in 3:14; 6:11. The point is to motivate the hearers to set their hearts fully on attaining the end that God has appointed for the constant and loyal, and to dissuade them from thinking that "shrinking back" is an advantageous course of action.

The majority of occurrences of this word group appear in a definitively cultic context. First, in 7:19, the author tells the audience that the Torah was unable to "perfect" anything (οὐδὲν . . . ἐτελείωσεν), but the better hope allows them to "draw near to God." The contrast is meaningful if the "better hope" now enables what the Torah did not enable. Under the Old Covenant, the worshiper could not "draw near to God," but now the better hope enables this drawing near. "Perfecting," then, refers to the cultic process by which a person is enabled to draw near to God. We will recall that "perfecting" could be used for "consecrating" and "cleansing" in cultic contexts, such that the adjective "perfect" could refer to those who had passed through a rite of passage (or cleansing or ordination) and arrived at the "other side" of that ritual. This idea will be further developed in 9:9–10:18.

The author describes the restrictions on access to God's presence in the tabernacle (the prescriptions of Torah), affirming that access to God ("drawing near") is never broadened because "gifts and sacrifices are being offered that are unable to perfect the worshiper in regard to the conscience (μὴ δυνάμεναι κατὰ συνείδησιν τελειῶσαι τὸν λατρεύοντα)." The way into the holy places is not open as long as the first chamber, in which ineffective sacrifices are offered, enjoys cultic standing. The desert tabernacle becomes a parable for the author of the lamentable condition of the unbridgeable distance between the worshiper and the holy God. The distance remains because the sacrificial system is incapable of "perfecting" the conscience of the worshiper so that it can stand in the very presence of God.

This situation is precisely what Christ overcomes, as the author celebrates Jesus' achievement: if animal blood suffices to cleanse the body from defilement, "how much more will the blood of Christ . . . cleanse our conscience (καθαριεῖ τὴν συνείδησιν) from dead works to serve the living God?" "Perfecting the conscience" and "cleansing the conscience" are set parallel to one another — this is what Torah cannot achieve but what Christ has achieved.[52] The intensely cultic context of Hebrews 7–10 upholds a cultic un-

---

52. Peterson (Hebrews and Perfection, 166) attempts to read these verses from the framework of his vocational understanding of perfection: "The object of the verb in 9:9 and 10:1 suggests that τελειοῦν was being applied to believers in a 'vocational' sense: they are perfected as would-be worshipers, as those who would draw near to God, through the work of Christ." The problem with this reading, however, is that it ignores the author's clue that "per-

derstanding of perfection in these chapters, not because the word had become a "technical term" for consecration[53] but because the word, surrounded by words like "sacrifice," "cleanse," "those who draw near," and the like, is placed squarely in a cultic discourse.[54] It would be unnatural for it not to take its meaning here from these cultic bearings.

These terms are informed by Israel's purity map, which the author imports together with his arguments from the OT cultus. The worshiper is not merely profane (i.e., the normal state that is the unmarked counterpart to "holy"), but polluted (the marked, abnormal counterpart to "clean").[55] The sins that one has committed against God have defiled the conscience, which cannot now come into the presence of the holy God, before whom nothing unclean (i.e., defiled or "unwhole") survives. Richard Nelson, borrowing an image from nuclear physics, speaks of the "danger of bringing the holy into contact with the unclean and provoking the catastrophic unclean-holy fusion reaction."[56] The fire of the Lord's holiness breaks out against the unclean thing. Only if the worshiper can be made clean from defilement and sanctified (i.e., pass from the profane state to a state of holiness), can he or she approach God.

Jesus' sacrifice, the author avers, cleanses the conscience from these defilements.[57] In effect, the blood of Jesus repairs the conscience from the ravages of sin and makes it whole again, thus "whole," "perfect." Such parallelism is appropriate to a purity map where lack of wholeness signals defilement. This reading is further reinforced by 10:1-2, where lingering "consciousness of sin" reveals the failure of the Law to "perfect those approaching," and "once having been cleansed" reveals the implications of the "perfecting" that the Law cannot achieve.

Perfecting, however, involves more here than merely cleansing (moving the polluted back into the category of the clean). It also involves sanctification (moving the profane

---

fection" is to be read as "cleansing" (specifically from defilement) in these passages, hence within the framework of cultic rituals designed to move persons or objects across a boundary to their ritually appointed end.

53. Although Silva ("Perfection and Eschatology," 61) adduces Lev. 21:10 as evidence that the "head word" in the idiom "perfect the hands" could carry the meaning of the whole idiom on its own. It appears not to have been suggested before that the author may have the idiom itself strongly in mind, substituting "conscience," however, for "hands" in chapters 9 and 10 as an implicit reinforcement of his explicit contrast between ablutions that cleanse the exterior body and ablutions that are effective for the interior (9:10, 13-14).

54. Thus, rightly, Wikgren ("Patterns of Perfection," 159): "it is of course clear from the whole argument of the Epistle that the terms have a cultic-religious orientation."

55. Nelson, *Raising Up a Faithful Priest*, 19.

56. Ibid., 24. See also p. 33: "What had to be avoided at all costs, however, was contact between the categories of holy and unclean. These two powers generated an incompatible and dangerous combination"; Milgrom, *Leviticus I–XVI*, 261: "the impure and the holy are mutually antagonistic and irreconcilable."

57. Conceptualizing sin as defilement is well rooted in the tradition of the Jewish Scriptures. Psalm 51:1-17 is perhaps the most familiar and eloquent expression of this (see especially vv. 2, 7, 10-11, 16-17); Isaiah 6:1-6 is also a striking testimony to the joining of moral and cultic conceptions of sin and holiness, as Isaiah declares his lips "unclean," and the seraph touches his lips with the coal to take away his "iniquity" (seen clearly as the "uncleanness") and declare his sin forgiven.

into the category of the sacred).[58] The difference between cleansing and sanctifying is that the former merely restores one to the normal state of being clean, while the latter moves one from the normal state of being profane to the marked state of being holy. Those who are "holy" serve in the holy places (cf. Exod. 28:41; 29:1; 30:30), not merely those who are clean. Jesus' offering of himself is thus properly both a purification offering and a consecration offering (see Exod. 29). It restores the wholeness of (thus "perfects") the conscience (as well as repairs the damage done to the heavenly sanctuary by the sins of the people) and also fits the worshiper to cross the boundaries hitherto uncrossed in the history of the cult of Yahweh, as Hebrews 10:19-22 will bring out forcefully (although 4:14-16 has certainly already intimated this). Hebrews 10:10, 29 speaks of the blood not merely as cleansing but as sanctifying. The author of Hebrews has completely conflated what in the OT world were frequently two separate moves. Hebrews 9:13 especially attests to this conflation, where the defiled are rendered clean through a process of "sanctifying" rather than mere "cleansing." The OT is not devoid, however, of parallels to this, perhaps the most striking being Leviticus 16:19, where Aaron "cleanses [the altar] and sanctifies it from all the defilements of the children of Israel." "Perfection" of the one who approaches God through Jesus (7:25), then, signals at one stroke both the cleansing and the consecration of the worshiper, the accomplishment (completion) of two rites designed to bring an object to an appointed goal (cleanness, holiness).

Finally, in 10:14-18 the significance of "perfection" as erasure of the defiling memory of sin is developed. Christ's successful perfecting of the one being consecrated is proven from God's declaration in Jeremiah to remember no more the sins of the worshiper. Neither the worshiper conscience nor the memory of God retains "awareness of sins." Both, in effect, have been cleansed (the author thus provides an interpretation of cleansing the heavenly sanctuary's accoutrements: Jesus both cleansed the worshiper's conscience from the defilement of sin and washed the memory of it from the heavenly mercy seat). The goal achieved through this process is then celebrated in 10:19-25: people are at last able to approach God. In essence, the perfection here is the completion of a salvation-historical process of bringing humanity back to its proper, divinely appointed state of enjoying face-to-face fellowship with God.

Perfecting as Consummation

Two other passages, however, remain to be considered, both of which suggest that the perfecting of the believer is not merely a cultic *fait accompli* in Hebrews. There is another sense in which perfection still awaits the addressees. The author carefully balances present accomplishment with future accomplishment — both aspects of which should impel the hearers on to the full realization of the goal, the τέλος, of their Christian pilgrimage. Hebrews 11:39-40 claims that the OT saints "did not receive the promise" in order that "they might not be perfected apart from us." Here, "being perfected" is set

---

58. See Nelson, *Raising Up a Faithful Priest,* 20-21. Ellingworth (*Hebrews,* 511) claims that "perfecting" and "sanctifying" are "used interchangeably in Hebrews," but Peterson (*Hebrews and Perfection,* 167) is more correct to note that there is overlap between "perfecting" and "sanctifying" without the two being coterminous.

parallel to "receiving the promises," arriving at the promised goal for the people of God.[59] The fulfillment of their trust (taking "perfecting faith" in the sense of fulfilling promises) is the fulfillment of the Christian addressees' hope as well, all brought to that fulfillment by the same, better means (Jesus' priestly mediation). The "something better" is thus not the promise, but the means by which the promise is fulfilled, and those who hope attain what they hope for.

Abraham and the patriarchs died looking for God's city, the same city toward which the believers strive (11:13-16; 13:13-14). Perfection here means arriving at and entering into that which God has prepared — the New Jerusalem, the better, abiding realm. The righteous who have already joined that assembly have "been perfected" (12:23), and it remains for the whole people of faith to persevere so as to arrive at their own completion of their hope (3:14; 6:1, 11). Perfection in this sense, then, means going where Christ has already gone as our forerunner (6:19-20), arriving ourselves where formerly only our hope reached in. Here, then, the perfecting of Christ most closely anticipates the perfecting of the believers in terms of entrance into the unshakable, divine realm. The author underscores the proleptic or present enjoyment of perfection in terms of the cleansing (making whole) of the conscience, which enables the worshiper now to have access to the throne of God, to enter God's presence in the worship of the community of faith even before they enter the divine realm in person. They remain connected to that realm, indeed to the inner chamber of God's presence, by the tether of hope, and look forward to their own eventual arrival there, the perfection of the promise that brings them into their unshakable inheritance.

In this exploration of the language of perfection, I have attempted to show how the formal sense of "to perfect" (i.e., "to bring something to its proper, final state" or its appointed goal) provides the general sense that brings coherence to every specific occurrence of the word group. The author of Hebrews especially employs the term to speak of the end result of a rite of passage of some kind. The "perfect" is the "mature" (the adult, who has passed from being a child into the "complete," "whole" state of the human being), the "clean" (which has passed from defilement through a purgative rite, emerging "whole" on the other side), the "consecrated" (which has passed through a rite of sanctification, moving from the state of the "ordinary" to its ritually appointed destiny, the "holy") and also, rather prominently, the "translated" (Christ, brought to his divinely appointed finished state of exaltation and session at God's right hand through a rite of passage, that entailed the "liminal" state of incarnation, humiliation, and the suffering of death; the people of faith follow their pioneer on this journey).

The author is attracted to this word group because it reinforces so well his ideological agenda. Anthony A. Hoekema suggests that the author's "main concern" in his use of perfection language is "to point to the superior efficacy of the new covenant over the old."[60] I suggest that this concern is ancillary to the author's real "main concern," which is to motivate the hearers to press on toward God's goal and reward, to hold out until the end

---

59. It is surprising that Scholer (*Proleptic Priests,* 200), who elsewhere employs this method of interpreting perfection language through parallel expressions, resists understanding "perfection" as a present state (in a limited sense) and a state yet to be realized by believers, although he is correct to resist another reading that suggests that "perfection" of the conscience already gives believers access to the "rest," which clearly is eschatological.

60. Hoekema, "Perfection of Christ," 31.

of the process that began at their conversion (3:14; 6:1, 11), to break through to the other side of their rite of passage from this world to the next. The word group is used to encourage the audience to persevere in the liminal state of marginalization, humiliation, and rootlessness in this world in order to arrive at God's good goal.

The author's use of perfection terminology specifically focuses the hearers on two things. First, the perfection of Jesus and the perfection that awaits the hearers turns their attention to their final home in God's realm. In this regard, it impels them forward on their Christian pilgrimage, preventing them from succumbing to the contrary motions of drifting off, falling away, or turning away. Second, however, the perfection of their conscience, which now gives them access to the throne of God, allowing them to draw near to God, impels them inward toward the group (again, the centripetal impetus of the sermon), toward that sacred space that they find in the "assembling of themselves together" (10:19-25). Their center of gravity is thus fixed on God and the gathered worshipping community and anchors them to their hope during this liminal period of their earthly life.

As Richard Nelson insightfully observes, "sacred space provided the human mind with a fixed center, the solace of formed order in the midst of formless chaos."[61] Hebrews speaks at length about sacred space — specifically the heavenly sanctuary that is, for now, accessed in Christian worship — so as to center the believers on their communal identity and their hope. In the midst of their experience of rootlessness, rejection, and marginalization, they are being induced to seek their center and to renew their sense of order through a common focus on the goal of the Christian pilgrimage and on the sacred gathering of the believing community. Sacred space is always within the group (the community of the sanctified who serve before the living God) or "out there" beyond the visible creation.

At this point we can return to 10:14 and consider the tenses of that pithy sentence: "by a single sacrifice he has perfected forever [perfect indicative active] those who are being sanctified [present passive participle]." On the one hand, it would be possible to argue that the present participle does not truly create a contrast with the perfect verb, whether it be explained as a timeless present or, perhaps better, as an action that occurs at the same time as the main verb. Those who read the present participle as indicative of an ongoing process, however, are closer to perceiving the dynamic that Hebrews is creating. The decisive ritual that cleanses and consecrates the believer is accomplished ("by one offering he has perfected for all time"), but the liminal state that surrounds that sacrifice — the larger rite of passage that surrounds the ritual and actually signals transition — continues for the believers. The hearers belong neither to their former, normal state (their status and at-homeness in Greco-Roman or Jewish society) nor yet to their final, normal state (their status and at-homeness in the unshakable realm of God's city and homeland). To encourage the hearers to persevere the author elevates the decisive "perfecting" that Christ's sacrifice has effected *and* reinforces the certainty and surpassing value of "being perfected" in the final sense of arriving in God's real presence and abiding in that state forever.

---

61. Nelson, *Raising Up a Faithful Priest,* 27.

Summary

The author advances his rhetorical goal for the hearers by affirming the availability of great and timely resources to help them persevere unto the goal of their calling. No less a broker than Jesus has secured access for them to no less a patron than God himself. Rather than succumb to any pressure or hardship they face on the way to their eternal inheritance of honor and homeland, they have every cause to hold onto their confession. Jesus himself provides a model for their own struggle, since "in the days of his flesh" he, too, relied on a vital prayer life to sustain him in his commitment to obedience. The author wants the hearers to feel confident as they contemplate pursuing the course he commends to them, as well as grateful for the unparalleled benefits provided by the "great high priest."

The certainty, quality, and efficacy of Jesus' priestly mediation become the author's chief focus in 5:1-10 and 7:1–10:18. At the outset he reaffirms the fact of Jesus' appointment through a Christocentric reading of Psalm 110:4. In Jesus, the hearers have still the best qualities of any earthly high priest (namely, sympathy and gentleness) without the drawbacks (the sin and vulnerability to weakness by which earthly priests acquire their sympathy). As they remain obedient to, and associated with, this most effective of brokers of divine favor, the addressees are given the assurance of "eternal deliverance," the final (i.e., telic) benefit Jesus secures as a result of his placement in the cosmos at God's right hand. The author thus reinforces his presentation of what course brings the greater advantage: attachment and loyalty to Jesus now brings both access to God's help in the present and the assurance of reaching the divinely appointed destiny, the unshakable realm.

Bridging the Horizons

The opening verses of this passage rather straightforwardly impel hearers in every age to prayer. The "spiritual discipline" of prayer is a resource neglected by many believers, particularly, I suspect, in the Western world where a lack of belief in the supernatural has led many, perhaps unconsciously, to devalue conversation with God. Nevertheless, the author of Hebrews presents our access to the divine "throne of favor" as one of the primary benefits won for us by Jesus through the shedding of his own blood. As we read on in Hebrews, we hear about the perfecting of the conscience and the ritual acts performed by our great high priest on our behalf in the heavenly sanctuary — all of which serve the end of allowing us to approach God's holy presence in the expectation of favor rather than to remain at a distance from God out of fear or sense of defilement. The first word of this passage to us, then, is indeed to "approach the throne of favor," casting our burdens and cares before God and awaiting the words God will speak or the resources God will provide to enable our continued fidelity and obedience to his call. Together with the model of Jesus articulated in Hebrews 5:7-8, this provides us with direction for how to navigate hardships, how to find resources for persevering in our commitment to Jesus and to the works he commits to us, whether those be acts of love and service, witness, or even the endurance of the "hostility of sinners."

The sympathy of the priest toward those on whose behalf he mediates is no minor topic in this discourse (2:17; 4:15; 5:1-2). What was true for Jesus and, at least ideally, for the levitical priests should be true for all who minister in the name of Jesus, indeed all who represent Jesus to the world. The remedy for a harsh, judgmental spirit is reflection on our own weakness, on our liability to the power of sin, and on our utter dependence on God to avoid sin and to do what is pleasing to him. Out of such reflection comes a gentle spirit that knows how to love and help the sinner and that reflects the love and care of the great high priest who calls them.

Finally, Jesus' example provides a perhaps unexpected model for encountering hardships or sufferings endured as a result of our commitment to do God's will and work in this world. Jesus' experiences — his sufferings — became opportunities to "learn" obedience and to deepen his acquaintance with this core virtue. The author of Hebrews does not seek to sanctify (and thus perhaps legitimate) all manner of sufferings, to be sure. All suffering is part of the fallenness of creation in general and its human inhabitants in particular, and thus not divinely sanctioned. Some kinds of suffering are, indeed, never to be legitimated as "God's will" for the victim (e.g., domestic abuse of any stripe). Nevertheless, there are certain experiences of hardship or deprivation or suffering that can become episodes of divine training, opportunities for the Spirit to shape us and form in us the virtues that please God. Specifically, these are the hardships encountered as a result of answering God's call, of doing God's will, of witnessing to God's standards for human life and society in an unjust world. For many Christians, simply associating themselves with the name of Christ leads them into places of extreme deprivation and suffering. By enduring these sufferings, however, the value of their calling and their hope is deeply implanted into their souls, and the Godward orientation of their desires is strengthened. Through the fires of suffering, they arrive at a strong sense of the priorities of life and place obedience to God and partnership with Christ at the head of the list. So also the voices crying out for justice where injustice is the accepted norm (e.g., the voices of protest raised in South Africa against apartheid or in the United States against segregation) call down upon themselves the "hostility of sinners." In their refusal to mute their own witness to God's vision and will for human society so as to escape marginalization or worse, however, such believers "learn obedience," learn what it means to live for God and God's kingdom before all else. The assurance of Jesus' commitment to bring "eternal deliverance" to his obedient ones assists our courageous and even victorious perseverance. As for the first addressees, so for us, "obeying him" must become the primary agenda of our lives, for it is by *such* a commitment that we will know Christ as the one who delivers us from this age for an unshakable inheritance at the consummation.

Honoring God Necessitates Perseverance: 5:11–6:20

Overview

The exposition of Jesus' exercise of his priesthood "after the order of Melchizedek" (5:10) is interrupted by 5:11–6:20 and is resumed at 7:1 as the author considers the significance and qualities of Melchizedek himself, the founder of this new order. This interruption serves many purposes, with each paragraph moving the hearers strategically closer to adopting the author's agenda for their lives. First, it acts as a second call for an attentive hearing. *Rhetorica ad Herennium* 3.14.9 states that the orator needs to engage the hearers' attention throughout the speech, "for attention slackens everywhere else rather than at the beginning." Hebrews 5:11–6:20 as a whole may serve this function, but 5:11-14 in particular issues a sharp call for attentiveness to, and internalization of, the author's message. Second, 6:1-3 reinforces the author's proposed course of action, namely, moving ahead toward the goal of the journey that the hearers had begun with their conversion and elementary catechism in the Christian worldview. Third, 6:4-8, often considered one of the more difficult passages in Hebrews, provides an extended rationale for pursuing the course proposed in 6:1-3. The stark and uncompromising language of this passage also serves the purpose of amplification. It reveals the importance of what is being discussed and of making a wise choice in response, and it does so by examining the consequences of making a poor response (see discussion of 2:1-4, which effects a similar end). Fourth, the appeal to the emotion of fear in 6:4-8 is balanced by an appeal to the emotion of confidence in 6:9-12 (see discussion of the juxtaposition of 4:12-13 and 4:14-16), which palliates the hearers and orients them yet once more toward the course of action to which they are being exhorted. Finally, 6:13-20 effects a transition back to the theme of this central discourse by considering the significance of God's oath (leading specifically to the oath that appoints Jesus as "high priest forever" in Ps. 110:4) and the reliability such an oath provides for the believer's hope.

The first four paragraphs of this "digression" (which is nevertheless central to the author's rhetorical purpose) are held together by an *inclusio* formed by the words "you have become sluggish" (νωθροὶ γεγόνατε, 5:11) and "in order that you not become sluggish" (νωθροὶ γένησθε, 6:12). The transitional character of 6:13-20 is borne out structurally. First, it develops the final words of 6:12. The addressees are urged there to imitate those who "through faith and patient endurance (διὰ . . . μακροθυμίας) inherit the promises (τὰς ἐπαγγελίας)," and 6:13-15 turns to consider the example of one such heir, Abraham, who "having thus patiently endured (μακροθυμήσας) received the promise (τῆς ἐπαγγελίας)." Second, 6:13-20 takes the hearer back to the key words that closed 4:14–5:10:

> "appointed by God a high priest after the order of Melchizedek"
> (προσαγορευθεὶς . . . ἀρχιερεὺς κατὰ τὴν τάξιν Μελχισέδεκ, 5:10)

> "having become a high priest for ever after the order of Melchizedek"
> (κατὰ τὴν τάξιν Μελχισέδεκ ἀρχιερεὺς γενόμενος εἰς τὸν αἰῶνα, 6:20)

Hebrews 6:20 thus reconstructs the platform from which to launch into 7:1–10:18 (a platform temporarily closed, as it were, during 5:11–6:20).

Commentary

5:11-14

The author rouses the hearers once more to attention and hopes to impel them forward in their investment in the Christian group through an appeal to the emotion of shame.[1] Aristotle defines shame (*Rh.* 2.6.2) "as a kind of pain or un-

---

1. Numerous scholars have noted the author's use of shaming to motivate the hearers to some end in this passage. Moffatt (*Hebrews*, 70), for example, writes: "The author, himself a διδάσκαλος, as he is in possession of this mature γνῶσις, is trying to shame his friends out of their imperfect grasp of their religion"; so also Calvin (*Hebrews*, 58): "This reproof hath in it no little pungency to rouse the Jews [sic] from their state of sloth. He says that it is out of all character and a shame that they should be in the elements when they ought to be teachers. . . . To shame them all the more, however, he says the first principles, as if one said, the alphabet." These scholars rightly note the appeal to the emotion of shame, even though their decision to use this passage at the same time as an accurate read-

easiness in respect of misdeeds, past, present, or future, which seem to tend to bring dishonour." Vices, in particular, are held to be shameful (2.6.3-4), but also failure to achieve a "share in the honourable things which all men, or all who resemble us, or the majority of them, have a share in. By those who resemble us I mean those of the same race, of the same city, of the same age, of the same family, and, generally speaking, those who are on an equality" (*Rh.* 2.6.12). Thus, violating core values or failing to measure up to the standards set by one's peers or society can become sources of the feeling of shame.

Here the author charges the audience with having become "sluggish with regard to hearing" (5:11). The importance of hearing the word, a central topic throughout the sermon (2:1-4; 3:7-19; 4:12-13), is once again underscored. Hearing and heeding the word (the "report," ἀκοή) that God uttered through the Son, and receiving and responding obediently to "his voice," have been promoted as the sole path to honor and security, while lack of attentiveness to the message leads to certain punishment and degradation. The author is thus accusing the addressees not merely of nodding off during his sermon, but of failing to respond honorably and wisely to the message of God, of not giving that message its due attention with all diligence.[2]

In addition to this charge, the author claims that the hearers ought to have achieved more by this point in their Christian journey, "ought" to have "measured up" better. Specifically, the author suggests that they ought to have been teachers of each other (ὀφείλοντες εἶναι διδάσκαλοι διὰ τὸν χρόνον) rather than remaining at the level of needing the author's instruction and motivation. The fact that the author will indeed go on to deliver the "long and difficult-to-understand" message (7:1–10:18), and that he immediately proposes pressing on without laying again the foundational teachings (6:1-2), demonstrates that he has used hyperbole in describing them as "having need of someone to teach them the fundamental rudiments of the oracles of God," and requiring "milk and not solid food" (5:12). The author employs common

---

ing of the hearers' spiritual pulse (not to mention their delineation of the audience and the author's goal) is of questionable merit. Delitzsch (*Hebrews,* 259), Göttlieb Lünemann (*A Critical and Exegetical Handbook to the Epistle to the Hebrews* [New York: Funk & Wagnalls, 1884], 382), and Stedman (*Hebrews,* 66) also fall into the trap of regarding the passage as a precise diagnosis of the actual state of the hearers.

2. Arguing that there is a substantial difference between "becoming sluggish with regard to the ears" (5:11) and "becoming sluggish" (6:12), such that the alleged "contradiction" is resolved, ignores both the rhetorical nature of the sermon (i.e., dedication to motivation rather than rigid accuracy at the literal level — always a danger when encountering well-known rhetorical devices such as hyperbole and irony) and the all-encompassing importance of "hearing" in Hebrews. "Hearing" denotes the person's complete response to the message of God, and it is sluggishness with regard to this wholehearted response that is in view throughout 5:11–6:12.

metaphors for levels of education to drive his appeal home.[3] Milk versus meat, the infant versus the mature adult, were frequently used by philosophers to speak of stages of education or achievement in philosophy.[4] Particularly informative is the way in which a philosopher like Epictetus will use these images to motivate his audience to progress in their commitment to the way of life he promotes and to internalize more fully and completely its values: "Are you not willing, at this late date, like children, to be weaned and to partake of more solid food?" (*Diss.* 2.16.39); "you have received the philosophical principles which you ought to accept, and you have accepted them. What sort of teacher, then, do you still wait for, that you should put off reforming yourself until he arrives? You are no longer a lad, but already a full-grown adult" (*Ench.* 51.1).[5] The author of Hebrews uses these metaphors in a manner very similar to what we find in Epictetus, shaming the hearers for not "measuring up" to where they ought to be and motivating them to prove themselves "mature" by their readiness to meet the expectations articulated by the author for the "mature."

Hebrews 5:13-14 introduces a distribution, a rhetorical device that assigns roles and qualities to different groups (here, the infants and the mature; see *Rhet. Her.* 4.35.47): "every one partaking of milk is unskilled in the word of justice,[6] for he or she is an infant, but solid food belongs to the mature, who on account of constancy of habit have their faculties trained for the discernment of the good and the base." The distribution contrasts a less honorable state (in-

---

3. See, for example, Epictetus *Diss.* 2.16.39; 3.24.9 on milk; Seneca *Ep.* 88.20 on "elementary teachings"; and Epictetus *Diss.* 1.26.3; 2.18.27; Philo *De virt.* 18 on education in philosophy as "training." Paul also makes use of these metaphors in 1 Cor. 3:1-3, again in an effort to shame the audience out of some failure to measure up to the expectations Paul has for them or to the virtues of the Christian culture.

4. Thompson (*Beginnings*, 29-30) and Attridge (*Hebrews*, 158-61) especially bring out the cultural intertexture of philosophical texts and educational metaphors.

5. Quoted in Attridge, *Hebrews*, 159 n. 59; 158 n. 42.

6. Stedman (*Hebrews*, 67), following P. Hughes (*Hebrews*, 191), reads the "works-righteousness" versus "imputed righteousness" debate into 5:13 at this point: the "word of righteousness" becomes the word about the righteousness imputed to the believer through Jesus as opposed to attempts to "earn 'brownie points' with God to gain his acceptance." Here is yet another example, similar to his near-allegorical treatment of "rest" (*Hebrews*, 52-59), of imposing theological conviction (ideology) on the text rather than of truly reading the text; the author of Hebrews nowhere gives an indication of combating "works righteousness." The surest way to interpret the ambiguous "word of righteousness" is to note the intentional contrast between the infant and the mature in 5:13-14. The mature person is skilled in "discrimination between what is noble and what is base (or evil)." Skill in the "word of righteousness" leads to this discernment. The author distinguishes between the noble and the base response to God's promises throughout the sermon, demonstrating his case by means of the skillful exegesis of the LXX. The most natural understanding of the "word of righteousness" may thus simply be the "oracles of God" themselves, that is, the LXX.

deed a shameful one, since lack of knowledge of virtue is dishonorable) with a truly and fully honorable state, making the latter group the one with which the hearers will want to identify. The description of the "perfect," "complete," or "mature" person is the one that the hearer will want for his or her own description. Two aspects of this description merit special attention. First, the trained faculty arrives at that mature state through ἕξις, "a constant state of being or practice." Many translations throw the emphasis on "practice" (e.g., NASB; NRSV), but I would suggest that the element of "constancy" is more central both to the semantic range of the word and to the author's agenda (thus the NIV's "through constant use"). A central characteristic of the "mature," then, is their constancy in terms of their commitments, habits, and assessments of advantage. This issues a serious challenge to those who are wavering among the group, who show a lack of stability or constancy.

Second, the author embeds his description of the mature believer in topics associated with the virtue of wisdom, one of the four cardinal virtues promoted by Platonists and Stoics, and which thus entered the mainstream of dominant cultural ethics. He even incorporates a definition of wisdom found almost verbatim in pagan sources, describing it as "the discernment of the good and the base" (5:14). The author of *Rhetorica ad Herennium* (3.3.4-5), for example, defines the faculty of "wisdom" as "intelligence capable, by a certain judicious method, of distinguishing good and bad."[7] After charging the audience with being infants rather than mature adults, the author sharpens his charge by questioning the hearers' capabilities particularly with regard to their capacity for "practical wisdom." It is precisely the discernment of the good or evil course, of the noble and the base, and of the proper evaluation of advantages and disadvantages that is at risk among the wavering. The author shames the hearers for not yet adequately exercising this faculty of wisdom or for not zealously encouraging and teaching one another about the truly advantageous course.

The goal of this section is to provoke the addressees to acquit themselves of the charge that they are not ready for mature instruction and to direct them forcefully toward behaviors in which they show themselves capable of taking on the responsibility of teaching what they have accepted as true rather than requiring further persuasion and instruction in the certainty of the gospel.[8] The

---

7. Aristotle (*Rh.* 1.9.13) similarly defines wisdom as an intellectual capacity for deliberating well about good and bad and thus moves even closer to the decision-making function of wisdom.

8. Thus Attridge (*Hebrews*, 157) argues that 5:11-14 is "an ironic *captatio benevolentiae*. The stance that 'this material is difficult because you are slow-witted,' followed by the more positive remarks of 6:1-3 and 9-12, is designed to elicit the response, 'no, we are not dullards, we are ready to hear what you have to say.'" Jean Héring (*The Epistle to the Hebrews* [London: Epworth, 1970], 43) shares this view, pointing to the discrepancy between the au-

author wants them to see themselves as teachers, of course, so that they will become active participants in the maintenance of the counter-definitions and values of the Christian culture. A community of "teachers" means a community of individual members reinforcing one another's hold on the minority culture's values and goals, precisely the sort of community the author must shape if they are to persist in their journey against the current (and frequently the blasts) of the dominant culture and arrive at their divinely appointed goal.

This passage advances the author's ideological agenda by presenting expectations that the audience should be living up to. This is a strategic way to get their focus off the expectations of their non-Christian neighbors, if their attention has been "drifting" in that direction. While the author will seek to desensitize his addressees to the honor rating of the outside society, he also nurtures their desire for honor before God's court, and thus also their sensitivity to the opinion of those who form the truly significant others for the believers, the Christian group and its leaders. The society's censure is to be "despised," but his censure is expected to have a motivating effect. Where the society shames them for being too actively and openly "Christian," the author counters this by shaming them for not being sufficiently proactive in their profession of faith and reinforcement of one another's commitment. He is urging them in this way to show their maturity through correct discernment of what is noble and what is base (i.e., through embodying wisdom), which has immediate application to their current situation (i.e., perceiving that God's patronage and promises are worth enduring any hostility or disenfranchisement in this temporary order), and to show their maturity through taking on the role of community builders and sustainers of one another's commitment to the group's definitions of reality and goals (e.g., entering the rest of God, remaining committed to the "living God" in contrast to idolatrous expressions of religion, curbing one's desire for material gain or illicit sexual opportunities, looking out for one's fellow group members, and resisting the voices from outside the group calling for abandonment of their commitments to God, Christ, and one another).

---

thor's diagnosis of their spiritual immaturity and his decision to give them the "meat" of the teaching about Melchizedek as a sure sign that "no doubt he was trying to use a well-known pedagogic device [in 5:11-13] to stir them to some exertion." Lane (*Hebrews 1–8*, 135) interprets the passage also not as an actual description, but rather as "irony, calculated to shame them and to recall them to the stance of conviction and boldness consonant with their experience." Long (*Hebrews*, 70) similarly displays a fine appreciation for the author's rhetorical strategy here, although he should say more clearly that "shaming" the hearers serves positively the goal of "motivating" them. Long obscures this somewhat by suggesting that the "goal, of course, would not be to shame them, but to motivate them," whereas the author views the successful appeal to the pathos of shame as the way to motivate the hearers.

6:1-3

Having roused the audience to seek to acquit themselves of being seen as immature in their grasp of their responsibilities toward one another and in their grounding in the values and wisdom of the Christian culture, the author proposes that the hearers indeed "move on to maturity (τὴν τελειότητα, 6:1)," the very thing they will be eager to do after 5:11-14. The author here uses another expression that will reinforce the overarching agenda he has been proposing for the addressees from the beginning, namely, pressing ever forward toward the end of the journey begun at their conversion, baptism, and early catechesis in the Christian worldview (see 1:14; 2:10; 3:18; 4:11 and discussion of these in the commentary above). In all of these passages, the author chooses an expression that seeks to propel the hearers forward in the journey they have begun — appropriately, since this is the movement the advantages of which some have begun to question. The word "maturity" (τελειότης) is polyvalent, meaning also "completion" and "perfection" (in the sense of having arrived at the final state proper to one's being or calling; see "A Closer Look: Perfection in Hebrews," 194-204). The term plays on the adjective "mature" in 5:11-14 but also carries resonances with the other "perfection" terminology and so introduces more than "mature teaching" as the goal that the author proposes. This is clarified by the "argument from the contrary" that follows in 6:4-8, where the alternative to pressing on (6:1) is falling away (6:6). He urges them to move ahead to maturity in terms of exercising wisdom in their choices and discernment of relative advantage (5:14) and in terms of taking a more active role in the encouragement and reinforcement of others in the Christian culture's definitions of wisdom, but he also urges them to move forward simply to the "completion," the divinely destined final state of which their conversion was but the first stage.[9]

Even as he proposes moving on, the author reminds the addressees of the essential elements of the "foundation" of their secondary socialization into the norms of the Christian culture in 6:1b-2. Each basic tenet or ritual serves to reinforce those contours of church-shaped reality and makes the author's agenda

---

9. As Attridge (*Hebrews,* 163) aptly puts it, "the mature Christian is expected not only to 'ingest' the solid food but also to follow Christ on that path to final perfection, whatever the cost." Lane (*Hebrews 1–8,* 139) also rightly sees in this "maturity" the "goal of spiritual maturity" and "perfection." The author's clever juxtaposition of ἀρχ- and τελ- words in 6:1 (Διὸ ἀφέντες τὸν τῆς ἀρχῆς τοῦ Χριστοῦ λόγον ἐπὶ τὴν τελειότητα φερώμεθα), from roots denoting beginning and ending or goal, reinforces this impression of being impelled along to the final state to which one's conversion and instruction in the faith is meant ultimately to lead. The author's use of τελειότης parallels his use of τέλος in 3:14; 6:11. The point is to motivate the hearers to set their hearts fully on attaining the end that God has appointed for the constant and loyal, and to dissuade them from thinking "shrinking back" an advantageous course.

clearly the "wise" and advantageous course of action to follow, and all opposing courses foolish and disadvantageous. The metaphor of "foundation" is a common expression for elementary instruction, especially in philosophical schools,[10] referring to the basic tenets on which the entire edifice of a life lived in accordance with that philosophy can be supported. Hebrews 6:1-2 therefore provides us with an important window into the secondary socialization of the hearers (see discussion in the Introduction), the basic elements of which, being recalled, should make it easier for the hearers to reaffirm their commitment to the course of perseverance in this way of life.

The specific elements are rich with Jewish and Christian cultural references. It has been suggested that there is nothing specifically Christian about these six elements, which would also be appropriate as "a catalogue of Jewish catechesis."[11] The specific content of each element could certainly be filled out in a Christocentric manner, however, and need not refer to any pre-Christian experience of being socialized into Jewish culture. Gentiles coming into the church would be unfamiliar with many of these elements, but even Jews converted to belief in Jesus would need a basic reorientation to these tenets in terms of Jesus' role in, for example, the "resurrection of the dead and eternal judgment."

"Repentance" lies at the heart of the invitation to seek God. It was a mark of John the Baptist's preaching as well as of Jesus' preaching (Mark 1:4, 15) and became the basic summons of the early Church as portrayed in the sermons of Acts (see 2:38; 20:21). Precise identification of the "dead works" (νεκρῶν ἔργων) from which one repents is problematic, but the suggestion that these "dead works" refer to the "external regulations associated with the levitical priesthood in the earthly sanctuary" is definitely to be rejected.[12] The cultic regulations of the earthly priesthood are not themselves characterized as "dead works" from which repentance is required, but as an ineffective means of cleansing the conscience from "dead works" of some other sort (9:9-14). They are incapable of removing sin (10:1-4), not "sin" in themselves (for it is from "sin" that one repents). More attractive is the suggestion that "dead works" refer to idols. Both times they are mentioned (6:1; 9:14), these "dead works" stand in contrast to faith toward, or worship of, the "living God." Contrasting idol worship with worship of the one God is common in Jewish and Christian literature (see, e.g., Ps. 96:4-5; 97:7; 1 Thess. 1:9). Furthermore, the closest parallel to the expression (indeed, the only verbal parallel) occurs in the Wisdom of Solomon 15:17 toward the end of a long tirade against idolatrous worship: "being mortal, they make a dead thing (νεκρὸν ἐργάζεται) with lawless hands." Idols are fre-

---

10. See, for example, Epictetus *Diss.* 2.15.8; Thompson, *Beginnings,* 30.

11. Attridge, *Hebrews,* 163.

12. Lane, *Hebrews 1–8,* 140, in an uncharacteristic lapse of exegetical acuity; see also Stedman, *Hebrews,* 69.

quently denoted as "dead things" (νεκρά) in the Wisdom of Solomon (see 13:10, 18; "dead image," 15:5).

It has also been suggested that the phrase should be read as "works leading to death,"[13] but I would prefer to treat the adjective as truly qualifying the noun, as in "noble works" (6:9-10), which no one suggests should be read "works leading to nobility." For hearers familiar with the Wisdom of Solomon, the "idol" will be a strong, specific echo. Nevertheless, even Wisdom 15:17 articulates a general principle that pushes beyond one specific case. All the work of lawless hands is dead, without life and without beauty. The author reminds the hearers thereby of the contrast between what the addressees "did" as non-Christians and what they can do now as Christians. Their prior life (be it in idolatry and its accompanying sins or in transgressions against Torah) was a life of "dead works," works without value or life or honor. The works they do for one another — their "works of mutual love and service" — are "noble works," works that live in the memory of God and have great reward. Characterizing one's life prior to one's association with the Christian community as "dead" is a strategic way to reinforce commitment to persevere in the new community. It is a potent image assisting believers to dissociate themselves from their own pre-Christian selves, thus making a return to that life less appealing.[14]

Having to learn "faith in God" recalls the typical socialization of Gentiles into the Christian community (1 Thess. 1:9; Acts 14:15), but Jewish converts would also need to reorient their own trust in God to incorporate the role of Jesus in securing God's promises and favor. The One God, accessible through the One Mediator, became the focus of one's hope and the ground of one's security. Again this is a strategic reminder to those who are wavering, who are challenged not to return to their life of dead works "like a dog to its own vomit" and not to renounce their one ground of hope in order to seek their security and well-being from their society (in effect, to move their faith from God back to their pre-Christian networks and religious experience).

Identification of the referents of "washings" and "imposition of hands" remains elusive.[15] From what we know of the early Christian movement in gen-

---

13. Nelson, *Raising Up a Faithful Priest*, 146, calling attention to the "sin unto death" in 1 John 5:16.

14. The same technique is used, with varying purposes, in Rom. 6:17-18; 1 Cor. 6:9-11; Eph. 5:8; Col. 1:13; 1 Pet. 2:9-10.

15. Lane (*Hebrews 1–8*, 140) reaches certainty by assuming that the contrasts articulated within the "advanced instruction" of 7:1–10:18 replicate contrasts present in the initial teachings of the group. Thus the "teaching about washings" refers to the contrast between Jewish purificatory rites and purification "in Christ's blood," and the teaching about "laying on hands" refers to the contrast between priests appointed through laying on of hands in accordance with Torah and the high priest appointed by God's oath. The amount of speculation involved in making this identification is especially apparent in the second case.

eral, and Pauline Christianity in particular, baptism was a widespread ritual of initiation into the Christian group. It would be surprising, therefore, if this term (even if βαπτισμός is a more general and inclusive term for "washings" than βάπτισμα) failed to conjure up reminiscences of that boundary-making ritual. The plural form strongly suggests, however, that the author is not thinking of this ritual alone. While several commentators assume that he is alluding to some early teaching that contrasted pagan ablutions or Jewish purificatory washings with baptism,[16] we should consider the author's own conceptualization of the cleansing of the believer as this is articulated in 10:22. There the author speaks of two purificatory ablutions, one pertaining to the body and effected with "clean water" and one pertaining to the heart, which is "sprinkled clean from a bad conscience," recalling the effects of Jesus' blood in 9:11–10:18. This verse provides an interesting example of an early Christian's reflection on the limitations of what baptism can accomplish (contrary to any *ex opere operatum* view of the ritual). Even baptism is an external rite and sign; the cleansing of the heart is solely the work of Christ's sacrifice.

The second member of this pair, the "laying on of hands," is a well-attested practice of the early Church and serves a number of functions (healing, imparting the Holy Spirit, commissioning). Once again it is difficult to be certain of which function the author or audience would recall here, although the "basic" nature of the other elements would favor the most primary experiences of the imposition of hands, namely, confirmation of the rite of baptism, of the baptized person's reception of the Holy Spirit, and of God's anointing. Such reminders of the ritual acts that marked one's passage from the community of the godless to the community of "those who are about to inherit deliverance" (1:14) would again serve the author's goal of keeping the group boundaries intact and maintaining the commitment of those within the group who had experienced the liturgical reinforcements of their new allegiances.

The third pair, "resurrection of the dead and eternal judgment," lays out two elements of the Jewish and Christian worldview that are especially essential to maintaining commitment to the minority culture's way of life.[17] In light of

---

16. See Spicq, *L'Épître aux Hébreux,* 2.148; Moffatt, *Hebrews,* 75; Lane, *Hebrews 1–8,* 140. Attridge (*Hebrews,* 164) also suggests that the author may refer to purificatory rites other than baptism, which were in use in some churches.

17. Belief in the resurrection of the dead is common to several Jewish groups (see 2 Macc. 7; Dan 12:2) and is attested widely among the strains of early Christianity represented in the NT: Matt. 22:23-33; Luke 14:14; John 5:29; Rom. 6:5; 1 Cor. 15; Acts 4:2; Rev. 20:4-15. This particular view of individual eschatology is frequently replaced by some conception of the immortality of the soul due to assimilation of this hope to a Greco-Roman framework (as in Wis. 2–5; 4 Maccabees). "Eternal judgment" is similarly shared and well attested; see, for example, *1 Enoch* 1:9; Dan. 7:26-27; Matt. 25:31-46; Luke 16:19-31; 2 Cor. 5:10; Rev. 14:9-11; 20:4–22:5. The concept of postmortem judgment, rewards, and punish-

the conviction that advantage and disadvantage, the expedient and inexpedient, are not to be weighed merely in terms of temporal consequences, members of the Jewish or Christian group will frequently prefer death to defection from the values of the minority culture. Fulfillment of the Christian commitment brings the hope of "eternal reward"; violation of that commitment brings the threat of "eternal punishment." The author reminds the addressees here of these pillars of Christian commitment as part of an orchestrated attempt to fix their minds and deliberations on "eternal advantage" and on discerning what is "expedient" in the face of the coming judgment before God (see 1:14; 2:1-3, 10; 4:12-13; 5:9; 10:26-31, 36-39; 12:26-28; 13:4). The assurance of "eternal judgment" (κρίματος αἰωνίου, 6:2) should make it all the more expedient to pursue at any cost the course that promises "eternal deliverance" (σωτηρίας αἰωνίου, 5:9).

The author keeps the agenda proposed in 6:1 firmly in view by affirming his commitment to move forward to completion, and, through the use of the first person plural ending ("we"), by inviting the hearers to do the same: "and this we will do, if God permits" (6:3). More than just a conventional aside,[18] the acknowledgment of dependence on God to move forward at every step of this journey prepares the way for the claim that the author will make concerning the impossibility of the ingrate making a second start on this journey. If God's favorable disposition is required for progress on the journey and for arriving at the goal of the journey, alienating oneself from God's favor by insulting the Benefactor becomes the most inexpedient course of action.

6:4-8

Hebrews 6:4-6 confronts the reader/hearer with its argumentative texture from the opening phrase, Ἀδύνατον γὰρ. The whole sentence employs the topic of the "impossible" (one of the topics common to all genres of rhetoric; cf. Aristotle *Rh.* 2.19) in order to provide a rationale to support the course of action proposed in 6:1-3. The γὰρ shows the enthymematic nature of 6:1-6.[19] The au-

---

ments was, of course, also deeply rooted in Greco-Roman thought. Plato (*Gorg.* 526D-27D) provides an especially bold expression of this.

18. Expressions identical or similar to this one appear in the writings of both Jewish and Greco-Roman authors: 1 Cor. 16:7; Josephus *Ant.* 20.12.1 §267; cf. also Seneca *Ben.* 4.34.4: "if nothing happens to prevent" (*si nihil inciderit, quod impediat*).

19. There appears to be some lack of clarity on this point even in the best of commentaries. Attridge (*Hebrews,* 167), for example, rightly argues that Heb. 6:4-6 is not the rationale narrowly for the clause "if God permits," but applies more broadly to 6:1: "The author will 'move on' (6:10) because, while apostates cannot be restored, his community can be renewed." This leaves the connection, however, vague at best. Pfitzner (*Hebrews,* 98) comments

thor has just urged the hearers to move on to "perfection," to the completion of
that enterprise that began with their elementary socialization into the values
and worldview of the Christian culture (6:1-3). 6:4-6 seeks to support this exhortation through an examination of the contrary course of action,[20] "falling
away." The author strategically moves the audience to see no middle ground between pressing on to the goal and falling away (or falling short, shrinking back,
or drifting off). It remains for us to discover, however, the inner logic of this
statement of the impossible. The agricultural metaphor of 6:7-8 illustrates
rather than demonstrates the argument from the contrary. It presents an analogy that helps guide the hearer to an understanding of why restoration of one
who falls away (rather than one who accepts the author's advice and maintains
commitment to the group) should be impossible. One of the questions we must
ask, then, is whether or not there is socio-cultural information available to the
audience that would allow them to accept this "impossibility" as true, as a
given. How would they hear this argument, and within what contexts would the
argument be persuasive to the hearers?

The next facet of the text that strikes the reader is the string of participles,
which give shape to an unspecified group of people. This is an instance of repetitive texture and is frequently noted by investigators.[21] The debate often
hinges, however, on the attempt to determine whether or not this group of people has experienced "salvation."[22] Are they "saved" individuals who then "lose"
their salvation, or are they merely semiconverts who fall away, so that the doctrine of "eternal security" is not impugned by this passage? This debate demonstrates the ways in which the ideology of interpreters may override the ideology
of the author of the text, constructing a foreign framework that inevitably dis-
torts the author's meaning. The author of Hebrews does not operate with the
theology of Ephesians, where "being saved" is spoken of as a past fact, much less
with a complex theology of the stages of salvation constructed from a harmonization of Romans and John. Here the ideological presupposition that "any in-

---

that "the particle 'for' in 6:4a links verses 4-6 with the claim that only the teaching about
Christ provides a foundation for repentance and faith (v. 1)." This casts a wrong emphasis on
6:1 (which is not a doctrinal claim but an exhortation to move on to completion) and obscures the relationship between 6:4-6 and 6:1 as a supporting argument "from the contrary."
Ellingworth (*Hebrews*, 318) correctly observes that 6:4-6 provides the motivation to move
forward (although he limits this to passing "on to mature teaching").

20. The argument from the contrary was a basic building block of demonstration, being incorporated into the training of the young as part of the *progymnasmata*, specifically in
the exercise called "elaboration of the *chreia*." See the text of Theon in R. F. Hock and E. N.
O'Neil, *The Chreia in Ancient Rhetoric, vol. 1: The Progymnasmata* (Atlanta: Scholars Press,
1986), 176-77.

21. Compare Lane, *Hebrews 1–8*, 142.

22. See the review of this debate in Gleason, "Old Testament Background," 69-71.

terpretation is unscriptural if it conflicts with scripture"[23] prevents us from allowing the author of Hebrews to conceptualize the work of God or the life of the believer any differently from his more popular colleagues in the NT. The result is that the construct that is called "God's revealed plan of salvation" (the synthesis of the more popular texts like John, Romans, and Ephesians)[24] wins out over anything that the author of Hebrews might have to say about that plan. The dominance of the interpreter's ideology is especially apparent here, since no attempt is ever made to adjust the "plan" to the expressions of Hebrews, but always the reverse.

Are the people described in 6:4-5 "saved" individuals in the estimation of the author of Hebrews? They cannot be, since "salvation" is, for this author, the deliverance and reward that awaits the faithful at the return of Christ. Those who have trusted God's promise and Jesus' mediation are "those who are about to inherit salvation," a deliverance ("salvation") that comes at Christ's second coming (9:28), a deliverance ("salvation") thus comparable to that enjoyed by Noah (11:7). Noah was not saved when he began to build the ark; he was saved when he finished, stocked, and boarded the ark (and, even more especially, when he found himself still alive after the flood). The deliverance offered by the Son is indeed "eternal" (5:9), but this "eternal salvation" is what the obedient believers look forward to inheriting and enjoying, specifically on the day when the Son comes to judge the world and reward his junior sisters and brothers who have maintained their trust in and loyalty toward him in a hostile world.[25] "Eternal salvation" only becomes the "eternal security" of those who have been saved after one has decided that the formulations of Ephesians are more important to one's ideology than Hebrews.[26]

---

23. J. B. Rowell, "Exposition of Hebrews Six," *Bib Sac* 94 (1937): 321. What Rowell admits explicitly as a "necessary postulate in all Bible exegesis" many more recent scholars exercise implicitly. For an astounding example, see T. K. Oberholtzer, "Thorn-Infested Ground in Hebrews 6:4-12," *Bib Sac* 145 (1988): 328: "The inheritance cannot be soteriological, for eternal salvation is by grace through faith." Ephesians 2:6 thus not only determined what "eternal salvation" means in Heb. 5:9 (contra Heb. 1:14; 9:28; 11:7) but also determined what "inheriting the promises" can and cannot mean.

24. Rowell, "Exposition," 329.

25. The author of Hebrews is not alone in considering "salvation" as something that lies ahead of the believer. 1 Peter (1:5, 9-10; 2:3) also retains the more thoroughly "eschatological" use of this concept.

26. As in Gleason, "Old Testament Background," 90 (and n. 91). This conviction that "salvation" is a past experience for the believer (and therefore must be the same in Hebrews) even leads him to claim that "the author assured his readers that they *had* received 'a kingdom which cannot be shaken' (12:28), thus suggesting their eternal state was not in question" (emphasis mine). In 12:28, however, the author urges the hearers to "show gratitude" since "we *are receiving* an unshakable kingdom." Moreover, the response of gratitude is motivated by the claim that "our God is a consuming fire," suggesting that the author's interest in assur-

If the author would not characterize the people described in 6:4-5 as "saved" (or "unsaved" for that matter), how does he present them, and how would the hearers view them? They are people who have received God's gifts, who have benefited from God's generosity (God's "grace," meaning God's favorable disposition to give benefits).[27] Indeed, the author presents a striking accumulation of divine benefits, creating several categories of the experience of God's generosity so as to make that generosity all the more impressive and the obligation of gratitude all the more pressing. These gifts are described in terms that are informed by oral-scribal intertexture with Jewish Scriptures as well as by Jewish and Christian cultural intertexture.[28]

The subjects of 6:4-5 were "enlightened" (φωτισθέντας), a word that, together with other words using the root φωτ-, are common terms for reception of the message of the gospel and its positive effects on the hearers in Christian culture (John 1:9; 1 Cor. 4:5; 2 Cor. 4:4-6; Eph. 1:18; 2 Tim. 1:10; 1 Pet. 2:9;

---

ance is not as great as Gleason's. See also Oberholtzer, "Thorn-Infested Ground," 326, 328, for uses of the phrase "eternal salvation" that align not with Hebrews but rather a theological presupposition.

27. Readers seeking more information on this aspect of the cultural environment of the ancient Mediterranean may consult deSilva, *4 Maccabees*, 127-33; idem, *Despising Shame*, 226-44, 272-75. Essential works in this area include Saller, *Personal Patronage*; Danker, *Benefactor*.

28. Gleason's chief point is that the episode of Kadesh-barnea, the negative example expounded in Heb. 3:7–4:11, is the principal background for Heb. 6:4-6 ("Old Testament Background," 64, 66, 72-91). He argues that the plural substantival participles in 6:4-6 have the wilderness generation (also described by substantival participles in 3:10-11, 16-19; 4:2, 6) as their "antecedents." This sort of linkage is peculiarly specious. Would the substantival participle in 6:12 also apply to the wilderness generation? He goes on to expand on the experience described in 6:4-6 as applying to both the addressees and the experience of the wilderness generation (much of which is forced — for example, suggesting that "being enlightened" corresponds to the pillar of fire). The enterprise is, in one sense, certain to succeed since the author of Hebrews has already in 3:7–4:11 established the situation of some of the addressees as precariously close to that of the wilderness generation. It is precisely this correspondence drawn in 3:7–4:11, however, which makes me question the usefulness of insisting (where the author does not insist) that it be carried over into 6:4-8. I would have taken the appearance of the phrase "crucifying the Son of God" to be a decisive piece of internal evidence against forcing this "background," but Gleason sees in the shift from aorist participles to present participles justification for reading the aorist participles as applying to both the past generation and present addressees, and the present participles as pertaining to the present audience only. This ignores, of course, the fact that in nonindicative moods, aspect, and not time, is the pertinent feature of tenses. The obligations of clients, moreover, serve as a common denominator between the failure of the wilderness generation at Kadesh-barnea and the danger of apostasy in the addressees' situation. See D. A. deSilva, "Exchanging Favor for Wrath: Apostasy in Hebrews and Patron-Client Relations," *JBL* 115 (1996): 105-9.

2 Pet. 1:10).[29] This represents a distinctive advantage over those who remain "in the dark" about the requirements of God and the future of the world. Paul, for example, could encourage the believers in Thessalonica that their reception of the gospel gave them "insider knowledge," which enabled them to live wisely in light of God's coming judgment, while all their neighbors continued to pursue foolishly the course that would result in destruction and loss (1 Thess. 5:1-8). Psalm 34 (Ps. 33 in the LXX) may be informing the author, as both this verb and the next (γευσαμένους) appear together in Psalm 33:6, 8 (LXX): "Draw near to God and be enlightened. . . . Taste and see that the LORD is good (φωτίσθητε . . . γεύσασθε)."[30] It is noteworthy that both the psalm and Hebrews seek to promote continued hope in God, fear of the Lord, and obedience to God by means of this image of tasting God's goodness, which takes the specific form of being "rescued" or delivered from peril and having the assurance of enjoying "every good thing" (i.e., enjoying God's protection and patronage: Ps. 33:4-7, 11 [LXX]).

Reference to receipt of a gift ("the heavenly gift," τῆς δωρεᾶς τῆς ἐπουρανίου) takes us even more directly into the social intertexture of patron-client scripts. Where a gift is bestowed and received, an obligation is incurred by the recipient. A primary resource for entering into the cultural context of patronage is Seneca's *De beneficiis*. A repeated emphasis of this work is that the social order only works as long as people honor their reciprocal obligations to one another. Greco-Roman mythology depicts this through the image of the three Graces dancing hand in hand in a circle:

> There is one for bestowing a benefit, one for receiving it, and a third for returning it. . . . Why do the sisters hand in hand dance in a ring which returns upon itself? For the reason that a benefit passing in its course from hand to hand returns nevertheless to the giver; the beauty of the whole is destroyed if the course is anywhere broken, and it has most beauty if it is continuous and maintains an uninterrupted succession. (Seneca *Ben.* 1.3.2-3)

For Seneca, accepting a gift means accepting an obligation to the giver at the same time: "the giving of a benefit is a social act, it wins the goodwill of someone, it lays someone under obligation" (5.11.5); "the person who intends to be grateful, immediately while he is receiving, should turn his thought to repaying" (2.25.3). Patronage creates relationships, with reciprocal obligations and

29. Attridge, *Hebrews*, 169; Lane, *Hebrews 1–8*, 141.

30. Another connection with this psalm appears in Heb. 12:14, where "pursue peace" has long been observed to reflect Ps. 34:14b (LXX 33:15b): "seek out peace and pursue it (ζήτησον εἰρήνην καὶ δίωξον αὐτήν)." The author thus appears to have been thoroughly familiar with this psalm, as would be expected since the Psalter was the hymnal and frequent source for moral exhortation for both synagogue and church.

duties, including loyalty: "a benefit is a common bond and binds two persons together" (6.41.2).[31] Violation of this bond was considered an act of sacrilege, an act contrary to the demands of justice (Seneca *Ben.* 1.4.4; Dio *Or.* 31.37).[32] The author's discussion of the ways in which the subjects of 6:4-5 have been benefited is setting up certain expectations concerning their response.

"Becoming sharers of the Holy Spirit" refers to one of the principal benefactions of God for the early Church. Reception of the Holy Spirit as part of the experience of conversion was prominent in early Christian culture (John 14:15-17; 16:13-15). It could signify God's adoption of the believer (Gal. 4:1-7), God's consecration of the Gentile sinner while still a Gentile (Acts 10:44-48; 11:15-18; Gal. 3:1-5), and God's assurance of the future benefit of eschatological salvation (2 Cor. 1:22; 5:5). Whatever its particular significance for this community, there can be little doubt that it was regarded as a significant benefaction from God (cf. Luke 11:13, where this is elevated, in contrast to the more general Matt. 7:11, as the most important of "good things" that God could impart to those who ask).

This group has "tasted the good word of God" (καλὸν γευσαμένους θεοῦ ῥῆμα), a phrase possibly informed by Josh. 21:45; 23:15, which speak of Israel hearing τὰ ῥήματα τὰ καλά of God, there signifying the promises of God (as opposed to τὰ ῥήματα τὰ πονηρά, the curses). Here the connotation of "promise" is strengthened by the focus on the quality of those "powers" or "wonders" that the addressees have experienced as belonging and pointing to the "coming age,"[33] that essential aspect of Jewish and Christian cosmology. The phrase "powers of

---

31. Social inferiors who received benefits would repay their benefactors by honoring them, increasing their fame or reputation (see Seneca *Ben.* 2.22.1; 2.24.2), providing services, and remaining loyal to the benefactor. Aristotle (*Eth. Nic.* 1163b1-5) captures the essence of this exchange: "Both parties should receive a larger share from the friendship, but not a larger share of the same thing: the superior should receive the larger share of honour, the needy one the larger share of profit; for honour is the due reward of virtue and beneficence (τῆς μὲν γὰρ ἀρετῆς καὶ τῆς εὐεργεσίας ἡ τιμὴ γέρας), while need obtains the aid it requires in pecuniary gain." Seneca (*Ep.* 81.27) stresses the importance of loyalty, particularly when association with a particular benefactor brought hostility: "No one can be grateful unless he has learned to scorn the things which drive the common herd to distraction; if you wish to make a return for a favour, you must be willing to go into exile, or to pour forth your blood, or to undergo poverty, or, . . . even to let your very innocence be stained and exposed to shameful slanders." For more on the components of gratitude, see Danker, *Benefactor*, 436-86.

32. Such an ethos was not foreign even to ancient Israelite culture, as Ps. 116:12-19 dramatically demonstrates: "What shall I render to the LORD for all His benefits to me?" (NASB). The answer involves, for the psalmist, honoring God through public praise, sacrifices of gratitude, and the public testimony to God's benefits that "paying vows" conveyed.

33. Thus Craddock, "Letter to the Hebrews," 75; Attridge, *Hebrews*, 170. Lane (*Hebrews 1–8*, 133 n. "u" and 144) misses the significance of this intertextuality and proposes a translation of "goodness of God's word" despite the fact that "good" grammatically qualifies "word," defining the nature of the word received by the addressees as assurance and promise.

the coming age" recalls the addressees' own experience of the divine confirmation of the "good word," which was proclaimed to them (2:2-4) and was a widespread feature of early Christian proclamation and conversion (1 Cor. 2:1-5; Gal. 3:1-5).

The subjects of 6:4-5 are clearly described in terms of the reception of benefits. They have been graced by God in this variety of ways, being granted great privileges and promises, as well as proofs of their patron's goodwill toward them. The repetitive use of the plural participles to designate these people at once creates the impression of the wide variety of benefits they have enjoyed as well as the rich supply of those benefits. Repetitive texture here serves to underscore the extent of God's generosity toward them — the care and persistence with which God has cultivated their gratitude — and hence to amplify the disgrace and injustice of shirking the obligations of the patron-client bond that divine generosity has created. The social context of the expectations of reciprocity (patronage) will take us far toward understanding the logic of the "impossibility" being posited by the author here and illustrated by 6:7-8: it is impossible to restore to repentance those who, having enjoyed such gifts and foretastes of gifts yet to come, then act as if the gifts and promises are not worth the effort and temporal cost of keeping them. By such action they heap public disgrace on the one by whose mediation these gifts and promises were conferred.

The final participle that rounds out the description of the subjects of this "case study" presents an unexpected outcome. Those who have enjoyed the very great privileges, gifts, and promises of 6:4-5 — who have been granted every incentive and resource to remain connected with the giver of such gifts — should never "fall away" (6:6). Elsewhere in the letter this course is depicted as "neglecting such a great deliverance" (2:2), "turning away from the living God" (which entails distrust toward God, 3:12), "shrinking back" instead of manifesting trust (10:38-39), "falling short of God's gift" (12:15), and "selling [one's] birthright for a single meal" (12:17). The larger context of the sermon reveals that the motivation that might induce some to "fall away" is an unwillingness to endure society's hostility and to continue without society's approval and gifts (10:32-36; 12:1-11; see the Introduction). Peace with the host society could be purchased at the price of open association with the Christian group (10:25). "Falling away" here is not the result of some unavoidable misfortune: it is the result of a value judgment that sets more store in society's friendship than God's beneficence.[34]

---

34. Both P. Hughes (*Hebrews*, 218 n. 68) and Lane assert that the aorist tense of the participle "indicates a decisive moment of commitment to apostasy" (Lane, *Hebrews 1–8*, 142). This is problematic not only in the weight it puts on the significance of the aorist ("undefined") tense (see F. Stagg, "The Abused Aorist," *JBL* 91 [1972]: 222-31) but also in running counter to other images that the author of Hebrews uses for the same action, many of which suggest not a "moment of decision" but a process of "drifting away" (2:1, e.g.; see also 3:13 for "hardening," and 4:1 and 12:15 for simply "falling short" for the goal, none of which suggest the "decisive moment").

Because of this value judgment, this conscious choice of friendship with society and rejection of one's obligations toward God, "falling away" can be further described as "crucifying the Son of God to oneself" and "holding him up to public shame,"[35] which become the rationale for the impossibility of renewing to repentance those who fall away. In their slight regard for God's gifts and promises, they have made the vicious response of offering insult to their benefactor. This response was widely recognized as an unjust act that merited opprobrium. It provoked the injured party to seek satisfaction and to exclude the offender from future favor. Seneca, for example, writes that "not to return gratitude for benefits is a disgrace, and the whole world counts it as such" (*Ben.* 3.1.1). The ingrate, while not punished by law, is punished by the public court of opinion and by his own awareness of being branded as ungrateful:

> "What, then," you say, "shall the ingrate go unpunished?" . . . Do you imagine that qualities that are loathed do go unpunished, or that there is any punishment greater than public hate? The penalty of the ingrate is that he does not dare to accept a benefit from anyone, that he does not dare to give one to anyone, that he is a mark, or at least thinks he is a mark, for all eyes, that he has lost all perception of a most desirable and pleasant experience. (3.17.1-2)

Dio Chrysostom, the orator and philosopher from Prusa, also writes at length about the disgrace of insulting rather than honoring one's benefactors. Those who act so as to honor their benefactors "all people regard as worthy of favor" (*Or.* 31.7), but "those who insult their benefactors will by nobody be esteemed to deserve a favour" (31.65). Just as a person refuses to have dealings twice with a dishonest merchant, or to entrust a second deposit to someone who has lost the first one, so also a person will exclude from future favors those who act ungratefully (31.38, 65).

The people who reject their obligation to show honor, loyalty, and obedience to their patron when the cost of such witness and loyalty becomes too high are thus charged in Hebrews with bringing public shame on the Patron, making a mockery of his beneficial death as they cut themselves off from him.[36] Because the author has spent considerable space developing the honor and authority of the Son (Heb. 1:1-14; 2:5-9), he considers it a dangerous course of action to offer an affront to the Son. The Son occupies the most exalted position in the Jewish and Christian cosmos; he awaits the subjection of all his enemies and promises to return as judge. Those who "crucify the Son of God" will not

---

35. Compare H. Schlier, "Παραδειγματίζω," *TDNT* 2:32.

36. The closest and most illuminating parallel to the expression "to crucify to oneself" appears in Gal. 6:14, where Paul uses the figure as a expression of breaking off all ties between himself and the world.

merely lose a reward but will become the objects of divine vengeance.[37] Hebrews 6:8 hints at this, but 10:26-31 will make it explicit. The honor of the Son, assaulted by the disloyal clients, will be restored through the punishment of those who have made themselves the Son's enemies by their poor evaluation of temporary versus eternal advantage.[38]

The addressees, themselves familiar with the reciprocal expectations and obligations of patrons and clients, will therefore understand and accept the "impossibility" advanced by the author. It is unlikely that they would have inquired into the psychological state of the fallen one to explain the impossibility of renewing such a one to repentance (as does Philo *Spec. Leg.* 1.58).[39] The other instance of repentance in Hebrews (12:16-17) clarifies that the author does not have in mind an emotional experience or human act at all, for Esau

---

37. Even John Calvin affirms the appropriateness of this divine response: "For it is unworthy of God to hold up his Son to scorn by pardoning them that abandon him" (*Calvin's Commentary on the Epistle to the Hebrews* [London: Cornish & Co., 1842], 66).

38. Punishment is frequently understood in the ancient world as the means by which the honor of the injured or affronted party is restored. Thus Aulus Gellius (*Attic Nights* 7.14.2-4) writes: "κόλασις or νουθεσία is the infliction of punishment for the purpose of correction and reformation, in order that one who has done wrong thoughtlessly may become more careful and scrupulous. The second is called τιμωρία. . . . That reason for punishment exists when the dignity and prestige of the one who is sinned against must be maintained, lest the omission of punishment bring him into contempt and diminish the esteem in which he is held; and therefore they think that it was given a name derived from the preservation of honour (τιμή)." Aristotle (*Rh.* 1.10.17) also attests to this: "There is a difference between revenge and punishment (τιμωρία and κόλασις); the latter is inflicted in the interest of the sufferer [ostensibly for improvement?], the former in the interest of him who inflicts it, that he may obtain satisfaction."

39. It is possible that the author conceives of repentance itself as a gift of God (so Lane, *Hebrews 1–8*, 142). Philo understands repentance as something that God can prevent: *Leg. All.* 3.213: "Many souls have desired to repent and not been permitted by God to do so" (cited in Attridge, *Hebrews*, 168 n. 25). Wisdom 12:10 also speaks of repentance as an opportunity allowed by God: the Canaanites were judged "little by little" to give them this space for repentance (ἐδίδους τόπον μετανοίας; cf. Heb. 12:16). Moreover, the author of Wisdom cites as the source of hope for God's people the fact that "you give repentance for sins" (Wis 12:19). Isaiah 6:9-10, while not using the term "repentance," speaks of God deliberately blocking repentance until judgment is executed upon the sinners. One may also recall "early narratives about Pharaoh and the sons of Eli, which speak of God deliberately blocking their repentance (Exod. 7:3f.; 8:28; 10:1; 11:10; 1 Sam. 2:25)" (Milgrom, *Leviticus I–XVI*, 375). Repentance is something God can grant or withhold. It is widely seen in Jewish culture as a gift, not a given: those who make ill use of the gift the first time can by no means count on a second opportunity to receive and use the gift. If the author of Hebrews shares this view, "repentance" would mean more a welcoming back into favor than the internal experience of feeling guilty or the change of mind that "repentance" signifies for so many today (again, given Esau's experience of great sorrow and regret without it effecting "repentance").

"repented" of his decision in those terms. The point there is that, despite how sorry he was, however much he upbraided himself, the decision was made and the die was cast. After spurning God's gifts for temporal safety and approval, there is no expectation of a second chance at those gifts. After defecting from the relationship, the ungrateful clients could not expect to be able to begin that journey to God's promised inheritances again.[40] μετάνοια was the first word encountered in the author's description of the addressees' "foundation" in 6:1-3, the starting place of this journey where they went from being God's enemies to God's beneficiaries. That precious gift of a first repentance must itself be valued and preserved intact.

It is also unlikely that the hearers would have introduced a distinction here between what is impossible for human beings and what is impossible for God.[41] Rather, they would understand that such an affront to God as their patron would result in their exclusion from future favor (starting with the favor of a return to favor). Dishonoring the Son, they should expect to find themselves among the "enemies" whose subjection is awaited (1:13; 10:12-13, 27).[42] The lack of a subject for the infinitive in this sentence would not have invited them to supply one, but rather made the impossibility all the more absolute and stark.

---

40. Long (*Hebrews*, 73) imaginatively suggests that "when the Preacher says that restoration is 'impossible', he is . . . pointing to the actual and sad experience of his own church. . . . They found that no amount of pleading and praying, working and worrying, could bring these people back into the community. Speaking realistically, for all practical purposes it was impossible to restore them to the fold." Long thus implicitly supports the softening of "impossible" to *difficile* (found in the late fifth-century Latin manuscript d). The impossibility is practical, not theoretical. Not only would this be out of keeping with the author's other three uses of "it is impossible" (6:18; 10:4; 11:6) and the rhetorical context of the topic of the "impossible" (Aristotle *Rh.* 2.19), it neglects the internal logic that explains the "impossible" in 6:4-8. Long is correct to observe, however, that the author is not making a statement about limitations on God's favor. Attridge's unwillingness to assume any qualification to this impossibility remains the strongest reading (*Hebrews*, 167).

41. As does Oberholtzer, "Thorn-Infested Ground," 323: "Since God is sovereign and is able to do as He pleases in human affairs, it is incorrect to assume that God is the subject of the infinitive." Reading into the text a subject that the author has left unspecified is dubious enough; using a theological datum derived from other texts to limit how this text may be read is even more problematic.

42. Lane (*Hebrews 1–8*, 142) interprets 6:4-6 thus: "The ἀδύνατον . . . expresses an impossibility because the apostates repudiate the only basis on which repentance can be extended." This seems to make the warning less serious than the author intends, for if it were simply a matter of a right appreciation of Christ's redemptive work, the apostate surely could have a change of mind (as did Esau, Heb. 12:17). What Esau did not have, and what the author threatens that the addressees would not have, is a second chance *tout court*. The reason for this is to be found in their flagrant display of ingratitude for the gift the first time around. The one who "falls away," who chooses society's approval and gifts over God's, willfully alienates himself or herself from the divine patron.

The author of Hebrews supports his exhortation to remain committed to the Christian group, its values, and its confession ("to be borne along to perfection," 6:1) with an argument from the contrary, explicating the disgrace of, and danger that follows, the alternative course ("falling away," 6:6). Now he reinforces the argument from the contrary with an illustration from agriculture. The ground that makes a fair return for the gift of rain received a blessing from God;[43] the ground that returns "thorns and thistles" is "rejected" and ends up burned.

Interpreters have frequently searched for the OT oral-scribal intertexture that might inform this illustration. Isaiah 5:1-7 is prominent in the discussion, whether as a possible resonance,[44] as a text for general comparison of the use of the metaphor,[45] or as the specific source for Hebrews 6:7-8.[46] The parallels between the two texts, however, are not so close as to suggest oral-scribal recitation, and thus Verbrugge's more extreme position must be rejected.[47] Hebrews 6:7-8 speaks not of vines or grapes (a major feature of Isa. 5:1-7 and other illustrations that can rightly be said to *depend* on this text, e.g., Matt. 21:33-43), but rather vegetation in general. It is thorns and thistles, not sour grapes, that bring about the destruction of the ground. Moreover, the production of thorns and thistles is the cause of the cursing or burning in Hebrews 6:8 but the result of the divine verdict in Isaiah 5:6.[48]

That being said, however, the similarities between the dynamics of Isaiah 5:1-7 and Hebrews 6:7-8 are worth noting. The Isaiah text is informative as a similar employment of an agricultural illustration of the failure to respond appropriately to divine patronage. Isaiah speaks of the investment of time, resources, and energy spent by God on God's people (the vineyard). All of this effort was spent in expectation of the production of good grapes, but instead it produced bad grapes. The vineyard dresser's response of destruction of the vineyard is radical and final (it is certainly more appropriate at the level of interpretation than as a practical procedure for viticulture). God's care and tend-

---

43. On rain as a gift of God, see also Matt. 5:44-48; Seneca *Ben.* 7.31.4.

44. Craddock, "Letter to the Hebrews," 76.

45. Attridge, *Hebrews,* 172 n. 69.

46. V. G. Verbrugge, "Towards a New Interpretation of Hebrews 6:4-6," *CTJ* 15 (1980): 61-73.

47. His novel solution has been aptly critiqued by Attridge (*Hebrews,* 172 n. 69). Verbrugge's suggestion that Heb. 6:4-6 refers to the effects of communal apostasy rather than to the individual apostate is likewise specious, foundering on the observation that the author is precisely concerned with "each one" of the congregation (3:12; 4:1; 10:25; 12:15).

48. κατάρας . . . ἀκάνθας καὶ τριβόλους suggests oral-scribal intertexture with Gen. 3:17-18. Here also, however, the order of events (bearing of thorns and cursing) is reversed. The author incorporates the image so as to reinforce the notion of curse without asking that his analogy be read closely in light of the Genesis episode.

ing of Israel led naturally to God's expectation of a harvest of justice. Isaiah claims, however, that Israel did not make the proper return to God for his benefits. Instead, Israel's response offended and affronted the God who commanded justice among his people. Such a disobedient response would call down his punishment, specifically the cessation of his protection, tending, and other benefactions. God tends his people with the anticipation of a crop of righteousness and justice — this is the return or yield God expects for his troubles. Instead, violence and oppression spring up, and God destroys the community that has brought forth so noxious a return.

Resonances with Greco-Roman literature have been, not surprisingly, largely neglected. One of the virtues of socio-rhetorical interpretation, however, is its emphasis on the value of both Jewish and Greco-Roman texts and culture as resources that inform early Christian culture,[49] a movement that had its start in the Roman province of Judea and thoroughly Hellenized Galilee ("of the Gentiles" in Matt. 4:15), and that spread through the urban centers of the Greek and Roman world. James W. Thompson seeks to read 6:7-8 as an echo of agricultural metaphors in Philo regarding education and cultivating knowledge of virtue (especially in *Agr.* 9–18).[50] The context of Hebrews 5:11-14 would certainly invite an interpretation of 6:7-8 in terms of Greco-Roman theory of education were it not for the intervention of 6:4-6, which moves the audience from the realm of education to the sphere of reciprocity, giving no indication that one should read 6:7-8 in terms of the former discussion rather than the immediate one.

Just as agriculture provided analogies for education in the Greco-Roman world, so it also provided illustrations for patronage. Agricultural images are used frequently by Seneca in his discussion of reciprocity. The first cause of the degradation of the system of reciprocity is that "we do not pick out those who are worthy of receiving our gifts; . . . we do not sow seed in worn out and unproductive soil; but our benefits we give, or rather throw, away without any discrimination" (*Ben.* 1.1.2). This first agricultural metaphor speaks about the quality of the recipient using the analogy of sowing seeds on appropriate soil that will produce a good crop rather than prove "worn out and unproductive." The same thought is captured later (4.8.2): "we ought to take care to select those to whom we would give benefits, since even the farmer does not commit his seeds to sand." While Seneca cautions potential benefactors to choose well the soil in which they will plant their gifts,

---

49. Robbins, *Tapestry*, 99, 232-35.

50. *Beginnings*, 37-38. For a fruitful use of Greco-Roman agricultural metaphors for education in the interpretation of the parable of the sower, see B. L. Mack, *A Myth of Innocence: Mark and Christian Origins* (Philadelphia: Fortress, 1988), 155-60; B. L. Mack and V. K. Robbins, *Patterns of Persuasion in the Gospels* (Sonoma, CA: Polebridge, 1989), 145-60.

we never wait for absolute certainty [concerning whether or not a recipient will prove grateful], since the discovery of truth is difficult, but follow the path that probable truth shows. All the business of life proceeds in this way. It is thus that we sow . . . for who will promise to the sower a harvest? (4.33.1-2)

The benefactor thus gives the gift in the hope, but not the certainty, of a harvest of gratitude. Finally, Seneca advises that a single gift may be insufficient to cultivate a client or friend:

The farmer will lose all that he has sown if he ends his labours with putting in the seed; it is only after much care that crops are brought to their yield; nothing that is not encouraged by constant cultivation from the first day to the last ever reaches the stage of fruit. In the case of benefits the same rule holds. (2.11.4-5)

These examples from Seneca and Isaiah suggest that an agricultural illustration would be quite appropriate to reinforcing some point about fulfilling the obligations of reciprocity (without suggesting that either Seneca or Isaiah has served as a direct source here). As Hebrews 6:4-6 has articulated a scenario involving patron-client roles and expectations, so the illustration of 6:7-8 is likely to be heard by the recipients within that same sphere. The author of Hebrews uses the metaphor to remind the hearers of God's expectation of a fair return for the experience of his benefits enumerated in 6:4-5. The question facing the audience is, What kind of beneficiaries will the addressees prove to be — base or honorable, ungrateful or reliable? Will they prove to be fruitful soil and receive the greater gifts yet to come as fit recipients of God's ongoing favor, or will they prove to be bad soil, which produces plants unpleasant and even hurtful? Moreover, Seneca's insight into how clients and friends must be cultivated by ongoing nurture and several gifts suggests that the enumeration of benefits in 6:4-5 could create the impression that God has carefully cultivated these beneficiaries, has acted in every way as a thoughtful patron zealous to establish a firm bond between himself and the clients. Ingratitude would be all the more base, all the more unjust, and all the more dangerous.

    This illustration employs another unmistakable element of intertexture involving the opposition of εὐλογίας . . . καὶ κατάρας, although it is difficult to determine whether the author uses oral-scribal intertexture with a particular text or relies on a more general cultural knowledge of the significance of "curse" and "blessing" in the context of the covenant articulated in Deuteronomy and in literature influenced by Deuteronomy. Fred Craddock and Harold Attridge point to Deuteronomy 11:26-28 as an informative parallel.[51] Attridge also suggests Malachi 2:2. Both of these texts, upon further examination, show

---

51. Craddock, "Letter to the Hebrews," 78; Attridge, *Hebrews*, 173 n. 90.

close connections with the language and intention of Hebrews and thus suggest that the author's goals are richly informed by these texts.

By incorporating Psalm 95:7-11 (LXX) into his sermon (Heb. 3:7-11), the author has recited and recontextualized a text that itself recontextualizes Deuteronomy 11:26-28:

> I place before you today (σήμερον) blessing and curse (εὐλογίαν καὶ κατάραν): the blessing (εὐλογίαν) if you hear (ἐὰν ἀκούσητε) the commands of the Lord your God which I am commanding you today (σήμερον), and the curses (τὰς κατάρας) if you do not hear (ἐὰν μὴ ἀκούσητε) the commands of the Lord your God, as many as I command you today (σήμερον), and if you wander (πλανηθῆτε) from the way (ἀπὸ τῆς ὁδοῦ) which I commanded you, going off to serve other gods whom you did not know (οὐκ οἴδατε).[52]

The emphasis on "today" and "hearing" in Hebrews, introduced directly by the recitation of Psalm 95, begins to spin a web of resonances with the text in Deuteronomy, which the psalm has itself recontextualized in its liturgical application of the paradigm of the wilderness generation to new generations of Israelites. The psalmist cries out, "If today (Σήμερον) you hear his voice (ἐὰν . . . ἀκούσητε), do not harden your hearts" or follow the example of those who "are always wandering (πλανῶνται)" and "have not known (οὐκ ἔγνωσαν) my ways (τὰς ὁδούς μου)." This web of resonances is now advanced by the author of Hebrews in the alternation of "blessing" and "curse," different results determined in Hebrews as in Deuteronomy by the kind of crop that those taken into God's covenant produce. In Hebrews, as in Deuteronomy, it concerns mainly loyalty and obedience toward the divine patron as opposed to apostasy.[53] The covenantal associations of the terms, therefore, reinforce reading the passage in the context of patron-client obligations and "rules."

The author's decision to end his illustration of the fate of soil that makes a bad return for God's blessings with "burning" does not leave much hope for "new growth" and replanting, even if that is a known practice for soil renewal in the ancient world. "Burning" is a common image for God's punishment of the unrighteous. Fred Craddock looks to the effects and pre-

---

52. The same points of connection are present in Deut. 28:1-2, 15 (LXX).

53. Malachi 2:2, like Ps. 95, also shows its dependence on Deuteronomy, but it is useful to our investigation of Hebrews on account of the echoes it adds: "if you do not hear (ἐὰν μὴ ἀκούσητε) and if you do not set your heart (τὴν καρδίαν ὑμῶν) to give honor to my name . . . I will send upon you the curse (τὴν κατάραν) and I will curse your blessing (τὴν εὐλογίαν)." The point of contact here is the requirement that God's clients set their hearts on bringing honor to God's name, which contrasts sharply with the results of apostasy as delineated in Heb. 6:6 and 10:29, both of which depict "shrinking away" or "drifting" from commitment as a gross assault on the honor of the Benefactor.

sentation of other "fires" in Hebrews (notably 10:27, but also 12:25-29), arguing cogently against the possibility that this burning seeks to restore or renew the soil.[54] This argument is strengthened as we become aware of how this author is informed by Deuteronomy 29. Hebrews 12:15 quite directly recontextualizes Deuteronomy 29:17[55] and thus reveals that the author carries the latter text in mind as he formulates his sermon. The conclusion of this passage speaks of the burning of the land of those who do not keep the covenant, such that later generations, seeing the land burned over (κατα-κεκαυμένον, Deut. 29:22), have a perpetual reminder of the punishment that awaits those who break God's covenant (Deut. 29:21-26). Informed thus thoroughly by the Deuteronomic conception of covenant blessing and curse (εὐλογίας . . . καὶ κατάρας) and by the use of agricultural language (metaphorical, as in 29:17, and real, as in 29:22; 11:11), the author gives every hint of conceptualizing this "fire" as God's judgment rather than some form of "temporal discipline."[56] The example of Esau (12:16-17) reinforces

---

54. Craddock, "Letter to the Hebrews," 76; Lane, *Hebrews 1–8*, 143.

55. Hebrews 12:15: μή τις ῥίζα πικρίας ἄνω φύουσα ἐνοχλῇ; Deut. 29:17 (LXX): μή τίς ἐστιν ἐν ὑμῖν ῥίζα ἄνω φύουσα ἐν χολῇ καὶ πικρίᾳ.

56. Oberholtzer ("Thorn-Infested Ground," 319, 324-26) attempts to establish this fire as "temporal discipline," "divine discipline in this life and . . . loss of future rewards in the millennium" but not the eternal reward of heaven. Oberholtzer's article is an extreme example of what will happen when a synthetic, theological construct is used as the mold and template within which Hebrews must be read. The first glaring difficulty is the imposition of a foreign eschatological scheme on Hebrews, namely, the idea of a "millennial kingdom," which in the NT is a clear feature only of Revelation's eschatology. Should we assume that the author of Hebrews, although he writes before John, nevertheless shared all elements of John's eschatology (really, dispensational eschatology)? The distinctive eschatology of Hebrews is thus sacrificed to the theological construct.

The second glaring difficulty is the way in which Oberholtzer argues in favor of "temporal discipline" over simple "judgment." According to him, "the Old Testament cursings were temporal, not soteriological in nature and did not result in eternal damnation" ("Thorn-Infested Ground," 325). This creates, however, a false dichotomy within the Pentateuch, which makes no distinction between "soteriology" and temporal rewards and curses simply because it envisions only temporal rewards and curses. The notion of some "eternal" or otherworldly reward or punishment is a later development within Judaism. Ultimately, though, it is Ephesians that carries the day: "Believers' soteriological status is settled on the basis of grace through faith alone (Eph. 2:8-10; Titus 3:3-7). They will never be judged to determine their eternal destiny (John 5:19-29; Rom. 3:21-30; 8:1 [et al.])" ("Thorn-Infested Ground," 326). Again it is the conviction that all scriptural texts share a uniform frame of reference, and the unadmitted privileging of certain texts over other texts, that determines in advance what the author of Hebrews is or is not permitted to say. Rather than seek clarification from within the text of Hebrews, the voice is Hebrews is overridden by other NT voices for the sake of harmonization.

Reading the burning in Heb. 6:8 as "temporal discipline," moreover, leads repeatedly

this point,[57] namely, that thinking little enough of God's gifts and promises to give them up for the sake of easing temporary discomfort or tension proves one to be an ungrateful client, who should expect only punishment and exclusion from favor.[58] Those who seek to read this, then, as an extreme but still salutary treatment of the soil are going well beyond the author's use of the metaphor; they violate the point he is trying to make (a point clarified by 12:16-17, which certainly brooks no thoughts of renewal) and defuse the effect he hopes to have on the emotions of the hearers.[59]

Excursus: Is Apostasy the "Unpardonable Sin"?

The concept of an "unpardonable sin" is derived from Matthew 12:32, Mark 3:28-30, and Luke 16:10: "whoever speaks a word against the Son of Man will be forgiven, but whoever speaks against the Holy Spirit will not be forgiven, either in this age or in the age to come" (Matt. 12:32, NRSV). In Matthew and Mark, this pronouncement is prompted by the Pharisees' attribution of Jesus' miracles and exorcisms to the power of one of Satan's minions. Mark makes this interpretation explicit. In effect, Jesus is saying "you can slander me and gain forgiveness, but if you slander the power of God where it is at work, you have passed the point of no return." Luke dissociates this pronouncement from the confrontation with the Pharisees (recorded in Luke 11:14-23) and places it in a new context — the imperative to bear witness to Jesus in the world and the assurance to the believers that the Holy Spirit will give them the words to speak when they are brought to trial (Luke 12:8-12). Luke thus extends confidence to believers, who will know that the calumny they bear

---

to a misreading of Heb. 12:5-11 in this article ("Thorn-Infested Ground," 325, 326). Hebrews 12:5-11 does not regard the suffering of believers as punishment for their sins. The suffering that the author interprets there as educative is the hostility of non-Christians, and the passage serves to insulate the believers against that hostility by interpreting it as a sign of sonship to be embraced rather than avoided. The most impressive statement of this thesis can now be found in Croy, *Endurance*.

57. εὐλογία provides a verbal link between 6:7 and 12:17. Esau, like the soil that brought forth noxious plants, also loses the blessing and cannot regain it.

58. For a study that takes into account all of the warning passages in Hebrews and their mutually supporting agenda and use of patron-client expectations, see deSilva, "Exchanging Favor," 91-116.

59. The author's desire to heighten the sense of danger does not, however, lead him to presume to pronounce judgment on those who hide or deny their association with Jesus. Jewett (*Letter to Pilgrims*, 105), who reads this passage as a sign of author's horror at apostasy, and his "serious and, for the modern world, distressing moral realism," rightly points out that the "author does not define the moment along the slothful path when the point of no return is reached." The person who chooses that path is left "on the verge of curse" by the author, who leaves it to God to pronounce final sentence.

for the sake of Jesus does not leave them in a dangerous place before God, but rather puts their calumniators on slippery ground.[60]

Biblical theologians tend to broaden the applicability of these pronouncements to indicate "a hardened state of sin which forms an insuperable barrier," a state in which a person no longer desires forgiveness.[61] Such a broad statement, however, cannot pretend to derive from the Synoptic texts, one of which even ventures a much more limited and specific interpretation. George Bradford Caird sees in this episode the indictment of "blunting [one's] own moral faculty of distinguishing right and wrong and running the risk of being unable thereafter to recognize goodness. . . . To blaspheme against the Holy Spirit by calling His works evil is to deprive oneself of a standard of judgement for one's life, and thus to become incapable of repentance."[62] While Caird certainly keeps himself closer to the situation that gave rise to the saying, pointing out that calling good "evil" is central to the offense, the tendency to broaden the applicability must be supplied without any confirmation from the text itself.

Perhaps the meaning of "the unpardonable sin" needs to be more cautiously considered in the context of its commission. The critics of Jesus, in their attempt to discredit "the man Jesus," presumed also to deny God's beneficence as it was manifested in the liberation of a demoniac. In their envy and hatred, they had ceased to give first attention to recognizing and honoring the hand of God at work in their midst, and thus they found themselves excluded from God's favor. In effect, the pronouncement comes as Jesus' response to a challenge to his honor.[63] The Pharisees, in their attempt to counteract the honor being ascribed to Jesus by the crowd, claim that Jesus' power comes from the devil. Jesus' final response to this challenge to his honor is to say that challenges to his honor are ultimately unimportant and can be forgiven. The Pharisees, however, have challenged God's honor by attributing God's works to Satan. They have overreached, crossed the line, and now find themselves the targets for God's satisfaction of his injured honor.

The second text that enters into the discussion of "unpardonable sin" is the "sin unto death" of 1 John 5:14-17, a text highly problematic in its lack of specificity. Does the author speak merely of temporal consequences of sin rather than "pardon" and eternal destiny (still following the dominant OT view that sees sickness and the like as punishment for offenses against God)? Is this obscure text to be clarified by easy association with the Synoptic pronouncement? In the words of Raymond Brown, "to apply these Synoptic

---

60. Donald Guthrie (*New Testament Theology* [Downers Grove, IL: InterVarsity, 1981], 608-9), arguing against the view that Luke is warning disciples not to blaspheme the Spirit whereas Matthew and Mark were warning unbelievers, asks "since [the disciples] were promised the aid of the Spirit in confession before the authorities, what relevance has the blasphemy saying to them?" Luke, however, does not arrange these sayings without logical connection, and we can now see how the pronouncement would be meaningful to the disciple on trial (although, it is true, not as a warning but as an encouragement).

61. Guthrie, *Theology,* 580; cf. also G. E. Ladd, *A Theology of the New Testament* (Grand Rapids: Eerdmans, 1974), 155: "when a [person] is so spiritually blind that he cannot distinguish between the Spirit of God and satanic power and therefore attributes the power at work in Jesus to the devil, he has reached a state of obduracy that can never be forgiven."

62. *New Testament Theology,* ed. L. D. Hurst (Oxford: Clarendon, 1995), 117.

63. On the challenge-riposte scheme, see Malina and Neyrey, "Honor and Shame," 25-66, especially 29-32, 36-38, 47-52.

sayings to 1 John 5:16-17 is to define the unknown through the more unknown."[64] Suggestions abound for the content of this sin, the very variety of which testifies to the lack of solid contextual clues as to its precise meaning (assuming that the first hearers themselves would have known what John was indicating by "sin unto death").

Does the sin of apostasy warned against in Hebrews 6:4-6 and 10:26-31 give Christians the fullest and clearest exposition of the "sin unto death" and "unpardonable sin"? It is clear that the honor of God is at stake in both the blasphemy against the Spirit in Matthew 12 (and parallels) and in the negative witness of the apostate. The practice and attitude of at least some corners in the early Church shows, however, that it considered neither the Synoptic saying nor the guidelines of 1 John (if such an obscure text can be called a "guideline") to be applicable to the situation of apostasy against which the author of Hebrews warns. This comes out most clearly in accounts of persecution in which many Christians, fearing the tortures or execution that their bold, confessing sisters and brothers encounter, deny their connection with Jesus and so receive reprieve or pardon. Their act of apostasy — their public denial of Jesus! — does not, however, exclude them from repentance and from returning to the tribunal of the magistrate, now to make at their second trial the good confession that they failed to make at their first.[65] Even the apostate who brings public shame upon the name of Christ by denying him may have the opportunity to restore that honor through confession and martyrdom.

The *Shepherd of Hermas* allows for a second repentance of those who had apostatized earlier to avoid persecution (*Herm. Vis.* 2.2), calling them now bravely to endure the wave of persecution on the horizon and, in a manner very similar to Hebrews, warning against flinching in the present time since no further repentance will be granted. His "compromise" is but one example of the early Church's attempt to hold onto both the gravity of apostasy and the unfathomable mercy of God — a tension that makes it difficult indeed for mortals to draw the line that marks the extent of God's mercy and forgiveness. Ultimately, the NT itself leaves us living within this tension. As we shall see below ("A Closer Look: Patronage, Eternal Security, and Second Repentance"), it is a tension deeply rooted in the social context of the first-century circum-Mediterranean world.

---

64. Raymond E. Brown, *The Epistles of John* (AB 30; New York: Doubleday, 1982), 617.

65. See, for example, the extended narrative of the persecution in Gaul during the reign of Verus, preserved in Eusebius *Hist. eccl.,* 5.1-2. Most moving is the following excerpt: "through the living the dead were being brought back to life, and martyrs were bestowing grace on those who had failed to be martyrs, and there was great joy in the heart of the Virgin Mother [here, the Church], who was receiving her stillborn children back alive; for by their means most of those who had denied their Master travelled once more the same road, conceived and quickened a second time, and learnt to confess Christ. Alive now and braced up, their ordeal sweetened by God, who does not desire the death of sinners but is gracious towards repentance, they advanced to the tribunal to be again interrogated by the governor. . . . Christ was greatly glorified in those who had previously denied Him but now confounded heathen expectation by confessing Him. These were individually examined with the intention that they should be released, but they confessed him and so joined the ranks of the martyrs" (Eusebius, *The History of the Church,* trans. G. A. Williamson [Harmondsworth: Penguin, 1965], 200-201).

Hebrews 6:1-8 contributes powerfully to the author's agenda for the hearers, reorienting them to their situation from quite a different perspective, namely, the danger that confronts them not from the unbelieving society but from God should they choose to alienate themselves from him. There would be some "advantage" to breaking off associations with the Christian group, as this would reduce and quite possibly remove the tension that exists between the (ex-)Christian and his or her non-Christian neighbors.[66] The author replaces the alternatives that potential deserters consider (tension and loss in society versus acceptance again among neighbors) with a new set of alternatives (blessing versus curse, promise versus destruction) so as to maintain the integrity of the sectarian group.

Hebrews 6:1 proposes an overarching agenda for the addressees — being carried along to completion, the end of the journey begun by their conversion, baptism, and early catechesis in the Christian worldview (6:1-2). This is another way of expressing what the author has held forward as the essential significance of life in this world from the beginning ("inheriting salvation," 1:14; entering "glory," 2:10; "entering God's rest," 4:1-11). In all of these images, the author chooses an expression that seeks to propel the hearers forward in the journey they have begun. The images themselves convey the importance of "pressing on" and work to counter the consideration of the advantages of "quitting" or even "soft-pedaling" one's Christian commitments. Recalling the essential elements of the "foundation" of the audience's secondary socialization into the norms of the Christian culture cannot be accidental or merely ornamental. Each basic tenet or ritual serves to reinforce those contours of church-shaped reality that make the author's agenda the "wise" and advantageous course of action to follow, and all opposing courses foolish and disadvantageous. This is particularly true of the last tenets, the teaching on "resurrection of the dead" and "eternal judgment." The hearers must consider advantage and disadvantage not only in terms of this visible world but also in terms of the circumstances in which one may find oneself after death and for eternity.

Hebrews 6:4-8 underscores the necessity of accepting the author's agenda as proposed in 6:1. To those who ask, "why should we press on to the completion of this journey, this partnership, which continues to cost us so much in terms of our life among the non-Christian majority," the author has prepared a striking and uncompromising answer. Response to God's word, and now more broadly the complex of God's gifts and endowments that the hearers have hitherto enjoyed, emerges as the single most important consideration (i.e., what the author wants his audience to bear foremost in their minds) in their deliberations. Once again, the author moves into a consideration of the danger of *not*

---

66. On this aspect of the addressees' situation and the author's strategy for defusing society's shaming techniques, see deSilva, *Despising Shame,* chapter 4.

moving forward in trust and loyal obedience (see also 2:1-4; 3:7–4:13). This is now painted even more fiercely than in previous iterations in what has become celebrated as one of the hardest passages of Scripture. The author's depiction of the "contrary" is all the more striking when we consider that the addressees were not being asked to deny Christ in some public trial before a magistrate but were merely succumbing to the pressures quietly to hide their association with this minority group.[67] The author asserts that merely "drifting off" or "shrinking back" is as good as hoisting the Son of God up on the cross and inviting more mocking and jeering. Simply leaving the voluntary association called the "church" becomes an active assault on the honor of one's divine benefactor and mediator.

This rather more dramatic portrayal of the courses of action open to the addressees invites a number of what Aristotle called "special" deliberative topics, which the author now brings to bear in support of his exhortation (6:1).[68] Most prominently, he is appealing to the topic of justice, and particularly the subtopic of gratitude (obligations to one's benefactors).[69] Not making a fair return to one's benefactor was unjust; to act so as to inflict dishonor upon one who had been a benefactor was an even more egregious act of injustice. This leads the author to the topic of the expedient.[70] There is no recovery of the present goods for the one who, thinking the course of "falling away" to be advantageous, is willing to throw them away and thus shame the benefactor.[71]

---

67. See Attridge, *Hebrews*, 171 n. 58.

68. These topics were employed to make the alternative course seem unattractive and the proposed course seem more attractive. A course of action was promoted by demonstrating it to be any combination of just, expedient, lawful, feasible, honorable, pleasant, and necessary; an audience would be dissuaded from a course of action by showing it to be the opposite of these. See Aristotle *Rh.* 1.4-7; *Rhet. Her.* 3.2.2–3.4.9; *Rhet. Alex.* 1421b21-1423a12.

69. *Rhet. Alex.* 1421b37-1422a2: "What is just is the unwritten custom of the whole or the greater part of mankind, distinguishing honourable actions from base ones. The former are to honour one's parents, do good to one's friends and repay favours to one's benefactors; for these and similar rules are not enjoined on men by written laws but are observed by unwritten customs and universal practice"; *Rhet. Her.* 3.3.4: "We shall be using the topics of Justice . . . if we show that it is proper to repay the well-deserving with gratitude; . . . if we urge that faith (*fidem*) ought zealously to be kept; if we maintain that ties of hospitality, clientage, kinship, and relationship by marriage must inviolably be cherished; if we show that neither reward nor favour nor peril nor animosity ought to lead us astray from the right path. . . . By their contraries we shall demonstrate that an action is unjust."

70. *Rhet. Alex.* 1422a4-7: "What is expedient is the preservation of existing good things, or the acquisition of goods that we do not possess, or the rejection of existing evils, or the prevention of harmful things expected to occur"; cf. Aristotle *Rh.* 1.7 on relative expediency.

71. The exclusion of a "second" chance may also be read as an attempt to remove a potential motive for wrongdoing, namely, the possibility of an indulgence (Aristotle *Rh.* 1.12.15).

Such a person will "in reality" act contrary to what is expedient, exchanging present goods for future, certain evils (6:8). "Drifting away" is shown to be unjust and, ultimately, disadvantageous. The hearers, therefore, will be inclined toward what the author depicts as the just course of continuing as a loyal, trusting client of God (6:1) and making a fair return for God's benefits (6:7, 9-10), which will also result in the preservation of goods already enjoyed and the acquisition of greater goods.

The author also paints the course of "shrinking back," of failing to press on to the completion of the Christian pilgrimage, as unpleasant and unsafe: the fire of 6:8 (underscored at 10:26-31) becomes the danger that the disloyal client, who foolishly exchanged the pleasant experiences of God's goodness and favor (6:4-5) for the unpleasant experience of punishment, must face. Perseverance in commitment to God and the Christian group is depicted as the course that "ensures the avoidance of a present or imminent danger"[72] (imminent because of the apocalyptic expectations of this author and the early Christian community; see 10:25, 37), while hiding or setting aside one's open association with that group leads to danger at the arrival of "the coming one" (10:37-39; the fire of 6:8 and 10:27).

To those contemplating the advantages of not pursuing the Christian hope any further, the author holds up the irreversible exclusion from benefits that such a course would produce. The addressees are led to consider movement away from the Christian group not in terms of how this will decrease tension between them and the host society but in terms of how it will create and exponentially escalate tension between themselves and the Son, who awaits the subjection of his enemies. They are led to consider it not as a movement toward what their neighbors would consider just and pious but as a movement toward the utmost injustice and impiety toward one who had gone to the most extreme lengths (death itself) to bring them the benefits that they now so carelessly spurned. The agricultural metaphor goes further than 6:4-6 (the impossibility of restoration), positing fiery retribution and curse as the end stage of that course of action (a most striking contrast with "deliverance," "glory," and "rest").

The author gains substantial ground by insisting that leaving the Christian group will not mean escaping the Christian worldview or the consequences of their actions before God. It is not merely a matter of human relationships that they must consider, or of what human beings can do to them (see 13:5-6), but of what God is capable of doing to those who willfully spurn God's gifts and dishonor his Son. Leaving the Christian group does not mean leaving the sphere of God's reach, only the sphere of God's favor! It becomes apparent that the author

---

72. *Rhet. Her.* 3.2.3 on topics of "safety" or "security," the second of two major divisions of "advantage" in that author's arrangement of deliberative topics.

is herein also making an appeal to the emotions (an appeal to pathos), specifically using the arousal of fear to advance his goal.[73] Hearers who responded with ingratitude to (specifically, acting disloyally so as to bring dishonor upon) one who had already showered them with great gifts and privileges would justifiably arouse the anger of the Benefactor.[74] Hebrews 6:8 especially articulates "imminent evil that causes destruction or pain"[75] as the result of affronting the virtuous Benefactor. The impossibility of help (Aristotle *Rh.* 2.5.12), here the impossibility of restoring such a person "to repentance," also enhances fear through the removal of its opposite, confidence.[76] The author thus seeks to make the hearers afraid to take the path of dissociation from the Christian group and from open association with the name of Jesus, to make them "feel" as well as "reason" that such a path is disadvantageous (being both unjust and dangerous). This point will be amplified and reinforced in 10:26-31; 12:16-17, 25-29.

A Closer Look: Patronage, Eternal Security, and Second Repentance

While I am critical of the efforts of several authors who have attempted to integrate this passage into their theology, I am not unsympathetic to the troubling questions raised by Hebrews 6:4-8 that prompt such harmonizing and make this passage an enduring stumbling block to affirmations of God's mercy, love, forgiveness, and even sovereignty. Therefore, I am impelled to address the theological questions raised by this passage, hoping that doing so from the insights gained through socio-rhetorical analysis will afford a new perspective on the passage and the theological enterprise itself.

---

73. See Aristotle *Rh.* 2.5, for a discussion of ways in which a speaker might cultivate this emotional response in the audience.

74. Aristotle (*Rh.* 2.2.8, 17) introduces this as a general rule, and the interpretation of Num. 14 by Hebrews certainly introduces this principle into the sermon. Especially salient is Aristotle *Rh.* 2.2.23: anger can be roused against the ungrateful, as their slights are "contrary to all sense of obligation." This "anger" will reemerge as a more forceful motivator in Heb. 10:26-31.

75. Aristotle (*Rh.* 2.5.1) presents this as an essential ingredient for stimulating an emotional response of fear.

76. Long avers that "the Preacher's main goal seems to be to encourage his congregation, not to scare them" (*Hebrews,* 73); "the Preacher's real goal is to generate not fear but encouragement" (p. 110). While he is aware of the larger agenda of the author to frame a "motivational contrast" that will help the hearers "not to forfeit the great reward," there is no cause to subordinate appeals to fear to appeals to confidence. The two are equal and essential aspects in the author's strategy, and both equally serve the author's real "main goal," which is not creating feelings of fear or confidence but rather dissuading the hearers from breaking faith with God or hiding their association with Jesus and Jesus' family and encouraging them to bold perseverance in the face of society's attempts to "correct" them.

In an earlier article, I suggested that the rhetorical situation governed the application of this text (together with the other warning passages of Hebrews).[77] The author is addressing the hearers with this warning precisely to motivate them not to undervalue the benefits they have received and will receive from God, in order that that they might not reject these in favor of a return to the world's friendship. He is not addressing those who had withdrawn, as he would consider it, unreclaimably. Hebrews 6:9-10 itself makes this clear. Those who "hear his voice" and "do not harden their hearts" (Heb. 3:7) may still reach the good end that God has prepared for them. To use this passage, then, as a basis for trying to determine when someone has crossed the point of no return, or to apply it so as to bar from the church those who do in fact repent, would be to remove the warning from its rhetorical setting.

Further investigation of the ethos of reciprocity, however, leads me to bolder conclusions about Hebrews 6 and theological debate concerning both "eternal security" and the "impossibility of repentance" (or "unforgivable sin"). In his lengthy unfolding of the complex dynamics of patronage and reciprocity (and, particularly, how to act honorably within that relationship), Seneca frequently articulates what can only be described as a "double mind-set." He appears at many points not to let the right hand know what the left is thinking. Clients are advised to think one way, patrons another. If these mind-sets get mixed up or crossed, the beauty of reciprocity, the gracefulness of grace, becomes irreparably marred.

Speaking to the benefactor, Seneca says, "In benefits the book-keeping is simple — so much is paid out; if anything comes back, it is gain, if nothing comes back, there is no loss. I made the gift for the sake of giving" (*Ben.* 1.2.3). The giver is to adhere to the principle that benefits are given not with an eye to the giver's advantage. Beneficiaries are thus not to be chosen on the basis of who will make the most profitable return. However, this is independent from the question of the obligation of the receiver and the ugliness of ingratitude (*Ben.* 2.25.3; 3.1.1). The point is that the giver should only be concerned with giving for the sake of the other, while the recipient should be concerned with showing gratitude to the giver. If either viewpoint is compromised (i.e., if the client attenuates his display of gratitude based on the detachment the patron should keep from such considerations), reciprocity ceases to be noble and becomes ugly. This different set of "rules" for giver and recipient in the social "game" of reciprocity is made explicit in several passages:

> The one should be taught to make no record of the amount, the other to feel indebted for more than the amount (*Ben.* 1.4.3);

> In the case of a benefit, this is a binding rule for the two who are concerned — the one [the giver] should straightway forget that it was given, the other should never forget that it was received (2.10.4);

> Let the giver of a benefit hold his tongue; let the recipient talk (2.11.2).

In cases where a recipient has taken great pains to try to return a benefit but simply has not found a way to help one who is far greater than himself or herself, "the one [the giver]should consider that he has received the return of his benefit, while the other should know that he has not returned it; the one should release the other, while the other should feel himself bound; the one should say, 'I have received,' the other, 'I still owe'" (7.16.1-2). Seneca displays these different and even contrary mind-sets in order to

---

77. "Exchanging Favor," 116.

keep before us the public good; the door must be closed to all excuses, to keep the ungrateful from taking refuge in them and using them to cover their repudiation of the
debt. 'I have done all in my power,' says he. Well, keep on doing so. . . . You have done everything in order to make return; this should be enough for your benefactor, it should
not be enough for you. For, just as he is unworthy of being repaid with gratitude if he
permits all your earnest and diligent effort to pass as nothing, so, if anyone accepts your
goodwill as full payment, you are ungrateful if you are not all the more eager to acknowledge your indebtedness because he has released you. (7.16.2, 4)

The purpose of this lengthy inquiry of Seneca is to show that the author of Hebrews
moves in a social ethos in which recipients of benefactions are led to act with one set of
considerations in view: the importance of maintaining a response of gratitude and avoiding any course that would show ingratitude toward a patron. Benefactors, however, are led
to act with another set of considerations in view: an emphasis on exercising generosity and
magnanimity. This strengthens, I believe, my earlier observation that the rhetorical situation of Hebrews (as an address to clients of the divine patron urging the maintenance of
loyalty and obedience) must govern its application and appropriation.

On one crucial point, however, Seneca contradicts both Dio Chrysostom and Hebrews.[78] The latter authors assert that those who have insulted or affronted their benefactor will be excluded from future favors (Dio *Or.* 31.38, 65; Heb. 6:4-6; 10:26-31;
12:16-17). Seneca, however, promotes a willingness to help those who have shown themselves ungrateful in the past: "although we ought to be careful to confer benefits by preference upon those who will be likely to respond with gratitude, yet there are some that
we shall do even if we expect from them poor results, and we shall bestow benefits upon
those whom we not only think will be, but we know have been, ungrateful" (*Ben.*
1.10.5). He develops this later as the means by which a truly noble spirit shows itself —
by imitating the gods:

> "He has not repaid me with gratitude; what shall I do?" Do as the gods, those glorious
> authors of all things, do; they begin to give benefits to him who knows them not, and
> persist in giving them to those who are ungrateful. . . . Let us imitate them; let us give,
> even if many of our gifts have been given in vain; none the less, let us give to still others,
> nay, even to those at whose hands we have suffered loss. (7.31.2, 4)[79]

> If a person is ungrateful, he has done, not me, but himself, an injury. . . . What I have lost
> in the case of one, I shall recover from others. But even to him I shall give a second bene-
> fit, and, even as a good farmer overcomes the sterility of his ground by care and cultiva-
> tion, I shall be victor. . . . It is no proof of a fine spirit to give a benefit and lose it; the
> proof of a fine spirit is to lose and still to give! (7.32)

---

78. Significantly, Seneca also "contradicts" himself since he has already discussed the
plight of the ingrate as one who sees himself or herself as "marked" by society and unable to
participate in the social game of reciprocity (*Ben.* 3.17.1-2, quoted above). This shows that
the answer to the question, "Does the ingrate ever have another chance at gaining favor?" will
be different, depending on whether one is a patron or a client).

79. Compare also Matt. 5:44-48, which points to God's lavishing the gifts of rain and
sun on both the just and the unjust as a model for the hearers' own generosity. Continuing to
give even when not repaid is there presented as foundational to God's character and, on that
basis, the character of God's children as well.

What accounts for Seneca's affirmation of restoring the ingrate to favor, something that his near contemporaries regard as impossible? It is the different audience and rhetorical situation. Seneca is addressing benefactors in these passages, directing them to their models for generosity (the gods, who pour rain "on the just and the unjust") and to what would constitute honorable action for the givers. Dio, like the author of Hebrews, is addressing clients who are in danger of committing ingratitude against their benefactors. In such a situation, the *desideratum* is to motivate immediate remedies for ingratitude or pursuit of a response of gratitude. It would not serve in such situations to discourse on the ability of any high-minded benefactor to overlook slights and affronts, since such considerations would not spur the hearers on to the course which Dio and the author of Hebrews urge.[80]

Thus Seneca proves relevant to the ultimate question of sin and repentance apart from the rhetorical strategy of Hebrews 6. Seneca (*Ben.* 7.32) even employs an agricultural metaphor (now in a way quite different from *Ben.* 1.1.2 or Heb. 6:7-8) to motivate benefactors to continue to show generosity toward the ungrateful and to cultivate virtue in the ingrate by surprising generosity. But Seneca consistently distinguishes between what considerations ought to guide the benefactor and what considerations the recipient should keep before his or her eyes. This sort of social game preserves the nobility of the system and helps us resolve the problem of interpreting and applying Hebrews 6. The author was shaped by, and writes within, a world in which the relationship between clients and patrons, and by extension human beings and the ultimate patron, is described dynamically rather than systematically, in which the declaration that the ingrate is forever excluded from favor stands alongside the exhortation to benefactors to be generous even to the ungrateful, as if by some means surprising generosity may win the ingrate over to a noble response of loyalty, respect, and service. Both considerations, though apparently contradictory, serve what was for the authors of our texts the higher goal of sustaining commitment to act honorably within the system of reciprocity.

The doctrine of eternal security certainly crosses the line from the perspective of Seneca, for pondering the expectation that a patron will be lenient and indulgent threatens to foster half-heartedness in the clients, who can too easily excuse themselves from making a fair return (particularly if it becomes inconvenient or costly). To teach that God would never give even the apostate a second chance also crosses the line, for patrons remain free to show favor on whom they will. Neither doctrinal position is appropriate for Hebrews, which was formulated rather within the cultural context of patron-client scripts in a world where such roles were fundamental to the functioning of society. The author of Hebrews

---

80. In response to the question of Heb. 6 and the limits on God's mercy, Attridge (*Hebrews*, 172) says: "In taking this stance, our author unjustifiably limits the gracious mercy of God, and the church's later position on the possibility of repentance and reconciliation seems to be more solidly founded in the gospel message." Our exploration of Seneca suggests, however, that even such a balanced assessment may offer an inappropriate criticism of the author of Hebrews. He is not addressing the ultimate question of how far God's generosity extends since to do so would be to violate what is emerging as an important rule of the patron-client social game: the client is never to act so as to presume upon the patron's generosity or magnanimity. Both Dio (with regard to human patrons, whose favor would be "unjustifiably limited" by Dio by the same token) and Hebrews focus fully on what clients need to "know" in order to do their part: they have received favors and must respond with gratitude if they hope for future favors.

wants to motivate his hearers to remain loyal and honorable clients of the Lord who gave them unprecedented access to God (as well as other great benefits), and he arms them with the arguments and sentiments that will facilitate their completing their part of the reciprocal relationship nobly and reliably. Like Seneca (*Ben.* 7.16.2), the author wishes to close the door on every excuse for ingratitude, to eliminate every possible motive for responding to God basely and disloyally.

We should not make Hebrews 6:4-8 have less force than it did for its first hearers, and many discussions of the passage written from the perspective of a conviction of "eternal security" seek to do exactly that. The text assumes the possibility that a person can fall away after receiving God's gifts, and after participating as fully as anyone can in what blessings of the next age are open for our experience in this age. With the cultural context of patronage and reciprocity a course that brings open disgrace on the benefactor who has in all things acted reliably and nobly should be regarded as the ultimate crime against goodness, a vice for which there are no remedies nor sufficient penalties. We should, however, also not make Hebrews 6:4-8 say more than it does. It does not reveal the ultimate condition of the benefactor's mind, for he may always choose to extend forgiveness. Seneca shows us, however, that, when speaking to clients, one must promote one set of attitudes and trajectories, and that, when speaking to patrons, one may promote different attitudes (and these are, in Seneca at least, frequently contradictory).

These considerations are offered in the hope that a long-standing problem in biblical theology may be settled — in favor of not attempting to settle it! Once the tension is resolved one way or the other, the beauty of grace, both as God's favor and our response, is threatened. The enterprise of biblical theology, particularly when the goal is to reduce the dynamics of a living God's relating with his creation to a logical, systematic order, may be fundamentally at odds at this point with the creative and necessary paradoxes and tensions of living relationships. The author of Hebrews is not being disingenuous when he utters stern warnings outlining the terrible consequences of acting ungratefully, bringing dishonor upon the noble and generous Benefactor. From the perspective of the client, this is the face of reality. These same statements do not mean, however, that God is limited in extending forgiveness and restoring even the repentant ingrate to favor. From the perspective of the patron, this remains a noble option, but one on which the client cannot presume, any more than he or she should presume upon favor in the initial encounter. Favor is always fresh, always unmerited, always surprising, never to be taken for granted — and never to go unrequited!

6:9-12

Having spoken in strong, uncompromising terms and rousing fear in the hearts of his hearers at the prospect of responding inappropriately to their divine patron, the author moves in 6:9-12 to a different strategy. He turns to the prescribed remedy for such "frank speech" as was heard in 5:11–6:8:

> If Frank Speech of this sort seems too pungent, there will be many means of palliation, for one may immediately thereafter add something of this sort: "I appeal here to your virtue, I call on your wisdom, I bespeak your old habit,"

so that praise may quiet the feelings aroused by frankness. As a result, the praise frees the hearer from wrath and annoyance, and the frankness deters him from error. (*Rhet. Her.* 4.37.49)

The author is concerned first to reaffirm his goodwill toward, and favorable estimation of, the hearers (essential to persuading through his character, or ethos; cf. Aristotle *Rh.* 1.8.6; 2.1.3, 5),[81] but also to propel his hearers onward in the course he recommends by presenting it as the way to avoid the dire consequences articulated in 6:4-8 and to attain the "better things that accompany deliverance" (6:9). By affirming their past progress in this course, he gives them the grounds for a most welcome confidence after the appeal to fear, and he encourages them to persist in that which gives them this confidence: "the love that you showed in God's name, serving the saints and continuing to serve" (6:10). This paragraph is not meant to negate the impact of 6:4-8, as the *Rhetorica ad Herennium* passage shows. Rather, it is added to restore the sense of mutual goodwill and high estimation between speaker and audience while allowing the force of 6:4-8 to spur the hearers on to the behaviors elevated in 6:9-12. The author may believe "better things" of the hearers "even though we speak this way," but this will not erase the message or the danger that he articulated so forcefully in 6:4-8. The alternation of appeals to fear and confidence is again an effective way to draw the addressees into the author's reorientation of their evaluation of the "real" dangers to avoid and the "real" advantages to preserve.

The reason for the confidence the author claims to have in his audience, and thus the cause for their own confidence, is expressed in 6:10: "For God is not unjust to forget your work and the love that you showed in God's name, serving the saints and continuing to serve." The author begins to concretize the metaphorical language of 6:7-8, drawing out for the audience what the "real-life" counterparts to bearing suitable vegetation are. The hearers have already been producing "suitable vegetation" for those for whose sake they were being cultivated by means of God's gifts, namely, for their Christian family.[82] As they have made, and continue to make, a "just" return for God's benefits,[83] God will

---

81. Attridge (*Hebrews*, 174) notes that this is "a conventional rhetorical device, commonly used either to create a sense of obligation or, as here, as part of an attempt to persuade the hearers." He refers helpfully to 1 Thess. 2:19-20; Rom. 15:14; 2 Cor. 7:4, 16; 9:1-2; Gal. 5:10 as other examples of this technique at work. For fuller discussion, see Stanley Olson, "Pauline Expressions of Confidence in His Addressees," *CBQ* 47 (1985): 282-95.

82. The term "saints" (ἅγιοι) is common in Christian (and Jewish) culture as a reference to the members of that culture (see Rom. 1:7; 12:13; 15:25; 1 Cor. 1:2; 16:15; 2 Cor. 1:1; Eph. 1:1, 15, etc.), as is the obligation to show love toward and do good for one's fellow "holy ones."

83. On the specific idea that service rendered toward fellow believers is a service rendered to God (a response that God will not "forget" but rather reward), see Matt. 25:31-46;

not be "unjust" to forget their nobility as clients and to continue to show them his favor.[84] The passage in this way serves another prominent goal of the sermon: shaping the kind of community that fosters sufficiently strong internal bonds and effectively marshals aid to withstand opposition from outside the group.[85] Their service on behalf of one another is that which gives them a claim on God (perhaps better, their assurance of God's ongoing favor as opposed to being excluded from favor). Perseverance in such activity is linked with the outcome of "better things, the things having salvation" (cf. 1:14; 5:9), such that mutual edification, support, and service emerge as the course that avoids the "fire" of 6:8 and preserves the enjoyment of God as ally rather than destroyer.

By claiming that God regards their acts of love and service toward one another as virtuous, meriting remembrance and reward (6:10), as well as by affirming his own conviction that such behaviors lead to a noble end, the author introduces the topic of the "praiseworthy" into 6:9-12. Praise of an audience's past choices serves as a means of maintaining their goodwill, especially as "palliation" after "frank speech."[86] More importantly, however, it serves to stimulate the hearers' desire to persevere in their present course of bearing "suitable fruit." Acts of love and mutual service count as valuable in God's sight, not replacement of lost property nor restoration of lost honor in society's eyes. The author uses considerations of this sort to reinforce his attempt to displace the goals of the wavering Christians with the goals that sustain commitment to the group. It is certainly likely that by recalling their past acts of assistance to one another the author will reawaken or reaffirm the sense of gratitude and favor among the hearers as well as friendship. As the hearers are reminded of past acts of mutual help, their minds may go to specific occasions when they have helped or received help from another sister or brother (10:32-34 provides another such

---

Heb. 13:16 (also Attridge, *Hebrews*, 175 n. 110). Hebrews 6:7-8 facilitates this understanding of how one responds correctly to God's gifts, for the benefit of rain is given to produce crops to benefit the eaters, not the rain giver. God's beneficence reaches out in this manner in widening ripples rather than returning to him.

84. The affirmation that God will not act unjustly so as to fail to remember the hearers' beneficence toward one another (out of love for God) is all the more striking after a passage warning against being unjust toward him (i.e., "forgetting" the value of the benefits enjoyed from God's generosity such that one fails to live out one's obligations of gratitude). On "remembering" as an attitude of key importance in reciprocity, see Danker, *Benefactor*, 436-37.

85. See Heb. 3:12-13; 10:24-25; 13:1-3, 16. For further discussion, see deSilva, *Despising Shame*, 284-89, 310-11.

86. See *Rhet. Her.* 1.4.9 on praising past decisions or verdicts as a means of securing the goodwill of an audience. Attridge (*Hebrews*, 174 and n. 104, citing 1 Thess. 1:3; Rev. 2:19) identifies the recollection of the addressees' good works as a *captatio benevolentiae* in early Christian texts. We see here, however, that it serves several rhetorical goals at the same time.

opportunity). Stirring up such feelings will also support his exhortation to continued solidarity and support.[87]

Hebrews 6:11-12 defines this ongoing mutual support and aid as the course of action that leads the hearers away from the dangers announced in 6:4-8 and toward the "salvation" that awaits and is described in various ways throughout the sermon: "we want each one of you to show the same zeal until the end to the fulfillment of hope, in order that you become not sluggish but imitators of those who through trust (διὰ πίστεως) and patient endurance inherit the promises." Ongoing investment in one's fellow Christians is supported by a consideration of the consequences. By zealous service to one another, they will not slow down (or worse, "stop" and "fall short") in their forward progress to the completion of their journey toward God's promised benefits (the "eternal deliverance" and entry into the unshakable homeland).[88] Rather, in such an environment of mutual support they will find the resources to "imitate" those who have embodied those core virtues of "firmness in trust" and "perseverance" that bring their possessor to the desirable end.[89] This anticipates the fuller appeal to emulation (and the fuller definitions of trust and endurance) found in 10:32–12:3.[90]

Hebrews 6:9-12, then, underscores the expediency of persevering to the completion of the journey begun at conversion (6:1) and continuing the investment in one's fellow Christians along the way (6:9-11). By such a course the hearers would preserve God's recognition of their worthy reception of his benefits and thus stimulate him to continue to benefit them. This course would preserve existing good things (their relationship with God as patron) and eventually help the hearers attain greater goods (entry into glory, rest, an abiding city, and a homeland). Elevating their minds to consider "eternal deliverance"

---

87. Thus the author of *Rhetorica ad Alexandrum* (1439b15-18) advises: "If we are urging our audience to render assistance [βοηθεῖν] to certain parties, whether individuals or states, it will also be suitable briefly to mention any friendly feeling or cause for gratitude or compassion [φιλία ἢ χάρις ἢ ἔλεος] that already exists between them and the members of the assembly." Hebrews 6:9-10; 10:32-34; 13:1-3 certainly reflect this strategy.

88. The notion of "inheriting promises" occurs frequently in Christian culture, which portrays its members as entering into the inheritance of the children of Abraham, becoming the (rightful) heirs to the OT promises, and thus of eschatological deliverance and reward. See Gal. 3:15-18, 29.

89. Attridge (*Hebrews*, 176 and n. 128) reads the linking of "perseverance" and "faith" as informative for the meaning of faith in Hebrews as in other Christian texts like Rev. 13:10; 14:12; 2 Thess. 1:4. *Herm. Sim.* 9.15.2. The connotations of "firmness" and "constancy," which "faith" can carry, are certainly well pronounced in Hebrews.

90. Imitation is a common image for discipleship in both Stoic and Christian texts but is grounded in the broad cultural tendency toward emulation of those publicly praised as virtuous for the sake of attaining the honor that belongs to virtue.

and "eternal judgment" (5:9; 6:2), the author is able to replace the alternatives being contemplated by those who are wavering (continued deprivation or a return to a "normal" life) with the alternatives articulated in 6:4-12: exclusion from God's favor (leading ultimately to the "fire") and reception of "deliverance" and the "better" things enumerated throughout the sermon.

6:13-20

The conjunction of the words "trust" and "patience" in 6:12 recalls the figure of Abraham, celebrated for these qualities in the intertestamental period. *Jubilees,* a retelling of Genesis 1 through Exodus 14 from the early- to mid-second century B.C., for example, speaks prominently of Abraham's patience and trust:

> The LORD was aware that Abraham was faithful in all of his afflictions because he tested him . . . and in everything in which he tested him he was found faithful. (*Jub.* 17:17-18)

> And we [i.e., God and the angels] were testing him whether he would exercise self-control. . . . And he was found faithful, controlled of spirit. (*Jub.* 19:3, 8)[91]

This provides the author with a natural lead-in to 6:13-20, which moves from the example of Abraham and his response to the oath of God to the discussion of God's oath made concerning the mediation of Christ and the proper response of the Christian recipients of that oath. This forms a bridge back to the main topic of the "long and difficult" word of 7:1–10:18, which shall make the priesthood established by God's oath and our proper response its focus.

The cardinal point of this paragraph is to impress upon the audience the reliability of the message they have received and of the mediator in whom they have placed their trust. Not only God's promise but God's oath stands behind that mediator and guarantees the efficacy of Jesus' priesthood to secure God's favor and benefactions for the clients. This concept also explains how rejection of God's promise through dissociation from Christ, refusal to commit oneself in trust to the promise, and refusal to endure what is required to arrive at the promised outcome provoke God, since God, we are told, has committed his honor to this promise through the oath. The value and certainty of this promise are set beyond doubt, and any course of action that suggests a belittling of the promise or distrust of the one who promised is presented as an affront to God.

The example of Abraham is adduced to demonstrate how God uses a divine oath to give absolute assurance to the recipients of God's promises. Chris-

---

91. Translation from *OTP* 2:90, 92.

tian authors frequently turn to the story of Abraham as an instructive paradigm for the life of faith (see Rom. 4; Gal. 3:6-18; Heb. 11:8-19; Jas. 2:18-24). The elements of God's promise to Abraham (Heb. 6:13), that he would become the father of a great nation (Gen. 12:2-3; 15:5; 17:5) and would inherit the land of Canaan (Gen. 12:7; 13:4), would have been well known to the audience of Hebrews. The particular detail that this author now elevates is the oath sworn by God as recorded in Genesis 22:16-17, which is here given in an abridged recitation with a number of minor alterations.[92] God's oath enables Abraham to "patiently endure" and thus receive the promise (Heb. 6:15).

The author of Hebrews moves into the human sphere of oath taking with a general observation or principle — a "probability" that the audience will accept: "people swear by one who is greater,[93] and the oath is an end to all contradiction for them, leading to certainty" (6:16). Oaths are regularly offered as proofs in forensic speeches, alongside the evidence of witnesses, legal contracts, and the like.[94] While rhetorical handbooks do present the possibility of raising doubts, in a legal battle, concerning the reliability of oaths, it appears to have been a truism that oaths carried great weight toward the establishment of certainty with regard to the "facts" of a case. According to Philo (*Som.* 1.12), "the uncertain things are confirmed and the things lacking conviction receive confirmation (τὰ ἀβέβαια βεβαιοῦται καὶ τὰ ἄπιστα λαμβάνει πίστιν)" by means of oaths.[95]

This text from Philo helps to highlight the impact of Hebrews 6:13-20, elevating the overtones of "confirmation" and "reliability." A text from the Greco-Roman side of the equation also locates the terminology of Hebrews in the sphere of trust and promises. Dio Chrysostom cautions his readers to take great care in choosing those in whom they will place trust, if trust is to be well placed at all, "for with human beings there is no constancy or truthfulness at all (οὐ γάρ ἐστι παρ' αὐτοῖς βέβαιον οὐθὲν οὐδὲ ἀληθές; *Or.* 74.24)." Even if human beings use oaths deceitfully, however, God's oath will surely provide certainty (βεβαίωσις, Heb. 6:16). The addressees would indeed be reluctant to question

---

92. The Genesis text reads: "By myself I swore, says the Lord, because you did this thing, and have not spared your beloved son on account of me, I will indeed bless you, and I will surely multiply your offspring as the stars of heaven and as the sand that is by the seashore" (Gen. 22:16-17 [LXX]).

93. Literally, "against one who is greater," showing the adversarial quality of an oath. In effect, the oath invites the hostility and reprisal of the deity in whose name an oath is sworn should the oath be deceitful or violated, since the name and honor of that deity was taken as a surety. As one might take out a loan "against" some collateral in the present Western economy, so an oath was a "loan" of reliability taken out "against" the honor and reliability of a god.

94. See Aristotle *Rh.* 1.15.27-32; *Rhet. Alex.* 1432a33-37.

95. Attridge, *Hebrews*, 180 n. 26; Lane (*Hebrews 1–8*, 151) refers the reader to Cicero *Topica* 20.77; Philo *On Noah's Work as a Planter* 82.

the truthfulness of God when God takes an oath — the example of the wilderness generation, previously invoked, would inveigh heavily against alleging God's untrustworthiness or the unreliability of his promises.

That God should take an oath is somewhat problematic: oaths are administered on account of the possibility of deceitful speech, but God's every word must be received as true and reliable even without an oath.[96] Philo, who also wrestles with this question in his exploration of the Abraham story, perceives that the reason for God's oath is different from the reason oaths are taken in human dealings: specifically God hereby assists human trust (*Abr.* 273). This is precisely the purpose that the author of Hebrews will invoke to explain God's taking of an oath:

> God, wanting all the more to show to the heirs of the promise the unchangeableness of God's will, interposed an oath, in order that, through two unchangeable things in which it is impossible for God to prove a liar, we who fled might have strong confidence to seize the hope that lies before us. (6:17-18)

The addressees have already been introduced to the oath (Ps. 110:4 in Heb. 5:5), but the author had previously quoted this only as a declaration, not as an oath. In 7:21 he will quote the full text of Psalm 110:4, which begins, "the Lord has sworn and will not change his mind." "The unchangeableness of his will" (τὸ ἀμετάθετον τῆς βουλῆς αὐτοῦ) of Hebrews 6:17 corresponds to the claim "he will not change his mind" (οὐ μεταμεληθήσεται) found in the oath itself.

The author seeks thus to embed the reliability and certainty of the Christian hope (the promise of entry into the divine, unshakable realm, as well as the assurance of enjoying access to God now) in the truthfulness of God, something that should be beyond question in the minds of the hearers. He hopes that the hearers will be encouraged to continue to invest in their hope (i.e., continue to invest in one another and live out their witness to the One God and his Christ), knowing that the ground will not fall out from under them, that they will not be, at the last, disappointed and put to shame. The author issues, however, an implicit warning. Choosing actions that show a fear of investing in that hope and pulling back from bold association with Jesus and one's fellow believers enact distrust of the promises that God has confirmed on oath. Their actions, if not their lips, would suggest that God could be untrue to his word, and hence would dishonor him. Again, Hebrews 3:7-19 and 6:13-20 show themselves to be mutually reinforcing. Rather than act in such a destructive way, the hearers are urged to greet with full commitment and trust the divine patron

---

96. For another perspective on this problem, see Philo, *Sacr. AC* 91-94 (cited in Attridge, *Hebrews,* 179 n. 17).

who has committed his own honor to providing the salvation and benefaction he has promised to those who remain faithful clients and persevere in the household of God.

The final verses of this paragraph (6:19-20) explore the qualities of this "hope" that has been so thoroughly confirmed for the believers: "we have [this hope] as an anchor for the soul, one that is secure and reliable and that enters to the inner side of the curtain where Christ entered on our behalf, having become a high priest forever after the order of Melchizedek." Using the simile of an "anchor" to convey the significance of the believers' "hope" invites the addressees to regard the assurance of a heavenly homeland as the fixed point in their lives, as that which keeps them from "drifting" into danger (cf. 2:1-4), their source of stability in a storm — perhaps specifically the squall of cognitive dissonance, of living as children of God and as dispossessed and disenfranchised persons at the same time. For the wavering — those who are seeking to root their lives in some order again — the author says that "order" is to be reestablished through this hope. The Greek words ἀσφαλῆ and βεβαίαν are terms of certainty and reliability,[97] meant here to stimulate trust and dispel distrust. Once again a contrast with Dio Chrysostom's oration "Concerning Distrust" is informative. Dio (*Or.* 74.24) uses the image of a harbor as an analogy for safety in trusting (again negatively, in keeping with his theme of "distrust"): "havens free from billows can be found, trusting which men may safely ride at anchor, however high the gale may rise. But with human beings, the most temperate are like our summer anchorages, which afford shelter for the moment only." The author of Hebrews insists that the Christian hope is unlike hope placed in the word of human beings. This hope provides a firm and secure anchorage grounded in the oath of God.

It is the "hope" of the believer that enters into God's realm, into God's rest, or, here, into God's temple and holy place[98] ahead of the believer, even as Jesus entered it as a forerunner on our behalf. The description of Jesus as a "scout" (πρόδρομος), a military figure who goes ahead of the main body of troops, recalls the author's earlier presentations of Jesus as the one who goes before the main body of God's "sons and daughters," leading them to their God-

---

97. Compare 4 Macc. 17:4, where the author commends the mother of the seven martyred brothers because she "held firm (βεβαίαν) the hope of her endurance toward God"; Wis. 7:23, which predicates these qualities of wisdom, claiming it to be "reliable, certain" (βέβαιον, ἀσφαλές) and therefore a trustworthy guide through life; 3 Macc. 5:31; 7:7, wherein the Jews are commended for their "firm" loyalty to the monarchy. Most telling, however, is Dio *Or.* 74.4, in which the orator criticizes human beings for their lack of reliability: "with human beings there is no constancy (βέβαιον) or truthfulness at all."

98. τὸ ἐσώτερον τοῦ καταπετάσματος is a reference to the veil that separated the holy of holies from the holy place (Lev. 16:2, 12, 15; Exod. 26:31-35; 36:35 [LXX 37:3]; 40:3; Lev. 21:23; 24:3). The reference is now reconfigured and applied to an accoutrement of the heavenly temple.

appointed destiny of glory (2:5-10). The author raises again the expectation that where Jesus has gone the many believers will follow. For the present, however, "hope" is the only part of the believer that has entered, and as long as the believer holds onto that hope, he or she holds onto the lifeline by which to enter. This concept can impact the hearer in two ways. First, it can recall a topic of the possible, that is, that if the beginning of something is possible, so is its end (Aristotle *Rh.* 2.19.5). The awareness of this "hope" becomes, in a sense, the demonstration that it can (and will, given God's oath) be fulfilled. The addressees should be reassured of the feasibility of the Christian project and thus be enabled to accept perseverance in it more readily. Second, if entering where Christ has entered is seen as "desirable in itself" (and the eschatological destiny of the material realm makes entry into the divine realm essential for survival), then holding onto that which connects the believer to his or her destination and goal will be regarded as expedient.[99]

Hebrews 6:18-20 emerges, therefore, as a particularly effective strategy for moving the hearers closer to the author's goal for them. To those who feel rootless in the world, who have begun to feel the need for security and "place" again, the author holds out the lifeline connected to the anchor of hope, "firm and secure" in the unshakable realm of God's heaven. As the sermon will devolve, images that connect "home" with the goal of the Christian pilgrimage will multiply: "better and lasting possessions" (10:34); "a city having foundations, whose designer and artisan is God" (11:10); "a better, that is, a heavenly, homeland" (11:15-16); "the city of the living God" (12:22); "an unshakable kingdom" (12:28). The author urges the hearers to find their stability and their rootedness in their hope in God's promise rather than in acceptance by their neighbors and by reclaiming their place in the world that is passing away.

The potential impact of the designation of the hearers as "those who have fled" is also not to be underestimated, being quite apt for the situation being addressed. Those who are contemplating a return to their former lives, trying to find a way to reenter the larger society, are reminded that they formerly fled that world as if from some great danger. The author wants them to consider themselves coming to the church not as shoppers trying out a new philosophy, but as refugees, fleeing from the certified catastrophe of eschatological judgment (recalling the two pillars of the early catechism, "resurrection of the dead and eternal judgment," 6:2) and seeking protection and deliverance from that day of judgment (cf. 1:14). The author thus subtly reinforces one of his main strategies: reinforcing the addressees' perception of life in the world apart from

---

99. This presentation of hope as that which connects the believer to, and assures him or her of, the future benefaction will also emerge as an important aspect of "faith" in 11:1 — that virtue also provides the believer with possession in the present of what will only later be enjoyed in full.

the people of God as a life that faces the truly gravest dangers and assured eternal loss. Could they now consider it reasonable to desert their lifeboat to return to the burning ship?

Hebrews 6:20 returns to the "topic sentence" of 5:10, again employing a recontextualization of Psalm 110:4 with the significant change of "priest" to "high priest" (as in 5:10). The audience is ready now profitably to hear the "long and difficult account" of Christ's high priesthood and allow it to motivate them to press on to the completion of their journey (6:1).

Summary

The author breaks off his exposition of the "priesthood after the order of Melchizedek" (5:10; resumption in 6:20) in order to devote some attention to the ground in which this word is to be planted. He uses a number of bold appeals to the *pathē* (emotions) of the hearers in order to move them to accept the author's agenda for them: "moving on to perfection" (6:1), the completion of their journey and the fulfillment of their hope as well as the finished state of their personal formation in the Christian way of life ("maturity").

First, he attempts to arouse shame in the hearts of the hearers based on the charge that they have not lived up to what might reasonably have been expected of persons joined to the Christian group for so long a period of time (however long that is). He claims that they ought to have taken on responsibility for assisting one another's perseverance rather than waiting for another teacher (like himself) to come along with a word of exhortation. By questioning their maturity, he moves them to want to prove their maturity. They will respond to his challenge, the author hopes, by taking up more intentionally and energetically their group-maintaining responsibilities, their reminders to one another, and reinforcement for one another, of the Christian hope, the values of the group, and the definition of the "wise" and "honorable" path as shaped by the Christian worldview.

Knowing that they do not need a refresher in the "basic lessons of the oracles of God" (5:12), but only need to be spurred on in their investment in and commitment to the Christian enterprise, the author proposes yet again the main items on his agenda: moving forward in their journey to the end of their hope (rather than allowing any force to draw them to "drift away" or "turn away"). He supports this proposal with an argument from the contrary course of action: What will happen to those who, rather than press on, fall away (6:6)? The author's argument here is deeply embedded in the ethos of reciprocity (patronage) and derives its force from the strength of that cultural background. Since they have experienced God's favor and benefactions (6:4-5), any response of theirs that failed to "give back" to the benefactor would be disgraceful and ugly. All the more ignoble would be the response that held Jesus, the broker of God's gifts, up to public scorn. Withdrawal from the Christian community, or hiding one's association with Christ's family and clients, would bear witness to the non-Christian world that their friendship was of greater value than God's friendship, their favor worth more than God's favor. Such ungrateful clients would injure rather than enhance Jesus' reputation, and so must expect to suffer the consequences (here, exclusion from any return to the favor they spurned).

The goal of this warning is, on the one hand, to arouse fear in the hearts of the addressees of pursuing any path that would show lack of regard for God and his gifts and promises. The positive counterpart of this aim is that the addressees will be motivated to continue to bear the "suitable vegetation" that is the proper return for God's benefactions. Their choices will be shaped by the desire to sustain the circle of grace (reciprocity) and respond to God's generosity "beautifully" rather than with ugliness. The author specifically directs the hearers to "return" God's favor by showing love and performing acts of service toward their sisters and brothers in Christ. It is by so doing that they make a "just" return that the "just" God will not forget. Their commitment to making a fair return assures them of God's ongoing, future favor. By continuing in such a course, the addressees will come to the "fulfillment of hope" rather than fall into the danger of becoming "sluggish" in their response to God's word and favor (the sluggishness that would lead to "falling short of God's gift" [12:15] or "falling short" of God's rest [4:1]).

The author seeks to deepen trust and motivate perseverance by elevating God's oath, the topic that dominates 6:13-20 and will be developed in 7:21-28. Just as God's oath to Abraham enabled the patriarch to endure patiently in trust, so God's oath to the believers (recorded in Ps. 110:4; see Heb. 7:21) should be regarded as the sure and unshakable foundation of the new covenant, Jesus' priesthood, and of the believers' hope of receiving the benefaction of deliverance and entrance into the heavenly realm. God has committed his honor to bringing the believers to the completion of the journey begun at their repentance and turning to God (6:1), and the author has already held up the dangerous consequences of doubting the reliability of God's promises (3:7–4:11). The believers' hope connects them to their destiny, to the heavenly sanctum ("holy place") in the unshakable realm. The author asks the hearers to consider this hope their anchor, their fixed point, the source of their constancy in this life.

Bridging the Horizons

The author of Hebrews was not reticent to challenge his congregation (or congregations) to live up to that measure of Christian instruction which they had received. The apostle Paul likewise challenges his readers in Philippi: even if we are not yet "complete" or "mature," "let us at least fall in line with what we have attained" (Phil. 3:16). Many believers could profit from being pressed on this point. Do we live by what we confess with our lips or "know" in our heads to be the truth of our existence in this penultimate world? Do we live up to the vows we make at our baptism or confirmation? Do we live up to the promises we make at the baptism of others into our congregation to nurture and encourage them in the faith they have embraced (or will be moved to embrace, if they are baptized as infants and raised in a supportive and nurturing congregation)? Arguably, we only really "know" that which we are willing to live out, and we only truly confess something to be true when we take measures to act and chart our course by that truth. Hebrews 5:11-14 may challenge us precisely on this point, motivating those of us who have spent years or even decades in the faith to accept our status and responsibility as "teachers," that is, as those who take an active role in modeling the Christian way of life (living up to "what we know") and in encouraging, exhorting, and challenging others to pursue that road more intently and wholeheartedly.

This text may release the power of our congregations to become active and supportive "courts of reputation" that hold each individual member accountable to the standards revealed by God in Christ, reinforcing for one another the reality and ultimacy of those standards in the midst of a society that vociferously and effectively seeks to form in us standards of its own devising. Applied with care and wisdom, the text may be used by preachers to form communities that assist each individual Christian to exercise "wisdom" (discerning between the advantageous and disadvantageous, the noble and the base) in light of eternity first rather than to fall prey to the persistent temptation to "hedge our bets" with regard to seeking self-respect and success in this world as well as the next.

First, Hebrews 5:11–6:3 as a whole challenges us to press on to the final state of that journey of which our conversion and preliminary catechesis (or New Members' Class in many Protestant denominations) was but the larval state. The goal of this process is not conversion or membership in a church but arrival at our God-appointed destiny: transformation into the reflection of Christ, at the level of the individual (see 2 Cor. 3:18; Gal 4:19), and translation to the unshakable realm, at the level of eschatology and history. We are invited into a process of maturation, of learning "wisdom" by exercising constancy in our choice of doing what is in keeping with what we know of God and his desires for us as individuals and communities of faith. We are also invited into a pilgrimage of learning that this world, with all its offerings, its vaunted values, and its markers of status, is not our true home, not our final home. We are invited to live so as to bear witness to the unseen realities that lie at the heart of our hope. The author dwells so much on the goal of this journey, and on setting our hearts and minds on this goal, because he wishes to motivate believers in every age to live here so that they will not be ashamed when they meet God in that undiscovered country.

Second, 6:1-3 invites us to reflect upon the social-formation potential of how we take in new members or resocialize current members more fully into the Christian worldview and ethos. Each element mentioned in these verses carries with it high potential for highlighting the initiate's renunciation of old ways of thinking and living, assimilation to a new and distinctive group with its own understanding of "the way the world really is," and education into a new and "more enlightened" understanding of what one's aims in this life should be. Do we think intentionally about laying the foundations for group commitment to the values and goals articulated in the NT? If we content ourselves now with a basic introduction to how our denomination "works" or what our particular congregation has to offer, how can the early Church's model of more complete and thoroughgoing resocialization challenge us to use that time when people cross the threshold of the church more powerfully and effectively?

The early Church recognized the importance and potential impact of rituals of entry (in our text, "baptisms and laying on of hands"). How can we use rituals or liturgies to mark the entry of new members (and allow for current members' reaffirmation of their commitment)? In denominations that practice infant baptism, liturgical acts other than baptism may still be used to elevate the significance of joining the congregation (e.g., congregational laying on of hands). Human beings are symbolic beings, and those of us who are entrusted especially with the building up of strong congregations might do well to consider how to enhance commitment and a sense of solidarity through symbolic acts of renunciation of non-Christian ways and incorporation into the church.

The argument from the contrary in 6:4-8 is frequently drawn into debates concerning "eternal security," but this debate was far from the mind and intention of the author of those words. Indeed, insofar as modern theological topics such as "losing salvation" and "eternal security" determine our reading or dominate our discussion, the real impact the author seeks to have is pushed out of central focus. He is interested rather in elevating the absolute necessity of making a full, appropriate, and grateful return to God for the benefits God has already granted the believers. Viewed negatively, he wants to render unthinkable any course of action that violates the beauty of reciprocity between God and human beings, particularly from the human side of the relationship (where loyalty, commitment, and obedience are from time to time called into question). The author has cast the divine-human relationship in terms of the giving and receiving of benefits (patronage), and he simply holds up the expectation that we will behave as honorable, grateful recipients of God's gifts. The author's strategy here suggests that preachers and lay leaders should make it an aim of their ministry to arouse a deep appreciation for the value of God's gifts (i.e., the arousal of gratitude), as well as to give direction for the appropriate and necessary response of gratitude. Paul appeals to this dynamic quite forcefully in 2 Corinthians 5:15: "he died on behalf of all" — the beneficent act — "in order that the living should live no longer for themselves but for him who died on their behalf and was raised up" — the fitting and necessary response of the grateful heart, which seeks to return a favor as fully as it was given.

We might consider the usefulness of allowing 6:4-8 to have its full force as an incentive to discipleship. Preaching "cheap grace," as Dietrich Bonhoeffer phrased it so eloquently in his *Cost of Discipleship,* does not do our congregations a good service. Rather, the author of Hebrews challenges us to provide our congregations with opportunities to respond honorably to God with our service and obedience and to know truly the sublime attitude of gratitude by enacting a grateful response. By such an invitation, we call people to their divinely appointed destiny. To borrow from Ephesians, "we are his workmanship, created in Christ Jesus for good works, which God prepared in advance in order that we should walk in them" (2:10). Rather than shy away from Hebrews 6:4-8, therefore, we might view it as an invitation to deepen our sense of the value of God's gifts, to understand the obligation that such generosity puts on us, and to pursue the nobility, the self-respect, and the sense of Christian integrity that can come from responding to God's generosity with full hearts. The author calls us to value God's favor, not thinking lightly of now obeying, now disobeying, now attending, now neglecting God and God's commands. Gratitude has thus the potential to cure the spiritual disease of double-mindedness.

The direction the author gives for this flow of gratitude back to God, this bringing of God's generosity full circle (recalling Seneca's image of the never-ending circular dance of the three Graces), is specifically toward acts of love and service for one's fellow believers. God stands in need of nothing, and so the divine benefits call us to bear the fruits of gratitude to those whom God has designated (as the rain is given so that land will bear vegetation for the farmers and others dependent on the land — not for the rain giver). This author may thus provide us with the clearest and tightest model for holding together personal reception of God's favor (I hesitate to use the word "salvation" here, since the author does not use the term this way) and the response of good works and service to the worldwide community of faith: the gospel of conversion and the "social gospel," as it were. Indeed, he suggests that these are inseparable, just as reception of a gift and reciprocity for the gift go "hand in hand" in Seneca's dance. If we gave some attention to developing the congregation's sensitivity to forming "noble" rather than "ugly" responses to God's gifts, what resources for building up the church worldwide would we unlock!

Because "eternal security" is such an important doctrine for many Christians, for which reason so much space was given above to considering the theological implications of setting our NT texts fully in their cultural context, we must ask what advice the author offers to those who seek "security" in their hope of salvation. Strikingly, he offers not the assurance of Romans 8:38-39 but points rather to "your work and the love that you showed in God's name, serving and continuing to serve the saints" (6:10). It is their mutual nurture, their investment in one another, that the just "God will not forget," and that gives the author assurance that the "better things that hold salvation" will be the lot of the addressees. To those who might have felt fear at the warning of 6:4-8, the author offers this care and mutual service as the welcome source of confidence. As a Protestant author, I feel compelled to remind myself and my readers that this is not about "salvation by means of works."[100] Rather, the author is pointing to a different source for the believers' sense of "security" than the doctrinal, intellectual, noetic dimension so often elevated by Protestant Christians. He suggests that confidence comes from acting as noble clients of the just God, rendering to God an appropriate return for God's gifts to us. Clients who respond to their patron with loyalty, respect, and obedient service as the patron directs have every confidence that the grace relationship will continue secure and that the flow of benefits from the patron will be untrammeled.

The danger, of course, is that our scruples might take over and we might become engrossed in questions concerning: "How much is enough?" "When have I responded gratefully?" "Have I returned enough for the gift?" This is, of course, to fall afoul of the ethos of reciprocity. Even Seneca knew that it was not required for a client to match the patron's gift, but rather to match the patron's "grace" — to respond beautifully and fully to a beautiful act of generosity. The author's model calls for stimulating the heart to gratitude with the remembrance of great benefits (as listed in 6:4-5, for example), and channeling that gratitude into acts of loving service that delight God. It is not a burden placed on the conscience and not something we must do slavishly. We must keep God's gifts and favor before our eyes (and to do less is to "forget" a benefit, a most shameful thing) and reflect on the magnitude of God's generosity. Understanding that reception of such gifts calls us into a never-ending cycle of giving, we will take up our obligation as clients joyfully, knowing also that as the cycle continues we will again and again be recipients of God's benefactions and will again and again show our gratitude in the concrete ways God directs.

The final paragraph of this section aims at stimulating trust in God, which is foundational for continued investment in the Christian community and its goals (so many of which lie perpetually beyond sight and touch). The author elevates God's truthfulness and confirmation of his word in Christ as pillars of trust. If we don't find his application of Psalm 110:4 particularly compelling, there are certainly other divine pronouncements and confirmatory wit-

---

100. All the more as this phrase tends to signify "works of Torah" in most of its NT contexts rather than "good works."

nesses to consider that present Jesus as the ultimate revelation of God's values and guarantor of God's promises. The only two sentences spoken by God in each of the three Synoptic Gospels, for example, come to mind, in which God names Jesus as his Son and pronounces Jesus' way "pleasing" in his sight and Jesus' teaching as the divinely endorsed message to "hear" and heed (see Matt. 3:17; 17:5). Jesus' words are presented as, in fact, God's message to humanity, and the reliability of God's word makes Jesus' words the sure foundation on which to build a life that will withstand the storms of this life and the fire of the next. The fact that over 1950 years have elapsed since Jesus uttered those words does not render them false or indicate that God "changed his mind."

The closing image of the hope that gives us sure and safe anchorage resonates with the rootless, listless twentieth- and twenty-first-century hearer as it did for the first-century pilgrim. Hebrews 6:19-20 offers us an anchor line, a tether connecting us to our final and abiding home. As we lay hold of Christ, we discover that our hope does in fact enter the unshakable, heavenly sanctum, and that we, too, enter in the Spirit. The word of Hebrews calls us, during the time of our earthly pilgrimage, to acquaint ourselves with that holy space of God's full presence so that we come to know it as our home. Such a center for the soul becomes a welcome source of stability and constancy in the midst of the "swift and varied changes of the world."

Jesus, the Better-Qualified Mediator
of God's Favor: 7:1–8:13

Overview

Hebrews 7:1–10:18 forms a well-integrated exposition of the value and efficacy of Jesus' priestly ministry. Therefore we must consider the purpose of the whole as we also consider the goals and arguments of the two halves (7:1–8:13, which deals largely with the comparison of the two priesthoods themselves, and 9:1–10:18, which treats more directly the rituals performed by these priesthoods and the relative efficacy of these rites). The character of the sermon changes at this point, for there are no exhortations that break up this four-chapter block of argumentation until 10:19. Why does the author devote so much space to comparing and contrasting Jesus' priestly work and the cultic arrangements prescribed by Torah, pressing on every point for the superiority of the former over the latter? What goals or needs might this central exposition serve?

Scholars from the early to the modern period have frequently read these chapters as an antidote administered to addressees who were tempted to revert (or convert) to Judaism.[1] In this view, the author compares Jesus with the levitical priests specifically because some of his addressees think the latter a viable (and perhaps advantageous) alternative to approaching God. The author's discussion of the inefficacy of the Torah-prescribed cultic regulations seeks, then, to dissuade Christians from detaching themselves from the Christian group for the sake of attaching themselves to the synagogue or even the temple. We have become quite accustomed to reading these chapters as an exhortation not to "go back" to Judaism, but there are several important alternative goals

---

1. See, recently, Nelson, *Raising Up a Faithful Priest*, 142; Peterson, *Hebrews and Perfection*, 187; Pfitzner, *Hebrews*, 29.

that the author might seek to achieve through these same chapters. Accepting too quickly the hypothesis that the author seeks to prevent reversion to Judaism prevents us from penetrating deeper into the full spectrum of rhetorical effects this discourse achieves.

One purpose may be to make the priesthood of Jesus more real for the hearers. The author is, after all, describing events in the "life" or "career" of Jesus that are unavailable for human observation. That Jesus should be understood as a "priest" at all is probably a claim requiring demonstration. Arguments concerning the inefficacy of the first priesthood (and intimations in Scriptural texts like Ps. 110:4 concerning a new priesthood) serve to demonstrate the necessity, and hence the reality, of this new order of priesthood on which the hearers are asked to rely so completely and for which they are to risk so much. That Jesus was consecrated to priesthood after his ascension "through the heavens" (4:14), took his own blood into the heavenly holy of holies, cleansed that immaterial and invisible sacred place, and sat down at God's right hand certainly requires some substantiation. How indeed could the author know what Jesus does in heaven?

Rather than answering this question as a visionary who claims to see into the invisible realm, the author approaches it as an exegete. The author's discussion of the priestly ministry of Jesus alongside that of the levitical priesthood can be understood as an exercise in typology, whereby present and forthcoming acts of God (or God's agents) are understood in terms of past acts or instruments of God. Based on this principle, the author of Hebrews has access to knowledge about Jesus' post-ascension priesthood based on the patterns of priesthood known from the prototype discussed in the Torah. Contrasting an invisible priesthood with a visible one would be consistent with the Platonic pattern of arriving at knowledge of the ideal form from contemplation of the material representations of that ideal.

The second purpose involves elevating both the honor of Jesus (which was the principal function of *synkrisis* in rhetoric) and the advantages that Jesus' mediation has brought to the hearers. The author would find it strategic to amplify the achievement of Jesus since this would arouse gratitude in the hearts of the hearers (thus stir them up to act so as to honor this Jesus for his achievement and return loyalty and service for the great gifts Jesus makes available to them) and would remind the wavering that the truly expedient course of action is one that preserves friendly and favorable connections with this Jesus, who brings such advantages to his clients. Here again one finds epideictic topics (amplification of Jesus' merits and achievements) serving deliberative goals (promoting continued association with Jesus and the people called by his name).

A persistent feature of Hebrews scholarship is the assumption that the comparison between Jesus and the levitical priests implies a polemic against the latter figures. Why would the author be talking about the levitical priests if some in the audience were not contemplating defection from Christ to return to the older cultus? Attention to classical rhetoric leads to a promising solution. Encomia (speeches in praise of some person and his or her achievements) regularly included comparisons between the subject of the speech and other persons of renown.[2] The sole purpose of this comparison was to amplify the honor and achievement of the subject of the encomium.[3] Quintilian (*Inst.* 3.7.16) advises that "what most pleases an audience is the celebration of deeds which our hero was the first or only man or at any rate one of the very few to perform . . . emphasizing what was done for the sake of others rather than what he performed on his own behalf." Hebrews 7:1–10:18 falls within the parameters of rhetorical convention by demonstrating through *synkrisis* that Jesus was the "first" and "only" person to attain the benefit of direct access to God for humankind. Such a demonstration serves, in turn, the author's primary goal of leading his audience to perceive attachment to Jesus as the source of their greatest advantage (and forfeiture of this bond as the greatest inexpedience).

The author of Hebrews selects the levitical priests as material for his *synkrisis* for a number of reasons. They provide the "type" or "pattern" from which the priestly activity of Jesus beyond the heavens can be credibly "reconstructed." They are a revered part of the work of God in the past, and their limitations can be used to highlight the surpassing honor of Jesus and value of having this Jesus as one's mediator of divine favor. Additionally, a comparison with the levitical priesthood affords a salvation-historical perspective that will also amplify the value of Jesus' priesthood. Hitherto the author has been largely eschatological in his orientation (looking ahead to entering God's promised rest and the believers' final glory or to the judgment by God and subjugation of Christ's enemies, among which the addressees should not wish to find themselves). Now the author approaches the believers' favored place in God's unfolding plan by contrasting the access afforded to God's people in prior times with the access afforded the Christians "in these last days" through the Son's mediation. Such a consideration should again arouse gratitude and a deep sense of being privileged beyond any of their predecessors in the faith (see also

---

2. See Aristotle (*Rh.* 1.9.38-39): "And you must compare him with illustrious personages, for it affords ground for amplification and is noble, if he can be proved better than men of worth. Amplification is with good reason ranked as one of the forms of praise, since it consists in superiority, and superiority is one of the things that are noble"; *Rhet. Alex.* 1441a27-28: "you must also compare the distinguished achievements of other young men and show that they are surpassed by his."

3. As Attridge (*Hebrews*, 55) comments, the author's "basic interest is to establish the significance of Christ for the present and future of his addresees by indicating the superiority of the Son to any other agent of God's purposes."

discussion of 11:39-40), and thus make the choice of a course that showed ingratitude all the more unthinkable. It is primarily the value of Jesus' blood that
some are in danger of valuing too lightly (10:29), and the author has but one
scriptural means of demonstrating the worth of that blood and the unprecedented quality of the access to God that it affords: a contrast with the only other
God-ordained system of mediation.

As we consider these chapters in detail, then, we should remember that
the rhetorical goals they serve are much broader and more constructive than
polemicizing against desertion to Judaism. It is, also, in these alternative goals
that one will discover the continuing word of this exposition to generations of
Jewish and Gentile Christians alike.

Turning to 7:1–8:13, we find the author concerned first with comparing
and contrasting the character and qualities of the two priesthoods spoken of in
Scripture — the levitical priesthood (and the covenant on which it rests) and
the elusive "order of Melchizedek" (and its basis for legitimation). He begins by
considering the founder of this new order, who is presented in every way as a
"type" of the Messiah, demonstrating his superiority to the founder of the
levitical order, Abraham. The implication, of course, is that Jesus' priesthood is
more honorable than its venerated predecessor, the levitical priesthood. More
importantly, the author derives from a consideration of Melchizedek the principle that a person can hold the priestly office on the basis of an unending life
without possessing genealogical qualifications (7:1-10). This principle is then
applied to the setting aside of Torah, which appointed its priesthood by means
of genealogical requirements, and the introduction of the oath, which appoints
a priest on the basis of his "indestructible life" (7:11-25). The author contrasts
Jesus with the levitical priests on several points (mortal versus immortal, subject to sin versus not subject to sin) in order to heighten the advantages that
have accrued to the hearers, who are able to approach God through the "priest
after the order of Melchizedek," and to show how these advantages are incomparably better than those provided by the mediation of the only other priesthood legitimated by Scripture (7:19, 25-28).

As a final point of superiority, the author considers the respective quality of the place of mediation in which the two priesthoods exercise their ministry. The one serves in a material "copy and shadow" of the "true" holy place
in the heavens, and the other in that heavenly sanctum itself (8:1-6). A summary statement of the advantages of Jesus' priestly mediation (better ministry, better covenant, better promises, 8:6) leads to a lengthy quotation from
Jeremiah 31, introduced in order to demonstrate not only the legitimacy of
the author's claims about the obsolescence of the old covenant but also to announce the theme that will occupy the author in 9:1–10:18: God's provision
in these last days for the removal of the sins that kept people at a distance
from God (8:7-13).

Commentary

7:1-10

Hebrews 6:20, with its return to the theme of the "high priest after the order of Melchizedek" announced in 5:10 and in Psalm 110:4, leads naturally to a consideration of the founder of this new priestly order in 7:1-10. The author here amplifies Christ's honor by means of amplifying the honor of his "ancestor" in the priestly line, Melchizedek.[4] The fact that Melchizedek is "greater" than Abraham means that Melchizedek's priestly lineage is more honorable than the levitical priests' lineage, and thus that Jesus merits greater honor than even the levitical priests.

The founders of the levitical priesthood were held in high esteem in the Hellenistic period. Ben Sira gives a prominent place to Aaron, with whom the priesthood was established, and to Phineas, Aaron's grandson, who renewed the priestly covenant through his demonstration of zeal for God:

> He exalted Aaron, the brother of Moses, a holy man like him, of the tribe of Levi. He made an everlasting covenant with him, and gave him the priesthood of the people. He blessed him with splendid vestments, and put a glorious robe upon him. . . . He added glory to Aaron and gave him a heritage. . . .
>   Phineas the son of Eleazar is the third in glory . . . that he and his descendants should have the dignity of the priesthood for ever. (Sir. 45:6-7, 18-20, 23-24, RSV)

The author finds in Genesis 14, however, two indications that the new order of priesthood merits even greater honor than that accorded the levitical order.[5] The author supplies in 7:1-2a a compressed summary of Genesis 14:17-20, focusing attention on the salient features of those verses, which will be developed in the verses to follow. The crucial data from the episode in which Melchizedek "greets Abraham as he was returning from the slaughter of the kings" are, first, that Melchizedek "blessed him" and, second, that "Abraham apportioned to him a tenth of everything."[6] These will be used in 7:4-7 to "prove" that Melchizedek is greater than Abraham, and therefore greater than Levi.

---

4. See *Rhet. Her.* 3.7.13, which lists discussion of illustrious ancestors among the topics to be treated under "external circumstances" in an encomium. The same topic is included by Theon under the heading "Exterior Excellences" (see Marrou, *History of Education,* 272-73).

5. One might construe the introduction of Gen. 14 after the citation of Ps. 110:4 as an example of the exegetical technique of *gezera shawa,* but such a construal may be a little forced since Gen. 14 is the only text besides Ps. 110 where Melchizedek is mentioned in Scripture.

6. The dominance of δεκάτ- words in 7:1-10 (7:2, 4, 6, 8, 9 [bis]) underscores the importance of the "tithe" for the author's demonstration.

The rest of the information provided by the author about Melchizedek is used to intimate the typological relationship between this strange figure with his brief but alluring cameo appearance in Scripture and the Messiah of the church's confession.[7] Hebrews 7:2b introduces the etymology of the name "Melchizedek" and of his title, "king of Salem." These translations give Melchizedek strong messianic overtones as the "king of righteousness" and "king of peace." Prophetic and intertestamental literature frequently attributes the qualities of justice and peace (or safety, wholeness) to the Messiah and his reign.[8] The author includes these etymologies not merely for the sake of completeness[9] but rather in order to build toward the point he makes in 7:3, that Melchizedek was "made to resemble the Son of God." He wants to show how Melchizedek provides the type, or even prototype, of Jesus, the Messiah-Priest who would succeed Melchizedek in his priestly office.

The claim that Melchizedek was "without mother, without father, without pedigree" derives from the principle that the silences of Scripture are themselves eloquent. If something is not written in Torah, it has no counterpart in the real world. Genesis 14:17 introduces the figure of Melchizedek without any mention of his lineage — he simply "appears" on the scriptural stage. The author sees here an opportunity to underscore the fact that Melchizedek's priesthood is not based on any genealogical qualification, for, according to Torah, he has no genealogy. His "lack of pedigree" (ἀγενεαλόγητος) sets up a contrast with the levitical priests, who depended on their genealogy for their priesthood (see Lev. 21:17–22:2; Num. 3:5-13). The author also notices that Scripture is silent concerning both the birth and the death of this figure — he is presented as though "having neither beginning of days nor end of life."[10] At this point, after a long string of subordinate clauses describing Melchizedek, the author finally arrives at the main clause begun in 7:1: "Now this Melchizedek . . . remains a

---

7. For more on Melchizedek speculation during the intertestamental and early Christian periods, see Attridge, *Hebrews*, 192-94; Gareth Cockerill, *The Melchizedek Christology in Heb. 7:1-28* (Ann Arbor: University Microfilms International, 1979).

8. Texts celebrating the righteousness that characterizes the Messiah and his kingdom include Isa. 32:1; Jer. 23:5-6; 33:15-16 (safety and well-being is also a feature of this text); *Pss. Sol.* 17:21-22, 26-27, 29, 32; 4 Ezra 12:31-34; 13:37 (with regard to reproving unrighteousness); *T. Levi* 18:2, 9; *T. Jud.* 24:1, 5. The peaceful reign of the Messiah appears in Mic. 5:2-5a; Zech. 9:9-10; 4 Ezra 13:39, 47; *T. Dan* 5:11. A number of important texts hold peace and righteousness together as marks of the Messiah: Isa. 9:6-7; 11:1-9 (righteousness, 11:3-5; peace, 11:6-9); 32:16-18; 4 Ezra 13:37-39; *T. Levi* 18:2-4. Jewish cultural intertexture is particularly thick, therefore, on this point, such that the messianic significance of the etymologies in Heb. 7:2 would be difficult to overlook.

9. Lane, *Hebrews 1–8*, 164.

10. This is expressed in a classic chiasm: μήτε (A) ἀρχὴν (B) ἡμερῶν μήτε (Β') ζωῆς (Α') τέλος.

priest forever" (μένει ἱερεὺς εἰς τὸ διηνεκές). This echo of Psalm 110:4 high-lights Melchizedek's "unending life," which will become a primary qualification for his successor, Jesus.

Abraham's dedication of a tenth part of the spoils to this Melchizedek is adduced as evidence for "how great" the latter figure is. The author is reading Genesis 14:20 as Abraham's own acknowledgment of Melchizedek's greater honor and status, particularly as a "priest of God Most High." Giving the tithe was a material affirmation of the divinely ordained function of priests and Levites as mediators of God's favor. For Abraham to give a tithe to Melchizedek was, so the author avers, for Abraham to acknowledge the legitimacy and necessity of Melchizedek's priesthood as a channel for securing God's favor. The Levites would tithe their own kinspeople on the basis of having received a commandment from God (see Num. 18:21) — it was specifically their descent from Levi that permitted them this privilege.[11] One not having any genealogical credentials, however, both took the tithe from Abraham and "blessed the one having the promises" (7:6, referring to Gen. 14:19).[12]

At this point the author introduces something of a fallacious argument, claiming that "without any contradiction the inferior is blessed by the superior party" (7:7). The inferior, however, frequently blesses the superior, as when mortals bless God (even Gen. 14:20 shows Melchizedek blessing God immediately after he blesses Abraham; see also Deut. 8:10; Ps. 15:7; 25:12; 33:2; 65:8, et al.) or when subjects bless their king.[13] The author expects this claim to have the force of a probability, however, assured that the addressees will be able to think of enough examples to support the claim (e.g., fathers blessing their children, liturgical benedictions calling for God to "bless" the worshipers) without examining it so closely as to overthrow it.

Where 7:5-6 develops the contrast between those relying on genealogical qualifications to receive tithes and the unique priest who receives tithes without a genealogy, 7:8 returns to the point about Melchizedek's unending life: "here mortal beings receive tithes, but there he is given the testimony that he lives." This testimony, once more, is provided only by the silence of Genesis 14:17-20, the absence of a narrative about Melchizedek's death. The final, almost playful ("so to speak," ὡς ἔπος εἰπεῖν),[14] note of this paragraph suggests that Levi also paid tithes to Melchizedek, since the former was still in the "loins" of his ances-

---

11. Attridge (*Hebrews*, 195) correctly points out the dissolution here of the distinction between priestly and nonpriestly Levites, but both groups hold their respective offices on the same basis — genealogy.

12. Once again the author ornaments his argumentation with chiasm: (A) δεδε-κάτωκεν (B) Ἀβραάμ (B′) καὶ τὸν ἔχοντα τὰς ἐπαγγελίας (A′) εὐλόγηκεν.

13. Attridge (*Hebrews*, 196 n. 134) cites 2 Sam. 14:22 (Joab blesses David, his king) and 1 Kgs. 1:47 (the servants bless David) as examples of the latter class.

14. Thus rightly Attridge, *Hebrews*, 197.

tor when Melchizedek encountered Abraham (7:9-10). Such a statement highlights for modern readers the intensely group-oriented and collective notion of
"personality" in the ancient world, such that all of a person's descendants can
be said to share, in some sense, in the actions and the honor of their ancestor.
That "Levi" paid tithes to Melchizedek suggests not only the greater honor of
Melchizedek but also the secondary nature of the levitical priesthood. As a
whole, the author claims, it acknowledges its dependence on the greater priesthood of Melchizedek, who is the ultimate receptor of the tithes collected by
Levi.

Hebrews 7:1-10 thus begins to lay the foundation for the author's claims
about Jesus' priesthood. In Melchizedek, king of righteousness and peace, one
sees the prototype of Jesus, the Messiah whose reign is justice and peace — a
priest of God whose claim to priesthood rests not on a genealogical qualification but on a certain quality of life beyond the reach of death. Moreover, the author has begun to establish the relative honor and efficacy of the two priesthoods. First, the levitical order, while possessing great honor as mediators of
the One God, still takes second place to the "order of Melchizedek." Second, the
passing of tithes from Levi to Melchizedek suggests that the levitical order (and
its priestly mediation) is itself dependent on, and subordinate to, the order of
Melchizedek.

7:11-28

The next paragraph (7:11-19) focuses mainly on the rationale for the "change
of priesthood" and "change of law," which the Christian group affirms has occurred. The author pinpoints the problem with the levitical priesthood and the
covenant (Torah), which at one and the same time regulated the priesthood
and was preserved by the priesthood's activity: the failure of these instruments
to "perfect" or bring "perfection" to the worshippers (7:11, 19; the author underscores the importance of this concept by using the τελείωσις word group, as
well as the νόμος word group, to create an inclusion around this paragraph).[15]

The "perfection" of which the author speaks here is, in a more proximate
sense, the "cleansing of the conscience" from the defilement of sin so that the
human being may approach God face-to-face rather than remaining at a safe
distance from God's holiness (and the danger holiness presents to things unclean). As the author will go on to demonstrate in 9:1-10, the levitical priesthood failed to close the gap between the people and their God. Barriers and restrictions always remained in force so that at no time could the average

---

15. Ellingworth, *Hebrews*, 370. τελείωσις and νενομοθέτηται in 7:11 reverberate with
ἐτελείωσεν ὁ νόμος in 7:19.

worshiper — or even the average priest, for that matter — enter God's holy place. The Torah and its provisions were unable to cleanse what sin had sullied, unable to join what sin had sundered. This more limited sense of "perfection" extends naturally into its more eschatological sense: as the Torah and its priesthood could not usher in any worshiper save the high priest into God's presence, so they are unable to lead human beings into God's very presence in the unshakable, heavenly realm. The author has already indicated that Jesus' high priesthood (here the "better hope," 7:19) is quite different, insofar as he enters that heavenly sanctum not only as mediator and representative but also as forerunner (6:19-20), looking ahead to the entrance of the "many sons and daughters" (2:10).

With 7:11, the author is moving into a topic familiar from rhetorical handbooks (and thus from typical disputes in law courts or counsel chambers). When two contracts or covenants or laws exist, or when a new one is being drawn up, it must be determined whether one invalidates the other, whether the later one invalidates the earlier or whether the earlier retains its force, nullifying the later (see Aristotle *Rh.* 1.15.25). Paul and this author both use this topic, but rather differently. Paul argues that the Torah, the later contract, does not nullify an earlier agreement, the promise made by God to Abraham (Gal. 3:15-18); for the author of Hebrews, a later covenant negates the earlier contract, the Torah. Both Psalm 110 and Jeremiah 31 provide the author with scriptural data pointing to a new contract and a new priesthood. Ceslaus Spicq refers to the line of thinking that undergirds the author's logic as a "chronological argument," according to which the later word nullifies or limits the earlier.[16] The fact that God would establish a non-Aaronic priesthood on oath in Psalm 110:4 — centuries after the levitical priesthood was established by Torah — provides the author with a "token"[17] that demonstrates the limited role and purview of the levitical priesthood and, by im-

---

16. *L'Épître aux Hébreux*, 1:365. The author appeals to this principle of interpreting the OT at several critical junctures in his argument. He had used it first at 4:1-11, claiming the fact that Ps. 95 was uttered after the entry into Canaan under Joshua as proof that Joshua did not, in fact, give the people "rest" but that this "rest" was still a future goal. Similarly, we observe it here in 7:11-28 (the oath of Ps. 110 being given later than, and therefore superseding, prescriptions for levitical priests in the Pentateuch). The author will employ it again in 8:6-13, taking the later oracle of Jer. 31, which postdates Deuteronomy, as a sign that the "old covenant" is abolished, and in 10:1-10, where Ps. 40, which postdates the prescriptions for animal sacrifices in the Pentateuch, declares these sacrifices invalid and proposes another. The constant rule is that a later word nullifies, limits, or clarifies an earlier one. This principle may now be seen to be reflected in 1:1-2a: the word spoken through the Son clarifies, limits, or supersedes all earlier pronouncements of God.

17. This is a proof spoken of as an "irrefutable sign" in *Rhet. Alex.* 1430a14-16, comparable to the appearance of footprints "proving" that someone had walked at that spot previously.

plication, of the Torah as well. If these organs were able to bring "perfection," that is, able to bring people to God's appointed goal for people, why would God speak later of a different priestly order?

The author understands the levitical priesthood and the Mosaic Law as inextricably bound up with each other. On the one hand, "the people were given the law on the basis of" the levitical priesthood (7:11), and, on the other hand, "The law appoints as priests men subject to weakness" (7:28). The Law regulates the priesthood, prescribing who may or may not serve (the "fleshly" or genealogical qualifications the Law establishes for priests) and ordering which sacrifices the priests will offer, but the priesthood was also essential to the maintenance of the Law, atoning for transgressions against the Law (repairing breaches of the contract from the human side) and officiating at ritual displays of gratitude toward God — in short, keeping the two parties involved in the covenant together. Without the priests, the covenant would be broken without reparation. On the basis of this mutual interdependence, the author claims that it is "necessary" that a change of law accompany any change of priesthood (7:12). The author and his readers may already have in mind the famous prophecy of the "new covenant" (Jer. 31:31-34) that he will introduce at 8:7 as the legitimating scriptural text. Hebrews 7:11-12 underscores both the reality and the necessity of a new priesthood as well as new ways of acting as a priest (new cultic regulations of a new law or covenant). This line of argumentation makes room for a non-Aaronic priest to offer a sacrifice, which is very strange indeed from the perspective of Torah (a self-offering!) but which is wholly in keeping with the "new regulations" for the "new priesthood."[18]

Jesus, who has already been identified as the "priest after the order of Melchizedek" (a claim substantiated from the "family resemblances" drawn between Jesus and Melchizedek as well as the peculiarities of Jesus' postmortem activities), came from a tribe from which no one "officiated at the altar" under the levitical arrangements.[19] The author draws on the cultural knowledge that the tribe of Levi was the tribe of "priests," that no other tribe produced individuals who qualified to serve at the altar, and that Jesus was descended from the tribe of Judah (a fact passed along in many streams of Christian culture, as in Matt. 1; Luke 3; Rev. 5:5). The fact of Jesus' appointment to priesthood proves the obsolescence of the Torah, for the Torah's sustaining priesthood is limited

---

18. As a *coup de grace* for his cultic argument, the author will present the scriptural legitimation for even this strange sacrificial ritual — Ps. 40:6-8, "a body you have prepared for me," expounded in Heb. 10:4-10.

19. Attridge (*Hebrews,* 201) correctly observes that the author of Hebrews ignores numerous instances in Scripture of non-Levites (particularly the kings of Judah) performing some rite or other at the altar, although strictly from the standpoint of Mosaic legislation he is right to make this claim.

to the levitical tribe. He cannot be said to function as a priest for Torah, since "Moses says nothing about priests" with reference to Judahites. Jesus thus must function as the priest for a new covenant and new law.

That the change of law has already occurred is made "even more abundantly clear" by the qualifications brought forward by Jesus to serve as priest.[20] The author's investigation of Melchizedek's priesthood in 7:1-10 provides the first premise for the argument here. Melchizedek exercised his priesthood by virtue of his unending life ("having neither beginning of days nor end of life," 7:3, 8). Jesus, by virtue of his resurrection from the dead, bears the "likeness of Melchizedek" (7:15), living now an "indestructible life" (7:16). This is taken as a clear indication that the "priest after the order of Melchizedek" (now one "after the likeness of Melchizedek") has appeared on the scene to supplant the honored but limited levitical priests and their charter, the Torah. Just as Melchizedek exercised his priestly prerogatives (e.g., tithing) on the basis of his enjoyment of a life beyond the reach of death rather than on the basis of genealogical requirements, Jesus' priesthood is certified and established by his enjoyment of the resurrected life rather than his lining up with the requirements of the "fleshly commandment" (7:16) — "fleshly" specifically because it pertains to physical descent and lineage. Hebrews 7:17 reintroduces the quotation of Psalm 110:4 as a way to emphasize the divine legitimation of this characteristic as the qualification for the new priesthood. Remaining a "priest forever" is taken by the author to signify the priest's eternally continuing existence — an interpretative move that was not altogether obvious, as the use of the phrase in 1 Maccabees 14:41 to refer to the appointment of Simon (never more than a mortal) to the high priesthood demonstrates.

The author's discussion of Jesus' "indestructible life" introduces a standard encomiastic topos of physical advantage, namely, "physical strength."[21] It is, first, a mark of Jesus' superior excellence that he possesses a strength that is not shared by the levitical priests. The display of such physical superiority, however, remains insufficient: it is also necessary "to explain how, such being his character, he has used the advantages or disadvantages, physical or external circumstances" (*Rhet. Her.* 3.7.13). Physical superiority becomes truly virtuous and praiseworthy when it is exercised to benefit others or to display one of the spiritual or ethical virtues.[22] This is precisely what the author of Hebrews moves toward in the next paragraph (7:23-25, specifically), pointing to Jesus'

---

20. The "if" clause indicates that the topic being made "even more obvious" is the topic announced in 7:12, namely, the change of law.

21. This is treated in *Rhet. Her.* 3.7.14, as well as in Theon's discussion of the form of the encomium under "Bodily Excellences" (Marrou, *History of Education*, 272-73).

22. Thus also Quintilian *Inst.* 3.7.13: "the praise awarded to external and accidental advantages is given not to their possession, but to their honorable employment."

use of his "indestructible life" to bring benefit to his clients in a way that the levitical priests, mortal as they were, could not.

The author focuses the audience's attention in 7:11-19 on the advantage they enjoy from a salvation-historical perspective. They are now able to arrive at the "perfection" that had formerly eluded the people of God. The "weakness and uselessness" of Torah is reflected in the weakness of its priests (a topic that will continue to be developed through 7:28), but all the more in the petrification, rather than the bridging, of the boundaries separating the people from God (the main theme of 9:1–10:18, as well as the exhortation of 10:19-25). The author engages in this argument not only to reinforce the reality of the invisible priesthood from the scriptural "documentation" but also to provide another angle on the benefits that have come upon the addressees (and hence a claim of God and God's Messiah on their ongoing respect, loyalty, and service). Hitherto, the focus has been largely eschatological. Now, with a shift to a salvation-historical perspective, they can be made to see the amplitude of the benefits they enjoy compared to the more limited benefits enjoyed by the people of God before "these last days." They have witnessed the "entrance of a better hope through which" they may "draw near to God" in ways unprecedented. To relinquish such a hope for any temporal benefits would be an act revealing a disgraceful lack of wisdom (the failure properly to evaluate relative worth and expediency) as well as justice (the failure to acknowledge the value of a gift by a proportionate return of commitment and gratitude toward the giver).

The author had prepared the way for this exposition of Jesus' priesthood by urging the hearers to continue in trust and steadfastness toward the God they had met through Jesus, offering the "oath" of God as a foundation stone on which to ground their confidence. The author continues throughout chapter 7 to show his interest in heightening the hearers' sense of the reliability of the venture to which they pledged themselves at their conversion and in their joining of themselves to the Christian group. While he urges them to be confident in their hope, he also gives them many assurances of the reliability of that hope. The addressees, after all, have already endured significant temporal losses for this hope and are being called by this sermon to invest themselves in one another and in this hope even more completely. They need to know beyond the shadow of a doubt that the "contract" they have formed with God through Jesus is utterly reliable and able to bring them to the benefits of surpassing value, for which they are willing to continue to endure the loss of respect and comfort in this life.

The reliability of a contract or covenant depends on the reliability of the guarantor of such a contract (Aristotle *Rh*. 1.15.21). The author brings forward two considerations that establish Jesus as the "guarantor of a better covenant" (7:22). Both of these involve antithetical claims contrasting the priesthood of Jesus with the levitical priests and showing the greater reliability and value of the former. First, "those men have become priests without an oath, but this man with an oath by the one addressing him, 'the Lord has sworn and will not change his mind: you are a priest forever'" (7:20b-21). The recitation of Psalm 110:4 is expanded to include the introduction (Ps. 110:4a), which shows that these words comprise an oath that reveals "the unchangeableness of God's will" (6:17).[23] Insofar (καθ' ὅσον), then, as Jesus became a priest "not without an oath" (7:20), he is accordingly (κατὰ τοσοῦτο) the "guarantor of a better covenant" (7:22) — God's own commitment of his name and honor to this priesthood assures those who approach him through Jesus of their success.

Second, the author returns in a second antithesis to Jesus' superior "physical excellence," now drawing out the implications of that "indestructible life" for his clients: in the case of the levitical priesthood, "the many have become priests on account of being prevented by death from continuing" in their priestly office, "but he holds the priesthood without interruption on account of his abiding forever" (7:23-24).[24]

The hope for a priest whose ministry would be endless and uninterrupted is not unique to Hebrews. A striking expression of this same hope appears in the *Testament of Levi* 18:8, which looks forward to a good and just high priest who "will have no successor unto generations and generations forever" (οὐκ ἔσται διαδοχὴ αὐτοῦ εἰς γενεὰς καὶ γενεὰς ἕως τοῦ αἰῶνος). The change of high priest created instability in the system of mediation on which Jews relied in their covenant with God. Not all high priests were equally faithful to God and to their office. Memories of the hellenizing high priests of the mid-second century B.C. — Jason and Menelaus, and the unreliable Alcimus — may have made the succession of high priests a source of some tension or anxiety. What would the new incumbent be like? Would he indeed serve the covenant and diligently seek to preserve God's favor toward the nation, or would other interests guide his actions, leading to more severe alienation from God's favor? The importance of this office for the divine-human relationship explains why the author of the *Testament of Levi* might consider a virtuous, stable, immortal high priest as a great *desideratum*.

The author of Hebrews also finds the mortality of the levitical priests to be a weakness in their mediation. The reasons for this may only be gathered inferentially from what the author says about the advantages of having a high priest who is beyond the reach of death. In 7:25, the author shows how this be-

---

23. The unchangeability of God's mind, and thus the absolute reliability of God's word, are important parts of Jewish and Christian cultural knowledge (see especially Num. 23:19; Rom. 11:29).

24. μένειν may have cultural resonances with the character of God, expressed as "abiding" in Jewish culture, and with the character of the realm of the real, ideal world of the Platonists (see Attridge, *Hebrews*, 209).

comes advantageous for those who approach God through Jesus — such people have a mediator who will always be able to offer intercession on behalf of his clients, and who will thus be able to complete their deliverance himself. They will never need to fear a time in the future when there is no mediator at work to sustain the people's relationship with their divine patron (the dangers of an interregnum in the priesthood); they will never need to fear the exchange of a faithful and effective mediator for an unreliable one (as the replacement of Onias with Jason in 175 B.C. proved to be, to the sorrow of the nation; see 2 Macc. 3:1–4:17). They can count on their "faithful and merciful high priest" (2:17) continuing for all tomorrows to stand before God on their behalf. Christians enjoy, then, a great advantage in having Jesus as their mediator (see Rom. 8:34; 1 John 2:1 for other uses of this concept to strengthen Christian assurance). He is the "better hope through which we draw near to God" (7:19), for he is able effectively to intercede at all times and for all time for those who would wish to "approach God through him" (7:25).

Hebrews 7:26-28 provides a recapitulation, a drawing together of the main points of the preceding discussions of priesthood (5:1-10; 7:1-25; cf. *Rhet. Alex.* 1433b29-34 on recapitulation) and an enumeration in summary fashion of the advantages of Christ's mediation over the mediation of the levitical priests.[25] The author introduces this recapitulation with a topic of "suitability" reminiscent of 2:11, where he had claimed that "it was fitting" for God to perfect Jesus, as the one leading many to their divine destiny, through sufferings: "a high priest of such quality is well suited to us" (7:26a). The author means that Jesus is "well suited" to meet the need of the believing community for an effective mediator (for it is this that he goes on to affirm). That Jesus is "holy, blameless, undefiled" (ὅσιος, ἄκακος, ἀμίαντος) affirms his complete suitability for the office of priesthood, all the more so as these words are derived mainly from the cult and the background of purity (although the second appears frequently as an ethical term as well). There is in Jesus no offense or affront to the holy God, no obstacle that might stand in the way of his own relationship with God, on which his effective mediation depends.

This fact sets him apart from the "many" priests: "he does not have the daily necessity, as the [levitical] high priests, first to offer sacrifices for his own sins and then for the sins of the people" (7:27a). He is "set apart from sinners and has become exalted above the heavens" (7:26b). The author took pains to

---

25. These verses provide another example of the author's attention to rhetorical ornamentation in order to make his sermon more appealing to the ears of his hearers, and thus to maintain their delight and favorable disposition to hear the sermon. Hebrews 7:26, for instance, employs comma (described in *Rhet. Her.* 4.19.26 as sharp, staccato speech) with ὅσιος, ἄκακος, ἀμίαντος, as well as homoeoptaton (the same sound ending a series of words) extending through the whole verse: ὅσιος, ἄκακος, ἀμίαντος, κεχωρισμένος . . . ὑψηλότερος . . . γενόμενος.

underscore Jesus' solidarity with sinners in earlier chapters of this sermon so as to emphasize Jesus' favorable disposition and gentleness toward his clients. Here the author emphasizes that Jesus is distinguished from sinners — perhaps having in mind in the first instance these sinful people who served as high priests — in his unimpeded relationship with God and unblemished holiness and suitability for priesthood. This separation from sinners is interpreted spatially by the author as well: the fact of his entry into the unshakable realm also "separates" Jesus from all sinners, not so as to be inaccessible to them but so as to have complete access to God's own presence,[26] a presence that the levitical priests could access only by the secondary means of a "copy and shadow" of God's true sanctum.

The contrast between Jesus and the levitical priests with regard to personal sin offerings completes the earlier discussion of 4:15–5:3. The earthly high priest had to offer sacrifices for his own sins before he could effectively mediate on the people's behalf (5:3). The sinless Jesus (4:15), however, whose sympathy with his clients is rooted in shared testing but not the shared experience of sinning, has no such need (7:27). That the levitical priests have a "daily" need of sin offerings may reflect a sort of conflation of the Day of Atonement (which makes specific provision for this preparatory atonement; see Lev. 9:1-17; 16:6, 11-19) with the *tamid,* the morning and evening offerings (see Exod. 29:38-45), or with the tradition, attested also by Philo, that the meal offering, which accompanied the daily burnt offering, was a sin offering performed by the priests on their own behalf.[27] In this contrast, however, the author is also looking ahead to the topic that will dominate 9:1–10:14: the repeated, continual cycle of sacrifices performed by the levitical priests demonstrates their inability to "perfect" (i.e., cleanse and sanctify) the conscience of the worshiper, whereas the single, unrepeatable sacrifice of Jesus demonstrates its efficacy in this regard ("for this he did once-for-all, having sacrificed himself"; 7:27).

A Closer Look: Voluntary Death and Atonement

The book of Hebrews develops to the greatest extent a familiar and widespread Christian interpretation of the execution of Jesus — regarded by those outside the group as a legal punishment for seditious behavior, but within the group as a noble death accepted willingly and intentionally on behalf of others so as to bring them benefits of a great magni-

---

26. The author here introduces a datum that he will develop in 8:1-6 and 9:11-28, namely, Jesus' officiating in the "true" and "better" sanctuary.

27. *Rer. div. her.* 174 (cited in Attridge, *Hebrews,* 214): "In the oblation of fine flour, which the priests offer for themselves, and in that offered in behalf of the nation, consisting of two lambs."

tude. The Christian culture drew on Jewish martyrological traditions, which themselves had roots in the OT, in order to frame its understanding of Jesus' death. This tradition comes to its fullest expression in 4 Maccabees, which celebrates the death of the martyrs of the hellenizing crisis (166 B.C.) in terms of sacrifice and vicarious atonement.[28] Eleazar, an aged priest, remains loyal to the Torah to the point of death. On the basis of his voluntary acceptance of martyrdom (since he could have saved his life through transgression of the Torah), Eleazar prays: "Be merciful to your people, and let our punishment suffice for them. Make my blood their purification, and take my life in exchange for theirs" (6:28-29, NRSV). Near the close of the book, the author reflects on the achievement of the martyrs in terms of sacrificial language and confirms that Eleazar's prayer and offering were accepted: "the tyrant was punished, and the homeland purified — they having become, as it were, a ransom for the sin of our nation. And through the blood of those devout ones and their death as an atoning sacrifice, divine Providence preserved Israel that previously had been mistreated" (17:21-22, NRSV).

Leviticus 17:11 establishes the foundational connection of blood and the exchange of a life with the covering of sins: "the life of the flesh is in the blood. This blood I myself have given you to perform the rite of atonement for your lives at the altar; for, as life, it is blood that atones for a life." Leviticus has in mind, of course, animal sacrifices prescribed by Torah — a charter that leaves no room, one must add, for human sacrifice. As Israel lived with its sacrificial system over the centuries, however, two developments emerged. First, authors tended toward the "rationalization" of animal sacrifices (preferring praise or obedience or contrition to bloody offerings). This is a very frequent theme of the Psalms (see 40:6-8 or 51:16-17 for but two examples). Second, they tended toward the metaphorical extension of sacrificial language to other acts. The most striking expression of this is the servant song of Isaiah 52:13–53:12, in which the experience of humiliation and marginalization (even death) is recast in terms of a death suffered so as to free others from punishment, thus a vicarious atonement.

These two strands come together in Jewish reflection on the martyrdoms of Eleazar, the seven brothers, and their mother. First, commitment to obey Torah (even in the face of overwhelming opposition, even death) is believed to unleash sacral power. This corresponds to the rationalization of sacrifice, where obedience is counted as "better" or "more pleasing" in God's sight than hundreds of burnt offerings (i.e., for disobedience). Moreover, the metaphorical application of atonement and cultic terminology to human suffer-

---

28. The date of 4 Maccabees remains a disputed matter among scholars. Opinions tend to center on two options: the first half of the first century A.D. or the early decades of the second century A.D.. Arguments in favor of the earlier date focus on the conjunction in 4 Macc. 4:2 of Syria, Phoenicia, and Cilicia under the jurisdiction of a single governor, which mirrors Roman administration of those provinces from 18 to 72 A.D. Arguments in favor of the later date tend to give more weight to the similarities in style between 4 Maccabees and the writings of the Second Sophistic. For a fuller discussion, see my *4 Maccabees*, 14-18, which comes out in favor of the 18-72 A.D. range. Throughout the commentary I provide indications that the author of Hebrews knew 4 Maccabees, particularly given shared vocabulary that is otherwise rare in the NT, as well as similarities of phrases and even thought. For this discussion, it suffices that 4 Maccabees, in connection with 2 Maccabees (surely a pre-Herodian text), bears witness to developments of thought with regard to the beneficial death of the righteous martyr.

ing in the Servant Song of Isaiah provides a hermeneutical key to interpret the death of the obedient, righteous ones who suffer ignominiously because they refuse to break faith with God. Whatever the song's meaning in its original context, Isaiah 53 certainly opens itself to readings (and not only to Christian readers, at the beginning) that cast the death of the righteous person as a sacrifice that restores God's favor and averts divine wrath. The sufferings and mutilations (Isa. 52:14 and 53:3), the concept of atonement before God through the willing death of the righteous person (Isa. 53:4-6, 8, 10, 12b), the affirmation of the efficacy of this unconventional offering (Isa. 53:10b-11), and the final celebration of the greatness and victory of the suffering servant (Isa. 53:12a) all have counterparts in the way the martyrs are viewed in 4 Maccabees (and, to a slightly lesser extent, 2 Maccabees 7:1–8:6).

In 2 and 4 Maccabees it is not, of course, the human blood itself that atones[29] but obedience unto death, which God accepts as a perfect sacrifice. In the context of Deuteronomistic theology, it is obedience (the return to obedience by the people) that effects reversal of the curses (Deut. 30:1-5). 4 Maccabees combines the provisions of Deuteronomy for repentance and renewal of the covenant blessings (Deut. 30:1-5) with the sacrificial terminology of Leviticus concerning the sin offering, which restores the relationship between the sinner and God (Lev. 4:1–5:13). Eleazar's "obedience unto death," together with the deaths of his fellow martyrs, was the act that brought reconciliation with God so that Israel was preserved (17:22). It is a representative obedience, an obedience maintained on behalf of others (rather than a collective return to obedience such as Deut. 30:1-5 envisions). Indeed, their deaths take on more of the coloration of a sacrificial act. The martyr stands as a mediator between the people and God; the martyr becomes a broker, who restores the relationship between the wayward clients and the offended patron (17:22).[30] While not a sacrifice properly prescribed by the Torah, the obedience that remains steadfast even unto death is accepted by God "as" a sin offering. The results of the martyrs' deaths prove the effectiveness of their deaths as the "dynamic equivalent" of a sin offering (in much the same way as acts of piety are counted "as" cultic acts in Psalm 141:2: "let my prayer be counted as incense before you, and the lifting up of my hands as an evening sacrifice."

These precedents provide useful material for early Christian reflection on the death of Jesus. The claim that Jesus "offered himself" as an atoning sacrifice by enduring an execution occasioned by his obedience to God's will to the end is grounded in these deeprunning currents of Judaism (resonating also with Greco-Roman conceptions of the noble death, to be sure). Sam K. Williams argues that this observation carries with it an important implication for Christian soteriology. The martyrs' sacrifice was not merely effective as a cultic act but also as an example that set in motion a return to obedience and zeal for God's Torah.[31] Just as the martyrs both reconcile the people to God and revive observance of God's Law, so Jesus' death would be seen under this dual aspect of an act of atonement and a call back to obedience. Such a dual focus certainly resonates with the NT teaching that Jesus' death enables obedience, the pursuit of virtue and good works, or, in the lan-

---

29. This point is well made by Sam K. Williams, *Jesus' Death as Saving Event: The Background and Origin of a Concept* (HTRDS 2; Missoula, MT: Scholars Press, 1975), 169.

30. Thus rightly A. O'Hagan, "The Martyr in the Fourth Book of Maccabees," *SBFLA* 24 (1974): 103, 119.

31. Williams, *Jesus' Death*, 176-86.

guage of the author of Hebrews, the offering of the "sacrifices" of praise, sharing, and doing good (13:15-16). Jesus obedient death leads ultimately to the "people of God" as whole
doing "what pleases him."[32]

Hebrews 7:28 concludes this segment of argumentation with a well-
constructed antithesis, contrasting the levitical priests and Jesus on three points:

A   For the Law (ὁ νόμος γὰρ)
B   appoints as high priests human beings (ἀνθρώπους καθίστησιν
     ἀρχιερεῖς)
C   having weakness (ἔχοντας ἀσθένειαν),
A′   but the word of the oath that comes after the law (ὁ λόγος δὲ τῆς
     ὁρκωμοσίας τῆς μετὰ τὸν νόμον)
B′   [appoints as high priest] a Son (υἱὸν [καθίστησιν ἀρχιερεὺς])
C′   perfected forever (εἰς τὸν αἰῶνα τετελειωμένον).

The author emphasizes the superiority of Jesus' mediation, and hence the great
advantage of remaining attached to him, at each point. The word of the oath (a
reference to Ps. 110:4) supplants the Torah but also shows a more direct commitment by God (and indeed God's pledge of his own honor) to this new
priesthood. It is established on an infallible foundation, unlike the first priesthood, which was built on a contract that could be broken (i.e., by the unreliability of the human parties; see Heb. 8:8-9). The incumbent is not merely an
ordinary human being but one who enjoys an especially close relationship with
the divine patron whose favor is sought. One's chances of success in mediation
are proportionately greater as one stands closer in relationship with the patron.
   Finally, and climactically, the "weakness" of these human priests (which
results in their impermanency in the office) is contrasted with the eternal "perfection" of the Son. The weakness of these priests appears in their liability to sin
(5:2-3; 7:27) and in their liability to death, both significant obstacles to their
mediation (7:23-25, 27). "Perfected" here would be heard as Jesus' "removal
from the sphere of liability to weakness," his passing through to the eternal, unshakable realm. The earthly priests moved in and out of holiness on account of
their own sins (hence their constant need of purification offerings). With this
point of contrast in view, the "eternal perfecting" of the Son would again underscore Jesus' nonliability to weakness, his nonliability to moving back and
forth across the barrier that separates the clean from the defiled. In both cases,
perfection signifies breaking through and existing on the other side of a boundary that trips up every other priest, whether death or sin, crossing a threshold

---

32. For more on this topic, please see deSilva, *4 Maccabees*, 137-41.

that other priests were unable to cross, and arriving at a finished state that all other priests fail to achieve.

The author devotes much time and space to building up the value of what the addressees "have" in this Jesus so that they will be the less tempted to throw it away in favor of the temporal benefits they lack as long as they are seen to belong to this minority group. If he has succeeded in reorienting their sights on eschatological deliverance and judgment, then this discussion of one who is able to "deliver completely" (7:25) and function as an unfailing broker between them and God will be quite effective.

8:1-13

The author continues his exposition of Jesus' priestly ministry with an explicit statement of the "leading idea" or "main point" (κεφάλαιον) that the foregoing discussion has been driving at: the author and the hearers "have such a high priest" as the author described in 7:26-28, one "who sat down at the right side of the throne of the majesty in the heavens, a minister of the holy places and the true tabernacle, which God, and not a mortal, erected" (8:1-2). This statement allows for a refocusing of the argument, which will henceforth take up the particulars of Jesus' better priestly sacrifice in the better place of mediation. It also affirms for the hearers their enjoyment of the great advantages the author describes, and thereby their ground for hope and for continuing to invest in their earlier commitments to seek God's benefactions. The author draws out the practical implication of "having" this high priest in the exhortations that flank the central discourse (4:14-16; 10:19-25), exhortations that seek to focus the hearers' attention and energies centripetally toward one another and toward the Lord at the center of their confession and hope.[33]

The importance of Psalm 110, which the author recontextualizes (and paraphrases slightly) yet again in 8:1,[34] emerges in its combination of the no-

---

33. The author's discourse could be analyzed in terms of topics of encomia, for example, in his emphasis on Jesus achieving what no other priest had achieved. Here Jesus is celebrated as the only priest to enter the heavenly, true sanctuary (cf. Aristotle *Rh.* 1.9.38; Quintilian *Inst.* 3.7.16 on the topic of "being the first" or "only" person to achieve something noble or remarkable). The "leading point" of the discourse, however, again points to the primacy of topics of advantage ("we have such a priest," i.e., we enjoy this advantage) and thus to considerations of expediency ("let us hold fast to our confession" and the like so as to preserve our advantages and avoid loss of necessary advantages; 10:19-31), hence the deliberative aims of the whole.

34. Compare "who sat down at the right hand of the throne of the Majesty in the heavens" (ὃς ἐκάθισεν ἐν δεξιᾷ τοῦ θρόνου τῆς μεγαλωσύνης ἐν τοῖς οὐρανοῖς, 8:1) with "sit down at my right hand" (Κάθου ἐκ δεξιῶν μου, Ps. 110:1; Heb. 1:13).

tions of being appointed a priest by God and sitting down at God's right hand. Psalm 110:1 (the invitation to session) and 110:4 (the appointment to a new order of priesthood) are addressed to the same person and articulate the place and role that person will occupy at the same time. It would appear that, in the author's reading, this psalm itself suggests a heavenly priesthood — one that would be exercised from the vantage point of the right side of God's own throne in the invisible realm. The psalm functions thus as a perfect reflection of, and legitimation for, the claims being made about Jesus in the early Church and developed specifically in this sermon.

Hebrews 8:1-13 proceeds to develop the thesis statement of 8:1-2 along argumentative lines reminiscent of the pattern found in the elaboration of a *chreia* or in the "figure of thought" called "descanting on a theme" in the *Rhetorica ad Herennium* (4.43.56–4.44.57). "Descanting on a theme" involves a simple statement of the thesis, the presentation of a rationale that supports the thesis, and a restatement of the theme in new words (with or without reasons). The speaker would then present an argument from the contrary (if the theme is "the wise person fights for his country," the contrary would be "only the fool flees when his country is in peril"), an argument from comparison (analogy), a supportive example or testimony from antiquity, and finally a conclusion that returns to the thesis. A very similar pattern appears in the various *Progymnasmata*, the curriculum for the elementary education leading up to rhetorical training.[35] This pattern contains many of the basic building blocks of argumentation: as orators grew in their facility, they would improvise in the order of arguments and even subtly shift the arguments to confirm not only the thesis but also the rationales adduced in support of the thesis. A brief outline of the argumentative texture of 8:1-13, then, would be as follows:

> 8:1-2: thesis
> [8:3: postponed topic]
> 8:4-5: argument from the contrary, with a rationale
> 8:6: restatement of the thesis, with a supplement
> 8:7: confirmation of supplement through argument from the contrary
> 8:8-12: testimony from antiquity in support of argument from the contrary
> 8:13: concluding statement affirming supplement

The author, then, begins this demonstration by focusing the hearers' attention on the fact that they "have" the mediation of the one who is best quali-

---

35. Mack and Robbins (*Patterns of Persuasion*) provide an excellent discussion of this pattern, its place in classical education, and its presence as an organizational principle in many collections of Jesus' sayings.

fied in every respect to present their suits before God and secure a successful outcome. The aspect of his mediation now being developed is the place in which he functions as priest, namely, the heavenly sanctuary. The author employs antithetical phrases ("which the Lord pitched [ἣν ἔπηξεν ὁ κύριος], not a human being") to point out the superiority of the founder of the temple in which Jesus serves: it is better because it is built by a better architect.[36] The author has taken a phrase from Numbers 24:6 (LXX), where Balaam blesses the Israelites and calls their dwellings "tents that the Lord pitched" (ἃς ἔπηξε κύριος), and applied it to the one tent of the heavenly tabernacle (see below on 8:5) rather than the "tents of Jacob" in general.

The next verse introduces the sacrifices that are offered by this priest, a topic whose discussion will be postponed until later: "for every priest is appointed in order to offer gifts and sacrifices." This definition of the role and responsibility of a priest recalls the second part of the more complete definition given earlier at 5:1. The major occupation of priests in the prescriptions of the Pentateuch is the offering of sacrifices, so that for Jesus to act as priest it would be "necessary for him also to have something to offer up" (8:3). Hebrews 7:27 had already provided the content of this sacrifice, and the author allusively returns here to the topic so that the hearers can make the connections again themselves. The author will develop the topic of the nature, warrant, and efficacy of this sacrifice later, particularly in 9:12-14, 23-25 and, most clearly, in 10:5-10.

Hebrews 8:3, then, becomes a postponed topic, as the author returns in 8:4 to the thesis of 8:1-2 with an argument from the contrary, with rationale:

[Thesis: Jesus is a priest in heaven]
Contrary: if Jesus were on earth, he would not even be a priest
Rationale: for the law has already prescribed who would be priests here

Jesus, descended from Judah rather than Levi, has already been shown to stand outside of the Torah's qualifications for priesthood, based on genealogy as they are (7:13-14). The author assumes the priesthood of Jesus now to be established beyond the shadow of a doubt. This was probably part of their learned Christian culture, and he has strongly supported the concept with his reading of Psalm 110. Jesus' priestly status takes on the character of an underlying premise here: since Jesus was appointed a priest by God, we can conclude (though we cannot observe this) that he is officiating in the heavenly, "true" sanctum since he does not qualify for the earthly priesthood.

---

36. That material, earthly temples are inferior "holy places" since they are built by human hands is a frequent topic of critique of religion in the ancient world (see, for example, Acts 7:48-50; 17:24-25).

The priests whom the Torah appoints, offering their conventional sacrifices according to the Torah's prescriptions (τῶν προσφερόντων κατὰ νόμον τὰ δῶρα) in contrast with the very unconventional sacrifice offered by Jesus (10:5-10), carry out their mediation in an inferior meeting ground. The author introduces a recitation of Exodus 25:40 to prove the imitative, secondary quality of the earthly temple and the existence of an original, heavenly temple of which the former is but a copy: "these serve a pattern and shadow of the heavenly things, even as Moses was warned when he was about to complete the tabernacle, 'see that you make all things,' he said, 'according to the model (κατὰ τὸν τύπον) shown to you on the mountain'" (8:5). The author's interjection of "all things" (πάντα) into the recitation may be significant since he relies on a complete and pervasive correspondence between the accoutrements and procedures of the earthly tabernacle in order to extrapolate the details of the ministry of Christ in the prototype, the heavenly tabernacle.

The notion of a heavenly counterpart to the Jerusalem temple or desert tabernacle was common in Hellenistic Judaism, as was the appeal to an exegesis of Exodus 25:40 in support of this belief.[37] This is especially well attested in the apocalyptic traditions of Judaism and Christianity. In an early stratum of *1 Enoch* (perhaps late third or early second century B.C.), the apocalyptist speaks of a two-room "house" in heaven, with the throne of God in the second room (14:10-20). The layout of the heavenly abode of God is clearly a reflection of God's earthly "house" with its two "holy" places. *2 Baruch* (a Jewish apocalypse from around 100 A.D.) depicts God comforting Baruch concerning the fate of Jerusalem as its destruction by Nebuchadnezzar's forces draws near. God affirms the reality of the heavenly Jerusalem with its temple, which he showed to Adam and Moses (4:1-7). The book of Revelation also contains a wealth of allusions to the heavenly temple (3:12; 7:15; 11:19; 14:15, 17; 15:5-8; 16:1, 17) as well as its various furnishings (the altar, 6:9-11; the incense stand, 8:3-5).

The belief in a heavenly temple also appears in Jewish wisdom literature. Notable is Wisdom of Solomon 9:8. "Solomon" prays to God: "you said to build a temple on your holy mountain and an altar in the city of your dwelling, an imitation (μίμημα) of the holy tent that you prepared beforehand from the beginning." The author of Hebrews also believed in the existence of a tabernacle in God's realm, which was prepared "from the beginning" so that it is actually the prototype (τύπος, 8:5) of which the earthly tabernacle is the antitype (ἀντίτυπα, 9:24) and imitation (Heb. 8:5, "copy and shadow"). "Shadow" is a Platonic term for what belongs to the material world in contrast to the "real" and "true" types in the

---

37. For a fuller discussion of this concept and its Jewish precedents, see Attridge, *Hebrews*, 222-24; Aelred Cody, *Heavenly Sanctuary and Liturgy in the Epistle to the Hebrews* (St. Meinrad, IN: Grail, 1960), 9-46.

immaterial, ideal world (see especially Plato *Rep.* 7.515A-B). The use of Exodus 25:40 in Hebrews 8:5 affords "a happy opening by which the Platonic speculation enters our epistle,"[38] although the author is far from a Platonist. Platonic terms, and specifically the notion that invisible realities are superior to their material imitations, are placed within the framework of Jewish cosmology (the heavenly versus the earthly) and Judeo-Christian interest in the historical, unfolding drama of redemption. G. A.Williamson correctly observes that Jewish-Christian views of cosmology and God's redemptive activity in history intrude upon the static, unchanging notion of the ideal realm as found in Plato: "Plato's Ideal world is not a heaven that could be entered by Jesus; it can be penetrated only by the intellect."[39] Nevertheless, Jesus' resurrection is clearly interpreted as a translation from earthly realities to their heavenly types. From the abiding, heavenly realm, Jesus is now able to offer a superior service to his partners, who must continue on in the earthly realm until the eschatological "shaking" and "removal" of the material realm (12:26-28).

The author now returns to his thesis, using new words to express the same idea found in 8:1-2: "but now he has received a correspondingly more distinguished ministry as he is the mediator of a better covenant, which was legislated on the basis of better promises" (8:6). This restatement (with the "more distinguished ministry" containing the idea of "ministerial charge," namely, his installation in the heavenly tabernacle in contrast with the secondary, earthly tabernacle) is extended to include a supplement qualifying the cause and degree of the greater value attaching to this ministry. The author does not go on to defend the proportion or the correlation he is making.[40] He assumes that his audience will accept it based on a common axiom of cause and effect — what is produced by a greater cause will be a greater good (Aristotle *Rh.* 1.7.7). The ministry of Jesus is an effect of the new covenant, which is itself an effect of better promises. The author has already explained that better guarantees stand behind this priesthood: in particular, God's oath (and thus God's commitment of his own honor to this arrangement). He now goes on to articulate the scriptural proof for the supersession of the old covenant with a new and more efficacious one. The Jeremiah text also provides an indication of what those "better promises" are, a topic that the author will develop at length in 9:1–10:18. What follows in 8:7-13, therefore, is a confirmation of the supplement that also provides a transition to the next section of argumentation.

---

38. G. H. Gilbert, "The Greek Element in the Epistle to the Hebrews," *AJT* 14 (1910): 528.

39. G. A. Williamson, "Platonism and Hebrews," *SJT* 16 (1963): 419.

40. The vocabulary and syntax of 8:6 (διαφορωτέρας . . . ὅσῳ καὶ κρείττονός) recalls the proportional statement that ended the introductory paragraph and launched the author into his first expositional section (κρείττων . . . ὅσῳ διαφορώτερον, 1:4).

Referring to Jesus as a better "mediator" (μεσίτης, 8:6; also in 9:15; 12:24) sets the discourse again firmly in the context of patronage and, particularly, in ancient conceptions of priests as brokers or mediators between human beings (their clients) and God. As Richard Nelson aptly observes:

> Priests also provided the connections that brought divinity near and made life with Yahweh possible. . . . As an insulator, the priest could stand between Yahweh and the people to protect them from danger, as Aaron does in Num. 16:46-48. . . . As one who embodied connection to Yahweh, the priest has traditionally been described as a mediator, one who represents the community to God and in turn God to the community.[41]

The author's comparison of the levitical high priests and Jesus focuses throughout on the superior access to God and God's favor now made possible by means of the latter's brokerage.

Hebrews 8:7-12 presents the confirmation of this supplement: the better quality of the new covenant. The author approaches this with an argument from the contrary: if the first were adequate, God "would not have sought out a place for a second" (8:7), but the author is armed with Jeremiah 31:31-34 to prove that God himself did set aside the first covenant as ineffective, establishing a time in which he would make a new covenant that would be effectual and thus "better." Once again the chronology of God's oracles proves significant. Speaking through Jeremiah after centuries of the levitical priesthood's operation under the regulations of Torah, God is seen as setting aside an existing covenant in favor of one that he will make with his people in the near future.[42]

The author introduces this "testimony from antiquity" (the authoritative text that establishes the necessity of a new, better covenant) specifically as God's censure of those who failed to execute the first covenant with excellence: "for, finding fault with them, he says, 'behold, the days are coming . . .'" (8:8a).[43] The oracle from Jeremiah becomes a witness to the failure of the first covenant due to the lack of commitment and fidelity of those with whom it was made: "'they

---

41. Nelson, *Raising Up a Faithful Priest,* 85-86; see also pp. 107, 144.

42. Christians were alone, however, in reading Jer. 31:31-34 in this way. The concept of a "new covenant" plays a strikingly small role in the vast body of literature that has been preserved from the intertestamental and early rabbinic periods. Only the community at Qumran seems to share the early Church's interest in this oracle, but there, of course, the "new covenant" was not discontinuous with the old but rather its perfecting. The Torah, as taught by the Teacher of Righteousness, would now be fully and completely observed by the people of the covenant at Qumran. For a fuller discussion of the meaning of Jer. 31:31-34 in its original context, as well as its application at Qumran, see Susanne Lehne, *The New Covenant in Hebrews* (JSNTSS 44; Sheffield: JSOT Press, 1990), 32-61; Vermes, *Complete Dead Sea Scrolls,* 67-69.

43. Thus rightly Vanhoye, *Structure,* 143-44; Lane, *Hebrews 1–8,* 208.

did not persist in my covenant, and I took no thought for them,' says the Lord"
(8:9). Although the author does not develop the quotation in this direction, the
hearers may have heard the lection as a recapitulation of the admonitions the
author had given them thus far to persevere in their hope and confession until
they attained God's promised rest. Through Jeremiah the author takes the hearers back again to the generation that God led out of Egypt "by the hand," the
same group of historic figures that had served so powerfully as a negative paradigm for the audience's own behavior in 3:7-19.[44]

The author's recitation of Jeremiah 31:31-34 shows minor variations
from known LXX codices. While it is difficult to discern whether the differences
derive from the author's mind or were present in the text of Jeremiah he knew,
one variation plays very well into the argument he seeks to make. In Hebrews
8:8-9, the verbs for "making" a covenant are different. Known versions of LXX
Jeremiah have "make a covenant" (διαθήσομαι) in both verses to denote God's
actions in establishing both the new and the earlier covenants. The author of
Hebrews may have altered this verb (an act of shaping the text interpretatively
very much in keeping with the way the OT was handled by the Targumists, including the translators of the LXX) so as to highlight the difference between the
two covenants. When God makes the "new covenant," the author uses the verb
συντελέσω (8:8), a word that resonates with the language of "completion" or
"perfection" that plays such an important role in the sermon. In speaking of
God's initiative in establishing the first covenant, the author uses the simple
verb ἐποίησα ("I made").[45] The introduction of the new covenant and its
priesthood marks the final, complete state of mediation between human beings
and God.

At 8:10 the Jeremiah oracle moves from a critique of the old covenant to
the better promises upon which the new will be instituted. First, it speaks of an
internalization of God's commandments, an internal knowledge of, and commitment to do, God's laws. The author does not comment on this verse in the
exposition that follows, but it clearly resonates with his interest throughout the
sermon in the believers' living so as to "please" God and to avoid what he hates
(12:16-17, 28; 13:15-16, 21), fixing their hearts on God and his favor in loyal
trust (3:12-13; 13:9), obeying God's commands to them (4:11), and living out
the love of neighbor that is at the heart of God's law (6:9-12; 10:24-25, 32-36;
12:14; 13:1-3). The author affirms that, in the reception of the word spoken
through the Son, they have "received knowledge of the truth" (10:26) that has a
more binding claim on them than the law of Moses on the Israelites (10:28-29),

---

44. In light of this connection, it is quite possible that the author has in mind not only
transgressions of commandments but failures of trust in mind when he reads "they did not
remain in my covenant."

45. Attridge, *Hebrews*, 227.

and which must bear fruit in their lives. The image of the life that pleases God has in fact been engraved upon their hearts, and the author throughout his sermon calls them to reflect this image in all their behaviors and decisions. The second aspect of this promise, God's owning of the people as his own and the people owning God as their own, is reflected in the author's description of the direct access and the renewed relationship between human beings and God (4:14-16; 10:19-22).

Harold Attridge observes that Jeremiah 31:34a (Heb. 8:11) plays no further role in the exposition:[46] "each shall certainly not teach his or her fellow citizen (πολίτην), saying, 'Know the Lord,' for they shall all know me." In one sense, of course, the author does urge that the members of the audience "teach" one another. Hebrews 5:11-14 explicitly exhorts the believers to teach one another, to continue to reinforce for one another the worldview and ethos of the Christian culture, and the author calls for mutual exhortation throughout the sermon (e.g., 3:12-13; 10:25). There is, however, another sense in which the author might consider even this verse to be a mark of the community formed by the new covenant. In the experience of the Holy Spirit, the recipient comes to have direct and intimate knowledge of God (2:3-4; 6:4-5; cf. the development of Wis. 9:17 in 1 Cor. 2:11-12). The members of the Christian community already enjoy this knowledge of God through the distribution of the Holy Spirit, and they have no need to "teach" one another (their fellow citizens with regard to the city of God; 11:10, 16; 13:13-14) on this level. They need only exhort one another to be faithful to the knowledge of God they have received.

The final couplet from Jeremiah 31:34, "I will be merciful with regard to their misdeeds, and their sins I will certainly remember no more," emerges as a crucial point for the argument that follows. This same verse reappears in 10:17 as the conclusion toward which the whole of 9:1–10:18 drives. The decisive removal of those sins that rendered the conscience unclean (as well as attached themselves to the heavenly mercy seat) would mean that worshipers could approach the holy God without fear of God's holiness consuming them on account of their internal defilement. Worshipers could approach God in the full expectation of favor and help rather than in the expectation that God's holiness would protect itself from contamination by burning up the unclean one. In the following chapters the author will show how Jesus' self-sacrifice and offering of his blood effects this decisive purgation of sin and makes face-to-face access between God and Jesus' clients possible, in striking contrast to the limitations set on access to God under the old covenant (for the sake of the "safe handling" of God's holiness).

At the end of this lengthy quotation, the author brings the paragraph to a

---

46. Ibid., 228. It is even omitted from the recapitulation of Jer. 31:33-34 at Heb. 10:16-17.

close by affirming the limited duration of the first covenant. He proceeds by drawing out the implications of the text, specifically Jeremiah's use of the adjective "new" (ἐν τῷ λέγειν 'Καινὴν'). Calling the second covenant "new," the author reasons, renders the first one "old," which carries the secondary meaning of "annulled" since the covenant did not merely "age" but God "rendered it out-of-date" (πεπαλαίωκεν τὴν πρώτην). The author adds an observation of what it means to "grow obsolete and aged" — it means that something is on the way toward disappearing from this reality. Harold Attridge underscores the use of this language in legal settings. The old covenant is likened to a law that is outdated and practically out of use. All that remains is to erase it from the books.[47] From this general observation about aging as a precursor to disappearing (ἐγγὺς ἀφανισμοῦ), which the audience will accept as probable and accurate, the audience is able to fathom the temporary and passing nature of the first covenant.

Whether the author regards the first covenant as "near to disappearing" already by the time of Jeremiah's oracle[48] or at the time of Christ's coming and even the author's speaking[49] is a matter of dispute. Either choice, however, would affirm that the first covenant shares in the transitory character of this material creation.[50] In this respect, 8:13 is important beyond the discussion of the Torah. The author opened the sermon with an affirmation that the visible earth and heavens would themselves "grow old" like a worn-out coat (1:11-12a), and he will close the sermon with a dramatic image of God's forthcoming act of shaking the heavens and the earth so that the visible, material creation will be removed and only the unshakable realm will remain (12:26-28).[51] Even if the descendants of Levi still minister at the Jerusalem temple at the time this sermon is composed, those heirs of the only other priesthood sanctioned in God's oracles cannot offer deliverance from the cataclysm that will rock this age and all that belongs to it. There is but one avenue for deliverance — connection

---

47. Ibid., 228-29 and n. 47.

48. Ibid., 229.

49. Ellingworth, *Hebrews,* 419.

50. There is no need to infer from 8:13 an awareness on the part of the author of the impending doom of the Jerusalem temple (Stedman, *Hebrews,* 92). Such a claim severely limits the time period of the author (66-70 A.D.) and binds him too closely to events in Palestine. Rather, the author associates the cultic arrangements under Torah, and even Torah itself, with the weakness and temporality of the material creation (since it is ultimately defined as "regulations for the flesh" in 9:10), which the author knows will soon be shaken and disappear together with all that is seen (12:26-28).

51. This is a very important component of the Christian worldview, essential to sustaining group commitment. It is the conviction that the visible realm is temporary and close to dissolution that makes considerations of the relative weight of "temporary" versus "eternal" (hence the advantage of remaining associated with Jesus and his people) possible and potent.

to the one who has already passed into the unshakable realm, Jesus (6:19-20), the mediator of a better covenant with the promise of eschatological salvation.

Summary

Theon, an orator from the second century A.D., writes about the rhetorical device of comparison (or *synkrisis*), "we will compare their actions by choosing those which are more noble and the reasons for the numerous and greater blessings, those actions that are more reliable, those that are more enduring, those that were done at the proper time, those from which great harm results when they have not been done, those that were done with a motive rather than those done because of compulsion or chance, those which few have done rather than those that many have done, . . . those we have done with effort rather than easily" (*Progymnasmata* 10.8-12, 18-24). "Comparison" provides a helpful model for understanding the author's goals in Hebrews 7:1–8:13, in which chapters he intends to establish the ways in which Jesus' mediation is superior to the mediation between humans and God provided by the levitical priests. The practical implications of this comparison for the audience concern the tremendous value of the benefits they have through their association with Jesus and the completely reliable and efficacious brokerage to God's favor he can provide.

Jesus is a "better mediator" (8:6) first because he offers no affront to the God whose favor he seeks to win for his clients. He is "holy, blameless, undefiled," in contrast with the levitical high priests, who first had to atone for their own offenses against God before they could hope to appeal to him for favor on behalf of others (7:26-28). Second, Jesus' enjoyment of a life beyond the power of death means that he will always be living "to intercede" on behalf of those who depend on him for God's favor. The believers will never stand without a mediator or in doubt of finding an equally worthy successor for their mediator should he die, since Jesus "remains forever a priest." He can personally guarantee, therefore, that his clients will arrive at their destined goal, knowing that their fate will never fall to a successor to complete (7:23-25). Melchizedek had personally provided the paradigm or prototype for a priest whose qualification for office would rest not in possessing a certain genealogical pedigree but in possessing a certain quality of life (7:1-10, 13-17). Third, Jesus' appointment to an eternal priesthood is sustained by God's oath, God's pledge of his own honor to the permanence and effectiveness of this channel of mediation (7:20-22). The covenant made between God and human beings and sustained through Jesus is utterly reliable because of this oath (6:13-20), such that the believers may invest themselves fully in fulfilling their part of the covenant without fear of suffering loss. Finally, Jesus officiates in a "more perfect tabernacle"

(9:11), the archetype in the divine realm rather than its copy and shadow on earth (8:1-6). Jesus enjoys a more direct access to the divine patron than the levitical priests, and he can really accomplish what the levitical priests enact merely symbolically in their copy of the "true" holy places.

On the basis of Jesus' priestly mediation there is at last the hope of the "perfection" of the worshipers (7:11, 19) and of their "drawing near" to God. In demonstrating that Jesus effectively provides access to God surpassing anything envisioned by the former priesthood, the author sustains and develops his over-arching point that attachment to and friendship with this Jesus is the most valuable good — an advantage not to be relinquished for any temporal advantage since not even the second-best priesthood begins to come close to providing the access to God that the believers have already enjoyed since joining themselves to God under the new covenant (8:7-13).

Bridging the Horizons

The salvation-historical perspective that the author offers on the access to God enjoyed by Christians cautions us who live two millennia after Christ's death not to take this access for granted. Christian worship is not a chore but an astonishing privilege, and the Christian is assured of being able to draw near to God in worship and prayer at any time, in any place, in any condition, precisely because Jesus, who intercedes on our behalf, has been living at, and continues to live at, God's right hand.

Chapter 7 places heavy emphasis on Jesus' enjoyment of an indestructible life as his qualification for office. The examination of Melchizedek, the model, presses this point, and the remainder of the chapter keeps returning to it. This provides us with an insight into the ways in which the resurrection of Jesus was interpreted in, and why it was so important to, the early Church. The resurrection was more than an expression of God's vindication of Jesus' way as the way that pleases him. It also enabled Jesus to continue to act on behalf of humanity, particularly in his role as priest, for the relationship between God and humanity is not restored, and our complete access to God is not won, until Jesus, our intercessor and the living guarantor of our deliverance, enters "heaven itself" to cleanse those sacred spaces (7:25). The new covenant and its better promises are not inaugurated apart from this priesthood of Jesus (8:6-13). In an era in which it becomes more and more fashionable to liberate oneself from the "mythological" elements of the Christian religion, many find the resurrection of Jesus an embarrassing leftover from a prescientific worldview. I would suggest, however, that removing this one piece of the Christian confession radically affects the remaining structure. In Hebrews, for example, it appears to provide the pillar upon which the rest of the edifice of soteriology leans. From our study of the implications of Jesus' resurrection for the early Church and its confession in this one sermon, it would appear that the resurrection is not an isolated piece that can be rationalized or detached; rather, it is a fundamental building block without which there is no new covenant or hope.

The primary objectives of the author are to amplify the value of our attachment to Jesus and to shore up our confidence that God's promises in Jesus will not fail. Perhaps we would now choose a rhetorical strategy other than comparison with the levitical priests to achieve these goals, but the goals are themselves essential to building strong disciples and communities of faith. Many of us in the Western world are afflicted with the disease of empiricism and materialism — we trust and care more for what we can see, feel, hear, and the like than for what remains beyond the observation of our senses. In order to follow Christ with our whole heart, rather than attempt to divide our time between God and Mammon, we need to latch onto what the author lays out at the beginning (1:10-12) and end (12:26-28) of his sermon. The visible, material world is the unreliable one, while Jesus is the reliable foundation on which to build a life and from which to seek security. This world's rewards may seem more real than whispers of God's promises, but as long as we think and evaluate this way we will lack the singleness of heart that gives discipleship its power, integrity, and joy. The author tries to help us understand that God's oath will never fail, that God's promises will come to the faithful, and that Jesus will never disappoint those who rely on him. If his arguments do not establish this for us, let us seek out other conversation partners (including God in prayer) who can drive this essential point home.

The Decisive Removal of Sin's Defilement: 9:1–10:18

Overview

The argument turns from comparison of the "staff" of the two priesthoods (the order of Levi and the order of Melchizedek) to a comparison of the "cultic regulations" and the sacrifices enacted by these priesthoods. The first covenant's regulations for worship prevented all but the priests from approaching the holy place and all but the high priest from approaching the holy of holies. The author's fundamental critique of the arrangements under the first covenant is that the sacrifices offered "are unable to perfect the conscience of the worshiper," so that he or she could enter into the presence of the living God. The mass of God's people was kept at a distance from the holy God, unable to discover their entry into the "holy places."

This is precisely the condition that Jesus overcomes. Having entered that better and "more perfect" tabernacle, the abode of God beyond the material creation, Jesus effects the decisive cleansing (given as a synonym in 9:14 for "perfecting" in 9:9, which the expression parallels) of the conscience of the worshiper. His better blood ensures better and fuller expiation than the blood of animals, which provided a cleansing that was only skin deep. The author sees in Jesus' death the blending together of a sacrifice of atonement and a sacrifice that ratifies a covenant (9:11-22; see Exod. 24:3-8), such that Jesus' sprinkling of his own blood in the heavenly sanctum both "atones" for the mercy seat in heaven and bears witness in the divine realm to the inauguration and binding force of this new covenant prophesied by Jeremiah (Heb. 8:7-13).

The author critiques the annual sacrifices for atonement (on Yom Kippur), which he claims serve only to remind the people of their sin and never to remove sin as an obstacle between God and the people. These sacrifices are said to be in-

291

capable of "perfecting those who approach God" (10:1); their very repetition demonstrates their ineffectiveness. In an exegetical *tour de force,* the author appeals to Psalm 40:6-8 (LXX Ps. 39:7-9) as authoritative proof for his claims, first, that animal sacrifices are valueless before God and, second, that Jesus' sacrifice of his own body (by standards of the Torah a most inappropriate and even unthinkable ritual act) does accomplish God's will for the people, namely, their sanctification so that they can stand in God's very presence (10:5-10).

The decisiveness of Jesus' achievement is attested first by his "sitting down at God's right hand" (returning to the application of Ps. 110:1) in contrast to the earthly priests who remain "standing" for their ongoing duties. The eschatological element enters this exposition at a number of points. Here the author reminds the hearers that Jesus is simply awaiting the time when his enemies will be subjected under his feet (10:13; Ps. 110:1). Subjection of Jesus' enemies is balanced by the deliverance that will come to those who are "eagerly waiting" for Jesus' second appearing (9:28). The proximity of this time of reward and punishment is emphasized by the fact that Jesus' sacrifice itself had already taken place "at the completion of the ages" (9:26). This reinforces the expectation that, since the "completion" of time is, in essence, behind them, the hearers live at the threshold of the dawning of the Son's return. The reprise of the quotation from Jeremiah that closes this exposition (10:15-18) that provides the second "witness" to the final efficacy of Jesus' sacrifice. God's promise to "remember" the people's sins no longer — a promise fulfilled in the inauguration of the new covenant, which the author has already linked with Jesus' sacrifice — demonstrates that there remains no need for a sin offering beyond the sacrifice offered by Jesus and the sprinkling of his blood in the heavenly sanctuary.

This central exposition serves the author's rhetorical goals rather directly. The author's celebration of Jesus' achievement incorporates many recognizable epideictic topics, which will serve to reawaken or sustain gratitude and admiration within the group toward the group's founder and ongoing leader. It will also amplify the baseness of responding with ingratitude and irreverence, reinforcing the justice of God's vengeance against such unjust clients (10:26-31). Jesus purchases benefit for others "at great cost to himself," his own blood (9:12; 10:5-10); he is the first and only one to accomplish what the many could not (9:14; 9:23-26; 10:1-3, 10; 10:11-12, 14).[1] The author also directly under-

---

1. See Aristotle's prescription for an encomium: "We must also employ many of the means of amplification; for instance, if a man has done anything alone, or first, or with a few, or has been chiefly responsible for it; all these circumstances render an action noble" (*Rh.* 1.9.38); also Quintilian *Inst.* 3.7.19: "we must bear in mind the fact that what most pleases an audience is the celebration of deeds which our hero was the first or only man or at any rate one of the very few to perform . . . emphasizing what was done for the sake of others rather than what he performed on his own behalf." These topics are also recommended by Theon as topics for a eulogy or encomium (Marrou, *History of Education,* 272-73).

scores the voluntary and intentional nature of Jesus' self-sacrifice (10:5-10).[2] Theon adds that achievements that are "prompt and efficient" win admiration, and the author of Hebrews certainly appeals to these topics in his comparison of Jesus' mediation with the inefficiency of the levitical priesthood.

While the author focuses on the nobility of Jesus' achievement, hopefully arousing the level of gratitude that will motivate continuing loyalty toward and reverence for Jesus, he also devotes considerable attention to amplifying the value of Jesus' benefits, the advantages currently enjoyed by the hearers. The Christians are reminded that, prior to Jesus, access to God was extremely limited; now, however, the believers can approach God's "throne of favor with boldness," having been sanctified for such an approach. They enjoy an advantage previously unknown in the history of the people of God, being enabled to approach God directly and to seek God's help and favors face-to-face. The advantages of desertion or merely shrinking back are small in comparison with the advantages that would be lost.

Alongside the advantages presently enjoyed, which would be placed at risk by dissociation from the Christian community and from its Lord, the author reminds the hearers yet again of the eschatological framework within which advantage must be calculated. His discussion of the "end of the ages" and Christ's return "for the purpose of salvation for those who eagerly await him" (9:26-28) supports the imminence of the dangers of neglecting, and of the rewards for attending to, the proper response to the heavenly benefactor. Those who choose to remain connected with Jesus' enemies face great danger on that day when all the Son's enemies will be subjugated (10:12-13).

Hebrews 9:1–10:18 (or, better, 7:1–10:18 as a whole) thus provides the author with the fuel for his exhortations in 10:19-39. He will urge them to hold onto the incomparable and unprecedented advantages Jesus has gained for them, to make use of the access to God that Jesus has opened up for them, and not to exchange these present goods for future evils by spurning the gift and insulting the giver. The person who fails to continue in a loyal, open, and unabashed association with Jesus the Benefactor will not only lose the advantages articulated in this section but will fall into degradation and gravest danger at the hands of the living God, the judge of all (10:26-31). The "once for all" quality of the sacrifice of Jesus will be seen to have both a positive and a negative consequence: it assures the loyal and grateful client of his or her ability to come before the holy God (10:18); it warns the potentially disloyal that there will be

---

2. Thus the *Rhet. Alex.* 1426a36-1426b1: "Another possible way of magnifying good or bad actions is if you prove that the agent acted intentionally, arguing that he had long premeditated doing the acts, that he repeatedly set about doing them, that he went on doing them a long time, that no one else had attempted them before, . . . that he was acting willingly, that he was acting deliberately."

no further sacrifice for sins should they choose to turn away after their enlightenment (10:26).

The author's interest in establishing the superior quality and results of Jesus' priestly mediation over the levitical priesthood is frequently explained as an attempt to divert Jewish Christians from abandoning their association with Christ in favor of a return to the temple cult and a relationship with God based on the prescriptions of Torah. A more modest version of this theory asserts that the author of Hebrews is writing to people who are becoming nostalgic for the ritual of the temple. He wishes to assure them that they have lost nothing by joining themselves to Christ. As I have argued in the Introduction, such an interpretation of the situation is hardly necessary to explain the sustained contrast between the "old" and the "new" advanced by the author. We turn here to consider the "ideological" achievement of this lengthy exposition. John Elliott writes that "the function of such ideology is not only to interpret but to motivate. . . . Members 'will gain courage from perceiving themselves as part of a cosmic scheme' and undertake actions that 'now have the legitimacy which proximity to the sacred provides.'"[3] Hebrews 7:1–10:18 (together with such exhortations as 4:14-16 and 10:19-25) underscores quite directly the more privileged proximity to the sacred enjoyed by virtue of joining the Christian group, developing this by means of contrast with the proximity to the sacred attained by the sect's parent body. The assumption that the author would be interested in delegitimating the efficacy of Torah-prescribed sacrificial regulations because of a perceived need to prevent retroversion (or conversion) to Judaism fails to take into account the fact that a certain group will regularly speak about the inadequacy of other group ideologies simply to support ongoing commitment to one's own ideological stance as superior.

Setting aside Jewish ideology remained an important part of Christian self-definition and provided a useful mechanism for enhancing commitment. The literature of early Christianity frequently addresses this task. 1 Peter takes up a wealth of language and images traditionally associated with Jewish identity and applies them to the new community formed by believing Gentiles (2:11-12; 4:3-5 especially). Philippians uses polemical contrast with the Judaizing movement in order to reaffirm the distinctive qualities that give identity and unity to the Torah-free Christian movement. The *Epistle of Barnabas,* which goes far beyond Hebrews in its polemical contrast between church and synagogue, does not emerge in response to a rhetorical situation in which conversion or reversion to Judaism is an issue. Rather, it engages Jewish ideology as a vehicle for supporting the definition and legitimation of the Christian group

---

3. Elliott, *Home for the Homeless,* 105 (citing Edward Shils, "The Concept and Function of Ideology," in *International Encyclopedia of the Social Sciences* [New York: Macmillan and Free Press, 1968], 7:72).

as the "correct" manifestation of OT religion. Justin's *Dialogue with Trypho,* similarly, serves to affirm the legitimacy of the (now mainly Gentile) church as the true continuation of God's people and recipients of God's promises. This is all the more pressing in each new generation of Christians as we hold as authoritative a collection of texts that contain laws and sacrificial regulations we do not follow. Explaining this phenomenon in and of itself necessitates the kind of discourse we find in Hebrews 7:1–10:18 without the suggestion of reversion as the presenting problem.

The exhortations urge the hearers to press forward rather than warn them against reverting to weaker or less efficacious forms of religion (as in Galatians). The salvation-historical argument of 7:1–10:18 serves a positive rather than a dissuasive function, giving the hearers forward momentum in their Christian walk as they consider how God has brought the realities into effect of which the religion of the OT was but a "shadow." This would give the addressees the sense of being far along in God's process of providing deliverance and entrance into the unshakable realm, for which he has been preparing the faithful since before Abraham. It reinforces the image of being at the threshold of entering the promised homeland, the image the author had been creating in 3:7–4:11 and continues to develop in 10:32-39.

There is yet a third dimension to the meaning of this discourse. While this section exhibits argumentative texture, seeking to demonstrate the superior execution and effects of Jesus' priestly service, the author also describes Jesus' sacrifice and the heavenly liturgy at great length so as to reenact, in effect, the unrepeatable drama of that sacrificial liturgy before the eyes of the audience. The events described in these chapters were not part of the kerygma of Christ dying, being buried, rising, and coming again. Indeed, the events described are beyond the realm of human experience. Many witnesses are attested for the resurrection and even the ascension of Jesus, but there are no witnesses to his heavenly, priestly work (save the OT types from which the author "reconstructs" the better liturgy). The audience may be "witnessing" for the first time the drama of this divine liturgy, accessible to them only through the text that describes them, and we should attend to this dimension of ritual drama and its effects on the congregation as part of our investigation of the rhetorical effect and strategy of Hebrews.[4]

While the sacrifice of Christ is unrepeatable, every remembrance of his sacrificial rites, like the remembrance of the unrepeatable ritual of Christian baptism, potentially allows their effects to be reappropriated. Hebrews 9:11–10:18 therefore allows the hearers to experience anew the cleansing of their

---

4. Thus, perceptively, Nelson (*Raising Up a Faithful Priest,* 71): "Ritual, and specifically sacrifice, can be understood as a drama intended to have some effect on the universe, but also on the participants and their society."

conscience, the sanctification that enables them to approach the living God with every obstacle barring their way to the heavenly sanctum removed. The dramatic presentation of the voluntary victim (10:5-10) impresses upon them the beneficence of Jesus and the cost at which he won for them such benefits. The ritual closes by pronouncing them cleansed from their iniquities, with the memory of their sins erased (cf. Isa. 6:1-6!), so that they may accept the author's invitation in 10:19-25 to run to God's presence, having thus been made holy in body and heart. The liturgical reading of the details of the ritual, indeed, impels the hearers to accept this "altar call" as well as the author's strategic addition of exhortations with regard to holding onto their confession and engaging in community-building activity rather than community-eroding activity (10:23-25). The sacrifice they have just witnessed unites them into a sanctified body, a body of worshipers,[5] and makes these exhortations all the more easily accepted. It is also under the aura created by this ritual drama that the author issues the strong warning of 10:26-31, also framed in terms recalling the ritual (the unrepeatable nature of the sacrifice and absence of further provision for sin offerings; profaning now the blood by which the hearers were sanctified). The path of apostasy is all the more abhorrent since it means the violation of the holiness imparted to the hearers by such a costly and unique sacrifice.

Even as the old barriers and limitations to access to God are eliminated in Jesus' priestly mediation, new ones are strategically erected. The hearers are told that they are sanctified by Jesus' blood and purified for entrance before the very throne of God, and that they thus enjoy unprecedented access even to the heavenly sanctum. This image is used, however, to reinforce community and to dissuade individuals from apostasy in 10:19-31. The believers must now be concerned with maintaining their sanctification through steadfast commitment to Jesus and to the group; moreover, their access to God is to be enjoyed as a community. Their holiness, then, serves to augment the centripetal forces drawing the individual Christians together and to defuse any centrifugal motions away from that community, which would profane the sanctifying blood, leave the worshiper with no means of purification, and expose him or her to God's wrath.

---

5. Nelson (*Raising Up a Faithful Priest*, 73): "The horizontal community of the onlookers would be strengthened by the shared observance of a public performance in which they had an emotional stake. Sacrifice united them into an audience." We might profitably consider here also Gal. 3:1, in which Paul recalls his proclamation of "Jesus Christ publicly portrayed as crucified." Paul's original preaching united the hearers into a congregation through this re-presentation of the fundamental sacrificial ritual at the core of Christian religion.

Commentary

9:1-10

The quotation from Jeremiah that closes chapter 8 sets up a contrast between "first" (πρωτος) and "second" (δευτερος) that the author will use as he compares the mediation and access to God available under the levitical priesthood and Jesus' achievement. The pair is applied most frequently to the two covenants (where the qualifier "second" can be replaced by "new"), but also to the two chambers of the tabernacle, the two kinds of sacrificial offerings, and finally the two comings of Christ, which provide the primary coordinates for the Christian's worldview. The prominence of these terms — a strong instance of repetitive texture — gives the whole section coherence and sustains the hearer's awareness of "comparison" *(synkrisis)* throughout the exposition.

πρωτος		δευτερος
8:7	covenants	8:7
8:13	covenants	[καινος]
9:1	covenant	—
9:2	chambers	9:3
9:6	chambers	9:7
9:8	first chamber	["holy of holies," 9:8]
9:15	covenants	[καινος]
9:18	covenant	—
[ἅπαξ]	Christ's two comings	9:28
10:9	sacrificial systems	10:9

What was blameworthy about the first covenant (8:7)? The author has already hinted at this in 7:11 and 7:19: the inability of Torah's cultic regulations and of the priesthood that enacted those regulations to effect "perfection." Now he will provide an explanation of that charge by contemplating the "regulations for cultic service" and the layout of the "worldly shrine" that were decreed by the first covenant (9:1). The author presents a summary of the layout and furnishings of the tabernacle (9:2-5): a first tent or compartment houses the lampstand, a table, and the bread set before God's presence; a second tent or compartment, located behind a second curtain, houses the gold altar of incense and the ark of the covenant in which are kept a gold vessel full of manna, the rod of Aaron, and the two tablets of the covenant.[6] It is above the ark that one finds the "mercy seat," the

---

6. The contents of the ark are not explicitly described in the Pentateuch save for the two tablets of stone containing the ten commandments (Deut. 10:2; 1 Kgs. 8:9). The jar of manna (Exod. 16:32-34) and Aaron's rod (the blossoming of the rod being the divine sign that the tribe of Levi, and especially Aaron as the head of that household, would serve in

place representing God's throne and presence.[7] The author describes these furnishings only to declare that his interest in them is incidental; he delays developing a detailed discussion of these items piece by piece (κατὰ μέρος).[8] Rather, the author is more concerned with drawing attention to the significance of the separation of the first chamber from the second, and the progressive limitations on access to God that these chambers and their regulations enforce (9:6-7).

The place where God's presence was thought to dwell was entered only once each year by only one man, with the blood that covered first his own sins (recalling 5:3; 7:27) and then the sins of the people "committed in ignorance" or "unknowingly."[9] This is, of course, a reference to the ritual of the Day of Atonement, described at length in Leviticus 16 and standing ever behind the author's thinking as he reflects both on the activity of the levitical high priests and the achievement of Jesus. The remainder of the priests carried out their duties in the outer chamber, tending the lampstand (Exod. 27:20-21) and replacing the consecrated loaves (Lev. 24:8-9).[10] The design of the tabernacle, and

---

God's tabernacle; Num. 17:10) were to be placed within the inner sanctum as a perpetual "testimony," but the author of Hebrews actually has them stored within the ark (suggested perhaps by Exod. 18:21: "in the ark you shall put the testimony that I will give you").

7. Many of these details are taken from Exodus 25–26 (see especially 26:31-35 on the separating curtain and the placement of various items on one side or the other of that curtain), although there are some striking anomalies — most notably the placement of the incense altar, which is clearly located in the outer of the two chambers in Exodus (these anomalies are discussed at length in Attridge, *Hebrews*, 232-38; William L. Lane, *Hebrews 9–13* [WBC; Dallas: Word, 1991], 220-21). Attridge (*Hebrews*, 236) shows how an exegete of LXX Numbers could place the incense altar in the inner chamber. More problematic is the designation of the outer chamber here as "holies" and the inner chamber as "holies of holies" when elsewhere he will refer to the inner sanctum simply as "holies" (τὰ ἅγια, 9:8, 12; 10:19). The author may simply be inconsistent in his terminology, although Attridge argues at length for an emended reading of P46 as the original reading. He develops the possibility that a reader of the LXX could reverse the terminology, calling the outer chamber τὰ ἅγια τῶν ἁγίων and the inner chamber τὰ ἅγια, a reversal of terminology that P46 contains (except for the fact that the inner chamber is referred to in that manuscript as ἅνα, which Attridge takes to be a scribal error). This is an attractive suggestion, since it avoids an inconsistency on the author's part, but the lack of manuscript support (one manuscript, and that with a proposed emendation) and the cardinal rule of textual criticism (the more difficult, not the smoother and more harmonized, reading is to be preferred) speak against it.

8. Philo (*Vita Mos.* 2.97-100) does provide an example of what an item-by-item discussion of the significance of the tabernacle and its furnishings might look like.

9. This qualifier will contrast significantly with 10:26, the "intentional sin" of dishonoring and repudiating the divine benefactor, for which there is no sacrifice (Pfitzner, *Hebrews*, 125).

10. According to Exod. 30:7-8 (see Luke 1:8-22), the priests would also offer incense on the altar of incense, although the author's placement of this altar in the inner chamber would preclude him from understanding this activity to be part of their duties.

later the temple, reflected the care that had to be taken by the people of Israel as they sought to live before a holy God. The lay Israelite, the ordinary priest, and the high priest represented three levels of holiness, three levels of adherence to purity requirements, and with each level came the added privilege and danger of moving closer to the awesome presence of holiness itself. Richard Nelson is, of course, correct to affirm that the priesthood was not in itself a barrier to access to God,[11] but neither was it able to improve the access to God of the ordinary worshiper. They facilitated access, making it "possible for an unclean and sinful nation to live before a holy God,"[12] but at the same time reminded the worshiper of the limits on access. The cultic regulations of the "first" covenant, therefore, made sure that the nation kept its distance from God, building a hedge of punishments for encroachment and an aura of taboo around the holy of holies so as to protect the holiness of God — or, more accurately, protect the nation *from* the holiness of God.[13]

The author of Hebrews regards this arrangement as unsatisfactory since worshipers who desired to draw closer could not on account of the inefficacy of the sacrifices and the binding rules regulating access to the holy place and the holy of holies. In his eyes the promise of God "dwelling in the midst" of his people (cf. Ezek. 37:27; Zech. 2:11; 2 Cor 6:14–7:1) went unfulfilled. The author of Hebrews again has a kindred spirit in John the Seer, who looks forward to the New Jerusalem for the fulfillment of God's hope: "Behold, the tabernacle of God is among human beings. He will pitch his tent with them; they will be God's people, and God himself will be with them" (Rev. 21:3). He therefore comes to his point in 9:8-10: the cultic arrangements of the first tabernacle, with their perpetual maintenance of boundaries and barriers to God's presence, are a vehicle by which the Holy Spirit demonstrates that "the way into the holy places has not yet been shown while the first chamber still has cultic status, in which chamber gifts and sacrifices are being offered that cannot perfect the worshiper in regard to his conscience, and which chamber is a parable for the

---

11. *Raising Up a Faithful Priest,* 105.

12. Ibid., 82.

13. Thus Milgrom (*Leviticus I–XVI,* 45): the priests "taught the people that God's holiness stood for the forces of life and that only when approached in an unauthorized way (e.g., 10:1-2) would it bring death. Contact with the sancta would be fatal to the encroacher, that is, the nonpriest who dared officiate there (e.g., Num. 16:35; 18:3), but not to the Israelites who worshiped God in their midst." The worshiper was "safe" as long as he or she remained in the proper place without attempting to move too near the holy God without the proper credentials and purification. See further Jacob Milgrom, *Numbers = Ba-midbar: The Traditional Hebrew Text with the New JPS Translation* (Philadelphia: Jewish Publication Society, 1990), 342-43: the unauthorized person who tried to enter the spaces forbidden to a person of his or her holiness quotient was to be cut down by the temple guards "before God cuts down everyone else" (cf. Num. 1:53; 18:5).

present time" (9:8-10).[14] The "yet" is significant, for the author believes that he and his addressees live in a time in which the way into the holy places has in fact been opened up. The author will return to speak of the "new and living way" by which the believers have "entrance into the holy places" through a quite different "curtain" in 10:19-20.[15]

The problem with the first covenant's cultic arrangements is that all the gifts and sacrifices offered before and within the first chamber did nothing to bring the worshipers closer to God. Their place was always restricted to the spaces outside the holy place. Direct access to God was still limited to one man, once a year, with a lesser degree of access being enjoyed by a limited number of priests. The spatial arrangements and the limitations on participants the closer one got to God's mercy seat merely reinforced the consciousness of separation, of unholiness, of barriers between human beings and God. The cultus could not "perfect the worshiper in regard to his or her conscience," that is, could not bring the conscience to the divinely appointed goal of allowing the worshiper to stand in the very presence of God in anticipation of favor rather than in fear of destruction (9:11-14 and 10:1-18 will take up the question of how the unmet need of 9:9 was overcome).

Conscience is a person's internal moral faculty, the resource by which a person discerns right from wrong. This is formed within a person as he or she is socialized into a group and begins to internalize the group's definitions of right (and honorable) behavior and wrong (and shameful) behavior. On the one hand, then, conscience connects an individual to the group's values, but, on the other hand, it is not the same thing as being concerned about public opinion.[16]

---

14. Attridge, *Hebrews*, 240: "What the Spirit reveals is the lack of access to the true presence of God. Under the old covenant there has not been a decisive revelation of the means of approach to God, the 'way into the sanctuary.'" Following Lane (*Hebrews 9–13*, 224), I take both relative pronouns to refer back to the "first tent."

15. The term for the veil closing off the inner sanctum in 9:3 reappears in 10:19-20, which declares Jesus to be the new and living way into the holy place.

16. This is a mistake made in B. Malina and J. Neyrey, "First Century Personality: Dyadic, Not Individual," in *The Social World of Luke-Acts: Models for Interpretation*, ed. J. H. Neyrey (Peabody: Hendrickson, 1991), 67-96. These authors are correct to stress the connection of individual conscience with group values and group approval, but in an attempt to correct misunderstandings of "individualism" they go too far. First, they elevate "shame" to the exclusion of "guilt": "Failure or sin would bring social 'shame,' not internalized 'guilt'" ("Personality," 79), in spite of the detailed demonstrations by E. R. Dodds (*The Greeks and the Irrational* [Berkeley: University of California Press, 1966]) concerning the coexistence of "shame" and "guilt" as powerful forces from the Classical Age onward in Greece. Second, and more importantly, when Malina and Neyrey say "No one [in the first-century Mediterranean world] would understand something as nonsensical as 'Let your own conscience be your guide'" ("Personality," 80), they are not taking into account the development of moral autonomy in Hellenistic culture seen, for example, in the heroine of Sophocles' play *Antigone*, who

It is an internal knowledge of whether or not one has acted virtuously and honorable, and it is intimately connected with the juridical sense of "guilt." For Paul, for example, it is the "conscience" that acts as one's own defending attorney or prosecutor before the judgment seat of God (Rom 2:14-16).

The fact that the innumerable sacrifices left the worshiper still standing "outside" proves for the author the inefficacy of the whole system. While the worshipers might have been sufficiently cleansed externally to stand safely at a distance from God, they were not "perfected" (or "cleansed," 9:14) in terms of their conscience so as to move directly into the burning presence of God. The author criticizes the regulations of the first covenant as mere "regulations of the flesh" — prescriptions concerned with food (Lev. 11; Deut. 14), purificatory washings of the body (Lev. 15; Num. 19), and drink[17] — which are incapable of extending sanctifying power to the inner person.

These regulations are of limited duration, holding only until the "time of reformation" arrives. This "time of correction," however, has already come from the perspective of the author and his hearers, for Jesus the high priest has already entered the heavenly tabernacle and instituted the new covenant of Jeremiah 31. Hebrews 9:10 is phrased in a forward-looking manner not because the time of reformation is yet to come, but because in the development of the argument the author is leading the listener to consider first the conditions of the time under the first covenant and then, in 9:11–10:18, the reformation effected by Jesus. The "first tent" has already lost its cultic standing, as the author's exegesis of Psalm 40:6-8 will demonstrate.

The "first tent" is also said to have a metaphorical significance: it "is a

---

chooses social shame and execution as a criminal for the sake of being true to the values of kinship she had learned growing up in Thebes. In her case, the "honorable" thing to do will not result in recognition.

Two voices from the late first century help provide balance. First, Pliny the Younger (*Ep.* 3.20) laments that "very few people are as scrupulously honest in secret as in public, and many are influenced by public opinion but scarcely anyone by conscience." On the one hand, this confirms Malina and Neyrey's corrective emphasis that "social shame" is the dominant force behind motivation. On the other hand, Pliny's own ability to distinguish "public opinion" from "conscience," one clearly related to group opinion ("public") and the other committed to acting with virtue apart from opinion (in "secret"), attests to the possibility of a moral autonomy that acts independently of public opinion. The ethical philosophy of Epictetus, moreover, is based on the principle that the wise person follows his or her "governing principle" (the conscience) in explicit opposition to what the majority approves and values. Pliny and Epictetus would certainly have understood the saying "let your own conscience be your guide."

These developments have been well documented in Bernard Williams, *Shame and Necessity* (Berkeley: University of California Press, 1993).

17. While there are no clear OT referents here, Moffatt (*Hebrews*, 119) notes the linking of "foods and drinks" in Hellenistic Jewish texts that explain the Torah, such as *Aristeas to Philocrates* 128, 142, 158.

parable pointing to the present time" (9:9). The hearers, however, do not live under the jurisdiction of the first cultus, or in a period characterized by the limitations of the first tent in its cultic sense, for the work of Christ is done. They are not still waiting in their "present time" for the first tent and its sacrifice to be replaced by a sacrifice that can perfect the conscience of the worshiper so that all can enter the holy of holies, for this has already been achieved for them by Jesus, who leads them into the heavenly holy place. How is their "present time,"[18] then, symbolized by this "first tent"? I would suggest that the solution here lies in reading the expression "which is a parable for the present time" as a parenthetical remark, adding an important insight to be sure but basically interrupting the flow of thought in 9:8-10. This parenthesis interjects a cosmological dimension to the layout of the first tabernacle, one that will eventually be clarified by 12:26-28. The outer tent is a symbol of the present age when the visible creation itself still hides the entry into the heavenly, permanent, unseen realm. There is the implicit assurance (noted as early as Calvin) that the heavenly holy place exists even though we do not now see it, just as the holy of holies existed even though only one person a year ever saw it. The way will be made clear when the first chamber, that is, this visible creation, will be shaken and removed, "so that what is unshakable may abide" (12:27).

Hebrews 9:1-10, then, describes the limitations on, and obstacles to, face-to-face access to God (or really the "shadow" of God's presence, as the earthly inner sanctum was but the shadow of the true holy place) that existed under the first covenant and its arrangements, and which have now been overcome by the Son. This paves the way for the author's discussion of the "correction" or "reformation" that God provided in Jesus. The hearers stand at a point after this "time of correction" with regard to access to God, for the "new and living way" into the holy place (10:19-20) has been revealed to them, who may "approach with boldness the throne of favor" (4:14). The structure of the tabernacle, how-

---

18. The apparent linking between the "present time" and the offering of ineffective "gifts and sacrifices," while attractive as support for a pre-70 AD date, is more apparent than real. Grammatically, the "which (καθ' ἥν, a feminine pronoun)" in the clause "in which gifts and sacrifices are offered" can either describe the "first tent" (the feminine noun σκηνή) or explain the "parable" (the feminine noun παραβολή), but it cannot describe the "present time" (the masculine noun καιρός) of the author and the hearers. English translations often obscure this by reading "a parable of the present time, in which gifts and sacrifices are being offered." In the Greek, however, there is no grammatical agreement between the relative pronoun "which" and "time," indicating that the latter is not the referent of the former. It is probably best to regard both pronouns in 9:9 (ἥτις; καθ' ἥν) as introducing further description of the feminine noun "tent." The present tense of the verb "are being offered" (προσφέρονται) thereby becomes irrelevant for the question of dating, since it merely describes the ongoing and ineffective activity of the priests in the first chamber, all the more as the "time of correction" was itself already initiated in Jesus' sacrifice.

ever, also points beyond the cultic *fait accompli* to the cosmological *desideratum*, that is, the removal of the outer, created cosmos so that the believers may enter at last their unshakable kingdom, the realm of God's full presence.

9:11-22

Just as the "first" covenant had a sanctuary and cultic regulations, so the second is assumed to have its own sanctuary and sacrificial rites. The first covenant provides the language and framework for conceptualizing the death and post-ascension experiences of Jesus, although the author of Hebrews stretches and refashions that framework to fit the new rite (e.g., in assigning to Jesus the role both of priest and sacrificial victim).[19] The old culture map, as type, provides the raw materials, but these are combined in new and impossible ways by the new priest. This should not be troubling, however, since the author has already warned us that a new priesthood requires a new law as well (7:12).[20] A "clean" fit between what Jesus does and what one reads in Torah is obviated by this claim, such that the author is freed from a too-rigid application of the types to the antitype. To give due dignity and weight to his triumphant declaration of Jesus' accomplishment of that which was impossible under the first covenant, the author uses chiasm, antithesis, and a lesser-to-greater enthymeme:

> But Christ, having become high priest of the good things that came into being, entered once for all through the better and more perfect tent, which is not made by hands (that is, not of this creation), into the holy places, not through the blood of goats and cows, but through his own blood, inventing eternal redemption.[21] For if the blood of goats and bulls and sprinkled ash of

---

19. See Nelson, *Raising Up a Faithful Priest*, 148: "We see how the attempt to fit the extraordinary phenomenon of Jesus into the existing structures of the Jewish culture map required a stretching and even fracturing of older categories."

20. Ibid., 142.

21. Lane (*Hebrews 9–13*, 237) identifies the chiasm in this way:

A   "through the greater and more perfect tent"
    (διὰ τῆς μείζονος καὶ τελειοτέρας σκηνῆς)
  B   "not made with hands, that is, not of this creation"
      (οὐ χειροποιήτου, τοῦτ' ἔστιν οὐ ταύτης τῆς κτίσεως,)
  B′   "not with the blood of goats and cows"
      (οὐδὲ δι' αἵματος τράγων καὶ μόσχων)
A′   "through, rather, his own blood"
    (διὰ δὲ τοῦ ἰδίου αἵματος).

The outside elements speak of the "better" elements of the second covenant's rites, the inner elements of the limitations or secondary qualities of the first covenant's liturgical accoutrements. B′ and A′ also are cast in the form of antithesis.

a heifer sanctifies the defiled with regard to the purification of the flesh, how much more will the blood of Christ, who offered himself blameless to God through eternal spirit, cleanse our conscience from dead works in order to serve the living God? (9:11-14)

Having already demonstrated Christ's appointment to the high priesthood (5:5-6; 7:1-28), the author moves now into the high-priestly rite enacted by Jesus in this "time of correction." Like the high priest on earth, Jesus moves through the tabernacle all the way to the inner sanctum. Unlike the high priest, Jesus does his ministry in a superior locale — the "greater and more perfect tent, not made with hands, that is, not belonging to this creation."[22] This description supports, first, the understanding of "perfection" language as relating to crossing the threshold between the visible and eternal realms. The heavenly temple is "more perfect" in that it exists in the unshakable, abiding realm. Sec-

---

22. On Jewish and Christian speculation concerning the heavenly temple, see the numerous texts cited in the commentary on 8:5. Here we may simply recall the witness of *T. Levi* 18:6: "the heavens opened, and out from the temple of glory sanctification came upon him." Stedman (*Hebrews*, 96-101) develops a very strange interpretation of this heavenly temple. He suggests that what Moses saw on the mountain was "the whole person — body, soul, and spirit (Gen. 2:7; 1 Thess. 5:23)," which "would explain the threefold division of the tabernacle" (p. 96 note). He then proceeds to allegorize the contents of the tabernacle's chambers. He matches up the human spirit with the holy place, appealing to 2 Cor. 5:1 (which speaks of the resurrected body as our "dwelling not made with hands") to interpret the tabernacle that Christ entered, which was also "not made by human hands" (Heb. 9:11; *Hebrews*, 98). Stedman's argument provides a good example of the rabbinic method of *gezera shawa* (interpreting one verse by means of the same word occurring in another) at work, but it is also fundamentally a bad example of exegesis. First, he betrays an utter lack of interest in the first-century context of the author's thought, a context full of references to the conviction that the earthly sphere is but a shadow of the heavenly sphere, and, in particular, that the levitical tabernacle (and later temple) was a copy of the realm of God beyond the heavens. Acting without regard to this context, Stedman quickly collapses (one might say demythologizes) a cosmological dualism (which undergirds the author's whole thinking) into an anthropological quality — heaven becomes the human spirit. Revelation 4 and 5 (along with the passing references to the accoutrements of the heavenly temple throughout the apocalypse) even provides a canonical safeguard against this kind of reduction, and thus it is all the more surprising to find it in Stedman. Second, he fails to refine his reading in light of the literary context of the sermon itself, for the author is clear that Jesus "entered heaven itself" (Heb. 9:24), even using the emphatic pronoun to stress the destination of Jesus as that divine realm beyond the material cosmos (not within the inner reaches of the human being). Moreover, he misses the way in which the author of Hebrews has traced Jesus' trajectory as a means of charting the believers' own course. Stedman writes that "The entrance, by faith, of Jesus into the spirit of a believer gives this person access to the heavenly reality" (p. 101), but this ignores the way in which the author of Hebrews repeatedly calls the hearers to go where Jesus has gone — which is not back into ourselves, but into the unshakable realm of God's kingdom (12:28).

ond, the author's distinction between "this creation" and the realm into which Jesus has entered "as a forerunner for us" (6:19-20) supports a reading of 9:9 ("a parable for the present time") that involves more than the mere replacement of the OT cult. "This creation" itself stands between the believers and final, complete access to God. Thus Jesus must "pass through the heavens" in order to enter that abiding place of mediation which belongs not to this material, visible realm. The "way into the holy places" has indeed been revealed now: believers may follow into that space in prayer and collective worship and may follow in person when Christ returns a second time (9:28; cf. 12:26-28).

As the earthly high priest enters the holy place only with blood, so also Jesus takes blood into the heavenly sanctum. Blood (αἷμα), in fact, emerges as a prominent term in 9:11-22 (9:12 [*bis*], 13, 14, 18, 19, 20, 21, 22 [*bis*]), giving it thematic coherence. The author's interest in the power of blood will remain through the end of the exposition (9:25; 10:4) and extend appropriately into the exhortation based on this exposition. The salvific benefits of this blood may be appropriated unto the enjoyment of access to God in community with one's fellow believers (10:19) or spurned with dire consequences by the one who prefers the friendship of society to the friendship of God (10:29). The blood of the new covenant is, however, of incomparably greater value than the blood of the old, as expressed in the antithesis of 9:12: "not through the blood of goats and cows but through his own blood." The earthly high priest officiating at the annual rite of atonement used the blood of these animals as the medium for cleansing both himself and the people (9:7b), as well as the mercy seat in the holy place:

> Aaron shall present the bull as a sin offering for himself, and shall make atonement for himself and his house. . . . He shall take some of the blood of the bull, and sprinkle it with his finger on the front of the mercy seat, and before the mercy seat he shall sprinkle the blood with his finger seven times. He shall slaughter the goat of the sin offering that is for the people and bring its blood inside the curtain, and do with its blood as he did with the blood of the bull. (Lev. 16:11, 14-15, NRSV)

The purificatory medium of the second covenant is far more costly, since it involves the death of the very Son of God (hence the greater danger that will accompany profanation of this blood by thinking too little of the benefits it has brought, 10:29).

The better blood, taken into the better shrine, effects better results. The single act of Jesus (his death, resurrection, and ascension into the unshakable realm) — the entry "once for all" into the heavenly sanctum — contrasts with the annual entry of the high priest into the earthly sanctum, unable ever to achieve decisive removal of sins (10:1-4). The "once for all" aspect of Jesus' sacrifice is reflected in the quality of the "redemption" he obtains. It is "eternal" because it lasts forever and needs no repetition (for this author, repetition is the sign of inefficiency and inefficacy).

In 9:13-14, the author introduces a lesser-to-greater enthymeme based on the antithesis of animal blood versus Jesus' own blood in 9:12, by means of which he seeks to clarify the significance and meaning of "eternal redemption." In linking together the "blood of goats and cows" with "the sprinkled ashes of a heifer," the author blends together the sacrifices offered on Yom Kippur with the procedure outlined in Numbers 19 for the preparation of the medium that removes the impurity contracted by corpse defilement. The author of Hebrews links the sacrifices of Yom Kippur with this purity regulation (the only purification rite that involves the death of an animal) in order to transfer the purely ritual and external significance of the latter onto the former. He associates them so as to advance his claim that the old covenant had the power only to deal with external defilement, being thus "regulations for the flesh" that could not pierce through to the removal of the contamination of the conscience (9:9-10). This linkage allows him to relegate the sacrifices of Yom Kippur to the level of "purification of the flesh" (9:13).

If the material substance is sufficient for the sanctification of the exterior person, the blood of Christ — offered "through [the] eternal spirit" — will surely suffice for the cleansing of the interior person. The author connects the rites that pertain to animal blood or dust with efficacy in the material realm and hence the cleansing of the "body" of the person; the rites that involve the "spiritual" offering, however, have the potency to effect purification in those untouchable, immaterial reaches within the human being. At this point, we should recall that the author is speaking about a crucifixion and its unique aftermath in the case of Jesus. He is using cultic, objective language to describe a most unusual sacrifice. How far should we take his objectifying language? Should we imagine that Jesus does, in fact, take some of his own blood into the immaterial, heavenly sanctum (eventually to cleanse those spiritual realities with material blood)? The author's awareness that Jesus' sacrifice takes place "through eternal spirit" may indicate that the author would not have us cling too tightly to the material aspects of Christ's death as we ponder the effects of that death in these cultic terms. He uses objective language to assist the subjective appropriation of this good news in terms that the hearers, well versed in the prototype (the relationally restorative rites in the OT), can grasp and apply now to their standing before God. Jesus' death on our behalf and his ascension into God's presence mean that the believers have been accepted by God for Jesus' sake into God's household and enjoy the benefit of Jesus' living and interceding "for them" at God's right hand (7:25; cf. Rom. 8:34; 1 John 2:1-2). The type of the OT cultus provides powerful language for grasping the fact that all obstacles standing between a holy God and an unholy humanity have been removed: the sins that defiled the conscience (which made the human being afraid to come before a holy God) as well as God's sanctuary (which remained as an affront to God's honor in God's own memory).

The "dead works" here are most assuredly not the cultic regulations of the OT.[23] How could faithful performance of the Torah actually defile the conscience?! The criticism that the author levels at the rites of Torah is not that they are themselves a source of defilement needing cleansing but that they have not the power to remove the defilement that exists in the inner person on account of some other, and prior, transgression. These are the dead works about which the convert learned and from which the convert repented (6:1), works that lead to death. Possibly the phrase carries connotations of idol worship, for "dead works" contrast here with serving the "living God," although "dead works" will refer also to all works that stain the conscience and prevent one from coming into the presence of a holy God, whose holiness breaks out against defilement, consuming the adversary (this aspect of Exodus and Leviticus is potently preserved in 10:26-31).

The author understands sin itself as a defilement that extends to the inner person, the conscience. The OT taught that people are defiled not just by contact with things unclean but by moral lapses and lapses in performance of the covenant. A poignant testimony to this appears in Isaiah 6. Isaiah stands before God and fears destruction on account of his "uncleanness." This uncleanness is not external but moral (Isaiah is particularly conscious of the pollution brought on by impure words). The defilement is removed with the announcement that "your iniquity is taken away, and your sin is forgiven." The emphasis on forgiveness of sin in Hebrews 10:14-18 as the decisive removal of the defilement of the conscience of the worshiper echoes Isaiah quite strongly at this point.

Jesus' death and ongoing intercession for the believers should provide the assurance, therefore, that the thoughts, words, and deeds that formerly came between us and the holy God need trammel up that relationship no longer. While the old rites could not "perfect the conscience of the worshiper" (9:9), the blood of Jesus does "cleanse our conscience" so that we can "serve the living God." The author's use of parallel phrasing here (enforced by the broader parallels he has been drawing between the rites and results of the old covenant in 9:7-10 and under the new in 9:11-14) clarifies what this internal "perfection" signifies — it is the fitting of the worshiper to come at last to the divinely appointed goal for him or her, the presence of God. The author criticizes the old cult because he assumes that this was God's goal for God's people from the beginning, a goal that went unrealized for centuries. Because the believers now have so great and so efficacious a mediator, however, they can "serve" in the very presence of the living God rather than remain at a distance. Indeed, their

---

23. *Contra* Lane, *Hebrews 1–8*, 140.

whole lives will become liturgical services, carried out not within human-made walls but wherever the believer finds himself or herself — in acts of worship, confession, sharing, and doing good (see 13:15-16).[24]

By means of his death, which effects "redemption for transgressions against the first covenant," Jesus, the "mediator of a new covenant" (returning to the language of Jer. 31:31), makes it possible for "those who have been called to receive the promise of an eternal inheritance" (9:15). Identifying the addressees, the beneficiaries of Jesus' death, as "those who have been called" (οἱ κεκλημένοι) serves to legitimate their association with the Christian group and its hope as a response to the divine initiative. It signals their privilege in having been singled out for this special destiny, as well as their piety in their obedient response to this call. The author points them again away from their present circumstances and their past possessions to the future inheritance that God has promised to bestow upon them, an inheritance of an "eternal" quality in stark contrast to the temporary and insecure goods they had enjoyed in the past (see especially 10:34). This promise has been, and will remain, an important focal point for the sermon (6:12, 17; 10:34; 11:39-40; 12:28; 13:13-14) as the author reminds the hearers of the greater good that is preserved through continued investment in the group and its values and is put in jeopardy by "shrinking back." Attaching the reception of this promise to Jesus' death, moreover, reminds the hearers of how much their mediator (or broker) was willing to give of himself in order to secure this benefaction for them. To throw away the promised inheritance now for temporal ease would be to reenact the folly of Esau (12:16-17) and offer a dangerous insult to an all-powerful Patron (10:26-31).

Joining the word "covenant" with "inheritance" allows the author to begin to play on the dual meaning of διαθήκη as both "covenant" and "testament" (i.e., will).[25] In this way, he can hold together the affirmation of Jesus' death as a covenant inauguration sacrifice and as the passing away of a testator that enables the property of the testator to fall to the heirs (making God's "will" valid for those who have been named his heirs). The new covenant is thus closely bound to the future inheritance of the unshakable kingdom by the believers. The author continues, then, with an observation from general legal practice: a testament that bequeaths an inheritance does not actually have force until it can be demonstrated that the testator has died. Since God, of course, cannot die, Jesus' death is brought forward as the death that makes the law of inheritance effectual for the heirs. This is, as Attridge rightly notes, a rhetorical con-

---

24. "Liturgical service" (λατρεία/λατρεύω) appears frequently in this central exposition as a description of what the earthly priests do (8:5; 9:1, 6), but it is applied also to the worshiper who has limited access under the old covenant (9:9; 10:2). It eventually becomes a term that summarizes the activity of Christian believers (9:14; 12:28; 13:10).

25. Paul also finds it useful to exploit the double meaning of διαθήκη in Gal. 3:15-18.

ceit,[26] but it serves the author's goal of making Jesus' death a sort of surety or proof of the addressees' future inheritance, so as to provide yet another prop for their continued confidence and perseverance in that hope. Testamentary language (linked with the language of promised inheritance, which was common in Pauline Christianity and which has already been used in this sermon) is employed to repeat the point derived exegetically earlier in this sermon in the reading of Psalm 8 (Heb. 2:5-10): the Son's death and exaltation assures the hearers of their own future exaltation and inheritance of "glory."

The author weaves across the line between covenant and will again in 9:17: "for a covenant (διαθήκη) is confirmed on the basis of dead bodies (ἐπὶ νεκροῖς βεβαία), since it does not have force while the testator lives." The introduction of "dead bodies" as the basis on which a διαθήκη is "confirmed" or "made binding" recalls covenant-making services. The covenant made between God and Abraham (Gen. 15:9-21) was established in the midst of animal corpses cleaved in two, the sign of God's own oath to see his part of the covenant through "on his life." With this expression, then, the author moves the hearers back from a legal to a cultic framework for reflecting on the significance of Jesus' death, although 9:17b returns to topics of testamentary law as if to complete the braiding and intertwining of these two frameworks of meaning.

The author wants to link the shedding of blood and death of a victim with a covenant inauguration, and the conceit of testamentary law helps him make this point. The main point this argument serves is that Christ's death accomplishes the inauguration of the covenant spoken of in the Jeremiah quotation (Heb. 8:8-12). Focused solely on his first/old versus second/new typology, a contrast encoded in the Jeremiah passage, the author shows no interest in the

---

26. *Hebrews*, 254. Lane (*Hebrews 9–13*, 242-43), however, reads this still purely as a covenant ratification, based on the precedent of Gen. 15:9-21, in which dismembered animals represented a self-imprecatory curse by the one making the covenant if he or she should prove unfaithful. This does well to explain the strange formulation ἐπὶ νεκροῖς βεβαία: the covenant has force "on the basis of dead bodies," which is also true for Exod. 24:1-8 (the ratification ceremony for the "old" covenant), but then we must accept without explanation the representative nature of these dead bodies for the "ratifier," whose death must also be demonstrated.

It thus seems better to read this passage as moving into the world of inheritance and wills (Attridge, *Hebrews*, 254-56), a move facilitated by the bivalence of the word for covenant/will as well as the author's identification of the purpose of the redemptive death as enabling "those who have been called to receive the promise of an eternal inheritance" (9:15). This verse thus effectively plays off both aspects of διαθήκη — the death of Jesus was a redemptive death atoning for sins committed under the first covenant, as well as a death that makes God's "will" valid for those who have been named heirs of the living God. In this reading, Lane's insight about the phrase ἐπὶ νεκροῖς βεβαία pertaining to a "covenant" (being an awkward reference to the binding force of a "will") would still have force, as it signals the move back into the world of covenant-inauguration rituals.

many covenants that are in fact ratified without bloodshed. The significant point is that the Sinai covenant, the "first" covenant, was inaugurated with bloodshed, so that a decisively new act of blood-shedding such as Jesus' death provided would become a "probable sign" of a new covenant inauguration.

Hebrews 9:18-21 summarizes and modifies the ceremony of Exod. 24:1-8, in which Moses took the blood of bulls, sprinkling half on the altar and half on the people after he read the laws of the covenant and they agreed to abide by that covenant. Just as the Day of Atonement ritual illumines Jesus' work in 9:7-14, so now the historic ratification of the Mosaic covenant will illumine another dimension of Jesus' death and ascension.[27] The aspersion of blood was a witness to the people and to God that the covenant was now indeed binding on both parties, once they had all agreed to it. The blood came from animals that were, significantly, offered up as peace offerings, sacrifices performed with a view to securing God's favor for the people, assuring their well-being. This is a prominent aspect of Jesus' offering of himself, an act that has directly brought the many believers into the household of God and under the aegis of his patronage.

The author of Hebrews adds details to the Exodus episode: the water, scarlet thread, and hyssop are absent from Exodus 24, as is mention of the sprinkling of "the tent and all the liturgical vessels." As in 9:13, so here, the author conflates rites from different places in Torah prescribed for different occasions and purposes to stress both the exterior nature of these acts[28] and, by virtue of having included many different rites in his comparison, the supersession of the whole cultic system in the rite of the new covenant. Finally, the author has modified slightly his recitation of Moses' words in Exodus 24:8. Rather than "behold the blood of the covenant," the author has Moses say "this is the blood of the covenant," words that resonate with the words of the institution of the eucharist (Matt. 26:28; Mark 14:24).[29] While the author makes nothing of this connection, it would be in keeping with his typological reading of the OT, and, indeed, reflection on that rite may have stimulated his reflection on the meaning of the "body" and "blood" of Jesus offered "for us."

The exegetical observation that Moses cleansed not only the people but also the sanctuary with the blood of bulls (9:21) will lead the author to the point of direct contrast between the priestly work of the antitype with the types

---

27. As Nelson (*Raising Up a Faithful Priest*, 148) observes, "His death becomes both an atonement sacrifice and a covenant inauguration sacrifice (9:15, 20)." The author of Hebrews bears witness to a striking exegetical approach to the Torah. On the one hand, Jesus is held up as the antitype of which the key personnel and rites of Torah were but hints and prefigurations; on the other hand, it is these figures and rites that provide a vocabulary and grammar as the author seeks to give meaning to a death on a cross.

28. Lane, *Hebrews 9–13*, 244; Attridge, *Hebrews*, 247.

29. Pfitzner, *Hebrews*, 131-33.

— both Moses in the covenant inauguration ceremony and the levitical high priest in the Yom Kippur rites. A shared conviction that God's arrangements for mediation and deliverance in the past prefigure God's eschatological arrangements (typology) supports that author's claim that the antitype also has occurred, namely, Christ's cleansing of the heavenly sanctuary with better blood (9:23). The fact that, according to the Law, hardly anything is cleansed except with blood (9:22a) suggests that the same will be true for the new arrangements, save with better blood. With a maxim the author returns to the primary theme of forgiveness: "without shedding of blood, forgiveness does not come about." This maxim reflects general Jewish cultural knowledge that what removes sins is the application of the blood of a sacrificial victim (Lev. 17:11, the pillar text of the sacrificial system). The author accepts this maxim, but he holds alongside it the affirmation that "it is impossible for the blood of bulls and goats to remove sins" (10:4). Together, this will create the necessity for what is in effect a human sacrifice to achieve remission of sins, a sacrifice supplied in the death of Jesus.

9:23-28

Just as the author responded to his discussion of the type in 9:1-10 with a presentation of the achievement of the antitype in 9:11-14, so here again the discussion of the old rite in 9:18-22 sets up the author's exposition of the counterpart in the new liturgy of the better high priest (9:23-28): "It was necessary, on the one hand, that the shadows of the realities in the heavens be cleansed by means of these sacrifices, but for the heavenly realities themselves to be cleansed with better sacrifices than these" (9:23). The author accepts the necessity of cleansing the earthly tabernacle with blood, which was a prominent feature of the Yom Kippur ritual (Lev. 16:11-20, 33) as well as the covenant inauguration service of Exodus 24:1-8. The prescriptions calling for the ritual cleansing of the holy place, the place of mediation between God and humanity, indicate that the ancient Israelites understood sin — the violation of a commandment, moral or ritual — to affect not only the sinner but also to adversely affect the innermost sanctum.[30] Jacob Milgrom has called this the "Priestly *Picture of Dorian Gray*. . . . While sin may not scar the face of the sinner it does scar the face of the sanctuary."[31] As Richard Nelson aptly observes, "human sin defiled holy space and holy things and, unless cleaned off

---

30. Nelson, *Raising Up a Faithful Priest*, 77: "Israel believed that uncleanness and sin present among the people automatically entailed the pollution of the sanctuary and altar (Lev. 15:31; 20:3; Num. 19:13, 20). This pollution created a hazard for the entire community."

31. Milgrom, *Leviticus I–XVI*, 49.

or covered over,[32] threatened to generate the 'holy-unclean fusion reaction'
and bring on Yahweh's wrath."[33] An alternative conceptualization of this
wrath is the departure of the holy God from the polluted sanctuary and thus
Israel's loss of divine patronage and protection, thereby spelling national
ruin.[34]

The medium for cleansing the affronting defilements from the place of
mediation was blood, the repository of the "life" that, once spilled, became a
detergent capable of removing ritual and moral pollution.[35] The author of Hebrews constructs an antithesis in 9:23 that recalls the "lesser to greater" argument of 9:13-14: just as the new rites involved cleansing the conscience (rather
than the surface) of the sinner with a more effective blood, so also the better
sanctuary is to be cleansed by means of the better blood as well. The author of
Hebrews would not expect God to leave his own realm because of human sin,
but the defilement of the heavenly sanctum signals the abiding reminder of human affronts against God before his very throne (his heavenly mercy seat, as it
were; cf. 4:14-16 for the author's invitation to the congregation to approach this
heavenly reality as their place of mediation, the place where God's favor and
timely gifts can be secured). Jesus' cleansing of the heavenly sanctum is the rit-

---

32. Mary Douglas ("Atonement in Leviticus," *Jewish Studies Quarterly* 1 [1993-94]:
117-18) argues that "to atone means to cover, or recover, cover again, to repair a hole, cure a
sickness, mend a rift, make good a torn or broken covering . . . it means making good an
outer layer which has rotted or been pierced." Applied to the mercy seat in the holy of holies,
this would suggest that the sins of Israel, in effect, eroded the symbolic representation of "the
protective covering of God's righteousness" (p. 123), and that the application of blood acted
as a sort of reparative sealant, a kind of ritual mortar that annually repaired that covering and
prevented God's holiness from "breaking out" against Israel. Douglas's argument is certainly
unassailable as far as Leviticus is concerned, but the author of Hebrews appears to stand at
some remove from understanding atonement as "covering," shown by his frequent use of the
verb "cleansing" (καθαρίζω, a term that highlights the "washing" off of dirt from a surface)
both for the conscience of the worshiper (9:14) and the effect of Christ's blood on the heavenly sancta (9:23-24).

33. Nelson, *Raising Up a Faithful Priest*, 75.

34. Thus Milgrom, *Leviticus I–XVI*, 43: "Humans can drive God out of the sanctuary
by polluting it with their moral and ritual sins. All that the priests can do is periodically
purge the sanctuary of its impurities and influence the people to atone for their wrongs." See
also Milgrom, *Numbers*, 447: "Although the merciful God will tolerate a modicum of pollution, there is a point of no return. If the pollution continues to accumulate, the end is inexorable: 'The cherubs . . . lifted their wings' (Ezek. 11:22). The divine chariot flies heavenward
and the sanctuary is left to its doom." Nelson (*Raising Up a Faithful Priest*, 150) includes both
divine holiness breaking out to consume the people and the departure of God from God's
sanctuary as dangers avoided by cleansing the holy place.

35. Nelson, *Raising Up a Faithful Priest*, 70.

ual enactment of God's promised resolution to "remember sins no more" (Jer. 31:34, cited in Heb. 8:12; 10:15-18).

Hebrews 9:24 develops a second antithesis between the lesser, earthly, material sanctuary and the locale of Jesus' ministry, which is the very presence of God in the heavenly realm: "for Christ did not enter into the holy places crafted by hands, antitypes of the genuine articles, but into heaven itself, now to appear before the face of God on our behalf." In calling the earthly tabernacle the "antitype," the author calls attention again to the fact that the heavenly temple existed prior to the building of the earthly copy (see 8:5), so that the relationship between the heavenly cult and the earthly rites are reversed at this point. The sanctuary serviced by the levitical priests is merely a copy made by human hands, while Jesus has entered the "real thing," the true place of God's dwelling and therefore locus of mediation. The Yom Kippur ritual lends meaning both to Jesus' passion, by which he cleanses the people (13:12), and to Jesus' ascension, by which he removes the memory of sin from God's presence, the memory that has stained and constrained human access to the divine. Not only is his death "for us," but his ascension is thus also "for us."

The author has also appealed to the rite of covenant inauguration, however, in his development of the significance of Jesus' priestly ministry. The death of Jesus, spoken of here with the ritual language of the application of blood to both people and sanctum, is at once an effective atonement and the solemnization of the new covenant spoken of by Jeremiah. The connection between atonement and covenant is facilitated by the fact that Jeremiah's "new covenant" is specifically about God's remembering sins no longer. The death of Jesus is thus taken by our author as a "witnessing" to both parties that this new covenant is in effect (a testimony appropriately carried out in both Exodus 24:1-8 and here by the mediator of the covenant).

The author's focus throughout this central exposition on the heavenly cult, apart from conveying convictions about the death and ascension of Jesus, draws the audience's attention away from the life of the world into an alternative reality, the reality of which is reinforced even as the author describes the events and landscape there — particularly as he describes those events and places as more "real" or "genuine" than earthly realities.[36] An essential component of his ideology is the belief that this world is far less important and lasting than the heavenly realm, the locus of the addressees' hope. That world must be more real to the hearers than this world if they are to endure the loss of many

---

36. "Real" is not to be taken as synonymous with "material," however, as if human blood was taken into the unshakable realm and spattered on God's throne. The author uses this ritual model to indicate the meaning of Christ's death and ascension. The earthly rite does not determine what Jesus must *do* in the divine realm, but rather indicates what Jesus' entrance there means for the believers.

components of "happiness" here for the sake of their hope. When the author describes as "real" the events of Christ's priestly acts in the heavenly sanctuary, this may help to secure the hearers' conviction of the reality of that realm he wants them to value. The use of Platonic categories to establish the relative worth of the heavenly realm and the visible realm in chapters 8–9 (types, shadows, and copies as opposed to the genuine articles, the originals, and the like) similarly supports this ideology.

A third antithesis follows in 9:25-26, which returns to the contrast between Christ's single sacrifice and the annual sacrifices of the levitical high priest: Jesus entered heaven itself "not in order to offer himself many times, as the high priest enters the holy places annually with the blood of another, since then it would have been necessary for him to suffer many times from the foundation of the world: but now he has appeared at the consummation of the ages to do away with sin once for all through the sacrifice of himself." The author has already noted that Jesus' once-for-all sacrifice accomplishes what the annual rites of Yom Kippur could not (9:7-14), and he now begins to return to this point of contrast at greater length (10:1-4 will focus on this exclusively). As opposed to the high priests, who enter their holy place every year with blood not their own, Jesus decisively entered the true holy place once. The distinction between "another's blood" and the "sacrifice of himself" shows not only the greater quality of Jesus' sacrifice but also the greater degree of investment of Jesus in this task of mediation. He literally poured himself out to restore his clients' access to God's favor. Any observer would agree that Jesus was a unique individual whose appearance on earth and whose death occurred only once in history. The historical dimension of the incarnation becomes now proof that Jesus' single sacrifice is all that his priesthood required.

At this point the eschatological dimension enters into the cultic argument (as it will again in 10:13). Jesus' priestly act occurs not only within history but at the end of history. The church is not the only group fed by the streams of Judaism to consider the decisive removal of sin as an important feature of God's end-time activity. The author of the *Testament of Levi* also looks forward to the messianic priest doing away with sin: "on the basis of his priesthood, sin will cease" (*T. Levi* 18:9). The prophecy of Jeremiah quoted in Hebrews regards both the forgetting of past sins and the doing of present righteousness as features of this new covenant and messianic era. "Sin will cease" not only because sins are forgiven and forgotten but also because human beings are effectively equipped to bring forth the fruits of righteousness, living lives pleasing to God (see Heb. 11:6; 12:18; 13:16, 21). Reminding the hearers that Jesus' appearance was an eschatological event reinforces the impression that the author would make on them from the beginning to the end of this sermon: they stand at the threshold of their inheritance, of their entry into their "rest" and "unshakable kingdom." The time for rewarding the loyal and subjugating the contrary is at the door, and Christians have only to hold fast to their commitments "yet a very short while" (see especially 10:36-39).

The introduction of the inauguration of the end time with the life and death of Jesus impels the author to include the consummation of these end-time events within his cultic exposition: "Just as it is in store for human beings to die once, and after this the judgment, so also Christ, having offered himself once in order to bear away the sins of many, will appear a second time (without connection with sin) for the deliverance of those who are eagerly waiting for him" (9:27-28). The first half of this sentence has a maximlike ring to it, related to such apophthegms as "human beings die once" (Homer *Od.* 12.22).[37] The maxim about death followed by judgment reinforces the author's strategic warning that leaving the group does not mean escaping danger, specifically in the form of being held accountable by the God whose Son they spurned. Given the near-universal acceptance of this maxim, which could be accepted from a Jewish, Christian, or Greco-Roman worldview,[38] the believers should have their eyes firmly fixed on meeting that crisis successfully rather than allowing their gaze to drift away out of concern for the relatively minor crises brought on by the hostility of sinners.

This truism serves as an analogy that will prove (or at least elucidate) the following claim about Jesus: just as the pattern of death followed by judgment is established as an absolute for all humanity, so also Christ dies once and then comes into the judgment. The difference, of course, is that Jesus will come not to face judgment but to act as judge of the contrary and rewarder of the faithful. The author again describes Jesus' death as a "bearing away of the sins of many," a phrase recontextualized from Isaiah 53:12, showing that the author reads that text also as a witness to the meaning of the cross.[39] Those who have received that act of beneficence and responded with loyalty and gratitude will enjoy the gift of deliverance (σωτηρία) at the time of Christ's coming the second time.[40] The author's use of the term "salvation" for the

---

37. ἅπαξ θνῄσκουσ' ἄνθρωποι, cited in Lane, *Hebrews 9–13*, 249.

38. Attridge (*Hebrews*, 265) seeks to link the postmortem judgment here with the immediate judgment of the soul recounted in Greek myths rather than an eschatological judgment. While this could be predicated of the maxim on its own, the context of 9:27-28, which concludes with the second coming of Christ (a key event in Christian eschatology, leading up to judgment), argues in favor of eschatological judgment here.

39. Compare Heb. 9:28, εἰς τὸ πολλῶν ἀνενεγκεῖν ἁμαρτίας, with Isa. 53:12, ἁμαρτίας πολλῶν ἀνήνεγκεν. The idea that the death of the faithful, Torah-observant Jew could atone for the sins of the nation and restore God's favor is prominent in 4 Macc. 6:29-31; 17:21-22, which may represent an intermediate step between the Isaianic servant song and Christian cultural reflection on the meaning of Jesus' death (see "A Closer Look: Voluntary Death and Atonement," 275-78 above; deSilva, *4 Maccabees*, 137-45).

40. Brooke Foss Westcott (*The Epistle to the Hebrews: The Greek Text with Notes and*

benefit that believers will receive on the day of Christ's appearing is quite different from the use of the term in Ephesians, for example, to describe a *fait accompli*. The pastoral need that the author addresses, namely, stimulating a forward-looking attitude that will endure unto the end, is well served by calling the hearers' attention to the future dimension of God's "deliverance" of those who are in Christ Jesus. Collapsing the breadth of what the NT authors consider "salvation" into any one facet of that process of salvation (reconciliation with God through "accepting Christ," joining the people of God through baptism, or being delivered from the cataclysm that will end "the present, evil age" and being brought into the kingdom of God) weakens the impact that the biblical concept of "salvation" can have on Christians' lives, pointing us not only backward to what God has done in our lives but also forward, making us long for what God will yet do for the faithful ones who live out their response of gratitude and reverence.

The hearers live between the first appearance, when Jesus sanctified them by his blood, and the second appearance, when he shall reward the faithful (and judge the disobedient). If the addressees accept this depiction of the principal coordinates between which they must chart their course through this life, they will accept it as expedient and thus live to preserve what Christ has accomplished for them, lest they face judgment instead of reward. The author will appeal to these considerations explicitly in 10:26-31. Possession of a cleansed conscience (9:14) will be a most valuable benefit in light of the judgment that is coming (4:12-13), as well as in light of one's enjoyment of the current access to God's very presence.

10:1-18

The author returns to consider the cause of the inability of the first covenant sacrifices to "perfect those drawing near" (10:1),[41] a phrase directly recalling 9:9, where the author describes the "gifts and sacrifices" offered in the first tent

---

Essays [London: Macmillan, 1920], 278) and Lane (*Hebrews 9–13*, 250) find that a close correspondence can be discerned between the rites on Yom Kippur and the career of Jesus: the people awaited the high priest's return from the inner sanctum with eager expectation, since his reemergence would signal that God had accepted the sacrifice. While this may linger in the background of the author's mind, he does not draw attention to this connection explicitly and, indeed, has himself moved away from describing Jesus' ministry through an analogy with the Yom Kippur rites (thus rightly Attridge, *Hebrews*, 266) by explicitly introducing the analogy from the experience common to all humanity in 9:27.

41. "Perfect" here retains the connotations of removing awareness of sin from the conscience of the worshiper (9:9, 14) as well as ending the limitations on access to God so as to bring "those who draw near" across the threshold into the true holy place.

as "unable to perfect the worshipers with regard to the conscience":[42] "For the Law, holding a shadow of the good things that were about to come and not the very likeness of those things, can never perfect those drawing near by means of the same annual sacrifices that they offer perpetually" (10:1). "Shadow," once applied merely to the earthly copy of the heavenly tabernacle (8:5), is now extended to describe the nature of the whole cultic law. It lacks efficacy because it lacks real "substance," vaguely pointing away from itself to that rite which possesses the necessary substance to remove sins. Hebrews 10:1-10 will confirm the "shadowy" nature of the old rites, the climactic proof being an oracle from Scripture itself that describes the relationship between first and new cultus (Ps. 40:6-8 [LXX 39:7-9]).

The Platonic categories of "shadow" and "reality" continue to reinforce the necessity and reality of the new priesthood. That is, if the nature of the first covenant as "type" is accepted, then that covenant and its apparatus becomes a proof, in effect, of the "realities" of the new covenant (just as the observation of many chairs demonstrated for Plato the reality of an ideal chair, something that existed in the province of the mind that captured the essence of a chair and enabled all its copies to be recognized as such). The ministry of Jesus provides the "image" of which the old rites were but shadowy representations. The term used for "image" here (εἰκών) is also used in the LXX version of Genesis 1:26, where God determines to make humanity after his "image." The author of Hebrews departs from Platonic thinking, however, in his temporal frame: the Law is the shadow of the real things that are, in respect to Torah, future — the "good things about to come" and that "have come" in the high priesthood of Jesus (see 9:11, where Jesus is described as "high priest of the good things that came into being").

The fact that the sacrifices prescribed by Torah (and here the author thinks chiefly of the Day of Atonement rites) occur year in and year out is taken as a sign of their ineffectiveness. The author attempts to provide a proof of this from the contrary: if they were able to cleanse the conscience, "would they not have ceased being offered on account of the worshipers, cleansed once for all, having sins no longer on their conscience?" (10:2). The unstated assumption here is that cleansing the conscience should be a one-time act, that sins will not return to beset the conscience anew. Again, the two sides of the new covenant in Jeremiah's oracle, the removal of old sins and the living out of what pleases God (so as not to defile the conscience anew), may be in view.

The annual repetition of sacrifices — indeed, the legislated repetition — demonstrates the inefficacy of that system. The author therefore posits that the endless sacrifices achieve a different goal. Rather than remove sins, "in these

---

42. Hebrews 9:9 and 10:1 share the formula: negative particle + δύναμαι + τελειόω + participle for worshiper.

there is an annual reminder of sins" (10:3). This claim appears to be based on a
generalization of Numbers 5:15 (LXX),[43] the sacrifice that brings the sins of the
suspected adulteress to remembrance. The author takes the specific effect of the
sacrifice offered by a jealous husband to make his wife conscience stricken and
make her guilt come into the open and applies it as a general principle even to
the Yom Kippur sacrifices. Such a generalization of a specific law was not
unique to this author. Philo, for example, uses this text as proof that the sacrifice of the nonvirtuous person, or the person whose heart is not in the rite, does
nothing but remind God of their sinfulness (*Plant.* 108).[44] Hebrews merely extends the principle even further: whether one is vicious or committed to virtue,
the sacrifices of Yom Kippur do nothing save to bring to mind one's stained
conscience year after year.

This is, of course, an ideologically motivated presentation of Yom Kippur,
which for its participants was more than a mere reminder of sins. The element
of remembering sins was for the express purpose of purgation, which was to be
accomplished annually. If *Ben Sira* 50 is a reminiscence of a Yom Kippur rite,[45]
it appears to have been festive and, one must assume, regarded by the participants as effective and even triumphant. Leviticus 16:30, moreover, gives every
indication that the ritual is supposed to "work": "on this day, atonement shall
be made for you, to cleanse you; from all your sins you shall be clean before the
LORD" (NRSV). The effects are aptly summarized by Jacob Milgrom:

> On each Yom Kippur, the high priest purged the entire sanctuary, including
> the adytum, of Israel's presumptuous wrongs (16:16) while, in the scapegoat
> rite, he purged a penitent Israel of all its sins (16:21). The purgative rites
> aimed not only to persuade the divine presence to remain in the sanctuary
> (i.e., with Israel) but also to repair the strained relations between a now re-
> pentant Israel and its God.[46]

The author of Hebrews might concede that the rites "repair" the relationship
but would assert that they do not particularly improve the relationship. Still decisive in his mind is the strict limitation on access to God under the first covenant and its rites. Yom Kippur perpetuated the limited, graded access to God
prescribed by Torah, but it never served to breach the barriers that separated Is-

---

43. ἀνάμνησις ἁμαρτιῶν in Heb. 10:3 bears a striking verbal similarity to ἀνα-
μιμνήσκουσα ἁμαρτιῶν in Num. 5:15 (LXX).

44. Cited by Attridge, *Hebrews,* 272-73.

45. So J. G. Snaith, *Ecclesiasticus* (Cambridge Bible Commentary; Cambridge: Cambridge University Press, 1974), 251. In light of the critique of this reading in F. O Fearghail,
"Sir 50, 5-21: Yom Kippur or the Daily Whole Offering?" (*Bib* 59 [1978]: 301-16), this connection must remain tentative.

46. *Leviticus I–XVI,* 55.

rael from God. In an ultimate sense, then, it never made the people truly "clean before the LORD" (Lev. 16:30).[47]

To prove this radical negation of Yom Kippur's efficacy, the author adduces the principle that "it is impossible for the blood of bulls and goats to take away sins" (10:4), that is, to cleanse or perfect the conscience of the worshiper (9:9, 14). This rationale for the claims made in 10:1-2, however, will itself need to be demonstrated from an appeal to ancient authority. What defense can the author offer in the light of the possible objection that Leviticus 16:30 (a verse from the very chapter that has been supplying the author with much of his imagery) supports the efficacy of animal sacrifices, as does Leviticus 17:11, the backbone of Torah's sacrificial system: "the life of the flesh is in the blood; and I have given it to you for making atonement for your lives upon the altar; for, as life, it is the blood that makes atonement" (NRSV)?

Critique of animal sacrifices is common in the Israelite prophets, who are mainly concerned that sacrificial rituals not be regarded as a medicine against the consequences of unmitigated dedication to oppression and injustice. These prophets already begin to elevate the value of obedience over sin offering, stressing the importance of the internalization of the positive values of love and mercy in one's dealings and the avoidance of injustice and exploitation (Hos. 6:6; Amos 5:21-24; Isa. 1:16-17). Oracles of God speaking about God's dissatisfaction with — even loathing and rejection of — the performance of rites without the accompanying dedication of heart and life abound.[48] Isaiah 1:11-13 is typical: "'what to me is the plethora of your offerings,' says the Lord. 'I am full of the burnt offerings of rams and the fat of lambs, and I do not want the blood of bulls and goats (αἷμα ταύρων καὶ τράγων)'. . . . bringing offerings is useless." This passage is particularly important on account of the evidence of oral-scribal recontextualization: the author of Hebrews has used the phrase "the blood of bulls and goats" (αἷμα ταύρων καὶ τράγων) twice during his exposition

---

47. A change in anthropology — a move from the more integrated, ancient Israelite conception of the human being in which interior and exterior aspects of a person were not radically distinguished toward a post-Hellenistic conception that posited a bifurcation between the external and the internal reaches of a human being — seems to stand behind the author's critique of levitical rites. It would not have occurred to the compilers of Leviticus to draw a line between cleansing of the skin and cleansing of the heart: a single rite cleansed the *person*. The author of Hebrews, stepping into history having the benefit of the prophetic critique of priestly ritual and centuries of Hellenization behind him, can now question Lev. 16:30 as to the degree of cleansing of the person it provides and conclude that it is a mere external rite (9:9-10, 13).

48. See also Jer. 7:21-23, in which God even denies giving commands about sacrifices when he delivered the Hebrews, calling rather for obedience to God's voice; Hos. 6:6. Psalm 51:16-19 goes even further, replacing the desirability of animal sacrifices in God's sight with the desirability of the interior sacrifice of a "broken and contrite heart."

(9:13; 10:4). What was in the prophetic texts an attempt to safeguard the integrity of the sacrificial system becomes in Hebrews a declaration of the inefficacy of the system itself.

While the author of Hebrews has many contemporary allies in his critique of animal sacrifices,[49] he relies on exegesis of Scripture rather than popular sentiment to demonstrate his point. In 10:5-10, he introduces an interpretation of Psalm 39:7-9 (LXX; MT 40:6-8), a text that provides the perfect solution for his needs since it can be read as an oracle of God decreeing the replacement of the animal sacrificial system with the voluntary offering of a single human victim. Only the version of this psalm preserved in the LXX would be useful for the author's argument. The MT reads: "sacrifice and offering you do not desire, but ears you have dug for me; you have not required burnt offering and sin offering. Then I said, 'See, I come. In the scroll of the book it is written concerning me; I delight to do your will, O my God; your law is within my heart.'" The psalmist's confession, "ears you have dug for me," suggests that obedience to Torah (the provision of ears to hear and heed God's commandments) is to replace the transgression of Torah, which makes the animal sacrifices (still regarded as effective) necessary. The LXX translators render "ears you have dug for me" as "a body you have prepared for me." It is impossible to enter the mind of the translator, but this change might have been introduced as a more aesthetically pleasing image, the "digging of ears" being a potentially ugly image. Whatever the rationale, the MT and LXX represent precisely the same meaning — obedience to Torah (being given a body with which to perform God's covenant stipulations) pleases God, whereas transgression followed by atoning sacrifices will not please God (although it may secure forgiveness).

The author of Hebrews, however, finds a very different interpretation when he applies this psalm to the lips of Jesus (an exegetical practice already encountered in 2:12-13). Combining his conviction that certain Scriptures find their true meaning when placed on Jesus' lips and his understanding that a later word from God can correct, clarify, or nullify an earlier one, the author finds in this psalm strong scriptural support for the claim that the first kind of sacrifice is set aside in order to make room for the second (see his application of Jer. 31:31-34 to the two covenants):

> Therefore when he comes into the world he says, "you did not want sacrifice and offering, but you prepared a body for me: you are not pleased with whole burnt offerings and sin offerings. Then I said: 'Behold, I come — in the chapter of the book it is written concerning me — to do your will, O God.' Saying

---

49. See Thompson, *Beginnings*, 103-15; Harold W. Attridge, "The Philosophical Critique of Religion under the Early Empire," *ANRW* 2.16.1 (1978): 45-78; Everett C. Ferguson, "Spiritual Sacrifice in Early Christianity and Its Environment," *ANRW* 2.23.2 (1980): 1151-89.

higher up that "sacrifices and offerings" and "whole burnt offerings and sin offerings you have neither wanted nor take pleasure in," which things are offered according to the law, then he says, "Behold, I come to do your will." He removes the first in order to make the second to stand, by which will we have been sanctified through the offering of the body of Jesus Christ once for all. (10:5-10)

The author's shaping of his quotation, together with a few glosses, leads the reader rather unobtrusively to arrive with the author at the confirmation of his point. The introductory phrase, "therefore when he comes into the world he says," subtly sets the hermeneutical context for interpreting the Psalms passage. Jesus — specifically in his incarnation — becomes the speaker of this oracle. The preparation of a body is now heard as the Son taking on the same "flesh and blood" shared by the many sisters and brothers (see Heb. 2:9, 14). The author heightens the psalm's language with regard to the burnt offerings and sin offerings. In the known versions of the LXX, God either "did not ask for" these or, in two important manuscripts (S, A), "did not seek" them. Now the more neutral language becomes an announcement of God's displeasure with such rites. The author has strategically truncated his quotation in the second half, where the speaker's own response to God is discussed. Psalm 39:9 (LXX) reads "I have decided to do your will (τοῦ ποιῆσαι τὸ θέλημά σου ὁ θεός μου ἐβουλήθην), O my God, and your law is in the midst of my bowels." By omitting the main verb "I have decided" (ἐβουλήθην), the author of Hebrews now makes the doing of God's will the object of the verb "I come" (ἥκω . . . τοῦ ποιῆσαι τὸ θέλημά σου), a connection that will be reinforced explicitly in 10:9. This contributes to the incarnational reading of the psalm, wherein the assumption of a body and the "coming" of the Son into the world are the means for the accomplishment of God's "will." Omitting the second half of Psalm 39:9 (LXX), of course, serves to divorce the text from its original sense (performing God's Torah as the way to please God) and free it for its new witness to the work of Jesus.

After his recitation of the text (with modifications) in 10:5-7, the author works through the text a second time with interpretive glosses and a final conclusion. In 10:8, the author rearranges the synonymous parallelism of the actual quotation, conflating the two lines that deal with the animal sacrifices (the objects and verbs of the different clauses are now joined in a single clause). The gloss ("which are offered according to the Law") is added here in order to introduce a striking contrast between the prescriptions of Torah and the prescription of God's will, the topic of the second half of the quotation (10:9). Even though the Pentateuch clearly envisions God ordering these sacrifices, the weight of the prophetic critique (in both the prophetic writings and certain psalms) allows the author to drive a wedge between God's will and the sacrificial system. The restatement of Psalm 39:8-9a (LXX) brings a sharper focus to the quotation, leaving out the extraneous line ("in the chapter of the book it is written concerning me"):[50] "I have come to do your will." The author then draws the pregnant conclusion, which has now been facilitated by his rearrangement of the information of the psalm neatly into a "first" grouping of rites that God neither wants nor finds pleasure in (the animal sacrifices, the "blood of bulls and goats") and a "second" rite that speaks now of Jesus' presentation of his own body as the means for effecting God's will. The first cultus is "removed" by the testimony of the Scripture itself in order that the second cultus might be established.

The meaning of doing God's will in the psalm is clarified in 10:10: "by means of this will (θελήματι) we have been sanctified through the offering (προσφορᾶς) of the body (τοῦ σώματος) of Jesus Christ once for all." The author recontextualizes three key words of the Psalms quotation (προσφορά, σῶμα, θέλημά), embedding them in his decisive interpretation of the text. Since the quotation has been placed on the lips of Jesus rather than the typical worshiper who might sing the psalm, the body that accomplishes God's will can be seen in strict parallelism to the animal sacrifices that do not please God (i.e., do not accomplish God's will). In Hebrews, therefore, this psalm is transformed from a declaration of commitment to Torah observance as the better means of pleasing God into an oracle announcing the means by which God's will for the worshipers will be fulfilled — by the self-sacrifice of Jesus' body, prepared for him by God for this very purpose. Scripture thereby provides the warrant for the strange sacrifice that the early Church believes Christ's death to be. The affirmation here of the effect of Jesus' single sacrifice, the completed cleansing of the believer, will become the topic for the final section of this central exposition.

By drawing Psalm 110:1, a verse that has enjoyed tremendous prominence in this sermon (1:3, 13; 8:1; 10:12-13; 12:2), into the discussion of priestly work, the author is able to confirm his assertions about the once-for-all efficacy of Jesus' sacrifice in a surprising way:

> And every priest stands daily, ministering and offering frequently the same sacrifices that are never able to take away sins, but this one, having offered a single sacrifice on behalf of sins, sat down permanently at the right hand of God, for the time that remains waiting until his enemies are made a footstool for his feet. For by a single offering he has forever perfected those being sanctified. (10:11-14)

In terms of exegetical devices used by first-century readers of the OT, the author is "leading out of the implications" of Psalm 110:1, namely, the "sitting

---

50. Extraneous, that is, to this argument. While the author does not develop this line of the psalm, it is hardly a stretch, given his interpretation of the OT throughout, to imagine him reading it quite plainly as a testimony to the fact that the OT oracles concern the work of Jesus.

down" of Jesus. First, the author constructs an antithesis (emerging as one of the favorite rhetorical devices of this preacher) to contrast the priests, who stand daily officiating at their ineffective sacrifices, with Jesus, who offered one sacrifice and then "sat down." "Standing" (ἕστηκεν) was known as the posture of serving in the tabernacle. Deuteronomy, for example, speaks of the tribe of Levi as those set apart "to stand before God to serve" (παρεστάναι ἔναντι κυρίου λειτουργεῖν, Deut. 10:8). The Levites are described as those who "stand to minister there before the Lord" (οἱ Λευῖται οἱ παρεστηκότες ἐκεῖ ἔναντι κυρίου, Deut. 18:7).

In the priestly career of Jesus as the author reconstructs it from his Christocentric exegesis of key OT texts, Jesus first offers his life as the only acceptable sacrifice (Ps. 40:6-8), passes through the heavens to enter the holy place with his blood (analogy with the rites of Yom Kippur and covenant inauguration), and is then invited to sit down at God's right hand (Ps. 110:1). Significant, however, is the fact that even this session is envisioned as part of his priesthood (for Ps. 110:4 is the text that was used to demonstrate his appointment to the office of high priest). The author can therefore read the psalm as envisioning a priesthood that would not engage in repeated cultic activity, an activity that would require "standing," but a completed priestly act, after which the incumbent could "sit down permanently." Since he does not need to rise repeatedly to perform this sacrifice, it must have achieved decisive effects for the relationship of human beings and the holy God.

The recontextualization of Psalm 110:1 in Hebrews 10:12-13, both in terms of Jesus' session at God's right hand and in terms of the future subjection of his enemies as a footstool, highlights the completedness of Jesus' priestly service. The levitical priests must always return to the posture of standing because their work is never completed. There remains nothing more for Jesus to do, however, save to await the final subjugation of his enemies. By returning to this second component of Psalm 110:1, the author also returns to the eschatological chord that he struck in 9:26-28. Here, however, he highlights the second side of Jesus "appearing a second time" (9:28). It will not just be for rewarding those who eagerly await him, but also for the subjugation of those who oppose the Son rather than become his partners and "friends." For those committed to Christ and investing themselves fully in the hope of God's kingdom, this will be a welcome assurance that God will at last vindicate the honor of Jesus and his clients against those who have viciously opposed both (see 10:32-34; 12:2-3). For those wavering in that commitment, however, who are deliberating the advantages of withdrawing from open association with the name, these alternatives will help them to remain with the Christian group.

The exhortations that follow will reinforce the starkness of these alternatives. One may either enjoy the purification of the conscience, which allows unprecedented access to the very presence of God (and connection with this God as one's personal patron, 10:19-25; 4:14-16), or one may go to the opposite extreme and encounter the Son as enemy and God as judge and agent of punishment (10:26-31). For the addressees, the choice is posed thus: remain in the enjoyment of the benefits provided by the Son or break faith, show yourself ungrateful, and await subjugation and punishment hereafter. Once again, the author's strategy of keeping the hearers focused on the Son emerges as a dominant part of his plan for maintaining group commitment. It is their relationship with him that must dominate their deliberations, whatever this means for their relationship with the unbelieving population.

The author has framed 10:14 specifically as the answer to 10:1. Three shared terms or phrases mark this strongly as an *inclusio*. While the sacrifices prescribed by the Torah, which "they offer (προσφέρουσιν) perpetually (εἰς τὸ διηνεκὲς)," are unable "to perfect (τελειῶσαι)" those drawing near to God (10:1), Jesus has "by a single sacrifice (προσφορᾷ) perfected (τετελείωκεν) forever (εἰς τὸ διηνεκὲς)" the worshipers approaching God through him (10:14). In terms of epideictic topics, the author is again underscoring Jesus' honor and the nobility of his achievement, since he performed it first, alone, and completely (see Aristotle *Rh.* 1.9.25). Additionally, the amplification of the favor Christ has done for the believers should amplify as well the favor the recipient of Jesus' unparalleled gift of access to God feels in return (leading also to a heightened sense of the baseness of showing ingratitude and the necessity of living out a grateful response). The climactic point of this argument is also the climax in the author's development of the theme of the "perfection" of the believer (see "A Closer Look: Perfection in Hebrews"). The old covenant's rituals were a perpetual reminder of the restrictions on access to God, and access to the holy place was never broadened to the worshipers no matter how many sacrifices and sin offerings were performed. The fact that the priests remained outside the holy of holies and the people remained barred from both holy places was proof for the author that the animal sacrifices and other purificatory rites never achieved the level of cleansing for the people that God desired. They might make the people "clean before the Lord" (Lev. 16:30) with regard to their proper places outside direct contact with God's holiness, but they could not so cleanse the people that they could all come before the mercy seat together with the high priest. This, the author declares, is the sad state that necessitated the new covenant with its new rites, and that was overcome by Jesus' single offering. The first exhortation following this lengthy exposition (10:19-22) will urge the believers to retain the advantages brought to them by the new and fuller cleansing that Christ has effected. This exhortation, however, is already an echo of 4:14-16, such that, in essence, the argument of 5:1-10 and 7:1– 10:18 has served to show why the exhortation of 4:14-16 can be acted upon by the hearers — why the hearers can indeed be assured of their access to God's presence and God's timely help for their perseverence in their Christian pilgrimage to their better city and homeland.

In a concluding paragraph the author returns to the foundational text announcing the new covenant, introducing a second recitation of Jeremiah 31:33-34 (see Heb. 8:8-12) to round out his exposition. Recitations of this particular oracle thus form an inclusion surrounding the whole discussion of 9:1–10:14. This reprise serves as a sort of scriptural *"Q.E.D."*[51] for the author's exposition, which has shown how this prophetic oracle was fulfilled in Jesus' death and postresurrection life. No lesser authority than the Holy Spirit is brought in to "bear witness" to the truth of what the author has been expounding:[52]

> And the Holy Spirit also bears witness to us: for after saying "this is the covenant that I will make with them after those days, the Lord says: setting my laws upon their hearts, I will write them even upon their minds, and their sins and their transgressions I will certainly remember no longer." Where there is forgiveness of these, there is no longer an offering for sin. (10:15-18)

The fact of the new covenant's inauguration (a premise basic to Christian culture and not likely to be disputed among the hearers) means, according to the oracle in Jeremiah, the decisive forgiveness of sins. The author has now spent considerable time presenting Christ's death as the sacrifice that inaugurates the new covenant and effects the decisive purgation of sins so that God will no longer "remember" them (Christ's entry into the heavenly sanctum to "cleanse" the genuine mercy seat of the defilement of human sin would correspond to the removal of human sin from God's awareness).

Once again the author's shaping of the recitation is apparent. First, he reads the covenant as being made by God "with them" rather than with "the house of Israel," perhaps to remove the ethnic and historic limitations on the oracle, easing its direct application to the mixed body of Jews and Gentiles in the church.[53] Second, he omits several components of Jeremiah 31:33b-34a: the words about God and the people belonging to one another, the cessation of the need for one to teach his or her neighbor, as well as the promise of being merciful. Rather, the focus is solely on the writing of the laws in the hearts and minds and on the forgetting of sins (underscored by the author's addition of the synonymous "and their misdeeds," καὶ τῶν ἀνομιῶν αὐτῶν). The author may have omitted the reference to no longer teaching one's neighbor because he specifically directs the congregation to engage in mutual "teaching" (5:11-14), reminding one another of the hope and promise that should urge them all for-

---

51. *Quod erat demonstrandum*, "which was the thing to be proven." Logical and mathematical proofs employ this abbreviation at the close of the demonstration, upon the derivation of the theorem that was stated at the outset of the proof as the hypothesis to be tested.

52. The author's conviction that the Spirit of God speaks through the words of the OT is evident from the introduction of Ps. 95:7-11 in Heb. 3:7 and Jer. 31:33-34 here.

53. Thus, suggestively, Attridge, *Hebrews*, 281.

ward in their journey. The omission of the other elements appears to have no motivation other than to focus the oracle on the internalization of God's Law and the removal of sins from God's own memory.

Some scribes introduced at 10:17 the words "he adds" in order to balance "after he says" in 10:15. Several commentators follow the ancient scribes' division of the oracle into two parts, the second beginning at 10:17.[54] The author, however, may very well use words from the quotation itself to provide this balance:

> "After saying" (μετὰ γὰρ τὸ εἰρηκέναι, 10:15)
> "The Lord says" (λέγει κύριος, 10:17).[55]

Such a division, together with an inventory of what components of the oracle the author chose to include, would underscore the dual promise of the new covenant: not only God's promise to remove the sins that stood as an obstacle between God and his people, but also God's promise to equip the people with an interior awareness of what pleases God in order that the people would be able to live obediently and in such a manner as pleased God. The author further exhorts the congregation to take hold of both benefits provided under the new covenant: he calls them to seize the advantage of going boldly to the very throne of God (4:14-16; 10:19-25), and he calls them to live out lives that God regards with approval (6:9-12; 12:28; 13:1-21).

Since the single act of Jesus provided the decisive cleansing that makes possible the decisive removal of sins ("forgiveness" [ἄφεσις] of sins replaces the "remembrance" [ἀνάμνησις] of sins under the first covenant), a fact attested by God's own declaration to forego future remembrance of sins, there is no more place for a sin offering. On the one hand, this statement can be read positively, as an affirmation of the decisive efficacy of Jesus' death on our behalf. On the other hand, the author will return shortly to the lack of provision for future sin offerings as part of his most threatening warning not to depart from the one who has made the decisive and final sin offering (10:26-31).

Summary

While the author of Hebrews is willing to acknowledge that the animal sacrifices and other rites performed by the levitical priests effect a certain "external" cleansing (Lev. 16:30), he perceives from the ongoing operation of those sacri-

---

54. Ellingworth, *Hebrews*, 514; Lane, *Hebrews 9–13*, 254 and note dd.
55. Michel, *Der Brief an die Hebräer*, 341; Attridge, *Hebrews*, 281.

fices that a deeper, fuller cleansing awaited the people of God. The Torah-prescribed sacrifices, repeated every year without end, continually left the worshipers outside the holy places. This signaled for the author their failure to "cleanse" or "perfect" the inner person, the "conscience." While they may have been cleansed from external defilement so as to survive at some distance from the holy God, they were not cleansed from their interior defilement so that they might come into the very presence of God. The author's underlying conviction is that human beings were meant, in the purpose of God, to travel "the way into the holy places" and be fitted to enter. "Perfection" language throughout Hebrews 7–10 is connected with this divine purpose: the Law and all its apparatus was unable to "perfect" those drawing near to God, unable to achieve that fitting of the conscience to stand in the presence of the holy God (7:11, 19; 9:9; 10:1). Its inefficacy is made only more evident by the endless repetition of the "same sacrifices" (10:1-4, 11).

The new covenant announced by Jeremiah, however, promises the removal of sins from the very memory of God and the implanting of the way to please God upon the human mind and heart. It is the core conviction of the early Church that Jesus inaugurates a new covenant between God and humanity. The author of Hebrews finds in the rituals of Yom Kippur and of the ratification of the Sinai covenant the language to express the significance of Jesus' death as the sacrifice that inaugurates the new covenant, specifically as this is formulated by Jeremiah. The author presents the coming of the Son of God to take on our flesh and blood, the offering up of this body by the Son, and the ascension of the Son into the divine realm as the witness to us and to God that the sins that polluted the inner person were removed and that divine favor toward the believer was fully restored. The worshiper would at last be "cleansed" throughout and able to come into God's very presence (as 10:19-25 will invite the hearers to do). Both aspects of the covenant — the removal of the obstacles to approaching God and the inscribing of the way of God upon the heart — are fulfilled in Christ's ministry, for the believers have been purged from "dead works" and are newly equipped "to serve the living God" (9:14), a service that will be developed throughout the following exhortation.

Of special interest is the way in which the author has grounded the work of Jesus in the texts of the OT: even while the first covenant is "obsolete" (8:13) in terms of a means of approaching God, the "oracles of God" remain the essential foundation for legitimating and comprehending the new arrangements. Thus the rites of Torah, understood as forward-looking types of the new rites, legitimate the death of Jesus as a necessity in the divine plan, the fruition of shadowy revelations. Specific oracles such as Psalm 39:7-9 (LXX; MT 40:6-8) are read as authoritative proof that God has set aside the rites of the OT as inadequate and has prepared a body for the Son with which to accomplish at last God's will for the perfecting of his people, bringing them to that state in which they can enter their divinely appointed goal. The conjunction of the discussion of sacrifice with the messianic reading of Psalm 110 provides a "proof" of the complete and permanent effectiveness of Jesus' sacrifice from the fact that he "sits down" at God's right hand at the completion of his single offering. Such a *via demonstrationis* shows clearly the relationship of Christian culture to Jewish culture. The two cultures agree that the OT contains the abiding revelation of God's will; the Christian culture develops its own reading to display how it enjoys the true fulfillment of that revelation.

This central exposition has highlighted the nobility of Jesus' death and achievement in a number of ways that are immediately recognizable as topics of encomium, so as to deepen and reinforce the hearer's admiration for and gratitude toward Jesus. The rhetorical goal of this section, however, tends even more strongly toward deliberative topics: the author has developed a lengthy exposition of the unprecedented advantages and present goods that the hearers enjoy on account of Jesus' priestly mediation (his brokerage of God's favor). They have received the purification and access to God toward which the entire history of God's dealings with his people has been moving. The exhortations (10:19-39) that the author builds upon this expositional foundation ask the Christians to weigh the advantages they enjoy now on account of their connection with Jesus (as well as the promises of benefits yet to come) against the advantages of returning to the unbelievers' world, and to weigh the danger and loss that dissociation from Jesus and his people would entail against the continued endurance of the hostility of sinners. These central chapters are calculated to impel the hearers closer to the throne of favor (and thus closer to one another, finding their center in their Christian fellowship and shared hope), and to counter any centrifugal forces that might lead them to exchange such unparalleled advantages for eternal degradation and exclusion from favor. Having shown them how they stand in greater proximity to the sacred and to the world that alone is "real" and "abiding," the author has equipped them ideologically to sustain their existence socially as a distinctive group culture.

Bridging the Horizons

If the limitation of access to God and the holy places maintained under the old covenant rites was the "imperfect" state of affairs in God's sight, overcome at great cost to Jesus, we need to take care that we, as the people of the new covenant, do not fashion our religious life after the pattern of the earthly sanctuary. Our author calls the old order "obsolete," but the pattern of the mass of worshipers leaving prayer, intercession, praise, and ministry to the "professionals" persists in many congregations. The good news announced by this author is that every believer — not only those Christians set apart for full-time ministry — has been given the unparalleled honor of coming before God at any time and of carrying out the service that God has appointed for him or her.

The life of the believer is conceived in sacral terms by the author of Hebrews. "Drawing near" to God (7:25), moving across the threshold into the "holy places" (10:19-20), being "sanctified" (9:14; 10:14), and, in light of the background of Exodus 29, even being "perfected" are all actions done by or to those who are priests.[56] The emphasis on Jesus as our "forerunner" underscores the fact that believers can now in prayer, and later in person, enter the heavenly sanctum and stand in God's very presence. The description of Christian activity as "service" and "worship" (λατρεύειν, 9:14; 12:28) again sets the believers in the role of priests, enjoying a better access to God than even the priests of the first tabernacle (8:5; 13:10). Finally, the fact that believers are called to offer "sacrifices" of worship, witness, and love and service (13:15-16) casts their daily activity in the language of priestly activity.

The author of Hebrews, however, falls short of ever calling the believers "priests," something that the authors of 1 Peter and Revelation are not reticent to do (1 Pet. 2:9-10; Rev. 1:5-6; 5:9-10). It has been suggested that the author of Hebrews does not take this step so as not to obscure the unique priestly role of Jesus and the efficacy of his single sacrifice.[57] I think the reason is more profound than this. The author's point in these chapters appears to be the obliteration of the distinction between priest and lay in Christ's sacrifice and under the new covenant. It was precisely this distinction that reinforced the graded access to God under the old covenant. While Isaiah (61:1-7) enjoyed the vision of all Israel serving as priests on behalf of the nations — already a notable broadening of priesthood beyond genealogical bounds and qualifications — even this vision still maintains the distinction between those who can have direct access to God and those who can have only mediated access. For Isaiah, God's kingdom would see all Israelites functioning as priests for all the nations. The author of Hebrews does not use this image to describe the Christian community. The new covenant breaks beyond even the considerably more generous boundaries of Isaiah's vision. God's perfect vision for the unshakable kingdom has no room for the maintenance of any graded access to God's presence and favor.

In light of this announcement, then, it is incumbent upon all Christians

---

56. Nelson, *Raising Up a Faithful Priest,* 61: "It was only the priest who dared 'draw near' and cross into sacred space to effect the sacrificial movement from the profane to the sacred. The Hebrew Bible, therefore, defined priesthood by the issue of 'access' (Lev. 10:3; Ezek. 44:15-16). Priests were those who could stand before Yahweh to serve (Deut. 10:8), those who might approach Yahweh (Exod. 19:22), enter Yahweh's presence (Exod. 28:35), or go up to the altar (1 Sam. 2:28). This pivotal right of access was denied to the blemished priest (Lev. 21:23) and to laypeople and Levites (Num. 16:40)."

57. Ibid., 152.

to take up the privileges that have been won for them by the death and life of Jesus, and upon the professional clergy to equip and empower their sisters and brothers for the full spectrum of ministries to which we are called (see further Eph. 4:11-13; 6:18). The removal of all barriers now to our access to God calls us to diligent ministry in prayer and outreach, joining in the work of priests, which is the announcement of the reconciliation of God and human beings and the calling of others into the new and intimate way of relating to God, which Jesus has opened up for us (2 Cor. 5:14-15, 18-20).

A second word that the author of Hebrews speaks across the centuries concerns the reliability of Jesus and the certainty that his death has brought God and humanity together in complete reconciliation. The church has throughout the ages sought models and images that helped to convey the significance of Jesus' death for our relationship with God, from judicial models of Jesus bearing our punishment in our place to more relational models of Jesus' death as the visible expression of God's love for us. The author of Hebrews digs deep into the OT heritage of the Christian Church to discover models that will help his congregation understand what Jesus' death means for them, selecting the models of the Day of Atonement ritual and the covenant inauguration rites. By this model he can highlight Jesus' personal investment in securing a renewed relationship between believers and God (he pours his own body and blood into the task); he can suggest that, in Jesus' death in our realm and ascension to God's realm, there is the assurance of removing the defilement of transgressions not only from our consciences but from God's memory as well (a witness to us that we are now completely "right with God"); through contrast with the layout of the OT tabernacle, he can indicate the level of intimacy with God now possible. When the hearers of this sermon (in any age) look at Jesus, the author wants them to see the proof that, in every sense, all is right between them and God, and that God is open to hear their petitions and favorably disposed to meet them at their place of need. Whatever circumstances they find themselves in — in the midst of illness or ostracism or loss or any of those situations that may suggest divine disfavor — God wants them to be assured of his favor, and that he will lead the steadfast home to a better end.

The author of Hebrews also emphasizes the future aspect of salvation, the consummation of our journey in faith when we will be brought into the "rest" of the "homeland" and the "city" that God has prepared (1:14; 4:1, 11; 11:16).[58] Many Christians are accustomed to think of salvation as something we already

---

58. He differs in this regard from the author of Ephesians, who views salvation as a completed action — "by grace you have been saved" (Eph. 2:5, 8). In various contexts, Paul can speak of salvation as an ongoing process, describing believers as "those who are being saved" (1 Cor. 1:18; 2 Cor. 2:15), as well as pointing ahead to a future deliverance (Rom. 5:9-10; 13:11).

possess, something that already happened. The salvation that God has prepared for us, however, is not exhausted by the gifts we presently enjoy. Hebrews speaks at length of the forgiveness of sins and the renewed relationship with God as our parent and patron (Heb. 4:14-16; 10:1-22) — components of what other authors label "salvation." He focuses us, however, on the final attainment of salvation in order to promote endurance and diligence among his hearers, to fix their hearts in their shaky and unsupportive world on that goal and hope which alone brings peace and stability to their walk.

Our task in the interim is to remain faithful to our reconciled divine patron and committed to the people called by God's name, to show loyalty in the face of an incredulous, sometimes mocking, sometimes hostile society, and to wait eagerly for Christ (9:28). This waiting means choosing our activities, setting our priorities, and shaping our ambitions in light of that day when Christ shall appear a second time. In this way, as we pour ourselves into witness, worship, and acts of love and sharing, we fulfill the law written in our hearts and minds, living lives "pleasing to God" (12:28; 13:16, 21). Honoring the cleansing and forgiveness that Jesus has gained for us at no less a price than his blood and suffering, we commit ourselves to avoid new defilements of the conscience.

Draw Near to God and to Each Other: 10:19-39

Overview

The remainder of the sermon "to the Hebrews" consists of the author's exhortation to the believers concerning their proper response to Jesus' ministry on their behalf, the response of steadfastness made possible by the confidence, hope, and assurance that they have been given. These exhortations seek to orient the hearers to the world so that they will persevere within the group and witness to the distinctive hope of the Christian confession. As the author urges them to take advantage of their access to God by drawing near to him in assembling themselves together for worship, he establishes the Christian assembly as the hub or center of their lives in this world. Motion away from this hub (i.e., defection or "shrinking back") signals motion away from the divine center of the cosmos. The unbelievers are "outside" this center, but their attempts at reclaiming their Christian neighbors are now seen as attempts not at drawing believers "back" toward a normal life but at drawing them "away" from their God-given privileges and destiny. The believers' eyes will be fixed by the author on this destiny, and even if they cannot see the end of their journey (the heavenly homeland, city, or unshakable kingdom), they can "look to" their pioneer on that journey and press on to glory.

As this climactic exhortation opens in 10:19-25, the author supplies an unmistakable echo of the exhortation in 4:14-16 that preceded his "long and difficult word." He thus creates a major *inclusio* around the central expository section:[1]

---

1. This *inclusio* was developed in Nauck, "Zum Aufbau des Hebräerbriefes," 200-203; Guthrie (*Structure of Hebrews*, 79-80) refined and extended the parallels.

4:14-16	10:19-23
4:14 Ἔχοντες οὖν ἀρχιερέα μέγαν	10:19, 21 Ἔχοντες οὖν . . . ἱερέα μέγαν
"Having therefore a great high priest"	"Having therefore . . . a great priest"
4:14 Ἰησοῦν	10:19 Ἰησοῦ
"Jesus"	"Jesus"
4:14 κρατῶμεν τῆς ὁμολογίας	10:23 κατέχωμεν τὴν ὁμολογίαν
"Let us hold fast the confession"	"Let us hold fast the confession"
4:16 παρρησίας	10:19 παρρησίαν
"Boldness"	"Boldness"
4:16 προσερχώμεθα οὖν μετὰ	10:22 προσερχώμεθα μετὰ . . .
"Let us draw near then with . . ."	"Let us draw near with . . ."

The author thus underscores the particular advantage enjoyed by the hearers from their relationship with the unfailing mediator of divine favor, Jesus, and from the course of action that should follow from such enjoyment, that is, the continued profession of trust in Jesus and hope for the eternal benefactions. The movement of the hearers' ambitions, hopes, and even bodies must be toward the God whose favor has been secured and who is approached together with the whole body of the consecrated daughters and sons.

Hebrews 10:19-25, then, outlines the suitable response to Christ's costly gift of access to God and reiterates the exhortation of 4:14-16, adding specifically the communal aspect of this response (10:24-25). Hebrews 10:26-31 supports the exhortation of 10:19-25 by depicting the dreadful consequences that follow upon the ignoble, ungrateful response of ignoring or throwing away this costly gift (interpreting movement away from the group strategically as the "intentional sin" for which there is no sacrifice). Hebrews 10:32-39 invites the hearers to continue in the path they had so nobly pursued in earlier times (and were, to some extent, still pursuing, 6:9-10) and concludes with a citation of ancient authority confirming the salutary effects of remaining loyal and firm and the deleterious effects of "shrinking back" or "falling away." The hearers are explicitly invited to identify themselves with the former stance.

The identification of "faith" or "trust" (πίστις) as the quality that, in opposition to "shrinking back," leads to the "preservation of the soul" (10:39) invites the author to develop the meaning and posture of "faith." Thus the encomium on πίστις is embedded in this exhortation (11:1–12:3), as the author develops first through a definition and then through a host of examples how this particular virtue manifests itself. Hebrews 12:1-3 provides the exhortation that closes the encomium on "faith" (Jesus' example completing the list of examples of faith), segueing directly into a sequence of related exhortations (12:4-29). The sermon closes (13:1-25) with moral instructions and exhortations that develop how one is to fulfill the exhortation of 12:28, namely, that the believers hold onto gratitude, "through which we worship God in a well pleasing manner." Mutual service (13:1-4, 16), trust in the divine patron (13:5-6), loyalty to Jesus (13:11-14), and worship (13:15) are all essential aspects of this manifestation of gratitude for what the believers are "receiving" at the eschatological shaking (12:26-28).

Commentary

10:19-25

The author of *Rhetorica ad Alexandrum* (1433b29-34) writes that

> recapitulation is a brief reminder. It should be employed both at the end of a division of a speech and at the end of the whole. In summing up we shall recapitulate either in the form of a calculation [i.e., drawing conclusions] or of a proposal of policy [i.e., an exhortation to the audience to bear something in mind or to do something] or of a question or of an enumeration [i.e., of the points proven so far].

Hebrews 10:19-25 provides a recapitulation in the form of a proposal for policy. On the one hand, these verses bring together the principal points of the preceding exposition, that is, the advantages enjoyed by the Christian community and the beneficial effects upon the worshipers of Jesus' sacrifice; on the other hand, they directly urge that certain actions be taken and certain courses be avoided on the basis of these principal points:

> Therefore, sisters and brothers, since by means of the blood of Jesus we have boldness for entrance into the holy places by the new and living path he opened up for us through the curtain (that is, through his flesh),[2] and since we have a great priest over the household of God, let us draw near with a true heart in the certainty of trust, having sprinkled our hearts from a bad conscience and having washed our body with clean water: let us hold unwavering the confession of hope, for the one who promised is reliable, and let us consider one another unto an outburst of love and good works, not abandoning the gathering together of one another, as is the habit of some, but encouraging one another — and this all the more as you see the Day drawing nearer. (10:19-25)

---

2. Lane (*Hebrews 9–13*, 275-76, note j) argues convincingly that this parenthetical remark clarifies not the content or material of the "veil" but rather the "way" in which the believers may enter that holy place. It stands as a parallel to "by means of the blood of Jesus" in 10:19. "Flesh" is metonymy for Jesus' sacrificial use of that flesh (see 10:5-10).

Jesus' effective sacrifice on the addressees' behalf, cleansing their consciences and not merely effecting an external purification, has "perfected" them, bringing them to their complete, whole, and therefore "holy" and "integrated" state. They have been granted what no previous age enjoyed: the sanctification that will allow them to cross the thresholds of the holy place and the holy of holies and to stand in God's very presence.[3] Because of the weighty restrictions on access to God and the severe consequences that descend upon the "encroacher" — the one who dares to go nearer to God than his or her holiness would allow — the addressees' "boldness" (παρρησία) is truly a significant and new endowment from God. They may enter openly, daringly, confidently those inner places where God dwells. παρρησία historically referred to the "boldness of speech" that was the right exercised in the Greek *polis* by the free citizen. It is a virtue that continued to be celebrated by the philosophers as an image of the freedom of the wise person who refused to cringe before a tyrant and exercised his or her "free speech" in bold defiance of the tyrant's power to compel acquiescence or flattery. The author reminds the Christians that they, too, have been granted a special, ennobling privilege to come before God as welcome children rather than cringing suppliants standing afar off.[4] This is a great good and an advantage to be preserved at all costs.

This "boldness" is conceived in specifically cultic terms, for the believers are equipped to "enter the holy places." The hearers have been consecrated to go where only priests and the high priest can go, and they have thus become boundary crossers,[5] priests in practice. The fact that the hearers will be called upon to offer sacrifices to God in 13:15-16 reinforces this definition of the worshiping body of the church as a community of those who have been consecrated to carry out sacred duties before God. The emphasis, however, should lie here not specifically on their ordination to priesthood (for the author never calls them priests, even though other NT authors are not reluctant to use that term; cf. 1 Pet. 2:6-10; Rev. 1:5-6), but on their breaking through of the boundaries to God's presence represented by the architecture and personnel of the earthly sanctuary, and, indeed, on the sacralization of all aspects of the life of the believer, for whom both worship in the assembly and acts of service or confession in the "profane" world are equally "sacrifices with which God is well pleased" (13:15-16).

The believers' possession now of the boldness "for entering the holy places" (εἰς τὴν εἴσοδον τῶν ἁγίων) recalls Christ's earlier entrance "into the

---

3. Entering the "holy places" is a metonym for entering God's presence: the author refers to the content or occupant by means of the container or dwelling.

4. See the helpful discussion of this term in Thompson, *Beginnings*, 32-33.

5. See the discussion of priests as "boundary-crossers" in Nelson, *Raising Up a Faithful Priest*, 83, 144.

holy places" (εἰς τὰ ἅγια, 9:12, 24-25). The earlier claim that Jesus is truly our forerunner in regard to his entry into the divine, unshakable realm (6:19-20) is being developed in 9:1–10:22. Jesus passed "behind the curtain," and the believers' hope follows after him (6:19-20); now the author celebrates the discovery of that "new and living way through the curtain" (10:20), the "way into the holy places" (τὴν τῶν ἁγίων ὁδὸν, 9:8), which had formerly been obscured under the first covenant. The "curtain" through which Jesus passed and the believers are now equipped to pass is not, however, the same as that second "curtain" separating the first from the second tent in the earthly model of the true sanctuary (9:2-4). The holy place they approach is certainly not the earthly sanctuary but the heavenly sanctum, the same "heaven itself" that Christ entered on their behalf (9:23-24). We would be mistaken, therefore, if we collapse "entry into the holy places" completely with that holy space created where the believing community gathers for prayer, worship, and mutual edification. The "way into the holy places" has now been revealed to the Christian community: they traverse that path proleptically in their communal worship but must wait until the eschatological "shaking" (12:26-27) to cross that threshold in an ultimate sense. They approach God's presence now in prayer openly and confidently, but still press on to "enter" the rest of God, the heavenly homeland, the abiding city, which holds their lasting and better possessions.[6] The author tells them, however, that they have already the full confidence to make that journey into the "real" realm, having been cleansed by the better sacrifice to go where even the levitical high priests could not.

The second good that the believers possess is "a great priest over the household of God" (10:21),[7] an expression that recalls the major theme of the exposition, first articulated at 2:17 and prominent throughout 4:14–10:18. The "Son over the house" in 3:6 now becomes a "great priest over God's house," but both terms underscore the same advantage for the hearers: the access to God's favor provided by the Mediator. Jesus' better priesthood means

---

6. Scholer (*Proleptic Priests*, 201) has drawn attention to the author's careful use of "entering" versus "approaching" or "drawing near" in the context of the heavenly holy places: "The careful distinction maintained in Heb[rews] is, therefore, a matter of life and death. Those living draw near or approach God. They have been granted the access to God which is appropriate to their still tangible, corporeal form of present, earthly existence. They have access to God 'as far as the conscience is concerned' (Heb. 9.9), that is, through prayer and worship . . . they approach the holy of holies. The deceased — the first-born who are enrolled in heaven, the spirits of just men made perfect — who are currently gathered around the throne (Heb. 12.22-24) have 'entered' into the heavenly holy of holies, i.e., into God's very presence (12.23)."

7. The expression "great priest" refers to the "high priest" in the LXX of Lev 21:10; Num 35:25, 28. The author is not therefore taking a step back from his naming of Jesus as "high priest" earlier in this sermon.

for the believers, however, a superior level of access to God's favor than previously available to those who approach God. Because of this "great priest," the believers may even now "approach the throne of favor with boldness" in order to "receive mercy and find favor for timely help" (4:16). The author underscores, then, the believers' access to God as their personal and communal patron,[8] who will provide them with the assistance they may need along their journey so as to persevere unto the reception of the benefactions promised at the end of that pilgrimage. The reappearance of the term "household of God" to describe the Christians reminds them of their kinship bonds with, and obligations toward, one another (this will become the direct basis for exhortation in 13:1-3), the nobility of their household, from which their individual honor derives, and the security that they have in the world from having God as the head and protector of this house and guarantor of the honor of its members.

By speaking so grandly of their access to God and embeddedness in God's household, the author seeks to engender confidence in the believers, giving them a hopeful orientation toward the world. Aristotle (*Rh*. 2.5.16) defined confidence as "the contrary of fear and that which gives confidence of that which causes fear, so that the hope of what is salutary is accompanied by an impression that it is quite near at hand, while the things to be feared are either non-existent or far off." Through Jesus, the believers are brought into the presence of God, near to one who has the will and power to provide help.[9] Thus the believer may say with the psalmist:

> The Lord is my light and my salvation; whom shall I fear? The Lord is the stronghold of my life; of whom shall I be afraid? . . . Though a host encamp against me, my heart shall not fear; though war arise against me, yet I will be confident. (Ps. 27:1, 3, RSV)

In emphasizing this benefit won by Christ for his clients, the author has moved to the topic of security, according to the author of the *Rhetorica ad Herennium* the other component of "advantage" and the goal of deliberative oratory (together with honor).[10] Their allegiance to Christ gives them access to the resources that will help them in the face of the exigencies of their life as Christians in society.

Given the advantages they enjoy, the author urges the believers to "draw

---

8. Compare Epictetus *Diss*. 4.1.91-98 for a Greco-Roman evaluation of the worth of such a privilege.

9. Compare Aristotle *Rh*. 2.5.17: People may be made to feel confident "if there are means of help, either great or numerous, or both."

10. *Rhet. Her*. 3.2.3: "Advantage in political deliberation has two aspects: Security and Honour *(tutam, honestam)*. To consider Security is to provide some plan or other for ensuring the avoidance of a present or imminent danger."

near" (10:22; cf. 4:14-16).[11] This is precisely the opposite of "shrinking back," the alternative course of action, which the author fears some hearers have in view (cf. 10:37-39) and others have begun to enact (10:25). They are to draw near with a "true heart in the full assurance of trust" (μετὰ ἀληθινῆς καρδίας ἐν πληροφορίᾳ πίστεως). The believer should be confident that Jesus has achieved the cleansing of the whole person of the Christian, fitting him or her for this final approach to the unshakable realm, as well as be fully assured of the reliability of the God who promised the believers an abiding homeland in the divine realm (10:23 will underscore this second aspect). They have prepared themselves to come before God's burning presence by means of their appropriation of the benefits of Jesus' sacrifice, having been cleansed in both body and heart for this confident approach to God. The blood of Jesus has, metaphorically speaking, sprinkled their hearts to cleanse them of the pollution of a bad conscience (the primary topic of 9:1–10:18).

The outward and visible sign of this interior cleansing[12] is the washing of their bodies "with clean water." The appearance of water suddenly as an agent of washing is rather unexpected, especially as the author had been discussing the use of animal blood for the ritual cleansing of the flesh (9:13).[13] Here, however, the text displays interaction with the Christian cultural phenomenon of baptism, the rite of entrance into the Christian community.[14] Baptism is frequently interpreted in the NT as a symbol for the appropriation of the purifying effects of Christ's sacrifice (Rom. 6:4; 1 Pet. 3:21), and since it would have been the common experience of the addressees (particularly if they are part of the Pauline mission), they would most naturally relate this past "washing" of which the author speaks with their own past experience of coming to the water of baptism.

---

11. The verb προσερχώμεθα often appears in cultic contexts to speak of approach to God (thus Nelson, *Raising Up a Faithful Priest*, 151; Scholer, *Proleptic Priests*, 91-149). Here, in the context of entering the holy places and going behind the curtain, the resonances with the cult are strong.

12. James D. G. Dunn, *Baptism in the Holy Spirit: A Re-examination of the New Testament Teaching on the Gift of the Holy Spirit in Relation to Pentecost* (Philadelphia: Westminster, 1970), 211-14.

13. The expression he uses, however, bears close resemblance to OT texts that prescribe ritual bathing as a prerequisite for priestly service or consecration (see, *inter alia*, Exod. 29:4; Lev. 16:4). Attridge (*Hebrews*, 289 n. 61) suggests that the washing with "clean water" may recall specifically Ezekiel's description of God's future act of renewing his people: "I will sprinkle clean water upon you, and you shall be clean from all your uncleannesses, and from all your idols I will cleanse you. A new heart I will give you. . . . And I will put my Spirit within you and cause you to walk in my statutes" (Ezek. 36:25-27, RSV). This OT text resonates with Jer. 31:31-34, which we have seen to be central for our author, on the important point of God's setting his law in the interior person.

14. Thus Moffatt, *Hebrews*, 144; Spicq, *L'Épître aux Hébreux*, 2:317; Bruce, *Hebrews*, 250-51; Attridge, *Hebrews*, 289; Lane, *Hebrews 9–13*, 287.

The addressees, then, are reminded of their identity as those who have been cleansed by baptism and the blood of Jesus from every external and internal defilement that bars safe access to God. They have been made "holy," having crossed the boundary between the profane and sacred, separating the defiled from the clean. The author's application of purity language at this point will reinforce the differences, and hence boundaries, between those "inside" the group and those "outside," who remain defiled by the "dead works" that characterize their lives. Since they have been prepared and consecrated, they should continue to act on that consecration rather than show contempt for it by turning away (10:26-29) and refusing to press on in the journey for which Jesus' death has prepared them.

"Drawing near" (10:22) is a rather vague suggestion for a course of action, but it serves to concentrate the hearers on "approaching" God, taking further steps toward God and the end of their Christian pilgrimage (cf. 6:1). The author will assist the hearers to concretize this course of action in the exhortations that follow, which provide specific components of what it means to "draw near." First, he calls the hearers yet again to "hold unwavering the confession of hope." The author had already called them to "hold onto the confession" (4:14) as well as to hold fast to the "boldness and claim to honor that belong to hope" (3:6). The repetition demonstrates the importance of this exhortation to "hold on" to the core beliefs and expectations of the Christian culture. William Lane translates this phrase so as to put the emphasis on hope, which should be kept unwavering: "let us continue to hold fast the hope we profess without wavering."[15] The author has chosen, however, "the confession of hope" rather than "the hope of our confession." The author's expression allows for the subjective dimension, which Lane highlights, but also opens up the possibility of reading the verse as a call to the public confession of this hope without vacillation.[16]

Such a reading would be in keeping with other uses of the word in the later Pauline mission (1 Tim. 6:12-13), as well as with the awareness that those who receive benefits from a patron should not be reticent about publicizing that benefit. Seneca put this quite sharply (*Ben.* 2.23.1): "a debt that you are ashamed to acknowledge you should not accept." The author is concerned elsewhere with the public testimony that Christians give, particularly with the negative witness that the apostate bears to the outside world concerning Christ and the value of his

---

15. *Hebrews 9–13*, 288.

16. That the accent should fall upon the "confession" (τὴν ὁμολογίαν) is underscored by the fact that the adjective "unwavering" (ἀκλινῆ) agrees with it, and not with "hope." Believers are called to bear a constant testimony to their hope both internally (I would not wish to lose the subjective aspect highlighted by Lane), never wavering in this testimony to themselves, and externally, bearing a constant witness to this hope through continued investment in the Christian group despite any countermeasures unbelievers may throw their way.

gifts (6:4-6). The subjective dimension of holding onto the "confession of hope" must manifest itself in the visible witness to that hope, especially in terms of continued, open association with the "people of God," who live for that hope (as opposed to hiding or terminating those connections so as to escape the negative consequences of association with the name of Jesus, 10:25, 37-39).

The rationale for "holding on" is the faithfulness or reliability of God, "the one who promised." This recalls the topic of 6:13-20 rather directly, where the author sought to amplify the reliability of the believers' hope through God's promise and his oath (the "two immutable things about which it is impossible for God to lie"). The author affirms the reliability of the believers' divine patron and calls them to affirm God's reliability as well through their continued open association of themselves with the hope of receiving God's promised benefactions and with the group that shares this hope. Hiding one's confession of hope (or, to approach this again from the subjective dimension, giving up on this hope) signals distrust of the God who promised. The author's use of the negative example of the wilderness generation, which distrusted God's promise, wavered in its confession of hope, and fell short of God's gift, has already prepared the hearers not to make such a poor choice.

Second, the author urges the hearers to consider one another (κατα-νοῶμεν), to look at and observe one another. The result is outbursts of love and good works as one believer discovers another to be in need or comes to appreciate another's distinctive contributions to the body. Several English translations render this verse "let us consider how to provoke one another to love and good deeds" (NRSV; see also NASV; RSV; NIV). The exhortation pertains more to doing good works and showing love as the addressees look around at their fellow believers, observing their situations and persons attentively.[17] The author may, moreover, seek to establish an emulative environment: "paying attention to one another" will not only lead to seeing and responding to need, but also will involve seeing one's sisters' and brothers' noble deeds and becoming zealous to emulate them, such that doing good stimulates more well-doing. The author approaches the congregation first by urging them to look at each other, to see each other, to notice one another. He does not merely exhort them to preach well-doing, but to be engaged in it first, and then perchance to stimulate it and be stimulated into well-doing by mutual example. This connects with the author's exhortations throughout Hebrews (3:12-14; 12:15-17; 13:1-3, 16) to create the sort of intra-group relationships and support structures that make it possible, even preferable,

---

17. So rightly Lane, *Hebrews 9–13*, 273; Ellingworth, *Hebrews*, 526. The NKJV and NJB provide better translations at this point: "Let us be concerned for one another, to stir a response in love and good works" (NJB); "Let us consider one another so as to stir up love and good works" (NKJV).

to put up with the snubbing and hostility from without rather than to give up the love and fellowship and mutual regard that exist within.

The remainder of the exhortation strengthens this point, using antithesis to contrast the wrong course of action with the advantageous course of action: "not abandoning the gathering together of yourselves, . . . but encouraging one another . . ." (10:25). The author acknowledges that some Christians have pulled back from open association with the community — some are in the habit of forsaking the gathering of the church. Some have considered, in effect, that the cost of holding onto God's promises is greater than those promises are worth (an evaluation that will provoke the warning of 10:26-31). They can no longer withstand their neighbors' shaming techniques and are now beginning to feel ashamed of that which once gave them confidence. Such withdrawal, however, is contrary to all sense of gratitude, which involves declaring openly one's debt to the giver and praising publicly the benefactor who has given great gifts (cf. Seneca *Ben.* 2.23.1; 2.24.4).

Withdrawing from the community does not merely mean that the individual falls short of God's gift; withdrawing discourages those who remain and diminishes the group as a whole. To paraphrase John Donne's well-known apophthegm, "each member's defection diminishes me" and my determination to hold on to the costly hope. When one's fellow believers begin to defect, it makes one wonder about the value of the enterprise and the wisdom of remaining faithful. The other believers enjoyed the same advantages and knew the same God through the same mediator. Now they decide that society's acceptance is worth more after all. On what basis should I persevere when our common experience was not sufficient to make them regard perseverance as the advantageous (or self-evident) course of action?

Rather than draw back, they are urged to become more forthright in encouraging others to hold fast. Rather than divest, they are to invest their energies more and more. The ultimate motive adduced by the author? The ultimate "day" draws nearer. As the eschatological clock ticks on, the believers should become more fervent rather than less fervent. The reference to the "day drawing nearer"[18] reminds the audience yet again (see the intrusions of this same day at 9:28 and 10:13) of the eschatological pole of their worldview. This will be a day of reward for the trusting and loyal, and contemplation of its proximity sustains commitment and investment in the interim. It will also be a day of punishment for the contrary, an occasion for "eternal judgment" (6:2), as the following passage will develop (10:26-31; also 10:35-39).

---

18. There is a widespread expectation in Christian culture as well as (other) apocalyptic circles of Judaism of the soon-approaching "Day of the Lord," when rewards and punishments will be meted out and the new order of God's rule activated; see 1 Thess. 5:1-9; Matt. 24–25; Acts 17:31; 2 Cor. 1:14; Rev. 1:7; 11:18.

Movement away from the group (10:25) is particularly what the author wants to avoid (see 3:12; 4:1; 6:6; 12:15-17), and he urges group members to interact with one another so as to prevent this exodus. It is a bad choice precisely because it is movement away from God, and one that, as the next passage will develop, actually shows cutting disregard for the beneficence of Christ, which cost the Mediator so dearly.

The author has focused the audience's attention now on the unique and unprecedented privileges that have been granted them thanks to the mediation of Jesus on their behalf. Cleansed within and without of every defilement that could make an encounter with God an occasion for fiery consumption rather than reception of favor, they have "boldness" to enter his very presence. In light of this astounding benefit, the author urges the hearers to "draw near" to God (rather than "turn away," 3:12, "shrink back," 10:38-39, or "drift away," 2:1). As they continue in their confession of Christ and in the hope to which that confession bears witness, as they continue to assemble with their fellow believers, and as they continue to grow in love and service toward one another, they also continue in the presence of God, who hears the prayers of his household and supplies them with help now and the promise of entrance into an unshakable kingdom at the dissolution of the material creation. Such a course of action, the author avers, would be feasible indeed since the believers have been prepared and equipped to arrive at the end of this journey. The author also hopes that the addressees will accept it as the expedient course, allowing them to maintain the advantages and goods won for them by Jesus and to attain yet greater goods.

10:26-31

The author supports his positive exhortation with a consideration of the alternative course: returning to a lifestyle of which the unbelieving neighbors would approve, withdrawing from visible associations with the Christian fellowship (2:1, 3; 3:12; 4:11; 6:12; 10:23, 25; 12:3, 16). In language strongly reminiscent of 6:4-8,[19] he censures the path of separating from the people of God for the sake of the "temporary pleasure of sin" (cf. 11:25) and posits its ultimate disadvantage as the course leading both to eternal dishonor and to the greatest of dangers (thus undermining the considerations of honor and security that might lead to that course):

---

19. Lane (*Hebrews 9–13*, 296-97) charts these similarities in a helpful table. Hebrews 6:4-8 and 6:9-12, with their alternation of appeals to fear and confidence, are both closely parallel to 10:26-31 and 10:32-36, respectively.

For if we intentionally continue to sin after receiving the knowledge of the truth, there remains no longer a sacrifice for sins, but a fearful expectation of judgment and of a zealous fire that is on the verge of consuming the opponents. Anyone violating the law of Moses dies without mercy on the word of two or three witnesses: of how much worse punishment will he or she be deemed worthy who tramples the Son of God underfoot and regards as common the blood of the covenant (by which he or she was sanctified) and insults the spirit of favor?! For we know the one who said "Vengeance belongs to me; I will pay back," and again "the Lord will judge his people." A fearful thing — to fall into the hands of the living God! (10:26-31)

The paragraph opens by naming the alternative course as an unjust one. Holding onto the confession of the Christian hope, intently looking to one another's needs and worth so as to arouse love and awaken good works, and faithfully gathering together for mutual confirmation and encouragement are all necessary if the believer is to complete the journey from the life he or she left behind at repentance and conversion to the life he or she is yet to possess beyond the visible creation. Failure to take up this course of action is strategically interpreted by the author as the "willful sin" for which no sacrifice exists. Hebrews 10:24-25 qualifies how 10:26 will be heard by the addressees — it will not be heard as a general reference to ongoing sins against which the believer might struggle, but more specifically as a reference to those who, despite knowing the truth of the deliverance and hope God provides (see 6:4-5), nevertheless choose the temporary benefits of hiding or abandoning their connection with the believing community (10:25; see 6:6). They prefer the friendship of sinners and the temporary enjoyment of sin (11:25) to the hardships that the people of God must endure in this world (11:25) on account of the hostility of sinners (12:3).[20]

The author alludes to Numbers 15:22-31, where Moses distinguishes between sins committed "unintentionally" (ἀκουσίως), for which there are prescribed sacrifices, and those committed arrogantly ("with a high hand"), for

---

20. Stedman (*Hebrews*, 111) is correct to affirm that this sin "is not the normal falterings of a Christian still learning how to walk in the Spirit," but he does not seek a contextual understanding of this sin in 10:26, preferring to describe it as "choosing to live for self behind a Christian veneer and refusing to be delivered from sin's reign. . . . Their life may appear to be fairly respectable when judged by the world's standards, but what it is like in God's sight is described in verses 28-30." Stedman has clearly abandoned commentary on Hebrews at this point, moving instead into preaching to a twentieth-century Western audience. The addressees themselves would have been most concerned to shed the "Christian veneer," for that is what made them unacceptable to their neighbors. Hebrews 10:28-30 describes, at least in the intention of the author, not the person who is Christian on the outside but refuses to be transformed on the insid; rather, it describes the person who shrinks back from being seen as Christian on the outside because of what that identification costs in a hostile society.

which there is only punishment.[21] This is recontextualized in the context of Christians who have come to the knowledge of what God requires and then have deliberately violated the patron-client bond. There remain no cultic provisions for a second cleansing since Christ's offering was a once-for-all event: the same affirmation that provided proof of decisive forgiveness and cleansing in 10:18 is now employed to underscore the importance of maintaining the relationship once formed. The censure of intentional wrongdoing is equal on the part of Greco-Roman authors. A course that involves the deliberate commission of evil is an "injustice" for which the severest punishments should be inflicted.[22] The adverb Ἑκουσίως, "willfully," brings this topic of injustice out forcefully,[23] as the action is shown to be voluntarily chosen, not compelled.

This might raise a significant issue for those believers who are especially wearied by society's pressures. They might well be reasoning that God would forgive their capitulation to such pressures. The author of 4 Maccabees, reflecting on the story of the tyrant Antiochus IV's attempts to compel an aged priest and seven youthful brothers by torture to break the Torah, places on the lips of the king this consideration: "whatever justice you revere will be merciful to you when

---

21. Milgrom (*Leviticus I–XVI*, 50) argues that "priestly legists [i.e., framers and interpreters of the legal code] . . . permit sacrificial expiation for a deliberate crime against God (knowingly taking a false oath) provided the person repents before he is apprehended." Rabbinic traditions testify to the later application of this principle. Milgrom (*Leviticus I–XVI*, 373) cites the following: "R. Simeon b. Lakish said: 'Great is repentance, which converts intentional sins into unintentional ones'" (*b. Yoma* 86b); "Because he has confessed his brazen and rebellious deeds it is as if they become as unintentional ones before him" (*Sipre Ahare* par 2:4, 6). He reads these principles as based on the precedent of Lev. 5:20-26 and Num. 5:6-8, whereby the Priestly writer "postulates a new category of jurisprudence: repentance as a factor in the mitigation of divine retribution" (*Leviticus I–XVI*, 375). The author of Hebrews, however, reveals no knowledge of such mitigating legislation (even within Torah, let alone later developments). Even if he does know of such provisions, he certainly expects no one among his audience to know them. Still working with Num. 15 (quite natural after his extensive excursion into Num. 14 in Heb 3:7–4:13), he expects the principle to go unquestioned and to have its full force.

22. Demosthenes attests this for classical Greek culture. In the speech "On the Crown" (*De corona* 274), he expresses as a truism that the one who "sins wilfully" (ἀδικεῖ ἑκών) receives "wrath and punishment" (ὀργὴν καὶ τιμωρίαν) while the one who "sins unknowingly" (ἄκων) receives "pardon in the place of punishment." The author of *Rhetorica ad Alexandrum* (1427a31-35) also elevates the important difference between intentional and unintentional crimes: "Define injustice as the deliberate commission of evil, and say that for offenses of that sort the severest penalties should be inflicted; declare that a harmful action done unwittingly is an error."

23. See Aristotle *Rh.* 1.10.3: "Let injustice, then, be defined as voluntarily causing injury contrary to the law. Now, the law is particular or general. By particular, I mean the written law in accordance with which a state is administered; by general, the unwritten regulations which appear to be universally recognized. Men act voluntarily when they know what they do, and do not act under compulsion."

you transgress under compulsion" (8:14); "consider this: if there is some power watching over this religion of yours, it will excuse you from any transgression that arises out of compulsion" (5:13). A small thing it would have been, perhaps, to save one's life by eating a mouthful of pork. By their courageous endurance of torture unto death, however, these martyrs (together with the mother of the brothers) showed a zeal and devotion to God that awakened the nation's loyalty to God and their ancestral ways and that lit the torch of faith for centuries to come. They decided that "no compulsion is more powerful than our obedience to the law" (5:16). The author of Hebrews seeks to lead his congregation to a similar stance (all the more given the fact that they have not yet had to resist to the point of martyrdom, 12:4). The defector, apostate, or cowardly believer is not allowed the unction of thinking that she or he yields to necessity by hiding his or her faith. Such a course remains a voluntary, willful violation of a compact (the universal law of being just and grateful to benefactors).

No "sacrifice for sins remains" for the willful sinner not only because of the once-for-all nature of Jesus' offering of himself, but because of the grave affront to God the Mediator, and to the blood itself, by the person who thinks such gifts not worth the cost of keeping them openly. Having received true knowledge about the fate of the world, the judgment of God, and the promises made to those who seek to please God, they nevertheless spurn these priceless advantages and choose to suppress the truth and deny their patron by "blending in" again with their non-Christian neighbors. All that is left for such people is God's judgment, the "expectation of an eager fire on the verge of consuming the adversaries" (10:27). The author employs the device of "vivid description," almost capturing the animate quality of fire "eating" the opponents. This is a recontextualization of Isaiah 26:11, "jealousy will take an uneducated people and now fire will eat the adversaries":

ζῆλος λήμψεται . . . καὶ νῦν πῦρ τοὺς ὑπεναντίους ἔδεται (Isa. 26:11)
πυρὸς ζῆλος ἐσθίειν μέλλοντος τοὺς ὑπεναντίους (Heb. 10:27)

The author of Hebrews has chosen to condense the Isaiah text by describing the fire as "jealous" and leaving out the remainder of the first of the two clauses, and to heighten the imminence of God's judgment (imminence being crucial to the arousal of the emotion of fear)[24] by changing the future tense of the verb ("will eat") to a verb expressive of "forthcoming" action (μέλλω).

---

24. Thus Aristotle, *Rh.* 2.5.1: "Let fear (φόβος) be defined as a painful or troubled feeling caused by the impression of an imminent evil that causes destruction or pain." Proximity of the evil is stressed: considerations will arouse fear "only if they appear to be not far off but near at hand and threatening. . . . The fearful thing itself appears to be near at hand, and danger is the approach of anything fearful" (2.5.2).

Those who refuse the course of action proposed by the author find themselves, then, facing the grim prospect of judgment, a forthcoming reality the severity of which is enhanced by 10:28-29, a classic lesser-to-greater argument.[25] The lesser case is provided from a generalizing reference to (and inexact recitation of) Deuteronomy 17:6: willful infractions of the Mosaic covenant resulted in execution "upon the testimony of two or three witnesses." The premise here left unstated is that Jesus is worthy of greater honor than Moses (Heb. 3:1-6).[26] The conclusion, expressed in the form of a question, posits proportionately greater punishment for willful infractions of the new bond between Jesus and the believers.[27] This enthymeme actually heightens the appeal to fear, since now a "punishment worse than death" is prescribed for the person who acts so as to embody rejection or devaluation of the gift.[28]

The author presents this act of violating the bond of gratitude toward Jesus and God in the most striking of terms. His strategy is to set drifting away from firm commitment to the group in the starkest of terms, making it so appalling that the wavering will "wake up" to the "real" nature of the course they contemplate, as if saying: "Look at what you're really doing if you withdraw from the group, if you value your neighbors' acceptance more than God's favor!" The alternative course is portrayed as a threefold offense against the honor of God, particularly heinous because such an assault violates the patron-client relationship, returning not gratitude but insult to the divine benefactor.[29]

---

25. Compare Héring, *Hebrews*, 94: "If rebellion against the Law of Moses entailed in certain cases capital punishment, those who show contempt for Christ must expect the worst for stronger reasons. It is another example of the well-known argument *a minore ad maius*, very much in vogue among the Rabbis, and which had already been used in 2:2 in order to give an almost identical proof."

26. A similar premise undergirds the lesser-to-greater enthymeme at 2:1-4, namely, the greater honor of the Son as messenger of the deliverance God has prepared (compared to the status of the angels, the messengers of the first covenant).

27. Attridge (*Hebrews*, 293 nn. 24-25) helpfully points to Philo's use of similar lesser-to-greater arguments underscoring the greater punishment and absence of an opportunity for repentance for the blasphemer: Moses "as good as proclaims . . . that no pardon must be granted to a blasphemer against God. For if those who have reviled mortal parents are led away for execution, what penalty must we consider that those have merited (τίνος ἀξίους χρὴ νομίζειν τιμωρίας) who take upon them to blaspheme the Father and Maker of the universe" (*Fug.* 84); "if he who swears a wrongful oath is guilty, how great a punishment does he deserve (πόσης ἄξιος τιμωρίας) who denies the truly existing God?" (*Spec. Leg.* 2.255).

28. Contrary to the advice of Aristotle ("And whenever you wish to arouse emotion, do not use an enthymeme, for it will either drive out the emotion or it will be useless," *Rh.* 3.17.8), the author of Hebrews embeds an enthymeme within an appeal to pathos. In this particular case, Aristotle's caveats about the effectiveness of one being muted or destroyed appear to be groundless.

29. Calvin (*Hebrews*, 132-33) insightfully underscores this aspect of the passage: "Now

First, the apostate is "one who has trampled upon the Son of God." The reminder that Jesus' title is "Son of God" (cf. Heb. 1:1-13; 3:1-6) both heightens the impudence of the offense and sets the affront within the context of God's own honor[30] and hence his desire to obtain satisfaction from the offenders.[31] The verb itself is an expression of contempt in keeping with the tendency to describe acts of honoring and dishonoring through physical representations. It is, in effect, the opposite of worshiping, of placing oneself at the feet of the Master (cf. the προσκύνησις of 1:6). Rather than taking one's proper place in submission and obedience to the Son of God, one treats him with the utmost scorn.[32] The author, in suggesting that the apostate "tramples upon the Son of God," creates a strikingly ironic and inappropriate image designed to make the hearers shrink from enacting such an affront. Indeed, the one who may be scorned now, and thus trampled, is the one at whose feet all his enemies will soon be brought into subjection (1:13; 10:13, 37).

The second and third phrases pertain more directly to a disregard for the gifts of God and a rejection of the patron-client relationship established with God through the brokerage (mediation) of Jesus. The one who continues in sin (i.e., abandons the people of God, cf. 11:25-26) "has regarded as profane the blood of the covenant with which he or she was sanctified." This "blood of the

---

it is more heinous to trample underfoot than to despise, and far other is the dignity of Christ than that of Moses. . . . He enhances this ingratitude by a comparison of benefits. It is an exceeding great indignity to count an unholy thing the blood of Christ, which is the material cause of our salvation; but this do they that revolt from the faith. . . . To do despite to Him [the Spirit of grace], by whom we are gifted with so many and so great benefits, is an impiety passing heinous. . . . Wherefore no marvel if God avenge so severely blasphemies of this kind; no marvel if he show himself inexorable to them that have trodden underfoot Christ the Mediator, who alone prevails with him on our behalf; no marvel if he stop the way of salvation to them that have spurned from them the one only guide, even his Holy Spirit."

30. Compare John 5:22-23, NRSV: "The Father . . . has given all judgment to the Son, so that all may honor the Son just as they honor the Father. Anyone who does not honor the Son does not honor the Father who sent him."

31. Delitzsch (*Hebrews*, 188) also appears to understand this passage in the context of a challenge to honor: "To trample Him under foot — the gracious and almighty Heir of all things, who is now seated at God's right hand — what a challenge to the Most High to inflict the severest and most crushing penalty!"

32. Delitzsch, *Hebrews*, 188: "Καταπατεῖν is not merely to reject or cast away as something unfit for use which men carelessly tread upon (Matt. v.13; Luke viii.5), but to trample down with ruthless contempt as an object of scorn or hatred (Matt. vii.6)." See also Spicq, *L'Épître aux Hébreux*, 2:324: "In trampling Jesus, the apostate has professed the most injurious and flagrant contempt for the person of the Son of God. καταπατέω is a verb of scorn," used also in Matt. 7:6 of salt that has lost its savor, denoting metaphorically the scorn that shall be earned by the disciple without fervor. For Josephus (*J. W.* 4.262), honoring and trampling form a pair of antonyms: the temple is honored (τετιμήμενος) by foreigners but trampled on (καταπατεῖται) by the Zealots.

covenant" (a phrase shared by Exod. 24:8 and Matt. 26:28, recited by the author already at 9:20) constitutes the means by which believers were decisively restored to divine favor, by which the sins that stood between people and God were removed from the very mind of God, and by which the consciences of the worshipers were at last perfected. The mention of blood and sanctification recalls most explicitly the central discourse on Jesus' offering of himself once-for-all — his death on the cross (12:2) in obedience to God (10:5-10) — on behalf of the addressees. The offense against this blood is described as a faulty evaluation[33] manifested in the abandoning of the Christian community and assimilation into the unbelieving society. Those who do not persevere in loyalty to Christ, but rather dishonor him by manifesting distrust and forsaking the confession of hope, show that they do not value his blood as that which has gained access for them to the greatest of benefits and the greatest of benefactors.[34] Such a failure to appreciate the worth of this gift would constitute a provocation of the benefactor, who would be slighted by this ingratitude and contempt for his gifts.[35]

Finally, the one who decides that the Broker's benefits (the greatest of which is access to God as patron) are not of sufficient value to merit bearing up with the society's abuse and scorn, bearing public testimony to this in his or her defection (see 6:6), "has outraged the Spirit of grace (τὸ πνεῦμα τῆς χάριτος ἐνυβρίσας)."[36] Ceslaus Spicq comments that "one could not make a more striking contrast than that between ὕβρις and χάρις,"[37] and indeed meeting favor and the promise of benefaction with insult is at once highly inappropriate and foolish. Dio expresses the larger society's condemnation of such a return, going

33. Spicq, *L'Épître aux Hébreux*, 2:324-25: "This scorn is completely conscious; the apostate has made a value judgement. ἡγέομαι does not have here its ordinary sense of 'drive, conduct,' but rather 'believe, think' (XI, 11) and more precisely 'esteem, evaluate' (XI, 26). . . . The renegade has considered common or profane the blood of Christ which has sealed the new covenant." See also Michel, *Der Brief an die Hebräer*, 236: "Whoever despises Christ also fails to appreciate the value of his blood."

34. Stedman (*Hebrews*, 112) equates "regarding as common the sanctifying blood" with the attitude that affirms that "religious activities ought to be enough to satisfy God." Once again, a "works versus faith" debate is being forced onto Hebrews, which gives no indication that such was the position of the addressees.

35. Regarding the benefactions of a great person lightly or of little value could easily provoke the wrath of the benefactor, whose honor alone should make every gift valuable. Hence the reaction of Brutus to the Xanthians (Plutarch *Brut.* 2.6-8): "The Xanthians ignored my benefactions, and have made their country a grave for their madness."

36. Compare Chrysostom (NPNF[1] 14:458; *PG* 63:144): "'And done despite unto the Spirit of grace.' For he that accepts not a benefit, does despite to the benefactor (ὕβρισε τὸν εὐεργετήσαντα)."

37. Spicq, *L'Épître aux Hébreux*, 2:325. His impression is confirmed by Seneca (*Ben.* 3.22.1): "Benefit and injury are the opposites of each other *(inter se contraria sunt beneficium et iniuria).*"

so far as to call it "impiety" (ἀσέβεια): "to commit an outrage against good men who have been the benefactors of the state (εὐεργέτας ὑβρίζειν), to annul the honours given them and to blot out their remembrance, I for my part do not see how that could be otherwise termed" (*Or.* 31.14).

This act is shameful in and of itself since it enacts ingratitude (the basest of vices). Such a show of ingratitude is not, however, without more pressing consequences. The client who insults rather than honors his or her benefactor and who responds with disloyalty rather than reliable service will be excluded from future benefits or any return from favor, and may even experience the wrath of the insulted patron (see discussion in 6:4-8). That the ingrate, and even more the one who returns insult for favor, merits "punishment" is commonplace in the first century.[38] The challenge to the honor of God and the Son results in God's vindication of their honor in the punishment of the offender. In this case, the omnipotence of the patron makes this threat fearsome indeed. God's choice of punishing would be considered nobler than "coming to terms" with those who have assaulted his honor, at least by Aristotle (*Rh.* 1.9.24) and other representatives of the dominant culture. The very word chosen by the author (τιμωρία) is also explained by Aristotle (*Rh.* 1.10.3)[39] and Aulus Gellius as particularly related to the restoration of the honor of the one assaulted through the degradation of the offender:

> It has been taught that there are three reasons for punishing crimes. One of these, which the Greeks call κόλασις or νουθεσία, is the infliction of punishment for the purpose of correction and reformation, in order that one who has done wrong thoughtlessly may become more careful and scrupulous. The second is called τιμωρία. . . . That reason for punishment exists when the dignity and prestige of the one who is sinned against must be maintained, lest the omission of punishment bring him into contempt and diminish the esteem in which he is held; and therefore they think that was given a name derived from the preservation of honour (τιμή). (Aulus Gellius *Attic Nights* 7.14.2-4)[40]

The punishment to be inflicted by God upon the ingrate is not to correct the ingrate but to restore God's slighted honor and perhaps to warn others not to

---

38. Seneca *Ben.* 4.16.2: "Who does not loathe the ungrateful man, a person who is unprofitable even to himself? And tell me, when you hear it said of someone: 'He is ungrateful for very great benefits,' what are your feelings? . . . I imagine you count him a worthless fellow, who should have, not a guardian, but punishment."

39. "There is a difference between revenge and punishment; the latter is inflicted in the interest of the sufferer [ostensibly for improvement?], the former in the interest of him who inflicts it, that he may obtain satisfaction (ἵνα ἀποπληρωθῇ)."

40. I am indebted to J. Neyrey for drawing my attention to this passage.

make the same mistake. Those who seek therefore to rehabilitate their image and worth in the eyes of their non-Christian neighbors by forsaking their open allegiance to the Son who brought them to God and made them fellow heirs of a great hope face a more weighty evaluation of their worth than society's. God, whose approval or censure should always be foremost in the believer's mind since it carries eternal weight, will think them "worthy" (ἀξιωθήσεται) of this degrading punishment in the company of all God's "opponents" (10:27), and God has the power and authority to enforce the appraisal.[41]

The passage seeks to remove several motives for what the author (though not the unbelieving neighbors) would consider "wrongdoing" and to undermine any case for actually pursuing the course of apostasy as advantageous. Aristotle (*Rh.* 1.12.1) writes that people "do wrong . . . when they think that their action will either be undiscovered, or if discovered will remain unpunished; or if it is punished, that the punishment will be less than the profit to themselves or to those for whom they care." The author of Hebrews appeals to the core belief in divine judgment to rule out the first motive and heightens the severity of the punishment (10:28-29) to counter the second. God is not a suitable choice of victim for injustice since there is no "chance for obtaining a merciful consideration" (*Rh.* 1.12.28): "there no longer remains a sacrifice for sin" (10:26; cf. 10:18), and thus the means of atonement are completely lacking. There is left only the expectation of a sentence to be carried out. The author has also cast the contrary course of action in the most unfavorable light possible: it is now an act of injustice perpetrated against the guilty person's benefactor, thus doubling the crime.[42] Amplification of the magnitude of the wrong is certainly also the effect of the triple description of the charge in 10:29 and of the suggestion that no adequate punishment can be imposed for this particular affront (one must at least go beyond the death penalty to find such a punishment).[43] A justly merited and inevitable destruction, then, will be the fate of those who outrage God's favorable spirit by rejecting his gifts and bringing shame upon the name of his Son.[44] As God's ene-

---

41. Delitzsch, *Hebrews*, 188: "In ἀξιωθήσεται we are to understand God Himself as the ἀξιῶν by whom all actions are weighed and their worth determined, and the measure of penalty needed to vindicate the majesty of the law laid down." Compare also Bernhard Weiß (*Der Hebräerbrief in zeitgeschichtlicher Beleuchtung* [Leipzig: J. C. Hinrichs, 1910], 540), who understands this verb as a divine passive denoting God's eschatological judgment.

42. Aristotle *Rh.* 1.14.6: a crime is greater "when committed against one who has been the guilty person's benefactor, for in that case, the wrongdoer is guilty of wrong twice over, in that he not only does wrong, but does not return good for good."

43. Aristotle *Rh.* 1.14.1-2: "Wrong acts are greater in proportion to the injustice from which they spring. . . . A wrong act is greater when there is no adequate punishment for it, but all are insufficient."

44. Josephus (*J.W.* 3.371-72) also uses this strategy in his attempt to dissuade his troops from carrying out their suicide pact: "And God — think you not that He is indignant

mies, they can look forward only to ascribed disgrace (i.e., "punishment") before the court of God on the day appointed for judgment.[45]

The impact of the appeal to fear and the reality of the author's threatened consequences are both sustained by citations of authoritative tradition, derived from the Song of Moses recorded in Deuteronomy 32. The author adduces these texts to emphasize his point that God avenges violations of his honor, which is the topic of the whole Song of Moses. He begins with a recitation of Deuteronomy 32:35: "for we know the one who said, 'Vengeance belongs to me; I will repay'" (Ἐμοὶ ἐκδίκησις, ἐγὼ ἀνταποδώσω). The author provides a version of Deuteronomy 32:35 that represents a conflation of the MT ("Vengeance is mine, and retribution") and LXX ("In the day of vengeance I will repay"). This was originally a promise by God to vindicate his own people after they were trodden upon by their enemies. Here it becomes a warning directed toward God's people. The author presents Deuteronomy 32:36 as a second quotation rather than as a continuation of the first ("and again, 'The Lord will judge his people'"). In the MT this verse clearly looks forward to God's vindicating the people: "The LORD will vindicate his people, and will have compassion on his servants." While the LXX version retains the synonymous parallelism that would support this same meaning, the choice of the word "judge" opens up the possibility of reading the verse as a warning of God's forthcoming judgment of the people. The author's separation of the two consecutive clauses as now two separate sayings would further support this threatening meaning. The terse, forceful statements from the Song of Moses concerning God's judgment are now brought to bear on the potential apostate, who must be reminded that "to fall into the hands of the living God is a fearful thing" (10:31). This conclusion continues to resonate with the Song of Moses, as God declares in Deuteronomy 32:39 that "there is none who shall deliver out of my hands." The ultimate danger that any human being could face is to encounter God, the judge of all, as an enemy. The addressees are reminded that there is one to fear, the one with power to inflict the punishment that is greater than death:

---

when people treat His gift with scorn (ὅταν ἄνθρωπος αὐτοῦ τὸ δῶρον ὑβρίζῃ;)? For it is from Him that we have received our being, and it is to Him that we should leave the decision to take it away. . . . How can he who casts out from his own body the deposit which God has placed there, hope to elude Him whom he has thus wronged (ἀδικούμενον)?"

45. See 2 Esdr. 8:56-61, RSV: "They despised the Most High, and were contemptuous of his law, and forsook his ways. Moreover, they have even trampled upon his righteous ones, and said in their hearts that there is no God — though knowing full well that they must die. . . . They themselves who were created have defiled the name of him who made them, and have been ungrateful to him who prepared life for them. Therefore my judgment is now drawing near." Compare also 2 Esdr. 9:10-12, RSV: "As many as did not acknowledge me in their lifetime, although they received my benefits, and as many as scorned my law while they still had freedom, and did not understand but despised it while an opportunity of repentance was still open to them, these must in torment acknowledge it after death."

the friendship of this one is worth maintaining even in the face of the hostility of "those who can kill the body but cannot kill the soul" (Matt. 10:28).

The author brings together an impressive array of rhetorical stratagems in his attempt to dissuade his hearers from withdrawing from their open commitment to the group and the Christian hope. Hebrews 10:26-31 is unmistakable as an appeal to pathos, specifically the emotion of fear (indeed, the culmination of a series of appeals to fear; see 2:1-4; 4:12-13; 6:4-8). The repetition of the word "fearful" (φοβερὰ, φοβερὸν) in 10:27 and 10:31 merely reinforces the effect created by the topics employed in this passage. Aristotle (*Rh.* 2.5.1) defines fear (φόβος) as "a painful or troubled feeling caused by the impression of an imminent evil (κακοῦ) that causes destruction or pain." The author has provided the prerequisite for fear in his depiction of the coming of God as judge and avenger, particularly as he underscores the imminence of this encounter (the modification of Isa. 26:11 in 10:27; the modification of Hab. 2:3-4 in 10:37-38). Aristotle suggests (*Rh.* 2.5.3, 5) that fear can be aroused also by signs of impending danger, such as the "enmity and anger (ὀργή) of those able to injure us in any way . . . and outraged virtue (ἀρετὴ ὑβριζομένη) when it has power, for it is evident that it always desires satisfaction." In showing a low estimation of the value of keeping the gifts provided by the Son of God, one knowingly incurs the wrath (ὀργή) of God, as anger is the expected response to a slight (all the more when one is slighted by those whom one desired to benefit; see Aristotle *Rh.* 2.2.8). The apostate has outraged the embodiment of the virtue of favor and generosity in insulting the Spirit of grace and thus can expect to be visited by an act of God's power seeking satisfaction. Fear is again heightened by the declaration of the impossibility of restoration (10:26), for after the transgresser has rejected the brokerage of Jesus there remains no mediator who can regain God's favor.[46]

This appeal to fear stands after an exhortation laden with appeals to the pathos of confidence (10:19-25), an emotion to which 10:32-35 returns. Each appeal to an emotion supports the author's goal of moving the recipients to commit themselves to "faith," that is, loyalty and trust, so as not to "shrink back unto destruction" (10:39). As the addressees are made to feel fear at the consequences of a certain course of action, they will recoil from the prospect of taking that course;[47] as they are made to feel confident and emboldened while con-

---

46. Aristotle *Rh.* 2.5.12: Fear is aroused "also when there is no possibility of help or it is not easy to obtain."

47. For those who are not seriously contemplating a course that would compromise loyalty and reverence for the One God, the words of 10:26-31, and 10:29 in particular, would have the potential to rouse indignation. As Aristotle avers, "if virtuous people do not obtain what is suitable to them, we feel indignant" (cf. *Rh.* 2.9.11). Here a just and honorable patron is not receiving what he deserves, but rather the opposite. This would reinforce the unwillingness of many hearers to go that route, since they are stirred up to understand how deeply unjust it would be.

templating the course of perseverance, they will choose to maintain that course. The horror and baseness of offending the divine patron should outweigh the temporary disadvantages of offending society through continued Christian commitment and rejection of such central values of the society as participation in idolatrous cults or ruler cult.

The dissuasion does not work on the emotions of the hearers alone, however: the emotional responses only serve to reinforce the author's appeal to *logos* (reason) as he demonstrates how deeply disadvantageous such a course would be. He interacts with quite a number of deliberative topics identified by the authors of *Rhetorica ad Alexandrum* and *Rhetorica ad Herennium*. Once again the topic of justice is prominent (see 6:4-12): returning injury to one who has shown favor is a primary topic of injustice, compounded here by the emphasis on the intentionality of the act ("willingly sinning after receiving knowledge of the truth"). Because it is unjust, such a course is inherently dishonorable. Equally prominent here, however, is the topic of security. The one who enacts ingratitude stands in imminent danger of suffering the vengeance of the God who acts to restore his honor and that of his Son (10:27, 29-31). This renders "drifting away" inexpedient to a high degree (recalling the importance of expediency — the preservation of existing goods and avoidance of evils — among the deliberative topics in *Rhetorica ad Alexandrum*). Violating the relationship with God through the Son leads to the expectation that extremely harmful things will occur (eternal judgment, a basic component of the Christian worldview, cf. 6:1-2). The harm is amplified as most final and ultimately will mean the utter degradation of the ingrate before the court of God (thus addressing the topic of honor as well). It is a much greater evil than the hostility of sinners endured but temporarily as the price of loyalty to the divine patron. Wisdom[48] should dictate, so the author will hope, that the hearers accept the course recommended in 10:23-25 (as in 10:35-36 and throughout the positive exhortations of Hebrews) as the honorable and only advantageous course.[49] The passage thus strongly serves to make the path of faithfulness (outlined in the immediate literary context of 10:19-25 and 10:32-39) more desirable, honorable, and advantageous, hence the path that the hearers are likely to choose.

---

48. See Aristotle *Rh*. 1.9.13: "Practical wisdom is a virtue of reason, which enables people to come to a wise decision in regard to good and evil things, which have been mentioned as connected with happiness."

49. Two other topics — that of the "pleasant" and the "necessary" — may also be at work as ancillary devices. The author's description of the experience of God's fiery vengeance briefly reminds the hearers of the unpleasantness of the consequences of affronting the living God. Contemplation of God's punishment of those who align themselves with the wicked is an important feature of apocalypticism (cf. Synoptic Gospel texts on "weeping and wailing," on the fire experienced by the rich man in Gehenna; Revelation), and the path the author opposes is certainly presented as the course with greater unpleasantness attaching to it.

The author's ideological strategy is also quite apparent in this paragraph. He turns the focus of the hearers once again from their visible circumstances and all those considerations that might move them to defect from their bold confession of clientage to Jesus toward their obligations to the divine patron and the dire consequences of dishonoring that one who looks on from above. Deciding that friendship with the world is more valuable than friendship with God, the author avers, is not merely a matter of withdrawing from a voluntary association that no longer "works" for the individual. It is an affront to the living God, whose Son gave his life in order to bring eternal benefactions to people. Those who have once tasted those gifts and then acted out their disregard for the gift and the Giver would meet with the punishment that reaffirms the honor and value of the gift and the giver. Once again the potential apostate is warned that leaving the group does not mean getting out from being under hostility and danger — it means exposing oneself to the greatest danger and loss. Leaving the group does not mean having nothing more to do with God, whose day of judgment and reward draws ever nearer. The real threat to the believer's honor is not continued association with the Christian group, even though this will mean continued lack of honor in the world's eyes. Rather, apostasy from the group poses the real and lasting threat to honor.

The passage concludes with a reaffirmation of what the addressees truly need to be fearing — not falling into the hands of their neighbors, but falling into the hands of the living God in God's capacity as judge and avenger (10:30-31). There lies the one danger to avoid at all costs, and no lesser danger should seduce one into a path that leads to the greater danger. The individual's relationship with God, therefore, remains in the forefront of the author's strategy — he seeks at every turn to focus their attention on the quality of that relationship as the leading consideration that should guide their actions and investments.

10:32-39

Hebrews 10:32–12:3 provide the addressees with a host of exemplars of the virtue of trust and firmness (πίστις). Aristotle long before had noted the close relationship of praise and advice: "Praise and counsels have a common aspect; for what you might suggest in counseling becomes encomium by a change in the phrase. . . . Accordingly, if you desire to praise, look what you would suggest; if you desire to suggest, look what you would praise" (*Rh.* 1.9.35-36). The author therefore sets out to praise those who have embodied the course he is advising. The effect of this encomium should be the arousal of the emotion of emulation: the hearers are encouraged and even made ambitious to embody the same virtue as these figures who have attained a praiseworthy remembrance. Significantly, the first example is not Jesus nor Moses nor even Abel. Rather, the hearers are pointed to their own past worthy conduct (10:32-36) as the best pattern for their imitation in the present.[50] The hinge between the preceding exhortations and the famous "faith chapter" is the author's appeal to the congregation to live up to their own example.

Appeals to a group's own past achievements often served as a basis for encouragement to future endeavors. At the climax of Tacitus's *Agricola* (33-34), the general rallies his troops with the words:

> The long road we have traveled, the forests we have threaded our way through, the estuaries we have crossed — all redound to our credit and honour as long as we keep our eyes to the front. . . . I would quote the examples of other armies to encourage you. As things are, you need only recall your own battle-honours, only question your own eyes.

The rhetorical effect is threefold. First, the appeal instills a sense of confidence that, as the group succeeded in performing what was required before, it would have the resources and stamina to succeed again.[51] Second, there is a reluctance to abandon an enterprise in which so much has already been invested. Finally, the general instills a sense of fear lest former achievements and honor be marred by failure to act and persevere in the present. Dio highlights the third of these in his paraphrase of the story of Philoctetes (*Or.* 59.2): "This thirst for glory (φιλοτιμία) is what leads even me to bear unnumbered woes and live a life of toil beyond all other men, accepting every fresh peril, fearing to mar the glory won by earlier achievements."[52]

The author of Hebrews, in drawing the addressees' attention to their former endurance and faithful action, harnesses the threefold power of this rhetorical device. John Chrysostom, commenting on 10:32, emphasizes the aspect of encouragement: "Powerful is the exhortation from deeds [already done]: for

---

50. Praising the past conduct and choices of the hearers will also serve to retain their goodwill toward the speaker (*Rhet. Her.* 1.4.9). Both 6:9-10 and 10:32-34 serve to reinforce the appeal to ethos by following up a strong episode of "frank speech" with words of reassurance and palliation. Stedman (*Hebrews,* 113) is incorrect to read this as an indication that "most of those he addresses are not apostate, as he describes in verses 32-34." While it is true that the writer has high hopes for his hearers, 10:32-34 has nothing to do with their present spiritual health. Even those who are now neglecting the assembly of the believers (10:25) had made it through those earlier troubles, but they have since allowed the poison of lingering social pressure to work upon their hearts.

51. In this regard, the author's attention to this episode of past history functions as an example or "narration" in a deliberative speech (Aristotle *Rh.* 3.16.11), in which one reminds the hearers of the past so that they can take better counsel with regard to the future.

52. For a similar use of holding up a group's past as a model for reforming its present course of action, see Dio *Or.* 31.66-68.

he who begins a work ought to go forward and add to it. . . . And he who encourages, does thus especially encourage them from their own example."[53] Calvin, himself trained in the classics and art of rhetoric, perceives the force of the appeal to the addressees' desire to preserve honor:

> For it is shameful, having begun well, to faint in the midst of the course; but baser still to go backwards when you have already made great progress. . . . Moreover, he increases the effect of the exhortation by saying that they had performed glorious exploits even then when they were as yet raw recruits: the more shame then would it be if they should faint now after having been exercised by long practice.[54]

The author intensifies this by pointing out how the achievement of the goal is in clear view, within the grasp of the addressees if only they persevere (10:35-36).[55] He thus makes it a mark of honor for them to continue in, and a mark of dishonor to abandon, their former course of action. When perseverance is at stake, this is an effective technique indeed.

Hebrews 10:32-39 is one of the few passages that give us a window into the history of the community being addressed by Hebrews. The contours and significance of this earlier experience of rejection and disenfranchisement endured by the believers has already been treated in the Introduction, to which the reader may wish to return.[56] Two aspects of the author's treatment of this experience remain to be elevated here: the endangered "happiness" of the believers and the author's remedy, as well as the author's preparation of the hearers to continue to resist society's shaming techniques by praising and recommending their past bold rejection of society's censure.

The Christians' "happiness" as it is defined by the dominant culture had been severely jeopardized by their new commitments to the Christian group. Aristotle observed that people acted with a view to obtaining or keeping "happiness" or one or other of its component parts, avoiding whatever was destructive to happiness as a whole or any of its parts (*Rh.* 1.5.1). "Happiness" could be defined as "well-being combined with virtue" (*Rh.* 1.5.3), and its components listed as "noble birth, numerous friends, good friends, wealth, good children,

---

53. NPNF[1] 14:461; *PG* 63:148-49.

54. Calvin, *Hebrews*, 135, commenting on 10:32.

55. Compare Josephus *J.W.* 6.38: "For shameful were it (αἰσχρὸν γὰρ) that Romans . . . should be outdone, either in strength or courage, by Jews, and that when final victory is in sight and we are enjoying the co-operation of God." The author of Hebrews likewise points to the availability of help from God, a topic intended to evoke confidence (cf. Aristotle *Rh.* 2.5.21), throughout the letter, notably at 4:15-16 and 10:19-23.

56. A more detailed treatment of 10:32-34 as historical reminiscence can be found in my *Despising Shame*, 154-64.

numerous children, a good old age; further, bodily excellences, such as health, beauty, strength, stature, fitness for athletic contests, a good reputation, honour, good luck, virtue" (*Rh.* 1.5.4). The experiences described in 10:32-34, however, speak directly to the loss of several of these components:

> But remember the earlier days, during which, after being enlightened, you endured a weighty contest of sufferings, in part being made a public spectacle by means of reproaches and hardships, in part showing partnership with those who were being thus treated. For you even showed sympathy with those who were in bonds and you welcomed the plundering of your possessions with joy, knowing yourselves to have better and lasting possessions.

Wealth (the enjoyment and security of land and movable possessions) and reputation ("being considered a person of worth by all," *Rh.* 1.5.8) were directly lost. For such hardships to be inflicted in such a variety of ways, however, it is clear that the believers' networks of friendship and protection (i.e., patronage) were also severely weakened.[57]

In order to defuse the growing desire to regain these components of happiness among those who begin to waver in their commitment to this group (i.e., who may finally be considering the group as a "bad investment"), the author reconfigures the definition of "happiness," such that the losses suffered by the believers do not in fact jeopardize what they should regard as their "true" happiness. Such a reconstitution of one's definitions of happiness is common among philosophical writers, who must distinguish their definition of happiness and its constituent parts from that happiness which the majority seeks:

> For he went on to praise philosophy and the freedom it gives, and to ridicule the things that are popularly considered blessings — wealth and reputation, dominion and honor, yes and purple and gold — things accounted very desirable by most men, and till then by me also. I took it all in with eager, wide-open soul, and at the moment I couldn't imagine what had come over me; I was all confused. At first I felt hurt because he had criticized what was dearest to me — wealth and money and reputation — and I all but cried over their downfall. (Lucian *Nigrinus* 3-5)

---

57. See Aristotle *Rh.* 1.12.24: "those who are friendless" are suitable choices for victims of crimes, since they lack the protection as well as the power for reprisal. The slander to which the Christians were subjected would have made the unofficial plundering of their possessions (i.e., looting) easier since the believers would lack the recourse to the courts. It would also have made the manipulation of the courts (e.g., to win fines and other material judgments from Christians) a possibility as well. See again Aristotle's analysis of what makes people suitable victims for injustice: "Those who have been slandered or are easy to slander; for such men neither care to go to law, for fear of the judges, nor, if they do, can they convince them; to this class belong those who are exposed to hatred and envy" (*Rh.* 1.12.22).

> [Riches, titles, and power] are not praised because they ought to be desired, but they are desired because they have been praised; and when the error of individuals has once created error on the part of the public, then the public error goes on creating error on the part of individuals. (Seneca *Ep.* 81.29)[58]

The author of Hebrews, like leaders within Christian culture generally, reinforces throughout his sermon the group culture's conception of happiness so that the wavering believers will be convinced that true expediency lies in persevering with the group rather than seeking to regain their former "happiness" and its constituent parts.

"Better and abiding possessions" therefore replace insecure, transitory possessions (10:34) as a component of happiness. Again we see the influence of Platonic categories (mediated thoroughly by means of Jewish cosmology and eschatology) on the author's expression of the Christians' goal. The possessions that belong to the earthly, visible realm are of less value than those that are afforded in the heavenly realm precisely because only the latter will "abide" or survive the eschatological removal of the "things that can be shaken" (12:27). Earthly possessions afford only "temporary" (πρόσκαιρος, 11:25) honor and enjoyment. The believers are called, therefore, to keep their hearts set on the "better and lasting" wealth reserved for them in the "abiding" city (13:14). In addition to wealth, reputation is being reconfigured (*Rh.* 1.5.8). Lost utterly in the eyes of their neighbors (10:32-33), their good reputation steadily increases in the eyes of Christ and the witnesses of faith (12:1-2) as they continue to persevere and invest in serving one another, and it will be immeasurably increased in the heavenly realm (2:10). Similarly, while they have lost formerly valuable friendships, the author's depiction of this earlier struggle underscores the new friendships that have been gained within the community as believers acted selflessly and sacrificially to care for the needs of their partners pilloried and abused by a hostile society (see also 6:9-10; 10:24; 13:1-3).

The Christians' neighbors had attempted to shame the deviants back into conformity (*Rh.* 2.6.26, 27), a shame that lingers as the Christians remain before the eyes of their neighbors day after day (*Rh.* 2.6.18, 27), continuing to live among those who witness their disgrace and even inflict such disgrace. Their neighbors want attachment to the Christian group to be a cause for shame (*Rh.* 2.6.25, 26) in order that the believers will withdraw from the shameful involvement. Such verbal attacks on the believers' honor and character appear to have been the common property of Christians in a number of social settings:

---

58. Seneca thus displays a beginning grasp of the process of the "social construction of reality" two millennia before Peter L. Berger and Thomas Luckmann displayed this process so thoroughly and insightfully in *The Social Construction of Reality* (New York: Anchor, 1967).

> If you are reviled in the name of Christ, you are honored, because the Spirit of glory and of God rests upon you. Let none of you suffer as a murderer or thief or evildoer or meddler, but if as a Christian do not be ashamed, but rather honor God in that name. (1 Pet. 4:14-16)

> Blessed are you when people revile you and persecute you and utter all kinds of evil against you falsely on my account. (Matt. 5:11, NRSV)

> Blessed are you when people hate you, and when they exclude you, revile you, and defame you on account of the Son of Man. (Luke 6:22)

In all these cases the verbal assaults and insults are linked directly with association with Christ. The assigning of disgrace and censure to the name of "Christian" indicates widespread rejection of this group by the society.[59] Their commitment to Christ exposed this particular community not only to censure, defamation, and jeering (all falling under the heading of ὀνειδισμοί) but also to physical abuse and other forms of inflicted hardships (θλίψεις). Public disgrace and the physical violation of their person constituted a comprehensive assault on their honor. Because the Christian community refused to accommodate itself to full participation in Greco-Roman life, the society responded with negative sanctions — shame — against the community's behavior and withdrawal.

The author of Hebrews must reverse this, so that the Christians will not only be insulated from the society's deviancy-control techniques but will regard brave endurance of such techniques as a source for honor within the group. He begins by reinterpreting the hearers' earlier experience of disgrace and abuse — the experience that initially marked their marginalization — as a "great contest." John Chrysostom finds the choice of metaphor significant as a means for ennobling that experience and encouraging the hearers to view their endurance of shame and hostility for their Christian confession as a competition that allows them to display honorable virtues such as courage and endurance: "Moreover, he did not say 'trials' but 'contest' (οὐκ εἶπε πειρασμοὺς ἀλλὰ ἄθλησιν), which is an expression of commendation and of very great praise."[60] Sensitive himself to matters of honor, Chrysostom perceives the author's strategic use of this image, by which he turns an experience of disgrace and marginalization into a competi-

---

59. The fact that the Christians, by the very nature of their monotheistic confession and their overt rejection of idolatrous forms of worship, showed contempt for what was dear to many of their neighbors — indeed central to many aspects of life in the Greco-Roman city — would have invited such rejection and hostility (see Aristotle *Rh.* 2.2.13). Dio's remembrance of the charges that led to the demise of Socrates (*Or.* 43.9) is informative: "Socrates is guilty of . . . not honouring the deities whom the city honours (οὓς μὲν ἡ πόλις θεοὺς τιμᾷ μὴ τιμῶν) but of introducing other new divinities." The Christians were similarly visible in their rejection of their cities' gods and in the worship of their "own" deity.

60. Chrysostom on 10:32, NPNF[1] 14:461; *PG* 63:149.

tion for honor. The application of athletic imagery to the hardships endured by members of a minority culture[61] resonates broadly with Stoic and Cynic literature, Jewish martyrological literature, and Jewish "philosophical" literature such as Philo's "Every Good Person is Free." The athletic metaphor is a common way for minority cultures to subvert and even invert the meaning of such sufferings as the dominant culture intends this message to be received (see "A Closer Look — Athletic Imagery and Moral Exhortation" below). Rather than regard the censure and abuse suffered at the hands of outsiders as a reason to desist from pursuit of the group's goals and further association with that group, the addressees are invited to orient themselves toward this hostility as wrestlers against their opponents. Persevering against the blows of opponents becomes the manifestation of courage and the path to victory, while yielding or giving up signals defeat and shame. The very path that would lead back to esteem in the eyes of unbelievers is thereby transformed into a path of cowardice and "true" disgrace, an admission of weakness and defeat. The author will return to this image extensively in 12:1-4: the hearers are urged to view their life in this world as a contest against sin and sinners, a striving to attain the prize of victory (the "hope set before them," 6:19-20), engaged in plain view of the many who have contended bravely and successfully throughout sacred history — it is for the approval of such "a cloud of spectators" that the hearers will be urged to contend, rather than to gratify their antagonists by giving in.

A Closer Look — Athletic Imagery and Moral Exhortation

The athletic contest in the Greco-Roman world afforded competitors an opportunity to achieve great distinction and prestige in their society. While monetary prizes were often given at games, the most valued prizes were the wreaths and proclamations given the win-

---

61. B. Malina criticizes my application of this term to the audience of Hebrews (review of *Despising Shame: Honor Discourse and Community Maintenance in the Epistle to the Hebrews, JBL* 116 [1997]: 379). Malina quotes a definition of "minorities" that applies the term to "groups that lack power, are regarded with contempt by the majority, and are insulated or placed on a socially or culturally inferior level." He does "not believe any of these characteristics of modern minorities apply to the group addressed in Hebrews." Even a cursory reading of 10:32-34, however, reveals that several of these characteristics do apply: the contempt in which the Christians were held is most clear; their lack of power is also evident in the extent of the abuse and injuries they suffered; their loss of reputation and property left them "on a socially inferior level." While it is true that early Christians should not be conceptualized *tout court* as facing analogous situations to "modern minorities" (e.g., a Christian can always leave the minority group, whereas a member of an ethnic minority cannot leave behind his or her ethnicity), the application of the term itself — by the very definition cited — remains defensible.

ners, by which their reputations were greatly enhanced. It is not surprising, therefore, that the athletic contest became a metaphor commonly used by spokespersons of minority cultures.[62] By means of athletic imagery they could portray the pursuit and achievement of the goals valued by their alternative culture as a path to acclaim and honor and, for those within the minority group, turn experiences of hardship and deprivation into a noble endeavor. Just as athletes endured much pain and even humiliation on the way to victory, so members of a low-status minority group could regard their suffering and humiliation as a sort of training for an honorable victory.

Athletic imagery is a favorite for Epictetus, who encourages the aspiring Stoic to endure hardships with courage and without dismay, since these hardships are but the result of Zeus matching one up with a wrestling partner for training, the result of which will be a great victory: "It is difficulties that show what you are. Consequently, when a difficulty befalls, remember that God, like a physical trainer, has matched you with a rugged young man. What for? someone says. So that you may become an Olympic victor; but that cannot be done without sweat" (*Diss.* 1.24.1-2). Reputation, abuse, and even praise are among those aspects of human experience listed as obstacles, which can be thrown in the athlete's way but which are despised and passed by on the way toward becoming "the invincible athlete" (ὁ ἀνίκητος ἀθλητής, *Diss.* 1.18.21).[63]

Both Epictetus and Dio Chrysostom speak of the life of the Cynic also as an athletic contest. Far from the normal channels of advancement in reputation and prestige (indeed, quite the opposite), the Cynic's experience is nevertheless ennobled as an "Olympic contest" (Epictetus *Diss.* 3.22.52); and his hardships, seen by more mainstream members of the Greco-Roman culture as tokens of his depravity, are interpreted by him as training ordered by Zeus (*Diss.* 3.22.56). Dio (*Or.* 8.11-13) describes the lifestyle of Diogenes of Sinope as that of one who competes in a contest, in which the antagonists, hardships, are of the most difficult sort.[64] While the Cynic endures the loss of his reputation and status within society, he remains a "noble person":

---

62. For a detailed discussion, see the classic study by Victor C. Pfitzner, *Paul and the Agon Motif: Traditional Athletic Imagery in the Pauline Literature* (Leiden: Brill, 1967), and now also the excellent treatment of this motif with specific regard to Hebrews in Croy, *Endurance,* 37-77, 167-82.

63. Epictetus returns often to the problem of the experience of losing honor and encountering revilers, as again in *Diss.* 3.20.9: "Is it possible, then, to derive any advantage from these things? Yes, from everything. Even from the man who reviles me? And what good does his wrestling-companion do the athlete? The very greatest. So also my reviler becomes one who prepares me for my contest; he exercises my patience, my dispassionateness, my gentleness." Seneca also employs athletic imagery to orient the "wise person" toward adversity, regarding the latter even as a desirable element in the life of the sage since constant exercise prevents the atrophy of virtue (*De prov.* 2.3-4; cited in Croy, *Endurance,* 52). Rather than shy away from adversity, the virtuous person regards "all hardships as exercises" (*De prov.* 2.2).

64. "And when a certain man asked whether he [Diogenes] too came to see the contest, he said, 'No, but to take part.' Then when the man laughed and asked him who his competitors were, he said with that customary glance of his: 'The toughest there are and the hardest to beat, men whom no Greek can look straight in the eye; not competitors, however, who sprint or wrestle or jump, not those that box, throw the spear, and hurl the discus, but those that chasten a man.' 'Who are they, pray?' asked the other. 'Hardships,' he replied, 'very severe

The noble man (ὁ γενναῖος) holds his hardships to be his greatest antagonists [which he engages] not to win a sprig of parsley . . . nor a bit of wild olive, or of pine, but to win happiness and virtue all the days of his life, and not merely when the Eleans make proclamation, or the Corinthians, or the Thessalian assembly, . . . disclosing no weakness even though he must endure the lash or give his body to be cut or burned. Hunger, exile, loss of reputation, and the like have no terrors for him; nay, he holds them as mere trifles, and while in their very grip the perfect man (τὸν ἄνδρα τὸν τέλειον) is often as sportive as boys with their dice and their coloured balls. (*Or.* 8.15-16)

Athletic imagery was also in common use within the Jewish minority culture as a means of transforming the disgraceful and status-degrading experiences of faithful Jews into an honorable competition that resulted in a reward before God. Athletic metaphors are particularly common in 4 Maccabees, an encomium of the martyrs that transforms their degrading experience of torture into a contest (ἀγών) and the tyrant's hall into an "gymnasium" of hardships (γυμνασία πόνων, 11:20).[65] The seven brothers are praised as "athletes" (ἀσκήτας) of religion and "combatants" (ἀγωνισταί) competing for virtue. By means of this metaphor, the disgrace of punishment and mutilation becomes a contest for honor, in which even to compete is noble: "My sons, noble is the contest (γενναῖος ὁ ἀγών) to which you are called to bear witness for the nation. Compete zealously for the ancestral law!" (16:16). 4 Maccabees 17:11-16 offers an extended athletic metaphor comparable in scope to Hebrews 12:1-4: In the "divine contest" (ἀγὼν θεῖος), Eleazar was the "first contestant," the mother of the seven brothers also "competed," the seven brothers "participated in the contest," and the tyrant "was the antagonist." Piety itself "crowned," that is, honored, the victors. Also like the author of Hebrews, the author of 4 Maccabees (in the mouths of the seven brothers, 13:15) places only two options before his audience: "for great is the soul's contest (ψυχῆς ἀγών) and great the danger of eternal torment lying before those who transgress the commandment of God." One either strives for honor before God or, yielding to the pressures of society (and its own promises of honor and approval, 4 Macc. 8:5-7), incurs the danger shared by those who provoke God through disobedience.

The use of contest or athletic imagery opens up the way for an author's use of rhetorical *topoi* pertaining to courage, harnessing this greatly admired Greco-Roman virtue for the cause of perseverance in Stoic or Jewish or Christian community and activity. According to the author of *Rhetorica ad Herennium* (3.2.3), "courage is the reaching for great things and contempt for what is mean; also the endurance of hardship in expectation of profit." The latter part of this definition describes a prominent part of the exhortation of the author of Hebrews. He urges "endurance" in the face of ongoing tension with the society (10:36) as the way in which the addressees will attain "great reward" and "what was promised" (10:35-36), just as Jesus "endured" the cross and arrived at the great "joy set before him," namely, session at God's right hand and exaltation in the unshakable world (12:2). By means of this imagery, the author strategically turns endurance of reproach and

---

and insuperable for the gluttonous and folly-stricken men who feast the livelong day and snore at night, but which yield to thin, spare men, whose waists are more pinched than those of wasps.'"

65. Compare Thompson, *Beginnings,* 64: "Both Philo and 4 Maccabees belong to a minority culture which was subject to persecution and acts of violence. Because they identified with this minority culture, the image of the contest was a useful way of giving a positive interpretation of the fate of their people."

hostility into a wrestling match in which yielding to the course society promoted is a shameful defeat and persevering against its blows is courageous endurance and victory (10:32-35; 12:1-4). Hebrews is thus resonant with a broad range of philosophical and Hellenistic Jewish literature, which has permeated far into Christian moral exhortation and interpretation of the exigencies of perseverance as a Christian.[66]

The author transforms the past actions and commitment of the addressees — their former acts of courage and generosity toward one another,[67] their wisdom in reckoning worldly goods to be of less worth than heavenly, abiding possessions — from sources of shame (society's estimation of them) into sources of praise and self-respect so as to move them to continue in the same course of action. Significantly, the addressees are commended specifically for their endurance of this experience of dishonor and suffering (10:32). In the face of degradation and reproach, they chose to endure society's assaults of their honor rather than "shrink back" from the course that faith required; they persevered in the confession of Christ and solidarity with those who belonged to Christ. It is precisely the preservation of this course that the author recommends.

The author's use of topics of friendship and enmity in 10:32-34 will begin to promote this course before the author even arrives at his explicit injunctions so to do (10:35-39). The outside world is portrayed here for the first time. The author presents nongroup members as hostile and the cause of many calamities for the believers. Recalling the harsher past hostilities of the society may reinforce the desire to endure in the Christian path and not capitulate to outside pressures. Part of the message of this episode is "remember their hatred, their abuse, their injustice." Such recollection will reinforce the boundary between society and the group.[68] Positively, the hearers are reminded of the mutual help and acts of support shown within the group, which will stimulate the feeling of friendship now, helping to move the addressees forward to committing themselves anew to one another (rather than to seeking their individual welfare through abandoning the cause). Reawakening mutual "favor" and friendship supports the author's many calls for ongoing mutual help.[69] Those who were

---

66. Attridge (*Hebrews*, 354-55) refers the reader to Acts 20:24; 1 Cor. 9:24-27; Gal. 2:2; [5:7]; Phil. 1:30; 2:16; [3:13-14]; 1 Thess. 2:2; 1 Tim. 6:12; 2 Tim. 4:7 for further examples of this metaphor at work in the NT.

67. The hearers themselves acted most nobly in their rallying to each other's aid: they acted "in the public interest," "at great cost to themselves, "braving risks and dangers" — all topics of praiseworthy behavior regularly featured in encomia.

68. Aristotle (*Rh.* 2.4.6-7) observes the force of recollecting mutual enemies on the arousal of friendship and solidarity within an audience.

69. Thus *Rhet. Alex.* 1439b15-18): "If we are urging our audience to render assistance (βοηθεῖν) to certain parties, whether individuals or states, it will also be suitable briefly to

helped are roused to gratitude, old partnerships are rekindled, and those who helped before are stimulated to help again.[70]

The earlier response of the hearers to outside pressure to "give up" their new commitments — their "confidence" in God's promises, their "boldness" brazenly to identify with their targeted sisters and brothers, and their "despising shame" in the form of society's attempts to pull them away from their new obedience to God[71] — becomes the path for them now to attain the greater "happiness" that God has promised:

> Do not, then, throw away your boldness, which holds a great reward. For you have need of endurance in order that, after having done the will of God, you may receive the promise. (10:35-36)

"Boldness" (παρρησία) is a quality that has appeared several times before in the sermon in reference to the addressees' confidence with regard to open access to God mediated through Christ (4:14-16; 10:19-22). This "boldness," this right of free expression and access, is certainly in jeopardy among those who "shrink back," who act ungratefully toward their patron and bring dishonor upon his Son (6:4-6; 10:26-31). Its usage here, however, develops a second, complementary side: the boldness or open declaration of their hope reflected in their endurance of the society's shaming techniques (10:32-33), a boldness that extends even to their open association with those especially singled out by society for deviancy control (10:34). After being "enlightened," they openly and confidently demonstrated the importance of the gifts they had received from God through Christ and the benefactions for which they yet hoped.[72] "Boldness" (παρρησία) often appears in opposition to "shame" (αἰσχύνη; see Phil. 1:20; 1 John 2:28), and the choice of this antonym elsewhere is informative for the

---

mention any friendly feeling or cause for gratitude or compassion (φιλία ἤ χάρις ἤ ἔλεος) that already exists between them and the members of the assembly."

70. See Seneca *Ben.* 4.15.3: "How often will you hear a man say: 'I cannot bear to desert him, for I have given him his life, I have rescued him from peril. He now begs me to plead his cause against men of influence; I do not want to, but what can I do? I have already helped him once, no, twice.' Do you not see that there is, inherent in the thing itself, some peculiar power that compels us to give benefits, first, because we ought, then, because we have already given them? . . . We continue to bestow because we have already bestowed."

71. Each of these elements will be developed in the exemplars of "faith" in 11:1–12:3.

72. The author creates a verbal echo between φωτισθέντες (10:32) and φωτισθέντας (6:4), thus inviting the hearer to recollect the earlier, powerful passage about making the right response to the gifts provided by God, the first of which was this "enlightenment," or sound "knowledge of the truth" (10:26). This response entails bold witness to the unsupportive society about the value of these gifts shown through the believers' ongoing commitment to their divine patron and Christian family despite all the dissuasive hardships society might throw at them.

meaning of "boldness" here. The community had been "bold" in the face of society's disapproval and its sanctions of reproach and punishment. Rather than
hold up Jesus to public shame by succumbing to the pressures exerted upon
them by their neighbors, they flouted society's attempts at compulsion[73] by
their endurance and perseverance in commitment to one another. Such is the
παρρησία that the author desires the addressees to continue to exhibit: they are
called to continue in that "boldness" in their confession and their open association with the name of Jesus, with other Christians, and with their hope so that
they may receive God's reward.

The call to have endurance (ὑπομονή, 10:36), a familiar topic of courage[74]
that the use of the athletic metaphor invites, becomes a prominent feature of
this final exhortation. The believers formerly exhibited this quality of endurance (10:32), will be invited to consider Jesus' example of endurance so that
they will not "grow faint" in their relatively lighter contest (12:2-3), and will be
repeatedly called to endure (10:36; 12:1, 7). The course of capitulation to society's shaming and hostility is painted as a failure of nerve, a cowardly course of
action. The hearers should feel shame at choosing such a course. Rather than
yield to the pressures from outside, they are called to stand and not be diverted
by these hardships from their noble pursuit and their commitments to God and
one another.

Moreover, the author depicts the work, the larger part of the investment
to be made, as complete. They "have done the will of God" and now must
merely hold on and receive the reward.[75] The author introduces here a brief appeal to the topic of "feasibility" or the "ease of accomplishment" of the course
he proposes: the author minimizes the difficulties of maintaining their com-

---

73. "Boldness" in speech was particularly held to be the behavior of "free" people or
citizens in a democracy (see, e.g., Philo *Quod Omn.* 48). The enemy of democracy in the ancient world was, of course, tyranny, and tyrants were especially hostile toward those who
clung to democratic "boldness" in their presence. In 4 Maccabees, Antiochus IV attempts to
compel capitulation to his edicts against Torah by a tyrant's typical strategies, namely, promises of favor and applications of torture. When the young Jews refuse to be persuaded by either promise or threat, but rather speak their mind and bear witness to the "truth" like free
people, he is enraged (see 10:2-5, in which it is specifically this "boldness" again that provokes the tyrant). "Boldness" — clinging to and bearing witness to one's principles in the face
of any compulsion from without — becomes the mark of the free and noble mind, an ideal
especially beloved by the philosophers. Thus the words of Epictetus (*Diss.* 3.24.71): "Therefore, the man over whom pleasure has no power, nor evil, nor fame, nor wealth, and who,
whenever it seems good to him, can spit his whole paltry body into some oppressor's face and
depart from this life — whose slave can he any longer be, whose subject?"

74. Thus Aristotle (*Nic. Eth.* 1115b12: "Courage endures fearful things for the sake of
what is noble."

75. The author employs metonymy in the expression "receive the promise," using the
term "promise" for "things promised" (the cause for the result).

mitments to God and one another, saying, in effect, that they have already fought the battle and need only wait until the victors are rewarded (10:36). This would make it seem all the more foolish for them to give up now, since their investment has already been made, their labors are complete, and all that remains is to receive the benefits after "yet a very short while" (10:37). This depiction of the addressees' position heightens their sense of having arrived at the very threshold of the inheritance (see 3:7–4:11 and the author's application of the wilderness generation's "threshold experience"). The repetition of the phrase "receive the promise" in 11:39 will compound the hearers' sense of standing on the verge of receiving God's eternal benefactions.[76] The parade of the heroic exemplars of trust in God's promise "did not receive the promise in order that they might not arrive at the goal apart from us" (11:39-40). The addressees stand, as it were, at the culmination of a long line of the faithful — the last generation, as it were — who will all cross the threshold of the unshakable realm together.

The author's description of their conduct and endurance in the experiences described in 10:32-34 as "doing the will of God" is also strategic. This designation validates those past experiences as well as their present disenfranchisement as a path of obedience to God's will (and not as signs that they are out of favor with God or that they are base persons). Their prior contest was one in which they pleased God by their endurance, by their display of faith toward God and toward one another. As they maintain their "upper hand" in the contest against society's attempt to make them capitulate, they persevere in the secure knowledge that they are acting exactly as God would have them act; they are not swayed by their opponents either to the right or to the left.

The author reinforces his exhortation to persevere in trust and resist "shrinking back" in the face of society's hostility with an appeal to OT Scripture:

> "For yet a little while, the coming one will arrive and will not delay: but my righteous one will live by trust. And if he or she shrinks back, my soul takes no pleasure in him or her." But *we* are not characterized by shrinking back unto destruction but rather by trust unto the preservation of life. (10:37-39)

Contrary to his custom, the author does not give any indication that these words are a quotation from an older text. Rather, he weaves them directly into the fabric of the exhortation. Moreover, he combines two different texts without giving any indication to the hearers of this blending. The author introduces a quotation from Habakkuk with a few strategic words from Isaiah 26:20: "yet a little while"

---

76. Compare ἵνα . . . κομίσησθε τὴν ἐπαγγελίαν (10:36) with οὐκ ἐκομίσαντο τὴν ἐπαγγελίαν (11:39).

(μικρὸν ὅσον ὅσον). These three words, in their original context, speak of the length of time that God's people are instructed to hide away in their chambers until God's punishment of the inhabitants of the earth runs its course. In this new context, they serve to stress the proximity of the forthcoming visitation of God or of Christ (the subject now of Hab. 2:3) and to facilitate maintaining commitment "just a little while longer." The author hereby reinforces the references to the coming "Day" in 10:25, 31 to create a sense of the nearness of both reward and dangerous judgment. This imminence is essential to the arousal of fear, but also of confidence. It provides proof, moreover, for the claim of 10:36 that the reward is very near. Isaiah reinforces the sense of being at the threshold of that inheritance, right where the wilderness generation was when it faltered and became forever a pattern of base distrust and disobedience.

It is the LXX version of the Habakkuk oracle, and not the MT, that provides the author with the support he requires. The MT of Habakkuk 2:3 speaks of "a vision for the appointed time; it speaks of the end, and it does not lie. If it seems to tarry, wait for it; it will surely come, it will not delay." The LXX version shifts the focus from the "vision" that will "come and not delay" to the "coming one": "there is yet a vision for the end and it will come to light at last, and not in vain: if it/he tarries, wait for it/him, for the coming one will arrive and will not delay." The ambiguity of the pronoun and pronominal suffix in 2:3b already invites a personal reading, which is then made explicit by the introduction of "the coming one." A second significant difference sets the MT apart from the LXX. The MT of Habakkuk 2:4 reads: "Look at the proud! Their spirit is not right in them, but the righteous one lives by faith"; this is transformed by the LXX translators into "if he shrinks back, my soul has no pleasure in him; but the righteous one will live by faith." The censure of the proud turns into a statement about the "coming one," namely, that if he shows cowardice he will not be pleasing to God.

The author of Hebrews further transforms the meaning of this text by transposing the order of Habakkuk 2:4a and 4b (LXX). The phrase "if he shrinks back" applies no longer to the "coming one" but to those who wait for God's deliverance. Those who await it in trust and firmness will "live," while those whose hearts fail will not please God. The way in which this transformation serves the author's pastoral goal is evident. The Habakkuk text can now serve to outline two courses of action — that of trusting and remaining firm and that of shrinking back. The former explicitly leads to "life," while the latter is censured by God, who takes no pleasure (οὐκ εὐδοκεῖ) in that path. "Pleasing God," however, becomes an essential virtue extolled and exhorted in 11:1–13:21 (although expressed with a synonym: see 11:6; 12:28; 13:16, 21). The Habakkuk quotation reinforces the starkness of the alternatives facing the addressees as the author wants them to formulate these alternatives (in order to make desertion from the group and a return to the embrace and supportive networks of the non-Christian society less appealing rather than more appealing).

Hebrews 10:39 concludes this section with a distribution — the figure of thought that assigns different roles or qualities to different groups[77] — framed as an antithesis.[78] Two key terms of Habakkuk 2:4 ("shrinking back" and "faith/trust") are recontextualized into a concluding statement. The affirmation that the hearers are people "exhibiting trust" rather than "shrinking back" seeks to bring into existence the very commitment to "trust" that it affirms. The author's transposition of the clauses in 2:4 allows him now to distinguish between two groups and their properties — those who show trust and firmness, who preserve their lives, and those who show cowardice and distrust, who fall into destruction.[79] Some intermediate exegetical steps are presupposed. "Living" is read by the author as eschatological salvation, and failing to please God is taken to signify eschatological destruction. Reading both Isaiah 26:20 and Habakkuk 2:3-4 as oracles of end-time deliverance has made these moves possible.

The hearers are thus explicitly led to identify with the group who are marked by "trust" rather than by "shrinking back," and the consequences of both courses of action are again expressed so as to reinforce the hearers' desire to identify with "faithfulness/trust." Once again the author's interest in the topic of expediency comes to the fore. The audience is led to consider how they might preserve the "better and lasting possessions," whose preservation motivated their earlier endurance. They must press on in trust if they hope to enjoy these better possessions, which they receive as they enter God's rest, the heavenly and abiding realm, God's city, their heavenly homeland (4:1-11; 6:19-20; 11:10, 13-16; 13:13-14). If they hold onto their boldness (rather than mute their witness and hide their association with the people of God), they will enjoy the great reward and receive the promised benefactions (10:35-36). It would be

---

77. *Rhet. Her.* 4.35.47: "Distribution occurs when certain specified roles are assigned among a number of things or persons, as follows: 'Whoever of you, people of the jury, loves the good name of the Senate, must hate this man, for his attacks upon that body have always been most insolent.'" The instructor's first of many examples shows how the figure of thought can be used to steer the hearers into accepting a role or course of action. In this example, the desirability of being a preserver of the honor of the Senate would lead a hearer to consider favorably the act of hating the defendant. So also in Heb. 10:39, the desirability of "preserving life" rather than coming to "destruction" leads the hearers to consider favorably the choice of a course of action that demonstrates "faith" or "trust."

78. This artfully crafted conclusion also develops chiasm with 10:38: πίστεως . . . ὑποστείληται (10:38) . . . ὑποστολῆς . . . πίστεως (10:39).

79. This "shrinking back" would entail the only true disgrace before the court of reputation formed by God and the believers. Epictetus uses this sanction in his encouragement to persevere in the calling of the philosopher (*Diss.* 2.2.13): "Far be it from you to receive many blows and yet at the last give in!" Such a capitulation would be αἰσχρόν (2.2.14). Similarly, he urges would-be philosophers (*Ench.* 29.1-3) to count the whole cost of the enterprise they are contemplating, lest they find it too difficult and "give up disgracefully" (αἰσχρῶς ἀποστήσῃ) or "turn back like children" (ὡς τὰ παιδία ἀναστραφήσῃ).

inexpedient at this point, having suffered the loss of earthly goods, also to surrender their claim to the eternal goods for which they originally surrendered the temporal goods. The path of trust in and loyalty toward God leads to enjoyment of the greater goods and avoidance of anticipated harm (the imminent danger posited again in 10:38), whereas shrinking back leads to the full experience of punishment.

Summary

The contemplation of Jesus' once-for-all sacrifice and the unprecedented access to God that it opens up for "those who are being sanctified" fuels the author's exhortation to "draw near" to God and "hold onto" the witness to the hope that Jesus has granted. The Christians enjoy two distinct blessings — a mediator who is able to see them through to the journey's end and the "boldness" or "confidence" to enter holy spaces never before accessible to human beings save for Jesus. The ministry of Jesus has opened up the unshakable, divine realm for the believers, who have been enabled to enter that "rest." In light of the gifts that have been given already, the provisions God has made for their journey, and the certainty of the promise that lies before them, the addressees are called to hold onto their confession of hope, to gather around one another to reinforce this hope, and to create a supportive community that assists the individual to persevere (in terms of material and emotional support, but also in terms of reinforcement of the individual's orientation and ambition toward attaining the hoped-for reward). The author seeks to rouse their confidence in this hope on account of the divine help and the open access in prayer to God's "throne of favor" as well as on account of the social support that exists for the believer in the church.

The alternative course of action is presented as unthinkable. Those who "forsake the gathering together" of the Christian assembly do so for a number of reasons, but a prominent cause in the addressees' setting is the reproach and hostility directed at the Christian group from outside. Those who withdraw from openly associating with the church show more concern now for the friendship of "sinners" (cf. 12:3) and for the approval of God's opponents than for the friendship and approval of God. Choosing the company of sin rather than solidarity with the people of God (11:25), however, entails a deliberate affront to God, which leads to encountering God as judge. Choosing the approval of sinners rather than the cost of belonging to the company of the redeemed, moreover, acts out a response of ingratitude of the basest sort. One tells God, in effect, that his gifts, provided at such cost to his Son, are not worth temporary deprivations and the "hostility of sinners." The promise is not worth the perseverance. The author intends for his readers and hearers to be struck by the hor-rifying ugliness of making this kind of statement to God and, echoing other NT voices like Matthew 10:28, reminds the believers that honoring God and his gifts is far more crucial than honoring society's demands for conformity. The author calls them to remember their obligation of gratitude and to respond honorably to one who has lavished upon them so generously and graciously such costly gifts and certified promises of future benefaction.

In the third segment of exhortation, the author holds up before his hear-ers the picture of their earlier "contest" and of the way in which they coura-geously strove for victory over the world. The believers had shown complete disregard for the shaming tactics of the unbelievers, courageous endurance in the face of hostility, and uncompromising support for fellow Christians — this is precisely the model for their ongoing attitude and conduct. If they will keep their "boldness" (παρρησία, 10:35) vis-à-vis society, witnessing through word and deed to their patron the value of his gifts and promises and the solidarity of believers, they will keep enjoying their "boldness" (παρρησία, 10:19; cf. 4:16) vis-à-vis God. The importance of the eschatological dimension for the Chris-tian's evaluation of advantages comes through again at the close of each seg-ment of this exhortation, as perseverance in trusting God and remaining firm in commitment to him and his people is set forth as the way to "preservation of the soul," while "shrinking back" from bold association with God, Jesus, and the believing community leads to "destruction." The believer is called to con-sider what would be advantageous not only for *this* life but also for encounter-ing God on *that* day when he comes as judge (10:25, 30-31).

The community's past example embodies the "faith" that brings safety for eternity (10:37-39). They are called to continue to identify themselves with the virtues of trust and fidelity toward the divine patron, and they will now be given multiple examples of how "faith" acts in its quest for the reward — faith as enacted by Abraham, Moses, the martyrs, and Jesus in the examples that will follow (11:1–12:3).

Bridging the Horizons

The author emphasizes the privilege of entering God's presence in confident expectation of favor and help enjoyed by Christians in prayer (4:14-16; 10:22), a foretaste, in effect, of our final entry into the unshakable realm and the full, unmediated presence of God (10:19-20; 12:18-28). This gives a focus to our times of prayer and worship not simply as a place where we can find strength for our daily life or solutions for temporal needs, but also as a portal through which we can begin to see and even experience the end of our journey. The author reminds us as well that "being in the world but not of the world" entails the awareness that our destiny is beyond the realm of what we can see and touch and measure. We are to set our hearts and ambitions "there where true joys are to be found" (to borrow again from the *Book of Common Prayer*), to live first and foremost not for what goals we would attain for ourselves in this life but for that goal which God has appointed and Christ has secured for our lives.

While we may "draw near" to God in our own times of private prayer, the author especially highlights our approach to God in the company of our brothers and sisters in Christ. The author calls us to form vital communities of faith where the holiness and wonder of God's presence is known, and where each member takes a share in the ministry of encouragement and support. From childhood we are daily assaulted by messages urging us to adopt worldly goals and values, to desire what this world offers, to seek temporal and all-too-temporary goods and achievements. We are continually being drawn, lulled, and pulled away from a pure commitment to the way that Jesus has opened up for us in his example and teaching and from a clear focus on the truly "needful" things. Knowing how these voices work their way into believers' hearts and rob them of the prize of endurance, the author calls us to remind our partners in Christ of the goal for which we strive and of the wisdom of choosing Christ over the "temporary enjoyment of sin" (Heb. 11:24-26). He calls us to offset the enticements of the world by boldly encouraging one another to seek what God values and to "love and do good" to one another (10:24-25). We need one another's strength in order to stand firm against all assaults on our commitment to God (Phil. 1:27-28). If our obedience to God takes us into dangerous territory (e.g., into the experience of the hostility of unbelievers), we need to know that we can count on our sisters and brothers to help us materially and personally as well as emotionally and spiritually (10:32-34; 13:3). Bold discipleship and prophetic witness require strong support by the faithful: our collective attention to one another can greatly multiply our individual growth in Christ, in witness, and in service.

Hebrews 10:26-31 especially challenges us to live in such a way that we honor the Giver and his gifts. For us who have known God's goodness, his Spirit, his love and forgiveness, and the hope of his future, showing ingratitude now — to act in such a way that shows a slight estimation of the value of the gift and the Giver — should be an unthinkable, horrifying prospect. Having gained intimate fellowship with God and knowledge of what he approves, we would dishonor him if we allowed fear of the world's hostility to keep us from bearing witness to what Jesus has done for us or from pursuing whatever course God called us to walk. If we drag our feet along the way of the cross out of regret for our lost friendship with the world, we again dishonor the Giver and the value of God's friendship. If we begin to think that following Christ means "giving up" too much, we show slight regard for the privileges and advantages that following Christ has brought us. Rather, our lives must reflect the great value of the gift we have received, which means responding to our divine benefactor with a gratitude that embraces heart, mind, body, and desire.

If we care more about "success," "respect," or being "wise" as this world defines it (see 1 Cor. 1:18-31), if we keep following its rules and set our ambitions on its promises, we trample upon Jesus. We set too little value on his blood if we refuse to walk in that life for which he freed us. We insult God's favor if we seek to secure the world's favor first and then, as far as the world will let us, God's promised benefits. If our first thought is for keeping our neighbors' or coworkers' or fellow citizens' approval, and if we seek to live out our Christian life within the parameters of the kinds of behaviors or words that will not "offend" the unbelievers, we show by our lives whose approval really matters to us, and we insult God. A special danger faces the Christian in the modern, secularized world (i.e., a world in which religion is but an optional component of a full life). Our tendency is to attend dutifully to everything else our society tells us is important and *then* to give to religious concerns any leftover time, resources, and energy. Again, such an approach to life says to God, "your gifts and call are not of the first order of importance in my life." The author of Hebrews calls us to let our choices, actions, and ambitions reflect the true value of things and to pursue God's promises with our full vigor, in full trust and firm commitment ("faith"), letting no worldly trifle detour or delay us (see Matt. 6:25-33; 13:44-46). First, we are called to contemplate what God really has given us and to seek out the full enjoyment of all the gifts the author listed in such passages as 4:14-16 and 6:4-5. From that awareness, we are to reorient our lives to be expressions of gratitude to God, recalling that gratitude entails revering him with our whole lives, showing fidelity to him at any cost, and serving consistently as he directs.

The author labels defection (or quiet slipping away) from the Christian community as an intentional choice of sin over obedience and grateful response. He chooses, however, a highly general expression to make this point — "if we intentionally continue to sin after receiving knowledge of the truth" (10:26). The generality of the category "willful sin" has occasioned many debates about the author's meaning. Does he claim that postbaptismal sin lies beyond forgiveness and incurs the wrath of God? The celebration of Jesus' ongoing intercession for the believer (7:25) would seem to rule out this position, and our consideration of the author's pastoral goal has shown that he has a very specific course of action in mind here as the "willful sin." Nevertheless, something can be learned about resisting any intentional sin from the author's treatment of the specific one of withdrawing from association with Jesus under duress. The apostate is stopped in his or her tracks by the memory of the value of God's gifts and the obligation to respond honorably to so generous and selfless a giver as Jesus. This same consideration may help anyone who is contemplating doing something contrary to the values and goals of the Christian group.

The contemplation of the immenseness of the gifts we have received from God may provide a powerful medicine against temptation. In light of the cleansing Jesus has effected for us, the intimate access we have with God, the daily friendship of the Holy Spirit, and the destiny God has appointed for the faithful, do we really want to give ourselves over to this sin that will offend God? Do we want to return bitterness to God, who has given only goodness to us? This passage suggests that we weigh the value of God's gifts and the response of gratitude when faced with a serious dilemma, or when contemplating an action that, though easy or profitable in the short run, is sinful.

The concept of "boldness" has been prominently featured twice in this hortatory section, and it may provide a sort of summation of the challenge of Hebrews 10:19-39 to us. First, we are assured of our "boldness" with regard to our final entry into the heavenly realm. Using the cultic imagery of sacrifice, sanctification, and entrance into the holy places, the author assures us that Jesus' death means that those who persevere in relationship with him will arrive at the heavenly, eternal realm. This boldness, however, makes us courageous in our approach to worship now, in our willingness to invest ourselves fully in our eternal hope (not hedging our bets in terms of laying up both with God and with Mammon!), and in our interaction with fellow believers (boldly encouraging one another, sharing our emotional and material resources with one another, and calling one another to live so as not to be ashamed on that day).

Second, we are also summoned to "boldness" in our encounter with the world outside the church. There are many pressures that trammel up "free speech" (the original sense of παρρησία in the democratic Greek city-state) with regard both to Christian witness and bold enaction of Christian values. In America, for example, the privatization of religion has created a culture in which "speech" about God is only appropriate in certain places (church, home, and the like). Secularization creates a climate in which some investment in religious pursuits is appropriate (though optional) but too much investment is regarded with suspicion. Materialism (the view that the tangible world is the primary world) breeds a culture in which it is far easier and more comfortable to speak of temporal concerns. Thus, weather, politics, movies, and the like are more frequent topics of conversation than our experiences of God in our times of prayer and meditation, than our progress in the struggle against certain sins, than our perceptions of God's challenges and call. And, of course, "academic" culture fosters critical study of religion but not conversation about direct encounter with God or living for God.

These are obstacles to παρρησία in the Western world; obstacles in Islamic countries, for example, are far more daunting. Whatever means the unbelieving world selects to promote its own culture and dissuade the open and radical pursuit of alternative cultures, the word of Hebrews is clear. "Do not throw away your boldness," or, if you have yet to exhibit it, discover your freedom to bear witness in word and deed to the God who redeemed and delivered you. Once again the importance of fellow Christians becomes clear. It is first in our churches, in the company of other Christians, that we can learn to be bold, to speak openly about our experiences of God, our spiritual struggles, our perception of God's vision for our lives, our churches, and our world. Let us renew our churches as places where this kind of "boldness" is welcome and honored, and then we will find ourselves equipped to exhibit this boldness in the sight of unbelievers as well.

Faith's Orientation in the World: 11:1–12:3

Overview

The addressees have been told that having "faith" or "trust," the salutary quality set forth in 10:37-39, is the way to "preserve life" on the day of Christ's appearing and the judgment of all. This provides the author with an opportunity to show more fully what "faith" is and how "trust" in God manifests itself in real-life situations. He therefore supplies in 11:1–12:3 something of an encomium on faith. After a definition of "faith" itself, the author proceeds to amplify the value and nobility of acting "by faith" through the narration of the stories of the figures commemorated and honored in the sacred scriptures. While the majority of commentaries discuss 11:1-40 as a distinct unit, treating 12:1-3 together with 12:4-29, the separation of 12:1-3 from 11:1-40 is not helpful. Encomia and example lists frequently end with a brief exhortation and are incomplete when considered apart from the parenetic purpose to which the author puts the exempla. Furthermore, the example of Jesus in 12:2 is shaped in such a way as to capture the essence of the major examples of "trust" in 11:1-40. It crystallizes the "many" examples into one overarching pattern. While 12:4-11 certainly grows out of 12:1-3 (my division will lead to similar infelicities on the other side), I find it more valuable to extend the "encomium on faith" to include its rhetorical conclusion in 12:1-3.

Hebrews 11:1–12:3 bears marked similarities with other lists of examples found in both Jewish and Greco-Roman texts.[1] Previously passed over in discus-

---

1. See the classic study of Cosby, *Rhetorical Composition,* in which the attention given to rhetorical ornament by the author of Hebrews is carefully displayed and compared with other example lists from antiquity.

sions of the form and purpose of example lists, Seneca's *De beneficiis* provides such a list and has several impressive points of similarity. First, after posing the question whether or not it is possible for children ever to "give back" to their parents more than they have received, Seneca (*Ben.* 3.36.2–3.38.3) provides a list of examples of those who succeeded in besting their parents in the "contest" of reciprocity. He begins with an exhortation to his imaginary audience: "To your task, young heroes! A glorious contest is set before you. . . . Nor, in this glorious struggle, will there be any lack of leaders to encourage you to do as they did, and bid you follow their footsteps to the victory that often ere now has been won from parents." This is very similar to the form and imagery of Hebrews 12:1-2, which uses athletic (contest) metaphors to frame an exhortation to the audience to "join" in the contest that many have run before. The difference, of course, is that Hebrews concludes with an exhortation while Seneca introduces his list with one.[2] There follow detailed examples of how Aeneas, certain Sicilians, Antigonus, and Manlius showed such filial devotion as to have conferred on their parents greater benefits than they received. These are all marked by the rhetorical device of anaphora (*Vicit Aeneas. . . . Vicere Siculi. . . . Vicit Antigonus. . . . Vicit . . . Manlius*), again remarkably similar to the use of anaphora in Hebrews 11 (the repetition of "By faith," Πίστει). To close his list, Seneca presents an accumulation, an impressionistic pastiche of ways in which children have returned and surpassed their parents' beneficence: "There are countless instances of others who have snatched their parents from danger, who have advanced them from the lowest to the highest station, and, taking them from the nameless mass of commoners, have given them a name that will sound throughout the ages." The author of Hebrews similarly ends his list with an impressive collection of images of faith in action in 11:32-38. Like Hebrews 12:1-3, Seneca closes with a concluding exhortation: "Struggle on, I beg of you, and, even though wearied, renew the fight. Happy they who shall conquer, happy they who shall be conquered."[3]

The author of Hebrews shares with authors like Seneca a careful attention

---

2. Concluding an encomium with an exhortation to take up the stance or imitate the virtues of the fallen, however, was quite common. See Thucydides *Hist.* 2.43.4; Dio *Or.* 29.21; 4 Macc. 18:1.

3. Seneca will use a second example list (*Ben.* 5.16.1–17.3) in order to provide images of ingratitude toward one's homeland. Again the list is marked by anaphora: "Ingratus est Coriolanus. . . . Ingratus Catalina. . . . Ingratus C. Marius. . . . Ingratus L. Sulla. . . . Ingratus Cn. Pompeius. . . . Ingratus ipse Pompei hostis ac victor. . . . Ingratus Antonius. . . . Ingrati publice sumus." Noteworthy is the last paragraph before the conclusion: "The day will fail me to enumerate those whose ingratitude resulted in the ruin of their country. Equally endless will be the task if I attempt a survey of how ungrateful the commonwealth herself has been to its best and most devoted servants." This is followed by a concise accumulation of the fates of Rome's champions. The same hyperbolic introduction to the concluding accumulation appears in Heb. 11:32.

to the rhetorical composition of his example list, employing anaphora throughout, but also alliteration, homoeoptaton, assonance, comma, and a wealth of other ornaments. Michael Cosby justifiably concludes that "the author of Hebrews considered the success of his message to be largely dependent on the way it sounded to his audience. As he preaches to them, his many efforts at oral artistry in the construction of his utterances are not peripheral but central to his purpose."[4] The purpose, moreover, is also quite similar to Seneca's in *De beneficiis:* the author of Hebrews wants to motivate the hearers to make the embodiment of faith their goal, to implant this virtue and the ways in which it will direct their decisions deep into their minds.[5]

In terms of content, however, the list created by the author of Hebrews shares more in common with those lists found in the texts of writers who take not secular or recent history, but sacred history, as their resource for finding suitable examples. A noteworthy example comes from 4 Maccabees 16:16-23:

> My sons, noble is the contest to which you are called to bear witness for the nation. Fight zealously for our ancestral law. For it would be shameful if, while an aged man endures such agonies for the sake of religion, you young men were to be terrified by tortures. Remember that it is through God that you have had a share in the world and have enjoyed life, and therefore you ought to endure any suffering for the sake of God. For his sake also our father Abraham was zealous to sacrifice his son Isaac, the ancestor of our nation; and when Isaac saw his father's hand wielding a sword and descending upon him, he did not cower. And Daniel the righteous was thrown to the lions, and Hananiah, Azariah, and Mishael were hurled into the fiery furnace and endured it for the sake of God. You too must have the same faith in God [better, "faithfulness toward God"] and not be grieved. It is unreasonable for people who have religious knowledge not to withstand pain. (RSV)

In order to support the particular course of action of choosing to remain obedient to God's commandments even under pain of death, the speaker (the mother of the seven martyred brothers) introduces several examples from the OT. Just as Abraham and Isaac, Daniel, and the three companions of Daniel chose courageous endurance in loyalty toward God (expressed in obeying God's orders) over continued enjoyment of the pleasures of this world, so the seven brothers are to act in their situation, embodying "the same faithfulness."

---

4. *Rhetorical Composition,* 91.

5. Cosby (ibid., 108) observes that Greco-Roman lists "are less likely to use famous people . . . as models of behavior to imitate or avoid. They are more prone to use examples to prove or illustrate concepts without regard to the moral virtues of the people they list." The first list from Seneca examined here certainly adds another "exception" to the two noted by Cosby.

The example list provided by the author of Hebrews, therefore, is calculated to rouse emulation by praising the figures of the past who have attained
an honorable memory (see Aristotle *Rh.* 2.11.1, 4, 7). The praiseworthiness of
the lives of the exemplars proves the nobility of the way of faith. That Noah,
Abraham, and Moses have been remembered all these centuries shows the way
of "faith" to be the path to receiving the character witness of God that a person's
life has been honorably lived (see *Rhet. Alex.* 1429a25-28; Aristotle *Rh.* 1.9.25).
The examples themselves outline what faith looks like in action,[6] and several
appear to resonate quite pointedly with the audience's past experience and
choices (10:32-34) and ongoing situation. That is to say, the author has selected
and shaped his examples to address the specific situation of his hearers and to
support his exhortation to them.[7] In particular, Abraham, Moses, the martyrs,
and Jesus will affirm to the hearers that they have already been enacting this
quality of faith, and will instruct them further on what faith would "do" in their
situation. Hebrews 11:1–12:3 provides a litany of those people who "through
faith and patience inherit the promises" (6:12), thus filling out the picture of
the model the author had held up for the addressees' imitation ("become imitators," μιμηταὶ) so that they would not become "sluggish" but rather attain the
reception of the promises.[8]

Hebrews 11:1–12:3, then, will seek to answer the questions: What does it
mean to say "we are characterized by trust [faith] unto the preservation of the
soul" (10:39)? How, as people who embody faith, will we live in this world?
What does the life of a person of faith look like? Although the examples are not
all shaped with the same mold, a common pattern does arise from the exemplars that are most fully treated by the author, a pattern that is always supported
in some way by the briefer examples.[9] People who exhibit trust look forward to

---

6. "After exhorting his audience to faith in 10:19-38 and affirming the existence of
their faith in 10:39, in Hebrews 11 the author provides an extended series of examples to illustrate the characteristics of faith that please God" (ibid., 89).

7. See Croy, *Endurance,* 73: "There is the issue of shaping the *exemplum* to meet the
needs of the situation. Quintilian (5.11.6) advises that 'we must consider whether the entirety of the *exemplum* is similar or only part, in order that we might know whether to employ the whole or only those parts which are useful.'" Not only has the example of Jesus been
thus shaped, but all the examples of faith have been shaped to meet the pastoral needs of the
addressees and serve the rhetorical strategy of the author.

8. The addressees will thus be given a "pattern of trust" to follow, even as they received
a "pattern of disobedience" and "distrust" to avoid in 3:7-19.

9. For a fuller examination of specifically this pattern in Heb. 10:32–12:3, see my *Despising Shame,* 165-208. Eisenbaum (*Jewish Heroes,* 178-83) provides another fine attempt to
discern a "profile" of these heroes, which intersects at crucial points with, and reinforces, the
one developed here. Particularly useful is her elevation of the forward-looking (future) orientation of the people of faith, as well as their loss of status and marginalization.

God's reward and the coming to pass of his promises and admonitions. They orient themselves to their life in this world wholly on the basis of their knowledge of God's future. They make their choices based on what course is expedient for the attaining of God's promised benefactions, even if that course of action means loss of status, homeland, honor, wealth, even life in this world. No hardship, however, deters them from pursuit of the goal God has appointed for them. Whether the path of loyalty and obedience toward God brings them fame or disrepute, deliverance or torment, that is the path they pursue. They consider this world to be but the land of their sojourning, looking ever ahead to the city and homeland God has prepared for his people (the unshakable realm, the city "with foundations" that cannot be shaken) and ever living here so as not to jeopardize their welcome there. Like Abraham, the addressees are being called to persevere in their pilgrimage to that unshakable realm and not to look back wistfully to the homeland they left behind (socially if not spatially); like Abraham, Moses, the many martyrs, and the marginalized people of God throughout history, and like Jesus himself, they are challenged to hold of no account the opinion of those who embody the values of society rather than God and to embrace disgrace before unbelievers in order to receive the attestation of God and a share in the honorable destiny of the people of God.

Commentary

11:1-7

The author begins by formulating a definition of "faith" (πίστις) rich with rhetorical ornament.[10] Many scholars have documented the definition formula and the way in which Hebrews 11:1 follows it,[11] although they debate the quality of this "definition." Paul Ellingworth, for example, draws back from calling the verse an actual definition "especially in the absence of any immediate reference to God or Christ."[12] A definition — something that must be true in general — need not include so specific a reference, however. It is not "Christian faith" that the author defines but "faith" in general, and in a manner equally

---

10. Note especially the assonance created by the repetition of the -στ- sound in the first half of the definition and the -πι- or -πο- sounds throughout the definition: Ἔστιν δὲ πίστις ἐλπιζομένων ὑπόστασις, πραγμάτων ἔλεγχος οὐ βλεπομένων. Homoeoptaton appears in the repetition of the -ις and -ομένων terminations. Alliteration is evident in the repetition of the initial ἐ- /ἐλ- sounds.

11. Attridge, *Hebrews,* 307; Ellingworth, *Hebrews,* 564. Others, such as Spicq, *L'Épître aux Hébreux,* 2:336, to be sure, object to calling this a definition.

12. Ellingworth, *Hebrews,* 566.

well suited to defining "trust" in God and "trust" in a human being (as in Dio *Or.* 73, 74). What makes the author's "faith" Christian is not its kind but its object (God as the patron whose favor is secured by Jesus).[13] Harold Attridge is surely correct to point out that 11:1 provides "not . . . an abstract definition of faith, but . . . a programmatic remark for the encomium that follows."[14] The author attempts not a comprehensive definition but a definition that will focus the hearers on the elements of "trust" that are central to his exhortation. As a starting point, we can note the orientation of the faithful person toward things hoped for and unseen — certainly an aspect of living "by faith" that will repeatedly emerge in the examples that follow.

The author's definition is, as Ellingworth aptly describes, a case of clarifying obscure things by means of even more obscure words:[15] "And trust is the ὑπόστασις of things hoped for, the ἔλεγχος of unseen things." In equating "faith" or "trust" with ὑπόστασις, the author is choosing a term that has a va-

---

13. Erich Grässer (*Der Glaube im Hebräerbrief* [Marburg: Elwert, 1965]) contended that "faith" in Hebrews was a marked step backward from the Christocentric conception of faith in Paul's letters, and that it represented a return to an OT conception of faith as well as a reflection of the virtue of faithfulness. He concludes from his intensive investigation of "faith" words in Hebrews that the text reflects a late first-century church setting, and he places our author on the threshold between apostolic witness and the postapostolic era (p. 184). His work has been rightly criticized on numerous points (see especially the critique offered by G. Hughes, *Hebrews and Hermeneutics,* 137-42), most importantly on the fallacy of comparing the usage of a word group between two authors as a reliable index of overall theological position. Much could be made of the Christ-centeredness of discipleship in Hebrews, and of the parallels in thought (if not expression) between this author and Paul on numerous points. For example, "faith in Christ" in Paul moves the apostle to seek a close identification with Christ in his sufferings, so as to share also in Christ's resurrection (cf. Phil. 3:8-11); the author of Hebrews uses few of the same words, but the elevation of "bearing Christ's reproach" as the path to enter into "glory" (11:24-26; 13:12-14; cf. 2:10) surely expresses a similar model for discipleship.

"Faith" in Hebrews certainly bears marked resemblance to the language of "trusting" in the Greco-Roman world as well as "firmness" or "fidelity" in Hellenistic Judaism (e.g., 4 Maccabees). This does not mean that the life of faith, that is, the life of the disciple, is any less Christ-centered, or that a personal connection with Jesus is any less vital to the Christian vision of the author of Hebrews, even though he may choose language other than "faith" terms to bring this out. However, the theocentric character of faith in Hebrews reminds us that, ultimately, Christian faith is God-centered faith: Jesus' benefits toward us all serve the goal in Hebrews, as also in Paul, of restoring humankind to its intimate communion with God (cf. 2 Cor. 5:18-21, particularly if the "in Christ" phrase is read as a dative of means: "God was, in Christ, reconciling the world to himself"). There is at this point an essential continuity between "faith" in the OT, Hellenistic Judaism, and the early Church that Grässer is in danger of devaluing.

14. Attridge, *Hebrews,* 308.

15. Ellingworth, *Hebrews,* 566: "*obscura per obscuriora.*"

riety of meanings. In philosophical language it can signify the "substance" or "underlying essence" of something. Hebrews uses it in this sense in 1:3, where Jesus is the reflection of God's very being (God's essential character and substance). The same term, however, carries the everyday legal or business connotation of "title deed" or "guarantee," as attested by numerous papyri as well as classical texts.[16] Attridge objects to this second meaning being adopted at Hebrews 11:1 since the philosophical rather than the legal connotation was previously exploited in both 1:3 (essence, being, substance) and 3:14 (confidence, ground for confidence). He opts instead for the philosophical connotation once more.[17] David R. Worley, Jr., however, argues that the definition of "faith" in 11:1 speaks directly to the believers' loss of property attributed in 10:34 to their loyalty to Christ and the Christian group.[18] Given this immediate context, ὑπόστασις should be heard in the sense of title deed in 11:1, linking the discussion of faith more closely with 10:32-36 and the Christians' loss of property.

Elevating the philosophical over the legal connotation (or vice versa) is, however, both unnecessary and, ultimately, undemonstrable. Both senses underscore the impression that the definition is not a subjective one, talking about what faith "feels like" (e.g., "assurance of things hoped for") or establishes in the mind (e.g., "firm conviction of things unseen"). Rather, it reveals what "trust" or "faith" (πίστις) is in and of itself, and thus the significance of "having faith" or "trusting." Those who trust have in their possession, in effect, the title deed to what the person they trust will provide. They already have the "essence" of the thing they seek. All they still lack are the accidents, the material form, of that thing. For those who hope to enjoy their "better and lasting possessions" (10:34), then, "trust" becomes especially important. If they have trust, they have the thing they are hoping to receive; if they cease to trust, they relinquish their grasp on that which they would have otherwise come to enjoy. The definition is calculated to motivate the hearers to hold onto their trust in God's promises rather than lose everything through distrust, as did the wilderness generation. The author affirms that trusting is, in essence, possessing now what shall be enjoyed later. If "trust" means a certain present possessing of what is still hoped for, walking in "trust" toward God is the path to securing the enjoyment of those goods, hence the expedient course.

In this reading, πίστις in Hebrews is being understood very much within

---

16. *P. Oxy.* 1.138, 26; 3.488, 17; 10.1274, 15; Sophocles *Phil.* 813; *Oed. Col.* 1632. See the fine discussion in Spicq, *L'Épître aux Hébreux*, 2:337, who rejects subjective interpretations of this term based on the rather more objective usage in nonbiblical literature; see also Attridge, *Hebrews*, 309.

17. Attridge, *Hebrews*, 309-10.

18. Worley, "God's Faithfulness to Promise," 87-92.

the context of patronage or friendship.[19] After a client receives the patron's promise that a certain benefaction will be given to him or her, or entrusts a request or need to a patron, "trust" is all the client has. If the patron is honorable and reliable, however, having "trust" is as good as having the promised item itself.[20] Conversely, showing "distrust" toward the patron means letting go of the grasp on the promised item not only psychologically (because distrust produces anxiety) but in reality (as "distrust" manifested itself in "disobedience," which caused the wilderness generation to lose their possession of the promised land; 3:7-19).

The second half of the definition calls faith an ἔλεγχος, which the *Rhetorica ad Alexandrum* (1431a7-10) describes as an irrefutable or necessary fact. It is a datum that cannot be overturned by the opposition and that establishes one's case in the court or council chamber. Since πίστις also had the meaning of "proof" in the law courts, this half of the definition would carry a natural meaning in the context of argumentation: proof is the establishment beyond doubt of things no one in the jury actually saw (but upon which they must deliver a verdict) or of things that the audience in the council chamber has not yet seen (but must plan for in advance). However, what does the second clause mean in the context of the first, which laid down that "faith" or "trust" is the part of things hoped for that the one who "trusts" currently possesses? Since those who distrust their patron are in jeopardy of not receiving the goods for which they once hoped, there appears to be a kind of reciprocal relationship between trust and these as-yet-unseen realities. The latter substantiate the former (proving "trust" to be well founded), but the former also establishes the latter (bringing them into visible existence). Without "trust," the latter never materialize, whereas "by trust" the reality of the as-yet-unseen goods is demonstrated. "Trust," then, is the demonstration of things not seen. These hoped-for, unseen goods already exist in the unshakable realm; they are future realities only from the perspective of those who live in the material creation, who do not yet have "sight" of that better realm which is yet to be disclosed.[21]

The definition of faith in 11:1 and the discussion of hope in 6:19-20 serve the similar function of motivating the hearers to invest themselves fully in this hope and persevere unwaveringly in this trust. In the earlier passage, "hope" is what enters the heavenly realm where Jesus has gone. Hope is our mooring or an-

---

19. This is in keeping with the use of the term in contemporary nonbiblical literature, such as in Dio's orations on "trust" and "distrust" (*Or.* 73 and 74).

20. Dio raises serious questions about the merits of trust on account of the untrustworthiness of so many human beings. Distrust was, for him, frequently the mark of the wise person. The author of Hebrews does not share in this skepticism because the object of the Christian's trust, the One who promised, is supremely reliable and trustworthy (6:13-20; 10:23). It is God's reliability that gives Christian trusting its absolute and irrefutable character.

21. See also Attridge, *Hebrews*, 311.

chorage in that heavenly harbor. To hold onto hope, therefore, is to hold onto our moorings in the heavenly homeland and the one thing that allows us passage into that harbor — the line, as it were, by which we are pulled along into the ultimate realm and our final destiny. Similarly, "trust" represents all that we currently possess of our "better and lasting possessions. "Trust" is the beginning of which "full possession and enjoyment" is the end. The formulation of 3:14, namely, that believers remain Christ's partners "if we hold the first installment of the ὑπόστασις firm unto the end," is reinforced and clarified now by this definition of "trust." If we have trust, the author says, we have the down payment and essence of that for which we hope because God is absolutely reliable — he will follow through in delivering what he promised. If we have hope, we are already anchored and moored in that abiding realm which we hope to enter.

Faith is the way to gaining "attestation" (μαρτυρία). Appended to the famous definition of faith in 11:1 is the phrase "for by this [i.e., faith] the elders[22] received approval" (11:2). While defined in LSJ primarily as a forensic term (i.e., testimony in a law court), the verb acquired a sense of "give recognition to" and the noun a sense of "favorable recognition" or even "praise." Frederick Danker's study of inscriptions to benefactors reveals the frequent use of this word group to express endorsement by Roman authorities of a person whom a local assembly wished to honor. It represented approval of the authorities that the candidate was worthy of receiving honors (and was politically reliable).[23] Danker then adduces numerous NT examples of the use of this word carrying the sense of "bearing favorable testimony" and thus "spreading a good reputation."[24] Noteworthy among these is 1 Timothy 3:7, in which one of the qualifications for the bishop is given as a good reputation ("it is necessary for him to have a noble reputation," μαρτυρίαν καλὴν) among outsiders. The concentrated use of μαρτυρεῖσθαι in the opening verses of the litany of faith (11:2, 4, 5) and the reoccurrence of this term at the transition from encomium to hortatory peroration (11:39) suggest that the author wishes to emphasize that perseverance in faith will result in a similar recognition of the addressees before God's court, a testimony to their worth and a grant of honor.

This "attestation" refers directly to the witness borne them by means of the incorporation of their stories in the oracles of God, the sacred history of God's people in the LXX. The sacred texts forever commemorated the honor

---

22. The very term "elders" may have been chosen to signify their honored status: the term is used to refer not merely to the aged but to those worthy of honor and held in esteem (see Philo *Sobr.* 16; cited in Attridge, *Hebrews*, 314).

23. Danker, *Benefactor*, 442-43.

24. Ibid., 443-47. Rather surprisingly, Danker does not cite any of the occurrences of this term in Hebrews, although he opened this section speaking of the importance of enjoying the favorable testimony of the gods.

and virtue of those who showed faith in and toward God. This testimony includes, however, God's approval, God's witness that the faithful one did well, chose wisely, acted nobly[25] — in short, "pleased" God (11:5-6), in stark contrast to the one who shrinks back, in whom God has no pleasure (10:37-38). God becomes the character witness for these people, the witness being recorded and available for posterity in the Scriptures.

The next verse poses something of a structural dilemma. The first appearance of the anaphoric refrain "by faith" in 11:3 appears to signal to the hearer that the list of examples has begun,[26] yet the hearer encounters not the first example of faithful behavior but rather a conviction about the origin of the cosmos held by "us," that is, the author and his audience:[27] "by trust we consider the ages[28] to have been established by the word of God, so that what is visible came into being from things unavailable to sensory experience."[29] The author's interest here is merely to affirm that the material, visible cosmos came into being by means of causes beyond and above the realm of what can be experienced by the senses, the principal cause of which was the "word of God."[30] This belief, however, is certainly a principle taken by the author and his audience on "trust" since no one was present to witness it. In this sense, the second

---

25. Attridge (*Hebrews,* 314) correctly observes that the author "will emphasize the incomplete achievement of many of the heroes of old. Hence the 'proof of the unseen' that their faith provides must come, in part at least, not from the immediate results of their fidelity, but from God's attestation that they were indeed on the right track." It is their commendation in the sacred texts that demonstrates the wisdom and nobility of their lives and choices, rather than the fact that they achieved the goal toward which they walked in faith.

26. Hence Cosby's grouping (*Rhetorical Composition,* 41) of this verse with those that follow. In favor of this grouping is the possibility that the author is merely seeking to be universal in his scope: rather than provide just a few examples, he relates everything from Genesis through 2–4 Maccabees to his survey of "trust" in God's promise and word.

27. The appearance here and in 11:39-40 of the first person plural pronoun leads Eisenbaum (*Jewish Heroes,* 147) to see an *inclusio* marking off 11:4-38 as the body of the example list (and thus 11:1-3 as an introduction).

28. The author refers to the created order using the plural "ages," showing his connection with the Jewish apocalyptic worldview (cf. Matt. 12:32; Mark 10:30; Gal. 1:4; Eph. 1:21; also Heb. 1:2, "through whom he made the ages").

29. The word order in the expression τὸ μὴ ἐκ φαινομένων is "normal in classical Greek" for "from things unseen" (Ellingworth, *Hebrews,* 569, helpfully points out that early Latin, Syriac, and Armenian translations of the Greek already understood the phrase this way). The negative particle is probably to be taken as negating the participle φαινομένων and not the infinitive γεγονέναι. See 2 Macc. 7:28 for a similar construction, which must likewise be construed.

30. 2 Macc. 7:28, however, very distinctly affirms the position of creation *ex nihilo,* a position that P. Hughes (*Hebrews,* 443) finds in Heb. 11:3 by taking the negative particle with the infinitive (which is certainly a possibility, though the classical Greek idiomatic word order, which reached as far as 2 Maccabees, still remains the more probable guide here).

half of the definition of "trust" (where trust provides the demonstrative proof of things unavailable to sensory inspection) is more immediately relevant. Because we trust the reliability of the oracles of God (i.e., Gen. 1:3, 6, 9; Ps. 33:6, 9; Wis. 9:1), we can "consider" this proposition a fact. Trusting in the reliability of God's word as "reliable report" and as "promise" is hardly a significant difference.

To what end does the author introduce this proposition? Significantly, 11:3 affirms the ultimate dependence of the visible on the invisible, and thus the superiority and ultimacy of the latter. It reinforces the author's axiological claim that the visible realm is secondary to, and less valuable than, the invisible realm. The invisible realm both predates (11:3) and postdates the visible realm (12:26-28). Given the absolute reliability of the scriptural witness concerning the origins of the material cosmos, 11:3 may also serve to make the visible creation a proof for the invisible realm from which it sprang (if the effect exists, the cause must also exist), and in which the addressees are called to place their hope and seek their home.[31] This invisible realm will be a major focus of many exemplars of faith.

Faith takes into consideration the unseen and future realities in charting its course of action. This is a repeated theme of chapter 11 (vv. 3, 7, 10, 16, 20, 22, 26b, 27b, 35b), in which the heroes of faith make the proper evaluations and choices only because they are able to see past the visible, material, sensory world. Reference to the unseen and future realities relativizes the importance of the visible and present — at the very least it sets it within a different perspective.[32] Because unbelievers do not share this perspective and the commitment that ultimate reality consists not in the present world but in the unshakable kingdom of God, their opinion and evaluation are unreliable. Only the person of "faith" can properly evaluate advantages and disadvantages. Indeed, this criterion (developed throughout 10:32–12:3, not merely by 11:3) appears to function in a manner similar to that posed in Plato's *Crito* (49C-D):

Then we ought neither to requite wrong with wrong nor to do evil to anyone,

---

31. The use to which 2 Macc. 7:28 puts the concept of creation *ex nihilo* is strikingly similar. There, the mother of the seven martyred brothers exhorts the last surviving one to consider that, just as God brought the visible creation out of nothing and thus brought the race of humankind into existence, so God was able to restore the life of the faithful martyrs. The introduction of this consideration in Hebrews may also encourage the release of temporal goods in favor of the invisible, unshakable possessions that God was able to supply.

32. Compare 2 Cor. 4:16-18: "So we do not lose heart. Even though our outer nature is wasting away, our inner nature is being renewed day by day. For this slight momentary affliction is preparing us for an eternal weight of glory beyond all measure, because we look not at what can be seen but at what cannot be seen; for what can be seen is temporary, but what cannot be seen is eternal" (NRSV).

no matter what he may have done to us. And be careful, Crito, that you do not, in agreeing to this, agree to something you do not believe; for I know that there are few who believe or ever will believe this. Now those who believe this, and those who do not, have no common ground for discussion, but they must necessarily, in view of their opinions, despise one another (ἀλλήλων καταφρονεῖν).

Indeed, it is by regarding the unseen as visible that the figures of Noah, Abraham, Moses, and the martyrs can endure the loss of status and prestige that the actions of faith bring in the eyes of unbelievers, and thus can attain life and honor before God and in the memory of the community of believers.

We shall never know what made Abel's sacrifice better than Cain's, but the author of Hebrews uses that obscure episode first to connect "trusting" with attaining the reputation of a "just" person (see also 11:7): "by faith Abel offered to God a greater sacrifice than Cain, through which he received the attestation that he was just, God bearing witness concerning his gifts, and through it [faith] he still speaks, even though he died." The role of "faith" is, of course, the author's addition: Genesis 4:2-10 (MT) does not mention faith, nor does it explain that Abel's sacrifice was "greater" or "better" either in terms of quality or quantity. The LXX already tends toward such an interpretation of Genesis 4:7 (MT). The LXX explicitly says "if you had offered it correctly, but you did not divide it correctly, you would not have been sinning, would you?" Philo (*Sacr. AC* 52, 57, 88) refers frequently to the superior quality of Abel's offering and the second-rate quality of Cain's offering. Hebrews's description of Abel's offering as πλείονα shows some awareness of this line of understanding. That the author of Hebrews ascribes the presence of a virtue as important for the sacrifice's acceptability (here, "trust") is also significant, since speculation about the relationship of Abel's and Cain's moral qualities to the acceptability of the respective offerings is also attested (Josephus *Ant.* 1.2.1 §53; 1 John 3:12). It is then, perhaps, the presence of "trust" or "faith" that makes Abel's sacrifice "greater" than Cain's, which also leads to Abel's enjoyment of that reality which he trusts God to provide (i.e., life after death).

Abel is not actually attested "to be just" in the LXX, but δίκαιος becomes a common epithet for Abel and a frequent description of his lifestyle (Matt. 23:35; 1 John 3:12; Josephus *Ant.* 1.2.1 §53). The author appears to share in this tradition of ascribing "justice" to Abel. It is perhaps this common evaluation of Abel as "just" that leads the author to deduce that he conducted himself "by faith," a connection inherent in the Habakkuk quotation in Hebrews 10:38, "my righteous one will live by faith." God "bears witness concerning the gifts" perpetually in the scriptural record of the acceptability of Abel's sacrifice and rejection of Cain's sacrifice.

Genesis 4:10 (LXX) spoke of Abel's blood crying out to God from the ground. This, of course, was meant figuratively in both the MT and LXX — a sort of biblical "murder will out" rather than a suggestion of Abel's ongoing existence. This verse has now been interpreted, however, as a signal that Abel, though dead, still lives beyond death and has the capacity to "speak."[33] As Harold Attridge aptly surmises, Abel is the first example of one who, by faith, "lives" even beyond the grave,[34] just as all who trust God shall "live" (Hab. 2:3-4; cf. 4 Macc. 7:18-19: "they do not die to God but live to God"; also 4 Macc. 16:25). Both the examples of Abel and of Enoch underscore the transcendence of death as the result of a life of trusting God, a theme that will continue to echo throughout the encomium (11:4-6, 11-12, 17-19, 35). This reinforces a crucial pillar in the construction of the Christian world: Christians must evaluate choices and weigh alternatives with a view to the next life.

The second exemplar of faith is the shadowy figure of Enoch:

> By faith Enoch was translated in order not to see death, and he was not found because God translated him. For before the translation he was attested to be pleasing to God. And without faith it is impossible to be pleasing, for it is necessary for the one drawing near to God to trust that God exists and that he becomes a rewarder to those seeking him out. (11:5-6)

The example of Enoch is confined to 11:5, with 11:6 drawing out a general principle for the addressees' benefit. Most of the author's words are a recontextualization of the LXX version of Enoch's story in Genesis 5:22, 24, NRSV. Genesis 5:22, 24 (MT) reads: "Enoch walked with God after the birth of Methuselah three hundred years. . . . Enoch walked with God; then he was no more, because God took him." The LXX interprets "walked with God" as "pleased God" (εὐηρέστησεν δὲ Ενωχ τῷ θεῷ). After pleasing God for three hundred years, Enoch "was found no more, because God translated him."[35] As with Abel, the author interjects the quality of "faith"[36] and provides an interpretation of "translation," taking it to signify specifically the bypassing of death. As did Abel's, Enoch's example elevated the value of faith as a quality that brings one

---

33. The author is still, contra Lane (*Hebrews*, 335), alluding to Gen. 4:10 as the locus of this witness, as the explicit reference to the blood, which speaks in Heb. 12:24, will render highly probable.

34. Attridge, *Hebrews*, 317.

35. Given the availability of expansions on the story of Enoch in the intertestamental period (e.g., *1 Enoch*), it is astounding that the author shows so little interest beyond what he can read about Enoch in Genesis. Wisdom 4:10-11 contains a generalized version of the story of Enoch as a paradigm of God's preservation of the virtue of the righteous person through an untimely departure from this world — one that, however, leads to a good destiny in God's company.

36. Perhaps the author reasons that Enoch can justly be said to exercise "faith" because he is said to have "pleased God," and "without trust it is impossible to please God."

to the enjoyment of life beyond death and beyond this visible realm. The author postpones the significant LXX detail that Enoch was "pleasing to God" so
as to highlight the cause and effect between pleasing God and the transcendence of death. The recontextualization of Genesis 5:22 and 24 (LXX) introduces the uncommon word εὐαρεστῆσαι, "to be pleasing," into the text, and
this word will continue to reverberate through 13:21 (11:6; 12:28; 13:16, 21).
The author seeks to develop "pleasing God" as a primary value for the believer,
particularly since it brings the reward of crossing over from death into life and
receiving God's eternal benefactions.[37] This well suits his strategy of detaching
Christians from the opinion and approval of outsiders (which would draw
them away from attachment to the group) and focusing them more completely
on God's approval (which leads them toward behaviors that sustain the group
and enact its values).

The key term of Genesis 5:22, 24 (LXX), "pleasing God," allows the author
to embellish briefly what "pleasing God" entails. Just as the example of the wilderness generation showed how distrust displeased God, the author now adduces the contrary, explaining why "trust" would be a necessary prerequisite to
pleasing God. In order to please God, one must trust that the invisible God exists (see 11:27) and that this God will prove a reliable and beneficent patron (a
"rewarder")[38] of those who seek out God's favor. This is the prerequisite to
pleasing God (which will involve worship, witness, service, reliability in one's
familial obligations to brothers and sisters in God's household; 13:1-3, 15-16)
and the necessary foundation in order to make the sorts of investments and
choices that will lead to a life pleasing in God's sight.

The author concludes his sweep of antediluvian worthies with an extremely concise reference to the trust and firmness exhibited by Noah in the extensive narrative of Genesis 6–9: "By faith Noah, having been warned concerning events not yet seen and responding reverently, prepared an ark unto the
salvation of his household, through which he condemned the world and became an heir of the righteousness that comes with trust" (11:7). Noah is introduced in Genesis 6:9 (LXX) as "righteous" and "pleasing to God" (δίκαιος . . .
τῷ θεῷ εὐηρέστησεν). The "warning" to which the author refers is given in Genesis 6:13, and Noah's reverent obedience, in Genesis 6:22. The focal point for

---

37. The importance of "pleasing God" was also recently reinforced by the author's recitation of his altered version of Hab. 2:4 and its interpretation in Heb. 10:37-39. "Shrinking
back" means not pleasing God, and it leads to destruction. For God to "take no pleasure" in
one has eternal repercussions.

38. The author uses what appears to be a word of his own devising — μισθαποδότης
— to describe God. This is closely related to another extremely rare word, μισθαποδοσία,
used at 2:2; 10:35; 11:26. The author's repetition of this unusual compound word reinforces
the focus throughout on the eternal consequences (the "payback") of the addressees' choices
and commitments here.

the author is that, given a warning by God concerning what was yet to come to pass, some event entirely unavailable to Noah's senses and experiences, Noah nevertheless trusted God's word and acted accordingly. Because he planned his agenda in light of the future realities announced to him by God, even though there was no observable confirmation along the way that this agenda was sound and profitable, he gained safety ("salvation," σωτηρία) for his whole family.

The analogies between Noah's position and the position of the hearers as the author has depicted it are striking. Just as Noah lived on the eve of judgment, so the addressees live just before the dawn of that coming "Day" (10:25, 37-38) when the corresponding eschatological judgment shall take place. The audience, too, has been warned about future things (9:28; 10:12-13, 25, 37-39), and the author invites them to imitate Noah, to trust the word about God's coming to judge the contrary and reward the loyal, and to act in their present situation so as to condemn the world by their ongoing witness to God's Law and standards, to God's sole claim on worship, and the like. Like Noah, the addressees are to use their time and resources in this life to prepare for salvation at the day of judgment, at the return of Christ, and to pour themselves into meeting that crisis. Thus they will attain the "salvation" or "deliverance" that God prepared for them (1:14; 9:28), namely, entrance into the world that "abides," and rescue from the world that will be catastrophically "shaken" (12:26-28), even as Noah attained "salvation" for his household by acting in accordance with trust in God and God's warnings. Noah's example shows that expediency resides in acting on the basis of God's declarations about the future, things not yet seen but certain to come into being.

The author includes two other significant comments in his shaping of Noah's example. First, Noah's trust was the means through which "he condemned the world." There was a widespread tradition that Noah, along with building the ark, preached a message of repentance in light of the impending judgment (a message that the audience rejected, of course).[39] If the author had this tradition in mind, however, it is surprising that he does not make more of it as a means of encouraging the addressees to witness boldly concerning the coming day of salvation and judgment. He leaves such "witness" implicit and undeveloped. The author may rather assert that Noah's commitment to trust God's word and preparations to grasp the opportunity of salvation that God announced in themselves condemned the world, which went on with its injustice without regard for God's judgment. Similarly, the addressees who walk in the way of Noah may regard their trust and preparation as a condemnation of the world — a striking concept given the ways in which the believers have been made to feel condemnation by the unbelieving society. The author raises them

---

39. See 2 Pet. 2:5; *Sib. Or.* 1.125-36; *1 Clem.* 7.6. Attridge (*Hebrews*, 319) and Lane (*Hebrews 9–13*, 339) both suggest that the author of Hebrews has this tradition in mind.

from being concerned with society's judgment on their commitment to Jesus and to one another to being empowered by the realization that their ongoing perseverance in the upward call of God "condemns" the world that sees no value in such a call.

The second comment involves a "superficially Pauline" expression,[40] "the righteousness which is according to faith" (τῆς κατὰ πίστιν δικαιοσύνης) of which Noah "became an heir." Harold Attridge helpfully suggests that this phrase describes not "being reckoned righteous on account of faith" (as Abraham is in Rom. 4), but rather the acting out of what is righteous because one is guided by trust in God.[41] The phrase is directly informed by 10:38-39 and 12:11, where the righteous person does not "shrink back" and where the child of God endures the training that produces righteousness as its fruit. "Faith" here signifies bold perseverance, trust, and firmness with regard to God's promises and warnings: the person who walks in line with "faith" of this kind will find the virtue of righteousness formed within himself or herself by the end of the journey.

11:8-22

The first example to receive substantial treatment is that of Abraham together with his immediate descendants, Isaac and Jacob. The common association of these three patriarchs stems from the shared condition of their existence as well as God's explicit identification of himself to Moses as "the God of Abraham, the God of Isaac, and the God of Jacob" (Exod. 3:6; see Matt. 22:31-32). The first three patriarchs thus become connected by more than the Genesis narratives, specifically in God's willingness to identify his name with them (Heb. 11:16).[42] This example is divided into two parts, the first half emphasizing the posture of the person of faith in this world, the second half the ability of God's promise to transcend death and the forward-looking quality of trust. Both parts, however, do contain as a minor theme the major theme of the other part.

> By faith Abraham, being called to go out into a place that he was about to receive as an inheritance, obeyed, and he went out, although he did not know where he was going. By faith he sojourned in the land of promise as if in a land not his own, dwelling in tents with Isaac and Jacob, fellow heirs of the same promise: for he was awaiting the city having foundations, whose

---

40. Attridge, *Hebrews,* 320.

41. Ibid.

42. See, for example, the association of these three names in 4 Macc. 7:19, NRSV: "they believe that they, like our patriarchs Abraham, Isaac, and Jacob, do not die to God, but live to God."

craftsperson and builder is God. By faith — Sarah herself being barren — he received power to procreate (and far past the age!), since he considered the one who had promised to be reliable. Therefore from one person were engendered — and these from a dead man! — descendants as numerous as the stars of heaven and as the innumerable sand beside the seashore.

These all died in a state of trust, not receiving the promised goods but seeing and greeting them from afar and confessing that they were strangers and resident aliens on the earth. For people who say such things show they are seeking a homeland. And if they had in mind that land from which they had gone out, they would have had an opportunity to return. But now they reach out for a better — that is, a heavenly — homeland. Therefore God is not ashamed of them to be called their God, for he has prepared a city for them. (11:8-16)

This portrayal of Abraham's faith emphasizes not, as in Paul, the firm conviction that God would fulfill his promise to give Abraham offspring (cf. Gal. 3:15-18; Rom. 4:13-21). Rather, it is his departure from his native land in obedience to God's call (11:8-10) that the author highlights in 11:8-10, 13-16. The author's comment on the example underscores their confession to be "strangers and exiles on the earth," which bears witness to the city of God and wins them association with God (11:16).

In 11:8, the author succinctly brings together the salient features of Genesis 12:1-7. The author infers that Abraham obeys before he knows the way from the precise order of the OT text, in which God first gives unspecified directions ("to the land which I will show you," Gen. 12:1), then Abraham immediately obeys (Gen. 12:4), and then, only after the journey, God indicates that the land they presently occupy will be theirs for an inheritance (Gen. 12:7; cf. 13:15; 15:7; 17:8). Once again the author's reserve in terms of using solely the LXX witness to Abraham's faith is striking, since there were available during the first century a wealth of legends concerning Abraham's experiences in "coming to faith" in the One God before leaving Ur.[43] The author portrays the patriarchs' existence in this "land of promise" (see Gen. 15:7 and 17:8, where Canaan is clearly identified as this promised land) not as citizens in their own country but as a "sojourning as in a land not their own" (παρῴκησεν εἰς γῆν . . . ὡς ἀλλοτρίαν). The first component of the depiction of these people of faith is that they willingly leave their place in their native land in order to follow in obedience the call and promise of God, accepting the status of "aliens" and "foreigners" in any earthly locale.

When the faith of Abraham and his family, then, motivates them to embrace the life of "foreigners and resident aliens" (ξένοι καὶ παρεπίδημοί, 11:13),

---

43. These are discussed in David deSilva and Victor Matthews, *Untold Stories of the Bible* (Lincolnwood, IL: Publications International Ltd., 1998), 34-48.

this would be heard as a deliberate choice to live a life of lower status liable to dishonor and danger. Whether or not Abraham suffered any of these ills in his sojourning, the cultural context of the hearers suggests that both author and addressees of Hebrews would have understood Abraham's choice as embracing a loss of status for the sake of obedience to God's call.[44] In effect, the patriarchs willingly embraced a lower status in terms of the world's estimation in order to attain at length an honored status in God's sight and God's city.

A Closer Look: Citizenship and Sojourning

Greco-Roman and Jewish literature attest both to the importance of one's native land for one's sense of identity and to the trials that attended the foreigner and sojourner. Dio indicates in an address to his native city of Prusa that one's native land held a special place in the heart of its citizens:

> Fellow citizens, no sight is more delightful to me than your faces, no voice dearer than yours, no honours greater than those you bestow, no praise more splendid than praise from you. Even if the whole Greek world, and the Roman people too, were to admire and praise me, that would not so cheer my heart. For though, in truth, Homer has spoken many wise and divine words, he never spoke a wiser or a truer word than this: "For naught is sweeter than one's native land." (*Or.* 44.1)

The fellow inhabitants of one's native country or city formed one's group of significant others, one's primary reference group. Hence Dio would regard honor (praise) from his fellow Prusans as greater and more meaningful than honor from the people of other cities or countries. Therefore, to lose their respect would be of correspondingly greater pain.

Living away from one's native land, however, exposed one to a loss of status and to limited access to acquiring real honor. While philosophers consoling those sent into exile might argue that one could gain fame in a foreign land to make up for the loss felt by being denied a place at home, their argument was not convincing. Lucian, for example, records that

> Those who get on well [in a foreign land], however successful they may be in all else, think that they lack one thing at least, a thing of the greatest importance, in that they do not live in their own country but sojourn in a strange land; for thus to sojourn is a reproach (ὄνειδος). (*My Native Land* 8)

Plutarch (*De exil.* 17 [*Mor.* 607 A]) likewise gives evidence that to live away from one's native land exposed one to reproach and dishonor. Plutarch's imaginary interlocutor inter-

---

44. The element of choice is important, as Worley ("God's Faithfulness to Promise," 72-73) has underscored: "The depiction in verse 9 of Abraham living in tents, behaving like a person in a foreign land, is not the picture of a man victimized by circumstances, living the life of an alien unable to possess the promised land. Rather, his life style is one of his choosing because of his expectations for a city of God. He lives in tents because he believes his inheritance to be elsewhere, in a city with permanent foundations designed and built by God."

jects into his discussion of enduring exile the objection: "But 'exile' is a term of reproach." Plutarch responds: "Yes, among fools, who make terms of abuse out of 'pauper,' 'bald,' 'short,' and indeed 'foreigner' and 'immigrant' (τὸν ξένον καὶ τὸν μέτοικον)." What is important to observe here is not Plutarch's objection to the use of these terms as insults, but the fact that such a use is current and common. Ben Sira provides a similarly dismal picture of the life of the stranger (Sir. 29:24-28, RSV).

> It is a miserable life to go from house to house,
>   and where you are a stranger you may not open your mouth;
> you will play the host and provide drink without being thanked,
>   and besides this you will hear bitter words:
> "Come here, stranger, prepare the table,
>   and if you have anything at hand, let me have it to eat."
> "Give place, stranger, to an honored person;
>   my brother has come to stay with me; I need my house."
> These things are hard to bear for a man who has feeling:
>   scolding about lodging and the reproach of the moneylender.

Living as a stranger in a foreign land implies that the foreigner has not been enfranchised in the new location, possessing neither citizenship nor the rights that accompany such status. Lack of citizenship in the ancient world also left one vulnerable to disgrace and loss. Dio (*Or.* 66.15) paints this picture of those who have lost their citizenship, which may also apply to those who never possessed it: "To the disenfranchised (ἀτίμοις) life seems with good reason not worth living, and many choose death rather than life after losing their citizenship, for whoever so desires is free to strike them and there exists no private means of punishing him who treats them with contumely." Rescinding the citizenship of the Alexandrian Jews was a prelude to the disasters that stripped them of honor, property, and life, as Philo (*Flacc.* 53-55) describes:

> When his attack against our laws by seizing the meeting-houses without even leaving them their name appeared to be successful, he proceeded to another scheme, namely, the destruction of our citizenship (πολιτείας), so that when our ancestral customs and our participation in political rights, the sole mooring on which our life was secured, had been cut away, we might undergo the worst misfortunes with no cable to cling to for safety. For a few days afterward he issued a proclamation in which he denounced us as foreigners and aliens (ξένους καὶ ἐπήλυδας) and gave us no right of pleading our case but condemned us unjudged. . . . And then to the first two wrongs he added a third by permitting those who wished to pillage the Jews as at the sacking of a city. . . .

Citizenship brought security, a solid "mooring" within a society; lack of citizenship left one adrift, as it were, an easy prey to abuse and insult. It was a far less comfortable position even if one never did suffer outrage, for the defenses against such outrage were much weaker than for the citizen.

In the description of the patriarchs' lifestyle and lack of rootedness in Canaan, the author brings together details from the LXX record (dwelling in Canaan in tents, Gen. 12:8; sojourning, Gen. 13:18; 17:8; 23:4) in order to emphasize a point not envisioned by the authors of Genesis. Abraham dwelt in

Canaan, the "promised land," as a sojourner,[45] "in tents," precisely because he knew he was looking not for any earthly region as his abiding dwelling place, but rather for the heavenly homeland (11:13-16). He was not merely looking forward to upgrading his living quarters and status in Canaan. Even when he arrived in Canaan he was still looking for a better homeland, understanding that to be the subject of God's promise. The fact that Abraham did not call Canaan "home," but explicitly refers to himself as a sojourner and stranger (Gen. 23:4) after his arrival in Canaan, is taken by the author of Hebrews to mean that Abraham was looking beyond an earthly homeland to the heavenly, abiding homeland as the true object of God's promise to him and to his children.[46] The promise to Abraham is being interpreted as heavenly rest, which the Christians also strive to enter. The addressees, therefore, are also in effect "fellow heirs of the same promise" (see Heb. 10:34; 12:28; 13:13-14), a point which will be made explicit in 11:39-40.

The author explains that Abraham intentionally assumes the posture of "foreigner and alien" precisely because "he was awaiting the city having foundations, whose architect and builder is God" (11:10). This description of the goal of the pilgrimage of the people of faith borrows qualities assigned in the OT to the first Jerusalem. God is frequently said to have "laid the foundations" of Jerusalem (Ps. 86:5 [LXX]; Isa. 14:32). Noteworthy is Psalm 47:9 (LXX): "God laid her foundations for ever" (θεὸς ἐθεμελίωσεν αὐτὴν εἰς τὸν αἰῶνα). The fate of the earthly Jerusalem in 70 A.D. led to increased attention among Jewish authors to the heavenly counterpart to the city of God, the "heavenly Jerusalem," which 2 Apocalypse of Baruch 4:1-7 significantly claims God revealed to Adam, Abraham, and Moses. Such a tradition may undergird the author's assertion that Abraham's real goal was the heavenly city prepared by God (Heb. 11:11, 16). That the final, eschatological goal for the people of God was already being conceptualized in terms of a heavenly Zion is already attested by Paul in Galatians 4:21-31.

The author of Hebrews returns to this image throughout the remainder

---

45. Lane (Hebrews 9–13, 344) reads παρῴκησεν εἰς γῆν as meaning "migrated to the land" rather than "sojourned in the land," found in the major translations and defended by Ellingworth (Hebrews, 583), who points to the nearby κατοικήσας to support the usual translation. If Lane is correct, Canaan is simply not in the author's presentation at all: Abraham is depicted as a pilgrim migrating to the land of promise, the heavenly city prepared by God. The phrase "as in [a land] not his own," which qualifies παρῴκησεν, should be decisive, however, in favor of Ellingworth's reading: it is Abraham's decision to regard Canaan as "belonging to another" that signals the otherworldly object of his quest.

46. This parallels the author's earlier argument that Joshua did not give the people the promised "rest" when they took possession of Canaan at long last (4:1-11). God's design was always to lead his people to a place in the unshakable realm, and people of faith live in this world in the knowledge that it is not their "home."

of his sermon (11:10, 16; 12:22; 13:14) as a meaningful image for the destiny of the believers themselves.[47] Unlike the earthly Jerusalem, destroyed by Nebuchadnezzar in 587 B.C. and prey to all manner of violence, corruption, and profanation throughout history (e.g., the episodes under Antiochus IV in 167-164 B.C. and Pompey in 63 B.C.), this heavenly city truly does "have foundations" that will not be shaken. Indeed, that city's foundations will enable it alone to stand after the eschatological "shaking" that will destroy every earthly city along with the removal of the visible cosmos itself (12:26-28; cf. 13:14: "here we have no lasting city"). Naming God as the craftsperson and builder of this city corresponds to the remarks about the superior quality of the tabernacle made by God and not by humans (8:2). These two details concerning the city's "fortifications" and "founder" correspond directly to common topics employed by orators praising a city's greatness.[48] Quintilian (*Inst.* 3.7.26) prescribes: "Cities are praised after the same fashion as human beings. The founder takes the place of the parent, and antiquity carries great authority. . . . The advantages arising from site or fortifications are, however, peculiar to cities." The superior prize for which Abraham contended allowed him to endure loss and hardship along the way, for he knew that citizenship in God's city entailed greater honor and security than citizenship in any earthly homeland. The addressees are encouraged to have the same mind as their spiritual ancestor.[49]

Following the order of the biblical narrative, the author arrives at a feature of the faith of Abraham and Sarah that he cannot bypass, even though it temporarily interrupts his focus in 11:8-16 and anticipates his focus in 11:17-22. In a few words, he adds to his sermon the leading features of the narrative of Genesis 17 and 18 — the promise that Sarah would bear a son (Gen. 17:16, 19, 21; 18:10), the advanced age of the parents (Gen. 18:11-13; 21:7), and the steril-

---

47. The author skillfully changes and develops the images for the final destiny of the believers and the content of the promise as the context of his discussion changes. Thus in chapters 3 and 4, in the context of the example of the wilderness generation, the promise is conceived of as "rest"; in the context of the presentation of Jesus' work and the hearers' advantage in cultic imagery, the goal becomes the heavenly "holy of holies." Now, as the author more directly addresses the believers' experience of loss and abuse in their current city, the image is again transformed into a secure city and homeland where they shall enjoy perpetual honor in God's presence.

48. They also correspond to topics of broader application when one desires to demonstrate superiority: it was formed by a greater "cause" (Aristotle *Rh.* 1.7.7) and possessed a greater ability to endure (Aristotle *Rh.* 1.7.26); it is therefore a "greater good" than earthly cities.

49. See Thucydides *Hist.* 2.42.1, where Pericles rouses the hearers to take up their place in defense of Athens based on the value of that city in comparison with others: "It is for this reason that I have dwelt upon the greatness of our city; for I have desired to show you that we are contending for a higher prize than those who do not enjoy such privileges in like degree."

ity of Sarah's womb (Gen. 11:30). Scholars are divided over the grammatical position of Sarah in this sentence. Is "Sarah, herself sterile" the subject who, by faith, receives the "power to beget offspring"? The nominative case of the three words strongly points in this direction, and thus one might find in this section on Abraham's faith a counterpart to the appearance of Rahab in the section on the faith of Moses and his generation.[50] Such an interpretation, however, remains problematic. First, the pronominal references in the following verse clearly point back to Abraham, and a shift in subject in 11:11 would make the flow of 11:10-12 rather disjointed. Second, the idiom "power for begetting" (εἰς καταβολὴν σπέρματος) is commonly attested as a reference specifically to the male contribution to conception.[51] This idiomatic usage (the conjunction of the two nouns rather than merely the association of σπέρμα with male seed, which can of course also refer more neutrally to offspring)[52] makes it awkward indeed to read Sarah as the subject.[53] Such a conclusion, however, does not alter the fact that Sarah is not forgotten in this list of examples, and her vital role in accepting and obeying God's promise is not hereby minimized.

Abraham received "power to engender children" in the face of Sarah's barrenness and his advanced age because he "considered reliable the one who promised" (πιστὸν ἡγήσατο τὸν ἐπαγγειλάμενον). This expression strongly recalls Hebrews 10:23, where the hearers are exhorted to hold onto the confession of their hope for the same reason. The believers are not to consider their hope any less possible for God than for a ninety-year-old woman to conceive and bear a child. The patriarchal couple's "impossible dream" became reality because of trust in God's promise; the same favored outcome will befall Christians who remain steadfast in their trust toward God.

Life in the form of countless offspring (the author joins together similes from Gen. 22:17 and 32:13 to highlight this vast progeny) came "from one who had died" (ἀφ' ἑνὸς . . . νενεκρωμένου, 11:12). The tendency to translate this verse "from one who was as good as dead" takes a step backward from the stark language of the Greek, in which Abraham is described as, simply, "one who had become dead" or "lifeless." The same term appears in Romans 4:19, which un-

---

50. Thus Eisenbaum, *Jewish Heroes*, 158.

51. Epictetus *Diss.* 1.12.3; Marcus Aurelius *Med.* 4.36; Galen *On the Natural Faculties* 1.6; *On the Use of the Parts of the Body of Man* 14.7; Philo *Op. Mund.* 132; *Cher.* 49; *Ebr.* 211; see J. Swetnam, *Jesus and Isaac: A Study of the Epistle to the Hebrews in Light of the Aqedah* (Rome: Pontifical Biblical Institute, 1981), 98.

52. Eisenbaum, *Jewish Heroes*, 158.

53. The words might be profitably construed as a nominative *pendens*, or, with Ellingworth, one might simply correct the words αὐτὴ Σάρρα στεῖρα to the dative case (a minimal scribal alteration, since to the ears the nominative and dative would be virtually indistinguishable). See the thorough discussion of the grammatical problems in Ellingworth, *Hebrews*, 586-88.

derscores even more fully the "deadness" both of Sarah's womb and Abraham's body. There "faith" was not impaired by the consideration of physical obstacles to the promise. Here the author's concern is to elevate the power of God to bring life from the dead, such that the emergence of generations from the "deadness" of Abraham's procreative parts echoes the earlier examples of Abel and Enoch transcending death (and will be further echoed in 11:19 and 11:35). The author is so keen on this point that he will strain the example of Isaac's sacrifice (11:19) to make it support God's life-restoring power. Rather than suggesting violent persecution of the hearers (topics of resurrection being prominent elsewhere in situations not involving violent persecution, e.g., 1 and 2 Corinthians), this emphasis supports the author's goal of motivating the hearers to look beyond their present circumstances, even beyond this life itself, for the reward that God has promised.[54] Not even death is sufficient to hinder God's delivery of his promised benefits to those who trust him.

The author provides a commentary now on the examples of Abraham and his fellow sojourners. They died "faithfully" (Κατὰ πίστιν) or "in a state of trusting,"[55] not having received the promised good for which they were looking but not giving up on that hope for the lesser goods of enfranchisement in an earthly homeland. Here again the author of Hebrews will interpret the promises as a reference to the heavenly homeland, the city that God prepared, rather than the gift of a child (which was fulfilled for Abraham in the birth of Isaac) or innumerable progeny and possession of Canaan (which were also promised, but not yet fulfilled in the time of Abraham, Isaac, and Jacob). Significant is the "confession" made by these patriarchs with both their lips and their lives: that "they were foreigners and sojourners on the earth" (ξένοι καὶ παρεπίδημοί εἰσιν ἐπὶ τῆς γῆς, 11:13). This confession is an amalgamation of Genesis 23:4 and 24:37:

"I am a foreigner and resident alien among you" (πάροικος καὶ παρεπίδημος ἐγώ εἰμι μεθ' ὑμῶν);
"I am living as a foreigner in their land" (ἐγὼ παροικῶ ἐν τῇ γῇ αὐτῶν).

The singular confession of Abraham is made plural to represent the confession of the patriarchs as a group; "in their land" is modified easily to "upon the earth" so as to create the contrast between the earthly and heavenly countries in 11:13-15.

This confession implies, so the author avers, the search for a homeland

---

54. This conviction does, however, enable believers to give the last, full measure of devotion to God when martyrdom is in view.

55. Ibid., 592.

where their status as foreigners will be converted to that of citizens. Important for the author is that patriarchs did not "turn back" to the homeland and the citizenship that they had left behind when they accepted God's call and set out in trust (13:15). Astoundingly, they persisted in bearing the lower status of "foreigner" and "resident alien," embracing this status until their deaths rather than desisting from their search for the homeland God promised and seeking reenfranchisement in their native land. In his treatment of Abraham, Philo (*Abr.* 86) similarly emphasizes the fact that Abraham didn't turn back even though he was weighed down by the loss of his former homeland and associations and by the difficulty of pressing on through continued sojourning and rejection. For both authors, Abraham becomes an example of perseverance and commitment to attain the end that God promises.

The description of the patriarchs' goal as "a better, that is a heavenly, homeland" (11:16) encapsulates a Jewish-Christian revision of Platonic dualism. Platonism divided reality into the "phenomenal" world and the "noumenal" world, the former being "characterized by movement, change, and corruption — and, therefore, only partial knowledge" — and the latter being characterized "by changelessness and incorruptibility because it is not material but spiritual."[56] The noumenal world is more real than the phenomenal, holds greater value, and allows for a truer perception of reality.[57] Platonic dualism could readily be modified into the spatial dualism of the Jewish cosmos: heaven and earth.[58] Heaven, the abode of the eternal God, was a realm superior to that of earth. It possessed a greater value and, within the temporal framework of Jewish eschatology, a permanence not shared by earthly realities.[59] In the peculiar eschatology of the author of Hebrews, the "unshakable" and "abiding" realm is not simply coterminous with "heaven" but exists beyond the material and visible heavens. The homeland toward which the believer reaches does not

---

56. Luke T. Johnson, *The Writings of the New Testament: An Interpretation* (Philadelphia: Fortress, 1986), 420.

57. Ibid., 420: "The distinction is metaphysical: one realm of being is denser and more 'real' than the other. It is epistemological: the world of change allows only approximate perceptions, therefore, 'opinions'; but ideas can truly be 'known.' The distinction is also axiological: the noumenal world is 'better' than the phenomenal."

58. Johnson (ibid., 421) adduces several examples from Philo to show how Platonic dualism could be appropriated in scriptural exegesis. Noteworthy is Philo's exegesis of Exod. 25:40, which is cited by our author in Heb. 8:5 with much the same result.

59. After the important studies of C. K. Barrett ("The Eschatology in the Epistle to the Hebrews," in *The Background of the New Testament and Its Eschatology,* ed. W. D. Davies and D. Daube [Cambridge: Cambridge University Press, 1954], 363-93) and Williamson ("Platonism and Hebrews," 415-24), it is impossible to claim that the author was a true Platonist. We can only explore how Platonic categories are reinterpreted by or give expression to aspects of the Jewish and Christian worldview.

come into being after the destruction of heaven and earth at the end of time in favor of the "new heavens and the new earth" (Isa. 66; Rev. 21); it already stands prepared in the invisible realm.

The patriarchs exhibit wisdom in their evaluation of the advantages and disadvantages of returning to their native land versus continuing to live as exiles in the world and looking for the land God has prepared for the faithful. Because they correctly perceive that the latter course is more expedient, God "is not ashamed of them to be called their God" (11:16). This is a reference to God's identification of himself as the "God of Abraham, God of Isaac, and God of Jacob," which amounts, in effect, to his confession of, or witness to, the patriarchs as people worthy to be identified closely with his own name (see Exod. 3:6; Gen. 28:13; Matt. 22:32). This phrase ("he is not ashamed to be called their God") appears earlier in Hebrews 2:11, where Jesus is said not to "be ashamed to call them his sisters and brothers." Those who trust God and perceive the surpassing value of his promises receive divine attestation to their honor through God's (or Christ's) open association with them,[60] an association that will lead eventually to the trusting person's arrival at the divinely appointed goal, "for God has prepared for them a city." Philosophers in the Greco-Roman world had long confronted the pain of exile with considerations of claiming citizenship in the city of God.[61] The Christian minority culture also lays claim to this better citizenship as a means of compensating for, and persevering in, loss of a place and status in the non-Christian world.

The author has fastened onto aspects of the ways in which the patriarchs' "faith" was enacted that correspond most nearly to the condition of the audience, particularly in light of the experiences detailed in 10:32-34. Like Abraham, the addressees left behind their homeland and status in their native city in order to follow God's call and reach out for God's promised benefactions. While there is no clear indication that they had physically moved from their native land,[62] they were at the very least socially removed from their native land through the open degradation they suffered at the hands of their neighbors. One might even have cause to reevaluate John Elliott's claim that the political

---

60. See Michel, *Der Brief an die Hebräer*, 266: "ἐπαισχύνεσθαι in the context of an act of confession answers the ἀρνεῖσθαι of Matt. 10:33. οὐκ ἐπαισχύνεται is thus an old circumlocution for confession, for a bold and open declaration, and not a psychological feeling. God thus becomes a witness (= μαρτυρεῖ) for the patriarchs, in that God calls himself by their names (Gen. 28:13; Exod. 3:6)" (translation mine).

61. Compare Musonius Rufus, who asserts that a virtuous person regards himself or herself as a πολίτης τῆς τοῦ Διὸς πόλεως (A. C. van Geytenbeek, *Musonius Rufus and Greek Diatribe* [Assen: Van Gorcum, 1963], 145). Compare Epictetus *Diss.* 1.9.1; Plutarch *De exil.* 5 (*Mor.* 600F), 17 (*Mor.* 607C-D); Seneca *Ep.* 24.17.

62. Lane (*Hebrews 1–8*, lxiv-lxvi) argues forcefully, however, that this was indeed the case.

terms "foreigner and resident alien" (ξένοι καὶ παρεπίδημοί) are purely metaphorical in Hebrews, whereas they are to be literally and legally applied to the addressees in 1 Peter.[63] The author infers that the patriarchs rejected the option of returning to their native land, that is, to enfranchisement and the protection from dishonor and danger that that brings (11:15). So focused were their hearts on God's promise, so firm were they in trusting God's reliability to deliver what he promised, that they preferred a lifetime of disenfranchisement in order to persevere in the quest for the "better, heavenly homeland" (11:16). Thus the author urges the addressees to persevere in their endurance of censure and abuse, preferring the prize promised by God to the apostasy that would provide the surest route back to favor and status within the unbelieving society. In the final analysis, God's witness to the honor of Abraham, Isaac, and Jacob shows that the choices they made were the advantageous and wise ones. The hearers should set their hearts to do likewise for the sake of lasting honor and a place in God's realm.

The mind-set that this world is not our home is central to early Christian self-definition. Philippians 3:20; 1 Peter 1:17; 2:11; and *Hermas, Similitudes* 1 all use this language to distance their audiences from investing themselves or rooting themselves in the dominant culture (or even desiring such rootedness). *Epistle of Diognetus* 5.5 is quite striking: Christians "inhabit their own native lands, but as resident aliens; they take part in all things as citizens, but they endure all things as aliens (πατρίδας οἰκοῦσιν ἰδίας, ἀλλ᾽ ὡς πάροικοι· μετέχουσι πάντων ὡς πολίται, καὶ πάνθ᾽ ὑπομένουσιν ὡς ξένοι). Every foreign land is a fatherland, and every fatherland a foreign land." Hebrews contributes in an important way to this emerging strategy for directing Christians' focus and sense of belonging toward the group itself as an enclave or colony of citizens of the heavenly homeland. They are, in effect, to make the patriarchs' confession (11:13) their own, and to make up their minds to press on in trust toward the heavenly city rather than turn back to retake their place in their earthly society. Their refusal of "at-homeness" within the world manifests their loyalty to God and their commitment to God's call. In this regard, Dio's claim (*Or.* 44.6) before his native city is informative:

> I have given practical demonstration of this [civic loyalty] too. For although many people in many lands have invited me both to make my home with them and to take charge of their public affairs, not merely at the present time, but even earlier, as the time when I was an exile — and some went so far as to

---

63. Elliott, *Home for the Homeless*, 55 n. 75. Attridge (*Hebrews*, 330 n. 26) similarly takes exception to Elliot's statement: "The 'alienation' involved here may not, however, be purely spiritual. Similarly, the alienation involved in 1 Peter may well be a social one occasioned by the addressees' Christian confession, without being strictly legal."

send the Emperor resolutions thanking him for the honour he had done me
— yet I never accepted such a proposal by so much as a single word, but I did
not even acquire a house or a plot of ground anywhere else, so that I might
have nothing to suggest a homeland (πατρίς) anywhere but here.

Dio's refusal to accept enfranchisement in any other city, and thus his perseverance in the status of exile and foreigner, serve as proof of his devotion to his native land, a devotion that he expects will win him greater approval and honor
there where he most desires it. Similarly, the early Christians are urged to remain detached from earthly possessions (*Herm. Sim.* 1) so that their loyalty to
their true homeland will remain strong. Their refusal to "turn back" to gain the
trappings of status and place in their earthly city will win them an honorable
welcome into that heavenly homeland which God has prepared.

The remainder of the space given to Abraham and the patriarchs changes
its emphasis to feature two other important components of living "in trust"
unto eschatological deliverance: (1) the promise of God is more powerful than
death and (2) the person of faith looks even beyond death to the fulfillment of
those promises:

> By faith Abraham, being tested, offered up Isaac, and the one who had re-
> ceived the promises was about to offer up his only child, with regard to whom
> it was said, "from Isaac shall your descendants be called," considering that
> God was able to raise up even from the dead — whence, figuratively speak-
> ing, he did receive him back. By faith Isaac blessed Jacob and Esau even con-
> cerning things yet to come. By faith Jacob, when he was dying, blessed each of
> the sons of Joseph and worshiped at the head of his staff. By faith Joseph, at
> his passing, considered in his mind the going forth of the children of Israel
> and gave commands concerning his bones. (11:17-22)

Hebrews 11:13-16 might appear at first glance to present a premature conclusion or comment on the trust or faith of the patriarchs Abraham, Isaac, and Jacob. Since 11:17-21 says something about their trust reaching beyond their
deaths, however, the placement of these verses after 11:13-16 (which speaks of
their dying without receiving the promises during their lifetime) is significant
rather than ill-planned.

The contemplation of Abraham's binding of Isaac (11:17-19) returns to
the theme of God's power to fulfill promises even after and beyond death (see
11:4-5, 11-12). The author captures in brief the episode recounted in Genesis
22,[64] highlighting the nature of the episode as the test of Abraham (Gen. 22:1)
and Abraham's ready compliance (Gen. 22:10), which was regarded as the su-

---

64. See Swetnam, *Jesus and Isaac,* 23-80 for the history of telling and interpreting this
story in early Judaism.

preme sign of Abraham's fidelity toward God (Sir. 44:20; *Jub.* 17:15-18; 18:9-11).[65] The author searches for the rationale that would have allowed Abraham to kill his "only" son,[66] the vessel of the promise (given prominent place here by the full recitation of Gen. 21:12, "your offspring shall be named through Isaac"), and finds it in Abraham's confidence in God's power "to raise up even from the dead." From the author's version, one would think that Abraham expected God to restore Isaac to life after this sacrifice, so that God's promise would not prove invalid. The sacrifice of Isaac is thus read as evidence of Abraham's trust in the irrevocability of God's promise, rather than as a test of Abraham's love for God (as Gen. 22 leads the reader to expect, preserved in Sir. 44:20; *Jub.* 17:15-18; 4 Macc. 16:18-20).

The next two, very brief examples (11:20-21) both involve the passing on of the "blessing" across the generations. The promise that was not received during the patriarch's lifetime became the patrimony bequeathed to his offspring. In the case of Isaac, the promise was passed on to Jacob rather than Esau (see Heb. 12:16-17), and the content of the "blessing" was a prophecy about the future of each son (the author refers to Gen. 27:27-29, 38-40). Jacob, in turn, blesses the two sons of Joseph and "worships at the top of his staff." Here the author has recontextualized the LXX version of Genesis 47:31, where "worshiped at the top of his staff" departs from the MT "bowed at the head of his bed" by means of a simple revocalization of the Hebrew word for "bed."[67] The author has also transposed the order of this "bowing" and the blessing of Joseph's two sons in order to hold closer together the two "blessing" stories for mutual reinforcement and in order to close with the image of Jacob, the perpetual sojourner. Worshiping God at the head of his "staff" signifies Jacob's persistence in embracing his identity and reaffirming his hope as a pilgrim and sojourner.

Including Joseph in this list provides a smooth passage from the patriarchal period to the Exodus, which will frame the discussion of Moses' "faith." The author passes over countless examples of Joseph's steadfastness, virtue, and, indeed, faith, being interested only in Genesis 50:24-25, where Joseph reaffirms the reliability of God's promise and oath to bring Israel's descendants into "the land which God swore to our fathers, to Abraham, Isaac, and Jacob" and gives the surviving members of the family instructions to carry his bones out from

---

65. *Jubilees*, intriguingly, gives Mastema, the Satan figure, credit for coming up with this test. A heavenly court scene patterned after Job 1–2 is thus made the setting for the tests that Abraham endured.

66. Isaac was not, of course, Abraham's only son at this point in the story: his special value came not from his being the sole son but from being the designated channel of the promise of progeny more numerous than the stars.

67. *Hamittâh*, "bed," is read by the LXX translator as *hamatteh*, "staff" — an easy mistake given the fact that the translator would have had only *hmth* to go on.

Egypt.[68] Joseph on his deathbed also "reflected on"[69] God's future acts on behalf of God's people, and oriented himself in hope for the fulfillment of God's promise, the Exodus being the next step. So certain is he of God's future acts that he gives specific instructions concerning the final resting place of his bones. This is quite significant, since the twelve patriarchs and their families had become quite at home in Egypt and might not naturally have been expected to entertain notions of leaving. Joseph still understands, even from his exalted position in the kingdom of Egypt, that they live merely in a place of sojourning and have no permanent abiding place in Egypt. This is the posture of faith — to resist the temptation to see the place where one is as one's home, as the place finally to settle down. Even in lush Egypt, Joseph looks for a better homeland.

From these aspects of the patriarchs' life, the addressees are to learn that God's promise is more certain than death, and that the person of faith need not flinch before any hardship. There is nothing, in effect, that can separate the trusting and faithful client from the reception of God's promises. The promises of God become the prominent focus of the person of faith; even at the shore of death, the Christian looks ahead to the certain fulfillment of God's word and acts accordingly.

11:23-31

The second figure to receive detailed attention in this encomium is Moses. While Stephen in Acts 7:17 says that the Exodus occurred as "the time of the promise drew near," the author of Hebrews regards Moses as another forward-looking person of faith whose choices are made not in light of the fulfillment of God's promise in his present circumstances but rather "looking ahead to the reward" that was yet to come. For this author, the dawning of the promise occurs in the present of the hearers, as all the company of faith "receive the promise" together (11:39-40).

> By faith Moses, after he was born, was hidden for three months by his parents, because they saw that the child was gifted and they did not fear the

---

68. The closeness of the author's interaction with the LXX is shown in his choice of the word for Joseph's "dying." Rather than repeat the one he used for Jacob's passing, he uses the same verb as the one in Gen. 50:26 (ἐτελεύτησεν) to describe Joseph's end.

69. Attridge (*Hebrews*, 336 n. 50) offers this translation of ἐμνημόνευσεν here, finding it chronologically impossible for Joseph to "remember" the Exodus. Jacob, however, had already affirmed to Joseph that God would bring his descendants back to the land of Canaan (Gen. 48:21), so that Joseph could still "remember" this going forth in a certain sense, namely, as a remembrance of his father's pronouncement (which he repeats for his own family on his deathbed in Gen. 50:24).

king's edict. By faith Moses, having grown up, refused to be called a son of
Pharaoh's daughter, choosing mistreatment along with the people of God
rather than the temporary pleasure of sin, because he estimated the reproach
of Christ to be greater wealth than the treasures of Egypt — for he was looking away to the reward. By faith he left Egypt behind, not fearing the king's
anger, for he persevered as one seeing the Invisible. (11:23-27)

As with Abraham and the patriarchs, the author shapes his description of Moses' faith to suit the needs of the situation of his addressees. Moses' fame as the
giver of the Law and mediator of the covenant is nowhere mentioned, as might
rather be expected in a Christian document that stresses the supersession of the
nomistic covenant.[70] What is central to the author's depiction of Moses' faith is
his renunciation of a place of honor in the world's eyes and his choice of solidarity with the people of God even if such association brought a radical loss of
worldly status and any potential for advancement. The choices of Moses as they
are presented here (see especially 11:25-26) have been replicated in the community's past (10:33-34) and are held up as a pattern for imitation in the community's present (13:3).

The example of Moses is introduced by the example of his parents, who
also enacted trust in God in the face of oppression. The author derives most of
the content of 11:23 directly from Exodus 2:2 (LXX): "but seeing that he was
gifted, they sheltered him for three months" (ἰδόντες δὲ αὐτὸ ἀστεῖον ἐσκέ-
πασαν αὐτὸ μῆνας τρεῖς). Exodus 2:3 (LXX) speaks of the parents' hiding the
child, thus supplying our author with the more common verb (κρύπτειν). The
detail that the parents "did not fear the command of the king" is not explicit in
Exodus, but was also inferred and explicated by Philo (*Vita Mos.* 1.9): "his parents resolved, as far as was in their power, to disregard the proclamations of the
king." Both Jewish and Christian cultures have strong traditions of preferring
reverence for God's commands over reverence for the commands of human
(and often ungodly) rulers (see 4 Macc. 14:13; Matt. 10:28; Acts 5:29), and the
example of Moses' parents reinforces these priorities. The child's "beauty" is a
sign of divine favor (something perhaps captured better by the translation
"gifted"). The decision of Moses' parents to hide him for three months is
prompted not merely by natural affection but by a special awareness of God's
promises being fulfilled through this child.[71] Again, the author of Hebrews

---

70. Moses is not, however, denigrated by the author of Hebrews, who uses him as a
positive model here and as an esteemed figure in comparison with whom he may establish
Christ's greater dignity in 3:1-6.

71. The expansions on the biblical narrative on this point in Ps-Philo's *Biblical Antiquities* strongly move in this direction. There Pharaoh's oppression is even more severe: male
children are to be killed, females made into concubines and breeders for the Egyptian slaves.
When all the Hebrew elders decide that it would be better not to have any more children,

shows a striking reserve concerning the incorporation of nonbiblical details, finding it a sufficient sign of trust that they shelter the infant for three months in direct violation of the secular power.

After mentioning the faith of Moses' parents in 11:23, the author presents Moses' first enactment of faith as his refusal "to be called a son of a daughter of Pharaoh" (11:24). Presented as a member of the royal family of Egypt, and possibly regarded by the author, as by Philo and Josephus, as the heir of Egypt's throne,[72] Moses occupied a place of exceptionally high status and honor. Remaining Pharaoh's grandson and looking to Pharaoh as *paterfamilias*, patron, and benefactor would have afforded Moses the power and status of a ruler of a great kingdom and access to the "treasures of Egypt" (an endless storehouse of worldly honor as the repository of the potential benefactions at his disposal). Nevertheless, led by faith Moses renounces these highest of worldly honors and promises of honor and rejects — even spurns[73] — Pharaoh as a source of honor and benefits. He exchanges his adoptive inheritance for the inheritance of the faithful. The author's shaping of the biblical material is especially bold at this point. "Moses, having grown up" (Μωϋσῆς μέγας γενόμενος), is a recontextualization of Exodus 2:11 (μέγας γενόμενος Μωϋσῆς) but with a very differ-

---

Amram announces his trust in God to liberate the descendants of Abraham and save God's own children. He and Jochebed therefore agree to have children. Because of their confidence in God's promise, God decides that one of their children will be the deliverer of the Hebrews from bondage.

72. Philo *Vita Mos.* 1.13: "The king of the country had but one cherished daughter, who, we are told, had been married for a considerable time but had never conceived a child, though she naturally desired one, particularly of the male sex, to succeed to the magnificent inheritance of her father's kingdom (τὸν εὐδαίμονα κλῆρον τῆς πατρῴας ἡγεμονίας), which threatened to go to strangers if his daughter gave him no grandson." Compare also Josephus *Ant.* 2.9.7, §232-34. "Thermutis . . . carried Moses to her father . . . and said to him, 'I have brought up a child who is of divine form, and of a generous mind; and as I have received him from the bounty of the river, in a wonderful manner, I thought proper to adopt him for my son and the heir of thy kingdom.' And when she had said this, she put the infant into her father's hands; so he took him, and hugged him close to his breast," thus signaling his acceptance of the child into his household.

73. Several commentators see in Moses' refusal a note of disdain or contempt for the honor offered by human courts of reputation. See, for example, Lünemann, *Hebrews*, 684; Spicq, *L'Épître aux Hébreux*, 357: "Moses had been raised by the daughter of Pharaoh, who treated him as a son. He could have claimed all the honors and advantages of his royal station and insisted upon his official title. What glorious prospects for an adopted child! But when he came to adulthood, Moses rejected and disowned these advantages of which he was beneficiary; . . . the personal decision, it seems, contains a nuance of scorn or disdain." Josephus (*Ant.* 2.9.7 §233) also attributes to Moses contempt for the offer of Egypt's honors: "on his daughter's account, in a pleasant way, (Pharaoh) put his diadem upon [Moses'] head; but Moses threw it down to the ground, and, in a puerile mood, he wreathed it round, and trod upon it with his feet."

ent sequel. Exodus 2:11 introduces the story of Moses' visitation of his fellow Hebrews in their misery and his murder of the violent taskmaster. Here the author passes over the details of this episode, interpreting it in such a way as to make it more relevant for the hearers (as well as to resonate more closely with the example of Abraham): Moses renounced a destiny that was his by virtue of his being a member of the unbelieving, dominant culture (his earthly heritage) in favor of a new, spiritual heritage that came from belonging to the people of God.

Moses casts off worldly honors in favor of "mistreatment together with the people of God." He left behind the honors of the throne of Egypt in order to join himself to slaves, people of the lowest status and subject to insult and physical outrage (expressed in the single word, συγκακουχεῖσθαι). The pleasure of the Egyptian court, however, is qualified by two terms. First, it is "temporary" (πρόσκαιρος), a term that stands in stark contrast to "abiding" (μένων), the word frequently used in this climactic exhortation to describe the lasting quality of the inheritance of the faithful (10:34; 12:27; 13:14). Once more the author's amalgamation of Platonic categories and Jewish and Christian cosmology becomes apparent: he borrows the Platonic distinction between the changing, impermanent material realm and the eternal realm of ideas and interprets this through the Jewish and Christian apocalyptic view of history and the cosmos. Thus the "visible" realm remains "temporary" and inferior because it is destined for removal at God's coming intervention in history; the "abiding" realm already exists, but as the realm of God that will be the sole remaining realm after this "shaking." Thus, the honor or ease this temporary enjoyment of worldly status and wealth bestows has no lasting value and is subject to being transformed into lasting disgrace and pain at God's visitation.[74]

This result is made all the more certain by the second qualification: the identification of such pleasure as "sin" (ἁμαρτία). Several scholars have argued cogently that the author intends "sin" to signify more than a transgression of God's law. Otto Michel, for example, defines it as the refusing to live in solidarity with the people of God: "The content of this sin was separation from the people of God: 'see, then, how he calls it sin not to endure the like injuries together with one's brothers and sisters.'"[75] This interpretation helps the long-

---

74. So Delitzsch, *Hebrews*, 261: "One of Moses' reasons for refusing the enjoyments and the splendours of a courtly life in Egypt is hinted at in the word πρόσκαιρον. He knew them to be but temporary, and to have an eternally bitter end in prospect. . . . Therefore he suffered not himself to be dazzled by all the honours and luxury which his position offered him."

75. Michel, *Der Brief an die Hebräer*, 273, quoting Theophylact (*PG* 125:356): Ὅρα δὲ πῶς ἁμαρτίαν ὀνομάζει τὸ μὴ συγκακουχεῖσθαι τοῖς ἀδελφοῖς. So also Weiß, *Hebräerbrief*, 605: "What is here called ἁμαρτία has thus a concrete form: the refusal of solidarity with the 'People of God' who are suffering maltreatment" (translation mine). Käsemann (*Wandering*

standing theological problem of Hebrews, namely, the view of the impossible restoration of one who "sins" after coming to faith, and relates the term specifically to the crisis facing the addressees. Sin occurs where fellowship with the people of God is refused or discontinued on account of the temptation to seek place or pleasure in the society of unbelievers. Sin occurs when one values the worth of God's friendship less than the world's friendship, when one abandons "ill-treatment with the people of God" for the sake of honor as Christ's enemies define it and bestow it. Moses manifests faith in that he chooses maltreatment and dishonor in the world's eyes over honor before the human court, destined as it is to be overturned.

Temporary versus eternal advantage is a prominent topic in Jewish and Christian argumentation (see 4 Macc. 15:2-8, 23; 2 Cor. 4:16-18) and is rooted in the very cosmology and worldview promoted within those cultures. In deliberation, it allows an orator (preacher) to minimize the advantages of aligning oneself with the unbelieving world and maximize the disadvantages of shrinking back from the fellowship of believers (topics of amplification and diminution). These terms became a powerful instrument for motivating group members to persevere in those behaviors valued within the church or synagogue, even if loyalty to the values of the group lead to the extreme penalty of martyrdom. Moses' choice reinforces the Christian cultural estimation of the relative value of earthly and heavenly wealth, reputation, and the like, and aids the addressees' acceptance of their losses as an investment made to attain a "better" happiness and its component parts (cf. Aristotle *Rh.* 1.5) in God's promised city. Moses' astounding reputation, and the honor in which he is held, demonstrate the wisdom of his choice and facilitate the making of a similar choice.

Moses' choice is motivated by his evaluation of the respective worth of the "treasures of Egypt" and the "reproach of Christ" (11:26). With his eyes firmly fixed on the reward (11:26b), he found that the latter constituted a greater treasure. Faith causes one to evaluate worldly realities in light of eternal realities, such that even reproach and dishonor before the world's court (endured on account of walking in obedience to God) can be transformed into the path to honor before God's court and be itself valued as possessing greater worth than worldly treasures. The meaning of the phrase "the reproach of Christ" (τὸν ὀνειδισμὸν τοῦ Χριστοῦ), especially in light of the apparent anachronism of allowing Moses to shoulder up this particular reproach, is far from obvious. Scholars have offered many solutions, but none is definitive (nor do I

People of God, 46) extends the meaning of "sin" in Hebrews to "slackening" in perseverance in faith. While such a slackening certainly puts one in jeopardy of "sin," the author appears to have in mind not a lack of rigor but a lack of regard for God's gifts and an unwillingness to endure what is necessary to attain them.

expect my words to provide the final solution).[76] The phrase appears to have
been formulated from several words in Psalm 88:51-52: "Remember, O Lord,
the reproach (τοῦ ὀνειδισμοῦ) of your slaves; how I bear in my bosom the insults of many peoples, with which your enemies taunt, O Lord, with which they
reproach (ὠνείδισαν) the exchange-price of your anointed (τοῦ χριστοῦ σου)."
The psalm laments the condition of Israel and the weakness (or absence) of a
Davidic monarch. He calls for God's remembrance of his covenant with David
to restore the kingdom to a state of strength. The psalmist suffers reproach by
virtue of belonging to a nation that has come into hard times. Moses' choice to
join himself to this same people of God at a much earlier time, but still a time
of great hardship, places him in a similar position to that of the psalmist. How
much Psalm 88:51-52 (LXX) influences the author's meaning (let alone the audience's understanding), however, is not clear. That is to say, the meaning of
Hebrews 11:26 may not be directly clarified by an analysis of how Moses' situation relates to that of the full text of the psalm.

More useful may be the observation that the addressees themselves are
called upon to bear the "reproach of Christ" (τὸν ὀνειδισμὸν αὐτοῦ, 13:13) in
their own circumstances. The example of Moses is being adapted to the pastoral needs of the audience in order to serve as a model for their own enactment
of faith, and this adaptation may have led the author to portray Moses, in
something of a literary conceit, as making the very same evaluation of faith that
the addressees must make. Moses accepts for himself the reproach that connection with Christ brings in the world (connection with Christ mediated through
connection with the historic people of God), the reproach that comes from
heeding God's call. Moses' evaluation recalls the former experience of disgrace
that the addressees endured on account of their commitment to Christ. Hebrews 10:33 specifically included reproaches (ὀνειδισμοί) resulting from associ-

---

76. Lünemann (*Hebrews*, 684) suggests that "the sense is: *the reproach, as Christ bore it,*
inasmuch, namely, as the reproach, which Moses took upon him to endure in fellowship with
his oppressed people at the hand of the Egyptians, was in its nature homogeneous with the
reproach which Christ afterwards had to endure at the hands of unbelievers, to the extent
that in the one case as in the other the glory of God and the advancement of His kingdom
were the end and aim of the enduring." Moses bore "the reproach of Christ" in that both Moses and Christ bore reproach for the same cause (such that Christ could also be said to have
borne "the reproach of Moses"). Moffatt (*Hebrews*, 180) understands the phrase to refer to
the "special obloquy in being connected with Christ," which, however, does not help much in
understanding how Moses could have associated himself with Christ so as to bear the reproach of this association. Héring (*Hebrews*, 105) suggests that the author "sees in the suffering of the people a prefiguration of or an allusion to the suffering of Christ." Thus, in joining
himself to the people of God, who were suffering disgrace, Moses joins himself to a type of
the future reproach of Christ. A survey of several other positions advanced may be found in
Attridge, *Hebrews*, 341-42.

ation with the name of Christ, which was a common occurrence in many Christian communities (cf. 1 Pet. 4:14-16; Matt. 5:11; Luke 6:22). In this regard, the complaint of the author of Psalm 68:8, 10 appears to come closer to the heart of our author's meaning:

> For it is for your sake that I have borne reproach (ὀνειδισμόν), that shame has covered my face. . . . For zeal for your house has consumed me, and the reproaches of those who reproach you have fallen on me (οἱ ὀνειδισμοὶ τῶν ὀνειδιζόντων σε ἐπέπεσαν ἐπ' ἐμέ).

The connection of this psalm with the ministry of Jesus is seen already in the Synoptic Gospels, which see the LXX version of Psalm 68:10 enacted in the indictment of the temple. Jesus himself bears reproach and abuse as a result of his obedience to God's call, as the author of Hebrews will underscore in 12:2-3 (using a different word for "reproach" than used here). "Bearing Christ's reproach" may signal a call to partnership with Christ in the agelong witness of the obedient servants of God bearing the hostility of those who refuse God and remain his enemies. In this regard, Moses and the addressees may equally choose to share "the reproach of Christ." In light of the promise ("for he was looking away to the reward"), Moses chooses to embrace the reproach of Christ, that is, he chooses the course of obedience to God even at the expense of being dishonored in the eyes of the world.[77]

Like his parents, Moses shows a lack of "fearing the anger of the king" and displays his lack of regard for those who have power over life and death by "leaving Egypt behind" (11:27). Scholars have difficulty deciding whether or not this departure from Egypt corresponds with Moses' departure for Midian after murdering the Egyptian or with his departure at the head of the Hebrews at the Exodus itself. Identification with the flight to Midian is problematic at first glance since Moses did in fact make that journey precisely because he did "fear the wrath of the king" (Exod. 2:14-15). There is ample evidence, however, that Jews "rewrote" the story of Moses at this point, embellishing it so as to exculpate Moses for the murder as well as to eliminate the motive of cowardice. Josephus (*Ant.* 2.11.1 §254-57),[78] for example, claims that it was rather Pha-

---

77. As scholars have observed, however, Moses is credited with being a visionary (Mary Rose D'Angelo (*Moses in the Letter to the Hebrews* [SBLDS 42; Missoula, MT: Scholars Press, 1979], 95-149; Attridge, *Hebrews,* 341), and the author may be making the claim that, just as the patriarchs looked ahead to the fulfillment of the promise, so Moses was able to look ahead with the eyes of faith to Jesus and the final outworking of God's promise to bring the people of God into their homeland (Eisenbaum, *Jewish Heroes,* 169). Such a reading would only strengthen the parenetic connection between Moses and the addressees outlined above.

78. Cited helpfully in Attridge, *Hebrews,* 342 n. 70.

raoh who was afraid of Moses and who sought to assassinate him. Moses' departure becomes merely the act of a wise person who takes thought to preserve his life, and the flight is an occasion for him to exhibit courage and endurance. Artapanus also tells the story of Pharaoh's jealousy and assassination attempt: it is the assassin that Moses kills in self-defense.[79] It is possible, therefore, that the author would not associate "fear" with Moses' initial departure from Egypt. Identifying this departure with the Exodus itself, in which Moses certainly did not show a fear of Pharaoh's might but rather moved with full confidence in God's power over Pharaoh, presents a problem with the chronology in Hebrews since the Passover follows in 11:28 (although we have seen in 11:8-19 how chronology is not inviolable in this presentation).

Rather than promote one reference over another, I propose that the author's focus here is simply on Moses "leaving Egypt behind" as Abraham left his homeland behind and as the addressees left their place in their society behind. The attempt to decide whether this was the flight to Midian or the Exodus itself misses the author's emphasis — his own lack of clarity shows his lack of interest on this point. Rather, he presents as a sort of conclusion to 11:24-26 the bare observation that Moses left his earthly homeland, status, and heritage behind. This is a prominent feature of the people of faith in every age — the patriarchal period, the Exodus period, and the addressees' own period. Moses was impelled to endure the lot of the wandering people of God because he had his mind's eye fixed on God and the recompense of fidelity to this God. He "endured as one seeing the Invisible" (τὸν γὰρ ἀόρατον ὡς ὁρῶν ἐκαρτέρησεν). The word "invisible" here is used elsewhere as an epithet for God (Col. 1:15; 1 Tim. 1:17) or for one of God's qualities (Rom. 1:20; Philo *Migr. Abr.* 183). While this may be derived from the tradition that Moses enjoyed a unique closeness to God (Deut. 34:10; Philo *Vita Mos.* 1.158), the author of Hebrews is interested in Moses as a paradigm for imitation, not in those aspects of Moses' life that are inimitable.[80] The focus of Moses' inner eye enabled him to make the right choices and to endure the hardships that those choices entailed. The addressees are challenged by his example also to fix their eyes on the "invisible One" and maintain unswerving their course toward the unshakable realm.[81]

Moses, like Jesus, "despised shame" by renouncing the worldly honors into which he had been born (or, rather, adopted) and, in a manner analogous to the pattern of Christ, by leaving a throne to take the form of a slave. He chose to be dishonored and reproached in the company of God's people, thus joining

---

79. The fragment is preserved in Eusebius *Preparatio Evangelica* 9.27.7-19.

80. Attridge, *Hebrews*, 343.

81. The contrast between having regard for Pharaoh's anger and looking to God recalls the frequent topic of Christian exhortation to "obey God rather than human beings" where these two are in conflict (Acts 5:29; cf. Matt. 10:28).

himself to their destiny, rather than to enjoy the pleasures afforded by a lofty status within the society of unbelievers, thus being joined with them in their destiny. Faith led him to choose temporary disgrace and to evaluate the honors of the world in light of God's reward, and thus to leave his adoptive patrimony behind. Philo, Josephus, and Artapanus do not depict Moses' departure from Egypt (or the murder of the Egyptian, for that matter) as the result of Moses' internal evaluations and conscious weighing of advantage.[82] The author of Hebrews, however, recasts the story of Moses to emphasize the evaluations and choices he made when he left the palace of Pharaoh for the hovels of Israel as the aspect of his faith most relevant for the confirmation of the addressees in their evaluations and choices.

Confronted with the praiseworthy example of Moses, the addressees may once more affirm their renunciation of their own status and accept the loss of their honor and place in society with joy, choosing to continue in their solidarity with the people of God by assembling together (10:25), ministering to their marginalized brothers and sisters (13:3), and "bearing Christ's reproach" (13:13). Moses' choices reinforce the standards of evaluation that the author wishes the community to maintain: what brings one closer to God's reward is always to be regarded as of "greater worth" than what leads one away from the path of loyalty, obedience, and perseverance. Even the very hardships the believers endured (10:32-34) and the deprivations with which they continue to live are elevated as being something valuable — indeed, more valuable than the status and wealth they have lost or could ever recover, since they now stand in God's favor to receive "the reward" (11:26).

The author moves smoothly from the personal displays of trust shown by Moses to the trust in God displayed by the people of Israel in the Exodus and the Conquest, concluding with the notable example of Rahab, the foreigner who recognized God's design for God's people and God's enemies and acted wisely in light of the coming judgment upon Jericho:

> By faith he kept the Passover and the sprinkling of the blood, in order that the destroyer might not slay their firstborn. By faith they crossed through the Red Sea as though through dry land: when the Egyptians attempted it, they were swallowed up. By faith the walls of Jericho fell after having been encircled for seven days. By faith Rahab the prostitute was not destroyed together with the disobedient, since she had welcomed the spies with peace. (11:28-31)

---

82. Philo *Vita Mos.* 1.32-33, however, comes close at one point: "Moses . . . still felt a desire for and admiration of the education of his kinsmen and ancestors, considering all the things which were thought good among those who had adopted him as spurious, even though they might, in consequence of the present state of affairs, have a brilliant appearance; and those things which were thought good by his natural parents, even though they might be for a short time somewhat obscure, at all events akin to himself and genuine good things."

The Passover meal was a celebration in advance of an emancipation declared already by God but still not declared by Pharaoh. The sprinkling of the blood (a reference to Exod. 12:7, 13, 21-23) was an act meant to protect the "firstborn" from "the destroyer,"[83] who was yet to make his way through Egypt, so thoroughly scourging Pharaoh that he would at last release God's firstborn, Israel. Both are done "in trust" or "in faith" because both pertain to future acts of God, to God's coming fulfillment of his promises. To the person not trusting God, how senseless would the Passover meal have appeared? How foolish the daubing of blood on doorposts? The Hebrews acting in trust, however, received the deliverance for which they hoped: their future reception of God's benefits prove the wisdom of the course of action they pursued, and their obedience to God's commands born from trust in God's word allowed them to experience those benefits. Their example speaks clearly to the hearers, whom the author wishes to be convinced firmly that God's future acts on their behalf (and against the impious, the "sinners" in 12:3) will show their course to have been wise.

The next example of acting in trust comes from Exodus 14:21-31, the actual crossing of the Red Sea.[84] As in 11:28, which linked the Passover and the coming of the destroyer, 11:29 also highlights elements both of salvation and judgment. Walking between two walls of water (Exod. 14:22) was an accomplishment of trust since the Hebrews placed their lives completely in the hands of the God who held back the waters. Their absolute dependence on God's goodwill and favor to them was never as clearly expressed; the reward for their dependence was the destruction of the Egyptians by those same waters. It is perhaps at the Red Sea that the wisdom of Moses' choice of company is most sharply manifested. On that day the value of belonging to the people of God was vindicated. Moses' earlier decisions to leave behind the wealth and power of Egypt allowed him to belong to the company that passed safely to the other side rather than to the one destroyed. The Red Sea becomes something of a type of eschatological judgment (together with the Flood in 11:7), prefiguring that day that at once spells salvation for the faithful and destruction for those who have not cast in their lot with the Christian group. With Moses, the addressees can truly gain a new perspective on their experience of hostility and shame. It is actually more valuable than the greatest worldly wealth, honor, and enjoyments if it is suffered as a result of belonging to the people of promise, who look ahead to God's deliverance and benefits.

---

83. The author refers specifically to Exod. 12:23, 29 (LXX), where the terms "destroyer" and "firstborn" appear. The "destroyer" appears again as the angel of death in Wis. 18:25 (whom Aaron turned back from destroying the Hebrews with plague).

84. The Greek forms for "Red Sea" (Ἐρυθρὰν Θάλασσαν) and "they were swallowed up" (κατεπόθησαν) are found in the hymn of Moses, Exod. 15:4; "as through dry ground" (ὡς διὰ ξηρᾶς γῆς) recalls the formulation of Exod. 14:22, 29 (LXX) (especially the latter, which reads διὰ ξηρᾶς).

The author shifts from Exodus to Conquest, the events in between having provided the pattern for the "distrust" to avoid rather than the "trust" to imitate. Trust was again exhibited at Jericho (the author now refers to Josh. 6:14-16, 20), for God gave instructions and the promise that the walls would fall by a most unconventional means. Trusting the promise of God, Joshua's troops spent seven days marching around the city — truly an exercise in stupidity to the disbeliever. Yet, the person who trusts God's promise obeys him and honors his commands even if "common sense" says that this is no way to win a battle. Within the walls of Jericho, moreover, lived a woman who would become a striking example of faith in the One God. Rahab, a prostitute, realized that her survival lay not within the fortifications of an earthly city but in partnership with the people of God. When the Hebrew spies make their way into the city of Jericho to gather intelligence on the fortifications for their general, Rahab welcomes the spies into her apartment (a reference to Josh. 2:1-21). She makes a surprising confession of faith that she knows that God will bring victory to his people and destruction upon the enemies of God and of God's people. Because she trusted God's promise to give the Hebrews the land of Canaan (Josh. 2:10-11), she became a traitor to her native city by giving hospitality and refuge to the representatives of God's people and by taking pains to help them escape from harm when they were discovered. Because she joins herself, in effect, to the people of God, her family alone is spared destruction (Josh. 6:17, 22-25).

The example of Rahab reinforces the view that every earthly city is unstable and impermanent. Like Jericho, they can fall by the word of God without a single stone being thrown. The worldly cities have no "foundations," and the wisest course one can take is to seek peace with God through joining God's people so as to escape the destruction that will fall upon "the disobedient" (τοῖς ἀπειθήσασιν). Each of the examples in 11:18-31 highlights, in some way, the starkness of the alternative destinies faced by God's people and those outside God's people: protection from, or vulnerability to, the "destroyer"; passage through, or annihilation by, the waters; deliverance from, or participation in, the fate of the disobedient. These examples continue to lead the hearers to choose the course that the author promotes as the one leading to "deliverance" at the final cataclysm. The value of their continued association with the name of Christ and the body of Christians is elevated immensely as their awareness of the eschatological divide is heightened.

11:32-40

The example list closes, as did the lists observed in Seneca's *De beneficiis* (3.36.2–38.3; 5.16.1–17.3), with an impressive accumulation of examples, compressed and abridged so as to make a vivid and strong impression of the endless parade of those whose example could be considered in greater depth "if time permitted":

> And why do I still speak? For the time would fail me to tell about Gideon, Barak, Samson, Jephthah, David and Samuel and the prophets, those who through trust conquered kingdoms, worked justice, received promises, closed the mouths of lions, quenched the power of fire, escaped the mouth of the sword, were made powerful from weakness, became strong in war, routed foreign armies. Women received their dead by resurrection; but others were tortured, refusing to accept release, in order to receive a better resurrection. Still others experienced mocking and beatings, and chains and imprisonment: they were put to death by stoning, they were cut in two, they were slaughtered by the sword, they went about clad in sheepskins and the hides of goats, hungering, afflicted, mistreated — people of whom the world was not worthy — wandering in wastelands and mountains and caves and in the crevices of the earth. And these all, having received attestation through faith, did not receive the promise, God having provided something better for us in order that they should not arrive at the goal apart from us. (11:32-40)

The expression "time will fail me" or "the day will fail" is a rhetorical commonplace by which one segues into a peroration.[85] The author calls to mind a host of examples even as he protests that he has not the time to do so.[86] Hebrews 11:32-35a, beginning with a list of names spanning Judges through potentially Malachi,[87] at least provides a summary of the achievements of faith through 2 Kings; Hebrews 11:35b-38 takes in the fates of the prophets and the Maccabean martyrs as well, thus rounding out the canonical history in addition to making reference to several legends about the deaths of the great prophets of Israel. The survey is structured cleanly in two parts. The first half (11:32-35a) speaks of those figures who, through trust in God, achieved what any person in the world would consider marvelous or miraculous things (military prowess, timely deliverance from death, resuscitation of corpses). The second half (11:35b-38) speaks of those who are, in the world's eyes, shamed and defeated losers but who, from God's perspective, are every bit as triumphant and honor-

---

85. Attridge (*Hebrews*, 347) notes Isocrates *Or.* 1.11; 6.81; 8.56; Philo *Sacr. AC* 27; *Spec. Leg.* 4.238 et al. Seneca *Ben.* 5.16.1–17.3 and Isocrates *Ad Dem.* 11 may now be added to that list.

86. Lane (*Hebrews 9–13*, 383) rightly identifies this section as an example of *paraleipsis*, in which "an orator pretends to pass over something which he in fact mentions."

87. The story of Gideon appears in Judg. 6–8; Barak in Judg. 4–5; Samson in Judg. 13–16; Jephthah in Judg. 11–12; Samuel in 1 Sam. 1–16; and David in 1 Sam. 16–1 Kgs. 2. The designation "prophets" encompasses a large number of individuals, from Nathan, Elijah, and Elisha (the so-called "former" or "earlier prophets") to the later prophets of the exilic and postexilic period.

able as the "heroes" of 11:32-35a. The message conveyed by this structure is that, regardless of external circumstances, it is the posture of loyalty to God and trust in God's word that marks a person's worth (a worth that the rest of the world failed to recognize, 11:38).

Commentators routinely expand at this point in their work on the stories of Gideon, Samson, Barak, and the others mentioned by name. While it may prove edifying to consider these examples at greater length,[88] we do not know what aspects of their stories he would have chosen to elaborate. In effect, he gives the hearers all they "need to know" about these figures in the verses that follow. Hebrews 11:33-34 provide a very terse collection of achievements of the "faithful," and the author has omitted articles and conjunctions (the device of asyndeton) to heighten the hearers' sense of compact enumeration. Moreover, the examples now appear to divide naturally into groups of three. "Those who conquered kingdoms" recalls in a general sense the military successes of the judges and David.[89] "Establishing" or "accomplishing justice" recalls the characterizations of David's reign in 2 Samuel 8:15 and Solomon's rule at 1 Kings 10:9. "They received promises" (again perhaps a metonymic reference to "things promised") provides a very broad reference to the reception of specific benefits promised by God to people who trusted him, as David received the promise of an heir to sit on his throne, a throne that God would make great.

The next three achievements of faith focus on deliverance from peril. References become quite specific in the first two phrases. Hearing of those who "shut the mouths of lions" (ἔφραξαν στόματα λεόντων), the addressees would no doubt recall at once the deliverance of Daniel from the form of execution appointed for him (Theodotion Dan. 6:23 uses the specific phrase ἐνέφραξεν τὰ στόματα τῶν λεόντων, and the next verse refers to his trust in God). Similarly, those who "quenched the power of fire" would call to mind the three companions of Daniel who, after being cast into the fiery furnace, emerged unscathed by the flames (Dan. 3). These four men were celebrated in Jewish culture for their steadfast loyalty to God shown in their uncompromising adherence to the first commandment (both the negative aspect of avoiding idolatry and the positive aspect of offering worship and prayer to God) in the face of the threat of death. The four are mentioned again by name in the exhortation of the mother to her seven sons in 4 Maccabees 16:21, where not their deliverance but their willingness to die is underscored for imitation (see also 4 Macc. 18:12-13). The author of Hebrews, however, will draw a contrast between these who were saved from death and the martyrs who were saved through death (11:35b-36): whether one's vindication by God comes within this life or in the

---

88. See, for example, the treatments in Lane, *Hebrews 9–13*, 383-85; Bruce, *Hebrews*, 320-22; contrast the reserve shown in Attridge, *Hebrews*, 347-48; Ellingworth, *Hebrews*, 623.

89. Thus Attridge, *Hebrews*, 348, and Lane, *Hebrews 9–13*, 385.

next, the person of faith can be certain that it will come and walk accordingly in the face of the "hostility of sinners." Finally, the author recalls those who "escaped the edge [figuratively, "mouth"] of the sword," which again could be true of a large number of prominent OT figures[90] and again will contrast sharply with those who "met death by the sword" (11:37).

The final three images return to the setting of Israel's victories over hostile peoples. "Those made powerful from weakness" certainly recalls Samson in Judges 16, whose strength is restored after he has been made weak. The author might have in mind (or his hearers might call to mind) others who achieved mighty acts by trust in and steadfastness toward God. The heroine Judith, although not historical per se, certainly provides a model of one who is considered weak but is empowered for a great act.[91] Both figures deliver the Israelites from a foreign power. "Those who became strong in battle" and "those who routed foreign armies" are descriptions of vast application from the judges to King David to the Hasmonean family and their armies. The judges routed the military armies (camps) of other nations (cf. Judg. 4:16; 7:15; 8:11), as did David and the army fighting under Judas Maccabaeus and his family.[92] The way the author has underscored the empowering of the weaker or lesser force in these descriptions calls to mind the way in which Israel, with inferior numbers and armaments, consistently defeated significantly larger and better-equipped armies. Although the addressees are not in a military situation, the witness to minorities overcoming majorities may be quite relevant and encouraging to them as they are braced to continue against the hostility of a distinctly larger and better-armed unbelieving world.

Hebrews 11:35 is the hinge verse between the two halves. The introduction of a new subject ("women") in the first half of this verse shows that it is not to be heard as a continuation of the previous list but as a new beginning. The author speaks first of women who received back their dead through resurrection. The author likely has in mind God's raising of the son of the widow of Zarephath through Elijah (recounted in 1 Kgs. 17:17-24) and the resuscitation of the son of the Shunammite woman through Elisha (found in 2 Kgs. 4:18-37). Their example provides yet another affirmation of God's power over death (see 11:4, 11-12, 17-19). The author presents these in mild contrast with those who remained loyal to the point of death in order to attain a "better resurrection,"

---

90. Lane (*Hebrews 9–13*, 386) and Attridge (*Hebrews*, 348) point appropriately to David (1 Sam. 17:45-47; 19:10-18; 2 Sam. 15:14, escaping Saul and Absalom), Elijah (1 Kgs. 19:1-3, escaping Jezebel), Elisha (2 Kgs. 6:26-32, escaping Jehoram), and Jeremiah (Jer. 26:7-24, escaping Jehoiakim).

91. Judith's prayer (Jdt. 9:9-11) is significant in this regard: "give to me, a widow, a strong hand to do what I plan. . . ."

92. The Greek words are particularly frequent in 1 Maccabees (see Attridge, *Hebrews*, 349 nn. 52-53).

that is, those who rose to life in the realm of God rather than those who were resuscitated to the life of this world.

"Those who were tortured" but who maintained their loyalty to God and trust in his reward of the faithful are frequently and rightly identified as the martyrs who suffered under Antiochus IV, whose story is vividly preserved in 2 Maccabees 6:18–7:42 and 4 Maccabees 5–18. The author's choice of the Greek ἐτυμπανίσθησαν recalls specifically the instrument of torture faced by the martyrs in 2 Maccabees (τύμπανον, 2 Macc. 6:19, 28). The persistent focus on resurrection sustained in 2 Maccabees 7 as the focus and expectation of each martyr (2 Macc. 7:9, 11, 14, 23, 29), and indeed as the motivation that allows them to remain faithful to Torah to the point of death, also provides a specific resonance with Hebrews 11:35b.[93] That the author of Hebrews should include among his examples of faith this group of martyrs is not at all surprising, for they had served an important function as examples of commitment to God and Torah in Hellenistic Judaism. Indeed, their role as examples of fidelity to be imitated introduces itself into the very narrative of their sufferings (see 2 Macc. 6:28, 31; 4 Macc. 1:7-8; 9:23; 12:16).[94]

The author of Hebrews thus also harnesses the power of their story to

---

93. The author of Hebrews may also have been familiar with the story as told in 4 Macc. 5–18. Hebrews resonates with the vocabulary of this text at several important points. For example, 4 Macc. 6:9 speaks thus of the stance of the first martyr, Eleazar: "he endured the pains and despised the external compulsions" (ὁ δὲ ὑπέμενε τοὺς πόνους καὶ περιφρόνει τῆς ἀνάγκης). This bears a striking resemblance to Heb. 12:2, where Jesus, persevering in obedience to God, "endured a cross [i.e., pain], despising shame" (ὑπέμεινεν σταυρὸν αἰσχύνης καταφρονήσας). Similarly, 4 Macc. 17:4, where the author by a literary fiction encourages the mother of the seven martyred brothers to persevere ("holding firm the hope of endurance toward God," τὴν ἐλπίδα τῆς ὑπομονῆς βεβαίαν ἔχουσα πρὸς τὸν θεόν) bears a certain likeness in thought and vocabulary to Heb. 3:6 ("if we hold the boldness and the boast of hope," ἐάν[περ] τὴν παρρησίαν καὶ τὸ καύχημα τῆς ἐλπίδος κατάσχωμεν) and Heb. 3:14 ("if we hold the first part of the substance firm until the end," ἐάνπερ τὴν ἀρχὴν τῆς ὑποστάσεως μέχρι τέλους βεβαίαν κατάσχωμεν).

Most significantly, however, the author of Hebrews gives the specific detail that these martyrs "did not accept release" from their torments, so that they might attain the better resurrection. In 2 Maccabees, the torments of Eleazar and the brothers commence only after they refuse to obey the tyrant. Once begun, they are uninterrupted: no opportunity for release is offered. In 4 Macc. 9:16, however, we do find the guards making the offer, "Agree to eat so that you may be released from the tortures" (καὶ τῶν δορυφόρων λεγόντων ὁμολόγησον φαγεῖν ὅπως ἀπαλλαγῇς τῶν βασάνων), and the third brother refusing this offer and urging the torturers to do their worst. Eleazar is also given a brief respite between tortures in which some members of the king's retinue seek to persuade him to eat and so save himself, an offer that is also refused (4 Macc. 6:12-23).

94. The martyrs continue to provide inspiration to Christians during the persecutions of the second and third centuries, as well as after the era of Roman persecution ended. For a brief survey of their influence, see my *4 Maccabees*, chapter 7.

drive his exhortation forward. Being tortured to death, besides being an experience of extreme pain, was an experience of utter degradation. The person was subjected to physical affronts involving a challenge to personal honor that left no possibility for satisfaction (the reparation of honor) in this life.[95] The martyrs die amid the scorn and mockery of their enemies, and thus by all accounts they die a shameful death. Nevertheless, they endure the pain and the shame. The author makes it clear that they had a way out from these extremities, a way back into ease and approval.[96] Like Abraham and the patriarchs, they had the opportunity to return and abandon the journey that obedience to God required, even to receive great honor in worldly estimation for their apostasy. With Abraham, Moses, and Jesus, however, the martyrs fix their eyes on the reward promised by God, here described as "a better resurrection."[97]

These martyrs are guided by different standards of worth and consider preserving obedience to God's Law and preserving themselves from sin or pollution (cf. 2 Macc. 6:19-20, 28), which would alienate them from God, to be of the greatest value. They provide an extreme example, then, of "obeying God rather than human beings" (Acts 5:29), and "fearing God" rather than "fearing the wrath of the king" or any other hostile power.[98] This, of course, resonates strongly with the heart of

---

95. 2 Maccabees 7 bears witness to this conjunction of pain and shame as the author notes the mocking, scornful atmosphere of the torture of the seven brothers. 2 Maccabees 7:7 (RSV) observes that "After the first brother had died in this way, they brought forward the second for their sport" (ἐπὶ τὸν ἐμπαιγμὸν; see Heb. 11:36a). Similarly, the author records that "after this, the third brother was the victim of their sport" (μετὰ δὲ τοῦτον ὁ τρίτος ἐνεπαίζετο).

96. In both versions of the story, Antiochus IV even promises tremendous socio-political advancement (i.e., honor) for those who comply with his demands. See, for example, 4 Macc. 8:5: "I encourage you, after yielding to me, to enjoy my friendship" (τῆς ἐμῆς ἀπολαύειν φιλίας), that is, his personal patronage, as his following remark makes clear: "I can be a benefactor to those who obey me" (δυναίμην . . . εὐεργετεῖν τοὺς εὐπειθοῦντάς μοι). 2 Macc. 7:24 and 4 Macc. 12:5 portray the tyrant repeating this offer to the youngest (and last-surviving) brother, promising even to make him "rich and enviable." No such considerations, however, will erode their constancy. They replicate in their lives the choice of Moses, who similarly relinquished the enjoyment of a patron-client relationship with a human king in order to attain God's benefactions.

97. Compare also Josephus Ap. 2.217-18: "The reward for such as live exactly according to the laws is not silver or gold; it is not a garland of olive branches or of smallage [i.e., leaves from any variety of celery or parsley], nor any such public sign of commendation; but every good man . . . believes that God hath made this grant to those that observe these laws, even though they be obliged readily to die for them, that they shall come into being again, and at a certain revolution of things receive a better life than they had enjoyed before."

98. 4 Maccabees 13:14-15 provides a fine witness to this choice: "let us not fear him who thinks he is killing us, for great is the soul's contest and great is the danger that awaits those who transgress God's commands."

the author's strategy, for he very much wants his hearers to have regard for God's honor and to fear provoking God through the disloyalty or disobedience that would result from valuing God's gifts too lightly. While in the eyes of Antiochus, other Gentiles, and even Hellenizing Jews the martyrs are behaving contrary to standards of rationality and the love of honor, the martyrs seek honor in the sight of God and of the patriarchs who have lived and died faithfully: "if we die in this way, Abraham, Isaac, and Jacob will welcome us and all the patriarchs will honor us" (4 Macc 13:17; see also 17:5). Again their own mind-set reinforces the outlook the author wishes the addressees to adopt: seeking honor before the "cloud of spectators" described in Hebrews 11 and the approval of God (12:1-3, 28; 13:16, 21).

The remainder of the examples expand specifically the company of those who endured shame and hostility in this world for the sake of their trust in God's promises, rather than abandon those promises for "release" from shame or marginalization in this world. The author combines a wide array of images, each of which contributes to the overall picture of a group that is marginalized in the extreme, having no place in society and exposed to every form of disgrace at society's hands. Hebrews 11:36 speaks of those who were tested by "mocking, scourging, chains, and imprisonment." All of these experiences are signs of the dominant culture's disapproval and rejection of those upon whom the shame is inflicted, and all of the specifics collected in this verse have strong connections with the addressees' own past and ongoing experience (see 10:32-34; 13:3). The hearers will see themselves closely reflected in this picture (as also in the experience of those who were "mistreated," κακουχούμενοι, a term that reappears in 13:3).

The author is, however, also drawing heavily on images that resonate with the conditions endured by the prophets of Israel, connections that become even clearer in 11:37. Jeremiah is particularly marked for taunting (Jer. 20:7-8) and beating (Jer. 37:15) and is noted for being frequently imprisoned and put in bonds (Jer. 20:1-3; 37:15-18; see also the fate of Micaiah ben-Imlah in 1 Kgs. 22:24-28). While the deaths of the prophets go largely unmentioned in the OT, Jewish legends arose to fill in these essential details. Thus Jeremiah was stoned, according to the tradition in *Lives of the Prophets* 2.1, as was Zechariah son of Jehoiada (2 Chr. 24:20-22; cf. Matt. 23:35-37). Both *Lives of the Prophets* 1.1 and the *Ascension of Isaiah* 5:1-14 preserve the tradition that Isaiah was sawn in two.[99] The prophet Uriah is slain with the sword (Jer. 26:20-23).

The remaining descriptive phrases outline life lived at the margins of civilization. The images are inspired chiefly by the accounts of the attire and frequent abodes of Elijah and Elisha, as well as by the *apochoresis* (the "heading for the hills") of those faithful Jews who left Jerusalem to avoid the "defilement" as

---

99. For the traditions on Jeremiah and Isaiah, see deSilva and Matthews, *Untold Stories,* 98-114.

well as the persecution during the Hellenization Crisis (2 Macc. 5:27), as a result of which the Maccabean Revolt began.[100] They live at, even beyond, the fringes of civilization. The description of the garments worn by some in this group speaks to the placement of these individuals at the margins of society: linen garments come from the realm of the craftspersons and merchants, but animal skins place the wearers outside of that ordered society.[101] The description of their location places them far from the populated places like cities, towns, or even farms and in places that signify the opposite of social order and in many cases specifically the rejection of society or the experience of tension and antagonism with the powers that be. The addressees are able to set their experience within the context of the larger people of God, who have always moved away from being "at home" in this world toward being "at home" with God: they will be explicitly urged to join in this movement away from at-homeness within society near the end of the exhortation (13:12-14).

In the midst of describing these people who are exposed to dishonor and who have lost all place in society, the author reminds the addressees of who is evaluating whom. The prophets and other people of faith are not persecuted, executed, or expelled because they are "undesirables" who are unworthy of a place in the world. Rather, the way the world has mistreated and marginalized those who embody God's values and who remain steadfast in their orientation toward God shows that "the world is not worthy of them" (ὧν οὐκ ἦν ἄξιος ὁ κόσμος, 11:38).[102] The child and follower of God is not to be evaluated by the

---

100. Going about in sheepskins (ἐν μηλωταῖς) recalls the garb of Elijah (1 Kgs. 19:14 [LXX], ἐν τῇ μηλωτῇ; also 2 Kgs. 2:8, 13-14). Numerous prophets hide from the persecution of Jezebel in a cave (1 Kgs. 18:4); Elijah lives out in the wilderness (1 Kgs. 17:1-7), in a cave (1 Kgs. 19:4-9), and once on a hilltop (2 Kgs. 1:9). During the Midianite oppression, the Israelites were forced to live in hiding in the wilderness and its caves (Judg. 6:2), as again very prominently in the early stages of the Maccabean Revolt (1 Macc. 2:27-38; see Pss. Sol. 17.17 on this period: "They wandered in deserts so as to preserve their lives").

101. Compare Neyrey, "Poverty," 3 n. 12: "As the saying goes, 'clothing makes the man.' There are many examples of honor and status displayed in public by the clothing worn: the Essenes at Qumran symbolized their pursuit of radical purity by wearing the 'white robe' (Josephus J.W. 2.129; Philo Vita Cont. 66). Conversely, prophets like John the Baptizer identified their roles on the margins of society by wearing garments of skin, not cloth woven in households (Mark 1:6; see Heb. 11:37-38; Zech. 13:4; Josephus Life 11)." So here in Heb. 11:37b, the clothing carries associations with a specific social location.

102. See Weiß (Hebräerbrief, 623-24), who sees here a reminiscence of Noah's "condemnation of the world" (11:7). The author's proximity to the strategies employed by Greco-Roman philosophers attempting to detach their students from the standards of the nonphilosopher is striking. Compare Epictetus Diss. 1.29.50-54: "the one who has authority over you declares, 'I pronounce you impious and profane.' . . . If he had passed judgement upon some hypothetical syllogism and had made a declaration, 'I judge the statement, "If it is day, there is light," to be false,' what has happened to the hypothetical syllogism? Who is being

standards of the dominant culture (specifically, the Greco-Roman culture); instead, the outside world is evaluated by the way it has treated the faithful in its midst. The addressees may be assured in their situation that the censure and abuse that befalls them as a result of their commitment to honor and obey the One God signals not their own disgrace but the disgrace of the unbelievers.

The final sentence may strike the first hearers as a bit of a surprise. "All these" noble exemplars of trust did not receive the greater good that God had promised[103] and for which they lived their lives. The faithful had, of course, received many benefactions that God had promised to them (see 11:33 explicitly): for example, the promises to Abraham of a son and a numerous heritage. The author has shifted the focus from any temporal promise (hence also his downplaying of the significance of the entry into Canaan and the Conquest) to the "promise of an eternal inheritance" (9:15) for and toward which, in his view, all the people of God have striven together.[104] This is the "heavenly homeland" or "unshakable kingdom" yet to be revealed, the promised good that the author introduced so vividly into the presentation of Abraham and the patriarchs (11:8-21).[105]

The cause of their failure to attain the promised benefaction during their lifetime is not any fault or deficiency on their part but rather the plan of God.[106] God's provision for bringing the many, trusting, faithful clients to the promised benefit of a heavenly homeland involved the sacrifice of Jesus, which "perfects forever" those who "draw near" to God (cf. 11:6). The patriarchs look forward to entering the same rest that lies open for the hearers (4:1-11; 11:13-16; 13:13-14), but this "new and living way" could not be opened up until, in the fullness of time, God's Son performed his priestly

---

judged in this case, who has been condemned? The hypothetical syllogism, or the man who has been deceived in his judgment about it? . . . But shall the truly educated man pay attention to an uninstructed person when he passes judgement on what is holy and unholy, and on what is just and unjust?"

103. "Promise" is used metonymically for "what was promised." According to the author of Hebrews, they received the promise that good and abiding benefactions were coming, but they did not receive the fulfillment of the promise.

104. So aptly Lane, *Hebrews 9–13*, 392; Pfitzner, *Hebrews*, 169. I would disagree at this point with Eisenbaum's suggestion that "the promise here . . . means salvation effected [by] Christ" (*Jewish Heroes*, 177), or at least would ask her to explain more fully what "salvation effected [by] Christ" includes. The "promise" is not the same thing as the "something better" (Jesus, the high priest and efficacious sin offering for the cleansing of the conscience) by which God's benefactions will be secured, but the entrance together into God's realm, the "perfecting" of all the people of faith together.

105. The author's comment in 11:13 that "they all died trusting, not having received what was promised" is echoed plainly in 11:39 (thus rightly Attridge, *Hebrews*, 352; Ellingworth, *Hebrews*, 634).

106. Thus Attridge, *Hebrews*, 352; Lane, *Hebrews 9–13*, 392; Pfitzner, *Hebrews*, 169.

work. This is left vague in 11:40, but the κρεῖττόν τι is articulated in an environment in which Jesus is at the heart of everything "better" — a better mediator of a better covenant founded on better promises (8:6), bringing the hearers to their better possessions (10:34) in their better country (11:13-16). The forerunners of faith must wait for the addressees, as it were, in order to cross the finish line together. The "perfecting" of the OT worthies is the same as the "perfecting" for which the addressees themselves wait — not the fitting of their conscience to come into God's presence but their actual entrance into the unshakable kingdom, their "ultimate transfer to the actual presence of God in the heavenly sanctuary."[107]

This concluding sentence lends a special urgency to the exhortation that follows. God's forethought for us (περὶ ἡμῶν . . . προβλεψαμένου) amplifies God's beneficence[108] insofar as God has shown special favor toward the Christian generation, which has seen the fulfillment of the promise of a new covenant and which has already been consecrated to approach God's very presence. They are closer to the goal than any of the exemplars of faith ever were, and they have seen the means whereby God brings the promise to its ultimate fulfillment. Their gratitude and loyalty should be all the greater since God has given them a special place in the fulfillment of his promise to all the people of faith. However, their responsibility is likewise greater.[109] Will they, at the very end of the relay race, drop the baton that has been passed to them in plain sight of the many who have already run the race so well and honorably (see 12:1)?

The hearers have the advantage of living after the ministry of the "perfecter of faith," and having his example as the crowning paradigm of trust in action. Those who now respond in trust respond to the "something better" that brings all the people of faith to the eternal inheritance. Those who lived and died in faith without that benefit now watch those who live in faith with that support and assurance. The hearer should be moved to emulate those who have succeeded in embodying the virtue of faith and received God's attestation and should be ashamed to quit now, having all the advantages as well as all the eyes of former winners watching their race. The author is supporting his exhortation in this way with appeals to two complementary emotions (shame and emulation).

---

107. Lane, *Hebrews 9–13*, 393. See also Kögel, "Begriff," 55-56; E. Riggenbach, *Der Brief an die Hebräer* (Leipzig: Deichert, 1922), 383.

108. Danker, *Benefactor*, 359-60.

109. Lane (*Hebrews 9–13*, 394) captures this effect quite well: "The privileged status of Christians as those who have shared in the fulfillment of God's promise should motivate them to be more willing and equipped to endure the testing of faith than were their predecessors."

This passage completes the delineation of the people of faith, the people of God's favor, as a people living at the margins of human society, pushed out to the fringes and even beyond, being exposed to society's deviancy-control techniques and hostility in every imaginable way. The author's evaluation of this situation, however, is that nonbelievers are showing their own lack of worth in this process. The people of God, from Noah to Abraham to Moses to these martyred and marginalized believers, are merely suffering the onslaughts of a condemned world as they themselves go out and on to the better homeland, the city of God. The addressees are asked to see society's hostility against them as a token of society's unworthiness, not a mark of the believers' lack of value or honor. The world is a place of dishonor, and association with the "world" is what ultimately brings one dishonor. Association with the much-pressed people of God remains honorable and assures honor and safety on the day of God's visitation.

Once again, the author sets the addressees' situation in salvation-historical perspective: they stand at the special place in God's unfolding plan where "something better" has been given, the means by which the whole procession from Abel to the very hearers is enabled to "be perfected," that is, to arrive at the goal of the unshakable kingdom. Again, the author wants them to see themselves standing at the very threshold of fulfillment so that they will have that additional incentive to persevere in their commitment to the group and to renew their efforts to assist one another make it across the finish line.

12:1-3

Having traced the line of the people of God, the people of faith, from Abel down to the hearers themselves, the author moves back into the mode of direct exhortation. He summons the hearers to persevere in the "contest" waged by the faithful for the prize of God's approval and entrance into God's realm.[110] The supreme example of faith, Jesus, is woven into this hortatory peroration:

> Having, therefore, so great a cloud of spectators surrounding us, let us also run with endurance the race laid out before us, putting off every weight and the sin that easily ensnares, looking away to the pioneer and perfecter of faith — Jesus, who, for the sake of the joy set before him, endured a cross, despising shame, and has sat down at the right hand of God's throne. Consider him

---

110. It was typical for encomia to include exhortations to contemplate and imitate the subject of the encomium, or to take up their place in a race that others have run, taking up the spots vacated by them. See especially the conclusion to Dio's eulogy for the boxer Melancomas (*Or.* 29.21).

who had endured from sinners such hostility against himself,[111] in order that you may not become faint, growing weary in your souls. (12:1-3)

The exhortation is couched in terms of athletic imagery (see "A Closer Look: Athletic Imagery and Moral Exhortation," 361-64 above), in which the address-ees' Christian experience is cast as a "race," the course of which is laid out ahead of them (ostensibly by God). Their performance in this race is being witnessed not merely by a crowd of flaccid spectators but by the assembly of those who have themselves run the race before them, and have run it well. They are there-fore called to run "with endurance," that is, persevering in the face of the pains and fatigue that threaten to overcome any runner, and to cast aside anything that hampers them from running and finishing well. Finally, they have the ex-ample of Jesus, who ran ahead of them and gave them a shining example of en-durance to fortify them against giving up or growing weary.

A metaphor does not merely "stand for" or "represent" the reality it re-places; it also interprets that reality, bringing to it a new perspective gained from setting it in the light of some other known reality. As observed above, the points of connection between athletic competition and the experience of social and physical deprivation were widely recognized by authors writing from a subcultural or countercultural location (e.g., Judaism, Cynic culture,

---

111. The textual variants at this point are significant. An impressive number of manu-scripts, including P13 and P46, read "hostility from sinners against themselves," thus under-scoring the self-defeating results of rejecting Jesus. Moffatt (*Hebrews*, 198) lists several paral-lel texts that attest to the tradition of highlighting the damage that vicious people do to themselves in assaulting the good person, but, as Croy (*Endurance*, 189-90) rightly points out, the parallels' "clarity of expression of self-destructiveness" make the obscurity of the variant reading all the more striking. It seems preferable (contra Lane, *Hebrews 9–13*, 416-17) to read this variant as an early scribal alteration of Hebrews, by means of which the scribe sought to introduce the philosophical conception of the self-destructiveness of attacking the just person into the text. Lane's defense of the more difficult reading involves an appeal to Heb. 6:6, in which one finds the expression "crucifying [again] the Son of God to their own disadvantage." Lane's reading of 6:6 is unimpeachable, but the importation of that concept here would actually distract the audience from the point the author is making: "the clear im-plication for the audience is that if they were to relinquish their commitment to Christ under the pressure of persistent opposition they would express active opposition against themselves (as in 6:6!), just as did Jesus' tormentors" (Lane, *Hebrews 9–13*, 417). The author, however, has been leading the hearers from 10:32 on to disregard society's hostility and censure as any indication of their lack of honor or correctness. The focus here is on the hostility endured by Christ from unbelievers and his persistence in the face of such "contradiction" or "hostility" as a model for the addressees' response to the hostility they experience at the hands and lips of "sinners." If one were to adopt the variant "against themselves" as the reading, the "clear implication for the audience" would be that society's hostility harms not the Christian but the persecutor, while the very hardships inflicted become a source of benefit to the Christian as the endurance of divine training (12:4-13).

Stoic culture, and the like). In both the race or contest and membership in an essentially voluntary group, a person willingly chose to endure physical discomfort, to submit to the reproaches of a trainer, to curb luxury, and to turn aside from many delights enjoyed by the nonathlete or the fully participating member of the dominant culture. The metaphor of athletic competition, however, also brings something to the experience of the minority culture. It provides for the recipient of society's censure and hostility an essential reorientation to that experience, turning a victim into a competitor and raising his or her dignity correspondingly. Athletic imagery turns debilitating experiences into endurable ones since there is now the prospect of victory,[112] even if that victory is to be attained not by turning the tables on opponents but by merely enduring to the end of the contest.[113] In the end, victory is attained insofar as the one suffering external assaults (censure, physical violence, and the like) does not allow them to alter his internal convictions and commitments to do what he or she knows to be just and right.[114] For the author of Hebrews, this means persevering in a lifestyle that manifests gratitude to the divine benefactor and to Jesus, the broker of that relationship — in short, maintaining a just response to God in view of prior gifts and future benefactions already promised.

The Christians' exposure to insult and hardship, then, is not an experience of victimization that should lead them to falter in their convictions and yield to the pressures of the outside world, but rather an opportunity to compete for the prize of virtue, conceived in Hebrews as God's approbation and an unending life in the abiding realm. The author first calls the hearers' attention to the exemplars of faith. They are no longer examples from a book or even witnesses to God; they are spectators, "witnesses" now of the audience's performance in this relay race of persevering in trust in God and looking always to the promise. This usage of μάρτυς is well attested in contemporary Greek literature.[115] Wisdom 1:6, for example, speaks of God thus: "God is a witness

---

112. See Aristotle *Rh.* 1.11.14-15: "Victory is pleasant . . . for there is produced an idea of superiority, which all with more or less eagerness desire." Aristotle goes on to speak of sports as pleasant, since competition implies victory. While one should not suppose this will render the addressees' experience truly "pleasant," it certainly provides them with the hope of being able to overcome their opponents and, indeed, this prospect will spur them on to endure assaults on their honor and persons with a courageous attitude and demeanor.

113. See the very helpful application of this image in Philo *Quod Omn.* 26-27.

114. A wide range of literature attests to this principle; see 4 Macc. 5:16; 7:4; 9:18, 30; 11:20-21 (these speak of the "victory" achieved by not yielding to the compulsions brought to bear on the martyrs from without); Epictetus *Diss.* 3.24.71; 4.1.60, 87; Philo *Quod Omn.* 30; Seneca *Constant.* 5.6-7; 9.5.

115. The first three texts are listed in Attridge, *Hebrews,* 354 n. 19, and are developed in greater detail in Croy, *Endurance,* 58-61; the position taken by these two scholars stands

(μάρτυς) of the inmost feelings, a true observer (ἐπίσκοπος) of their hearts and a hearer of their tongues." The parallelism suggests that "witness" is being used here in the sense of "onlooker," depicting God as the watchful observer of our thoughts and attitudes. That author wishes to underscore the importance of living for God's approval at every level of our being, in deeds of the body as well as thoughts and desires of the heart. A second informative source is Josephus, whose *Jewish War* 4.134 and *Antiquities* 18.299 use the term to speak of witnesses who "observe valor or wrongdoing with the intent, or at least the potential, of honoring or blaming."[116]

A crucial insight emerges from this discussion: the author uses the strategy of drawing attention to the presence of spectators who will witness one's performance either for praise or censure. Aristotle's discussion of appealing to the pathos of shame is thus most apt for understanding 12:1. Making the heroes of faith into a cloud of spectators who "witness" the contest run by Christians creates a court of reputation before which the hearers will be ashamed to fail in their race, since they highly esteem these figures.[117] The technique of conjuring, in effect, a specific crowd of spectators in whose sight a decision must be rendered or action carried out is a sufficiently common strategy used to motivate hearers to choose a particular course of action. There is a textbook example in Aristotle (*Rh.* 2.6.24): "Cydias, when haranguing the people about the allotment of the territory to Samos, begged the Athenians to picture to themselves that the Greeks were standing round them and would not only hear, but also see what they were going to decree." Looking at their decision in light of what the other Greek city states would think of Athens would be presumed to move them toward the choice Cydias favored.[118] The strategy has the effect of reminding the hearers of who is watching their choices and whose opinion really matters regarding their choices. Left to make their choice in the awareness only of what their pagan neighbors would think of them, the Christians would surely be moved to return to their idolatrous or non-Christian Jewish way of

---

opposed to the position adopted in Lane (*Hebrews 9–13*, 408) and Stedman (*Hebrews*, 135), who view these "witnesses" merely in terms of the testimony they bear about the life of faith, thus missing an essential elements of the rhetorical force of the passage.

116. Croy, *Endurance*, 59.

117. Aristotle *Rh.* 2.6.14-15: "People feel shame before those whom they esteem, . . . whose opinion they do not despise" (μὴ καταφρονεῖ τῆς δόξης).

118. Croy (*Endurance*, 59) points also to Pseudo-Longinus *On the Sublime* 14.2, where the author speaks of his own approach to writing as undertaken while imagining "the ancient masters of style, Homer, Demosthenes, *et al.*, being present to judge his writing. This imaginary assembly is referred to as a θέατρον (theater) made up of μάρτυ-ρες. . . ." The use of the latter term is here explicitly "witness" in the sense of "spectator" in the arena or theater, and the person "on stage," as it were, performs so as to please the spectators imagined present.

life. Mindful of the opinions of the heroes of faith and God, however, they will be much more likely to persevere in their race of faith.[119]

The author is at work creating an image for the hearers that should provide their specific and strategic orientation toward their life in the world. Verbal repetition reinforces the creation of the image as the author speaks about what "surrounds" them (περικείμενον) and what "lies ahead" of them (προκείμενον, 12:1; see the use of this word in 6:18 for the "hope lying before us"). Who surrounds them and whose approval should they seek? Rather than seeing themselves surrounded by a cloud of unsupportive, censorious, and hostile neighbors who want them to resume living by the world's standards, the author wants the Christians to see themselves surrounded by the host of the faithful in every age, who have run the race with excellence and whose lives bear testimony to the reality of the prize for which they all strive together. What lies ahead of them that should present the primary agenda for their daily lives? The author wants them to see not improvement of their living conditions in this age, not "getting ahead" or "getting by" in this world, but rather the goal of arriving at God's eternal kingdom. It is this goal that must guide every decision along the way, even as the runner must keep his or her mind fixed on arriving at the goal, permitting nothing to distract him or her from that goal.

The "race set before us" (τὸν προκείμενον ἡμῖν ἀγῶνα) is a "fixed classical expression" for a race whose course is determined by the masters of the games.[120] The author is not suggesting a strictly predestinarian understanding of existence. He has already shown, however, that Jesus' course conformed to the needs that God knew the "many sons and daughters" would face (2:10-18). That is to say, God, having knowledge of the conditions in which his children would find themselves along their journey home, fitted Jesus beforehand to be their pioneer and helper by means of sending him through the course first. The "course set before us" is thus the same course that Jesus ran ahead of us, and this connection leads the author to introduce Jesus in 12:2 as the prime example of how to run. The way in which Jesus encountered opposition on the way to the goal provides the many children with a model for successful perseverance in the race.

The Christians are to run this race "with endurance" (ὑπομονή). By casting the Christian life as an athletic contest, the author is able to harness

---

119. 4 Maccabees again provides a significant parallel usage of this technique. The martyrs encourage each other to die amid torture and degradation by pointing one another to the opinion that the supra-temporal community of faith will have of them: "Abraham, Isaac, and Jacob will welcome us, and all the patriarchs will praise us" (4 Macc. 13:17).

120. Attridge (*Hebrews*, 355) refers to Euripedes *Or.* 847; Plato *Laches* 182A; Epictetus *Diss.* 3.25.3; Josephus *Ant.* 19.1.13 §92. Croy (*Endurance*, 66) adds Plato *Phaedrus* 247b; Dio *Or.* 13.118.

the dominant cultural descriptions of the virtue of courage to fuel the forward movement of the church. Aristotle repeatedly speaks of the manifestation of courage as "enduring" hardships and terrible experiences because it is honorable to do so and dishonorable not to do so. For example, one's duty to one's city involves fighting for that city when it is threatened. The battlefield is a place of horror, pain, and the most terrible things, yet the honorable person must face and endure those hardships in order to be true to his duty to the city-state. To choose not to endure those hardships would be a dereliction of duty and a violation of sacred obligations and trust. Thus, courage is elevated as a cardinal virtue, and those who act courageously act honorably since they set moral obligation above physical safety and comfort.[121] Wherever hardship was the price of remaining committed to a group's values and to doing those things that preserved the group over time, topics of courage would be a helpful tool for motivating ongoing commitment. The author of 4 Maccabees, for example, uses topics of courage within his narration of the martyrs' deaths. He promotes ongoing commitment to Jewish values (keeping Torah even in the midst of a Hellenized world that looks down on Jews as superstitious, atheistic, and misanthropic) by claiming that Torah is the best teacher of the virtues prized even by the Greco-Roman world. Torah "teaches courage, with the result that we endure all hardships willingly," Eleazar explains to the tyrant Antiochus, and Eleazar's protracted death allows him to demonstrate the truth of this claim (4 Macc. 5:23).[122] The image of the "contest" orients the hearers to the opposition of their pagan neighbors now in such a way that perseverance in Christian commitment and witness in the face of censure and abuse becomes the "noble" and "courageous" path, and yielding to the shaming techniques of the outside world, the "ignoble" and "cowardly" path. This is an astounding coup, since the author is turning the continued endurance of censure into an honorable course of action.

Running a race effectively requires running unencumbered. The image

---

121. Aristotle *Eth. Nic.* 1115b12: Courage "endures fearful things for the sake of what is noble" (ὑπομενεῖ τοῦ καλοῦ ἕνεκα); 1115b23-24: "The courageous man endures the terrors and dares the deeds that manifest courage, for the sake of that which is noble"; 1117a17-19: "the mark of the courageous man, as we have seen, is to endure things that are terrible to a human being and that seem so to him, because it is noble to do so and base not to do so." See also *Rhet. Her.* 3.3.5: "When we invoke as motive for a course of action steadfastness in Courage, we shall make it clear that . . . from an honorable act no peril or toil, however great, should divert us; death ought to be preferred to disgrace; no pain should force abandonment of duty; . . . for country, for parents, guest-friends, intimates, and for the things justice commands us to respect, it behooves us to brave any peril and endure any toil."

122. See also the linking of "courage" and "endurance" in 4 Macc. 1:11; 5:23; 17:17, 23. 4 Maccabees 7:22; 9:30; 16:17, 19, 21 also use topics of courage to praise the martyrs' commitment to Jewish values. See deSilva, *4 Maccabees*, 82-84.

itself invites the author to urge the addressees to "lay aside every weight" and obstacle, one notorious hindrance being sin. What "weight" does the author have in mind? Anything that would keep one from running forward. Particularly in the hearers' past situation, their reputation became a "weight" that might have made them stumble if they tried to keep it intact — to keep carrying it, as it were. Instead, they threw it aside for the sake of running to Christ. Their physical well-being became a "weight" that again, if they had been inclined to keep their bodies free from harm, might have caused them to stop running altogether. Again, they threw off that weight and kept running forward. Their property became a weight when they were caught between keeping it and keeping Christ; again, they chose the "better part" and laid the weight aside. And, of course, prior to these weights there were the sins that filled their lives prior to conversion — sins revealed to them as such by the gospel, but which were just an accepted way of life before (e.g., idolatry). All these weights they cast aside, but as time goes on the runner becomes encumbered again (as are those who are wavering, or who have already drawn back from open fellowship). The call to such believers, as to all, is to keep laying aside everything that threatens forward progress in the race. In situations of persecution, the words of Martin Luther's hymn remain fitting:

> Let goods and kindred go,
> this mortal life also;
> the body they may kill,
> God's truth abideth still.

In situations of lesser tension between church and society, the weights may become more insidious. The desire to serve God and Mammon is always menacing, particularly in times of prosperity. Whatever threatens running well, that is the weight to cast off.

The race is to be run "looking off to Jesus (ἀφορῶντες εἰς . . . Ἰησοῦν), the pioneer and perfecter of faith."[123] Hebrews 12:2 provides the climactic example of living by faith, one that will be posed in direct contrast to the negative example of Esau in 12:16-17. Jesus' example is of a different order than Abraham's or Moses', since here we read not only about the orientation of faith in this world but also about the reward of faith at the end of the race. Jesus is the pioneer of faith in that he runs ahead of the believers (recall the earlier image of "forerunner" in 6:20), leading the host of the many sons and daughters to glory (2:10 is the other place where Jesus is called a "pioneer"). As pioneer, Jesus emboldens the hearers to endure hardship and despise the world's attempts at shaming

---

123. See 4 Macc. 17:10: the martyrs endure the torments and achieve victory in their competition "looking to God" (εἰς θεὸν ἀφορῶντες).

them for the sake of the joy that has been set before them. The "end" of his story shows his attitude toward the world's opinion to be correct. His exaltation becomes the proof that walking as he walked will lead the "many children" also to glory.

The meaning of "perfecter" (τελειωτής) is harder to determine since the term is extremely rare. In the one other text not dependent on Hebrews that uses the term,[124] the noun τελειωτής appears as an antonym of "inventor" (εὑρετής, synonymous with ἀρχηγός in other texts). The text refers to the fact that one person will invent a style while others will refine and perfect it. Reading Hebrews 12:2 in this light suggests that Jesus is presented as the one who has displayed trust or faith in its complete and perfect form, and the placement of Jesus at the very end of this list of examples would support such a reading. A second possibility, however, may merit consideration. Hebrews 11:39-40 left the heroes of faith in the posture of awaiting their "perfecting," something that would only occur after the "something better," namely, the ratification of the new covenant and the effective removal of sins from the conscience of the human being and the memory of God. Their "trust," like the trust of the believer in this world, remains unfulfilled. Jesus might then be seen as the one who perfects the trust of others, that is, brings others to the fulfillment of the thing they were trusting to receive.[125] Which reading represents the intent of the author or the hearing of the first-century audience lies beyond adjudication: both readings would be possible, and the literary context is equally amiable to either.

The example of Jesus is framed succinctly and powerfully: he "endured a cross, despising shame, and has sat down at the right hand of God's throne." The form of execution called crucifixion was calculated to leave the victim utterly stripped of dignity and worth in the eyes of this world.[126] It was the vilest, most degrading death possible, as the crucified was hung up before all the world precisely as an example of how not to act. A shameful death was the most feared of evils among many ancients[127] since it left one with no opportunity to regain one's honor. The last word on one's life was a judgment of worthlessness. As Jewish authors transformed the deaths of the Maccabean-era martyrs from

---

124. Dionysius of Halicarnassus *On Dinarchus* 1, first presented by Croy, "Note," 117-19.

125. In neither case, however, would it mean that Jesus makes the trust of believers stronger or better, as in the common translation "perfecter of *our* faith" (found in Stedman, *Hebrews,* 137; Long, *Hebrews,* 128). See the explanations given in Lane (*Hebrews 9–13,* 399 n. k).

126. See the careful study of crucifixion by Martin Hengel, *Crucifixion in the Ancient World* (Philadelphia: Fortress, 1977), for a horde of helpful primary materials on grasping the obloquy of the death on the cross.

127. See Epictetus *Diss.* 2.1.13: "it is not a fearful thing to die, but to die shamefully."

experiences of degradation into "noble deaths,"[128] so the early followers of Jesus quickly came to understand that his death on the cross, too, was a "noble death" and not a shameful one.[129] The author of Hebrews has reinforced this Christian-cultural understanding of Jesus' death as noble. It is a voluntary death endured on account of a commitment to virtue (here obedience to God; 10:5-10); it is a beneficial death suffered in order to bring benefit to others (2:9-10, 14-15; 4:14-16; 5:7-10; 7:11–10:18). The addressees, having been brought into the Christian group, will understand Jesus' death on the cross as a death suffered "for them," and thus one that must arouse their gratitude and respect rather than their contempt and disgust. Calling attention to the sufferings or hardships endured by a patron is common in the inscriptions surveyed by Frederick Danker.[130] This verse, therefore, is not merely a recital of Jesus' passion; it uses language that enhances his honor as a benefactor and the beneficiaries' awareness of debt.

Jesus "endured" (ὑπέμεινεν) hardship in the extreme, but he did so armed with a certain mind-set. He "despised shame" (αἰσχύνης καταφρονήσας).[131] This entails more than simply enduring the experience of disgrace rather than shrinking from it.[132] "Shame" (αἰσχύνη) is more than the experience of being dishonored: it signifies the sensitivity toward public opinion that moves people to do certain things that will be approved by the majority and to shrink from doing other things that will be censured by the majority. Aristotle (*Rh.* 2.6.26) tells us that "there are many things which people either do or do not do owing to the feeling of shame which other people inspire." Jesus is free to act in complete obedience to God, and thus to attain the very desirable and honorable end that God has set before him, because he is free from sensitivity to other people's opinions of his actions. The only literary parallel to the phrase in Hebrews 12:2 appears in an oration by Dio (*Or.* 7.139) in which the orator, in his role now as

---

128. See my *4 Maccabees*, 93-96. For an excellent study of the "noble death" and its component parts (a voluntary death, a death endured for the sake of some virtue, and a death endured so as to bring benefit to others), see David Seeley, *The Noble Death: Graeco-Roman Martyrology and Paul's Concept of Salvation* (JSNTSS 28; Sheffield: Sheffield Academic Press, 1990).

129. The ways in which Matthew and John effect this transformation is the subject of my *The Hope of Glory: Honor Discourse and New Testament Interpretation* (Collegeville, MN: Liturgical Press, 1999), chapters 2 and 3.

130. Danker, *Benefactor*, 363-64.

131. Again compare the portrayal of Eleazar's martyrdom in 4 Macc. 6:9: "but he endured the pains and despised the compulsions" (ὁ δὲ ὑπέμενε τοὺς πόνους καὶ περιεφρόνει τῆς ἀνάγκης).

132. Delitzsch, *Hebrews*, 306: "despising, disdaining to shrink from any kind of shame"; Lane, *Hebrews 9–13*, 414: "καταφρονεῖν, 'to scorn,' acquires in this context a positive nuance: 'to brave,' or 'to be unafraid' of an experience in spite of its painful character."

moralist, censures the rise in adultery by pointing out how it paves the way to even worse abuses of families and individuals: winking at adultery with inappropriate partners (i.e., social inferiors) is "paving the way to hidden and secret assaults upon the chastity of women and boys of good family, such crimes being only too boldly committed when modesty (shame, αἰσχύνης) is openly despised (καταφρονουμένης)."[133] The complete disregard for public opinion (shame, modesty) poses, for Dio, a menace to the fabric of society.

"Despising shame" is very much synonymous, then, with "despising opinion" (καταφρονεῖν δόξης), a phrase that appears far more frequently in the literature. All human beings value the opinion of some people (e.g., their neighbors, their kin, other honorable and virtuous human beings, fellow-citizens, and the like), and live their life in such a way as will gain the approbation of such people and avoid their censure.[134] People are not, however, sensitive to just anyone's opinion. Aristotle frequently observes that adults carry on their business with no regard for the opinion children or animals have of them: they have no "shame" before such beings because they "despise the opinion" of children or animals. The reason for this is that children and animals are considered to have no grasp of the "truth," so that any opinion they form about an adult's action is going to be unreliable and worthless.[135] This principle could be extended, however, to exclude people who value different things from one's "court of reputation," that group of significant others whose esteem one values.[136] Thus, the noble person committed to virtue might "despise" equally the esteem and the contempt that might be offered by the "common people" (Aris-

---

133. Discovered by J. J. Wettstein, *He Kaine Diatheke: Novum Testamentum graece* (Amsterdam: Dommer, 1751-52), 2:434. A fuller discussion of this concept may be found in my *Despising Shame*, 168-73, and also in chapter 3 of that book (passim).

134. Aristotle *Rh.* 1.11.16: "Honour and good repute are among the most pleasant things, because everyone imagines that he possesses the qualities of a worthy man, and still more when those whom he believes to be trustworthy say that he does. Such are neighbours rather than those who live at a distance; intimate friends and fellow-citizens rather than those who are unknown; contemporaries rather than those who come later; the sensible rather than the senseless; the many rather than the few; for such persons are more likely to be trustworthy than their opposites."

135. *Rh.* 2.6.23: "[People] are not ashamed . . . before those whose opinion in regard to truth they greatly despise — for instance, no one feels shame before children or animals" (οὐκ αἰσχύνονται ὧν πολὺ καταφρονοῦσι τῆς δόξης τοῦ ἀληθεύειν); see also *Rh.* 1.11.16: "As for those for whom men feel great contempt, such as children and animals, they pay no heed to their respect or esteem"; *Rh.* 2.6.14-15: "People feel shame before those whom they esteem, . . . whose opinion they do not despise" (μὴ καταφρονεῖ τῆς δόξης).

136. See Seneca *Constant.* 11.2–12.1: just as one does not take offense at (i.e., regard as truly insulting) a child's actions, since children are inferior, the wise person takes "the same attitude . . . toward all whose childhood endures even beyond middle age and the period of grey hairs."

totle *Eth. Nic.* 4.3.14; Dio *Or.* 24.4). Greco-Roman philosophers seized on this idea as a means of taking their students' minds and hearts off the approval and the disapproval of anyone who did not follow that philosophy:

> In the same spirit in which he sets no value *(nihilo aestimat)* on the honours they have, he sets no value on the lack of honour they show. Just as he will not be flattered if a beggar shows him respect, nor count it an insult if a man from the dregs of the people, on being greeted, fails to return his greeting, so, too, will he not even look up if many rich men look upon him. For he knows that they differ not a whit from beggars. . . . (Seneca *Constant.* 13.2)

The goal of such teaching was to free students from being distracted by anxiety over what "people might think" regarding their pursuit of virtues and fulfillment of moral obligations. The nonphilosopher does not pursue or know the truth or the true nature of what human beings are meant to be. Their estimation of the philosopher, therefore, will be valueless.

When the author credits Jesus with "despising shame," he signals that Jesus affirmed the unreliability of evaluations of honor and dishonor made by human beings. They were not in full possession of the facts, and therefore their approval and censure were not worthwhile guides for conduct. That is to say, Jesus acted without regard for public opinion, one way or the other. In saying that he "despised" shame, the author point outs that Jesus understood public opinion to be based on error and ignorance.[137] Such a reading also makes Jesus' example extremely relevant for the hearers. Like the philosophers who pursue what they know to be honorable without being distracted by praise or reproach from nonphilosophers, the Christians, too, are to "despise shame."[138] They are not to allow themselves to be swayed to the left or to the right in their race by any sensitivity to the praise or censure of non-Christians. It is only the approval of God, Christ, and the community of faith across the ages that should determine their choices and actions. In the words of John Chrysostom, Jesus died disgracefully "for no other reason than to teach us to count as nothing the opinion of human beings."[139]

Jesus endures hardship for the sake of arriving at a noble goal or, in the words of this author, "for the sake of the joy set before him" (ἀντὶ τῆς προκει-

---

137. The early church fathers took the verse in this direction as well. Origen (*Fragmenta in Psalmos* 37.12.4-5), for example, provides a paraphrastic translation of this verse that makes explicit the difference in value between human opinion and, implicitly, God's evaluation: "having despised disgrace from human beings." Gregory of Nyssa (*Contra Eunomium* 3.5 [*PG* 45:708 B 4-6]) explicates this more fully: Jesus "despised a disgraceful reputation among human beings on account of him being the lord of glory."

138. See Weiß, *Hebräerbrief,* 639; Attridge, *Hebrews,* 357-58.

139. NPNF[1] 14:493; *PG* 63:194.

μένης αὐτῷ χαρᾶς). Jesus' choice was made because, like Moses (who similarly chose hardship and extreme loss of status) and Abraham, he was looking ahead to the reward that God had set for the faithful one. It is not immediately apparent to every commentator that the preposition ἀντὶ in this phrase is to be read "for the sake of." The preposition can also mean "instead of," such that Jesus endures a cross "instead of the joy set before him."[140] My preference for the first reading,[141] therefore, calls for some defense. First, the complete lack of a referent for this joy that Christ renounced presents a substantial difficulty with reading the preposition here as "instead of." Does the author give any awareness elsewhere of the content of this nebulous "joy"? The author is very clear, however, on the joy that came to Christ as a result of his endurance of the cross, both in the broad (the exaltation in 1:5-14) and the immediate (the session at God's right hand in 12:2) literary context. In a sense, pondering two "joys" that could be received — the one as a result of obedience, the other as the result of disobedience — would also work against the author's ideological strategy. He does not want the addressees to think that they have two viable alternatives, or that "joy" in any sense awaits the one who refuses to endure hardship and who begins to care about the opinion of outsiders. The best they could have is "the temporary pleasure of sin," but surely not "joy."

Second, the usage of the preposition in 12:16 suggests even more forcefully that "for the sake of" is the proper sense of ἀντὶ in 12:2. The structure of these two examples is very similar, such that the author appears to provide an intentional contrast to the wise and honorable choice of Jesus in the foolish and dishonorable choice of Esau, "who for the sake of (ἀντὶ) a single meal sold away his inheritance as firstborn." Jesus chooses temporary hardship for the sake of eternal honor, but Esau chooses temporary relief at the cost of lasting honor as the bearer of the promise.

Third, the pattern of Jesus' example is cast in terms very similar to Aristotle's paradigm of the courageous person (*Eth. Nic.* 3.1.7) who gains praise by "submitting to some disgrace or pain as the price of some great and noble object" (αἰσχρόν τι ἢ λυπηρὸν ὑπομένωσιν ἀντὶ μεγάλων καὶ καλῶν). In both Hebrews 12:2 and this excerpt from the *Nicomachean Ethics* the authors speak first

---

140. This position is defended by Paul Andriessen, "Renonçant à la joie qui lui revenait," *NRT* 107 (1975): 424-38; Lane, *Hebrews 9–13,* 413. D'Angelo (*Moses in Hebrews,* 53) also prefers it as a way of reading Jesus' example as more strictly parallel with Moses' example, which included the renunciation of a life of pleasure and power in Pharaoh's court. On this point, however, there is still a parallelism with Moses if the preposition is read as "for the sake of," since Moses chose hardship and loss of status for the sake of the "reward" to which he was looking (11:26).

141. A preference shared by Moffatt (*Hebrews,* 196), H. Windisch (*Der Hebräerbrief* [2nd ed.; Tübingen: Mohr, 1931], 109), Spicq (*L'Épître aux Hébreux,* 2:387), Michel (*Der Brief an die Hebräer,* 434), P. Hughes (*Hebrews,* 523-24), and Attridge (*Hebrews,* 306).

of enduring pain and disgrace and, second, of the attainment of some great or noble goal. Aristotle observes that, in effect, an honorable goal or achievement renders honorable even the experience of disgrace, which certainly also fits our author's presentation of Jesus' passion.

Decisive proof has now been supplied by Clayton Croy, who investigates the trail blazed in a footnote of Harold Attridge's commentary.[142] He investigates the many occurrences of the phrase "prizes set before" the athlete (προκείμενα ἆθλα or γέρα).[143] Josephus (*Ant.* 8.302) provides an exceptionally illuminating use: "Those before whom a prize has been set . . . do not cease striving after it." He determines that, given the thoroughgoing athletic image that governs 12:1-4, the most natural way to read "the joy set before him" is to read it in light of the athletic idiom, "the prize set before him." As a final interpretive move, Croy attempts to analyze the ideology of the interpreters, which leads some to resist this reading:

> No one takes issue with Jesus' exaltation following his suffering. The discomforting feature is the portrayal of Jesus having subsequent joy as a *conscious motive,* or perhaps even compensation, for enduring the cross. . . . Modern notions of altruism and selflessness may make us demur at the thought of Jesus' having joy in view while suffering the cross. . . . The relevant question is whether *the author of Hebrews* demurs at a certain portrayal of Jesus.[144]

Ancient notions of heroism and beneficence did not preclude the quest for honor on the part of the hero or giver. The quotation from Aristotle above shows that the motive of a noble goal is essential to "justifying" the subjection of oneself to disgrace. Moreover, Seneca bears witness that a beneficiary is not to think less of a benefactor who confers a benefit in order to enhance the estate of both giver and recipient:

> I am not so unjust as to feel under no obligation to a man who, when he was profitable to me, was also profitable to himself. . . . nay, I am also desirous that a benefit given to me should even be more advantageous to the giver, provided that, when he gave it, he was considering us both, and meant to divide it between himself and me. . . . I am not merely unjust, I am grateful, if I do not rejoice that, while he has benefited me, he has also benefited himself.

Particularly after the author has already dwelt so long on how Jesus voluntarily endured death in order to benefit the believers, the first-century Christian

---

142. Croy, *Endurance,* 66-67; 177-85; Attridge, *Hebrews,* 357 n. 65.

143. See Josephus *Ant.* 1.proem.3 §14; 8.7.7 §208; Polybius 3.62; Pausanias 9.2.6; Plutarch *Mor.* 8D; 156A; Plato *Rep.* 608C; Philo *Praem.* 13; *Mut.* 88.

144. Croy, *Endurance,* 185.

would not at this point in the sermon think less of Jesus running his course with God's reward in view. Moreover, the parenetic or exemplary function of Hebrews 12:2 also necessitates a change in focus, since the hearer is to imitate the posture of this exemplar.[145] We, too, are called to look ahead to the "joy" that God "set before us" as an incentive to endure in costly discipleship. The "joy" for which Jesus endured is thus none other than his session at God's right hand, as the closing words of Hebrews 12:2, recontextualizing Psalm 110:1 yet again, make explicit. The honor with which Jesus was rewarded proves the nobility and wisdom of his course of action[146] and confirms as well the nobility of the one who imitates his choices.

The next verse applies 12:2 to the hearers' situation. They face hostility and contradiction from sinners just as Jesus did (though their wrestling match is less brutal than Jesus endured, as the author will remark in 12:4). Jesus' endurance of substantially greater hostility, pain, and censure at the hands of "sinners" should embolden those on whose behalf specifically he suffered those things not to "grow weary" in their running of the race. There is a strong potential for considerations of reciprocity to enter the hearers' minds at this point. Growing weary would mean, in effect, breaking faith with the one who endured infinitely more to bring them benefit in the first place. They have not yet begun to pour themselves out for Christ as Christ did for them. The introduction of the label "sinners" for those who show hostility toward Jesus helps to reinforce the group boundaries and the exclusion of nonbelievers from the "court of reputation." The very resistance of nonbelievers to the believers, as with their spiritual predecessors' hostility toward Jesus, shows them to be on the wrong side of God's values. Once again the abuse offered by outsiders is to be taken as a sign of the outsiders' moral and spiritual depravity, not a sign that the believers should reconsider their commitments. They may instead gain strength in times of hardship endured for the sake of fellowship with Jesus that sharing in his sufferings brings. The experience of hostility from outside becomes an occasion to identify more closely with Jesus, but also to identify with the final outcome of Jesus' sufferings — entry into "glory" (cf. Phil. 3:10-11).

---

145. Croy (ibid.) also makes this excellent point: "Secondly, we must remember that we are, in fact, dealing with a *portrayal* of Jesus. The psychological state of the historical Jesus as he contemplated and endured the cross was no more recoverable for the author of Hebrews than it is for us. The issue is the *paraenetic use* of the Jesus tradition." Hebrews 12:2 may be less problematic if we regard it in this manner rather than read it back into the mind of the historical Jesus.

146. See Aristotle *Rh.* 1.9.16: "Those things of which the reward is honour are noble; also those which are done for honour rather than money."

Summary

Having summarized the essence of the Christian's posture as one of "trust" or "faith" (πίστις) at the conclusion of the hortatory material in 10:19-39, the author provides in 11:1–12:3 a picture of how "faith" lives in this world. This picture is thoroughly shaped to address the pastoral needs of the hearers, showing them by example what their response of "trust" should look like. The experience of trusting God is the present possessing of the future benefits yet to be conferred, as well as the irrefutable demonstration of the existence of those as-yet-unseen benefits (as well as of the invisible realm as a whole). The person of faith looks to God as to a beneficent patron, understanding that the visible, material realm is merely secondary and subordinate to the permanent realm of God's dwelling. Based on this trust in God, the heroes of faith memorialized in the oracles of God acted always with a view to the invisible and the future, understanding that this world was transitory and not their home. Their hearts were fixed on entering the city and homeland that God prepared for them and on being found on the right side of God when God intervened to judge the godless.

Because of this fixedness of their hearts, they were willing to leave behind their status and wealth as worldly people would define these, choosing instead a humble or even humiliated condition of life in this world so as to join themselves to God's people and to obey God's call, knowing that this would lead them to enjoy the promised benefactions. Their own condition in this life never caused them to falter in their trust. They knew that even their death in this world could not prevent their reception in God's time of God's promises, for God was able to give life to the dead. Thus they were emboldened to act without any view to worldly persons' estimation of their honor or their decision, looking solely to the approval of the God who called them out and promised them an abiding homeland — and never looking back to the worldly honor and goods they left behind, as if to seek their restoration.

These virtuous people, who have received God's testimony to their wisdom and worth through their inclusion into sacred history, now form the circle of spectators before which the addressees must make their choices and live their lives. The author wishes the audience to be sensitive to what the people of faith in every age will think about them, rather than to be concerned for their honor rating in the eyes of unbelievers, those who consistently act unwisely in light of God's judgment and promises. The hearers are to fix their mind's eye on Jesus, who pioneered the trail to eternal honor before them and showed them that obedience to God's call, even though it should mean a cross, is always the noble and rewarding choice. Committed to the highest virtue of rendering God the gratitude, honor, and obedience that is his due, the follower of Jesus may also consider worthless the opinion of those who are not committed to these values.

To yield to the shaming tactics of "sinners" — those who stand under God's censure and judgment — would be for the addressees a dishonorable defeat. Endurance in the face of such antagonism is the path to an honorable victory over the world.

Bridging the Horizons

Followers of Christ are still called to be people of "faith," and in many ways the horizons of the first century and twenty-first century converge quite closely when contemplating this section. That is to say, the author seems to speak to us as directly as to those believers for whom he felt a personal pastoral responsibility. Before we consider how we are led to act "by faith" through the words of this encomium, we must discover in ourselves a prerequisite: Do we have "trust" in God and God's promises? The more certain our grasp of God's reality (i.e., God's presence and friendship), the more complete our own investment in God's promises can be, and the more single-hearted our concern for honoring God and serving God's will can be. What is "real" for you as you move through a typical day's activity? Are the agendas imposed by worldly concerns foremost in your thoughts and energy, or is it the agenda imposed by God's spirit as you attend to those other, secondary concerns? Are the tangible rewards of your labors (property, home, some measure of luxury, financial security for the future) more real, or the intangible rewards of your pursuit of God? How we deploy our time, talents, energies, and resources will tell us something about where we fall along this continuum. Whose company we keep throughout the day will also be quite revealing. Do we keep company mainly with ourselves and the internalized voices of worldly ambitions and priorities, or do we keep company with God?

A prominent strain of Christian spirituality involves the "practice of the presence of God" throughout the week, even throughout the day. Spiritual guides like Brother Lawrence, Thomas à Kempis, and Jeremy Taylor all bear witness to the value and importance of this spiritual discipline, namely, the cultivation of a heart and mind that is ever attentive to God's presence and promptings throughout the course of everyday life. However it may be attained in your life, or the lives of those to whom you minister, a vibrant life of faith requires a constant and consistent awareness of the reality and the friendship of God. In the cradle of conversation with God and meditation on God's word, trust in him and his promises is nurtured; in the life lived in the midst of the everyday world from this place of centeredness, faith is matured. The prerequisite to faithful living, then, is truly to know the One "who exists and who is the benefactor of those who diligently seek him" (11:6). This relationship is the bedrock of every act of faith, every living testimony to the realm that is beyond.

Faith orients our ambitions to seek God's approbation: "pleasing God" in all that we do becomes a core value, and thoughts, words, actions, or omissions of action are weighed in terms of whether or not God will regard our decisions with approval or disapproval. What "pleases God," of course, is learned through prayerful reflection on the "oracles of God," the Scriptures. The introduction of examples of faith that involve the judgment, indeed the destruction, of those who do not live out of a regard for God underscores the importance of God's approbation. The warning that God was sending judgment upon humanity led Noah to devote his full attention to preparing for deliverance from that judgment. He did not work on the ark merely as his more pressing business allowed (or only on Sunday mornings). Obeying God's instructions for deliverance became the project that ordered his life until it was completed. Early Christian authors frequently linked the first judgment with the last judgment, seeing in the Flood a sort of type of the judgment to come when the elements would be dissolved not with water but in fire (see 2 Pet. 2:4-9; 3:5-7; Matt. 24:37-39; 1 Pet. 3:18–4:5). The NT speaks to us as well both of the promise of deliverance (salvation) and warning of judgment, calling us to respond faithfully, that is, with a trust that orders all our being and doing. In the words of Paul, "we are therefore ambitious . . . to please God, for it is necessary for us all to appear before the judgment seat of Christ, in order that each might receive the recompense for the deeds done in the body — whether that recompense be good or evil" (2 Cor. 5:9-10).

Like Abraham and Moses, the person of faith recognizes himself or herself to be a foreigner to this world rather than a rooted citizen. Such people are also called to leave their native land in the sense of renouncing their education in its values and priorities, and reshaping their desires and ambitions according to God's priorities (see Rom. 12:2). This takes some conscious, intentional work as we examine how our values, our priorities, and our sense of worth have been shaped by voices that do not look to God's reward but rather to temporal rewards, and as we resocialize ourselves and one another in the body of Christ into those values and priorities that God praises, even though our neighbors — even our family members — think us foolish. Our life, like the lives of the patriarchs, will witness to a better homeland as we compete not for the things that the world so prizes according to its rules, but rather for the prize that God holds before us — the city whose inhabitants enjoy true peace, mutual respect, and mutual service in love and in the light of God's uneclipsed presence.

Like Moses, we have two destinies before us. We are born into one destiny; we are groomed by our upbringing and our secular peers to be dependable members of our society, to enjoy its promised gifts, and to be mirrors of its values; we fulfill this destiny as we live out our primary socialization in the values of the world. Like Moses, however, we are called to recognize that even if such a destiny includes a life of wealth, fame, and power as this world counts it, our ultimate destiny would be regret and remorse when God comes to judge those who have despised his promises for the sake of temporary goods. By faith we are born to a new hope (see John 1:12-13; 1 Pet. 1:23–2:2) and called to invest ourselves fully in pursuit of that prize as our true destiny. The choices made by Moses teach us that even the disgrace that comes upon us as we follow Jesus is of greater worth than honor from those who are alienated from God. Whether the pursuit of our eternal destiny leads to great prosperity or adversity in this life is, ultimately, immaterial. The author teaches that true greatness is not determined by the visible outcome of faith as worldly eyes would evaluate it. There is no room for a "prosperity gospel" in his theology, for prosperity comes too often from accommodation to the ethics and values of the world, nor is there glorification of suffering for its own sake. Greatness comes solely from remaining loyal to God and following the path that maintains that relationship, whether it be to victory and remarkable achievements (which even the unbeliever cannot but praise) or to a life far from the limelight of society — even to deprivation, contempt, and ridicule.

Whether our unbelieving neighbors respect our lives because of our visible successes or try to rehabilitate us because of our Christian excesses makes no difference. Our worth comes from our firmness ("faith") with regard to God's commands and promises, not from the outward circumstances in which we find ourselves because of that commitment (see Dan. 3:17-18). When a person despises us for being "weak" (perhaps for seeking reconciliation rather than stabbing back) or "careless" in our finances (perhaps for sharing too much with those in greater need) or "foolish" (perhaps because we do not pursue our advantage at another's expense), their judgment shows only their own alienation from God (v. 38a). We remember instead Jesus' evaluation of greatness as loving service, of wisdom as being "rich toward God," of true life as living out his example (Matt. 20:25-28; Mark 8:34-38; Luke 12:13-21).

Examples of people who have lived by faith, who have turned aside from the trivial pursuits of temporal prizes to the pursuit of the "peaceful fruit of righteousness," could be multiplied endlessly — and should be multiplied! If the author of Hebrews found it helpful to surround his congregation with this crowd of spectators, we, too, could benefit from surrounding ourselves and our fellow believers with an ever-burgeoning cloud of those whose faith testifies to the reality of our shared goal and whose life choices can rouse our ambition in holy directions. Such an endeavor is all the more necessary as those other voices around us — the voices of the media or of easily impressed acquaintances — seek to flood the stands with examples of another sort, namely, those who are "success stories" in this world's eyes. The author of Hebrews reveals how important it is to form a godly image of heroism, for those whom we admire (or even envy) we desire to emulate. We cannot help but feel some tug to internalize the values and ambitions that brought success and glory to the "hero," so choosing these heroes well is crucial to running the right race. Do we admire those who make $20 million for a single film, or those who minister in virtual anonymity mending lives and mentoring children in the inner cities? Are we impressed by titans of industry, or by entrepreneurs of service to the poor, the sick, the "unbeautiful"? Do we follow the careers of professional athletes or the pacings of those imprisoned for their identification with Jesus?

It would therefore be useful for us to surround ourselves with examples of faith rather than examples of "self-made people," to turn away from "Lifestyles of the Rich and Famous" and look rather to the "Lifestyles of the Rich toward God." The history of the church is replete with stunning exemplars of faith, but we need not reach beyond our present decade to discover those whose fight for the faith should rekindle our own passion for God. A great cloud of witnesses is to be found in the survivors and the martyrs from behind the Iron Curtain, now rent from top to bottom.[147] Time would fail me to tell of Alexander Ogorodnikov, Alexander Men, Anatoly Rudenko, and Irina Ratushinskaya, whose commitment to Christ led them to endure brutality, degradation, and, in Men's case, even death. Their resistance, now known and narrated freely in the West, is mirrored in Islamic countries from North Africa to Pakistan, where Christians face the full range of their societies' deviancy-control techniques. Their brothers and sisters in the West should investigate their stories and should learn of the battles even now being waged for faith's sake and of the extremes of marginalization and martyrdom experienced for the cause of God now. The description of the faithful in Hebrews 11:35b-38 is not past history only, and the calm of the West should not make those living in and enjoying that calm oblivious to the state of the body of Christ elsewhere.

Others, by faith, devote themselves to ministry in places that more "sensible" people would flee. The world knows of Mother Theresa's ministry among the outcasts of India; many more minister in relative anonymity, taking hope to the inner cities of America by means of mentoring and drug rehabilitation programs. Here, too, Christians put their safety and even their lives at risk in order to obey God's call. Truly great works are being accomplished, even though no worldly media voice or sound byte cares to draw our attention to them. Let the stadium of our minds be filled with such people, the people of faith from every age and every part of this globe. Then let us run in our time and our place like them!

---

147. See the outstanding collection of these stories in Barbara von der Heydt, *Candles behind the Wall: Heroes of the Peaceful Revolution That Shattered Communism* (Grand Rapids: Eerdmans, 1993).

In Training for the Kingdom: 12:4-29

Overview

While it is advantageous to read 12:1-3 as part of 11:1-40, it is also admittedly disadvantageous to read it as if it were disconnected from the exhortations that grow out of it so organically in 12:4-29. The author has woven his concluding exhortation together so tightly that every division is truly artificial — an act of bowing to the necessity of treating manageable blocks of text *seriatim*. In the following exhortations, the author continues to orient the addressees toward their experience of social tensions but segues from athletic images (12:1; 12:4) to educative metaphors (12:5-11) in order to move the exhortation forward. The two images are closely related, "endurance" of unpleasant circumstances providing a strong common thread. The hardships suffered at the hands of their unbelieving neighbors are now cast as the parental discipline of God. The experience of rejection by the world is thus strategically transformed into a sign of the believers' adoption into God's family (God is treating them as sons and daughters) and as the means by which God shapes their characters and fits them with the virtues appropriate for future citizens of the city of God, the kingdom they are on the threshold of receiving. The experience of censure becomes, in effect, a sign of one's honored and favored status in God's sight.

After giving the believers specific instructions on how to press on (12:12-14) and menacing pitfalls to avoid (12:15-17) in their journey, the author contrasts the way in which God had formerly been approached, namely, amid severe taboos and with much fear and trepidation (12:18-21), with the celebratory and confident approach to God's eternal city with which he has privileged the addressees (12:22-24). After a final lesser-to-greater warning (12:25) urging the hearers not to turn away from the one speaking to them "from heaven," the

445

author presents his eschatological expectations for the removal of the visible, shakable realm and the believers' reception of the abiding, unshakable kingdom (12:26-28). In light of the coming, promised benefactions, the only appropriate response is "gratitude" (12:28), a response that 13:1-21 will flesh out in rather practical and explicit terms. If the addressees maintain a response of gratitude, they are showing due reverence for God, which is the only wise course of action given that "our God is a consuming fire" (12:29).

Commentary

12:4-11

After presenting the climactic example of faith — Jesus' endurance of a cross for the sake of God's reward — the author points out to the hearers: "you have not yet resisted to the point of blood in your contending against sin" (12:4). This is more than merely an indication of the extent to which the addressees have suffered for their Christian convictions. As David Peterson has aptly noted, "the writer is . . . *shaming* them: their sufferings are much less than Jesus had to bear, and they are apparently ready to 'lose heart and grow faint.'"[1] Hebrews 12:4, then, may very well appeal to the emotion of shame. Failure to live up to the examples of those honored within the Christian minority group (most notably Jesus) provides a basis for feeling shame, just as following the example of those honored yields the praise of the other members of the community and the hope of honor before God. Moreover, the addressees are conscious that Jesus endured such extreme hardship specifically on their behalf. It would be both cowardly and unjust to quit the contest now. The injunction to "consider" Jesus' contest with hostile sinners (12:3) should embolden the hearers to endure the same hostility and not to shy away from showing even the same measure of devotion to Jesus as Jesus did to them (although they appear only to be called to suffer less on his behalf than he on their behalf). These two verses together (12:3-4) may also speak to the topic of feasibility: Jesus' endurance of greater hardship assures the hearers that it is possible for them to endure the lesser hardships that stand between them and their goal.

This verse continues the athletic metaphor begun in 12:1, seen especially in the participle ἀνταγωνιζόμενοι ("contending against"). The metaphor moves more toward that of a wrestling match, with the opponent being "sin." This personification of "sin" creates a vivid picture for the audience's interpretation of their difficulties. The author's labeling of the opposition as "sin" casts the be-

---

1. Peterson, *Hebrews and Perfection,* 174; see also Croy, *Endurance,* 194.

lievers' detractors and abusers in a strategic light: they are to be seen as agents of sin (the same as the hostile "sinners" in 12:3). The very way of life toward which the neighbors try to reassimilate the addressees then comes to be viewed as that which alienates from God. The possibility of resisting "to the point of blood" shows that, while the addressees must battle the internal temptations to yield to social pressures, the contest is not strictly internal. This ideologically loaded portrayal of the situation, moreover, makes resistance to social pressures all the more urgent. Giving up their forward movement toward God's promise means allowing "sin" to conquer them. Making peace with the nonbeliever (on his or her terms of withdrawal from association with the Christian group and its confession) becomes giving up disgracefully in the struggle against sin. The metaphor of "contest" continues here strategically to undercut any growing tendency to consider cooperation with society.

Hebrews 12:5-11 is dominated thoroughly by παιδεία ("education," "discipline") and related forms (2:5, 6, 7, 8, 9, 10, 11). The persistent repetition of the παιδεί- or παιδεύ- stems impresses firmly yet another image into the addressees' minds, one that will allow them to regard the cost of their association with Christ and the church in a positive and honorable light:[2]

> You have also forgotten the exhortation that speaks to you as sons and daughters: "My son, do not value too little the discipline of the Lord, nor grow faint when being reproved by him, for the Lord disciplines the one whom he loves, and he chastises every son whom he receives." Endure for the purpose of educative discipline — God is behaving toward you as to his sons and daughters. For what son or daughter is there whom a father does not dis-

---

2. T. K. Oberholtzer presents an unfortunate misreading of Heb. 12:4-11 throughout his five-part series of articles, seen, for example, in the following quotation: "The wilderness generation forfeited their possession of Canaan (they experienced temporal discipline). Likewise the present readers of Hebrews were in danger of experiencing temporal discipline (cf. Heb. 12:3-13) and of losing eschatological rewards" ("Kingdom Rest," 195); see also "Kingdom Rest," 196: "Failure to persevere may result in temporal discipline (12:4-11) along with the loss of future rewards and authority to rule with Jesus in the millennium." A critical error here is Oberholtzer's assumption that Heb. 12:4-11 threatens the believers with "temporal discipline" if they disobey or show distrust. Rather, in Heb. 12:4-11 the author ennobles the sufferings the addressees *have experienced and are experiencing* — the pressures, contempt, abuse, and poverty that society inflicts on them specifically because they have been responding to God with trust and obedience by continuing to associate with the name of Jesus — by means of the image of God's parental training. By this rhetorical *tour de force*, the Christians are able to look at the shaming techniques of the non-Christian society as actually a token of their honor, their place in God's family as legitimate sons and daughters whom God trains toward the formation of his own holiness in them (see deSilva, *Despising Shame*, 295-96). Moreover, this discipline is formative and not punitive, as has been since demonstrated by Croy, *Endurance*.

cipline? But if you are without discipline, in which all have become partakers, then you are bastards and not legitimate children. Since we had our biological fathers as our discipliners and paid heed, shall we not all the more submit to the Father of Spirits and live? For they disciplined us for a short while as seemed best to them, but he disciplines us to our benefit in order that we might have a share in his holiness. And all discipline seems to be not joyful but grievous for the present time, but later it gives the peaceful fruit of righteousness to those who have been trained by it. (12:5-11)

The educative process, like athletic training and competition, involved unpleasant experiences, but the author sets those experiences in a more positive light. Not all discipline, moreover, was punitive (i.e., punishment for doing something wrong). Educative discipline also involved the endurance of rigorous exercises that trained the mind, soul, and body, and it is this second aspect that the author highlights both in his selection of terms to expand upon from the quotation of Proverbs and in his return to the more athletic image of "being exercised" (γεγυμνασμένοις, 12:11) by this discipline. This second image will reinforce the effect of the athletic metaphor in 12:1-4, turning society's censure and abuse into an experience to be valued for its positive effects and implications rather than avoided (i.e., at the cost of continued association with the Christian group).

The author introduces the quotation from Proverbs 3:11-12 as the "exhortation that addresses you as sons and daughters (ὡς υἱοῖς)." This anticipates one of the salient points that will follow: endurance of divine discipline is a sign of divine sonship.[3] The author creates a significant repetitive texture through 12:5-8 using the word "son" (υἱός, 12:5 bis, 6, 7 bis, 8) to support his association of their experience of hardship specifically with their honored status as children in God's household. They are experiencing God's parental training. The quotation from Proverbs supplies the authoritative warrant for the claim the author makes about these difficult experiences. The Greek version followed by the author differs from the MT at one especially significant point. In the final clause, the MT reads "like a father [chastens] the son in whom he delights." The LXX transforms this into "he chastens every child whom he receives." The LXX thus obscures the quality of analogy inherent in the MT, and the verse becomes testimony to actual adoption by God ("every child God receives") rather than a useful analogy for describing God's chastening ("like a father . . ."). This modification makes the LXX version more useful for the author's purposes.

---

3. Hebrews 12:3 had already begun building this bridge, where the negated participle "growing weary" (μὴ ἐκλυόμενοι) anticipated the negated imperative in Prov. 3:11: "do not grow weary" (μηδὲ ἐκλύου). See Vanhoye, *Structure*, 199.

Proverbs clearly articulates a punitive model of discipline, one that is shared by many Palestinian Jewish authors.[4] Clayton Croy has provided a compelling demonstration, however, that the model contained in the OT text is not the same as the model framed by the author of Hebrews in his recontextualization of Proverbs 3:11-12.[5] Greco-Roman authors and Jewish authors removed from Palestine tended to favor an understanding of God's discipline as formative or educative rather than punitive. One of the more striking discussions of endurance of hardships as divine parental discipline that was recovered for this conversation in Croy's survey is Seneca's *De providentia*. In *De providentia* 1.6, the sage is described as God's "pupil, imitator and true progeny, whom that magnificent parent, no mild enforcer of virtues, educates quite sternly, just as strict fathers do." God "'rears' *(educat)* the wise person like a son (2.5). . . . God 'tests, hardens, and prepares' the sage for Himself (1.6)."[6] Most impressive is *De providentia* 4.7: "Those whom God approves and loves, God toughens, examines, and exercises."[7] Seneca goes so far as to compare the paternal training of God with the way in which Spartan fathers whipped their children in public as a demonstration of the child's attainment of the prized virtue of endurance (4.11-12).

This is a remarkable comparative text from the Roman background, showing that the argument in Hebrews 12:5-11 would have been as much at home in Seneca's parlor as in the synagogue. In both Hebrews 12:5-11 and Seneca, hardships are a sign of God's parental training, God's preparing the disciple for some great destiny ("God's own self" in *De providentia*, "a share in God's holiness" in Heb. 12:10). Subjection to hardship is a sign that one is God's legitimate progeny ("true progeny" in Seneca; this is stated from the contrary in Heb. 12:8). More significantly, however, in both Seneca and Hebrews there is the complete absence of the sense that these hardships fall upon the sufferers because they have done something wrong. Rather, the emphasis is on the positive fruits that the courageous endurance of such trials will produce in the trainee. The author's conjunction of athletic and educative imagery in 12:1-13, moreover, will lead the hearers away from any punitive understanding of this "discipline" toward an understanding of their circumstances as trials that "exercise" their faith, endurance, and faculty of moral choice (cf. 5:14).[8] Moreover, the author's selective use of vocabulary

---

4. A fine survey of this literature is provided in Croy, *Endurance*, 83-133. I would take issue with him only in his treatment of 4 Maccabees, in which the suffering is not punitive or educative but solely probative — the endurance of those tortures proves that training in Torah (prior to the tortures) yields the perfection of the virtues of courage and the like.

5. See ibid., 196-214.

6. Ibid., 149.

7. Ibid., 150.

8. The author introduces athletic images back into the second half of this passage at

from his OT quotation also directs the listeners to a nonpunitive interpretation. In the verses that follow the recitation of Proverbs 3:11-12, the author
will repeatedly speak of "discipline" (παιδεία) but will never reintroduce the
aspects of the OT text that lead in a punitive direction ("being reproved,"
ἐλεγχόμενος; "chastens," μαστιγοῖ).[9]

On the basis of this authoritative pronouncement, the author frames
an exhortation that recontextualizes the two key words from Proverbs 3:11-
12 and sets the tone for the expansion that will follow: "endure for the purpose of formative discipline (παιδείαν);[10] God is behaving toward you as toward sons and daughters (υἱοῖς)." The emphasis of the exhortation remains
on "endurance" (ὑπομένετε), which the author has held up before the addressees' eyes repeatedly (10:32, 35; 12:1, 2, 3).[11] Both perspectives on hardship being developed by the author in Hebrews 12:1-13 aim at motivating
the hearers to adopt the course of action he recommends — perseverance in
their Christian confession and solidarity with one another. It is essential for
both the exegesis and the application of this passage to understand what
sufferings the author has in mind. He is not speaking of disease or illness,
domestic abuse, poverty, or subjection to an oppressive regime. He is speaking particularly of the censure, insult, abuse, and deprivations suffered by
the believers as a result of their association with Jesus and the people of
God. These are the same trials as the "hostility from sinners" endured in the
course of contending against sin, the continuation of that noble contest
which the believers endured in the past (10:32). If the hardship is not encountered as a result of remaining faithful to Christ, it is not included under this heading.

This involves an important reinterpretation by the author of the circumstances that have been and are being endured by the addressees. The deprivations
faced on account of their commitment to Christ and to one another are actually
core courses in God's curriculum. They train the believers as God's own children,
forming and shaping them for their citizenship in the New Jerusalem. The author
supports this interpretation by means of a general analogy with the experience of
all children raised by human fathers, "for what child is there whom a father does

---

12:11 and 12:12-13. For other texts that weave together discussions of training and competing (indeed, specifically training for the demonstration of one's prowess in competitions),
see Seneca *De prov.* 1.5–2.4; Epictetus *Diss.* 1.29.33-35; 4.4.30-32; Polybius 1.1.2.

9. Croy, *Endurance*, 198-99.

10. The language of 12:7a recalls *Pss. Sol.* 10:2b; 14:1: "The Lord is good to those who
endure discipline" (τοῖς ὑπομένουσιν παιδείαν); "The Lord is faithful to those who love him
in truth, to those who endure his discipline" (τοῖς ὑπομένουσιν παιδείαν αὐτοῦ).

11. The author thus maintains that the "right" or "virtuous" course is to press forward
in their Christian walk, since to do so manifests courage (enduring hardship for the sake of
honorable gain, 12:7a, 10-11).

not train?" (12:7b). The wisdom traditions of Israel develop the topic of the father's responsibility for discipline (both corrective and formative),[12] but the early experiences of the addressees in their families of origin, or now as parents, would also attest to the truth of this general proposition.

Hebrews 12:8 provides an argument from the contrary: "if you are without such training in which all children share, you are illegitimate children and not genuine children." The author thus makes the experience of reproach and loss suffered for the sake of Christ a sign of favor and honor, and, more astounding, the lack of such hardship a sign of disfavor and dishonor! Those who shrink back so as to avoid these experiences find themselves shamed because they no longer experience what all children of God share in common.[13] At this point the hearer may recall that Jesus, the Son, also shared in this discipline (5:7-10; see 2:10-18 for the author's rationale for Jesus' experience of hardship and 12:2-3 for the nature of his curriculum). The hearers are called to share in it so that they may have the benefits of sharing also in the Son's honor and virtue — insofar as they are "partakers" (μέτοχοι) of discipline, they are also partners (μέτοχοι, 3:14) with Christ in the final state of glory. They will endure a less rigorous version of Christ's training (12:4), but it is still a constant exercise, namely, the endurance of the scorn and hostility of sinners.

The author returns to the lesser-to-greater argument, one of his favorite enthymemes, in order to support his exhortation that the hearers persevere courageously and appreciatively under the Lord's training exercises. The lesser case is the observation that human beings tend to bear the discipline of human fathers, which should lead the hearers "all the more" to submit to the discipline of the "Father of Spirits" and thus arrive at "life" (12:9). The identification of God as the "Father of Spirits"[14] supplies an embedded rationale that assumes the superiority of the "spirits" to the "flesh." God, as a "parent" in a greater and more ultimate sense, is correspondingly more worthy of our reverent submission to his training.[15] The result of such submission is that "we shall live," and

---

12. See Bertram, "παιδεύω, etc.," *TDNT* 5:596-625.

13. See Aristotle *Rh.* 2.6.12 on how this topic arouses the emotion of shame.

14. This epithet for God was possibly derived from Num. 16:22; 27:16 (LXX), where God is identified as "the God of spirits and all flesh," where "spirits" probably refers to an order of being different from and above "fleshly" creatures, as in *1 Enoch* 37:2-4; 38:4, etc., which refers to God as the "Lord of spirits." The language is therefore traditional, but its referent (i.e., to the human soul, engendered by God) is new.

15. This enthymeme appeals to several deliberative topics at once. The hearers are urged to accept God's discipline first on the basis of justice. Since it is a "duty imposed by nature" to respect temporal parents and be subject to their discipline, it is even more just to submit to God's discipline: God is greater than earthly parents and thus merits more our submission, and God's discipline is more assuredly beneficial (12:9-10). The hearers may also perceive an appeal

the hearers will perhaps hear "life" here in the same sense that it was presented in 10:37-39. There the righteous person "lives" by faith in that only those who are of faith will be delivered from the eschatological cataclysm and "live" with God in the unshakable realm.

By means of antithesis the author further supports the exhortation developed by the lesser-to-greater argument of 12:9. The hearers' earthly parents disciplined the hearers "as seemed best to them," but God's discipline is absolutely "for our benefit." There is no hint of doubt as to the value of this discipline, unlike the discipline of earthly parents, which is sometimes on the mark and sometimes off the mark. Training under earthly parents is also short-lived. The expression that it lasts "for a few days" may suggest the incompleteness of this preparation. No parallel expression of duration appears in the second half of the antithesis, again giving a sense of the "absoluteness" of God's training (it lasts as long as necessary to bring us to the goal). The end result of God's training is a share in God's holiness,[16] which is in essence the fulfillment of God's injunction to "be holy as I am holy" (Lev. 11:44-45; 19:2). Aristotle (*Rh.* 1.9.14) observed that whatever produces virtue is considered to be noble. The ascription of virtue-producing power to the hearers' experience of disgrace and abuse at the hands of their disapproving neighbors ennobles these very experiences of rejection. The result will be that the addressees will see in these experiences not society shaming them, but God shaping them.

The author brings closure to this paragraph with a paraphrase of a well-attested maxim: "all discipline seems for the present time to be not joyous but grievous, but later it yields the peaceful fruit of righteousness to those who have been trained by it" (12:11). Isocrates is credited with saying that "the root of education (παιδεία) is bitter but its fruit (καρπός) is sweet." This witty saying became a favorite, not surprisingly, of educators, who used it frequently in their lists of *chreiai* (sayings) and in their examples of how to execute the rhetorical embellishment of a *chreia,* turning a saying into a complete, if short, speech.[17]

---

to the "feasible." As they survived their parents' upbringing, even though it was unpleasant, the connection between that experience and their present exercises may suggest to them that it would also be feasible to endure their current training, even though it, too, is unpleasant. Hebrews 12:7-8 suggests also that such submission and perseverance are "necessary." Just as parental discipline is taken as an unavoidable fact of life, so being trained under the watchful hand of God should be accepted as necessary for those who have become God's children. Those who refuse to endure remove themselves, in effect, from the legitimate line in God's household.

16. With regard to the purpose for God's discipline, namely, the full association of the one who exercises with the virtues and character of God, see Seneca *De prov.* 1.6: God "tests, toughens, and prepares [the good person] for Himself."

17. See Hermogenes "On the Chreia" 35-59; Priscian *De usu.* 35-64; Aphthonius "On the Chreia" 23-77; Nicolaus of Myra "On the Chreia" 72-73, 83-84, 133-34 (all references are to the editions provided in Hock and O'Neill, *The Chreia in Ancient Rhetoric*).

This saying was so popular and widespread that it was attributed to several different authorities (Diogenes Laertius, e.g., attributes it to Aristotle; see *Vita Phil.* 5.18). The author's appeal to this generalization, or maxim, allows the hearers to see their experiences of hardship within the context of beneficial, necessary training in the virtues required of the citizen, virtues that lead to an honorable life and praiseworthy career. As in other areas where discipline's present grief contrasts with its future benefits, so also the current grief endured by the hearers will bear noble fruit.[18] The truth of the maxim being widely accepted, the hearers are more likely to accept the application of this maxim as an interpretational framework for their experiences, and thus to accept the call for endurance.

The athletic metaphor enters again with the word "training" (γεγυμνασμένοις),[19] a verbal echo of the γυμνάσιον ("gymnasium"), where the future citizens of the Greek city-state trained for the development of physical prowess and strength.[20] The goal of these exercises for the Christian is the formation of "righteousness" or "justice" (δικαιοσύνη) in his or her soul and life. This is one of the four cardinal virtues celebrated alike by the Greek dominant culture, Stoic ethical philosophy, and Hellenistic Jewish works; it is also, of course, a core virtue of the OT tradition. This sentence is informative for the earlier description of Noah as "an heir of the righteousness that is according to faith" (11:7), showing us perhaps a different aspect of the Christian life than Paul's "justification by faith." This is a righteousness that is inherited through perseverance and trust, specifically perseverance in the discipline in which all children (i.e., heirs) of God share. Through these training exercises, the moral faculty of the believers is formed and strengthened, so that the believer learns how always to choose to honor God and to honor his or her obligations to fellow be-

---

18. The maxim is a particular species of the general argumentative topic of contrasting the temporary or short-lived nature of toils and the eternal or long-lasting nature of their prize (cf. 2 Cor. 4:16-18). The author of the Wisdom of Solomon (3:5) uses this topic to recast death — even the explicitly shameful death endured as a result of persecution by the godless — as divine discipline that tests and proves the worth of an individual. The final result is not disgrace in the eyes of society but profit in being benefited by God and honor in being proven worthy of God: "having been disciplined a little (ὀλίγα παιδευθέντες), they will be greatly benefitted (μεγάλα εὐεργετηθήσονται), for God has tested them and found them worthy of himself (ἀξίους ἑαυτοῦ)" (RSV with modifications). The author of Hebrews shares this conviction as he urges the believers to cherish their marginalization and censure by society as a process by which their worth is proven (and will one day be manifested to all) and by which they come into the closest possible relationship with their benefactor.

19. See Héring, *Hebrews*, 113; Spicq, *L'Épître aux Hébreux*, 2:395.

20. Epictetus frequently speaks of the experience of reviling, insult, and physical violence as the "exercises" by which God trains a person in the philosophical virtues. See "A Closer Look — Athletic Imagery and Moral Exhortation," 361-64 above.

lievers. The outcome, the author avers, of their perseverance will be the formation of this prized virtue in their hearts and lives: they will be fitted to live as
honorable citizens of the city that God has prepared for them.

The author very skillfully turns society's deviancy-control techniques
into a demonstration of God's adoption of the hearers as his own sons and
daughters and as a divinely appointed vehicle for the formation of their virtuous and honorable character. Once again what is meant to turn the hearers
from their commitments is recast and reinterpreted so as to spur them on to
endure in those commitments since their eternal honor depends on it.[21] The
recitation of Proverbs 3:11 in this context, then, urges the hearers not to "value
too lightly" or "fail to esteem" the discipline of the Lord.[22] That is, the "exhortation that addresses them as sons and daughters" calls them to turn bravely toward these training exercises and run the course that strengthens and stretches
their commitment to righteousness, rather than to shrink away from such
training or regard it as something to be avoided rather than embraced.

Encomia regularly included some praise of the education of the subject
of the eulogy; the author here praises the "education" that the hearers are receiving at God's hands, an education at the best, unfailing academy. As the
Christians commit themselves to persevere under this training, allowing God
to shape and train them using the hostility of society, they are building their
own encomium. Their own honor as sons and daughters of God depends on,
and is manifested by, their experience of this discipline. By continuing to face
the hardships and remaining steadfast in commitment to the Christian
group, the addressees are in fact being shaped and molded by God so as to
share God's virtuous character (holiness and righteousness). Society is serving God's goals, as long as the believers refuse to give in to the pressure to

---

21. What Elliott (*Home for the Homeless,* 143) writes concerning the role of "suffering"
in 1 Peter is thus applicable also to Hebrews (especially 12:1-13 and 11:24-26): "1 Peter repeatedly stresses that suffering for obedience to God is a hallmark of Christian uniqueness, a
unifying and purifying experience for those who remain faithful. Suffering . . . is not to be
avoided, therefore, but embraced as a sign that the fullness of salvation is at hand." Suffering
therefore functions to reinforce "distinctiveness, solidarity and commitment." The salient
difference is that 1 Peter uses the experience of suffering as a sign that the last judgment is at
hand, while the author of Hebrews, who also lays great stress on the proximity of judgment,
does not link the believers' experience of hardship with that proximity as a sort of eschatological "birth pangs" motif.

22. Calvin, *Hebrews,* 171, commenting on 12:5, recognizes the connection between the
signs of God's adoption and God's benefaction displayed in the believers' experience of suffering, such that he can accuse those who wish to avoid this marginalization as "unthankful"
in light of the great benefits that they stand to receive by enduring: "If the chastisements of
God testify to his love towards us, it is shameful that they should be regarded with disdain or
aversion. For they must be exceedingly unthankful that endure not to be chastened of God to
salvation; nay that spurn a token of his fatherly loving kindness."

abandon their noble pursuit. The "expedient" course — the one that preserves and augments their honor — is thus not to eschew, but to embrace these formative exercises.

If some believers choose to conform to society's wishes for them, they will indeed escape the experience of continued deprivation and hardship, but will that actually mean that their status has improved? The author claims that, to the contrary, deserters will find themselves without the parental discipline that assures them of their legitimate derivation from God. Those who do not experience hardship are actually "bastards"; they lose their honorable status as legitimate sons and daughters. Hebrews 12:1-11, then, uses two powerful images to neutralize the pressures that can pull members away from the group. It orients the hearers positively toward enduring those same pressures as the means to attain honor in the sight of God, Christ, and the faithful members of the people of God who have gone before.

12:12-17

The connection between "educative discipline" and "training" forms a bridge back to the athletic language that characterizes the resumption of direct exhortation: "Therefore make straight the drooping hands and weak knees, and make straight paths for your feet in order that what is lame may be healed rather than disjointed" (12:12-13).[23] The language is very closely influenced by LXX texts. Hebrews 12:12 recontextualizes Isaiah 35:3 (LXX): "Be strong, drooping hands and weak knees."[24] Isaiah encourages the hearers on the basis of an oracle of divine deliverance concerning the blossoming of the desert and the highway to be prepared through it to bring the "ransomed of the Lord" back to Zion amid songs of celebration (35:1-10). Just as Isaiah encouraged his hearers to stiffen their resolve and raise their hopes in view of God's forthcoming deliverance, so the author of Hebrews is leading the new people of God to do the same in light of the eschatological deliverance (12:26-29) for which God is currently training the hearers (12:5-11). They are to continue in their race to the celestial city,

---

23. Attridge (*Hebrews*, 364) correctly observes that the language is "appropriate" to an athletic context, though not, strictly speaking, specific to an athletic context since the terminology comes from Isaiah. Other scholars have also seen the close connection between this exhortation and the athletic imagery of 12:1-4 (see Bruce, *Hebrews*, 347; Weiß, *Hebräerbrief*, 658).

24. Compare Heb. 12:12 Διὸ τὰς παρειμένας χεῖρας καὶ τὰ παραλελυμένα γόνατα ἀνορθώσατε with Isa. 35:3, ἰσχύσατε χεῖρες ἀνειμέναι καὶ γόνατα παραλελυμένα. The author of Hebrews changes the main verb ("strengthen" becomes "straighten") and the case of the nouns (vocatives become accusatives). Sirach 25:23 uses these images, but to a very different purpose (the results to the husband of a displeasing wife).

where a festal gathering awaits, with their guard up (their hands raised in the posture of good pugilists in their match against sin)[25] and their forward motion unfaltering.[26]

Hebrews 12:13 incorporates verbatim the first part of Proverbs 4:26 (LXX): "make right paths for your feet and straighten your paths."[27] The context of Proverbs speaks of choosing paths that are just rather than wicked, a connection that might have led the author, who has been concerned with promoting what he perceives as the "just" course (in response to the divine patron) over against an unjust one, to incorporate this text. The author's gloss on this OT text commands attention, for he regards "walking justly" almost as a spiritual counterpart to the physical therapy that heals a lame joint through carefully guided and prescribed exercises (where careless walking would lead to complete "dislocation"). The author provides these prescriptions to avoid a certain danger: "in order that what is lame may not be disjointed (ἐκτραπῇ)." This Greek term may mean "be turned aside," and so refer to the danger of apostasy, the course to be avoided; more commonly the medical meaning of "be dislocated" is defended. The author may intend for the hearers to hear this as a double entendre: the latter meaning is certainly the more appropriate for the metaphor, but the former meaning is very appropriate for the situation that is being articulated with the metaphor. Those wavering in their trust and hope, by responding justly toward God now and walking forward in ways that maintain loyalty toward Jesus and the Christian family, will be strengthened and, in effect, healed.

The verses that follow begin to map out what paths are "straight" (12:14) and what paths lead to dislocation and even greater injury (12:14-17):

> Pursue peace with all and sanctification, without which no one will see the Lord, watching out lest any falls short of God's gifts, lest any root of bitterness springing up cause trouble and many become defiled through it, lest anyone be immoral or profane like Esau, who for the sake of a single meal gave away his birthright. For you know that also later, when he was desirous of inheriting the blessing, he was rejected, for he found no opportunity for repentance, even though he sought for it with tears. (12:14-17)

---

25. The author has mixed the metaphors of racing and wrestling in 12:1-4, and this recontextualization of Isa. 35:3 continues to resonate well with both kinds of athletic contest.

26. The absence of a personal pronoun in 12:12 (e.g., "strengthen *your* drooping hands and weak knees") suggests that the author is not calling the hearers to look out for their own spiritual condition first — as Stedman (*Hebrews*, 141) puts it, "get your own hearts right toward your troubles" — but is still looking out for everyone in the community, themselves included.

27. Compare Heb. 12:13, καὶ τροχιὰς ὀρθὰς ποιεῖτε τοῖς ποσὶν ὑμῶν with Prov. 4:26 (LXX), ὀρθὰς τροχιὰς ποίει τοῖς ποσίν.

There is a very fine balance to be noted in 12:14-15. The goals of "peace" and "sanctification" are set forth in 12:14, the latter being prerequisite to "seeing the Lord." The following verse presents the danger of the "root of bitterness," which has the power to threaten the community precisely with regard to its peace ("causing trouble") and sanctity ("and many become defiled through it"). Not "seeing the Lord" means "falling short of God's gift." These first exhortations may thus display a chiastic arrangement (in which the "A" elements could be further broken down into two parallel contrastive elements):

A   Pursue peace with all [A2] and sanctification
B   without which no one will see the Lord,
B′ watching out lest anyone fall short of God's gift,
A′ lest any root of bitterness springing up cause trouble [A2] and
      many become defiled through it.

Hebrews 12:14 begins with an abbreviated recontextualization of Psalm 33:15 (LXX): "Seek peace and pursue it."[28] What may seem a rather plain exhortation — "pursue peace with all" — has occasioned no small debate among commentators. Does the preposition "with" mean peace "toward" all, or are we enjoined to seek peace as a goal "along with all"? How wide a circle is drawn by "all" here? William Lane reads "peace" as a term signifying some "objective" reality, "a gift of eschatological salvation as well as a sign that points to the presence of the new age and to the future perfection."[29] The rather more developed expression "the peaceful fruit of righteousness," which is the outcome of persevering under God's formative discipline (12:11), is read as the immediate reference here. One might well ask, however, why the author does not make this connection explicit with a demonstrative pronoun ("pursue this peace"). Lane supports his reading by arguing that μετὰ πάντων must here mean that the believer seeks peace "in the company of all" rather than "peace toward all." He points appropriately to Romans 5:1 as a text where peace "toward" another being (there, God) is conveyed with the pronoun πρός, which is certainly preferable. Lane's claim, however, that "if the idiom meant to seek concord with others, the prep[osition] πρός would be demanded,"[30] is overstated. Another text from Romans (12:18) already uses μετὰ πάντων in an exhortation to "seek concord with others": "live peaceably with all people." This command is surrounded by exhortations not to take revenge or return evil for evil, to bless the persecutor, and the like (Rom. 12:14-21); rather than acting hostilely toward

---

28. Compare Heb. 12:14, Εἰρήνην διώκετε μετὰ πάντων with Ps. 33:14 (LXX), ζήτησον εἰρήνην καὶ δίωξον αὐτήν.

29. Lane, *Hebrews 9–13*, 449.

30. Ibid., 438 n. b.

others (even the hostile), believers are to act peaceably *toward* them. Similarly, in an even less ambiguous fashion, 3 Kingdoms 22:45 (LXX) uses the preposition μετά when recounting that "Jehoshaphat made peace *with* the king of Israel." Greek authors, to the consternation of every Greek professor, consistently ignore the limits we place on the semantic ranges of their prepositions.

It seems equally, if not more, likely that the addressees will hear this exhortation quite simply: "seek peace with all." Harold Attridge reads this "all" as denoting one's fellow Christians,[31] which would be in keeping with the interest of the author in promoting group solidarity. It is possible, however, that the author promotes peaceful relations with one's non-Christian neighbors as well (cf. Rom. 12:18; 1 Pet. 3:11): in this reading, "all" would really mean "all people."[32] The author of 1 Peter, a letter that addresses a similarly marginalized Christian community, is particularly interested in cultivating a response of nonretaliation and nonaggression toward hostile non-Christians. Even though peace with society will never be possible on society's terms (i.e., apostasy from the full confession of the faith), the author of Hebrews gives no indication of promoting a response of "abuse for abuse." The emphasis will always be, as Attridge rightly notes, on peaceful relations within the community. To draw an

---

31. Attridge, *Hebrews*, 367.

32. Harmony — seeking to live peaceably with one's fellow citizens — was considered an essential civic virtue, and disruption and civil strife were counted the worst of civic evils. Deliberative orations survive, such as the 48th oration of Dio, which attest to the importance of promoting an ethos of peace and concord within a city as a primary means of preserving the honorable reputation of the city and its citizens. Dio had the occasion to address his city before the arrival of their new proconsul from Rome. There were grievances, and Dio was anxious that the citizens not use the occasion of the governor's arrival to air their differences and show their divisiveness. Such would be merely to parade their shame before him:

> If a quarrel arises among yourselves and your enemies taunt you because you have wicked citizens and civil unrest, are you not put to shame? . . . It is truly a noble and profitable thing for one and all alike to have a city show itself of one mind, on terms of friendship with itself and one in feeling, united in conferring both censure and praise, bearing for both classes — the good and the bad — a testimony in which each can have confidence. . . . Accordingly I shall say only this much more — is it not disgraceful that bees are of one mind and no one has ever seen a swarm that is factious and fights against itself, but, on the contrary, they both work and live together, providing food for one another and using it as well? . . . Is it not disgraceful, then, that human beings should be more unintelligent than wild creatures which are so tiny and unintelligent?! (Oration 48, passim).

In an honorable city, its citizens are at peace, at unity among themselves, fomenting no divisions or unrest. Only thus could a city have a good reputation. The author of Hebrews urges the hearers to act honorably toward one another and even toward outsiders insofar as their allegiance to God would permit. In effect, their own commitment to "seeking peace" would show up the dishonor of the persecutors all the more sharply.

absolute (or even a visible) line there, however, would unduly limit the injunction to be a people promoting peace on God's terms with all other people.

The second goal believers are to pursue is "sanctification" (ἁγιασμός), which is a term of value throughout Jewish and Christian culture. Romans 6:22, for example, speaks of freedom from sin and service to God producing the "fruit" that leads to sanctification (εἰς ἁγιασμόν), the result of which is eternal life.[33] "Eternal life" in Romans may provide a synonym for "seeing God" in Hebrews, which happens when the believer "enters" God's presence at last. Matthew 5:8 also preserves a tradition in which purity of heart provides the necessary prerequisite to seeing God, again conceived as a future vision reserved for the pure in heart to enjoy at a later time.[34] The concept also reinforces the social boundaries of the community of "those being sanctified," for their fitness to come before God sets them apart from the unbelievers, who cannot stand before God save in the expectation of wrath and judgment.

Peace and holiness here are placed at the same level by the author, insofar as both are present goals for the hearers. The latter is a quality prerequisite to seeing God (i.e., arriving at the unshakable realm), so it is likely that the former is also a quality of life to be sought in this penultimate realm rather than a synonym for "salvation" or that "rest" of 4:1-11. The structure tends to support this interpretation: peace and sanctification are present qualities put in jeopardy by the apostate or the wavering in the midst of the community. These qualities are to be pursued in order that the threat of any "falling short of God's gift" may be neutralized.

As the believers run together straight for the finish line, the gates of God's city, they are again called upon to exercise watchful care over one another (ἐπισκοποῦντες), to keep an eye out for the endangered sister or brother who might be straying from the path that leads to life. The three negative images of 12:15-16 articulate the same danger of apostasy (be it overt or subtle, public or private: the effect is the same). Each image brings a particular facet to the danger presented to the individual and the group when a sister or brother chooses this course.[35] First, it means "falling short of God's gift"[36] (12:15a), which re-

---

33. See also 1 Thess. 4:3, where sanctification is presented as God's plan for the believer; 1 Pet. 1:2.

34. See also 4 Ezra 7:91, 98 (although the wicked also "see" God in 7:87, this is a cause for shame and fear).

35. This is all the more probable a reading given the absence of any coordinating conjunctions that might separate the three images into distinct dangers. The repetition of μή τις . . . μή τις . . . μή τις creates the impression that the content each phrase presents is a repetition as well. Deuteronomy 29:17 (LXX) has very similar syntax: two repetitions of μή τις, the second phrase providing a colorful and vivid image for the kind of person who would fit the description of the first phrase.

36. "Gift" is the second of three meanings of χάρις within the context of patronage:

calls the earlier exhortation "let us fear lest, while the promise to enter God's rest remains, any of you thinks to fall short" (4:1). Those who "shrink back" or "drift away" or "turn away" cease to pursue the promised benefit God has set before all believers, and thus "fall short" of entering that promised inheritance. Because of distrust, they dishonor their patron and are excluded from the benefaction that is yet to be conferred.

Second, the author introduces a recontextualization of Deuteronomy 29:17 (LXX), which warns the people of Israel to beware lest there be any in their midst who refuse to keep the covenant but rather cling to their idols. Such a person would be a "root of bitterness springing up to cause trouble." The LXX witnesses are divided on the exact reading of Deuteronomy 29:17,[37] and the author of Hebrews specifically chooses to comment on a word that is disputed. Some versions understand the root springing up to "cause trouble" (ἐνοχλῇ), others present the root as springing up "in wrath" (ἐν χολῇ). Hebrews follows the first variant. The wavering believer, and especially the apostate, disrupts the well being of the community and brings the danger of defilement (threatening the attainment of the necessary sanctification that enables one to enter God's presence and "see" God). That the apostasy of a few can defile the many would be a figurative way of expressing the disillusionment and weakening of resolve that would be felt by those who witnessed their former sisters and brothers give up the race (see discussion of 10:24-25).[38] As the remaining believers ponder the defection or the withdrawal of their sister or brother, the pollution of doubt will enter their own minds as well. The apostate knew what they were striving for; how could he or she give it up? Is the prize perhaps really not worth the cost?

The third element of this warning is an admonitory use of the example of Esau, whose foolish choice and lamentable fate puts the value of the course of

---

God's disposition to provide favor (e.g., timely help) was already the topic in 4:14-16, and the third meaning, "gratitude," will appear in 12:28.

37. The text of the LXX at this point is rather corrupt. Alexandrinus agrees with the wording of Deut. 29:17 provided in Hebrews, while several witnesses read "lest there be among you a root growing up in wrath and bitterness." The latter reading is closer to the MT, which may, however, then represent a correction of an earlier Greek [mis]translation. See discussion in Attridge, *Hebrews*, 368, who favors the hypothesis of a pre-Christian scribal corruption of the Deuteronomy text as the best explanation for what one finds in Hebrews as well as the LXX witnesses.

38. Stedman's assertion (*Hebrews*, 143) that "the root is unbelief which refuses to reckon on God's provision of righteousness because it feels confident it can produce an acceptable righteousness on its own" is a fine example of a reader's ideology imposing itself and reinscribing itself upon the text. "Justification by works" has never been an issue in Hebrews, but it is now read into Hebrews from the dominant grid of Galatians and Romans (via Reformation theology). The cause of apostasy is not seen in Hebrews as an arrogant desire to "be righteous apart from God's provision" but an attempt to avoid temporary shame and loss at the expense of eternal goods.

apostasy in perspective and reinforces the finality of the consequences of making so unwise and intemperate a choice. By considering Esau's decision and its consequences,[39] the author hopes to drive a final nail in the coffin of apostasy, underscoring the point made by the first major example in 3:7-19 and by the warnings of 6:4-8 and 10:26-31. Esau is presented immediately as a figure for nonimitation, a censurable person who is both "immoral" and "profane." The author first introduces a topic of intemperance: Esau is characterized as a fornicator, as one lacking control of his sexual urges; his choice later will betray him as a slave also to the feelings of hunger. He is not the master of his passions but their slave, and thus a degraded and sorry figure. While intertestamental literature develops a picture of Esau as sexually immoral based on his marriage to Hittite wives (Gen. 26:32),[40] the author may be using fornication as metaphor for faithlessness or distrust. The metaphorical use of the term in Numbers 14:33 — a chapter already shown to be of great significance for Hebrews (see 3:7-19) — would support this reading. There God decrees that the people "will bear your fornication until your bodies are spent up in the desert." Esau's parallel with the wilderness generation would thus extend to lack of regard for and trust in the promises of God, hence his faithlessness ("fornication"). While the author of Hebrews certainly does enjoin sexual continence (see 13:4), he may still be focused entirely on the driving issue of faithfulness to God versus unfaithfulness, distrust, and straying away.

Esau's "godlessness" or "worldly mindedness" is unquestionably a trait that is displayed in his choice and that shows that he values all too lightly God's promises and benefactions, represented here by his birthright as a son of Isaac, the son of Abraham. Thus Harold Attridge writes: "the second epithet (βέβηλος) . . . is readily comprehensible as a description of Esau, whose worldliness is manifested in a misplaced sense of value."[41] His incorrect evaluation manifests "a decisive contempt for the gifts of God."[42] The author of Hebrews refers, of course, to Genesis 25:29-34.[43] The choice of a single meal to sustain him in his hunger is a choice of temporary safety and enjoyment that people of faith refuse in favor of persevering unto the attainment of the promises of God. Esau stands as a foil to Moses, who rejects the "temporary enjoyment of sin" and chooses to endure hardship (11:25) in order to attain the reward (11:27). Esau makes the choice rejected by

---

39. On the proof provided by examples in deliberative oratory, again see Aristotle *Rh.* 1.9.40; 2.20.8; *Rhet. Alex.* 1428b12-17; 1429a25-28; Quintilian *Inst.* 3.8.36.

40. Philo, *Virt.* 208; *Jub.* 25:1-8 (cited in Attridge, *Hebrews,* 369 n. 48).

41. Attridge, *Hebrews,* 368.

42. Lane, *Hebrews 9–13,* 488.

43. The important interpretive retelling of Genesis 1 through Exodus 14 called *Jubilees* understands this selling of the birthright to mean that the seniority of the two brothers hereafter switched (*Jub.* 24:7): Esau gave up his right as firstborn and became as the second-born.

the seven martyred brothers (cf. 11:35), who for the sake of God's reward choose torture unto death. Faith values the promise of eternal reward over the attainment of temporary security. Esau enacts a lack of faith, providing for his safety today at the cost of eternal honor and blessing. Perhaps he stands most closely as a foil to Jesus, with whose example his own is linked by textual proximity (12:2) as well as syntactic parallelism. Jesus was presented in 12:2 as choosing to endure the pain of the cross in order to attain the honor and joy set before him by God: "who for the sake of (ἀντὶ) the joy set before him endured the cross, despising shame, and has sat down at the right hand of the throne of God." Esau, however, "for the sake of (ἀντὶ) a single meal gave away his birthright." Where Jesus is praised for submitting "to some disgrace or pain as the price of some great and noble object" (Aristotle *Eth. Nic.* 3.1.7), Esau is blamed for relinquishing a great and noble object, giving up honor before God for the sake of avoiding temporary hardship.[44]

By means of applying Esau's example (which speaks clearly to which good is greater or more valuable; see Aristotle *Rh.* 1.7.16) to the hearers' situation, the author sets up a strategic analogy. Society's goods stands in a value relation to God's reward similar to that of a single meal to a birthright. Esau's poor evaluation of the relative worth and advantage of a meal to his birthright has tainted his memory across the millennia, leaving him the ridiculous antiexample of evaluating wisely and virtuously. The addressees are invited to evaluate a bowl of lentil soup and a divine inheritance, and to understand that the choice being contemplated by the wavering is analogous to Esau's choice. For the addresses to choose temporary relief over constancy with regard to God's promises would reenact Esau's folly, and they should be ashamed for choosing as foolishly or acting as intemperately as Esau.[45] Those who would buy a few decades of peace and security among their nonbelieving neighbors are selling their eternal birthright (the hearers would no doubt recall the author's frequent mention of their own hope as their "inheritance"; 9:15; cf. 1:14; 6:12, 17; 11:7) for what amounts to a single meal. Would they be so foolish as to avoid a little discomfort and to buy such temporary relief from hardship at such an immense cost?! The wavering believers might be evaluating the alternatives quite differently, reflecting that they have seen very little return for their massive investments and now wanting to recover their losses before it is too late. The author persists strategically in leading such people from the beginning not to lose sight of the eternal consequences of

---

44. Thus Chrysostom (NPNF[1] 14:506; *PG* 63.214), commenting on 12:16: "'Who for one morsel of meat sold his birthright,' who through his own slothfulness sold this honor which he had from God, and for a little pleasure, lost the greatest honor and glory."

45. Aristotle (*Rh.* 2.6.3-4) observes that people are ashamed of committing acts of vice such as cowardice, injustice, and intemperance, and thus orators can use the association of a course of action with a particular vice to their advantage in dissuasion.

such a choice, and also to resign themselves to hardship in this world as the (small) price of eternal glory, enfranchisement, and safety.

The example of Esau, however, will also be used to amplify the importance of making a right choice in the addressees' present circumstances. The author "recalls" the consequences of Esau's choice, where the impossibility of restoring what was lost magnifies the importance of keeping hold of it now. In referring here to Genesis 27:30-40, however, the author draws a connection where the Genesis text does not. Esau's loss of the blessing was a sequel to the trading away of his birthright, but the patriarchal narrative by no means suggests that it was a consequence. In Genesis 27:36 Esau reveals an awareness that he had previously given away the birthright, but he shows no sign that this included the blessing. Rather, this is a second, separate act perpetrated by Jacob against his brother. The author of Hebrews appears to conflate birthright and blessing so as to make Esau also an example of the impossibility of regaining what one had previously devalued and thrown away. The lamentable scene of Esau with his father after Jacob had tricked the latter into blessing him creates a vivid impression of the "die being cast," although for a different reason. This is precisely the image the author wishes to connect with the consequences of trading in peace with God for peace with society. Like Esau, such people will find no "space for repentance" (μετανοίας τόπον). The phrase appears also in Wisdom 12:10, which speaks of God's generous treatment of the Canaanites, "judging them little by little" rather than all at once so that those who remained would have an "opportunity to repent" (τόπον μετανοίας). Repentance itself is God's gift to grant or withhold; it is dangerous indeed to presume upon God's favor by valuing it too lightly.[46] The aspect of Esau's example that is particularly developed by the author is the "lack of an opportunity for repentance," and this should definitely impact the way we recall 6:4-6; 10:26.

12:18-29

Having urged the hearers repeatedly to press on, to "straighten the drooping hands and weak knees" and run toward the goal, the author returns once again to providing an image for them of the goal toward which they are running. In 12:18-24, he provides an antithesis[47] that contrasts the quality of the Israelites'

---

46. Esau's example thus is made to reinforce 10:26-31 and 6:4-8; in particular, all three texts address the topic of removing a particular motive for committing an injustice, namely, the possibility of obtaining an indulgence (Aristotle *Rh.* 1.12.15).

47. "You have not drawn near to (Οὐ γὰρ προσεληλύθατε) . . . but you have drawn near to (ἀλλὰ προσεληλύθατε). . . ." Once again the author returns to what Aristotle (*Rh.* 3.10.5) observed to be a popular stylistic device.

approach to God at Mount Sinai with the quality of the approach to God being made by the Christians — specifically now the ultimate approach to God that marks the hearers' entrance into "glory" and their perfection, just as Christ was perfected through his entry into the unshakable realm:

> You have not drawn near to something palpable and burning, to fire and darkness and gloom and a whirlwind,[48] and to the reverberation of a trumpet and the sound of words — the hearers of that sound begged that the speech not be prolonged, for they could not bear[49] the command, "if even an animal touches the mountain, it will be executed by stoning." Indeed, so terrifying was the phantasm that Moses said: "I am afraid and trembling." But you have drawn near to Mount Zion and to the city of the living God, the heavenly Jerusalem, and to myriads of angels in a festal paean and to the assembly of the firstborn inscribed in heaven, and to God the judge of all and to the spirits of the perfected righteous, and to Jesus, the mediator of a New Covenant, and the blood of sprinkling that is speaking something better than that of Abel.

These two encounters with the living God contrast as follows: the first took place in the material realm, the second in the abiding, invisible realm; the first was marked by fear and hedged about with taboos carrying severe penalties, the second by celebratory worship of God. The author is pulling together a wealth of images in a very short space, seeking to make a cumulative effect of the images that goes beyond the individual meanings of each individual component (or the minute analysis of such details). That is to say, the first hearers, too, might not have known precisely what the "assembly of the firstborn" was, but they knew that the image contributed to the impression of a great heavenly celebration where hymns to God replaced fearful meteorological phenomena.

The author has drawn extensively on the accounts of the experience of meeting God at Sinai for his depiction of the encounter (see especially Exod. 19:12-19; Deut. 4:11-12, 25; 5:22-23; 9:19). The Nestle-Aland marginal notes suggest that the opening verb, "you have [not] drawn near" (προσεληλύθατε), echoes the Deuteronomic version of the theophany, where the Hebrews were told to "approach (προσήλθετε) and stand beneath the mountain" (Deut. 4:11

---

48. I follow here the recommendation of Ellingworth (*Hebrews*, 672), who proposes that the phrases be read as follows: ψηλαφωμένῳ καὶ κεκαυμένῳ, πυρὶ καὶ γνόφῳ καὶ ζόφῳ καὶ θυέλλῃ. This provides the best solution since the participles are taken as a pair and the nouns are taken together as a descriptive set. The balance of the whole is thus better established.

49. Most translators and commentators read the negated Greek imperfect ἔφερον here as an "Imperfect of Resistance or Refusal" (see H. W. Smyth, *Greek Grammar* [Cambridge, MA: Harvard, 1920], paragraph 1896), hence "could not bear" or "would not bear" rather than simply "were not bearing."

[LXX]), but forms of the verb "to draw near" (προσέρχομαι) have been promi-nent in the sermon, recurring here in the perfect tense as a sort of conclusion to the invitations to "draw near" (4:16; 10:22; cf. 7:25; 10:1; 11:6). The author's in-terest in the hearers' approach to God in Christian worship has thus led him to a much earlier, well-known approach in Exodus 19 (//Deuteronomy 4). That experience was "palpable" (ψηλαφωμένῳ), a rare word chosen by the author to contrast with the "heavenly" (and therefore beyond the material realm) aspect of the hearers' approach to God.[50] The remainder of the terms in 12:18 (the "burning," "fire," "darkness," and "whirlwind") are, save for the single word "gloom," derived from Deuteronomy 4:11 (cf. Deut. 5:22), clearly marking 12:18-21 as a reference to the Sinai epiphany even though Sinai is never named. The Exodus account of this event mentions the "echo of a trumpet" (Exod. 19:6), and the author returns to the Deuteronomic account with the "sound of words" (Deut. 4:12b).

Those who heard the voice of God asked that God speak no more to them (Exod. 20:19; Deut. 5:25). The verb translated here simply as "begged" (παρῃτήσαντο) will appear again in its purely negative connotation of "refuse" in 12:25.[51] In the next paragraph, the author will interpret this request for God to stop talking as a rejection of the speaker. The rationale for their request is here not the frightfulness of the voice itself (as in Deut. 5:25) but the severe re-strictions and taboos, which hedged the mountain round about and secured the sanctity of the place. Exodus 19:12-13 explicitly forbids human beings and animals to touch the mountain where God was coming down. The author of Hebrews preserves only the "lesser" case in his abbreviated recontextualization ("if even an animal touches the mountain, it will be stoned to death"), but the "if even" reminds the hearers of the "greater" case: the strong prohibition of hu-man encroachment into the holy place.[52] Once again the author reminds the hearers that, formerly, drawing near to God was strictly a matter of going so far and no farther: God's holiness in both tabernacle and mountain was "preserved by exclusion."[53] The author provides a stunning conclusion to this picture of the approach to God upon which the hearers are *not* embarking by presenting

---

50. Attridge, *Hebrews,* 372, who also suggests that this is derived from Exod. 10:21, the "palpable darkness" of the plague of darkness. The author may have borrowed that qualifier in order to give a "material" character to the darkness that shrouded Sinai, casting a pall of penultimacy over the whole Exodus experience. At any rate, the purpose for the characteriza-tion, whatever its actual source, is clear (see also Ellingworth, *Hebrews,* 672).

51. LSJ likens the verb to the Latin *deprecari,* "to avert by petition," "to beg off." It thus tends always to have a negative connotation.

52. See Milgrom, *Leviticus I–XVI,* 45: this prohibition stems from the earliest tradi-tions in the Pentateuch, in which holiness can still be contracted by lay people (sometimes, as here, with fatal results).

53. Attridge, *Hebrews,* 373-74.

even Moses, the mediator, as terrified at the vision. Moses' confession of fear, which appears only later in Deuteronomy 9:19, is taken quite out of context by our author. It had originally referred to Moses' trepidation concerning God's anger in the aftermath of the golden calf incident; it now is made the capstone of the author's presentation of the fearful and restricted access to God that has been broken through for the Christians by Jesus.

Set alongside the frightful picture assembled in 12:18-21, the author's vision of the goal of the Christian pilgrimage will appear all the more radiant. Not Mount Sinai but Mount Zion stands at the end of the journey. The author begins this portrait using language for any terrestrial pilgrimage of the people of God, who make their way to "Mount Zion and the city of the living God" for the festivals held annually in Jerusalem. The goal of this people's pilgrimage, however, is no mere earthly festival celebrated in the earthly Jerusalem, but the festal gathering of the angelic hosts in "heavenly Jerusalem" ('Ιερουσαλὴμ ἐπουρανίῳ). The ideology of Jerusalem as the city of God and the seat of God's kingdom is transferred to the eternal, lasting, heavenly counterpart. The prophetic texts and psalms concerning Zion and Jerusalem's eternal destiny provide the raw material for the depiction of God's eschatological kingdom — a kingdom truly not subject to the vicissitudes of fortune and international politics. The image of the heavenly city, the "New Jerusalem" (Rev. 21:1–22:5), or the "Jerusalem above" (Gal. 4:21-31) becomes widespread in early Christianity as well as in post–70 A.D. Judaism (see also 2 Apoc. Bar. 4:1-7; 4 Ezra 7:26; 8:52; 10:26-27; 13:36). For the marginalized believers addressed by the author of Hebrews, who have lost their "place" in their earthly city, the hope of a "lasting city" and the enjoyment of a citizenship that cannot be jeopardized serves as an especially apt conceptualization of God's promised benefaction (see Heb. 11:10, 14; 13:13-14).

The heavenly Jerusalem is a scene of worship. No fearsome and depressing meteorological phenomena surround this mountain, but the angelic hosts gathered in a panegyric, a festal song in praise of the ruler of the unshakable kingdom. "Myriads of angels" are a standard part of descriptions of the Sinai theophany and visions of God's judgment (Deut. 33:2; Ps. 68:17-18; Dan. 7:10; 1 Enoch 1:9), but here their activity is more specifically the offering of praise, which accords well with visions of God's court such as Revelation 4:8-11; 5:8-14. The angelic hosts are joined by "the assembly of the firstborn" (ἐκκλησίᾳ πρωτοτόκων).[54] Un-

---

54. Images of angels and human beings united in worship or in the community of the redeemed were widely shared in apocalyptic Judaism and Christianity. 1QS 11:5-9, for example, regards the human community of the elect to have been joined to the congregation of faithful angels: "God has given them [his mysteries and knowledge] to his chosen ones as an everlasting possession, and has caused them to inherit the lot of the Holy Ones. He has joined their assembly to the Sons of Heaven." Attridge (Hebrews, 375 n. 73) helpfully points to Rev. 7:8-12; 1 Enoch 39:5; 4QSîr as other instances of angelic and human creatures united in worship.

like Esau, who gave away the "inheritance of the firstborn" (τὰ πρωτοτόκια, 12:16), these people of faith have held on and have arrived at the reception of their "eternal inheritance" (9:15).[55] As Harold Attridge observes, "the 'firstborn' are those who share in the inheritance (12:16) of the Firstborn par excellence (1:6)."[56] The fact that these "firstborn" were "inscribed in heaven" recalls the Jewish notion of the names of the righteous being written in the "books" of heaven (Dan. 12:1; Rev. 13:8). Here, however, since no books are actually mentioned, the image may call up more strongly in the hearers' minds "enrollment" (i.e., as a citizen) in the city of the living God, the enjoyment of full participation for which the people of faith, now dead, had sought (11:13-16) and for which the hearers now are themselves being trained (12:5-11).

God himself is present at this festival, and his presence is fully enjoyed by the people of faith who have persevered. He is presented as "judge of all," reminding the hearers of the surpassing importance of God's evaluation of one's life in this world. Pleasing God at all times, no matter how that is viewed by others, is all the more necessary in light of the eternal effects of God's judgment. He stands at the center of the Christian's court of reputation, and others stand within that court only insofar as they demonstrate that they, too, have regard for God's approval first of all (see, e.g., 12:1). With God are the "spirits of the perfected righteous" (πνεύμασι δικαίων τετελειωμένων).[57] This phrase helps clarify the meaning of "make perfect" in Hebrews. These righteous ones have finally entered into God's presence, having gone themselves where Christ had gone as the forerunner. The OT people of faith and the NT people of faith are "perfected" together (11:39-40) as all are brought into the unshakable realm and the city of God. The placement of God in this list between the "assembly" and the "righteous" may not be haphazard, showing rather the final state of human beings enjoying God's intimate presence without any separating barriers, not even an angelic hierarchy interposed between the heirs of salvation and their God.

The final components of the author's description of this glorious goal are "the mediator of a new covenant, Jesus," and the "blood of sprinkling" that made possible the entrance of the people of God into his real presence. These

---

55. A perceptive connection made by L. R. Helyer, "The *Prōtotokos* Title in Hebrews," *Studia Biblica et Theologica* 6 (1976): 13; see also Lane, *Hebrews 9–13*, 469.

56. Attridge, *Hebrews*, 375. Such a reading is preferable to regarding the "firstborn" (plural) as angelic beings, particularly in a sermon in which the author has carefully distinguished the Son with his unique title from the angels (1:4-14) and in which he has sought to unite the path and destiny of Jesus with that of the "many sons and daughters" (2:10; 6:19-20).

57. *1 Enoch* 22:9 uses the phrase "the spirits of the righteous" (τὰ πνεύματα τῶν δικαίων) to describe the departed souls of righteous human beings, who are kept separate from the souls of sinners after death.

images recall the central exposition of the sermon, which spoke of the ratification of this new covenant, the effective cleansing of the worshipers from the internal defilement of sin (as well as the removal of sins from God's memory), and the access to God opened up for those who follow this Jesus to the goal and end of the journey begun at conversion. The blood of Jesus is simply said to "speak a better word than the blood of Abel."[58] Richard Nelson has noted: "the priest's role in representing Yahweh was primarily a matter of the spoken word. The priest was one who spoke for God, delivering blessings, oracles, and declarations."[59] Jesus' blood "speaks" a word of pardon in contrast to the blood of Abel, which cried out for justice and vengeance (see Gen. 4:10; Heb. 11:4). Jesus' blood speaks of the sanctification of the believers and the forgiveness of sins (cf. especially 10:15-18). The message of this priest, therefore, concerns the inauguration of the new covenant and the full provision made for its promises to be executed.[60]

Hebrews 12:18-24 reinforces the alternation between confidence and fear[61] before God that has marked this sermon and that has undergirded the author's attempts to motivate the hearers to hold onto their cause for confidence and assurance of favor in God's presence. The desirability of standing before God in full assurance of a favorable welcome into the abiding realm should make perseverance in the face of temporal hardship stand out as the advantageous course of action, even as the prospect of encountering God as judge and avenger has been used to dissuade the believers from seeking a peace with society at the cost of loyalty to God and the believing community. Hebrews 12:18-24 presents the good that lies in the sure possession of the hearers if they but continue to move forward. That good is an approach to God marked by festivity rather than fear, hedged in by celebration rather than taboo. Again this feeds the topic of expediency, as the hearers will be concerned to preserve these present advantages and not, by acting foolishly, exchange favor for wrath (12:25-29 will return to these deliberations explicitly).

The author informs the hearers that there is nothing lying ahead of them from which they need to "shrink back." Rather, ahead is a jubilant celebration in the heavenly city in the company of Jesus their mediator and all the righteous brought to their final home, beckoning them to continue their

---

58. The author employs a brachyology in the last phrase: the hearers of the phrase "than Abel" (παρὰ τὸν Ἄβελ) will be able to fill this out as "than the blood of Abel" from the mention of "blood speaking" (αἵματι . . . λαλοῦντι) in the preceding phrase.

59. Nelson, *Raising Up a Faithful Priest*, 87.

60. The author uses litotes here, but the hearers can fill in the expansiveness of this "better word" from the discussion in 7:11–10:18.

61. Appeals to the emotions of confidence and fear have alternated strategically throughout the exhortations of the sermon: 4:12-13 (fear); 4:14-16 (confidence); 6:4-8 (fear); 6:9-12 (confidence); 10:19-25 (confidence); 10:26-31 (fear); 10:32-36 (confidence).

forward movement to "perfection." The "hostility of sinners" has been transformed from something from which to shrink back to something bravely to engage and even value (10:32-39; 12:1-11). In a strategic way, the author has even let this hostility drop from sight after 12:3-4. The address-ees now see only God's means of training them (12:5-11, by means of these experiences, of course) and the good goal for which they are learning citizenship. They have every reason, then, to continue forward to seize the good gift that God has prepared.

The contrast of the spoken word on Sinai (12:18-21) and the better word from heaven (12:22-24) has also set up the final warning in 12:25, the final lesser-to-greater argument, which corresponds very closely to 2:2-3. The mediation of Jesus provides for a more joyful approach to God and a better one, an approach to the divine realm and the eternal realities themselves. This also entails, however, a more serious threat to those who refuse to hear and heed the one who now speaks:

> Watch out lest you refuse the one who is speaking to you; for if those people did not escape after refusing the one who was warning them on earth, how much more will we not escape when turning away from the one warning from heaven,[62] whose voice shook the earth at that time, but now has promised, saying, "only once more I will shake not only the earth but also the heaven." And this "only once more" signifies the removal of the shakable things (as things that have been manufactured), in order that the unshakable things may remain. Therefore, as we are receiving an unshakable kingdom, let us show gratitude, through which let us worship God in such a way as pleases him, with reverence and awe, for our God is indeed a consuming fire. (12:25-29)

This paragraph acts as a sort of recapitulation. It recalls the warnings that have run throughout Hebrews (especially 2:1-4 and 10:26-31), affirming again the fearful consequences of choosing to turn away from God; it focuses the hearers again on God's forthcoming fulfillment of his promise, which has also been a recurring topic (1:14; 4:1-11; 6:13-20; 11:39-40); it reinforces the message of the whole concerning the relative value of worldly, visible things over against heavenly, lasting things; and it proposes a response of gratitude (the content of which will be further developed in chapter 13) as the consequence of these considerations.[63]

---

62. The Greek is elliptical in the second clause. Brackets show what must be supplied from the first clause to complete the meaning: εἰ γὰρ ἐκεῖνοι οὐκ ἐξέφυγον ἐπὶ γῆς παραιτησάμενοι τὸν χρηματίζοντα, πολὺ μᾶλλον ἡμεῖς [οὐκ φεύξομεν] οἱ τὸν [χρηματίζοντα] ἀπ' οὐρανῶν ἀποστρεφόμενοι.

63. See *Rhet. Alex.* 1433b29-34 on what components might be expected of a recapitulation, or what forms it could take.

The Hebrews had "begged off" from hearing any more from God at the Sinai theophany (12:19). This is now recast using the same verb (παραιτη-σάμενοι) rather more negatively, as the author posits that "those people" at Sinai "did not escape" the consequences of "rejecting the one who warned them on earth." This presents the lesser case, strongly reminiscent of the lesser case in the argument of 2:2-3 (the confirmation of Torah, the "message spoken through angels," by means of the punishment of transgressors). The Christians are now warned not to "reject" or "refuse to obey" the "one who admonishes them from heaven." The language is directly reminiscent of 2:3 at this point, where the author asked "how then will we escape" when refusing to heed the salvation announced by the Son himself. The fate of the disobedient Hebrews recorded at various points throughout the Pentateuch provides proof from historical precedent of the grim consequences of slighting God by not heeding his word. Once again the author makes the point that departure from the Christian group does not place one beyond the grasp of an angry, slighted benefactor. "Fleeing" the consequences of desertion remains an impossibility. The path to avoid an expected danger (judgment) is to attend the God who is speaking to them, to refuse to "turn aside" from him. This warning offers a reminder of the appeals to fear that have punctuated the sermon and pushes them a final time away from the alternative course of "turning away" (ἀποστρεφόμενοι) from the God who called them in Jesus.

The following verses show why the stakes of heeding or not heeding God's word are so high, and ultimately why desertion for the sake of peace with society is a foolish choice. The author has multiplied words built on the root -σαλευ- ("shake") in 12:26-28 (12:26, 27 bis, 28), strengthening through repetition the content he wishes to convey through argument. Putting more stock in the conditions of one's life in this world than in the next is always going to be a bad investment, since this realm is subject to "shaking." The author wishes to call the hearers' attention to one forthcoming episode of "shaking" in particular. The recollection of the Sinai theophany in 12:18-21 and now again in 12:25 leads the author to consider the detail that "the voice of God shook the earth at that time" (see Judg. 5:4-5; Ps. 67:8 [LXX]).[64] The author then introduces a contrast between that shaking merely of the earth and God's declaration in Haggai 2:6, presented as a "promise" (an unfailing word of God), that "yet once-for-all I will shake the heaven and the earth." The author has modified the Haggai text for the sake of emphasizing the inclusion of heaven in the future shaking along with the earth; he adds the words "not only" and "but also" and inverts the order of heaven and earth in order to make the contrast evident. He

---

64. Other psalms connect the voice of God shaking the earth with other events in the Exodus story, for example, the parting of the Red Sea in Ps. 76:18 (LXX) or the Jordan in Ps. 113:7 (LXX).

finds the initial two words of the recitation, "only once more" (Ἔτι ἄπαξ) to provide the key to its interpretation. Since God will shake the earth and heaven "once for all," and not merely "again," the author reads this as a promise of the decisive shaking and removal of the visible creation, both the earth and the visible heavens.[65] He returns thus to themes he introduced as early as 1:10-12, which contrasted the temporal and mutable quality of the "heavens and earth" as "works of God's hands"[66] with the unchanging and eternal quality of the Son. All things created and shakable will be removed "in order that what is unshakable may abide."[67]

The eschatology of the author of Hebrews is somewhat different from that usually associated with Isaiah and Revelation: heaven and earth are not renewed, nor does the age to come "begin to be" after the passing of the present age.[68] Rather, the kingdom of God already exists beyond the material and visible creation, and it will simply "remain" after the removal of the temporary, secondary created order. Being part of the Christian community (and remaining a part) is vitally important for survival itself, which is perhaps one reason the author conceives of "salvation" as that which the believer is "about to inherit" (1:14), as the gift that comes with Christ's second "appearing" (9:28). It signifies deliverance from the material world that is slated for dissolution and entrance into the abiding realm that alone survives the "shaking."[69]

---

65. This is in keeping with his use of ἄπαξ elsewhere in the sermon, particularly in his discussion of the "once only" sacrifice of Jesus.

66. This same "manufactured," secondary quality of the visible cosmos is captured in the phrase "as things that have been created" (ὡς πεποιημένων, 12:27).

67. The language of shaking or the impossibility of shaking set up rich harmonic resonances with many texts from the Psalms as well as Isaiah. We have already seen how reflection on several such Psalm texts led the author to distinguish between the "earth" (γῆ), which can and will be shaken, and the "inhabited realm" (οἰκουμένη), which cannot be shaken (see commentary on 1:6). Salient here are those texts that, along with Hag. 2:6, distinguish between shakable and unshakable realities. Psalm 95:9-10 (LXX) enjoins the "whole earth" to "be shaken from before the face of God" (σαλευθήτω ἀπὸ προσώπου αὐτοῦ πᾶσα ἡ γῆ), while also positing a realm that "will not be shaken" (τὴν οἰκουμένην ἥτις οὐ σαλευθήσεται; see also Ps. 92:1 [LXX]). Psalm 45:6-7 (LXX) attributed to the "city of God" (meaning earthly Jerusalem in its initial utterance) the quality of not being able to be shaken ("it shall not be shaken," οὐ σαλευθήσεται). Those trusting in the Lord are compared to "Mount Zion," and the inhabitant of Jerusalem "will never be shaken" (οὐ σαλευθήσεται εἰς τὸν αἰῶνα, Ps. 124:1 [LXX]). Psalm 81:5 (LXX) and Isa. 13:13 both speak of the "foundations of the earth" being shaken in the future, the latter text explicitly in the context of the day of judgment. Reflection on such texts informs the peculiar eschatology of the author of Hebrews.

68. Thus rightly Attridge, *Hebrews*, 374.

69. Although the visions of the "unshakable kingdom" in Hebrews and the "new heaven and new earth" in Revelation are conceptualized differently, they are not incompatible. From the perspective of a biblical theology, the vision of Hebrews can refine our under-

The "removal of the things that are shaken" corresponds to the removal of the first chamber that blocks access to the holy place (see 9:9-10 and commentary). At this eschatological shaking, the visible creation, which stands as a barrier between the believers and their better, abiding, heavenly homeland — the presence of God in the unshakable heaven — will be removed. They will then enter into their promised, eternal inheritance, the "unshakable kingdom" that they are receiving. This expectation undergirds the author's consistent devaluing of worldly possessions, worldly citizenship, worldly status. All such things are guaranteed by God's promise to pass away, and only the believers' better possessions in God's realm will remain. It is in light of this conviction that one sees the wisdom of the choices of Moses and Abraham, and the folly of

---

standing of the "new heaven and new earth" in significant ways. First, it cautions against understanding the kingdom of God as a strictly future reality. From our perspective, of course, its in-breaking is future, but the realm of God's kingdom already exists. Just as the earthly tabernacle could be said to be but a shadow of the heavenly tabernacle, which served as its pattern, so the present heaven and earth can be said to be but a shadow and copy of that permanent realm of God's unmediated presence, which shall be experienced fully by those who are welcomed into the city that God has prepared (Heb. 12:22-28; Rev. 21:3-4, 22-23; 22:3-5). Second, the eschatology of Hebrews cautions us against an overly materialist interpretation of the vision of Rev. 21–22: the New Jerusalem, while described in terms reflective of this-worldly realities, is not part of this material creation, but belongs to the realm beyond the material and temporal.

Stedman's presentation of the eschatology of Hebrews is fundamentally flawed in this regard. He speaks repeatedly about the believers awaiting the appearance of the city of God on earth and is very specific about the location of this city coming *on earth* (*Hebrews*, 14, 37, 123, 133, 144). He is committed to reading "the coming world" (2:5) and "the unshakable kingdom" as a terrestrial millennial kingdom. Aside from the fact that Rev. 20:4-6 gives no sure indication that this reign of the martyrs would take place "on earth" as opposed to the heavenly realm, the author of Hebrews clearly does not share Stedman's evaluation of the material realm as somehow the more real realm. "The reference to *foundations* [11:10] indicates something material and earthly, rather than purely spiritual" (Stedman, *Hebrews*, 133). For the author of Hebrews, however, it is precisely the "material and earthly," that is, the visible, manufactured order, that is shakable and unreliable.

Another argument advanced by Stedman is worth discussing as an example of dangerous exegesis. He adduces Eph. 2:7 (*Hebrews*, 37), which speaks of "coming ages," in arguing that "at least two more ages lie ahead." Following a popular eschatological scheme, he proceeds to enumerate these as the restored Davidic monarchy on earth and then the new earth and heavens. The problem, of course, is that the plural of "ages" is frequently interchangeable with the singular. If we were to turn to Luke 18:10 or Mark 10:30, we could match proof text with proof text and say, "But Jesus speaks of only one coming age — 'in the age to come [my followers will receive] eternal life.'" Even Eph. 1:21 contrasts "this age" with "the *one* that is coming," so that it cannot be said on the basis of Eph. 2:7 that two ages are yet to come. That is turning a blind eye to the complexities of the texts themselves for the sake of rigid schematization.

the choice of Esau. The author now wants the audience to view their own situation from this perspective, so that perseverance in their trust and loyalty will appear the only wise and advantageous course to purse.

The "unshakable" is that which is truly reliable and secure. Dio (*Or.* 74.24) finds human beings to be unsuitable objects of trust since, even though they might be reliable under some circumstance, when others arise "you would perhaps not find him unshaken and trustworthy" (ἀσάλευτον καὶ πιστόν). By the same token, the author of Hebrews regards only the gifts of God to be worth holding onto and considers it wise to hold onto them at any cost in terms of worldly goods and comforts. Those who have lived so as to secure their investments in the material realm will ultimately suffer loss and disgrace; those who, by their loyalty to God and the people of God, invest themselves in their hope will exchange temporal goods for eternal goods, temporary honor for eternal honor, and eternal loss for eternal benefit in the "unshakable kingdom."

The believer has been made an heir of this eternal benefaction (see 6:17; 9:15), and in light of God's desire to confer so magnificent a gift on the people of faith (as well as all that has been done to prepare them for entrance and to help them along the way), the only proper response is to "show gratitude" (ἔχωμεν χάριν, 12:28). The author offers this exhortation as a suitable response to receiving a gift (the "unshakable kingdom"), so that χάρις refers most clearly to the response of the beneficiary to the Patron,[70] rather than to the Patron's disposition to give favors or the gift itself, two other possible meanings.[71] This becomes the basic summons of the whole letter, and indeed gratitude and ingratitude have been central to the author's depiction of the two courses of action open to the believers (see especially 6:4-10; 10:26-31 and commentary). The author has strategically couched the call to remain loyal to Christ and the Christian group in topics of justice. While the dominant culture would evaluate attachment to the Christian community as involving injustice (both toward the gods who merit grateful worship and toward the rest of their neighbors who merit the display of solidarity that public worship expressed), the author shows that continuing in association with that community is precisely the only way to

---

70. See the use of this word in Dio *Or.* 31.

71. Thus rightly Attridge, *Hebrews*, 382; Lane, *Hebrews 9–13*, 486; P. Hughes, *Hebrews*, 559. Attridge lists the following as evidence for this translation (indeed, for recognizing ἔχωμεν χάριν as idiomatic): Epictetus *Diss.* 1.2.23; 2 Macc. 3:33; 3 Macc. 5:20; Luke 17:9; Acts 2:47; 1 Tim. 1:12; 2 Tim. 1:3; Josephus *Ant.* 2.16.2 §339; 4.8.47 §316. Some of these are ambiguous (e.g., 3 Macc. 5:20), and others clearly do not refer to "gratitude" as much as "favor" (e.g., Acts 2:47). Nevertheless 2 Macc. 3:33 and Josephus *Ant.* 2.16.2 §339 definitely attest the meaning of "have gratitude," and, as with the term χάρις generally, the precise meaning can finally only be determined by which aspect of the exchange of a benefit is in view at the time. Here, since ἔχειν χάριν results in honoring God and pleasing God, and results from receiving a great gift from God, "gratitude" is the aspect that fits.

act in accordance with the demands of justice, especially in terms of the respect, loyalty, and obedience that great benefactors deserve from their beneficiaries.

A Closer Look — Gratitude in Greco-Roman Ethics

The person who received a benefaction in the ancient world received also the obligation to show gratitude. In the words of Seneca (*Ben.* 2.25.3), "the person who intends to be grateful, immediately while receiving, should turn his or her thought to repaying." Gift and obligation to respond are experienced together. Reciprocity was a core value of these societies[72] (Greco-Roman and Jewish authors[73] will both attest to these principles at work in their social relations), and "returning the favor" of a benefactor was an element of the cardinal virtue of justice.[74] Showing gratitude was considered a sacred obligation,[75] while ingratitude was ranked as one of the most vile of crimes.[76]

How was gratitude (the disposition to return favor toward the generous benefactor) to be expressed or manifested? One prominent component of this response was to bring honor to the benefactor. Frederick Danker, a pioneer in researching the importance of patronage for NT exegesis, cites a letter of Gnaeus Arrius Cornelius Proculus stating that "generous people are deserving of honor," and this was indeed the majority opinion.[77] Aristotle (*Eth. Nic.* 8.14.2) speaks thus of the mutual obligations in an alliance between patron and client:

> Both parties should receive a larger share from the friendship, but not a larger share of the same thing: the superior should receive the larger share of honour, the needy one the

---

72. Expressed beautifully in Seneca's "Allegory of the Three Graces" (*Ben.* 1.3.2-5): "Some would have it appear that there is one for bestowing a benefit, one for receiving it, and a third for returning it. . . . Why do the sisters hand in hand dance in a ring that returns upon itself? For the reason that a benefit passing in its course from hand to hand returns nevertheless to the giver; the beauty of the whole is destroyed if the course is anywhere broken, and it has most beauty if it is continuous and maintains an uninterrupted succession."

73. Psalm 116:12-19, for example, preserves an ancient testimony to the centrality of reciprocity, including the application of the patron-client (or lord-vassal) model to the divine-human relationship as well: "What shall I give back to the LORD for all his benefits to me?" The answer consists in public witness to God's generous response to the psalmist's plea for assistance and honoring God in worship.

74. See *Rhet. Alex.* 1421b37-1422a2, which holds it to be just to "repay favors to one's benefactors," which is "observed by unwritten custom and universal practice," and *Rhet. Her.* 3.3.4, which also mentions this as a subtopic of justice.

75. Dio *Or.* 31.37: "For what is more sacred than honour or gratitude (τί γάρ ἐστιν ἱερώτερον τιμῆς ἢ χάριτος;)?"

76. Seneca *Ben.* 1.10.4: "Homicides, tyrants, thieves, adulterers, robbers, sacrilegious men, and traitors there will always be; but worse than all these is the crime of ingratitude." See also *Ben.* 3.1.1: "Not to return gratitude for benefits is a disgrace, and the whole world counts it as such."

77. Danker, *Benefactor,* 436.

larger share of profit; for honour is the due reward of virtue and beneficence, while need obtains the aid it requires in pecuniary gain.

Friends exchanged reciprocal services, and such people enjoyed a mutual sense of partnership; between those who were not friends, the one party would enjoy the benefit, the other the "prestige" that came from "the ability to confer services which were highly valued and could not be remunerated."[78] That prestige was generated by the publicity afforded the patron by the clients, who increased the patron's honor not only in his or her own demeanor and actions, but in public testimony to the benefactor:

> The greater the favour, the more earnestly must we express ourselves, resorting to such compliments as: . . . "I shall never be able to repay you my gratitude, but, at any rate, I shall not cease from declaring everywhere that I am unable to repay it." (Seneca *Ben.* 2.24.2)

> Let us show how grateful we are for the blessing that has come to us by pouring forth our feelings, and let us bear witness to them *(testemur)*, not merely in the hearing of the giver, but everywhere. (Seneca *Ben.* 2.22.1)

Seneca sternly warns that one should never accept a gift if one would be ashamed to acknowledge the debt publicly (*Ben.* 2.23.1); a gift should be accepted if the recipient were willing to "invite the whole city to witness it." Such sentiments have direct bearing on how "public" the recipients of God's benefactions provided through Jesus' brokerage are willing to be about their association with the Patron. Withdrawing from the fellowship, they announce, in effect, that they are ashamed to be indebted any longer to the Patron, hence the outrageous insult to the God who was not ashamed to associate himself with them.

Gratitude involves more than a subjective feeling and more than words. The recipient of a favor seeks opportunities to be of service to the patron and should place loyalty to the patron above any considerations of personal advantage. Seneca (*Ep.* 81.27) provides a powerful picture of the intense bond created by the giving of favor toward the grateful person:

> No one can be grateful unless he or she has learned to scorn the things which drive the common herd to distraction; if you wish to make a return for a favour, you must be willing to go into exile, or to pour forth your blood, or to undergo poverty, or, . . . even to let your very innocence be stained and exposed to shameful slanders.

Gratitude such as Seneca describes involves an intense loyalty to the person from whom one has received beneficence, such that one would place a greater value on service to the benefactor than on one's place in one's homeland, one's physical well-being, one's wealth, and one's reputation. "It is the ungrateful person who thinks: 'I should have liked to return

---

78. J. D. M. Derrett, *Jesus's Audience: The Social and Psychological Environment in Which He Worked* (New York: Seabury, 1977), 41. The exordium of Ephesians could profitably be read in light of the expectation that generosity would redound to the increase of the fame and honor of the giver. The end result of God's provision in Christ is "the praise of the renown of God's gift that God freely bestowed on us (εἰς ἔπαινον δόξης τῆς χάριτος αυτοῦ ἧς ἐχαρίτωσεν ἡμᾶς) in the beloved" (1:6); the redemption of the believers as God's own people leads to "the praise of God's glory" (1:14). The believers are themselves called to enhance God's glory as a result of receiving the promise of the inheritance, which is thus again "for the praise of God's glory" (1:12).

gratitude, but I fear the expense, I fear the danger, I shrink from giving offense; I would rather consult my own interest'" (*Ben.* 4.24.2).[79] The author of Hebrews will call on the hearers to show this measure of gratitude to Jesus, going out to him "outside the camp, bearing his reproach" (13:13), considering not their temporal interests in charting their future course but only the considerations of what such a generous patron merits from those whom he has benefited.

The bond between client and patron (and, one should add, between friends who share mutual beneficence) is thus truly the strongest bond in Greco-Roman society.[80] Where the sanctity of gratitude is maintained, it becomes the one support that remains after all other values and valuables have crumbled. It is this bond that provides a sense of stability and safety in hard times, such that ingratitude is especially vicious, robbing a person of the loyalty and support he or she thought could be counted upon.[81] It is precisely this bond that the author of Hebrews promotes as the source of stability and security for the hearers in the midst of their troubles — "it is a fine thing for the heart to be made firm by grace," in the sum of all its aspects (13:9).

The immensity of the benefit God is conferring (an eternal homeland in which the beneficiaries will be enfranchised as citizens) requires a proportionate commitment to living gratefully.[82] This gratitude will express itself through "worshiping God with piety and reverent fear" in ways that are "pleasing (εὐαρέστως) to God." Words built on the stem εὐαρέστ- had been introduced in 11:5, 6 where "trust" was posited as the prerequisite to pleasing God, and will return in 13:16, 21. By returning to this root toward the end of the following chapter, the author signals that 13:1-21 will develop what gratitude toward God looks like in terms of the everyday activities of sharing with and doing good to one another in the believing community, engaging in that mutual support

---

79. See also *Ben.* 4.20.2: "There is advantage in being grateful; yet I shall be grateful even if it harms me. And what is the aim of one who is grateful? Is it that his gratitude may win for him more friends, more benefits? What, then, if a man is likely to arouse disfavour by it, if a man knows that, so far from being likely to gain anything by it, he must lose much from the store that he has already acquired, does he not gladly submit to his losses?"

80. See Seneca *Ben.* 1.4.2: benefaction is "a practice that constitutes the chief bond of human society"; 5.11.5: "The giving of a benefit is a social act, it wins the goodwill of someone, it lays someone under obligation"; 6.41.2: "A benefit is a common bond and binds two persons together."

81. Thus Seneca *Ben.* 4.18.1: "Ingratitude is something to be avoided in itself because there is nothing that so effectually disrupts and destroys the harmony of the human race as this vice. For how else do we live in security if it is not that we help each other by an exchange of good offices? It is only through the interchange of benefits that life becomes in some measure equipped and fortified against sudden disasters. Take us singly, and what are we? The prey of all creatures."

82. Paul beautifully expresses the measure of what would constitute a fair return to Jesus in 2 Cor. 5:15: "he died for all in order that the living might live no longer for themselves but for him who on their behalf died and was raised."

which makes resistance to society's assaults possible, and acknowledging God's beneficence — affirming to God, one another, and the unbelieving world that God's gifts are good and worth what they cost to keep (13:15-16). The exhortations that close the sermon are far from "general exhortation"[83] or a moral appendix but are in one crucial way the climax of the sermon. They reveal how one is to act justly and preserve the beauty of the circle of grace, and thus also how one will arrive at the promised kingdom. The response of gratitude thus appeals not only to topics of justice, but also to topics of expedience, specifically the acquisition of greater goods (the unshakable kingdom) and the prevention of certain harm (judgment and divine vengeance).

Seneca (*Ep. Mor.* 81.21) writes that gratitude is "an utterly happy condition of soul" that produces a great experience for the one who feels it. It is worth pondering here how the author might elevate the virtue of "gratitude" to provide medicine for the addressees' souls as well as direction for their steps. By urging them to "have gratitude," he reminds them that what they have gained is ever so much greater than what they have lost. Perhaps those who are wavering in their faith feel defeated. They are sick at heart with the losses they have sustained and the daily reminders of that loss. They are invited, rather than to succumb to the pressures of people who have not had the benefit of their encounter with the living God, to reflect on what knowing Christ has meant to them, on how they have experienced the timely help of God either directly or through the agency of their sisters and brothers, and on the good things yet in store for those who remain firmly fixed in Jesus. Gratitude may provide a starting point for the recovery of spirit as well as the course correction for a drifting heart.

Hebrews 12:29 rounds out the paragraph with a fitting image of God as a consuming fire, a recontextualization of words from Deuteronomy 4:24 with only a change of a pronoun (from "your God is a consuming fire" to "*our* God"). This image reinforces the warning of 12:25, specifically recalling 10:26-31, where the ingrate faced the prospect of the "eager fire ready to consume the adversaries." Hebrews 12:28-29 repeats in a nutshell the pastoral technique of the author throughout the sermon: to reinforce the injunction to offer God reverent and pious service and to show God the gratitude he merits through consideration both of the magnitude of his generosity and of the danger of his judgment upon the unjust.

---

83. Thus Buchanan (*To The Hebrews*, 228), who includes an imaginative hypothesis of how the "editor" put together this appendix.

Summary

With Hebrews 12:4-11, the addressees are insulated even further against the erosive effects of society's censure on their commitment to Jesus and one another. Not only is society's challenge to be endured courageously for the sake of victory (12:1-4), but the hardships become the means by which God shapes and forms the hearers' character. They are the training exercises by which the addressees' faculty of moral choice and virtues are refined and honed, preparing them for their enfranchisement in the city of God. What their unbelieving neighbors intend as corrective discipline meant to bring the Christian back into conformity with the dominant culture the author turns into a sign of God's special favor — the very proof of their adoption into God's family as daughters and sons and the path to being endowed with God's holiness and the "peaceful fruit of justice" (12:10-11).

Armed with this new perspective on their experiences, the addressees are urged to find their second wind and plunge forward in their Christian race with new vigor and dedication. Along the way they are to exercise watchful care over one another, strengthening one another's commitment and reaffirming one another in the wisdom of remaining openly attached to Jesus and the people of God. They are to guard against a repetition of Esau's foolish choice and are led to see temporal peace and restoration as a mere bowl of lentil soup in comparison with the glorious prize that has been awarded them, which they will receive if they but hold firm until the return of Christ and the dissolution of the material cosmos. The way opened up for them by Jesus in the inauguration of the new covenant is a road to splendor and celebration, an approach to God that is in every way superior to the encounter with God that accompanied the forging of the old covenant.

The author has consistently led the addressees to view everything around them (the society's rejection and antagonism, 12:1-11) and everything in front of them (their approach to God, 12:18-24) as a cause to move forward and bravely persevere. The final paragraph of this section reaffirms the eschatological conviction that makes this forward movement indispensable. The world around them and behind them is destined for demolition and removal. Moving back into the bosom of society means a return to the demolition zone. Moving ahead, running to the prize of deliverance, is the only option for those who believe God's promise concerning the removal of the manufactured cosmos. For those who do press on, however, this eschatological event will be "good news." It will mean the revelation of the "way into the holy places" of the abiding realm and the believers' reception of an "unshakable kingdom" (12:28). The way to attain this ultimate benefaction is also the only proper response to the God who has promised to confer it — to show gratitude. Justice demands of the recipients of God's former gifts (especially in light of Jesus' costly efforts at mediation) and of God's promises of future benefits that they live for the increase of the honor of such a patron, seeking also to return the favor through the performance of the services that will please God. As the following chapter will develop this response, pouring oneself and one's resources into the support of one's fellow Christians is an essential component of a grateful response, as is maintaining loyalty to Jesus even as this leads the hearers, too, to share in the reproach that Jesus endured on their behalf.

Bridging the Horizons

The author's words concerning discipline in 12:5-11 have led to some serious misconceptions about God as well as the appropriateness of corporeal punishment, which has in turn led to critique of this passage itself. Mary Rose D'Angelo, for example, censures the "abusive connection between punishment and love" that "puts a divine sanction behind the abuse of women and abusive child rearing."[84] Clayton Croy correctly analyzes this statement as an accurate response to the misapplication and misreading of the passage, but not an accurate critique of Hebrews 12:5-11 itself,[85] which in no way legitimizes domestic abuse. Neither does the passage reinscribe the common belief that suffering is somehow a punishment for sin: although this would be an appropriate assessment of the ideology of Proverbs, the author of Hebrews has muted those aspects of the text of Proverbs that speak of punitive discipline and moves instead in the direction of formative discipline.

Specifically, the author speaks in this passage only of the hardship that meets us when we step out in faith, speak out for God's values, and act to serve his ends (see John 15:18-19). The passage serves to empower the believer for continued resistance in the face of oppressive powers and for continued witness and service to Jesus and the household of faith in the face of the hostility of the world. Once the passage is removed from the pastoral context that it addressed, its meaning is open to grievous distortions.[86] Read in light of its pastoral context, however, it remains a powerful encouragement to those who have accepted loss or hardship on account of their commitment to Jesus and the witness of the church. The defenders of this world's way of life will seek to hinder the faithful, but what we suffer (and here we must remember the global commu-

---

84. Mary Rose D'Angelo, "Hebrews," in *The Women's Bible Commentary*, ed. C. A. Newsom and S. H. Ringe (Louisville, KY: Westminster/John Knox, 1992), 366.

85. Croy, *Endurance*, 222.

86. See ibid.: "The suffering lying behind the Epistle to the Hebrews is religious persecution experienced in reproaches, scorn, imprisonment, and confiscation of property. A facile application of the author's arguments to other kinds of suffering could be theologically risky and pastorally disastrous."

nity of faith, some of whom suffer far worse losses than even the first audience) at their hands can make us all the more committed rather than defeat our spirits and mute our confession of hope. It reminds us of our favored place in God's sight, since we are being trained even as the Son for our glorious destiny. When we are confronted with such losses and still choose to follow God rather than shrink back from him, our own moral faculty is strengthened, our character shaped (see Rom. 5:1-5), our commitment enhanced, and our values sharpened. Such hardship educates us in the vast differences between the world's ideology and the Christian life, as well as fits us for the exercise of citizenship in the City of God, cultivating in us God's own holiness and the "harvest of righteousness and peace" (12:11).

We must remember, however, that Hebrews 12:5-11 does not have in view every experience of suffering. Illness, oppression, domestic abuse, and the like are not within its purview, nor does it affirm that God is the orchestrator of such suffering. Even within the context of religious persecution, it does not legitimate such oppression that remains the "hostility of *sinners*," that is, those who act against God and his people, who are themselves not serving his will even though he can use for good what they intend for evil. Nor does it allow us to stand by idly and watch our sisters and brothers face hostility and hardship for their obedience to God's call. The duty of the Christian is always to critique the forces that resist God's purpose by resisting God's people (see Rev. 18:1-24), to alleviate suffering, to share aid, and to bear the other's burden (see Heb. 13:1-3, 16).[87]

In the next section, the example of Esau confronts us as powerfully today as it did the first audience. Christians in the former Soviet Union, for example, certainly faced choosing between their birthright as children of God and the temporary relief that would come from denying or hiding or compromising their Christian confession. Even in situations where "apostasy" per se is not the way to peace with society, we are still very much in danger of selling our birthright for what amounts to a single meal. The easy relationship of church and government in America, for example, may lead us subtly to give up our birthright as children of God for the sake of temporal goods. Unaware of the profound differences and even antagonism between the gospel of Christ and the *Zeitgeist* of our society, we may be following a pale shadow of Jesus, a Jesus who allows us to gather up our wealth and goods into bigger and bigger barns, who allows us to shop and hop from church to church with the same consumer mentality we take to car dealerships. Has our comfort and our commitment to comfort accomplished here what decades of brutal repression could not accomplish in the former U.S.S.R, namely, taming Christianity and making it a harmless, private, and fundamentally irrelevant religion that can be safely tolerated since it never interferes with business as usual?

---

87. See rightly ibid., 224.

To whatever degree this might be found to be true, it is not the fault of people outside the church. Rather, blame for lukewarmness rests on those of us within the church who have the form of godliness but have refused to know its power. A question that many of us might need to ask is, Have we sold our birthright and chosen rather to drink deep from the fountains of temporal goods and be satisfied with meager sips of God's living waters? Have we become content with a God who serves our needs when we need him rather than sought after the God who calls us to serve him and his vision for our community, our nation, and the world? Have we fashioned a savior who loves and tends us but is content to allow us to pursue our own goals and ambitions rather than calling us to serve his goals? Freedom from sin, empowerment by the Holy Spirit, intimate fellowship with God, and vision for extending God's love and justice to our fellow human beings — these are but a few elements of our birthright, not to mention our assurance of perpetual life and honor in God's presence. Have we seized this inheritance, or do we devote more of our time, energy, and desire to the things our society holds up as valuable? How often do our choices reflect our hunger for God, our love for God, our desire to be God's instruments in this world, and how often do our choices show contentment with this world's trivial entertainments and pursuits? Esau reminds us not to make the same poor choice he did, not only in terms of our ultimate destiny but in terms of our everyday choices. When we feel the pangs of our bodily appetites or of worldly desires and ambitions rising up within us (see 1 Tim. 6:9-10), will we choose to satisfy them at the cost of enjoying the greater inheritance? The author of Hebrews calls us to make our choices while holding before us the surpassing value of knowing Christ, the promise of finding perfect freedom through serving him in this life, and the deliverance unto eternal life he has opened up for us. We should allow no lesser appetite or ambitions to rob us of that joy.

The awe-inspiring vision of journey's end in 12:22-24 resonates with other scriptural depictions of the liturgy of heaven and the company of the redeemed in their eternal inheritance. Such visions were of great value and help to the early Church as they sought the larger picture that made their present situation bearable and even desirable. As the author of Hebrews urges us to live here so as to be welcomed there, the vision of the splendor of God's kingdom can become a source of power and boldness for Christian witness and service in this world, as well as a source of strength for making those choices that result in reduced temporal comfort or status but a more Christ-like walk. Do we connect with that, or a similar, vision? Do we make space in our prayer and worship together to connect with the larger body of God's faithful ones, angelic and human, so as to receive the strength and confirmation that come from that encounter? The ancient liturgy of the Eucharist (Holy Communion) moves into the "Great Thanksgiving" thus:

Therefore with angels and archangels, and with all the company of heaven, we laud and magnify thy glorious name, evermore praising thee and saying: "Holy, holy, holy Lord God of hosts: Heaven and earth are full of thy glory!"

Is our congregational or private worship a time in which our "reality" intersects with the larger reality of God's realm? Is the goal of the Christian pilgrimage as real and vibrant to us as the temporary world in which we sojourn (see also 12:26-28)? The authors of Hebrews and Revelation both insist that faithful living here is facilitated by contemplation of the larger entourage of God and the working together of all God's servants to arrive at the final consummation of the kingdom. Even centuries after the "Enlightenment" and decades after Rudolf Bultmann declared angelic orders and life after death to be but relics from an antique worldview,[88] we might still have reason to trust the instincts of our canonical writers and consider how our life and goals and investments in this world are clarified when seen in light of eternity and the realms beyond our senses and observation.

Finally, the focus on "gratitude" at the close of the chapter provides a promising overarching frame for our approach to our life in this world. First, the injunction to "show gratitude" invites us to seek out a full understanding of how favored we are by God. Particularly in the United States, the popular mind is either on what we "earn"[89] or on what our "rights" are, but rarely are we urged to contemplate what we are, what we have, and even *that* we are (see Rev. 4:11) as gifts from God for which we ought already wholeheartedly to be grateful and committed to show our gratitude. The more we fathom of the deliverance that Christ brings us and the riches of knowing God's friendship and guidance, the more we will know the extent of our debt of gratitude. Letting this gratitude toward God grow and allowing it to shape our lives brings integration to all we do and experience. All parts of our life come together in a reflection of that beautiful circle dance of the Graces, as we walk in the awareness of receiving from God and returning thanks to him through our reverence and service and our sharing of what he has given us with one another. The grateful Christian alone will understand Christian stewardship: the God who has given us our lives, our goods, and our eternal hope deserves the full expression of our thanks as we dedicate our own lives — our time, talents, and treasures alike — to "live no longer for ourselves but for Jesus, who died on our behalf and was raised up" (2 Cor. 5:15).

---

88. Rudolf Bultmann, "New Testament and Mythology," in *Kerygma and Myth by Rudolf Bultmann and Five Critics,* ed. H. W. Bartsch (New York: Harper & Row, 1961), 4.

89. Compare our situation here with Nebuchadnezzar's mistake in Dan. 4: do we look out over our homes, our financial portfolio, our business ventures, and say, "Is this not Babylon the great, which I myself have built . . . by the might of my power?"

Living In Gratitude to God: 13:1-25

Overview

The connection between chapter 13 and the rest of the sermon has not always been regarded as clear, and, indeed, the literary unity of Hebrews as we have it has been debated. The chapter begins with a simplicity of style and content that has struck some scholars as an indication that this section is at best an appendix of loosely connected exhortations, and perhaps even an addition made by a second author.[1] Several scholars have undertaken to show, however, the thematic connections between chapter 13 and the rest of the sermon,[2] with the result that the literary unity of Hebrews is rarely challenged today. As the commentary below will demonstrate, each exhortation is directly relevant to the pastoral need addressed by chapters 1 through 12, giving the hearers specific direc-

---

1. Héring (*Hebrews*, 119) advances the rather reserved hypothesis that chapter 13 was added by the writer of chapters 1–12 (although Paul may have authored chapter 13, which is now incorporated by the author of Hebrews 1–12) when he sent his sermon to a specific location. More speculative is the hypothesis of Buchanan (*Hebrews*, 229-45, 267-68), who suggests that the chapter was added by some member of the "committee on canon" to bring the fine sermon more in line with the literary genre of epistle, the expected genre of apostolic instruction, after the condemnation of Marcion. Even more imaginative is the argument made by E. D. Jones ("The Authorship of Hebrews xiii," *ExT* 46 [1934-35]: 562-67) that this chapter originally stood as the conclusion to the lost "severe letter" written by Paul to the Corinthian churches before 2 Corinthians.

2. The most comprehensive of these is Filson, *Yesterday;* see also R. V. G. Tasker, "The Integrity of the Epistle to the Hebrews," *ExT* 47 (1935-36): 136-38; Jukka Thurén, *Das Lobopfer der Hebräer: Studien zum Aufbau und Anliegen von Hebräerbrief 13* (Åbo: Akademi, 1973), 57-70 and passim.

tions concerning how they are to persevere in the face of a hostile society and arrive safely and unwearied at the goal of the "lasting" city that is to come.

Hebrews 13:1-21 outlines the response that shows gratitude to God and pleases God. The author's description of this response is bracketed and given thematic consistency by words related to the term "well pleasingly" (εὐαρέ-στως) found in the introductory exhortation of 12:28:

"Let us show gratitude, through which we worship God in a well pleasing manner." (εὐαρέστως, 12:28)

"Let us not forget to do good and to share, for with such sacrifices God is well pleased." (εὐαρεστεῖται, 13:16)

"working in you what is well pleasing (τὸ εὐάρεστον) before him through Jesus Christ." (13:21)

This repetition also recalls 11:5-6, where "pleasing God" was presented as an essential quality (one associated closely with the transcendence of death) attained by means of trusting God ("faith"). Exhortations to maintain that solidarity and support which allows individual believers to persevere in the confession of hope (13:1-4, 15-16) however marginalized they become (13:3), exhortations to remain disinvested from the pursuit of status and wealth in this world (13:5-6, 11-14), and exhortations to find one's firmness and place in Jesus and the relationship of grace established through him with God (13:7-10) show the way to live "in a well-pleasing manner," to make a just and fitting return to God for benefits received and benefits yet to come.

The sermon, which remains after all a written oration sent from a member of a ministry team to a specific congregation, closes with the epistolary postscript typical in Christian culture.[3] The author adds his own request for the addressees' prayers for God's action on his behalf (13:18-19), thus enacting with them the exhortation of Hebrews 4:16. He follows this with a benediction that encapsulates several important themes of the sermon (13:20-21a) and a formulaic doxology (13:21b). Indications of travel plans (13:22-23), greetings from the supralocal Christian community (13:24), and a final, formulaic wish for God's favor to remain with the hearers (13:25) bring to a conclusion this "brief word of exhortation" (13:22).

---

3. See Attridge (*Hebrews* 404-5), who lays out the form of the closings of Christian letters and shows the especially close parallels between the ending of Hebrews and the epistolary postscripts of Romans, 1 Thessalonians, 1 Peter, and 2 Timothy.

Commentary

13:1-6

Contrary to the assessment by James W. Thompson, who holds that "the exhortations in 13:1-6 are loosely placed here, and bear no relation to the rest of the epistle,"[4] I believe that the author comes in these verses to exhortations of primary importance for his solution to the pastoral needs of his hearers. Though the sentence structure is simple, this section is nonetheless artfully constructed. The repetition of the root φιλ-, "love of,"[5] provides linguistic and thematic cohesiveness as the author exhorts the hearers to engage certain forms of love and dissuades them from deleterious kinds of attachments:

> Let brotherly love continue. Do not forget to love guests, for through hospitality some have unwittingly entertained angels. Remember the imprisoned, as being imprisoned together with them, the mistreated as being yourselves in their skin. Let marriage be respected in all things and the marriage bed kept pure, for God will judge the fornicators and adulterers. Let your way be free from the love of money, being content with what you do have, for he himself has said: "I will never leave you nor abandon you," so that we are emboldened to say, "The Lord is my help; I will not fear — what can a human being do to me?!"

The first exhortations direct the addressees to pour themselves into building up a strong community base and network of support for the individual believers, creating the kind of group that can sustain the commitment of its members even when society brings its most fearsome weapons to bear on them.[6] The relationships among believers are to be marked by "the love that characterizes siblings" (φιλαδελφία, 13:1). Fostering an ethos of kinship within the Christian group was a widespread technique grounded in the conviction that the believers have become kin by the blood of Christ, being adopted into the one household of God as the many sons and daughters. Applying such a model to the voluntary group known as the church (which is called "fictive kinship") allows community leaders like our au-

---

4. Thompson, *Beginnings,* 143.

5. "Let brotherly love continue" (φιλαδελφία, 13:1); "Do not forget the love of guests" (i.e., hospitality, φιλοξενίας, 13:2); "Let your way be free from love of money" (Ἀφιλάργυρος, 13:5)

6. Elliott (*Home for the Homeless,* 149) writes concerning the strategy of 1 Peter: "Solidarity *among* the Christians . . . was encouraged not only through the collective terms which were used to express their unity and raise their group consciousness but also through direct appeal for brotherly love, hospitality, mutual service and the kind of conduct which insures group cohesion." These very words could have been written about Hebrews as well.

thor to fuel mutual support, solidarity, and aid by appealing to the obligations that family members have toward one another, and especially to the ethical ideals of how siblings ought to regard one another and care for one another.

The relationship between siblings was the closest, strongest, and most intimate of relationships in the ancient world. Aristotle considers brotherly love to be a special and augmented form of friendship: "Brothers love each other as being born of the same parents; for their identity with them makes them identical with each other (which is the reason why people talk of 'the same blood,' 'the same stock,' and so on). They are, therefore, in a sense the same thing, though separate individuals" (*Eth. Nic.* 1161b30-35). This sentiment is echoed four centuries later by Plutarch ("On Brotherly Affection" 5 [*Mor.* 480B-C]): "insofar as Nature has made [siblings] separate in their bodies, so far do they become united in their emotions and actions, and share with each other their studies and recreations and games." The relationship between siblings was, by nature, marked by agreement, cooperation, sharing, and harmony. Siblings are "to use in common a parent's wealth and friends and slaves" in the manner that "a single soul makes use of the hands and feet and eyes of two bodies" (*Mor.* 478C-D).[7] Solidarity and cooperation, rather than competition, should be the hallmark of their interaction: "Nature from one seed and one source has created two siblings, or three, or more, not for difference and opposition to each other, but that by being separate they might the more readily co-operate with one another" (*Mor.* 478E), even as multiple fingers of a single hand work together to accomplish a task.

It became common to place more emphasis on the similarity of character that bound siblings together rather than relationship by blood merely. 4 Maccabees 13:24-26 speaks of a common zeal for Torah and virtue binding the seven brothers together more closely than natural affections on their own, so that a common dedication to the same values strengthens natural kinship. A similar sentiment appears in Philo *De nobilitate* 195: "Kinship is not measured only by blood, but by similarity of conduct and pursuit of the same objects." It is a small step from here to the redefinition of kinship as that which is created not by blood but by this sharing of values and pursuit of a common goal, such as one finds throughout the literature of the Christian culture.[8]

7. Friends "hold all things in common" (Aristotle *Eth. Nic.*), so that it is all the more necessary for siblings to do the same.

8. See several Christian exhortations that seek to infuse the audiences with an ethos of sibling love as a means of shaping the relationships within the group: "love one another with brotherly affection (τῇ φιλαδελφίᾳ); outdo one another in showing honor" (Rom. 12:10); "But concerning love of the brothers and sisters (φιλαδελφίας) you have no need to have any one write to you, for you yourselves have been taught by God to love one another" (1 Thess. 4:9); "Having purified your souls by your obedience to the truth for a sincere love of the brothers and sisters (φιλαδελφίαν ἀνυπόκριτον), love one another earnestly from the heart" (1 Pet. 1:22); cf. also 1 Pet. 3:8; 2 Pet. 1:7.

The author of Hebrews has reinforced the addressees' identity as kin one with another by means of their common adoption into the "household of God" (Heb. 2:10-13; 3:6; 10:19-20), and he now brings together his many exhortations to watch out for one's fellow believers and to do good and show love to them (3:12-14; 6:9-10; 10:24-25; 12:15-17; 13:15-16) by means of topics of kinship in this last chapter. The conviction that siblings were so closely united as to be, in essence, "the same thing, though separate individuals" (Aristotle *Eth. Nic.* 1161b35), undergirds the exhortation to extend care to those imprisoned or physically abused for their association with Jesus. The conviction that siblings were to make common use of their inherited goods undergirds the exhortation to "benefit" and "share with" one another within the community (13:16; cf. 6:9-10; 10:24-25). Lucian bears witness that this attitude is thoroughly established among Christians by the second century in his satire "On the Passing of Peregrinus": "their first lawgiver persuaded them that they are all brothers of one another. . . . Therefore they despise all things [i.e., material goods] indiscriminately and consider them common property" (*Peregr.* 13). As siblings in Christ, the believers are to pull together in every way so that every member of the family arrives safely at the heavenly goal.[9]

Hospitality ("love of guest and stranger," 13:2) is also to remain the hallmark of this community. The relationship of hosts and guests was long considered a sacred bond, the preservation of which is a topic of justice (*Rhet. Her.* 3.3.4). Within the Christian culture, hospitality was also an important expression of the love of believers one for another, a living out of the ethos of kinship within the translocal Christian community:

> In addition to the poor, the outcasts, the dispossessed, the imprisoned and the widows and orphans who had to be cared for, there were, according to Hatch, "the strangers who passed in a constant stream through the cities of all the great routes of commerce in both East and West. Every one of those strangers who bore the Christian name had therein a claim to hospitality. For Christianity was, and grew because it was, a great fraternity. The name 'brother' . . . vividly expressed a real fact. . . . a Christian found, wherever he went, in the community of his fellow-Christians a welcome and hospitality."[10]

The importance of hospitality toward visiting brothers and sisters carrying on the work of the church is apparent throughout the NT. Missionaries, itinerant

---

9. Cf. Worley, "God's Faithfulness to Promise," 217: "What the author of Hebrews has attempted to do . . . is exhort his readers to a faithfulness before God and a dependability in brotherly love in the face of financial and social pressures, as well as a waning of Christian enthusiasms, which threaten the fellowship of the church and the readers' access to God."

10. Elliott, *Home for the Homeless,* 146, citing Edwin Hatch, *The Organization of the Early Christian Churches* (Oxford and Cambridge: Rivingtons, 1881), 43-44.

teachers, and leaders of the movement were especially dependent on the hospitality of their fellow believers along the way. 3 John, for example, praises Gaius for his hospitality toward visiting Christians (3 John 5-8) and censures Diotrephes for his refusal to extend hospitality and his attempts to prevent others from exercising this ministry (3 John 9-10). Paul, similarly, depends on the hospitality of converts for his travels (see 1 Cor. 16:5-6; Phlm. 22). The houses of the better-endowed believers became the meeting places for the local Christian community, which sustained the "constant intercourse and meeting . . . essential to preserve the Church's cohesion and distinctive witness," as well as provided a place where the distinctive Christian worship could be practiced.[11] Both for the ongoing nurture of the local community and for the sake of ongoing connectedness with the larger Christian culture — the supralocal family of God[12] — hospitality was a core value of the early Church.[13]

The rationale provided here for hospitality is a general reference to those biblical stories in which hospitality was extended unknowingly to angels.[14] The hearers might think first of the narratives in Genesis 18 and 19, in which Abraham and Sarah, then Lot, show hospitality to strangers who turn out to be angels of the Lord. Lot's dedication to hospitality is quite exemplary (if not without other difficulties), in that he places the well-being of his own daughters at risk in order that his guests' well-being not be violated while staying under his roof. One might also recall Tobit 5 and 12, which speak of Tobit's entertainment (and hiring) of Raphael, disguised as Azariah.[15] The notion that in entertaining a human being one actually extends hospitality to something greater is even more forcefully expressed by Jesus in Matthew 10:40: "those who receive you receive me, and those who receive me receive him who sent me."

The third injunction is introduced with "remember," offering an artistic balance to (and avoidance of repetition with) "do not forget" in 13:2. The ex-

---

11. E. G. Selwyn, *The First Epistle of Peter,* 2nd ed. (London: Macmillan, 1955), 218. See Rom. 16:3-5, 23; 1 Cor. 16:19; Col. 4:15; Phlm. 2; 1 Pet. 4:9.

12. With the exhortation to provide hospitality for traveling fellow believers, the author extends the court of opinion beyond the boundaries of the local Christian community to that of the broader Christian minority culture.

13. See further Meeks, *First Urban Christians,* 16-23, 107-10; M. B. Thompson, "The Holy Internet: Communication between Churches in the First Christian Generation," in *The Gospels for All Christians: Rethinking the Gospel Audiences,* ed. Richard Bauckham (Grand Rapids: Eerdmans, 1998), 55-56.

14. The author works in a pun in this verse, between "Do not forget (ἐπιλανθάνεσθε) hospitality" and "unwittingly (ἔλαθόν) entertained angels." Both words are built on the verb λανθάνω, meaning "escape notice."

15. Pfitzner (*Hebrews,* 192) also points to the stories about Gideon and Manoah and his wife in Judg. 6:11-21; 13:2-20.

hortation to "remember" those in prison and those being mistreated for their confession directs the hearers specifically to provide relief in the forms of material and emotional support to those believers who are experiencing the most pressure from outside the group. The kinship of Christians should lead the free believer to regard the sufferings of another as his or her own sufferings and to alleviate them as wholeheartedly and bravely as one would relieve one's own distress. They are, as kin, "the same thing, though separate individuals," and so should feel and respond to one another's needs in that spirit.[16] This exhortation specifically recalls 10:32-34, where the author lauded the believers for their relief efforts on behalf of one another (specifically, "showing sympathy toward the imprisoned") despite the negative attention that would draw from society. It also recalls 11:24-26, where Moses chooses solidarity with the mistreated people of God over comfort with the sinners. The verbal similarities between the example of the community's past,[17] Moses' example, and this exhortation are striking[18] and suggest that the author particularly wants to reinforce support for the marginalized, which is essential to maintaining group commitment among both those who are being targeted by society and those who fear that they might become marked for deviancy-control techniques in the future. The latter need to see that their new family will never desert them in their time of need, but will rather be for one another the visible and active manifestation of the promise of God that follows in 13:5. This is all the more pointed as some believers have already "abandoned" the assembly, whereas God promises never to "abandon" the believers (cf. 10:25 and 13:5).[19]

---

16. The strong sense of solidarity promoted here also recalls Paul's use of the human body as an image for the organic unity of the believers in 1 Cor. 12. Particularly striking is 1 Cor. 12:24-26: "God has so arranged the body . . . that there may be no dissension within the body, but the members may have the same care for one another. If one member suffers, all suffer together with it; if one member is honored, all rejoice together with it" (NRSV). Here again the intimate connection of believers should lead to mutual support, care, and cooperation, since the fate of each member is felt by all others.

17. "You sympathized with the imprisoned" (τοῖς δεσμίοις συνεπαθήσατε, 10:33); "remember the imprisoned" (μιμνῄσκεσθε τῶν δεσμίων, 13:3).

18. Moses chose "rather to be mistreated together with (συγκακουχεῖσθαι) the people of God" (11:25); "remember the mistreated (κακουχουμένων) as being in their body" (13:3).

19. The emphasis on solidarity with believers who are victimized by the outside society became a prominent feature of the Christian counterculture. During the journey of Ignatius from Antioch to his martyrdom at Rome, he was visited, attended, and given hospitality by Christians along the way. This shows the willingness of the believers to "remember those in prison as though imprisoned with them" (Heb. 13:3). The martyr himself testifies (*Smyrn.* 10): "My life is a humble offering for you; and so are these chains of mine, for which you never showed the least contempt or shame. Neither will Jesus Christ in his perfect loyalty show Himself ashamed of you." Lucian's famous satire on the charlatan Peregrinus also pro-

In 13:1-3, the author has appealed to topics of justice as a means of maintaining the unity, solidarity, and strength of the minority group. The fulfillment of the obligations of kinship (here, fictive) and ties of hospitality (13:2) are both featured prominently in lists of subcategories under the heading of justice.[20] As the author continues now in 13:4, he appeals to another topic of justice, namely, fidelity in marriage (13:4), which intersects with an introduction of topics on temperance, urging abstinence from illicit or excessive passions (here, specifically lust in 13:4 and greed in 13:5-6).[21] For a rationale to support the injunction to maintain conjugal fidelity, the author solemnly reminds the hearers of God's future judgment of adulterers and fornicators. The goal is to reinforce sanctions against the sort of activity that can bring legitimate stains upon the honor of the Christian group[22] or damage those intimate relationships between people who should rather be supporting one another in the Christian enterprise. Anyone who has witnessed

---

vides a window into the Christian community in the mid–second century. It is a view that would have greatly pleased the author of Hebrews:

> The Christians . . . left nothing undone in the effort to rescue [Peregrinus]. Then, as this was impossible, every other form of attention was shown him. . . . From the very break of day aged widows and orphan children could be seen waiting near the prison, while their officials even slept inside with him after bribing the guards. Then elaborate meals were brought in, and sacred books of theirs were read aloud. . . .
>
> Indeed, people came even from the cities in Asia, sent by the Christians at their common expense, to succour and defend and encourage the hero. They show incredible speed whenever any such public action is taken; for in no time they lavish their all. . . . (*Peregr.* 12; LCL)

20. See, for example, *Rhet. Her.* 3.3.4: "We shall be using the topics of Justice . . . if we urge that faith *(fidem)* ought zealously to be kept; . . . if we contend that alliances and friendships should scrupulously be honored; if we make it clear that the duty imposed by nature towards parents, gods, and the fatherland *(in parentes, deos, patriam)* must be religiously observed; if we maintain that ties of hospitality, clientage, kinship, and relationship by marriage must inviolably be cherished."

21. Compare *Rhet. Her.* 3.2.3: "Temperance is self-control that moderates our desires *(modesta est in animo continens moderatio cupiditatem)*"; 3.3.5: "We shall be using the topics of Temperance if we censure the inordinate desire for office, money, or the like." With the enjoining of temperance, the author has encouraged the believers to pursue all four cardinal virtues of the Greco-Roman society, although transposed into a Christian framework. The conviction that virtuous action leads to honor (cf. *Rhet. Her.* 3.2.3) has a place now within the believer's quest for honor, as the believer may still regard himself or herself as a virtuous person while remaining exclusively faithful to the minority culture.

22. The believers are to despise the opinion of outsiders with regard to criticisms of their commitment to one God, Jesus, and the like, but they should still safeguard the honor of the group with regard to legitimate claims that could be made against them, for example, that they shelter adulterers, thieves, and the like (see 1 Pet. 4:14-16).

the damage that adultery (particularly when committed by people in the same church) can do to the Christian walk of the individuals involved and to the vision and mission of the whole church will understand at once the author's concern here.[23]

"Love of money" in a setting where deprivation of money is one of society's deviancy-control techniques (cf. 10:34) obviously threatens single-minded commitment to the group. Indeed, it is precisely the lack of contentment with what they possess that leads some to waver in their commitment and to begin to dissociate themselves from the group, association with which has cost them dearly in terms of worldly honor and possessions. This has led them to forget the value of the gifts they have received from God, falling into what Seneca perceives to be a common trap (*Ben.* 3.3.1-2):

> busied as we are with ever new desires, we turn our eyes, not to what we possess, but to what we seek to possess. . . . We love someone, and look up to him, and avow that he laid the foundation of our present position so long as we are satisfied with what we have attained; then the desirability of other things assails our mind, and we rush toward those, as is the way of mortals, who, having got great things, always desire greater.

The exhortation to be content with what they currently possess (ἀρκούμενοι τοῖς παροῦσιν, 13:5) cannot fail to recall to the audience their loss of possessions (10:34). The author is not simply using a common topos of paraenesis but has carefully constructed his exhortation with the community's circumstances in mind. He thus urges them not simply to avoid greed, but rather not to seek to regain at the cost of losing their reward what they had lost for Christ's sake in previous times.[24] Their forbearance now will bring them better and lasting possessions in a country where their honor will be that of the children of God. The author knows, with the author of 1 Timothy 6:10, that "love of money" (φιλαργυρία) is the root of every evil, particularly dangerous as a cause for "wandering away from the faith." The author therefore seeks to "reinforce the de-

---

23. Sexual restraint was a common feature of Christian exhortation, as Christian culture wanted to distinguish itself in its dedication to continence (even as it frequently accused non-Christians of rampant lust; 1 Thess. 4:4-5; 1 Pet. 4:3-4). See 1 Thess. 4:1-7, which links sexual continence with the sanctification that is God's will for the believers; also Eph. 5:3-5, which combines exhortations against lust, greed, and covetousness (as does Heb. 13:4-5). Attridge notes (*Hebrews*, 387 nn. 45-46) that injunctions against greed and lust were frequently connected in Greco-Roman and Jewish ethical literature.

24. Thus, rightly, Ellingworth (*Hebrews*, 698): "one of the results of persecution has been the loss of property (10:34). In these circumstances, the Christian response is not to grasp all the more eagerly at material wealth, but to rely quietly on God's provision, even in the face of human opposition."

tachment from material goods," the lack of love of money (ἀφιλάργυρος), "that had previously enabled his community to suffer their losses gladly (10:34)."[25]

Hebrews 13:5b reminds the hearers of what they do in fact possess, that is, God's certain assurance of help: "I will certainly never leave you nor abandon you" (Οὐ μή σε ἀνῶ οὐδ' οὐ μή σε ἐγκαταλίπω). This is an inexact recitation of Deuteronomy 31:6, altered to conform to the more personal, first person singular form of God's statement in Genesis 28:15:[26]

> "Your God . . . will certainly never leave you nor abandon you" (ὁ θεός σου . . . οὐ μή σε ἀνῇ οὔτε μή σε ἐγκαταλίπῃ, Deut. 31:6).
> "I will certainly never abandon you" (οὐ μή σε ἐγκαταλίπω, Gen. 28:15).

This should remind the hearers of the proximity of divine help and God's personal commitment to hear and answer those who call upon him through his Son, which is their ground for confidence. The effect should be an arousing of confidence among the hearers.[27] The remembrance of God's past benefactions — God's investment in the hearers thus far — may itself be understood as a cause for assurance of God's continued favor and of his future investment in the faithful:

> How often will you hear a man say: "I cannot bear to desert him, for I have given him his life, I have rescued him from peril. He now begs me to plead his cause against men of influence; I do not want to, but what can I do? I have already helped him once, no, twice." Do you not see that there is, inherent in the thing itself, some peculiar power that compels us to give benefits, first, because we ought, then, because we have already given them? . . . We continue to bestow because we have already bestowed. (Seneca *Ben.* 4.15.3)

That God had given his own Son for the redemption of the addressees, had bestowed upon them the gift of the Holy Spirit, had lavished upon them the foretastes of the powers of the age to come, and the like gives added power to the author's application of this promise made by God to Abraham and the patriarchs, and now to the addressees as well.[28] The author has devoted much space

---

25. Attridge, *Hebrews*, 388.

26. Attridge (ibid.) suggests that the author was not the one who made this change, since the same quotation appears in Philo *Conf. ling.* 166. The change, however, is relatively simple such that both Hebrews and Philo could have made this alteration independently.

27. Aristotle writes that people feel confident when "remedies are possible" and when "there are means of help, either great or numerous," and "if it is well with us in regard to the gods" (*Rh.* 2.5.17, 21).

28. Attridge (*Hebrews*, 389 n. 74) draws a fitting contrast between 10:25 and 13:5: with regard to "leaving," God will never do to the believer what some believers are doing to the group and to God.

in this sermon to assisting the addressees to keep their enjoyment of God's benefits constantly before their eyes, so that desire for temporal goods will not hinder their commitment and loyalty and cause them to lose the greater friendship and wealth that God provides for eternity.

Armed with God's assurance, the believer should say with the psalmist, "The LORD is my help; I will not be afraid. What will a human being do to me?" (Ps. 117:6 [LXX], verbatim). The resolve not to be afraid of a human being recalls specifically the examples of Moses' parents and Moses himself, who followed God not fearing the decrees or anger of Pharaoh (11:23, 27), urging the hearers to adopt a bold stance toward the hostility of the unbelieving society. The addressees are to fear God (10:26-31) but not human beings.[29] Rather, they are to stand in the face of their neighbors' assaults (whatever form these will take), assured of God's "mercy and favor for timely help" (4:16). They can win their current contest, for their ally is none other than God, the judge of all.

The author has built his exhortations in 13:5-6 on several prominent deliberative topics. First, he grounds them in the virtue of temperance, censuring the desire for money (13:5) particularly in light of the "wealth" to which they do have access, namely, God's help (13:5-6). Temperance is emerging in these last chapters as an important ancillary resource for urging the hearers to remain committed to the group (12:16-17; 13:5-6), which requires them to refuse to seek pleasure now at the expense of the benefits that God affords and will confer for eternity. This blends easily into topics of expediency. Hebrews 13:5-6 articulates a very desirable good that the author claims the hearers presently enjoy. This is a good that is threatened by a believer's desire to "better" his or her position in society. Such a path must ultimately be inexpedient, even though some appear already to have begun down that road (10:25). Finally, the assurance of God's perpetual help shows that perseverance in commitment to the group, even if one never recovers one's earthly resources, is ultimately feasible as well, emboldening the believer to tackle the challenge of remaining faithful as indeed something well within his or her grasp (the boast of 13:6).

13:7-16

The next block of exhortations, while moving through a wide array of topics, never departs from the author's goal of moving the hearers to find the center

---

29. The author has strategically and clearly mapped out proper objects to fear and objects not to fear through his repetition of words built on the root φοβ- ("fear"). The addressees are to fear failing to enter the promised rest (4:1) and experiencing God's anger toward the ungrateful (10:27, 31) but are not to fear death (2:15), human powers and their demands (11:23, 27), or hostile human beings in general (13:6).

that gives them stability and firmness in their Christian hope, and thus also reliability in their relationship with, and obligations to, one another and Jesus:

> Remember your leaders, who spoke the word of God to you; looking to the end result of their conduct, imitate their trust. Jesus Christ is yesterday and today the same — and forever. Do not be swept along by diverse and foreign teachings, for it is a fine thing for the heart to be made firm by favor, not by foods. Those who follow such practices were not benefited by them. We have an altar from which those worshiping at the tent have no authority to eat. The bodies of these animals whose blood is taken into the holy places through the high priest for a sin offering are burned up outside the camp. Therefore Jesus, in order that he might sanctify the people through his own blood, also suffered outside the gate. Now then, let us go out to him outside the camp, bearing his reproach; for we have here no lasting city, but we are seeking the one that is coming. Through him, let us continually offer to God a sacrifice of praise, that is, the fruit of lips confessing his name. Do not forget doing good and sharing, for with sacrifices of such a kind God is well pleased.

The author begins by inviting the hearers to reflect on the model of their earlier leaders. Speaking "the word" or "the word of God" is frequently used to mean proclaiming the gospel,[30] and the author has already mentioned once before the addressees' experience of hearing this word through those who witnessed and heard Jesus (2:3). These leaders showed a "way of life" that was firmly committed to Jesus and to the hope announced in the gospel, and it is specifically the "outcome" (ἔκβασιν) of their way of life that the author lifts up for the hearers' consideration. This word may point the hearers to the idea of the heavenly goal that is the "result" of every life lived in trust and faithfulness toward God, but it frequently appears as a euphemism for "death." Like the heroes of faith celebrated in chapter 11, these figures lived and died as witnesses to the certainty of God's promises in Jesus. Now that they, too, belong to the assembly of the "spirits of the perfected righteous" (12:23) and have joined the "cloud of witnesses" (12:1), they are suitable models for the hearers' imitation. Their fixedness in trust and loyalty toward God led them to inherit the promises,[31] and now their "faith" is commended to the addressees as another prop for their own trust.

The leaders' firmness was made possible by the unwavering reliability of the object of their trust, Jesus. The argumentative significance of the declaration "Jesus Christ is the same yesterday and today and forever" (13:8) is some-

---

30. Attridge (*Hebrews*, 391 n. 19) cites Acts 4:29, 31; 8:25; 13:46; 16:32; Phil. 1:14 as examples of this.

31. Hebrews 13:7 (μιμεῖσθε τὴν πίστιν) recalls rather directly 6:12 (μιμηταὶ . . . τῶν διὰ πίστεως . . . κληρονομούντων τὰς ἐπαγγελίας).

times lost on commentators.[32] This conviction provides, however, the bedrock of the trust of the departed leaders as well as the trust that the addressees are called to exhibit if they are to attain the "preservation of their souls" (10:39). Jesus' perpetual "sameness" is more than a confessional declaration about the unchangeableness of Jesus. Here, as in 1:12,[33] "sameness" means "constancy" and is opposed to "changeableness" and "unreliability." Dio provides a very helpful comparative text in the context of his oration on "distrust" (ἀπιστία). Complaining that "with human beings there is no constancy (βέβαιον) or truthfulness at all" (*Or.* 74.4), he writes:

> What someone has said about Fortune might much rather be said about human beings, namely, that no one knows about any one whether he will remain as he is until the morrow (τὸ μηδένα εἰδέναι περὶ μηδενός, εἰ μέχρι τῆς αὔριον διαμενεῖ τοιοῦτος). At any rate, men do violate the compacts made with each other and give each other different advice and, believing one course to be expedient, actually pursue another. (*Or.* 74.21-22)

Because one can never be sure that a person will remain tomorrow (when it comes time to deliver in some area in which one has trusted that person) as he or she is today (when trust is first called for), it seems to Dio more prudent not to trust human beings insofar as one can avoid it. The author of Hebrews avers, however, that there is one man whose character and word do not change through the ages but who remains constant. Because of this constancy, the hearers may trust Jesus today and tomorrow even as "yesterday" their leaders trusted Jesus and were not disappointed. Jesus' favor, which is not here today and gone tomorrow but always present toward his faithful ones, becomes thereby the source of stability for the hearts of the addressees (see 13:9b).[34] This is an effective summary of a major thrust of the sermon, the reliability of the "one who has promised" (6:13-20; 10:23; 11:11).

As in Hebrews 1:10-12 and Dio's oration, sameness and constancy were

---

32. Ellingworth (*Hebrews,* 704), for example, remarks: "This apparently isolated statement has no syntactic connection with what precedes or follows; its content also seems general and unrelated to the surrounding exhortations."

33. Heaven and earth "will perish, but you remain. . . . They will be changed, but you are the same." The author has effectively bracketed the sermon with contrasts between the reliable foundation for trust, upon which to build one's happiness, and unreliable foundations, upon which those who build are destined for loss.

34. Attridge's insight (*Hebrews,* 393: "the emphasis is clearly on the eternal 'sameness' of Christ. Because Jesus Christ is an integral part of the eternal divine realm that is unchanging, he is now, for the Christian addressees, a sure foundation for their communal life [vs 7] and doctrine [vs 9]"), while certainly on track, can now be sharpened and refined in light of the Dio text. Filson (*Yesterday,* 50) and Pfitzner (*Hebrews,* 194) correctly read this verse as stressing the "loyalty," "steadfast integrity," and "constancy of Jesus Christ."

opposed to mutability and unreliability, so here the constancy of Jesus as a firm foundation for trust and self-investment stands in contrast to "strange and variegated teachings." In a sermon that has repeatedly contrasted the "many" (who are ineffective, weak, and unreliable) with the "one" (who is effective, indestructible, and completely reliable), the very multiplicity of these teachings is a strike against them when set alongside the single, unmovable focus on Jesus Christ (13:8). Many suggestions have been made concerning the content of these teachings that the author regards as "foreign" in contrast to pure trust in Jesus,[35] but James W. Thompson's conclusion on this point is wise.[36] He cautions us not to read 13:9-10 as a polemic against Christian heresies about which "we could only speculate," but rather as a final instance of the author's technique of using the levitical cultic system simply and rhetorically as a foil for expressing the great value of the provisions for worship and perseverance that Christians enjoy.[37] The rhetorical purpose of 13:9, therefore, is to provide a foil for the secure foundation for trust, Jesus, whom the community's founders found to be an ample and adequate anchor for their own hope's arrival at port. Any teaching that is older or newer or other than the teaching about Jesus' effective mediation of God's favor and the way in which to remain in favor threatens the hearers' own stability in Christ — following such inferior, human-made teachings threatens to see them "carried off," precisely the opposite of remaining in a "fixed" place of "firmness" (another translation for "faith" and a value elevated by the author in such places as 6:19-20, where he speaks of their secure anchor; 2:1-4, where "drifting away" rather than "holding" at port is the grave danger facing the community; and 10:23, where he urges the hearers to hold firm and unwavering the confession of their hope).[38]

The remainder of 13:9 presents a rationale for this warning against "strange and varied teachings": "for it is a fine thing (καλὸν) for the heart to be made secure by grace (βεβαιοῦσθαι χάριτι), not by foods by means of which those attending to them were not benefited (ὠφελήθησαν)." The attention in

---

35. Prominent among these suggestions are: (1) Judaizing tendencies, (2) ascetic regulations, often associated with (3) Gnostic tendencies, (4) syncretism, involving Christian participation in the mystery cults, and (5) celebrations of the eucharist involving harmful scruples about the bread and wine. For a fuller discussion, see the fine summaries in Filson, *Yesterday*, 50-52 and Attridge, *Hebrews*, 394-96.

36. See Thompson, *Beginnings*, 141-51, especially 150-51; Filson (*Yesterday*, 152) concurs.

37. The fact that the "food" that Christians have the right to ingest from their altar is never specified (one might say, never materializes) reinforces the impression that the author is, in fact, playing with "foods" entirely metaphorically. In fact, even the "food" of "those serving in the tent" goes up in smoke in the next verses (13:10-11).

38. Hebrews 10:23 is a significant verse that brings together quite directly the reliability of God as the foundation for the firmness or fixedness of the addressees.

this verse has been more directly on the reliability or fixedness of the Christian in response to the reliability and fixedness of Jesus (13:8), through which the departed leaders were able to remain steadfast throughout their lives. It is "grace" that enables the heart to be constant.[39] The lack of a specific referent here (it is not "God's favor" or "Christ's favor," but merely "grace") allows the term to embrace in general the complete orientation of the believer toward God as his or her patron and Christ as mediator. Discovering stability for one's life in the reciprocity of this relationship is "noble" or "honorable." Any other course is of "no benefit."

The "diverse and strange teachings" are relegated to the level of "foods." This term recalls 9:10 (the only prior reference to "food"), where food and drink and regulations for the body sum up the regulations for the limited access to God provided for under the first covenant. The author recapitulates his basic distinction between the character of the old covenant (external regulations of limited efficacy and scope) and the new covenant (the favor of God that has been gained for us by Jesus) in order to safeguard the addressees against modifications of, or additions to, the gospel that are bound to arise and perhaps have already drifted through — as at Colossae, where props of asceticism were promoted to strengthen one's relationship with God (cf. Col. 2:8-19). Rather than address these teachings in detail, the author finds it sufficient merely to associate them with the religiously impotent "foods" with which the old covenant was concerned. Just as the foods of the old cultus have not "benefited" those who "walk"[40] in them, not bringing them into God's real presence, so all external observances and rituals, however spiritual they may seem, only detract from the one thing that provides stability of faith. The exhortation in 13:7-9 becomes a way, in parting, to affirm the solitary way to God as the grace-relationship established by Christ. The importance of patronage scripts for the underlying logic of this passage is reinforced by the author's contrast between "grace" (χάρις) and the alternatives or additives that "do not benefit" (οὐκ ὠφελήθησαν) those who pursue them.[41] As the exhortation continues, the emphasis

---

39. The comment by Attridge (*Hebrews*, 393) that "the reference to grace . . . recalls a minor, but recurrent motif involving the assistance which comes from the divine throne (4:16), which characterizes the 'spirit' (10:29), and which the addressees have been warned not to lose (12:15)" shows the deficiencies of a lexical approach to "grace" in Hebrews. Our investigation of the extent to which patron-client roles, expectations, and obligations are applied in this sermon shows that it is really far from a "minor" motif in Hebrews.

40. "Walking" is a common metaphor in Christian literature for one's manner of conduct, specifically with regard to living in accordance with a body of regulations (Rom. 8:4; 13:13; 14:15; 2 Cor. 4:2; 5:7; 10:2; Gal. 5:16; Eph. 2:2; 4:1, 17; 5:2; Phil. 3:17-18; Col. 1:10; 2:6; 1 Thess. 2:12; 4:1; 2 John 6, etc.); cf. Jewish *halakha*, a term derived from the Hebrew verb *halak*, "to walk."

41. See Pfitzner, *Hebrews*, 197: "The simplest solution to the *crux interpretum* of verse

on "grace" will come full circle (recalling the circle dance of the three Graces) as the author returns once more to consider Jesus' endurance of hardship to bring us benefit (13:12) and then the response that the believer is honor-bound to make (13:13-16) to such a selfless patron.

Hebrews 13:10-16 continues to function as a fitting recapitulation of the argument and exhortations of the whole sermon. In these few verses the author reminds the hearers of the advantage gained by Jesus' priestly mediation (13:10; cf. 4:14-16; 5:9-10; 10:19-22); the act of Jesus' sacrifice and its effects for the people (13:11-12; cf. 9:1–10:18); the fitting response of loyalty, honor, and service by those who receive Jesus' benefits and are themselves consecrated to enter God's presence, expressed through the metaphors of sacrifice and cult (13:13-16; cf. 3:6, 12-14; 6:9-10; 10:19-25, 32-39; 12:1-4, 13-17); and the goal of the pilgrimage of faith (13:14; cf. 4:1-11; 6:19-20; 11:8-16; 12:22-24). Specifically, 13:13-14 urges a response based in a deep loyalty to Jesus, 13:15 calls for bringing public honor to the Patron, and 13:16 calls for obedient service directed toward one's fellow believers. All of this is interpreted as the worship that pleases God (13:16; cf. 12:28).

The declaration that "we have an altar from which those who minister at the tent have no authority to eat" (13:10) affirms the privilege that has been gained for believers by inverting the normal Jewish discourse about priests' rights to eat at certain tables in the temple, from which nonpriests cannot eat. Priests were entitled to eat the "bread of the Presence" (or the "shewbread") laid out before the Lord and apportioned specifically for the priests (Lev. 24:5-9), as well as portions of the meat of sacrifices (cf. Lev. 7:5-6 Num. 18:9-20). The author draws attention now to the altar that the Christians "have,"[42] at which the priests of the old cultus have no such prerogatives. This claim reinforces the impression that what formerly was accessible only to priests is now accessible to all believers, but it goes one step further to exclude those who serve under the old covenant. The "altar" is, as Harold Attridge observes,[43] deliberately ambiguous so as to recall the entire discussion of Christ's priestly sacrifice and its benefits for the Christian community.

The "altar" is significant in ancient Israelite religion (as in Greek and Ro-

---

9 is to read it in connection with 9:9-10: the old sacrificial system dealt with externals like 'food and drink,' things that could not purify the conscience. Only the sacrifice of Christ can purify the conscience (heart) and mediate heavenly grace." We have seen throughout the commentary how this nebulous expression "mediate heavenly grace" can be refined and clarified by means of reading the sermon in light of the social context of patronage.

42. It has been very important to the author to delineate for the addressees, who have lost much, what exactly they do "have." The list has included a "high priest" of a specific, exalted quality (4:14-15; 8:1), hope as a firm and secure anchor (6:19), boldness for entrance into God's realm (10:19), and a cloud of spectators (12:1).

43. Attridge, *Hebrews,* 396.

man religion) as the place of transaction between human beings and God (or the gods). Richard Nelson captures this significance beautifully:

> Human space consisted of the land from which Israel brought offerings and the temple courts. God's sacred space consisted of the temple building itself and heaven. At the intersection of the two was the altar. The altar was thus a marginal area, and area of overlap between the sphere of the human and the sphere of the divine.[44]

Jesus is now the place where the human and divine overlap, the place of intersection. This is not a claim made on the basis of four centuries of Christological controversy but on the basis of the first two chapters of Hebrews, the first of which presents the Son as sharing in God's essence and being the imprint of God's being, the second of which speaks at length about the Son's sharing in flesh and blood so as to take on the plight of the many sons and daughters. Hebrews 10:19-22 even goes so far as to speak of the point of entrance into the heavenly holy of holies as the flesh of Jesus, underscoring Jesus' place at the intersection, or at least the threshold, of the divine and human realms. Jesus is also the place in which other contradictory qualities that separate human beings from the divine are mediated and resolved: "mortal" and "immortal" (2:9; 7:16) and "subject to temptation" and "sinless" or "beyond weakness" (2:18; 4:15; 7:28). The author has presented a characterization of Jesus that prepares the hearers to understand him as the "area of overlap between the sphere of the human and the sphere of the divine," and hence the focus of mediation and means of access to God's favor.

The exclusion of the "ministers of the tent" from eating at this altar suggests, although by no means necessitates, that the believers do have the right to eat there. The eucharistic overtones of this verse have been much explored and debated.[45] Commenting on the eating of meat from sacrificial offerings, Richard Nelson writes: "Meat derived from violence has been transformed into food eaten in a meal, which establishes community. . . . The blood that had the potential to destroy relationships (Gen. 9:4-6) has become instead the mechanism to promote those same communal ties through atonement (Lev. 17:11)."[46] The eucharist is the ultimate expression of this principle, wherein a violent and bloody execution is transformed into a meal that provides a model for the new community of believers[47] and sustains that new community. For hearers accus-

---

44. Nelson, *Raising Up a Faithful Priest*, 61.

45. See Thurén, *Lobopfer*, 83-91; R. Williamson, "The Eucharist in the Epistle to the Hebrews," *NTS* 21 (1975): 300-312.

46. Nelson, *Raising Up a Faithful Priest*, 66.

47. Hence Paul's objections to reproducing the old community of the Greco-Roman society with its hierarchies and inequities within the context of this covenant meal (1 Cor. 11:17-34). See Theissen, *Social Setting*, 145-74.

tomed to participating in this ritual, an allusion to it here in 13:10 is unavoidable and has the potential to enrich their understanding of that meal and to safeguard them against an overly materialistic interpretation of its power and significance (as the author has laid ample stress on the once-for-all and unrepeatable quality of Jesus' sacrifice on the cross). Nevertheless, it is a resonance that the author will himself neither develop nor exclude — whether or not it is heard depends more on the hearer than the author, who is more directly concerned with the historic and decisive act of Jesus on behalf of "the people" (13:11-12). Hebrews 13:10 speaks allusively, then, of the unique privilege enjoyed by the addressees in terms of access to God's favor, recalling the central discourse of Hebrews. While others have the shadow, the addressees enjoy the real thing and should not relinquish this privilege for any lesser good.

The author moves on immediately to develop an analogy between Jesus' death and the Yom Kippur sacrifices that were not in fact eaten by the priests of the tabernacle but burnt up entirely. The levitical rule is that, if blood is taken from the offering for sprinkling the holy places, the rest of the body must be delivered to God as well (see Lev. 6:30; 16:27).[48] Hebrews 13:11 recontextualizes Leviticus 16:27 (LXX): "the bull for the sin offering and the goat for the sin offering, whose blood was carried into the holy places to effect expiation — they will carry them outside the camp and will burn them up with fire." While even the syntax of 13:11 recalls that of the underlying OT reference, the author does make a few significant alterations. The specific references to the cow and goat are replaced with the general term "animals," the reference to "making expiation" (ἐξιλάσασθαι) is tellingly deleted (since this is the effect of Jesus' sacrifice alone), and the role of the high priest as the bearer of the blood into the holy places is introduced explicitly, for the sake of clearer contrast with Jesus.

The phrase "outside the camp" (ἔξω τῆς παρεμβολῆς) provides the thread of continuity through 13:13. It provides a link with Jesus' experience of crucifixion "outside the gate" of Jerusalem (ἔξω τῆς πύλης), a reminiscence of historical fact.[49] The prescription for the disposal of carcasses of atonement sacrifices in Leviticus 16:27 provides a frame for interpreting Jesus' death "outside the camp" as a sacrifice "to sanctify the people" (13:12). The author demonstrates the superiority of Jesus' sacrifice over the levitical cultus in two ways: (a) the sacrifice involves "his own blood" rather than "the blood of the animals," thus a far more costly and self-invested medium of mediation (see 9:12-14, 25-26;

---

48. The "ministers of the tent" truly leave these verses empty and hungry, for they have no authority to eat at the Christians' altar, and even their own sacrificial animals here go up in smoke.

49. See John 19:17-20. So important was the tradition of Jesus dying outside Jerusalem that it affects Matthew's retelling of the parable of the wicked tenants, who first cast the son out of the vineyard and *then* kill him (Matt. 21:39; cf. Mark 12:8).

10:4-10); and (b) this sacrifice serves truly "to sanctify the people" (cf. 9:9-10, 14; 10:1, 14), whereas the animal blood was offered "concerning sins" but had a more limited purpose (9:13; 10:2-4). The crucifixion is thus once more grounded in the purpose of God for the preparation of the "many sons and daughters" to enter God's presence.

This reminder of Jesus' selfless act of beneficence leads directly to a call to render gratitude in equal measure (13:13) as the hearers are invited to make a like return to their Benefactor: "let us go out to him outside the camp." Gratitude should compel the hearers not to flinch from the cost of being loyal, reverent, grateful beneficiaries of Jesus' benefits.[50] Their debt to Jesus should lead them to leave the camp as he did for them and to bear reproach for his sake as he did for them — in short, to make this response of gratitude the most important agenda for their lives, which no other consideration will mute or diminish. Richard Nelson and Helmut Koester read this "going out" as a "balance" to the language of approaching and entering, a call "to leave the security of holy space for the cruciform 'disgrace' of profane space."[51] Such a reading, however, misses entirely the ideological strategy of Hebrews, which urges the hearers to accept that "drawing near to God" and going "outside the camp" to follow Christ are precisely the same move. The believers enter holy space as they leave behind their place in the camp, in human society, refusing with Abraham to look back (11:13-16) to their earthly city as they move toward the heavenly city that is also the heavenly sanctum and divine rest.[52]

The place "outside the camp" is ambiguous. On the one hand, it is a place of uncleanness, where lepers dwell (Lev. 13:45-46; Num. 5:2-4), the defiled wait out their purification (Num. 12:14-15; 31:19-20), and lawbreakers are executed (Num. 15:32-36). On the other hand, there are "clean places" outside the camp where sacrificial corpses are burned (Lev. 4:12; 6:11; 16:27) and, most strikingly, where God's presence is to be found (cf. Exod. 33:1-7). Harold Attridge finds "the tradition that the tabernacle was outside the camp (Exod. 33:7-11)"

---

50. Recall here the discussion of Seneca's description of the mind-set of the grateful (see "A Closer Look — Gratitude in Greco-Roman Ethics"), who willingly endure any loss rather than fail to show honor and loyalty to their benefactors (*Ep. Mor.* 81.27; *Ben.* 4.20.2). Worth hearing again is the characterization of the ingrate (*Ben.* 4.24.2): "It is the ungrateful person who thinks, 'I should have liked to return gratitude, but I fear the expense, I fear the danger, I shrink from giving offense; I would rather consult my own interest.'"

51. Nelson, *Raising Up a Faithful Priest*, 152; Helmut Koester, "Outside the Camp: Hebrews 13:9-14," *HTR* 55 (1962): 299-315.

52. Lane's (*Hebrews 9–13*, 544-45) critique of Koester ("Outside the Camp," 299-315) on this point is very apt: "The identification of 'outside the camp' with 'the realm of the profane' is an imposition on the text. The writer's concern is not to advocate a separation from the sphere of the cultic so as to embrace the secularity of the world, but rather the acceptance of the reproach of Christian commitment in a hostile environment."

to be "of marginal significance here."[53] This assessment is not accurate. Throughout the sermon the movement into the presence of God in the real realm has been presented as the movement away from security in and belonging to the earthly camp. The way "out" from rootedness in the temporal society becomes the way "in" to the unshakable realm of God. The Exodus tradition is most suited to this image: "Moses, taking God's tent, pitched it outside the camp (ἔξω τῆς παρεμβολῆς) far from the camp . . . and it happened that everyone seeking the Lord went out of the camp (ἔξω τῆς παρεμβολῆς) to the tent" (Exod. 33:7 [LXX]). The Exodus 33 narrative provides a sort of prototype for the overturning of traditional thinking about the relative value of inside and outside. The space "inside the camp" becomes the place of sin and unholiness against which a holy God might "break out" to consume the unrighteous; the place "outside the camp" becomes the place where one approaches God. The author affirms that the true sacred space is to be found "out there" in the realm of the invisible: the community has been sanctified to move toward and eventually enter that sacred space (10:19-22), and the life of the community is itself sacralized as it moves toward its goal, offering its appointed cultus of thanksgiving and mutual service along the way (13:15-16). They are not, however, leaving the sacred behind. They are leaving the profane (the temporary and shakable world) behind and moving toward the sacred (entering the rest of God and their heavenly city, 13:14).[54]

The hearers have throughout the book been urged to "draw near" (προσέρχομαι) and "go into" (εἰσέρχομαι) God's presence — now they are urged to "go out" (ἐξέρχομαι) of the society of humans, the "earthly city," which is not the believers' "abiding city." The three ἔρχομαι verbs ultimately all move in the same direction, creating a clear trajectory for the addressees. They are called to replicate the movement of Abraham (11:8), who also left behind his place in his city to journey toward the city that God had prepared for God's people (11:11-16), and the journey of Moses (11:24-27), who left behind the land of Egypt for the sake of the promise to be bestowed on the "people of God." Rather than withdraw or shrink back into society because of the pressure of human beings (10:25, 37-39), the hearers are being called to continue on their path out from society toward the "city that is coming" (13:14).

This journey entails "bearing Christ's reproach," a phrase that recalls Moses' willingness to do the same (11:25) for the sake of a reward.[55] Choosing to

---

53. Attridge, *Hebrews,* 399 n. 119.

54. So, rightly, Thompson, *Beginnings,* 147-50.

55. Compare Filson, *Yesterday,* 61: the author "urges the Christians addressed to break ties with whatever would prevent full loyalty to the Christ who offered himself as the once-for-all sacrifice for sins. . . . They must 'go forth,' and since that will bring them under criticism, they must willingly bear the reproach that will come to them as they live in this new sit-

bear Christ's reproach, however, is the wise and noble choice, as Moses demonstrated so long ago. That reproach means, in the end, greater wealth than the treasures of Egypt, for it is the mark of the one who has joined the people of God and thus come into the "eternal inheritance" of God's sons and daughters. Persevering in the course that leads to the experience of loss and reproach now for Jesus' sake is ultimately the expedient course, as the author reminds the hearers in the pun contrasting the lack of a "lasting" (μένουσαν) city here with the expectation of the "coming" (μέλλουσαν) city that will endure eternally. Investment in one's position in this world, especially if it means loss of a place in God's kingdom, is inexpedient. This world offers no security or happiness that can withstand the eschatological shaking (12:26-28) or conflagration (12:29). When this world is bracketed as "not lasting," its benefits or goods cannot compare to those of the unshakable kingdom.

Hebrews 13:11-14 articulates a particular ethos for the Christian community — one that the author has been promoting throughout the closing exhortation. It is an ethos best described as "permanent liminality," to use a phrase coined by Victor Turner to describe the way of life promoted by St. Francis of Assisi by means of dedication to complete poverty: "Francis appears quite deliberately to be compelling the friars to inhabit the fringes and interstices of the social structure of his time, and to keep them in a permanent liminal state, where, so the argument of this book would suggest, the optimal conditions inhere for the realization of communitas."[56]

From his study of rituals of status-transformation in primitive cultures (which Richard Nelson has, in turn, found extremely useful for considering ancient Israelite religion), Turner derives the following schema. The "liminal" state is usually a temporary state describing the intermediate step in a rite of passage that takes a human being from one "normal" state through a ritual transformation to a new "normal" state. Such rites of passage include, for example, the transition from childhood to adulthood, from lay person to priest (consecration), from citizen to king (coronation). On either side of the ritual lay two "normal" states of being: the ritual itself "breaks down" the subject's connection with the first state of being before creating the new state of being. The period of "breaking down" is the liminal state, during which the subject is often separated from the rest of society, suffers the loss of any status in society,

---

uation." Delitzsch (*Hebrews*, 389-90) also perceives a social component to the author's exhortation to go "outside the camp": "let us no longer continue in their society who have rejected the Lord Jesus, but go forth to Him outside the camp.... To forsake their company ... for His sake is to involve ourselves not merely in future but in present shame or reproach; but this reproach is the reproach of Christ, a shame which we share with Him, and in bearing which we are made like Him."

56. Turner, *Ritual Process*, 145.

is placed on an equal level with others also undergoing the ritual, and yet is often exposed to ritual impositions of pain or reproach by those performing or observing the ritual.[57]

At many points, such characteristics correspond to the state of the addressees. They have been undergoing an informal, but nonetheless effective, status-degradation ritual at the hands of their neighbors, being censured, reproached, and even physically abused and materially deprived for their "deviant" behavior. The author, however, has taken what society intends as status-degradation (and correctional procedures) and cast it more in terms of a status-elevation ritual. They have been separated from their former, "normal" identity as Jews or pagans, having suffered the loss of property and reputation and other such things as bind them to their former status in that society. They have been brought together into a community marked by cooperation, sharing, and equality, within which they are rendered sacred for intimate access to God and are being fitted for their new, glorious, "normal" state, which they shall "enter" at the eschatological shaking of the material realm. Like Abraham, Moses, the martyrs and marginalized, Jesus, and even their departed leaders, the hearers are called to embrace the liminal status they currently have in this world, to seek not to return to their former "normal" state but to press on to arrive at their perfected state (following their forerunner and pioneer), that is, their entrance into the abiding realm where their honor as God's children will be fully manifested.

Topics of justice continue to be employed to urge perseverance in the confession. Loyalty to the Benefactor, especially when it is costly, is part of the proper response to favor, especially when that favor has involved great cost on the part of the Benefactor (13:12-14). Calling for Christians, then, to go out to Jesus and to bear his reproach with him is a call to act justly. Hebrews 13:15-16, however, extends the topic of making a fair return for favors received, particularly with a view to bringing honor to the Patron and rendering the services that please him. This response of gratitude is expressed in cultic language, recalling thus both the cultic overtones of the exhortation to gratitude in 12:28 and the costly consecration of the hearers effected by Jesus, which has fitted them to offer these acceptable sacrifices. Cultic language, however, intersects directly with the language of everyday life in these verses, thus working out how the life of the community is in fact sacralized in its entirety.

The first component of the believers' offerings of thanksgiving is the "sacrifice of praise," which is described as the "fruit" or result of "lips confessing God's name" (13:15).[58] This sentence recontextualizes Psalm 49:14 (LXX), "of-

---

57. Ibid., 95-108.

58. These offerings are made "through Jesus," who remains ever the mediator between humanity and God.

fer to God a sacrifice of praise"[59] (see also Ps. 33:2 [LXX]), thus building on a long-standing tradition of the "rationalization" of sacrifice in Jewish religion, namely, the move away from material, animal sacrifices to offerings of another kind, like acts of worship or, as in 13:16, acts of service to others. Within this emerging tradition, praise of God's name was even celebrated as "more acceptable" than animal sacrifices (Ps. 63:31-32 [LXX]). The quotation above from Psalm 49 (LXX), in fact, immediately follows two verses about the irrationality of thinking to give God food and drink in animal sacrifices, presenting then "the sacrifice of praise" as the reasonable alternative. Praise is the "fruit of lips confessing God's name," a phrase that recalls Hosea 14:3. This text identifies the "fruit of our lips" as the appropriate tribute to "give back to God" for the good things God sends.[60] "Confession" of God's name is the response of expanding the honorable reputation of the Patron. The Greek word was frequently chosen by the LXX translators to render the MT "give thanks" (e.g., LXX Ps. 9:2; 17:49-50; 29:2-13; 34:17-18), stressing the public character of thanksgiving as testimony to the generosity of the God (see "A Closer Look — Gratitude in Greco-Roman Ethics" above). Within the setting of the community addressed by the author of Hebrews, this response would no doubt include the offering of praise and worship in the setting of the Christian assembly. The highlighting of "confession," however, underscores also the public dimension of this response — certainly at least in the form of being seen going to the Christian assembly, associating with other believers, and thus confessing the name of Christ. By word and deed, the addressees are called to confess that God's gifts are good and worth the cost of remaining loyal to such a marvelous benefactor, thus honor-

---

59. Compare Heb. 13:15, ἀναφέρωμεν θυσίαν αἰνέσεως διὰ παντὸς τῷ θεῷ, with Ps. 49:14 (LXX), θῦσον τῷ θεῷ θυσίαν αἰνέσεως. The author has changed the verb and added the adverbial expression "continually."

60. Compare Heb. 13:15, καρπὸν χειλέων with Hos. 14:3 (LXX), καρπὸν χειλέων ἡμῶν. This text, together with the translation of "thanksgiving offering" in Lev. 7:12 (LXX) as θυσία αἰνέσεως, "sacrifice of praise," helps us appreciate the resonance of a "sacrifice of praise" with the expectation of gratitude (cf. 12:28). Scholars of ancient Israelite ritual also help establish the context of reciprocity as the primary context for reading such injunctions to offer "sacrifices of praise." Compare Nelson, *Raising Up a Faithful Priest*, 63: "The names of the 'gift offering' and 'peace offering' both carry strong overtones of gift and tribute. . . . Gifts in human society establish or maintain an affinity between giver and recipient. They may also be proffered as tokens of gratitude or obligation." Bruce Chilton (*The Temple of Jesus: His Sacrificial Program within a Cultural History of Sacrifice* [University Park, PA: University of Pennsylvania, 1992], 31, 35) also speaks of ritual generating generosity from the divine and the provision of needful blessings. While this is indeed inherent in sacrifice both in the pagan and Jewish world, so is the thanksgiving offering. "I give so that you may give" has its counterpart in "I give because you gave." This is one avenue for the demonstration of gratitude toward the divine patron, and the demonstration of gratitude for past benefactions also serves to stimulate benefactors to continued generosity toward the loyal and grateful clients.

ing God and spreading his reputation. They are to maintain the "boldness," indeed the "bold witness," that marked their earlier confrontations with their unbelieving neighbors, in which they made an unambiguous confession concerning the goodness of God and God's gifts and the value of God's friendship (10:32-35).

They are also called to offer to God their services on behalf of one another, pooling their resources and looking for opportunities to assist one another as any has need: "do not forget to do good and to share, for with such sacrifices God is well pleased" (13:16). The author's thought is still very deeply rooted in Jewish reflection on what sacrifices God desires. The Israelite prophets frequently declared that animal sacrifices were unacceptable (Isa. 1:10-16; Jer. 14:11-12; Hos. 8:13). This critique of the sacrificial cultus led to proposals for what "sacrifices" and other religious observances (e.g., fasts) would be acceptable to God. Frequently, the prophets' answers tended in the direction of kindness and justice shown to one's fellow Israelite. Amos, for example, calls for an outpouring of just dealings and righteous acts rather than the ritual slaughter of animals (5:21-24); Isaiah calls for care for the poor and homeless as the fast that pleases God (58:3-9), summoning the people to look out for the interests of the poor, the orphan, and the widow so that the ritual sacrifices may again be acceptable (1:11-17). Christian culture widely accepted this sacralization of good deeds toward community members as the offering of acceptable sacrifices. Mark 12:33, for example, elevates love of God and neighbor as "more bountiful than all the burnt offerings and sacrifices"; Paul enjoins the believers to yield their lives in service to God and one another as a "living and holy sacrifice, well pleasing to God" (θυσίαν . . . εὐάρεστον τῷ θεῷ, Rom. 12:1) and commends the Philippian church's gifts to support him as an "acceptable offering, well pleasing to God" (θυσίαν . . . εὐάρεστον τῷ θεῷ, Phil. 4:18). Finally, the author of 1 Peter develops an ideology of Christian identity in which the believers are invited to see themselves collectively as a sacred temple wherein "spiritual sacrifices" that are "wholly acceptable to God" are offered up "through Jesus Christ" (1 Pet. 2:5).

The author of Hebrews also draws on this vast cultural intertexture. While we cannot repay God, who has need of nothing, we can, indirectly, repay God's generosity by extending it to one another (a point made most dramatically in Matt. 25:31-46). The author of Hebrews reinforces this connection between showing gratitude to God and giving assistance to one's sisters and brothers, between honoring God and serving others. Frederick Danker records an inscription in which service to the members of a guild is lauded as honor shown the patron deity of that guild.[61] Similarly, caring for the needy clients of God honors the divine Patron (cf. Prov. 14:31, where honor of God

---

61. Danker, *Benefactor*, 343.

must be reflected in one's relations to the poor and needy). The addressees offer these pleasing sacrifices whenever they show diligence in serving the saints as they have been doing (see 6:10-11). Gratitude toward God must be expressed in the believers' continued effort to build community and maintain solidarity, while withdrawal from fellowship (10:25) and failure to serve the marginalized and imprisoned saints constitute a violation of this basic virtue. Society's onslaughts can be endured if the family of God supports one another. Everyday life is thus made sacral wherever these sacrifices are offered to God — wherever confession of God and Christ are openly made rather than hidden, and wherever assistance is extended toward the fellow Christian, helping him or her to persevere in the group's partnership with one another and with Christ (3:1, 14). The hearers are summoned not to forget (μὴ ἐπιλανθάνεσθε, 13:16) the noble works and investments that God will not forget either ("for God is not unjust to forget," οὐ γὰρ ἄδικος ὁ θεὸς ἐπιλαθέσθαι, 6:9), but which will rather preserve the circle of grace unto the reception of eternal benefactions.

13:17-25

Harold Attridge has shown that 13:18-25 conforms very closely to the pattern for letter closings found in Romans 15:30–16:23; 1 Thessalonians 5:23-28; 2 Timothy 4:19-22; 1 Peter 5:10-14 (where the order of the components is exactly the same); and *1 Clement* 64-65. This pattern of request, benediction, doxology, news and announcements of travel, greetings, and final farewell shows an adaptation of the typical closings of letters in antiquity, particularly in the addition of the benediction and doxology. As with the way Christian leaders modified the epistolary opening formulas, this gives a distinguishing mark to letters within Christian culture. Structurally speaking, it is difficult to decide where to make a meaningful partition between the exhortations that precede and the letter's closing.[62] On the one hand, one might treat the closing as a unit (13:18-25), which would then present 13:17 as more closely connected with the preceding material. Such a division has much to recommend itself, since the injunction to obey church leaders is certainly not unrelated to the thrust of 13:7-16. Remaining firm and constant toward Christ and one another is facilitated by honoring the guidance of respectable leaders, particularly in an environment in which harmful modifications or additions to the gospel seek a hearing in local churches (13:9). The pilgrimage of the addressees out of the camp to

---

62. Attridge (*Hebrews,* 390) and Lane (*Hebrews 9–13,* 521) treat 13:7-19 as a unified block of exhortation, which is especially surprising given the former's excellent treatment of the components of a letter closing.

the abiding city thus would have been initiated by the leaders who brought them the word and now continued under the leaders who exercise watchful care over their souls (13:7, 17), forming a pleasing *inclusio*.[63]

Nevertheless, I consider this exhortation to be more closely related thematically to the closing material, which gives considerable attention to the leadership figures to whom the addressees ought to be looking for guidance and for the ascription of honor or censure — local leaders (13:17, 24), the author and his team (13:18-19, 22), God (13:20-21), and Timothy (13:23). These are the figures whose opinions should influence the addressees. The local leaders will "give an account" of the people with whose spiritual growth they have been charged (13:17); the benediction reminds the hearers a final time of the central importance of "pleasing God," assuring them that God is working in them to produce those qualities and fruits that please him (13:20-21); the author and Timothy both expect to visit the hearers in the immediate future, when they will affirm the faithful, censure the wavering in person (13:19, 23), and discover and reinforce the effects of the written sermon delivered in advance of their impending visit:

> Pray for us, for we are persuaded that we have a good conscience, in all things desiring to conduct ourselves nobly. I encourage you to do this all the more, in order that I may be restored to you quickly. And may the God of peace, who led up from the dead the great shepherd of the sheep by the blood of the eternal covenant — our Lord Jesus — make you complete in every good thing in order to do his will, fashioning in you what is well pleasing before him through Jesus Christ, to whom be honor forever. Amen. And I encourage you, sisters and brothers: bear with my word of exhortation, for indeed I have written to you briefly. You know that our brother Timothy has been released, with whom, if he comes quickly, I will see you. Greet all your leaders and all the holy ones. Those from Italy greet you. Favor be with you all.

This epistolary closing also contains several features that would fulfill the task of the *peroratio*, or the epilogue of an oration,[64] particularly with regard to leaving the hearers favorably disposed toward the speaker. Aristotle (*Rh.* 3.19.1) observes that perorations tended to address any number of four basic goals: "dispose the hearer favourably towards oneself and unfavourably towards the adversary; to amplify and depreciate; to excite the emotions of the hearer; to recapitulate." Hebrews 13, as we have seen, does recapitulate the major points and, especially, exhortations of the sermon, and the benediction of 13:20-21

---

63. Lane (*Hebrews 9–13*, 553) and Attridge (*Hebrews*, 401) both note this return to the interest in leaders, but neither one decides to highlight it by beginning a new section after 13:17, running on instead to 13:19.

64. Scholars need not choose between analyzing these texts as letters or as speeches, but they would profit from using both kinds of analysis side by side.

will also serve this end. Of the other functions, this author's closing serves mainly the first, the making of a final appeal to ethos. Since the pastoral situation is not an adversarial one, as Paul faced in Galatia, there is no place for vituperation against opponents (cf. Gal. 6:12-13). The *Rhetorica ad Herennium* provides several topics from which a speaker might arouse the goodwill of the hearers, one of which involves "the topic of our own person" (*Rhet. Her.* 1.4.8): "praising our services without arrogance and revealing also our past conduct toward the republic, or toward our parents, friends, or the audience.... likewise by setting forth our disabilities, need, loneliness, and misfortune, and pleading for our hearers' aid." The author of Hebrews includes several of these subtopics: he speaks of his noble motives and clear conscience with regard to his past conduct (13:18) and asks for the hearers' help in the form of earnest prayer (13:18-19). The pronouncing of the benediction also affirms his own goodwill toward the hearers (13:20-21).

The author enjoins the addressees to obey their leaders — those who now watch over their souls (13:17) as opposed to those leaders who brought them the gospel and the outcome of whose pilgrimage of faith is now a matter of record (13:7). The rationale provided by the author points to the function of these leaders as servants of God, watching over the people as stewards, that is, as those who must "render an account." This is a common expression for standing before the judgment seat of God: sinners "give an account" to God in Matthew 12:36; 1 Peter 4:5 (Acts 19:40 is similar, in that the citizens of Ephesus would be unable to "give an account" to the governing authorities for their riotous gathering against Paul). The usage here is more akin to the meaning of the idiom in Luke 16:2, where the steward must "give an account" of his management of the master's household. These leaders are, in effect, stewards in the household of God (3:6; 10:19), who exercise authority on the basis of their responsibility before God, a responsibility discharged now in the role of servant leaders who "lose sleep" in order to exercise oversight of the community of believers. While it is risky to infer too much about church polity from a single verse, the author's choice of rationale for obedience gives the impression of a less fully developed conception of church "offices" that would entail a complete routinization of authority, that is, a vesting of authority in a traditional office rather than in "function" before God.[65]

The hearers are to respond to their leaders' directions in such a way as to bring joy to the leaders rather than make them groan at their charge. The author suggests directly that it would be inexpedient for the community if their leaders' ministry is a cause for sorrow. Cooperation is to be the hallmark of the Christian community in every way — from treating one another as the best of

---

65. See F. Laub, "Verkündigung und Gemeindeamt: Die Autorität der ἡγούμενοι Hebr 13, 7.17.24," *SNTU* 6-7 (1981-82): 169-90.

kin, to the pooling of resources to help those in need persevere in their commitment to the group, and now to having a positive attitude toward those entrusted with the protection and direction of the group. Energy spent on conflict is energy unavailable for edification, something always needed when the church itself rests in a hostile environment. If the leaders receive the support and cooperation of their fellow believers, however, they can serve as a first line of defense against false teachings from without as well as weakening from within. The fact that the author mentions the inexpediency of making the leaders "groan" in close proximity to their impending account to God for their charge suggests more threatening admonition: not only will the community itself benefit less in the present time if their leaders' ministry is hindered by opposition within the group, but the hearers will fare worse when the leaders bear witness to the pride and disobedience of the insubordinate.[66]

Even while the addressees are to be mindful of those leaders in their midst, they are also enjoined to pray for itinerant leaders of the movement such as the author and those with him (13:18-19).[67] That the author is part of a team of some kind is evident in his alternation from first person plural pronouns ("pray for *us*," "*we* are persuaded," 13:18) to first person singular ("*I* exhort you," 13:19; see also 13:23). The author gives no direct information concerning his situation, save that he was formerly present with the addressees,[68] is currently separated from them, and wishes to "be restored" to them as soon as possible. Harold Attridge correctly surmises that the content of the author's prayer request is simply that he can return to them "sooner rather than later."[69] Hebrews 13:18-19 provides an instance of the sort of help one can expect from the "throne of favor" (4:14-16), and the hearers are urged to seek "timely help" for the speaker himself. The speaker's expectations that such prayers are indeed effective and that God will help reinforce the reality of the assistance available for

---

66. Thus Attridge, *Hebrews,* 402; Pfitzner, *Hebrews,* 202. There is no compelling reason to think, however, that the addressees have been showing disrespect toward, or acting antagonistically against, their leaders. Since the author devotes only a single verse to this topic, it is more likely that he is merely encouraging them to keep on doing a good thing by cooperating with their leaders, advocating their intentionality with regard to submission and willingness to be given guidance. Lane (*Hebrews 9–13,* 556), for example, reads more from this verse into the situation of the hearers than guidelines for mirror reading would warrant. This is all the more apparent when one compares Hebrews with texts where conflict over leadership was indeed problematic (e.g., 2 Corinthians, 3 John, and *1 Clement*).

67. Such requests for prayer were a common element of the closings of Christian letters (see Rom. 15:30-31; Col. 4:3; 1 Thess. 5:25; 2 Thess. 3:1).

68. Lane (*Hebrews 9–13,* 558) perceptively comments that the sermon was not originally anonymous — the hearers had intimate acquaintance with the author and knew his identity, even if posterity has not received this information.

69. Attridge, *Hebrews,* 403.

the hearers themselves. The author may, in fact, be counting on his ability to come visit them and encourage their perseverance in person. Within his request for prayer, the author affirms the noble conduct of himself and his team and the sincerity and nobility of their motives. They possess the "good conscience" (καλὴν συνείδησιν) before God that signifies the absence of obstacles between the speaker and the God who will grant their prayer, and between the speaker and the hearers whose mediation he seeks.

The benediction that follows weaves together several important themes from the earlier exposition (7:11–10:18) and exhortations (11:1–13:16). The reference to God as the "God of peace" has a distinctly Pauline ring, again suggesting some influence by the apostle upon this author.[70] God is further identified as the active cause of Jesus' resurrection from the dead, thus again as the one who has power to bring life from death, an emphasis running throughout Hebrews 11. This facet of the Easter event is frequently more significant in early Christian literature than the bare fact that "Jesus rose." Many hymns current in the church celebrate the fact that "He arose," but something is lost when this triumph over death is not seen particularly within the context of God's act on behalf of Jesus. In Acts 2 and 3 it is the sign of God's legitimation of Jesus as the teacher of God's ways, as Savior and Lord, counter to the opinion of most Jewish leaders; in Romans 1:4 it is the manifestation of God's affirmation of Jesus as his Son. In Hebrews 13:20 it signifies God's acceptance of the covenant established by Jesus' sacrifice.[71] Jesus is identified here as "the great shepherd of the sheep," whom God "led up from the dead." The author has framed this sentence on the basis of Isaiah 63:11, where God raises up Moses "from the earth" as "shepherd of the sheep" (τὸν ποιμένα τῶν προβάτων).[72] The author does not develop a comparison here, nor a polemic against Moses, but merely derives his language from this source, applying it to the mediator of the new covenant with some appropriate changes. First, rather than "raise up from the earth," the author says "led up from the dead," a reference to Jesus' resurrection. The change of verb is potentially significant, as it recalls 2:10, where God "leads the many sons and daughters to glory." Second, the title "great" is added, as it has been elsewhere in Hebrews (cf. 10:19): just as Jesus is the "great" priest or "great" high priest, so he is the "great" shepherd.

The author provides a new metaphor that informs the hearers about their relationship to Jesus. They are all ultimately under his care, even if they currently are also under the watchful supervision of their "leaders" (13:17). The description of Jesus as a shepherd is widespread in Christian culture (John

---

70. See Rom. 15:33; 16:20; 2 Cor. 13:11; Phil. 4:9; 1 Thess. 5:23; Attridge, *Hebrews*, 405.

71. Pfitzner, *Hebrews*, 205; Lane, *Hebrews 9–13*, 562-63.

72. Compare Isa. 63:11 (LXX), ὁ ἀναβιβάσας ἐκ τῆς γῆς τὸν ποιμένα τῶν προβάτων, with Heb. 13:20, ὁ ἀναγαγὼν ἐκ νεκρῶν τὸν ποιμένα τῶν προβάτων τὸν μέγαν.

10:11-14; 1 Pet. 2:25) and resonates with Jewish discourse about God as the shepherd of the people of Israel or the individual righteous person as well (Ezek. 34; Ps. 23). Although the metaphor has changed, the author still reinforces the trajectory developed in 2:10, as well as 6:19-20; 10:19-20; 12:2. Jesus as shepherd goes ahead of the flock, leading them and calling them toward their final destiny, even as he, in the role of pioneer, is seen blazing the trail of the many children who follow, or the consecrated hosts who are entering God's realm by means of the way he opened up.

God led Jesus back "by the blood of the eternal covenant" (ἐν αἵματι διαθήκης αἰωνίου, 13:20). This phrase recontextualizes Zechariah 9:11 (LXX), which celebrates God's act in freeing the exiles: "you, by the blood of the covenant (ἐν αἵματι διαθήκης), sent forth your prisoners out from the waterless pit." In the Zechariah passage, it becomes clear that the preposition "in" or "by" signifies "because of" or "by virtue of."[73] We should expect the same meaning in Hebrews 13:20, where the phrase provides the rationale for a different exodus. God, having accepted Jesus' death as the sacrifice that inaugurates the new covenant, signifies this by raising Jesus from the dead and exalting him to his right hand.[74] The difference between the covenant to which Zechariah appealed and this covenant is underscored by the addition of the adjective "eternal." The OT prophets looked forward to the "eternal covenant" (Isa. 55:3; 61:8; Jer. 32:40 [LXX 39:40]; 50:5 [LXX 29:5]; Ezek. 16:60; 37:26) that God would make in the future, which would reverse the misfortunes of Israel, make obedience to God a way of life, and usher in the long-awaited promise of Zion's exaltation over the nations. The author of Hebrews, sharing this view with Christian culture generally, finds these promises and predictions of an eternal covenant fulfilled in the ministry of Jesus (see Heb. 8:6–10:18).

The content of this closing prayer over the addressees is finally given in 13:21. The author invokes God to furnish the addressees with "every good thing," to "make them complete unto the doing of his will" (καταρτίσαι . . . εἰς τὸ ποιῆσαι τὸ θέλημα αὐτοῦ). Just as Jesus made the doing of God's will his central agenda (cf. Ps. 39:7-9 [LXX], applied to Jesus in Heb. 10:4-10), so now this is to become the focus of the addressees. This invocation of blessing reaffirms the central value that the author would instill in the hearers, namely, seeking from God the strength and resources required for the doing of his will, the doing of what will be pleasing (τὸ εὐάρεστον; cf. 11:5-6; 12:28; 13:16) to God.[75] Focusing the hearers on pleasing God rather than their unbelieving neighbors remains at the center of his strategy. The author stresses here again that the

---

73. Lane, *Hebrews 9–13*, 562-63; Pfitzner (*Hebrews*, 205) also stresses the importance of the Zechariah text for understanding Heb. 13:20.

74. Bruce, *Hebrews*, 388; P. Hughes, *Hebrews*, 589.

75. See Attridge, *Hebrews*, 407; Lane, *Hebrews 9–13*, 565.

course is ultimately quite feasible (by now a familiar deliberative topic) since God himself "furnishes" the addressees with everything required to persevere in the path to which the author has been calling them, and himself "works in them" what pleases him as they merely continue in their Godward orientation. As with all God's gifts, these too will be secured "through Jesus Christ," who remains thus in his role of broker of divine favor (see 4:14-16).

The doxology that closes the prayer, "to whom be glory forever, amen," is part of the liturgical heritage of Judaism. The same form can be found in 4 Maccabees 18:24 and Romans 16:27 (and with slight variations in Rom. 11:36; Gal. 1:5; et al.). The referent for the pronoun could grammatically be God or Jesus. While Harold Attridge is right to suggest that the proximity of Jesus to the pronoun makes him the more natural referent,[76] the theocentric character of the sermon weighs more heavily in favor of understanding God as the referent. It is to God that gratitude must be shown through reverent worship (12:28); it is "to God" that sacrifices of praise, confession, and service are offered "through Jesus Christ" (13:15-16). This would suggest that God is again the recipient of honor for the gifts he gives "through Jesus Christ," ever the mediator, to those who approach God "through him" (7:25).[77] Once more, it is impossible to be decisive, only suggestive.

The author makes a parting request for a favorable hearing, affirming that he has kept the message "brief" (διὰ βραχέων) so as not to strain their attentiveness (13:22). The fact that the sermon would take an hour or more to read effectively and emotively should not make us read this remark as disingenuous. Many of Dio Chrysostom's speeches would have taken three times as long to deliver! William Lane is correct to observe that this claim is a literary convention,[78] but we should not therefore discount every use of a convention as *merely* conventional. For example, 1 Peter 5:12; Ignatius *Rom.* 8:2; *Pol.* 7:3 all speak about writing briefly: these three letters, however, are truly short even by comparison with Hebrews. In Hebrews, as in these three letters, the words about "writing briefly" appear at the end — a point at which the hearers, if the assessment is too far from the truth, could object. Would it be rhetorically effective to invite such an objection at the close of a speech for no other reason than to include a literary convention? When, however, the author of the *Epistle of Barnabas,* a text twice the length of Hebrews, claims to be writing "briefly" (*Barn.* 1:5), we may suspect that the phrase is being used as an attempt to gain an attentive hearing rather than representing an accurate projection of length. Significantly, however, the claim appears there at the opening of the text. In *Barnabas,* it advances the purpose of an exordium. I would suggest, therefore, that all

---

76. Attridge, *Hebrews,* 407-8.

77. Lane, *Hebrews 9–13,* 565; Bruce, *Hebrews,* 412; Thurén, *Lobopfer,* 230-33.

78. Lane, *Hebrews 9–13,* 568-69.

such occurrences should not be lumped together, but each examined according to its rhetorical placement and purpose, which should qualify any comparison of *Barnabas* and Hebrews (with 1 Peter, et al.) on this point. The author's designation of his own work as a "word of exhortation" (λόγου τῆς παρακλήσεως) suggests that it belongs to the genre of "homily" or "sermon" (cf. Acts 13:15), as indeed the term comes to be used.[79]

News, travel plans, greetings, and a formulaic benediction close the sermon. First, the author passes on a report that "our brother Timothy has been released," which may already be "old news" ("you know that . . .") but which the author wishes to confirm. It is likely that this is the same Timothy who was Paul's traveling companion and protégé, and that the situation from which he was "released" was imprisonment,[80] a condition to which Christian leaders were frequently subjected. This imprisonment of Timothy is otherwise unattested in the NT, unless it is the one shared by Timothy with Paul (Phlm. 1). Timothy appears to be journeying to the author's location, and the author hopes to be able to wait for Timothy and travel together with him to the addressees' location. So pressing is the author's desire to see the addressees and to confirm and continue in them the work effected by his sermon that he may not wait. The addressees may look forward to the return of this leader and teacher, and the author may be stressing the haste with which he hopes to come as a means of raising their hopes that they will soon have his resources for the group's perseverance at their disposal in person.

The author asks the hearers to "greet your leaders and all the holy ones" and passes on the greetings of "those from Italy" (13:24). Because we know very little about the situation of the addressees, it is difficult to know precisely how the hearers would understand these greetings. If the author addresses a single house church within a city containing several house churches (like Rome or Corinth), then they might take this as the author's request that his greetings be passed on to the leaders and members of the other house churches.[81] It seems strange, however, that, if the author knows of Christian assemblies other than the one he addresses, he merely wants his greetings and not his word of exhortation passed along. Would only the one house church benefit from this sermon? One would expect a closing more along the lines of 1 Thessalonians 5:26-27: "Greet all the sisters and brothers with a holy kiss; have this letter read to all the brothers and sisters." Thus, in 13:24a the author doesn't simply address a

---

79. See L. Wills, "The Form of the Sermon in Hellenistic Judaism and Early Christianity," *HTR* 77 (1984): 277-99, esp. 280.

80. See Attridge, *Hebrews,* 409 n. 68 for an impressive collection of data favoring this understanding.

81. Thus Moffatt, *Hebrews,* 246; Spicq, *L'Épître aux Hebreux,* 2:438; Lane, *Hebrews 9–13,* 570.

segment of the Christian population[82] and then ask the hearers to bear his greetings to those "who are not expected to be present when the homily and its attached note are read aloud."[83] Rather, the greeting is accomplished in its reading to the gathered body of saints. Greeting the leaders specifically, even though they are included among the "saints," elevates their visibility within the community.

The second greeting, the one conveyed by the author from "those from Italy," has also figured prominently in reconstructions of the addressees' location. The greeting certainly suggests some connection with Italy, particularly the church at Rome, but it is impossible to decide whether the greeting comes from Italians present with the author in Rome to the author's congregation outside of Italy, to which the author will be returning later, or from Italians present with the author outside of Italy sending their greetings back home. If the former case is true, this greeting would remind the addressees in their local setting that they are not alone but are part of a growing, empire-wide movement. The minority culture is both supratemporal, as the cloud of witnesses shows, and supralocal, with chapters springing up across the Mediterranean. Believers in any one location may take heart in knowing that they are part of a much larger band, and not quite so small a minority as their local circumstances might make them think.

The sermon closes, as do most NT letters (see Rom. 16:20; 2 Cor. 13:13; Gal. 6:18; Eph. 6:24; Phil. 4:23; Col. 4:18; 1 Thess. 5:28, 2 Thess. 3:18; 1 Tim. 6:21; 2 Tim. 2:22; Titus 3:15; Phlm. 25; Rev. 22:21), with an invocation of God's favor (ἡ χάρις) to rest upon all the hearers (13:25). While the expression is clearly formulaic, it is nonetheless a singularly appropriate closing to this sermon, in which perseverance in the church has been promoted as the way also to remain within the sphere of God's favor, while defection has been condemned as the path to exclusion from favor. More than a mere formality, the final invocation leaves the addressees focused on the experience of God's favor, an inexhaustible source of help in time of need providing the believers with all the assistance necessary to help them remain firm in their confession of hope here, and to bring them at last to the ultimate benefaction that God has prepared for those who draw near to him through the Son — entrance into the rest and glory to be enjoyed beyond this decaying, manufactured world.

---

82. Thus rightly Attridge, *Hebrews,* 409.
83. Lane, *Hebrews 9–13,* 569.

Summary

Hebrews 13 very directly addresses the formation of the ethos of the community. An overarching topic for this ethos would be to pursue "reliability" in their relationships with one another, a reliability that will be grounded in the reliability of God and Jesus toward them. In 13:1-3, the author reminds the believers to remain constant in their "brotherly and sisterly love" and their "hospitality." Since they have been made kin one to another by virtue of being adopted as children into God's household (i.e., made what sociologists call a fictive kinship group), they are called to live out the obligations of siblings toward one another and to provide that constant network of support and help that natural kin would otherwise be expected to provide. This "love of the brothers and sisters" includes two particular, practical needs of the early Christian community. First, the addressees are called to continue to show hospitality toward traveling Christians (thus maintaining the bond of love across the supralocal Christian community) as well as toward their local Christian fellowship. Second, they are to direct their support especially toward those most dramatically targeted by society for deviancy control. Siblings, being "the same thing in different bodies," should feel deeply the needs of their imprisoned or abused partners in Christ and make haste to extend relief in every possible way, letting everyone in the church know that their new family will never leave them nor desert them.

The author also cautions against behaviors or inclinations that can erode the reliability and commitment of individual members and thereby the peace and solidarity of the group (13:4-6). Christian love giving way to sexual looseness cannot be tolerated, and the sanction of divine judgment is invoked to back this prohibition. Just as believers are to be reliable in the fulfillment of their kinship obligations one to another, so they are to remain reliable within the marital covenants they have made. Concern for temporal possessions, which could very easily draw people away from association with the group, is to be moderated in light of the greater resources that God has promised. The believer "has" all he or she needs, for he or she has God's promise to remain faithful and a present help (cf. 4:14-16). Proper fear of God, which has been a keynote of the sermon, should mean the enjoyment of the assurance of God's friendship and protection (13:5), such that fear of human beings is removed (13:6). The addressees once again are directed to have regard for God and their relationship with God, and not to jeopardize that priceless asset out of desire for worldly goods or fear of what unbelievers might think or do. Again, the goal of such exhortations is to reinforce their fixedness in faith, their firmness, and their dependability.

Ultimately, Jesus is completely reliable, and the hearers may count on him being "the same" tomorrow as they found him today, and as their former leaders had found him throughout their walk (13:7-8). They were enabled to remain firm in their commitment and trust by Jesus' trustworthiness, which provided them with a sure anchor and fixed compass point through all the vicissitudes of life. The hearers are also called to remain firm. It is by means of their "grace relationship" with God through Jesus that their hearts are nobly confirmed and secured. As they keep their minds and hearts and desires fixed on Jesus and the gifts of God he secures, they will themselves be firm and unmovable — no longer a prey to being tossed here and there by so many faddish teachings that have no more value than the "foods" that touch only the body and not the conscience (13:9).

Reminding the hearers once more of the tremendous privilege they have been given by Jesus, whose death and exaltation has perfected their consciences and who has become for them a sure and unfailing place of mediation between themselves and God, the author calls them again to make a fair return. They are called to show themselves reliable clients to this Jesus who has endured so much to bring them benefit; they are called to endure now for him, to show him gratitude. Hebrews 13:12-14 reinforces the sectarian consciousness of the group, reminding them that their proper place is on the "outside" of their society. Justice itself (in the form of loyalty and gratitude toward one's benefactor) requires that they accept disenfranchisement for the sake of their confession of this Jesus and attachment to his household. The author moves them by means of these images to see themselves, in fact, as outsiders to the society of unbelievers, and to embrace that identity rather than seek means of restoration to a place "inside" the camp, which would inevitably result in compromise of their confession and their attachment to their fellow Christians.

The place "outside," however, is also the better place to be, for it is the way out from the decaying, disintegrating city of the world and the way to the "abiding" city that God has prepared for those who seek his gifts and honor his Son. Rather than regret their loss of attachments to their earthly city and the status, privileges, or goods they enjoyed therein, the believers are encouraged that they have left behind just in time that which is already destined for shaking and destruction, and are traveling safely to a better, eternal homeland where their honor as God's children will be fully manifest rather than daily challenged. Their journey is a sacral one: even though "outside the camp," they are the ones who enjoy access to God and whose entire lives become sacred offerings to God as they worship him, spread his honor in the world, use their goods for the relief of others, and seek ways in which to assist one another (13:15-16). Their visits to their imprisoned sisters and brothers, their witness to the value of enjoying God's patronage, their acts of sharing — all these mundane works become beautiful thank offerings to God, who takes great pleasure in these liturgies. Cooperating with their leaders and enjoying God's provision for their doing what pleases him, the addressees have all they need to remain in "grace," to live gratefully, and, at the last, to attain the eternal benefactions God has prepared for the faithful.

Bridging the Horizons

Once again the text invites us to reflect on the kind of community the church is called to be for its members. We have heard throughout the sermon that a strong network of support among believers was deemed essential to the perseverance of individual Christians and thus to the health of the whole group (3:12-14; 10:23-25, 32-34; 12:15-17). Now the author introduces the term "brotherly love" to describe the quality of the relationship that should mark the bond between Christians. Application of the language of kinship to this voluntary association is universal in early Christian culture. (Jude is the only NT text not to use the term "brother" or "sister" to refer to a fellow believer.) In the Synoptic Gospels, the kinship of Jesus' followers is created by their common dedication to doing God's will (Mark 3:31-35 and parallels), and it becomes the compensation in this world for the loss of natural kinship networks suffered by believers (Mark 10:28-30 and parallels). In the remainder of the NT, various sources for the establishment of kinship between believers are cited, but the most prominent is their birth "from above" (see John 1:12-13) or their being "born anew into a living hope" and "imperishable inheritance" (1 Pet. 1:3-4). Adoption into the family of God as sons and daughters (Gal. 3:26; 4:4-7) makes Christians sisters and brothers one to another, and the author of Hebrews certainly shares this conviction (2:10-13; 12:5-11).

The fact that confession of Jesus could mean the loss of one's own kinship networks and could even invite the enmity of natural kin (as it still does today in Islamic countries, for example) meant that the church had to become family for one another, to provide sustained, committed, reliable support for one another. Where Christians are openly persecuted, this remains a necessary hallmark of the church. In Western Europe and North America, where this external exigence has not existed for some time, the vital essence of Christian brotherhood and sisterhood has, in many churches, been lost. The words "brother" or "sister" spoken in a religious context have come near to being clichéd expressions rather than reflections of mutual commitment and solidarity. While there is no longer the need, in the majority of cases, to speak of the church replacing natural kin or taking priority over natural kin (where such occurs, we normally speak of a cult mentality), there is a need for Christians everywhere to reclaim the larger family that the NT authors so diligently and uniformly promote. We have a tendency to draw a strict line around our natural families, considering them "our own" and regarding the rest of humanity as, to greater and lesser degrees, strangers.

The result is that even the "church family" becomes clearly distinguished from our "real family," and we interact with fellow believers with at least one set of defenses and barriers left erect. The latent notion that *our* blood, rather than *Jesus'* blood, defines our kin means that we deny ourselves and one another in the church a level of intimacy and mutual commitment that might otherwise open up the doors to real inner healing, growth in the spirit, victory over temptations, and powerful witness and work in the world. In Jesus' answer to Peter's question concerning the reward of those who have left all to follow Jesus, Jesus speaks of this larger Christian family as our inheritance in this present age. We are, in effect, one another's reward and treasure in this life, the resource given to one another for strength for the journey. Being born into a worldwide family that acts as a family in the best sense — encouraging, sharing, helping, risking — could be one of the greatest assets of the Christian Church, if only we would reclaim this ethos. Those Christian groups that do kindle a familial love among their members are frequently the most vital, suggesting a strong relationship between the degree of intimacy among fellow Christians and the spiritual energy of a congregation. The author of Hebrews perceived that people will risk according to their resources. If an individual Christian knows that the other members of a church are fully committed to seeking his or her well-being, wouldn't that believer risk the level of honesty and openness that allows deep personal and spiritual growth to occur? And knowing that the resources of a whole body of believers stand behind him or her, what vital ministries might he or she be enabled to pioneer, what bold outreaches of faith?!

If Jesus calls us his family and gives each of us to one another as family, we ought not to neglect this great gift. As family, however, we inherit obligations to our new family no less binding than those owed our natural kin. Our interactions with fellow believers must be shaped by our kinship in Christ and reflect the intimacy and unity that ancient ethicists attributed to the love of sisters and brothers growing up in a single household. Such relationships were marked by unity of values, purpose, and mutual favor. Competition, divisiveness, and neglect of one's kin were looked upon as the basest of vices. As we extend our frontier of intimacy from "home" to "church," we will look upon the needs of our fellow Christians as an opportunity for us to "take care of our own." We will replace competition and power struggles with a commitment to cooperation and the good of the other. We will not be selective in whom we choose to befriend within the church but regard all as our sisters and brothers, welcoming one another and including one another without reserve, "as Christ welcomed us" (Rom. 15:7). As Jesus' followers, we are called to be family to one another first, and then employers or employees, business partners or customers, professors or students, and so forth.

Even the best of families will have difficulties. Families will fight, and siblings will cause one another pain and frustration. The ideal for a family may be the absence of disagreements or injuries, but, failing that, the ideal is to work through these differences *as family*. Epictetus, the Stoic philosopher, said that there are two handles by which to hold on in any disagreement — by the issue that gave rise to disagreement, or by the fact that the contending parties are brothers or sisters (*Ench.* 43). There is some real wisdom that we Christians can learn from this Stoic. When we chafe against one another, we can hold onto the injury or onto our kinship in Christ. One choice leads to a rift in the family of God; the other opens up the door to reconciliation and an even deeper intimacy with one another. Every church of which I have been a part (and I trust there is no connection) has had some deep rifts between members, but when their fellow believers were able to bring them back to the essential focus of their kinship with one another in Jesus, reconciliation was possible.

It is not just for one another's well-being, however, that the church would do well to rekindle and maintain "brotherly love." A church that nurtures the ethos promoted by the author of Hebrews will be able to offer itself as family for those who do not have the support of natural kin, or, indeed, for those whose immediate family may be the problem (as in situations of domestic violence). The church can become a haven of support that people can rely upon for help, and having a reliable support could embolden many to leave harmful lifestyles and situations (from substance abuse to prostitution). To field that kind of support, however, requires the prior commitment of the believers within the church to be kin one to another and to assume the obligations and mutual commitment that entails.

The author of Hebrews calls us to extend this love also toward guests and strangers. We have seen the circumstances that made hospitality a necessity for the growth and maintenance of the early Church. In what ways is hospitality a needful practice today? Many churches are experiencing measurable revitalization and growth by means of small group ministries, which frequently requires, however, the willingness of a number of church members to open up their homes for these meetings. In this way, there is a call for the replication of the hospitality that made possible the regular meeting of the early churches. Hospitality is a vital quality for churches to possess as a whole toward the visitor or guest. Many readers will have no doubt experienced the sort of Christian community that makes one feel welcome, even honored, and the sort that makes one feel invisible or worse. We are called to welcome strangers, bringing them into the circle of love as sacred guests (for hospitality was considered a holy obligation in the ancient world). If any person has been led by God to visit one of our churches or study groups and the like, let that person not leave thinking it was a mistake! Because of the abundance of God's love for us, we have love to spare for the visitor, to give that person a taste of the love that exists between Christian brothers and sisters. Part of being the family of God still includes the willingness to open up the homes of our natural families to our spiritual family. Whether hosting a visiting minister or choir, giving lodging to a family that has lost its home in a disaster or crisis, or providing a safe shelter for a victim of abuse, the opportunities for hospitality arise, and we must be sensitive to using these opportunities for sharing the "love of sisters and brothers."

We are especially urged that our love for the family of God express itself in support for those of our family who face some danger, trial, or extreme situation — locally, nationally, and globally. "Remember those who are in prison, as imprisoned with them; those who are ill-treated, as also in their body" (13:3). Many sisters and brothers in Christ living today have had, or continue to have, their lives directly affected by persecution. The reports of the persecution and execution of Christians behind the Iron Curtain circulated before the fall of the Berlin Wall have proven in all too many instances to have been true and unexaggerated.[84] Not once, however, was the persecution of Christians mentioned from the pulpits of four of the five churches to which I have belonged — let alone any efforts at relief or support undertaken. I do not pretend to know why so many churches are silent about the plight of Christians worldwide. Whether it stems from denial or the ignorance that results from decades of being preoccupied only with our local and national conditions makes little difference. The author of Hebrews calls us to throw off our forgetfulness and "remember" these sisters and brothers.

The first course of action is, of course, to learn. Repressive regimes do not readily and openly admit to religious persecution, but several avenues for investigation remain. Many books have been published documenting the persecution of Christians globally. Many more web sites exist to raise public awareness of religious persecution as well as to coordinate relief efforts.[85] Some of these web sites provide information on every country where the persecution of Christians is known to take place; others gather relevant news releases and reports. Internationals residing in America can also provide firsthand testimony to the conditions faced by the church in their countries.[86] As you and your churches learn more about the contest of the brothers and sisters abroad, pray. The content of such prayers will be obvious from the needs you discover, rang-

---

84. See, for example, the collection of firsthand reports gathered by von der Heydt (*Candles Behind the Wall*).

85. For those with access to the web (even public libraries are now offering this, so access is broadened tremendously), the following sites may be worth perusal: www.persecution.com (the web site of "Voice of the Martyrs," a long-standing advocate for aiding the persecuted churches); www.persecuted.org; www.persecution.org; www.calebproject.org/persec.htm; www.erlc.com/rliberty/persecution. Such sites would be but starting places, of course, for deeper and more thorough investigation, but their utility as starting places should not be overlooked.

86. Ashland Theological Seminary has the privilege of having many international students. Two students — one from Nigeria and another from Indonesia — have been able to provide firsthand reports of the nature and degree of persecution faced by their families and churches. Contact with such students, who will return to their native land, affords Christians in the United States an opportunity to enter into long-term partnership with sisters and brothers fighting a fiercer struggle overseas.

ing from encouragement of the imprisoned, to provision for the families of the martyred, to relief from torture, to the conversion of the persecutors and their agents. The persecuted do not consider such prayers to be empty, so neither should we.[87]

In addition to praying, talk. The slogan "shatter the silence" is a fitting one, for silence is the persecutor's ally. Public awareness, however, can effect relief and release. The fear of bad publicity in the West led to the release of Anatoly Rudenko from the living hell of a psychiatric prison.[88] In a dramatic living out of the solidarity of sisters and brothers in Christ, as is expressed precisely in Hebrews 13:3, Anglican priest Richard Rodgers, hearing of the unjust imprisonment of Christian poet Irina Ratushiskaya, spent Lent 1983 raising public awareness of her predicament by living himself in a cage under the same harsh conditions as Irina endured. This began the process of garnering public outrage that led to Irina's release by Mikhail Gorbachev before an important summit in 1986.[89] Christians in over forty countries worldwide could benefit from such acts of devotion in the free world. While public awareness and political considerations are brought to bear on the conditions of the persecuted church, we are also called to act to relieve the suffering and want presently experienced. We need to discover ways by which to share our material resources — clothing, food, medical care, and, of course, Bibles — with those believers in need and with the families they leave behind. In astounding ways, we should expect to be recompensed by the spiritual resources possessed by the sisters and brothers we seek to help. Those who have endured the fire of persecutors have also persevered under the formative discipline of God (12:5-11), who has forged in them a strength of character and clarity of faith desperately needed by Western Christians, whose spiritual faculties have frequently gone underexercised, to say the least.

An individual pastor or lay person may feel the need of "the persecuted Church" to be overwhelming, but there are ways in which such an individual may meaningfully and significantly enter into partnership with a single church or small cluster of churches facing persecution. Dr. Grace Holland, Associate

---

87. Alexander Odorodnikov, who endured almost nine years in Russian prisons, provides this testimony:

> Alexander remembers one time that the fierce coldness of his cell was so piercing that he was desperate. There was no way to get warm, and no place to hide from the cold. So he prayed.
>
> "I felt warm breathing, and the lovely touch of a brother's hand," he recalls. "I cried like a child, and understood it was a prayer for me. It helped me to survive" (von der Heydt, *Candles Behind the Wall*, 38).

88. Ibid., 107.
89. Ibid., 131.

Professor of Missions at Ashland Theological Seminary (now retired), has committed herself to be in regular, personal contact with one missionary in Nigeria, communicating mostly through e-mail. In this way, she is able to serve as a resource person to a minister in an area where converts to Christianity face brutal persecution, to pray specifically for the needs of the converts as they arise, to provide encouragement, and to be available to hear specific needs and coordinate efforts to meet them, whenever help like a public voice or material resources "from outside" are required. No single Christian would, through this venue, eliminate persecution of Christians in the world, but if pastors, lay people, even congregations would commit to help a single Christian community facing persecution somewhere in the world, whether through a missionary, a contact from that community (e.g., an international student returning home), or the like, a tremendous first step will have been taken.

We cannot, then, neglect this summons to those of us who are not suffering oppression to discover ways in which to help our suffering sisters and brothers, to expose and keep before the public eye the inhumanity and persecution, to construct networks of aid and support, and to rally political and economic pressure against repressive regimes. The early Christians were known for their bold and lavish support of their partners in need — what a difference it would make if we personally revived that interest and sought ways to reach out in love to them! What an encouragement it would be to those who are persecuted now across the world for the gospel's sake to find their global family rallying to their support by all possible avenues! And what a disgrace to us if we do less.

The value of fidelity in marriage is also clarified by our author in view of the context in which he sets his injunction to "keep the marriage bed undefiled" (13:4). Violations of the trust relationship of marriage attacks the support base of all believers involved. The marital bond could be a tremendous resource for spiritual growth and vital ministry and outreach, and this higher purpose is thwarted when one party yields to adultery. Not only that, but it creates a deep rift in the larger family of God: the strength and solidarity of the whole church is weakened by a single act of adultery. If a leader is involved, the church is left with a wound to its ability to trust its leadership; whether it involves clergy or lay person, the act of betrayal extends beyond the injured spouse to the entire church family. While, of course, reconciliation and restoration should remain at the forefront of the church's agenda in such circumstances, this particular sin creates especially deep wounds since trust is especially difficult to restore.

Passion for material gain is no less dangerous to Christian faith than passion for illicit sexual encounters, although the former is rarely censured and too often encouraged. For the first hearers, desire for material gain would lead directly to hiding one's association with the Christian group or, at the least, compromising certain stands that were integral to Christian witness (e.g., complete avoidance of even the semblance of idolatrous worship). While such overt threats to Christian commitment are infrequent (though not absent) in the West, the other threats to mature discipleship remain undiminished. Greatest of these is the danger of double-mindedness, being drawn in two directions by our desire for God and our desire for comfort and security as these are defined by the world. Cultivating spiritual growth and attending to the work that God calls believers to accomplish require time, energy, and focus, but prayer and ministry are frequently the first things crowded out of a schedule filled with business concerns and driven by the quest for material gain (see, poignantly, Matt. 13:3-8, 18-23). People educated and living in capitalist countries have difficulty perceiving what is "enough," and rarely think to live with "less" in terms of this world's comforts and pleasures so as to seek "more" of what makes us rich in God's sight (see Luke 12:21, 33).

The author's censure of "love of money," moreover, shows that he perceived the amassing of material wealth to betray a certain lack of trust in God, an implicit confession that God's friendship and patronage were not a sufficient cause for confidence and security. Insofar as a person sees his or her security in laying up for a "sound financial future," he or she may be in danger of living out a practical distrust toward God. The person who first "takes care of business" and then attends to matters of the spirit, building up a relationship with God, and engaging in God's work in the world, completely reverses Jesus' priorities and stands in danger of sacrificing the second consistently for the sake of the first. Hebrews confronts us with the ultimate unreliability of what so many human beings seek to build their life upon, namely, this world and its riches (Heb. 12:26-28; 13:14; cf. 1 Tim. 6:17). However, this is a hard lesson for many North American and Western European Christians to digest, for it means rewriting some major components of our socialization (our education and upbringing). Yet so many passages of both testaments speak of the importance of getting these priorities correct that it would be impossible not to wrestle with these questions. Are we following Christ or trusting God when we "build bigger barns" (i.e., investment portfolios and the like) with our earnings in order to lay up for ourselves a secure financial future, while so many lack the daily necessities of life today? Passages like Luke 12:12-21 and 1 Timothy 6:7-9 would suggest not. Do we place more value on (i.e., "seek first") the acquisition of material possessions and assets than on the acquisition of spiritual wealth? The author of *Shepherd of Hermas,* a widely read early Christian apocalypse (early- to mid–second century), challenges his readers to consider whether or not they are so attached to their worldly goods that they are truly free to serve God and remain loyal to God's laws. Would they, for the sake of keeping and increasing their earthly goods, be willing to play by the rules of the prince of this age? Or do they so invest their material assets that they expect to enjoy an eternal yield in God's city? Are they so rich toward God that they live in readiness to leave this world and go to enjoy their eternal homes, lands, fields, and possessions in God's realm (*Sim.* 1)?

These are many of the same questions that the author of Hebrews asks of his hearers, and of us across the centuries. The answers are not easy, but the questions are unavoidable and need to be answered by each believer in her or his own conscience. If following Jesus and obeying God remain our first priorities (and our lives bear this out), if we regard our security to be grounded in God's provision, and if we think of our possessions not as our own insulation against want but as the resources of which God has made us temporary stewards to do his work, we may not be far from the kingdom of God.

The author of Hebrews urges Christians in every age to find their center, their anchor, their security, and thus their own source of reliability, in Jesus. Trusting Jesus means building our lives around our growing relationship with him in prayer, on the foundation of his words and commands, and on obeying his call to us day to day. If the real foundation of our life is something else, our "trust" in Jesus will be artificial, unreal. As we risk building on the foundation of his word and friendship, we discover, as generations of Christians have found (cf. 13:7), just how trustworthy he is. We learn that obeying Jesus' call is not, in the end, a risk at all, but a sure foundation. This summons to "risk" takes us back to the kind of church we seek to nurture, for the individual believer will learn more of Jesus' reliability and trustworthiness as he or she sees a deep level of reliability in fellow believers and allows that fellowship to support the risks he or she may take in following Jesus. Once again, the importance of a strong community of faith for the strengthening of individual trust is apparent.

Many have not built on this foundation, however, having been led by their primary socialization to build their lives around financial goals, to pass their time in many trivial and empty pastimes, and to look not to what is unseen but to what is seen (in a grim paraphrase, or parody, of 2 Cor. 4:18). As a result, many even within our churches feel empty. They become an easy prey to the "foreign and varied teachings" that fill the religion, occult, and self-help shelves at bookstores. Always looking for some "spiritual dimension" for their lives, they are easily "carried away" with the latest fad (secular or "Christian") and ultimately lack a fixed, firm, and stabilizing center. The author of Hebrews reminds us of the way to a centered, stable life — not stable in the sense of changeless and mundane, but in the sense of having such deep roots in Christ that "no adversity and no prosperity shall ever move"[90] us from God's love. "As those who are to give an account" (13:17), pastors and others charged with the nurture and care of believers (e.g., music ministers, youth directors, and directors of Christian Education) could find in Hebrews 13:1-9 an adequate challenge but also a helpful focus for their ministries, for here we are charged with

---

90. From a prayer by Thomas à Kempis.

leading believers into a deep trust and grace relationship with God through Jesus as well as with developing a very specific kind of community that will support its members locally and globally. Having such focus is especially helpful, since, in the multiplicity of programs and activities that a church can find itself getting involved in, the thread of purpose is often lost. A recovery of vision for what the church can be for believers worldwide, however, can act as a purifying flame, burning away those aspects of programming that simply spend time and resources without contributing in some meaningful way to the vision, and making room and resources for those ministries that will contribute directly to making a vital congregation that is capable of reaching out to the needs of community and global church.

The author soberly calls believers to "go out to Jesus outside the camp, bearing his reproach" (13:13), which is only our reasonable and fair return for what he bore for our sake. Believers persecuted for their association with Jesus, and often for their refusal to cooperate with unjust governments that suppress the truth, know what it is to bear this reproach for Jesus' sake, and as we stand in solidarity with them and support their contest we share with them in their noble acts of gratitude and loyalty. But even in the West we can be called to "bear his reproach," for example, when we protest the injustice by which many profit, when we stand against the prejudices that many hold dear, when we choose obedience to God's call when that means a loss in the goods that the society around us prizes. Where do we not go for Christ, for fear of bearing reproach for his sake, for fear of "giving up" something that is dear to us, or for fear of not attaining what our upbringing in the world has taught us is valuable? When our allegiance to God or obedience to God's call makes us bear this "reproach," the author of Hebrews emboldens us to embrace it since the way God is leading us brings us nearer the abiding city, our true home and goal, and further away from our entanglement in the worldly camp.

The sermon leaves us with the value of being "well pleasing" to God placed prominently before our eyes (13:16, 21). Every arena of life becomes an appropriate venue for offering our sacrifices of thanksgiving to God, and all of life is rendered sacral as it is lived out of the center of gratitude toward God. Again we are reminded that extending the honor and reputation of our Patron is an essential aspect of the response of gratitude. This prompts us not only to offer worship to God in the sacred spaces of our churches but to render sacred the public spaces where we also bear witness to what God has done for us. Our culture has, in subtle and not-so-subtle ways, made us uncomfortable with the idea of talking about God (or, more properly, acknowledging God's gifts to us and place in our lives) outside of the properly designated buildings. Nevertheless, the "sacrifice of praise" inside the sanctuary cannot be separated from the "confession of the name" in the marketplace. Were we to keep our religion hidden away behind the doors of churches and homes, we should become what the author of Hebrews urged his hearers so strongly not to become — Christians without "boldness," afraid or unwilling to speak about their connections with Jesus in the public hearing.

Our response of gratitude does not stop with honor, however; it should also move us to obedient service. This service is directed not toward the God who has need of nothing, but rather toward other human beings as an extension of God's generosity toward us and witness to the same. Every act of doing good or sharing with others what God has given us constitutes the liturgical offering that pleases God. Protestants in particular are sensitive to how "good works" fit into the Christian life, always on guard against "works righteousness." Hebrews gives us a sufficient model: good works are a necessary part of our response of gratitude to God for all his gifts to us. While they do not "earn" God's favor, they are a necessary return of favor to God. "Grace," as we have seen throughout this commentary, is a rich and multivalent concept that embraces the whole of the Christian life — from God's favor acquired for us by Jesus to our wholehearted commitment to live gratefully. If the circle is anywhere broken, the beauty of the dance of the Christian life that God set in motion is marred. As we deepen our understanding of the immensity of God's favor and the gifts God bestows and will bestow, we will also find our commitment to return favor deepened, to bring honor to this God and serve him in complete loyalty. For this reason, "grace" is commended as that which nobly and ably grounds the believer's heart (13:9), making him or her secure in Jesus' trustworthiness and a reliable member of the household of God.

Bibliography

Adkins, A. W. *Merit and Responsibility: A Study in Greek Values.* Oxford: Oxford University Press, 1960.

Ahern, A. A. "The Perfection Concept in the Epistle to the Hebrews." *JBR* 14 (1946): 164-67.

Anderson, C. P. "The Setting of the Epistle to the Hebrews." Ph.D. diss., Columbia University, 1969.

Anderson, H. "4 Maccabees (First Century A.D.). A New Translation and Introduction." In *The Old Testament Pseudepigrapha,* vol. 2, ed. J. H. Charlesworth, 531-64. Garden City, NY: Doubleday, 1985.

———. "Maccabees, Books of: Fourth Maccabees." In *ABD,* ed. D. N. Freedman, vol. 4, 452-53. New York: Doubleday, 1992.

Andriessen, Paul. "Renonçant à la joie qui lui revenait." *NRT* 107 (1975): 424-38.

Attridge, H. W. *The Epistle to the Hebrews.* Philadelphia: Fortress, 1989.

———. "The Philosophical Critique of Religion under the Early Empire." *ANRW* 2.16.1 (1978): 45-78.

———. "'Heard Because of His Reverence' (Heb 5:7)." *JBL* 98 (1979): 90-93.

———. "Paraenesis in a Homily (λόγος παρακλήσεως): The Possible Location of, and Socialization in, the 'Epistle to the Hebrews.'" *Semeia* 50 (1990): 211-26.

Barrett, C. K. "The Eschatology in the Epistle to the Hebrews." In *The Background of the New Testament and Its Eschatology,* ed. W. D. Davies and D. Daube, 363-93. Cambridge: Cambridge University Press, 1954.

Bateman, Herbert W., IV. *Early Jewish Hermeneutics and Hebrews 1:5-13.* New York: Peter Lang, 1997.

Beale, G. K. "Eschatology." In *The Dictionary of the Later New Testament and Its*

Developments, ed. R. P. Martin and P. H. Davids, 330-45. Downers Grove: InterVarsity Press, 1997.

Becker, Ernest. *The Denial of Death.* New York: The Free Press, 1973.

Berger, P. L. *The Sacred Canopy.* New York: Doubleday, 1967.

―――, and T. Luckmann. *The Social Construction of Reality.* New York: Doubleday Anchor, 1967.

Betz, Hans-Dieter. *Galatians.* Hermeneia. Philadelphia: Fortress, 1979.

Bloomquist, L. Gregory. *The Function of Suffering in Philippians.* JSNTSS 78. Sheffield: Sheffield Academic Press, 1993.

Boissevain, Jeremy. *Friends of Friends: Networks, Manipulators and Coalitions.* New York: St. Martin's, 1974.

Brown, R. E. *The Epistles of John.* AB 30. New York: Doubleday, 1982.

Bruce, F. F. *The Epistle to the Hebrews.* NICNT. Rev. ed. Grand Rapids: Eerdmans, 1990.

Buchanan, G. W. *To The Hebrews.* New York: Doubleday, 1972.

Büchsel, F. "Hebräerbrief." In *Religion in Geschichte und Gegenwart,* ed. H. Gunkel and L. Zscharnack. 2d ed. Tübingen: J. C. B. Möhr, 1928, 2:1669-73.

Bultmann, Rudolf. "αἰδώς." *TDNT* 1:169-71. Grand Rapids: Eerdmans, 1964.

―――. "αἰσχύνω, etc." *TDNT* 1:189-91. Grand Rapids: Eerdmans, 1964.

―――. "New Testament and Mythology." In *Kerygma and Myth by Rudolf Bultmann and Five Critics,* ed. H. W. Bartsch, 1-44. New York: Harper & Row, 1961.

Caird, G. B. *New Testament Theology.* Ed. L. D. Hurst. Oxford: Clarendon Press, 1995.

Calvin, John. *Calvin's Commentary on the Epistle to the Hebrews.* Tr. "by a Beneficed Clergyman of the Church of England." London: Cornish and Co., 1842.

Carlston, C. "The Vocabulary of Perfection in Philo and Hebrews." In *Unity and Diversity in New Testament Theology,* ed. R. A. Guelich. Grand Rapids: Eerdmans, 1978.

Charlesworth, J. H. *The Old Testament Pseudepigrapha.* 2 vols. Garden City, NY: Doubleday, 1983, 1985.

Chilton, Bruce. *The Temple of Jesus: His Sacrificial Program within a Cultural History of Sacrifice.* University Park, PA: University of Pennsylvania Press, 1992.

Cockerill, Gareth. *The Melchizedek Christology in Heb. 7:1-28.* Ann Arbor: University Microfilms International, 1979.

―――. *Hebrews: A Commentary in the Wesleyan Tradition.* Indianapolis: Wesleyan Publishing House, 1999.

―――. "Hebrews 1:6: Source and Significance," *BBR* 9 (1999): 51-64.

Cody, Aelrad. *Heavenly Sanctuary and Liturgy in the Epistle to the Hebrews.* St. Meinrad, IN: Grail, 1960

Collins, J. J. *Between Athens and Jerusalem.* New York: Crossroad, 1983.

————. *The Scepter and the Star: The Messiahs of the Dead Sea Scrolls and Other Ancient Literature.* Garden City, NY: Doubleday, 1995.

Cosby, M. R. *The Rhetorical Composition and Function of Hebrews 11 in Light of Example Lists in Antiquity.* Macon: Mercer University Press, 1988.

————. "The Rhetorical Composition of Hebrews 11." *JBL* 107 (1988): 257-73.

Craddock, F. B. "Hebrews." In *The New Interpreter's Bible,* vol. 12, ed. Leander Keck, 1-174. Nashville: Abingdon, 1998.

Crossan, John D. *The Historical Jesus: The Life of a Mediterranean Jewish Peasant.* San Francisco: HarperCollins, 1991.

Croy, N. C. *Endurance in Suffering: Hebrews 12:1-13 in Its Rhetorical, Religious, and Philosophical Contexts.* SNTSMS. Cambridge: Cambridge University Press, 1998.

————. "A Note on Hebrews 12:2." *JBL* 114 (1995): 117-19.

de Jonge, Marinus. *The Testaments of the Twelve Patriarchs: A Study of Their Text, Composition, and Origin.* Leiden: Brill, 1953.

de Ste. Croix, G. E. M. "Suffragium: From Vote to Patronage." *British Journal of Sociology* 5 (1954): 33-48.

D'Angelo, M. R. *Moses in the Letter to the Hebrews.* SBLDS 42. Missoula: Scholars Press, 1979.

————. "Hebrews." In *The Women's Bible Commentary,* ed. C. A. Newsom and S. H. Ringe. Louisville: Westminster/John Knox Press, 1992.

Daniélou, Jean "La symbolisme du temple de Jérusalem chez Philon et Josèphe." In *Le symbolisme cosmique des monuments religieux,* 83-90. Rome: Instituto Italiano per il Medio ed Estremo Oriente, 1957.

Danker, Frederick W. *Benefactor: Epigraphic Study of a Graeco-Roman and New Testament Semantic Field.* St. Louis: Clayton Publishing House, 1982.

Davis, John. *The People of the Mediterranean: An Essay in Comparative Social Anthropology.* London: Routledge & Kegan Paul, 1977.

Deissmann, A. *Light from the Ancient East.* Tr. L. R. M. Strachan. New York: Doran, 1927.

Delitzsch, Franz. *Commentary on the Epistle to the Hebrews.* 2 vols. Tr. T. L. Kingsbury. Edinburgh: T. & T. Clark, 1871-72.

Delling, G. "τέλος, τελέω, τελειόω, etc." *TDNT* 8:49-87.

Derrett, J. D. M. *Jesus' Audience: The Social and Psychological Environment in Which He Worked.* New York: Seabury, 1973.

deSilva, D. A. *The Hope of Glory: Honor Discourse and New Testament Interpretation.* Collegeville, MN: Liturgical Press, 1999.

————. *Despising Shame: Honor Discourse and Community Maintenance in the Epistle to the Hebrews.* SBLDS 152. Atlanta: Scholars Press, 1995.

————. *4 Maccabees.* Guides to the Apocrypha and Pseudepigrapha. Sheffield: Sheffield Academic Press, 1998.

————, and Victor Matthews, *Untold Stories of the Bible*. Lincolnwood, IL: Publications International Ltd., 1998.

————. "The Epistle to the Hebrews in Social-Scientific Perspective." *Restoration Quarterly* 36 (1994): 1-21.

————. "Investigating Honor Discourse: Guidelines from Classical Rhetoricians." *Society of Biblical Literature Seminar Papers* 36 (1997): 491-525.

————. "Exchanging Favor for Wrath: Apostasy in Hebrews and Patron-Client Relations." *JBL* 115 (1996): 91-116.

————. "Let the One Who Claims Honor Establish That Claim in the Lord: Honor Discourse in the Corinthian Correspondence." *BTB* 28 (1998): 61-74.

————. "Hebrews 6:4-8: A Socio-Rhetorical Investigation. Part I." *Tyndale Bulletin* 50/1 (1999): 33-57.

Dodds, E. R. *The Greeks and the Irrational*. Berkeley: University of California Press, 1966.

Douglas, Mary. *Purity and Danger: An Analysis of Concepts of Pollution and Taboo*. London: Routledge and Kegan Paul, 1966.

————. "Atonement in Leviticus." *Jewish Studies Quarterly* 1 (1993/94): 109-30.

Droge, A. J., and J. D. Tabor. *A Noble Death: Suicide and Martyrdom among Christians and Jews in Antiquity*. San Francisco: Harper, 1992.

Dunn, J. D. G. *Baptism in the Holy Spirit*. Philadelphia: Westminster, 1970.

Ehrman, Bart D. *The New Testament: A Historical Introduction*. Oxford: Oxford University Press, 1997.

Eisenbaum, P. M. *The Jewish Heroes of Christian History: Hebrews 11 in Literary Context*. SBLDS 156. Atlanta: Scholars Press, 1997.

Elliott, J. H. *A Home for the Homeless: A Social-Scientific Investigation of 1 Peter*. Minneapolis: Fortress, 1990.

————. "Disgraced Yet Graced: The Gospel according to 1 Peter in the Key of Honor and Shame." *BTB* 24 (1994): 166-78.

————. "Patronage and Clientism in Early Christian Society." *Forum* 3 (1987): 39-48.

Ellingworth, P. *The Epistle to the Hebrews*. NIGTC. Grand Rapids: Eerdmans, 1993.

————. "Hebrews and *1 Clement*: Literary Dependence or Common Tradition?" *BZ* 23 (1979): 262-69.

Fearghail, F. O. "Sir 50, 5-21: Yom Kippur or the Daily Whole Offering?" *Bib* 59 (1978): 301-16.

Fee, Gordon. *Philippians*. NICNT. Grand Rapids: Eerdmans, 1997.

Ferguson, Everett C. *Backgrounds of Early Christianity*. 2d ed. Grand Rapids: Eerdmans, 1993.

————. "Spiritual Sacrifice in Early Christianity and Its Environment." *ANRW* 2.23.2 (1980): 1151-89.

Filson, F. V. *'Yesterday': A Study of Hebrews in the Light of Chapter 13*. London: SCM, 1967.

Frankowski, J. "Early Christian Hymns Recorded in the New Testament: A Reconsideration in Light of the Question of Heb 1,3." *BZ* 27 (1983): 183-94.

Gaster, T. H. "Angels." In *IDB* 1:128-34.

Gilbert, G. H. "The Greek Element in the Epistle to the Hebrews." *AJT* 14 (1910): 521-32.

Gilmore, D. D. "Introduction: The Shame of Dishonor." In *Honor and Shame and the Unity of the Mediterranean,* ed. D. D. Gilmore, 2-21. Washington: American Anthropological Association, 1987.

Gleason, Randall C. "The Old Testament Background of the Warning in Hebrews 6:4-8." *Bib Sac* 155 (1998): 62-91.

Grässer, Erich. *Der Glaube im Hebräerbrief.* Marburg: Elwert, 1965.

Grundmann, W. "δεξιός." In *TDNT* 2:38.

Guthrie, Donald. *New Testament Theology.* Downers Grove, IL: InterVarsity Press, 1981.

Guthrie, G. H. *The Structure of Hebrews: A Text-linguistic Analysis.* Leiden: Brill, 1994.

Gyllenberg, R. "Die Composition des Hebräerbriefs." *Svensk Exegetisk Årsbok* 22-23 (1957-58): 137-47.

Hadas, Moses. *The Third and Fourth Books of Maccabees.* New York: Harper, 1953.

Hagner, Donald. *The Use of the Old and New Testaments in Clement of Rome.* Leiden: Brill, 1973.

Hamm, D. "Faith in the Epistle to the Hebrews: The Jesus Factor." *CBQ* 52 (1990): 270-91.

Hatch, Edwing. *The Organization of the Early Christian Churches.* Oxford and Cambridge: Rivingtons, 1881.

Hay, D. M. *Glory at the Right Hand: Psalm 110 in Early Christianity.* SBLMS 18. Nashville: Abingdon, 1973.

Hengel, Martin. *Crucifixion in the Ancient World and the Folly of the Message of the Cross.* Philadelphia: Fortress, 1977.

Héring, Jean. *The Epistle to the Hebrews.* Tr. A. W. Heathcote. London: Epworth, 1970.

Hewitt, Thomas. *The Epistle to the Hebrews.* Grand Rapids: Eerdmans, 1960.

Heyler, L. R. "The *Prototokos* Title in Hebrews." *Studia Biblica et Theologia* 6 (1976): 13.

Hock, R. F., and E. N. O'Neil. *The Chreia in Ancient Rhetoric. I. The Progymnasmata.* Atlanta: Scholars Press, 1986.

Hoekema, A. A. "The Perfection of Christ in Hebrews." *CTJ* 9 (1974): 31-37.

Hofius, Otfried. *Katapausis. Die Vorstellung vom endzeitlichen Ruheort im Hebräerbrief.* Tübingen: Mohr, 1970.

Holmberg, Bengt. *Sociology and the New Testament: An Appraisal.* Minneapolis: Fortress, 1990.

Hübner, H. "τέλειος" and "τελειόω." In *Exegetical Dictionary of the New Testament,* vol. 3, ed. H. Balz and G. Schneider, 342-45. Grand Rapids: Eerdmans, 1993.

Hughes, Graham. *Hebrews and Hermeneutics.* SNTSMS 36. Cambridge: Cambridge University Press, 1979.

Hughes, P. E. *A Commentary on the Epistle to the Hebrews.* Grand Rapids: Eerdmans, 1977.

Hurst, L. D. *The Epistle to the Hebrews: Its Background of Thought.* SNTSMS 65. Cambridge: Cambridge University Press, 1990.

———. "The Christology of Hebrews 1 and 2." In *The Glory of Christ in the New Testament: Studies in Christology,* ed. L. D. Hurst and N. T. Wright. Oxford: Clarendon, 1987.

———. "Eschatology and 'Platonism' in the Epistle to the Hebrews." *SBLSP* 23 (1984): 41-74.

James, William. *The Varieties of Religious Experience: A Study in Human Nature.* New York: Mentor, 1958.

Jewett, Robert. *A Letter to Pilgrims: A Commentary on the Epistle to the Hebrews.* New York: Pilgrim, 1981.

———. *Saint Paul Returns to the Movies: Triumph over Shame.* Louisville: Westminster/John Knox Press, 1998.

Johnson, Luke T. *Sharing Possessions: Mandate and Symbol of Faith.* Philadelphia: Fortress, 1981.

———. *The Real Jesus: The Misguided Quest for the Jesus of History.* San Francisco: HarperCollins, 1995.

———. *The Writings of the New Testament: An Interpretation.* Philadelphia: Fortress, 1986.

Jones, E. D. "The Authorship of Hebrews xiii." *ExT* 46 (1934-35): 562-67.

Kaiser, Jr., Walter C. "The Promise Theme and the Theology of Rest." *Bib Sac* 130 (1973): 135-50.

Kanter, R. M. *Commitment and Community: Communes and Utopias in Sociological Perspective.* Cambridge, MA: Harvard University Press, 1972.

Käsemann, Ernst. *The Wandering People of God: An Investigation of the Letter to the Hebrews.* Minneapolis: Augsburg, 1984.

Kee, H. C. "The Linguistic Background of 'Shame' in the New Testament." In *On Language, Culture, and Religion: In Honor of Eugene A. Nida,* ed. M. Black and W. A. Smalley, 133-48. The Hague: Mouton, 1974.

Kennedy, G. A. *New Testament Interpretation through Rhetorical Criticism.* Chapel Hill, NC: University of North Carolina Press, 1984.

Kittel, Gerhard. "δοκέω, δόξα." *TDNT* 2:232-55. Grand Rapids: Eerdmans, 1964.

Koester, Helmut. "Outside the Camp: Hebrews 13:9-14." *HTR* 55 (1962): 299-315.

Kögel, J. "Der Begriff 'τελειοῦν' im Hebräerbrief im Zusammenhang mit dem neutestamentlichen Sprachgebrauch." In *Theologische Studien: Martin Kähler zum 6. Januar 1905,* ed. F. Giesebrecht et al. Leipzig: A. Deichert, 1905.

Kuhn, H. B. "The Angelology of the Non-Canonical Jewish Apocalypses." *JBL* 67 (1948): 217-32.

Kümmel, W. G. *Introduction to the New Testament.* Nashville: Abingdon, 1973.

Ladd, G. E. *A Theology of the New Testament.* Grand Rapids: Eerdmans, 1974.

Lane, W. L. *Hebrews: A Call to Commitment.* Peabody: Hendrickson, 1985.

————. *Hebrews 1–8.* WBC 47A. Dallas: Word Books, 1991.

————. *Hebrews 9–13.* WBC 47B. Dallas: Word Books, 1991.

Laub, F. "Verkündigung und Gemeindeamt: Die Autorität der ἡγούμενοι Hebr 13,7.17.24." *SNTU* 6-7 (1981-82): 169-90.

Lehne, Susanne. *The New Covenant in Hebrews.* JSNTSS 44. Sheffield: JSOT Press, 1990.

Levick, Barbara. *The Government of the Roman Empire: A Sourcebook.* London: Croom Helm, 1985.

Levine, Baruch A. *Leviticus.* JPS Commentary. Philadelphia: The Jewish Publication Society, 1989.

Lincoln, Andrew T. "Sabbath, Rest, and Eschatology in the New Testament." In *From Sabbath to Lord's Day,* ed. D. A. Carson, 197-220. Grand Rapids: Zondervan, 1982.

Lindars, Barnabas. *The Theology of the Letter to the Hebrews.* Cambridge: Cambridge University Press, 1991.

————. "The Rhetorical Structure of Hebrews." *NTS* 35 (1989): 382-406.

Long, Thomas. *Hebrews.* Interpretation. Louisville: Westminster/John Knox, 1997.

Lünemann, Gerhard. *Kritisch-exegetischer Handbuch über den Hebräerbrief.* MeyerK 13. Göttingen: Vandenhoeck & Ruprecht, 1878.

Mack, Burton. *Rhetoric and the New Testament.* Minneapolis: Augsburg Fortress, 1990.

————. *A Myth of Innocence: Mark and Christian Origins.* Philadelphia: Fortress, 1988.

————, and V. K. Robbins, *Patterns of Persuasion in the Gospels.* Sonoma, CA: Polebridge, 1989.

MacMullen, Ramsey. *Paganism in the Roman Empire.* New Haven: Yale University Press, 1981.

MacRae, George W. "Heavenly Temple and Eschatology in the Letter to the Hebrews." *Semeia* 12 (1978): 179-99.

Malherbe, A. J. "Ancient Epistolary Theorists." *Ohio Journal of Religious Studies* 5 (1977): 3-77.

Malina, Bruce. *The New Testament World: Insights from Cultural Anthropology.* Louisville: Westminster/John Knox, 1993.

————, and J. H. Neyrey. "Honor and Shame in Luke-Acts: Pivotal Values of the Mediterranean World." In *The Social World of Luke-Acts: Models for Interpretation,* ed. J. H. Neyrey. Peabody: Hendrickson, 1991.

————, and J. H. Neyrey. "First-Century Personality: Dyadic, Not Individualistic." In *The Social World of Luke-Acts: Models for Interpretation,* ed. J. H. Neyrey. Peabody: Hendrickson, 1991.

————, and J. H. Neyrey. "Conflict in Luke-Acts: Labelling and Deviance Theory." In *The Social World of Luke-Acts: Models for Interpretation,* ed. J. H. Neyrey. Peabody: Hendrickson, 1991.

————, and R. Rohrbaugh. *Social-Science Commentary on the Synoptic Gospels.* Minneapolis: Fortress, 1992.

Manson, T. W. "The Problem of the Epistle to the Hebrews." *BJRL* 32 (1949-50): 1-17.

Marrou, H. I. *A History of Education in Antiquity.* New York: Mentor, 1956.

Marshall, I. H. "The Problem of Apostasy in New Testament Theology." *Perspectives in Religious Studies* 14 (1987): 65-80.

Marx, Karl, and F. Engels, *On Religion.* Ed. Reinhold Niebuhr. Atlanta: Scholars Press, 1964.

McCown, W. G. "Ο ΛΟΓΟΣ ΤΗΣ ΠΑΡΑΚΛΗΣΕΩΣ: The Nature and Function of the Hortatory Sections in the Epistle to the Hebrews." Ph.D. diss., Union Theological Seminary, VA, 1970.

McNicol, A. J. "The Relationship of the Image of the Highest Angel to the High Priest Concept in Hebrews." Ph.D. diss., Vanderbilt University, 1974.

Meeks, Wayne A. *The First Urban Christians: The Social World of the Apostle Paul.* New Haven, CT: Yale University Press, 1983.

Meier, John P. "Symmetry and Theology in Heb 1,5-14." *Bib* 66 (1985): 504-33.

Michel, Otto. *Der Brief an die Hebräer.* 12th ed. MeyerK 13. Göttingen: Vandenhoeck & Ruprecht, 1960.

Milgrom, Jacob. *Leviticus I–XVI.* AB. New York: Doubleday, 1991.

Moffatt, J. *Hebrews.* ICC. Edinburgh: T. & T. Clark, 1924.

Montefiore, Hugh. *A Commentary on the Epistle to the Hebrews.* New York: Harper, 1964.

Moxnes, Halvor. "Honor and Shame." *BTB* 23 (1993): 167-76.

————. "Honor, Shame, and the Outside World in Paul's Letter to the Romans." In *The Social World of Formative Christianity and Judaism,* ed. J. Neusner, E. S. Frerichs, and R. Horsley. Philadelphia: Fortress, 1988.

————. "Honour and Righteousness in Romans." *JSNT* 32 (1988): 61-77.

————. "Patron-Client Relations and the New Community in Luke-Acts." In *The*

Social World of Luke-Acts, ed. J. H. Neyrey. Peabody: Hendrickson, 1991, 241-68.

Nauck, Wolfgang. "Zum Aufbau des Hebräerbriefes." In *Judentum, Urchristentum, Kirche,* ed. W. Eltester. BZNW 26. Giessen: Töpelmann, 1960.

Neitz, M. J. *Charisma and Community.* New Brunswick, NJ: Transaction Books, 1987.

Nelson, Richard D. *Raising Up a Faithful Priest: Community and Priesthood in a Biblical Theology,* chapter 4. Louisville: Westminster/John Knox Press, 1993.

Newsom, Carol A., and Duane F. Watson, "Angels." In *ABD* 1:248-55.

Neyrey, J. H. "Despising the Shame of the Cross: Honor and Shame in the Johannine Passion Narrative." *Semeia* 68 (1996): 113-37.

———. "Loss of Wealth, Loss of Family and Loss of Honour: The Cultural Context of the Original Makarisms in Q." In *Modelling Early Christianity: Social-scientific Studies of the New Testament in Its Context,* by P. F. Esler, 139-58. London: Routledge, 1995.

———. *2 Peter, Jude.* New York: Doubleday, 1993.

———. "Poverty and Loss of Honor in Matthew's Beatitudes: Poverty as Cultural, Not Merely Economic Phenomenon." Unpublished paper delivered at the CJA Seminar in October 1992.

———. "The Symbolic Universe of Luke-Acts: 'They Turn the World Upside Down.'" In *The Social World of Luke-Acts: Models for Interpretation,* ed. J. H. Neyrey, 271-304. Peabody: Hendrickson, 1991.

———. "The Idea of Purity in Mark's Gospel." *Semeia* 35 (1986): 91-128.

Nickelsburg, G. W. E. *Jewish Literature between the Bible and the Mishnah.* Philadelphia: Fortress, 1981.

Oberholtzer, Thomas K. "The Warning Passages in Hebrews: Part 1: The Eschatological Salvation of Hebrews 1:5–2:5." *Bib Sac* 145 (1988): 83-97.

———. "The Kingdom Rest in Hebrews 3:1–4:13." *Bib Sac* 145 (1988): 185-96.

———. "The Thorn-Infested Ground in Hebrews 6:4-12." *Bib Sac* 145 (1988): 319-28.

O'Hagan, A. "The Martyr in the Fourth Book of Maccabees." *SBFLA* 24 (1974): 94-120.

Olbricht, T. "Hebrews as Amplification." In *Rhetoric and the New Testament,* ed. S. E. Porter and T. H. Olbricht, 375-87. JSNTSS 90. Sheffield: Sheffield Academic Press, 1993.

Olson, Stanley. "Pauline Expressions of Confidence in His Addressees." *CBQ* 47 (1985): 282-95.

Osiek, Carolyn, and D. Balch. *Families in the New Testament World.* Louisville: Westminster/John Knox Press, 1997.

Peristiany, J. G., ed. *Honour and Shame: The Values of Mediterranean Society.* Chicago: University of Chicago Press, 1966.

————, and Julian Pitt-Rivers, eds. *Honor and Grace in Anthropology*. Cambridge: Cambridge University Press, 1992.

Peterson, David. *Hebrews and Perfection: An Examination of the Concept of Perfection in the 'Epistle to the Hebrews.'* SNTSMS 47. Cambridge: Cambridge University Press, 1982.

Pfitzner, V. C. *Paul and the Agon Motif: Traditional Athletic Imagery in the Pauline Literature*. Leiden: E. J. Brill, 1967.

————. *Hebrews*. ACNT. Nashville: Abingdon, 1997.

Pitt-Rivers, Julian. "Honour and Social Status." In *Honour and Shame: The Values of Mediterranean Society*, ed. J. Peristiany. London: Weidenfeld and Nicolson, 1965.

Proulx, P., and L. A. Schökel, "Heb 6,4-6: εἰς μετάνοιαν ἀνασταυροῦντας." *Bib* 56 (1975): 193-209.

Reid, D. G. "Angels, Archangels." In *Dictionary of Paul and His Letters*, ed. R. P. Martin and P. H. Davids, 20-23. Downers Grove, IL: InterVarsity Press, 1995.

Riggenbach, E. *Der Brief an die Hebräer*. Leipzig: Deichert, 1922.

Robbins, Vernon K. *The Tapestry of Early Christian Discourse: Rhetoric, Society and Ideology*. London: Routledge & Kegan Paul, 1996.

————. *Exploring the Texture of Texts*. Valley Forge, PA: Trinity Press International, 1996.

————. "Rhetoric and Culture: Exploring Types of Cultural Rhetoric in a Text." In *Rhetoric and the New Testament*, ed. S. E. Porter and T. H. Olbricht. JSNTSS 90. Sheffield: JSOT, 1993.

————. "Socio-rhetorical Criticism: Mary, Elizabeth, and the Magnificat as a Test Case." In *The New Literary Criticism and the New Testament*, ed. E. S. Malbon and E. McKnight, 164-209. Sheffield: Sheffield Academic Press, 1994.

Roberts, K. A. *Religion in Sociological Perspective*. Chicago: Dorsey Press, 1984.

————. "Towards a Generic Concept of Counterculture." *Sociological Focus* 11 (1978): 111-26.

Robinson, William. "The Eschatology of the Epistle to the Hebrews: A Study in the Christian Doctrine of Hope." *Encounter* 22 (1961): 37-51

Rowell, J. B. "Exposition of Hebrews Six." *Bib Sac* 94 (1937): 321-42.

Rowland, Christopher. *The Open Heaven: A Study of Apocalyptic in Judaism and Early Christianity*. New York: Crossroad, 1982.

Sabourin, L. *Priesthood: A Comparative Study*. Leiden: Brill, 1973.

Saller, R. P. *Personal Patronage under the Early Empire*. Cambridge: Cambridge University Press, 1982.

Sanders, J. T. *The New Testament Christological Hymns: Their Historical Religious Background*. SNTSMS 15. Cambridge: Cambridge University Press, 1971.

Scheidweiler, F. "ΚΑΙΠΕΡ: nebst einem Exkurs zum Hebräerbrief." *Hermes* 83 (1955): 220-30.

Schlier, H. "παραδειγματίζω." In *TDNT* 2:32.

Schmidt, T. E. "Moral Lethargy and the Epistle to the Hebrews." *WTJ* 54 (1992): 167-73.

Scholer, J. M. *Proleptic Priests: Priesthood in the Epistle to the Hebrews.* JSNTSS 49; Sheffield: JSOT Press, 1991.

Seely, David. *The Noble Death: Graeco-Roman Martyrology and Paul's Concept of Salvation.* JSNTSS 28. Sheffield: Sheffield Acadmic Press, 1990.

Selwyn, E. G. *The First Epistle of Peter.* Second ed. London: Macmillan, 1955.

Shils, Edward. "The Concept and Function of Idealogy." In *International Encyclopedia of the Social Sciences.* New York: Macmillan and Free Press, 1968, 7:72.

Silva, Moisés. "Perfection and Eschatology in Hebrews." *WTJ* 39 (1976): 60-71.

Skehan, P. W., and A. A. Di Lella. *The Wisdom of Ben Sira.* New York: Doubleday, 1987.

Snaith, J. G. *Ecclesiasticus.* Cambridge Bible Commentary. Cambridge: Cambridge University Press, 1974.

Spicq, Ceslaus. *L'Épître aux Hébreux.* 2 vols. EBib. Paris: Gabalda, 1953.

Stagg, Frank. "The Abused Aorist." *JBL* 91 (1972): 222-31.

Stambaugh, J. E., and D. L. Balch. *The New Testament in Its Social Environment.* Library of Early Christianity 2. Philadelphia: Westminster, 1986.

Stedman, Ray C. *Hebrews.* Downers Grove, IL: InterVarsity Press, 1992.

Swetnam, James. *Jesus and Isaac: A Study of the Epistle to the Hebrews in Light of the Aqedah.* Rome: Pontifical Biblical Institute, 1981.

Tasker, R. V. G. "The Integrity of the Epistle to the Hebrews." *ExT* 47 (1935-36): 136-38.

Theissen, Gerd. *The Social Setting of Pauline Christianity: Essays on Corinth.* Philadelphia: Fortress, 1982.

————. *Untersuchungen zum Hebräerbrief.* SNT 2. Gütersloh: Mohn, 1969.

Thompson, J. W. *The Beginnings of Christian Philosophy: The Epistle to the Hebrews.* CBQMS 13. Washington, DC: Catholic Biblical Association of America, 1982.

Thompson, M. B. "The Holy Internet: Communication between Churches in the First Christian Generation." In *The Gospels for All Christians: Rethinking the Gospel Audiences,* ed. Richard Bauckham, 49-70. Grand Rapids: Eerdmans, 1998.

Thurén, Jukka. *Das Lobopfer der Hebräer. Studien zum Aufbau und Anliegen von Hebräerbrief 13.* Åbo: Akademi, 1973.

Thyen, H. *Der Stil der jüdische-hellenistischen Homilie.* FRLANT 47. Göttingen: Vandenhoeck & Ruprecht, 1955.

Toussaint, Stanley D. "The Eschatology of the Warning Passages in the Book of Hebrews." *GTJ* 3 (1982): 67-80.

Troeltsch, Ernst. *The Social Teaching of the Christian Churches.* 2 vols. London: George Allen, 1931.

Trotter, Jr., Andrew H. *Interpreting the Epistle to the Hebrews.* Grand Rapids: Baker Book House, 1997.

Turner, Victor. *The Ritual Process.* Ithaca, NY: Cornell University Press, 1969.

Übelacker, W. G. *Der Hebräerbrief als Appel.* Stockholm: Almqvist & Wiksell, 1989.

Vaganay, L. "Le Plan de L'Épître aux Hébreux." In *Memorial Lagrange,* ed. L. H. Vincent. Paris: Gabalda, 1940.

van Geytenbeek, A. C. *Musonius Rufus and Greek Diatribe.* Assen: Van Gorcum, 1963.

Vanhoye, A. *Le message de lÉpître aux Hébreux.* Paris: Cerf, 1977.

———. *La Structure litteraire de l'Épître aux Hébreux.* Paris: Desclée de Brouwer, 1963.

———. "L'οἰκουμένη dans l'Épître aux Hébreux." *Bib* 45 (1964): 248-53.

Verbrugge, V. G. "Towards a New Interpretation of Hebrews 6:4-6." *CTJ* 15 (1980): 61-73.

Vermes, Geza. *The Complete Dead Sea Scrolls in English.* Harmondsworth: Allen Lane/Penguin, 1997.

von der Heydt, Barbara. *Candles Behind the Wall: Heroes of the Peaceful Revolution That Shattered Communism.* Grand Rapids: Eerdmans, 1993.

Wallace-Hadrill, Andrew, ed. *Patronage in Ancient Society.* London: Routledge & Kegan Paul, 1989.

Watson, Duane F. *Invention, Arrangement, and Style: Rhetorical Criticism of Jude and 2 Peter.* SBLDS 104. Atlanta: Scholars Press, 1988.

———. "A Rhetorical Analysis of Philippians and Its Implications for the Unity Question." *NovT* 30 (1988): 57-88.

Weima, Jeffrey A. D. "What Has Aristotle to Do with Paul?" *CTJ* 32 (1997): 458-68.

Weiss, Bernard. *Der Hebräerbrief in zeitgeschichtlicher Beleuchtung.* Leipzig: J. C. Hinrichs, 1910.

Weiss, H.-F. *Der Brief an die Hebräer.* 15th ed. MeyerK 13. Göttingen: Vandenhoeck & Ruprecht, 1991.

Westcott, B. F. *The Epistle to the Hebrews.* London: Macmillan, 1920.

Wettstein, J. J. Η ΚΑΙΝΗ ΔΙΑΘΗΚΗ: *Novum Testamentum Graecum,* etc., vol. 2. Amsterdam: Dommer, 1752.

Wikgren, A. "Patterns of Perfection in the Epistle to the Hebrews." *NTS* 6 (1960): 159-67.

Wilken, R. L. *The Christians as the Romans Saw Them.* New Haven: Yale University Press, 1984.

Williams, Bernard. *Shame and Necessity.* Berkeley: University of California Press, 1993.

Williams, S. K. *Jesus' Death as Saving Event: The Background and Origin of a Concept.* HTRDS 2. Missoula, MT: Scholars Press, 1975.

Williamson, Ronald. *Philo and the Epistle to the Hebrews.* Leiden: E. J. Brill, 1970.

———. "Platonism and Hebrews." *SJT* 16 (1963): 415-24.

Wills, L. "The Form of the Sermon in Hellenistic Judaism and Early Christianity." *HTR* 77 (1984): 277-99.

Windisch, H. *Der Hebräerbrief.* Tübingen, 1913; 2d ed. 1931.

Winter, B. W. *Seek the Welfare of the City: Christians as Benefactors and Citizens.* Grand Rapids: Eerdmans, 1994.

Witherington, Ben, III. *Conflict and Community in Corinth: A Socio-Rhetorical Commentary on 1 and 2 Corinthians.* Grand Rapids: Eerdmans, 1995.

———. *Jesus the Sage and the Pilgrimage of Wisdom.* Minneapolis: Fortress, 1994.

———. "The Influence of Galatians on Hebrews." *NTS* 37 (1991): 146-52.

Worley, Jr., D. R. "God's Faithfulness to Promise: The Hortatory Use of Commissive Language in Hebrews." Ph.D. diss., Yale University, 1981.

Index of Modern Authors

Index of Texts Cited